50 Jahre im Bild
Years in Pictures

© 1999 Könemann Verlagsgesellschaft mbH
Bonner Straße 126, D-50968 Köln

Art Director: Peter Feierabend
Project Management: Ute Edda Hammer
Project Assistance: Jeannette Fentroß; Ingo Müller (Support)
Design: Peter Feierabend, Erill Vinzenz Fritz
Picture Editor: Ulrich Weichert, Bonn
Contributing Editor and Historical Consultant: Daniel Koerfer, Berlin
German Textediting: Wolfgang Stegbauer, Deggendorf
Translations: David E. Jenkinson, London
Contributing Editor for English: Hilary Heltay, Cologne
Production Management: Detlev Schaper
Production: Mark Voges
Reproductions: Typografik, Cologne
Printing and binding: Imprimerie Jean Lamour, Maxéville

Printed in France
ISBN 3-8290-2869-5
10 9 8 7 6 5 4 3 2 1

**Der Verlag dankt dem Presse- und Informationsamt der Bundesregierung
und der Bundesbildstelle für die kooperative Zusammenarbeit.**

The publishing house would like to thank the Presse- und Informationsamt
der Bundesregierung and the Bundesbildstelle for their cooperation.

Daniel Kosthorst   Ulrich Lappenküper

50 Jahre im Bild
Years in Pictures

Picture Editor: Ulrich Weichert

Bundesrepublik Deutschland
Federal Republic of Germany

KÖNEMANN

Inhalt / Contents

1945–1949

Besatzungsherrschaft im Zeichen der Teilung
Rule by Occupying Powers in a Land Divided

Auftakt zur Potsdamer Konferenz: Begrüßung zwischen Winston Churchill,
Harry S. Truman und Josef Stalin im Juli 1945.

At the beginning of the Potsdam Conference: greetings betweenn Winston
Churchilll, Harry S. Truman, and Joseph Stalin in July 1945.

Mit der bedingungslosen Kapitulation der deutschen Wehrmacht in Reims und Berlin-Karlshorst am 7./8.5.1945 endete der »totale« Zweite Weltkrieg in der totalen Niederlage. Weitgehend zerstört, militärisch erobert und von alliierten Truppen besetzt, hatte Deutschland aufgehört, ein handlungsfähiger politischer Faktor zu sein. Für viele Überlebende war das Ende der nationalsozialistischen Schreckensherrschaft keineswegs nur eine Befreiung, sondern auch eine grausame Enttäuschung. Deutschland war »erlöst und vernichtet in einem« (Theodor Heuss).

Am 5.6.1945 übernahmen die USA, Großbritannien, die Sowjetunion und Frankreich als Siegermächte mit der Berliner Erklärung die oberste Regierungsgewalt. Entsprechend den seit 1944 getroffenen Absprachen wurde Deutschland in vier Besatzungszonen aufgeteilt und einem gemeinsamen Kontrollrat der vier Oberbefehlshaber Eisenhower, Schukow, Montgomery und Lattre de Tassigny unterstellt. Zwei Monate später beschlossen die Staats- und Regierungschefs der Großen Drei, Harry S. Truman, Clement Attlee und Josef Stalin auf einer Konferenz in Potsdam, daß der »deutsche Militarismus und Nazismus ausgerottet« werden solle und Deutschland niemals mehr zur Bedrohung des Weltfriedens werden dürfe. Konkret einigten sie sich auf die Durchsetzung von vier Grundsätzen: Demilitarisierung, Denazifizierung, Dezentralisierung und Demokratisierung. Um den Sowjets einen direkten Zugriff auf das westdeutsche Industriepotential zu verwehren, machten Briten und Amerikaner im Abschlußprotokoll, dem »Potsdamer Abkommen« vom 2.8.1945, außerdem ein verhängnisvolles Zugeständnis. Sie stimmten der »ordnungsgemäßen Überführung« der Deutschen aus Ungarn, der Tschechoslowakei und den Gebieten jenseits von Oder und Neiße, der Unterstellung dieser Gebiete unter polnische Verwaltung sowie der Abtretung des nördlichen Ostpreußens an die Sowjetunion vorbehaltlich eines Friedensvertrages zu. Weitere wichtige Fragen hinsichtlich des zukünftigen Schicksals von Deutschland, wie die Grenzen oder die Reparationen, blieben ungeklärt.

Schon bald sollten die latent vorhandenen Differenzen über die innere Gestaltung des besiegten Deutschland offen ausbrechen. Bei der Ahndung der nationalsozialistischen Verbrechen, die zu den wichtigsten Zielen der Siegermächte gehörte, beschränkten sich die Siegermächte auf die Bestrafung der Hauptkriegsverbrecher vor dem Nürnberger Militärtribunal. Die Absicht, dem Verfahren weitere Prozesse unter gemeinsamer Gerichtshoheit folgen zu lassen, ließ sich nicht mehr realisieren, so daß es lediglich zu einzelnen Prozessen gegen Diplomaten, Generäle und führende Vertreter des NS-Regimes und der Wirtschaft kam.

Als wichtigen Besatzungszweck erachteten die Alliierten die Herstellung eines demokratischen Systems durch Entnazifizierung und Umerziehung. Doch auch hier führten die unterschiedlichen Interpretationen des Begriffes Demokratie schon bald zu tiefgreifenden Meinungsverschiedenheiten.

Nicht weniger umstritten war die in Potsdam in Aussicht genommene Bildung von deutschen Zentralverwaltungsbehörden. Sie scheiterte letztlich an der Forderung Frankreichs, zunächst das Ruhrgebiet zu internationalisieren und das Saarland wirtschaftlich angliedern zu dürfen. So grundlegend diese Differenzen der ehemaligen Verbündeten waren, bildeten sie doch nur einen Aspekt des nun ausbrechenden Kalten Krieges. Als der amerikanische

With the unconditional surrender of the German armed forces in Reims and Berlin-Karlshorst on May 7-8, 1945 at the end of the Second World War, "total war" ended in total defeat. Extensively destroyed, conquered on the battlefield, and occupied by Allied troops, Germany had ceased to be capable of independent political action. For many survivors the end of the national socialist reign of terror was by no means simply a liberation, it was also a cruel disappointment. Germany was "rescued and annihilated at the same time" (Theodor Heuss).

On June 5, 1945, with the Berlin Declaration, the victorious powers of the USA, Great Britain, the Soviet Union, and France assumed supreme governmental responsibility. As had been agreed since 1944, Germany was divided into four zones of occupation and placed under the authority of a joint Control Council consisting of the four supreme commanders Eisenhower, Zhukov, Montgomery, and Lattre de Tassigny. Two months later the leaders of the Big Three, Harry S. Truman, Clement Attlee, and Joseph Stalin, resolved at a conference in Potsdam that "German militarism and Nazism" were to be "expunged" and that Germany must never again be allowed to pose a threat to world peace. In concrete terms they agreed to implement four basic principles: demilitarization, denazification, decentralization, and democratization. In order to prevent the Soviet Union from having direct access to the industrial potential of western Germany, the British and the Americans made a fatal concession in the final Protocol of Proceedings, the "Potsdam Agreement" of August 2, 1945. They agreed that there should be an "orderly transfer" of Germans from Hungary, Czechoslovakia and the territories beyond the Oder and the Neisse, that these territories should be placed under Polish administration, and that the northern half of East Prussia should be ceded to the Soviet Union, subject to a peace treaty. Further important issues concerning the future fate of Germany, such as borders and reparations, were left unclarified.

It did not take long for the latent differences of opinion as to the internal shape to be taken by the defeated Germany to come out into the open. Punishment of the crimes of national socialism, one of the most important goals of the victorious powers, was limited to the major war criminals who came before the military tribunal at Nuremberg. The intention that further trials should follow under joint jurisdiction ceased to be feasible. As a result there were only individual trials of diplomats, generals, and leading representatives of the national socialist régime and the economy.

The Allies regarded the establishment of a democratic system through denazification and re-education as an important purpose of the occupation. But here too the differing interpretations of the concept of democracy soon led to far-reaching differences of opinion.

No less controversial was the creation of German central administrative authorities envisaged at Potsdam. It failed ultimately because of France's demand that the Ruhr region should first be internationalized and that France should be allowed to annex the Saarland to its own economy.

Fundamental though these differences between the former allies were, they merely constituted one aspect of the Cold War which now broke out. When, at the first session of the Council of the Four Foreign Ministers in the summer of 1946, American Secretary of State Byrnes put forward a plan to neutralize and demilitarize

Zerstörtes Kulturgut: Der Berliner Lustgarten nach den alliierten Luftangriffen vom April 1945.

Destruction of cultural assets: the Berlin Lustgarten after the Allied airraids in April 1945.

Außenminister Byrnes auf der ersten Tagung des Rates der Vier Außenminister im Sommer 1946 einen Plan zur Neutralisierung und Entmilitarisierung Deutschlands vorlegte, forderte sein sowjetischer Kollege Molotow statt dessen die Beteiligung Moskaus an der Ruhrkontrolle und die Umstrukturierung der deutschen Wirtschaft nach dem Vorbild der eigenen Besatzungszone. Anfang September 1946 kündigte Byrnes daraufhin die Abkehr von der bisher gültigen Deutschlandpolitik an und proklamierte das Ziel, den Deutschen einen »ehrenvollen Platz unter den freien und friedlichen Nationen der Welt« einzuräumen. Winston Churchill, der ehemalige britische Premierminister, tat es ihm nach und propagierte kurz darauf die Idee der »Vereinigten Staaten von Europa« unter Einschluß Deutschlands.

Vor dem Hintergrund der sich verschlechternden Wirtschafts- und Ernährungslage faßten Amerikaner und Briten wenig später den Entschluß, ihre Zonen zum Vereinigten Wirtschaftsgebiet zu verschmelzen. Diese »Bizone« sollte sich nach ihrer Gründung am 1.1.1947 zur Keimzelle des künftigen Weststaates entwickeln.

Das Scheitern der Moskauer Außenministerkonferenz der Vier Mächte im Frühjahr 1947 ließ den Graben zwischen Ost und West noch tiefer werden. Vor dem Hintergrund der kommunistischen Unterwanderung Griechenlands und der Türkei leiteten die USA eine politische und wirtschaftliche Offensive in Europa ein. Ein wichtiger Eckpfeiler dieser auf die weltweite »Eindämmung« der Sowjetunion gerichteten Politik war das vom neuen amerikanischen Außenminister Marshall Anfang Juni 1947 verkündete »European Recovery Program« (ERP). Es zielte darauf ab, die ökonomische Lage in Europa zu stabilisieren, um »Hunger, Armut, Verzweiflung und Chaos« zu überwinden. Dabei ging Marshall davon aus, daß der Wiederaufbau Europas nicht ohne die deutsche Wirtschaft gelingen könne.

Germany, his Soviet opposite number Molotov demanded instead that Moscow should have a part in the control of the Ruhr and that the German economy should be restructured following the example of his own zone of occupation. Byrnes thereupon announced, at the beginning of September 1946, that previous policies towards Germany had been jettisoned and proclaimed the aim of conceding to the Germans an "honorable place among the free and peace-loving nations of the world." Winston Churchill, the former British prime minister, followed suit and shortly afterwards gave currency to the idea of a "United States of Europe," to include Germany.

Not long after this, against the background of the deteriorating economic and food supply situation, the Americans and the British resolved to amalgamate their zones to form the United Economic Area. This "bizone," founded on January 1, 1947, was to develop into the germ cell of the future West German state.

The failure of the Moscow Four-Power Conference of Foreign Ministers in the spring of 1947 deepened still further the rift between east and west. Against the background of communist influence in Greece and Turkey, the USA launched a political and economic offensive in Europe. An important cornerstone of this policy, with its aim of "containing" the Soviet Union worldwide, was the "European Recovery Program" (ERP) announced at the beginning of June 1947 by George C. Marshall, the new American Secretary of State. Its aim was to stabilize economic conditions in Europe in order to overcome "hunger, poverty, desparation, and chaos." Marshall's premise was that the reconstruction of Europe could not be successful without the German economy.

While Stalin refused the offer of ERP resources for the Soviet Union and its satellite states, France, which had hitherto clung to the illusion that it could come to an understanding with the Kremlin, now increasingly adopted the Anglo-American line.

Demontage: Abtransport von Industrieanlagen der Essener Steinkohlewerke durch belgische Soldaten 1949.

Dismantling: industrial plant from the coal works in Essen being taken away by Belgian troops in 1945.

Während Stalin das Angebot von ERP-Mitteln für die Sowjetunion und ihre Satellitenstaaten ablehnte, schwenkte Frankreich,
das bisher an der Fiktion einer Verständigung mit dem Kreml fest-
gehalten hatte, nun mehr und mehr auf den angelsächsischen Kurs
ein. Der »seidene Vorhang« zwischen der französischen und der Bi-
Zone wurde allmählich durchsichtig.

Als Frankreich im Frühjahr 1948 auf der Londoner Sechsmächtekonferenz die amerikanische Weststaatskonzeption in Übereinstimmung mit Großbritannien und den Benelux-Staaten als Grundlage
künftiger Deutschlandpolitik akzeptierte, nahm die Sowjetunion
dies zum Anlaß, den Alliierten Kontrollrat zu verlassen. Zur offenen
Feindseligkeit geriet das Verhältnis der ehemaligen Verbündeten,
als Stalin Ende Juni eine totale Blockade aller Land- und Wasserwege zu den Westsektoren Berlins verfügte. Kurz darauf erzwang er
die politische und administrative Spaltung der ehemaligen Reichs-
hauptstadt. Doch der Versuch, den Westteil in den eigenen Machtbereich zu bringen, scheiterte am Widerstand des Westens und dem
Durchhaltevermögen der Bevölkerung, die zehn Monate lang nur
über die alliierte Luftbrücke versorgt werden konnte. Die Demarkationslinie zwischen den drei westlichen und der sowjetischen
Besatzungszone (SBZ) wurde im Kalten Krieg zur Front zwischen
den Machtblöcken.

Die psychologischen Auswirkungen auf Deutsche und Westmächte waren folgenreich. Stärker als je zuvor wurden die Amerikaner als Bewahrer der Freiheit angesehen. Im Gegenzug bewun-
derten sie die Standhaftigkeit der Berliner. Die Blockade ließ nicht
nur bei den Siegern des Zweiten Weltkriegs ein neues Deutschland-
bild entstehen; sie forcierte auch die Bereitschaft der Besiegten, auf
das Angebot zur Gründung eines westlich geprägten Teilstaats ein-
zugehen.

Zusammenbruch und Neubeginn

In der Bevölkerung interessierte man sich in den ersten Nachkriegsjahren gewiß nur wenig für Politik; für sie ging es vornehmlich um das nackte Überleben. Hoffnungslosigkeit und Erschöp-
fung, Hunger und Sorge um die Angehörigen bestimmten den
Alltag in der »Zusammenbruchsgesellschaft« (Christoph Kleßmann).
Viele Städte lagen in Trümmern. Zahlreiche Menschen, die den
Krieg überlebt hatten, vegetierten in Kellern, Baracken oder Well-
blechhütten. Aus den Ostgebieten strömten 12 Millionen Flüchtlinge oder Vertriebene und verschärften die Wohnungsnot. Drei-
tausend zerstörte Eisenbahnbrücken ließen den Güterverkehr und
damit auch die Energieversorgung zusammenbrechen.

Das staatliche Bewirtschaftungssystem des Dritten Reiches, das
von den Alliierten beibehalten wurde, erwies sich als völlig unzu-
reichend. Angesichts der relativen Wertlosigkeit von Geld und
Lebensmittelkarten kehrten die hungernden Menschen zum
Tauschhandel auf dem »Schwarzmarkt« zurück. Auf »Hamster«-
Fahrten versuchten sie, Nahrungsmittel zu ergattern.

In Anbetracht steigender Zahlen von Hungertoten und erhöh-
ter Kindersterblichkeit ermahnte der von 1945-1947 als Stellvertretender amerikanischer Militärgouverneur, dann bis 1949 als
Amtschef tätige General Clay seine Regierung, die Augen vor dem
Schicksal der Deutschen nicht zu verschließen.

Kampf gegen den Hunger: Amerikanische Lebensmittelhilfe verhinderte die
Katastrophe.

The fight against starvation: American food aid prevents a disaster.

The "silk curtain" between the French zone and the bizone gradually
became transparent.

When at the London Six-Power Conference in the spring of
1948 France, along with Britain and the Benelux states, accepted the
American conception of a West German state as the basis for future
policy towards Germany, the Soviet Union took this as grounds for
walking out of the Allied Control Council. The relationship between
the former allies became one of open hostility when at the end of
June Stalin ordered a total blockade of all land and water routes to
the western sectors of Berlin.

Shortly afterwards he brought about the enforced political and
administrative division of the former capital of the Reich. But his
attempt to bring the western part into his own sphere of control
failed thanks to the resistance of the West and the endurance of the
people, who for ten months were provisioned solely by the allied
airlift. The line of demarcation between the three western zones of
occupation and the Soviet zone became the front between the
power blocs in the Cold War.

Frostige Atmosphäre: Übergabe der »Frankfurter Dokumente« durch die Militärgouverneure Clay, Koenig und Robertson am 1.7.1948.

Frosty atmosphere: the "Frankfurt Documents" being handed over by the Military Governors Clay, Koenig, and Robertson on July 1, 1948.

Gehör fand er zunächst bei kirchlichen und karitativen Organisationen sowie Privatleuten, die die Not der Bevölkerung seit 1946 mit »Care-Paketen« (Cooperative for American Remittances to Europe) zu lindern suchten.

Im Schatten dieser vom Kampf um das tägliche Brot bestimmten Lage regte sich seit dem Sommer 1945 politisches Leben. Entsprechend dem Beschluß der Potsdamer Konferenz zur Dezentralisierung des deutschen Staatsgebietes entstanden 1945/46 eine ganze Reihe neuer, aber auch alter Länder. Je nach Gusto der jeweiligen Besatzungsmacht blieben sie politisch separat oder wurden miteinander verknüpft.

Parallel dazu kam es seit Sommer 1945 zum Aufbau von Verwaltungsorganen und politischen Parteien. Im Gegensatz zur sowjetischen Besatzungszone (SBZ) wurden sie im Westen zunächst nur im lokalen Bereich, seit der Gründung der Länder auch auf dieser Ebene zugelassen. Dabei traten neben den 1933 verbotenen Kommunisten und Sozialdemokraten auch neue Parteien auf die Bühne. In der Christlich-Demokratischen Union Deutschlands (CDU) etwa, die sich programmatisch wie organisatorisch als überkonfessionelle Sammlungspartei verstand, entwickelte sich Konrad Adenauer allmählich zur bestimmenden Figur. Seine Stellung als Vorsitzender der CDU in der britischen Zone half ihm dabei, den Führungsanspruch der Berliner Christdemokraten zurückzudrängen. In der SPD übernahm Kurt Schumacher diese führende Rolle. Auch er verfocht eine betont antikommunistische Linie, mit der er sich entschieden von der ostzonalen SPD absetzte, die im April 1946 unter massivem sowjetischen Druck einer Vereinigung mit der KPD zur SED zustimmte. Die Freie Demokratische Partei (FDP) rekrutierte sich vornehm-

The psychological effects on the Germans and the western powers had far-reaching consequences. More strongly than ever before the Americans came to be seen as the guardians of liberty. They in their turn admired the steadfastness of the Berliners. The blockade not only created a new image of Germany in the minds of the victors of the Second World War, it also increased the willingness of the vanquished to take up the offer to found a western-style state in half of Germany.

Collapse and New Beginning

In the early postwar years there was undoubtedly little interest in politics among the population. For them what mattered primarily was sheer survival. Hopelessness and exhaustion, hunger, and concern for their families dominated people's everyday life in the "collapsed society" (Christoph Kleßmann). Many cities lay in ruins. Numerous survivors of the war eked out a bare existence in cellars, huts or corrugated iron shacks. Twelve million refugees or displaced persons came flooding in from the eastern territories, exacerbating the housing shortage. With three thousand railway bridges destroyed, freight traffic, and with it the provision of energy, collapsed.

The state rationing system adopted during the Third Reich, which was retained by the Allies, proved wholly inadequate. Faced with the relative worthlessness of money and ration cards, hungry people reverted to barter on the "black market," and went foraging for food.

In view of the rising number of people dying of starvation and increased infant mortality, General Clay, who was deputy American military governor from 1945-1947 and then governor until 1949, called on his government not to close its eyes to the plight of the Germans. To begin with he gained the ear of church and charitable organizations, along with private citizens, who from 1946 attempted to alleviate the hardship suffered by the population with CARE parcels (Cooperative for American Remittances to Europe).

In the shadow of this situation dominated by the struggle for daily bread, the first stirrings of political life began from the summer of 1945 onwards. In accordance with the resolution of the Potsdam Conference that the national territory of Germany should be decentralized, a whole series of new Länder came into existence in 1945-46, along with some old ones. Depending on the liking of the particular occupying power they either remained politically separate or were joined together.

Parallel to this development, from the summer of 1945 onwards administrative bodies and political parties were created. In the west, in contrast to the Soviet zone, they were at first permitted only at local level, then at Land level after the Länder were established. Along with the Communists and Social Democrats, who had been banned in 1933, new parties also appeared on the scene. In the Christian Democratic Union of Germany (CDU), which as regards both its program and its organization saw itself as a party uniting Christians of all denominations, Konrad Adenauer gradually emerged as the leading figure. His position as party chairman of the CDU in the British zone helped him to fend off the bid for leadership by the Christian Democrats of Berlin.

lich aus den ehemaligen liberalen Parteien der Weimarer Zeit und wuchs zunächst hauptsächlich im Südwesten Deutschlands unter Theodor Heuss und Reinhold Maier zu einer politischen Kraft heran.

Obwohl es 1946/47 in allen Ländern zu Parlamentswahlen gekommen war, blieben die Zuständigkeiten der von den Militärbehörden eingesetzten Regierungen beschränkt. Dies zeigte sich in aller Deutlichkeit auf der Münchner Ministerpräsidentenkonferenz vom 6./7.6.1947, die zum Symbol der deutschen Teilung wurde. Sie war geplant, um Vorschläge an die Militärregierungen zur Linderung der wirtschaftlichen und sozialen Not auszuarbeiten und die Zusammenarbeit der Länder »im Sinne wirtschaftlicher Einheit und künftiger politischer Zusammenfassung« (Hans Ehard) zu stärken.

Doch die Konferenz scheiterte, noch ehe sie begonnen hatte. Als die ostdeutschen Vertreter am Vorabend der Tagung die sofortige Bildung einer deutschen Zentralverwaltung mit dem Ziel eines Einheitsstaates verlangten, mußten die westdeutschen Kollegen passen. Sie besaßen weder die Kompetenz noch die politische Macht, um einer solchen Forderung zuzustimmen. Die sofortige Abreise der ostdeutschen Delegierten wirkte wie ein Fanal der sich vertiefenden Spaltung Deutschlands. Ein Jahr später nahm sie konkrete Gestalt an.

Grundgesetz und Staatsgründung

Anfang Juni 1948 verständigte sich der Westen auf der Londoner Sechsmächtekonferenz darauf, Westdeutschland mit der Schaffung einer demokratischen Verfassung zu beauftragen. Gleichzeitig liefen unter strengster Geheimhaltung die Vorbereitungen für eine Währungsreform. Sie sollte die im Krieg zerrüttete Finanzwirtschaft in den drei Westzonen sanieren und somit die Basis für den vom Marshall-Plan anvisierten Aufbau der Wirtschaft schaffen. Zehn Tage nach der Währungsreform vom 20.6.1948 übergaben die drei westlichen Militärgouverneure den Ministerpräsidenten in zeremonieller Form und frostiger Atmosphäre die in London erarbeiteten »Frankfurter Dokumente«. Darin wurden die Ministerpräsidenten autorisiert, eine Nationalversammlung zur Ausarbeitung einer demokratischen Verfassung für eine föderalistische Regierungsform einzuberufen.

Die brutale Abriegelung Berlins durch Moskau bestärkte die westdeutschen Politiker, das Angebot aufzunehmen, das eine Verbindung zwischen der Vereinigung der Bizone mit der französischen Zone und der Gründung eines westdeutschen Staates vorsah. Um eine Antwort abzustimmen, kamen die Ministerpräsidenten Mitte Juli im Hotel Rittersturz bei Koblenz zusammen. Da sie befürchteten, die Teilstaatsgründung werde die deutsche Spaltung festigen, verlangten sie eine Einschränkung des alliierten Auftrags. So sollte keine Verfassung, sondern lediglich ein provisorisches »Grundgesetz« (Max Brauer) ausgearbeitet werden, und zwar nicht von einer Nationalversammlung, sondern durch einen von den Landtagen zu wählenden »Parlamentarischen Rat«.

Da die Militärgouverneure derartige Änderungen nicht wünschten, trafen sich die Ministerpräsidenten zu erneuten Beratungen auf Schloß Niederwald bei Rüdesheim. Nach einem energischen

In the SPD Kurt Schumacher took on this leading role. He too stood for an emphatically anti-Communist line, thereby setting himself decisively apart from the SPD in the eastern zone, which in April 1946 consented, under immense Soviet pressure, to a merger with the KPD (German Communist Party) to form the SED (Socialist Unity Party). The FDP (Free Democratic Party) was recruited mainly from the former liberal parties of the Weimar era and initially grew mainly in the southwest of Germany under Theodor Heuss and Reinhold Maier to become a political force.

Although parliamentary elections had been held in all the Länder in 1946-47, the powers of the governments installed by the military authorities remained limited. This was made abundantly clear at the conference of minister presidents of the Länder in Munich on June 6-7, 1947, which came to symbolize the division of Germany. The conference was planned in order to work out proposals to be put before the military governments for the alleviation of economic and social hardship and the strengthening of cooperation between the Länder "with an eye to economic unity and future political union" (Hans Ehard).

Ohne Nachtflugverbot: »Rosinenbomber« der USA und Großbritanniens sicherten während der Berlin-Blockade 1948/49 das Überleben der Stadt.

No ban on night flying: during the Berlin blockade of 1948-1949 American and British "candy bombers" ensured the survival of the city.

Plädoyer des Berliner Oberbürgermeisters Ernst Reuter für die Annahme der alliierten Offerte einigten sie sich mit den Militärgouverneuren in einer hochdramatischen Sitzung auf einen Kompromiß. Kurz darauf traf auf der ebenso idyllischen wie abgeschiedenen Herreninsel im Chiemsee ein Verfassungsausschuß zusammen, um Richtlinien für eine »freiheitliche und demokratische Grundordnung« festzulegen. Zur selben Zeit wählten die elf Länderparlamente in aller Eile den Parlamentarischen Rat, der sich am 1.9.1948 im Bonner Museum König konstituierte.

Nach teilweise harten Auseinandersetzungen beendete dieses Gremium seine Arbeit am 8.5.1949 mit der Verabschiedung des Grundgesetzes. Vier Tage später genehmigten es die Militär-

Ende der Berliner Luftbrücke: Mit »Freier Ware aus dem Westen« in den Schaufenstern ging der Einzelhandel auf Kundenfang.

The end of the Berlin airlift: retail traders tried to attract customers with "unrationed western goods" in the store windows.

gouverneure. Mit Ausnahme Bayerns wurde es anschließend von allen Landtagen gebilligt und am 23.5.1949 verkündet. Tags darauf trat es in Kraft und begründete die Bundesrepublik Deutschland als förderalistischen, sozialen Bundesstaat mit freiheitlich-demokratischer Grundordnung. Bald danach setzte der Wahlkampf zum Ersten Bundestag ein, in dessen Mittelpunkt das Ringen um den wirtschaftspolitischen Kurs der Bundesrepublik stand. Als die Stimmen nach dem Urnengang am 14.8.1949 ausgezählt wurden, lag die CDU mit knapper Mehrheit in Führung. In den anschließenden Koalitionsverhandlungen setzte Adenauer die Bildung einer Regierung mit den Liberalen und der niedersächsisch-konservativen Deutschen Partei durch.

Am 7.9.1949 trat das Parlament zu seiner ersten Sitzung zusammen. Fünf Tage später wählte der Bundestag den Vorsitzenden der FDP Theodor Heuss zum Bundespräsidenten, am 15.9.1949 Adenauer mit einer Stimme Mehrheit zum Bundeskanzler und beendete damit den westdeutschen Gründungsakt.

But the conference failed before it had even begun. When, on the eve of the conference, the representatives from eastern Germany demanded that a central German administration be set up immediately with the goal of a unified state, their colleagues from western Germany were unable to respond, as they possessed neither the authority nor the political power to agree to such a demand. The immediate departure of the east German delegates seemed to signal the deepening division of Germany. A year later this took on concrete form.

The Basic Law and Foundation of the Federal Republic

At the London Six-Power Conference at the beginning of June 1948 it was agreed that western Germany would be given the task of draw-ing up a constitution for a parliamentary democracy. At the same time, in the strictest secrecy, preparations for a currency reform were under way. Its purpose was to rehabilitate the financial sector of the economy, which had been severely disrupted by the war, in the three western zones and thereby to lay the basis for the economic reconstruction envisaged by the Marshall Plan. Ten days after the currency reform of June 20, 1948 the three western military governors, ceremonially and in a frosty atmosphere, presented to the minister presidents of the Länder the 'Frankfurt Documents' which had been drawn up in London authorizing them to convene a national assembly to draw up a democratic constitution for a federalist form of government.

Moscow's brutal blockade of Berlin encouraged the politicians in western Germany to take up the offer, which provided for a package deal linking the unification of the bizone and the French zone with the foundation of a West German state. The minister presidents of the Länder met at the Hotel Rittersturz outside Koblenz in mid-July to agree on a reply. Fearing that to set up a state in one half of Germany only would consolidate the division of the country, they asked for the task set by the Allies to be limited to drawing up not a constitution but merely a provisional "Basic Law" (Max Brauer), and for this task to be carried out not by a national assembly but by a "Parliamentary Council" to be elected by the Landtage.

Since the military governors did not want changes of this kind, the minister presidents met for renewed deliberations at Schloß Niederwald outside Rüdesheim. Following a vigorous plea by Ernst Reuter, the Mayor of Berlin, that the Allies' offer should be accepted, they reached a compromise with the military governors in a highly dramatic meeting. Shortly afterwards a constitutional committee met on the "Herreninsel" in the Chiemsee (a venue as idyllic as it was isolated) to lay down guidelines for a "fundamental order based on liberty and democracy." At the same time the parliaments of the eleven Länder, in great haste, elected the Parliamentary Council, which constituted itself on September 1, 1948 in the König Museum in Bonn.

After sometimes acrimonious deliberations this body completed its task on May 8, 1949 with the adoption of the Basic Law. This was approved by the military governors four days later. It was then approved by all the *Landtagen* with the exception of Bavaria and

proclaimed on May 23, 1949. It came into effect on the following day, laying the basis for the Federal Republic as a federalist state based on social responsibility, liberty, and democracy.

Soon after this the election, campaigning for the first federal parliament began, the central issue being the struggle over the direction to be taken as regards the economic policy of the Federal Republic. When the votes were counted after polling on August 14 the CDU led with a narrow majority. In the ensuing coalition negotiations, Adenauer managed to form a government with the Liberals and the conservative Deutsche Partei from Lower Saxony. Parliament met for its first session on September 7. Five days later parliament elected the party chairman of the FDP, Theodor Heuss, as federal president and on September 15 elected Adenauer as federal chancellor by a majority reached by a single vote, thus completing the process of founding the West German state. This was followed at the beginning of October by the second part of the "dual state foundation" (Christoph Kleßmann) which had been in preparation for some months.

A year earlier a German People's Council, created without democratic legitimacy, had put forward a preliminary draft constitution which was adopted in May 1949 as the constitution of the German Democratic Republic. However, the SED delayed the act of proclamation in order to uphold its self-styled image as the champion of German unity. It was not until October 7 that a new People's Council dominated by the SED constituted itself as a Provisional People's Chamber and brought the constitution into force.

With the election of Wilhelm Pieck as president and the confirmation by the People's Chamber on October 12 of the provisional government under Otto Grotewohl as Prime Minister, the establishment of the East German "counter-state" (Andreas Hillgruber) was complete.

Rittersturzkonferenz der westdeutschen Ministerpräsidenten: Die Fahne von Rheinland-Pfalz am Tagungsort im Juli 1948.

The "Rittersturz Conference" of West German Minister Presidents. The Rhineland-Palatinate flag at the conference venue in July 1948.

Anfang Oktober folgte der seit Monaten vorbereitete zweite Teil der »doppelten Staatsgründung« (Christoph Kleßmann). Schon ein Jahr zuvor hatte ein ohne demokratische Legitimation geschaffener Deutscher Volksrat einen Verfassungsvorentwurf vorgelegt, der im Mai 1949 als Verfassung der Deutschen Demokratischen Republik angenommen wurde.

Den Akt der Verkündung zögerte die Sozialistische Einheitspartei Deutschlands jedoch hinaus, um die Selbststilisierung als Vorkämpferin der deutschen Einheit aufrechterhalten zu können. Erst am 7.10.1949 konstituierte sich ein von der SED dominierter neuer Volksrat als Provisorische Volkskammer und setzte die Verfassung in Kraft. Mit der Wahl Wilhelm Piecks zum Präsidenten und der am 12.10.1949 erfolgten Bestätigung der provisorischen Regierung der Deutschen Demokratischen Republik unter Ministerpräsident Otto Grotewohl durch die Volkskammer war die Errichtung des ostdeutschen »Gegenstaats« (Andreas Hillgruber) abgeschlossen.

Ein freigewähltes Parlament als Zuschauermagnet: Die Eröffnungssitzung des Deutschen Bundestages am 7.9.1949.

A freely elected parliament as a magnet for spectators: the opening session of the German Bundestag on September 7, 1949.

70 Millionen Kubikmeter Schutt verstopften die Straßen. Am Brandenburger Tor türmten sich die Trümmer meterhoch.

The streets were clogged with 70 million cubic meters of rubble. At the Brandenburg Gate there were heaps of rubble meters high.

Trümmerlandschaften

Im »Nero-Befehl« hatte Hitler angeordnet, den Alliierten Deutschland als »Wüste« zu hinterlassen. Sein Wille sollte sich auf grausame Weise erfüllen. Mehr als 20% aller Wohngebäude lagen in Asche, 3 Millionen Deutsche waren obdachlos. »Das Dritte Reich bringt sich um; doch die Leiche heißt Deutschland«, schrieb Erich Kästner lakonisch. Besonders stark war Berlin in Mitleidenschaft gezogen. Sechzehn Stunden hatte die Schlacht gedauert, bevor am 30.4.1945 die Rote Fahne über dem Reichstag gehißt wurde. Von den 4,3 Millionen Einwohnern, die die Hauptstadt des Deutschen Reiches 1939 beherbergt hatte, lebten nur noch etwa 2,3 Millionen. Der Verlust an Wohnraum betrug fast 40%. Dem Beobachter präsentierte sich ein infernalisches Bild: Ruinen, Brände, hungrige Menschen in zerfetzten Kleidern.

Ruined Land

With his "Nero's command" Hitler had ordered that Germany was to be left to the Allies as a "wasteland." His wish was to be fulfilled to a horrifying degree. More than 20% of all residential buildings had been burned to the ground, three million Germans were homeless. "The Third Reich is killing itself, but the corpse is called Germany," Erich Kästner noted laconically. Berlin was particularly badly affected. The battle had lasted for sixteen hours before the Red Flag was hoisted over the Reichstag on April 30,1945. Of the 4.3 million inhabitants who had their homes in the capital of the German Reich in 1939, only about 2.3 million were still alive. The loss of housing amounted to almost 40%. The observer was confronted with an infernal sight: burnt-out ruins and hungry people in ragged clothes.

Angesichts geborstener Fluß- und Kanalüberführungen, hier die Louisen-Brücke, konnte der Schutt nur so schleppend beseitigt werden, daß die Aufräumarbeiten auch nach zwei Jahren noch nicht abgeschlossen waren.

With bridges over rivers and canals destroyed – here the Louise bridge – removing the rubble was such a slow job that even after two years the work of clean up work was still not finished.

(oben) Auch Köln wirkte in zahlreichen Stadtteilen wie eine Einöde aus Schutt und Asche. Über die Hälfte der Häuser war völlig, der Rest teilweise demoliert; nur 300 standen unversehrt. Die zerbrochene Hohenzollernbrücke blockierte nicht nur die Rheinschiffahrt, sondern verhinderte auch den Verkehr zwischen den Ufern.

(links) Kaum weniger betroffen waren die Großstädte im Westen Deutschlands. In Frankfurt am Main, hier der Römerberg mit der Paulskirche, waren 47% der öffentlichen Bauten und 33% der Wohngebäude beschädigt.

(above) Many districts of Cologne also were a wilderness of rubble and ashes. Over half the houses had been completely demolished, the remainder partly so; only 300 were left undamaged. The shattered Hohenzollern bridge not only blocked the way for shipping on the Rhine but also prevented traffic from crossing the river.

(left) The large cities in western Germany were scarcely less badly hit. In Frankfurt am Main, whose "Römerberg" with the Church of St. Paul is shown here, 47% of all public buildings and 33% of residential buildings were damaged.

(unten) Zu den schwerwiegendsten Beschlüssen der Potsdamer Konferenz gehörte die »Westverschiebung« Polens. Bis zur endgültigen Festlegung der Westgrenze Polens sollten die deutschen Gebiete östlich der Oder und der Lausitzer Neiße sowie der südliche Teil Ostpreußens unter polnische, der nördliche Part unter sowjetische Verwaltung kommen. Außerdem stimmten Briten und Amerikaner der »ordnungsgemäßen Überführung« der angestammten Bevölkerung nach Deutschland zu. Für viele Deutsche begann damit eine zweite Flucht.

(rechts) Schon im Januar 1945, nach Beginn der sowjetischen Offensive, waren Bauern aus Ostpreußen über das Kurische Haff vor dem russischen Einmarsch geflohen. Sie hofften auf diesem für Mensch und Tier mörderischen Weg, Sicherheit vor der sowjetischen Soldateska im bisher unbesetzten Gebiet zu erreichen.

(below) One of the most momentous decisions of the Potsdam Conference was the "westward shift" of Poland. Pending the final determination of Poland's western border, the German territories to the east of the Oder and the western Neisse were to be placed under Polish administration along with the southern half of East Prussia, whose northern half was to be placed under Soviet administration. Furthermore, the British and the Americans agreed to the "orderly transfer" of the ethnic German population to Germany. Many Germans thereby became refugees for a second time.

(right) Back in January 1945, after the beginning of the Soviet offensive, farmers from East Prussia had fled before the invading Russian army across the "Kurisches Haff," a murderous route for both man and beast, by which they hoped to reach territory that was as yet unoccupied where they would be safe from the rabble of Soviet soldiery.

Bis zur Potsdamer Konferenz hatten etwa 4 Millionen Deutsche ihre Heimat in den Ostgebieten verlassen. Nun wurden 5,5 Millionen vertrieben. In Trecks aus Pferdewagen, mit Traktorkolonnen, Bahntransporten oder zu Fuß zogen über 12 Millionen Menschen aus den polnisch oder sowjetisch besetzten Gebieten, aus der Tschechoslowakei und Ungarn mit ihren letzten Habseligkeiten nach Westen. Nach den Erhebungen der kirchlichen Suchdienste kamen rund 2,11 Millionen bei dieser Völkerwanderung um oder blieben vermißt.

By the time of the Potsdam Conference around four million Germans had left their homelands in the eastern territories. Now 5.5 million were expelled. In trains of horse-drawn wagons, in convoys of tractors, by rail and on foot, over twelve million people from the territories under Polish or Soviet occupation, from Czechoslovakia and Hungary moved westwards with their few remaining belongings. According to statistics compiled by the churches' missing persons tracing services, about 2.11 million people died or went missing during this great migration.

Trümmerfrauen / Rubble Women

1945 bedeckten ca. 400 Millionen Kubikmeter Schutt das ehemalige Reichsgebiet. Wohnungen und Transportwege waren weitgehend zerstört. Zum Wiederaufbau fehlten nicht nur Baumaterialien, sondern auch Maschinen und Arbeitskräfte. Da ein Großteil der Männer gefallen, verschollen oder in Kriegsgefangenschaft geraten war, mußte die Arbeit meist von Frauen geleistet werden, häufig ausgebombt, verwitwet, alleinerziehend. Ob ehedem Damen der Gesellschaft oder Arbeiterfrauen, das spielte jetzt keine Rolle mehr.

Oft war nicht der Stundenlohn von wenigen Pfennigen bei einem Schwarzmarktpreis von 350-550 RM für ein kg Butter der Grund, sondern die Aussicht auf eine bessere Lebensmittel-karte als die für Hausfrauen vorgesehene »Hungerkarte«. Mit Mut und Improvisationsgeschick begannen sie den Wieder-aufbau und wurden so zu Symbolfiguren des Neubeginns.

In 1945 the former Reichterritory was covered with about 400 million cubic meters of rubble. Housing and transport routes were largely destroyed. Not only the building materials for reconstruc-tion were lacking but also the machinery and labor. Because a large proportion of the menfolk had been killed in the war, or were either missing without trace or held as prisoners-of-war, the work had to be done by women, many of whom had been bombed out of their homes or had lost their husbands and were left with children to bring up alone.

Often their motive was not the wage of a few pfennigs per hour, when the price of a kilogram of butter on the black market was 350-550 Reichsmarks, but the prospect of a better ration card than the "starvation card" available to housewives. With courage and skillful improvisation they began the reconstruction and so came to symbolize the new beginning.

Unterbrochen nur von kurzen Ruhepausen, reinigte eine Frau im Durchschnitt 1200 Ziegelsteine pro Tag, stets von Gefahren wie herabstürzenden Mauern oder Blindgängerexplosionen bedroht.

Stopping only for brief rest breaks a woman cleaned on average 1200 bricks a day, in constant danger of walls falling down or unexploded shells going off.

(gegenüber) Allein in Berlin räumten 1946 60 000 Frauen ohne technisches Hilfsgerät oder Schutzkleidung schwerste Hindernisse wie Stahlträger aus dem Weg. Sie folgten entweder dem Aufruf der Besatzer oder beteiligten sich freiwillig an den Aufräumarbeiten.

(opposite) In 1946 in Berlin alone 60,000 women, without either technical equipment or protective clothing, cleared away the heaviest of objects, steel girders for example. Either they obeyed the call of the occupying forces or they joined of their own accord in the work of cleaning up.

Zunächst klopften sie Mörtel und Zement von den noch verarbeitungsfähigen Steinen.

First they removed mortar and cement from the bricks that could still be used.

Danach reinigten sie die Ziegel an Putzmaschinen.

Then they cleaned the bricks using cleaning machines.

Mit bloßen Händen schichteten die »Trümmerfrauen« schließlich die bearbeiteten Steine für den Abtransport auf.

Finally, with their bare hands, the "rubble women" stacked the finished bricks up to be taken away.

Alltag in Trümmern / Everyday Life in Shambles

Für Briefträger wurde die Postzustellung im zerstörten Deutschland zu einer detektivischen Aufgabe. Wenn überhaupt, konnten sie die Empfänger wie hier in der Trümmerlandschaft Berlins nur durch langwieriges Nachforschen ermitteln. Aber häufig mußte die Post mit dem Stempel "Adressat unbekannt verzogen" an den Absender zurückgeschickt werden.

For postmen, delivering letters in a devastated Germany was detective work. They were able to locate addressees, if at all, only by means of lengthy enquiries, as here in the rubble-strewn landscape of Berlin. But mail often had to be returned to the sender stamped "moved, address unknown."

Trümmer und Ruinen, so sah für die meisten Kinder in den Städten der späten vierziger Jahre die Freizeitkulisse aus. Spielplätze gab es nicht. Die Freude dieser barfüßigen Berliner »Rennfahrer« mit ihren selbstgebastelten Seifenkisten (1946) konnte über die Tristesse der Zeit nicht hinwegtäuschen. Nach dem Zweiten Weltkrieg gab es im Westen Deutschlands etwa 1 250 000 Kinder und Jugendliche, die ihre Väter durch den Krieg verloren hatten; 250 000 waren Vollwaisen. Ende 1947 besaßen allein in Berlin 125 000 Kinder kein einziges Paar brauchbarer Schuhe. Hunger, Wohnungsnot und Verwahrlosung führten zu einer steigenden Jugendkriminalität.

Rubble and ruins, this was the backdrop to children's spare time activities in the cities in the late 1940s. There were no playgrounds. The pleasure which these bare-footed Berlin "racing drivers" took in their home-made soapboxes (1946) could not conceal the dreariness of the times. In western Germany after the Second World War there were about 1,250,000 children and young people who had lost their fathers in the war, 250,000 of them were orphans who had lost both parents. At the end of 1947 in Berlin alone 125,000 children did not possess a single pair of serviceable shoes. Hunger, housing shortages and neglect led to an increase in juvenile delinquency.

(links) Selbst der Kleinstunternehmer mit einem Bollerwagen fand sein bescheidenes Auskommen.

(links unten) Ein Volk »auf Achse«. Obwohl es nur noch wenige Züge gab, reisten die Deutschen ausgiebiger als zuvor, nicht zum Vergnügen, sondern zum Überleben. Auf »Hamster«-Touren fuhren die Ausgehungerten in überfüllten Zügen, bisweilen auf Dächern, Trittbrettern und Puffern in tagelangen Expeditionen aufs Land, um Wertgegenstände gegen Nahrungsmittel einzutauschen. Müde, aber glücklich transportierten sie die Errungenschaften ihrer »Kompensationen« in Rucksäcken, Körben oder Koffern vom Bahnhof, hier Spandau-West, nach Hause.

(unten) Transportmittel waren in der Nachkriegszeit Mangelware. Die Deutschen entwickelten viel Phantasie, um mit Holzvergasern, Fiakern oder 1-PS-Eigenbauten die Defizite zu kompensieren.

(left) Even the humblest entrepreneur with a wooden handcart could make a modest living.

(below left) A nation "on the move." Although there were only a few trains, the Germans traveled more extensively than before, not for pleasure but in order to survive. Starving people in overcrowded trains, sometimes riding on the roof, the running boards, and the buffers, went foraging in the countryside for days on end in order to trade valuables for food. Tired but happy they carried the fruits of barter back home from the station (here Spandau-West) in backpacks, baskets or suitcases.

(below) In the postwar period, means of transport were in short supply. The Germans developed great ingenuity in bridging the gap with wood-fired or horse-drawn trucks, or 1 HP homemade vehicles.

Besonders in den Großstädten waren die Nachkriegsjahre von katastrophalen Versorgungsengpässen gekennzeichnet. Trotz der hohen Kriegsverluste stieg die Bevölkerungszahl in den vier Besatzungszonen durch den anhaltenden Strom der Vertriebenen und Flüchtlinge von 60 auf etwa 66 Millionen. Lag der tägliche Kalorienverbrauch im Februar 1945 bei 2100, so fiel er 1946 auf weniger als 1500. Mitunter sackte er auf unter 1000 Kalorien pro Tag. Von den drei kursierenden Währungen, der Reichsmark, dem von den Siegermächten seit August 1946 gedruckten Besatzungsgeld und den Zigaretten, besaß allein der »Glimmstengel« echten Wert, zumindest auf den Schwarzmärkten. Im System klaffte der Bewirtschaftung zwischen Angebot und Nachfrage eine große Lücke. Warteschlangen, hier vor einem Berliner Fischgeschäft 1946, gehörten zum alltäglichen Straßenbild.

In the cities especially, the postwar years were marked by disastrous shortages. Despite heavy losses in the war, the population figures in the four zones of occupation rose from 60 million to around 66 million as a result of the continuous influx of refugees and expellees. In February 1945 the daily calorie intake was 2,100, but by 1946 it fell to less than 1,500.

At times it plummeted to less than 1000 calories per day. Of the three currencies in circulation: the Reichsmark, the occupation currency printed by the occupying powers from August 1946, and cigarettes, only "fags" had any real value, at least on the black market. In the rationing system, in contrast, there was a yawning gap between supply and demand. Lines, here in 1946 outside a Berlin fishmonger's, were part of the everyday scene.

(rechts) Im Kampf gegen den Hunger wurden Grün- und Freiflächen – wie der Tiergarten in Berlin 1946 unweit des Brandenburger Tores – von den Bewohnern in Gemüsebeete umgewandelt. Bäume, die die letzten Kämpfe überstanden hatten, waren im strengen Winter 1945/46 abgeholzt und verfeuert worden. Die Arbeit oblag dabei erneut meist den Frauen, die sich nicht nur um die Erziehung der Kinder, sondern auch um das Überleben der Familie kümmern mußten.

(right) In the struggle against hunger, grassland and other open spaces – such as the Tiergarten Park in Berlin in 1946, not far from the Brandenburg Gate – were turned into vegetable patches by the local people. Trees which had survived the closing battles of the war had been cut down and used as fuel during the harsh winter of 1945/46. Once more the work fell for the most part to the women, who were responsible not only for their children's upbringing but for the family survival.

CARE-Pakete / CARE Parcels

(gegenüber) Um die Ernährungssituation der Jüngsten zu verbessern, wurde seit dem Frühjahr 1947 für 3,5 Millionen Kinder zwischen 6 und 18 Jahren in der amerikanischen und britischen Zone eine »Schulspeisung« durchgeführt, hier in Berlin im April 1949. Für viele bedeutete das fast ausschließlich aus Verpflegungsbeständen der Besatzungstruppen bereitgestellte Essen die einzige warme Mahlzeit am Tag. Bis zur Währungsreform im Juni 1948 mußten die Eltern einen kleinen Unkostenbeitrag beisteuern, danach stellten die Militärregierungen die erforderlichen Mittel zur Verfügung. Vom Mai 1949 an wurde die Schulspeisung auch auf die französische Zone ausgedehnt.

(opposite) In order to improve the nutrition of young people, subsidised school meals were introduced in the American and British zones from spring 1947 for 3.5 million children aged between six and eighteen, as seen here in Berlin in April 1949. For many, this meal, which was provided almost entirely from the food stocks of the occupying forces, was the only hot meal of the day. Until the currency reform of June 1948 parents had to contribute a small amount towards the cost; after the reform the military governments provided the necessary resources. From May 1949 free school meals were extended to the French zone also.

Bis Ende 1946 reichten die aus der Kriegszeit geretteten Vorräte für eine bescheidene Produktion noch aus. Dann zollten die drastisch verringerten Anbauflächen bei steigenden Flüchtlingsströmen ihren Tribut. Für den stellvertretenden amerikanischen Militärgouverneur General Clay wurde die unzureichende Lebensmittelversorgung zu einem zentralen politischen Problem im Kampf mit der Sowjetunion. »Wer als Kommunist 1500 Kalorien bekommt und als Anhänger der Demokratie nur 1000, hat keine Wahl«, lautete sein Motto. Seine Warnungen vor einer Hungerkatastrophe wurden zunächst von kirchlichen und karitativen Organisationen, aber auch Privatleuten erhört. Mit »CARE«-Paketen (»Cooperative for American Remittances to Europe«), die etwa 8,8 Pfund Fleisch, 5,8 Pfund Nährmittel und Kekse, 3,5 Pfund Zucker und Schokolade, 3,2 Pfund Marmelade und Pudding, 2 Pfund Gemüse, 1 Pfund Kakao, Kaffee und Getränkepulver, 350 Gramm Milch, 200 Gramm Butter und 200 Gramm Käse enthielten, suchten sie die Not in den drei westlichen Besatzungszonen zu lindern.

Up to the end of 1946 the stocks which had been salvaged from the war years were still sufficient for a modest level of production. Then, as the influx of refugees increased, the drastic decline in the area under cultivation began to take its toll. For the deputy American military governor General Clay, inadequate food supplies became a central political issue in the struggle with the Soviet Union. "However, there is no choice between becoming a Communist on 1,500 calories and a believer in democracy on 1,000 calories" was his motto. His warnings of famine were heeded by church and charitable organizations, and also by some private individuals. They attempted to alleviate the hardship in the three western zones of occupation by means of CARE parcels ("Cooperative for American Remittances to Europe") each containing about 8.8 lb of meat, 5.8 lb of cereal products and biscuits, 3.5 lb of sugar and chocolate, 3.2 lb of jam and desserts, 2 lb of vegetables, 1 lb of cocoa, coffee, and powdered drinks, 350 grams of milk powder, 200 grams of butter and 200 grams of cheese.

(oben) Die Ahndung der nationalsozialistischen Verbrechen gehörte zu den wichtigsten Zielen der Siegermächte. Am 20.11.1945 begannen vor dem Internationalen Militärtribunal im Justizpalast in Nürnberg, der Stadt der Reichsparteitage, Verhandlungen zur Bestrafung der »Hauptkriegsverbrecher«. Angeklagt wurden 24 führende Personen des Dritten Reiches und sechs »verbrecherische Organisationen«. Das Nürnberger Gericht war ein »Tribunal der Sieger«, aber im Hinblick auf die öffentliche Weltmeinung wohl »eine unerläßliche Maßnahme zur endgültigen Liquidierung des Hitlerschen Krieges« (Theodor Eschenburg). Göring entzog sich seiner Hinrichtung am 15.10.1946 durch Selbstmord (links).

(above) One of the most important aims of the victorious powers was to exact retribution for the crimes of National Socialism. On November 20, 1945, legal proceedings were opened before the international military tribunal in the Palace of Justice in Nuremberg, the city of the Nazi rallies, with the aim of punishing the "major war criminals." 24 leading personalities from the Third Reich and six "criminal organizations" were indicted. The Nuremberg court was a "victors' tribunal," but in view of international public opinion it was probably "an essential measure for the final winding up of Hitler's war" (Theodor Eschenburg). Göring avoided execution on October 15, 1946 by committing suicide (left).

Am 30.9. und 1.10.1946 verkündete das Gericht den Richterspruch: Zum Tode verurteilt wurden Reichsmarschall Hermann Göring, Reichsaußenminister Joachim von Ribbentrop, Generalfeldmarschall Wilhelm Keitel, Leiter des Reichssicherheitshauptamtes Ernst Kaltenbrunner, Reichsminister für die besetzten Gebiete Alfred Rosenberg, Generalbevollmächtigter für den Arbeitseinsatz Fritz Sauckel, Generalgouverneur für Polen Hans Frank, der Herausgeber des antisemitischen Hetzblattes »Der Stürmer« Julius Streicher, Chef des Wehrmachtsführungsstabes Alfred Jodl, Reichskommissar in den Niederlanden Arthur Seyß-Inquart, Reichsinnenminister Wilhelm Frick. Hitlers Stellvertreter Rudolf Heß, Reichswirtschaftsminister Walther Funk und Großadmiral Erich Raeder wurden zu lebenslanger Haft, Reichs-jugendführer Baldur von Schirach und Rüstungsminister Albert Speer zu 20 Jahren, Ex-Außenminister Konstantin Freiherr von Neurath zu 15 Jahren, Großadmiral Karl Dönitz zu 10 Jahren Gefängnis verurteilt. Der ehemalige Reichskanzler Franz von Papen, der Abteilungsleiter im Reichspropa-gandaministerium Hans Fritzsche und Reichsbankpräsident Hjalmar Schacht wurden freigesprochen. In der ersten Reihe von links: Göring, Heß, Ribbentrop, Keitel, Kaltenbrunner, Rosenberg, Frank, Frick, Streicher und Funk; in der hinteren Reihe von links: Raeder, Schirach, Sauckel, Jodl, Papen, Seyß-Inquart, Speer, Neurath, Fritzsche.

The court announced its verdicts on September 30 and October 1, 1946. The death sentence was passed on Reich Marshal Hermann Göring, Reich Foreign Minister Joachim von Ribbentrop, General Field Marshal Wilhelm Keitel, the Head of Reich Security Ernst Kaltenbrunner, Reich Minister for the Occupied Territories Alfred Rosenberg, the Procurator General for Labor Fritz Sauckel, the Governor General of Poland Hans Frank, the editor of the demagogic anti-Semitic paper "Der Stürmer" Julius Streicher, the Chief of Military General Staff Alfred Jodl, Reich Commissar in the Netherlands Arthur Seyß-Inquart and Reich Minister of the Interior Wilhelm Frick. Hitler's Deputy Rudolf Hess, Reich Economics Minister Walther Funk and Admiral Erich Raeder were sentenced to life imprisonment, Reich Youth Leader Baldur von Schirach and Armaments Minister Albert Speer to twenty years. The former Foreign Minister Konstantin Freiherr von Neurath was given fifteen years, Admiral Karl Dönitz ten years. The former Reich Chancellor Franz von Papen, the Departmental Head in the Reich Propaganda Ministry Hans Fritzsche and the President of the Reich Bank Hjalmar Schacht were acquitted. In the front row, from left to right: Göring, Hess, Ribbentrop, Keitel, Kaltenbrunner, Rosenberg, Frank, Frick, Streicher and Funk; in the back row, from left to right: Raeder, Schirach, Sauckel, Jodl, Papen, Seyß-Inquart, Speer, Neurath, Fritzsche.

(links) Während des Krieges hatten die Alliierten entschieden, die Deutschen der politischen Säuberung zu unterwerfen. Die »Entnazifizierung« erfaßte jeden Erwachsenen. Am konsequentesten durchgeführt und am schnellsten abgeschlossen wurde sie in der sowjetischen Zone. Rigoros gingen auch die Amerikaner zunächst vor. Mit beginnendem Kaltem Krieg verschwand ihr Elan. Für die Verfahren waren deutsche Spruchkammern zuständig. Bis zur Gründung der Bundesrepublik wurden in den drei Westzonen 3,6 Millionen Personen von der »Inquisition auf Papier« (Theodor Eschenburg) erfaßt. 1667 galten als hauptschuldig, 23 000 als belastet, 150 000 als minderbelastet, 1 000 000 als Mitläufer und 1 200 000 als entlastet. Die restlichen Verfahren wurden eingestellt. Im Dezember 1946 mußte sich der berühmte Dirigent Wilhelm Furtwängler vor der Entnazifizierungskommission in Berlin verantworten. Sie stufte ihn im Frühjahr 1947 als entlastet ein und ermöglichte ihm damit die umjubelte Rückkehr ans Dirigentenpult der Berliner Philharmoniker.

(left) During the war the Allies had decided to carry out a political purge of the Germans. "Denazification" involved every adult. It was carried out most thoroughly and concluded most speedily in the Soviet Zone. The Americans also tackled the matter energetically to begin with, but their enthusiasm dwindled as the Cold War began. Denazification proceedings were the responsibility of denazification tribunals. In the three western zones during the period up to the foundation of the Federal Republic, 3.6 million people were dealt with by the "inquisition on paper" (Theodor Eschenburg). 1667 of them were classified as major offenders, 23,000 as offenders, 150,000 as lesser offenders, 1,000,000 as followers and 1,200,000 were exonerated. In the remaining cases proceedings were abandoned. In December 1946 the famous conductor Wilhelm Furtwängler was required to give an account of himself before the denazification commission in Berlin. In the spring of 1947 they classified him as exonerated, thereby making it possible for him to return amid jubilation to the rostrum of the Berlin Philharmonic.

(rechts) Trotz schwierigster äußerer Bedingungen führte der in zwölf Jahren geistiger Isolierung aufgestaute Nachholbedarf in den ersten Nachkriegsjahren zu einem regen Kulturleben. Theater, Musik, Film und Dichtung boten vielen Deutschen eine tröstende Zuflucht. Erheblichen Einfluß gewannen die Werke deutscher Emigranten wie Bertolt Brecht oder Thomas Mann. Aber auch ausländische Autoren wie Ernest Hemingway, Arthur Miller oder Jean-Paul Sartre wurden begeistert aufgenommen. Daß der Hohepriester des Existenzialismus bereits im Oktober 1947 mit seiner Lebensgefährtin Simone de Beauvoir zu einem Schriftstellertreffen nach Berlin kam (Mitte und rechts), gab der aufstrebenden neuen deutschen Literatur Reputation und internationales Flair.

(right) In the years immediately after the war, notwithstanding the extremely difficult material conditions, the need to catch up after twelve years of intellectual isolation produced a vigorous cultural life. Theater, music, films, and literature offered many Germans a consoling refuge. The works of German émigré writers such as Bertolt Brecht and Thomas Mann came to have considerable influence. But authors from abroad such as Ernest Hemingway, Arthur Miller and Jean-Paul Sartre were also welcomed enthusiastically. The fact that the high priest of existentialism and his companion Simone de Beauvoir (center and right) came to a meeting of writers in Berlin as early as October 1947 lent prestige and a cosmopolitan aura to the aspiring new German literature.

Zentrale Persönlichkeit der neuentstehenden Christlich-Demokratischen Union Deutschlands (CDU) wurde Konrad Adenauer. Ab 1917 Oberbürgermeister von Köln, nach 1918 Mitglied des Preußischen Herrenhauses, seit 1920 Präsident im Preußischen Staatsrat, hatten die Nationalsozialisten den Zentrumspolitiker 1933 von allen Funktionen entbunden. Anfang Mai 1945 setzten die Amerikaner ihn wieder in sein Amt als Oberbürgermeister ein. Doch schon wenige Monate darauf, am 6.10.1945, wurde Adenauer vom britischen Militärgouverneur für das Rheinland, Brigadier John Barraclough, wegen »Unfähigkeit und mangelnder Pflichterfüllung« fristlos entlassen und der Stadt verwiesen. Sein Traum, noch einmal politische Bedeutung zu gewinnen, schien zerplatzt. Später äußerte sich Adenauer sogar froh über die Absetzung, weil er ihr die Ernennung zum Bundeskanzler verdankte. Von links: Adenauer, der Oberpräsident der Rheinprovinz Hans Fuchs und Barraclough.

In the newly created Christian Democratic Union (CDU) Konrad Adenauer emerged as the central personality. As a politician of the Center Party he had been Mayor of Cologne from 1917, a member of the Prussian Upper House from 1918 and President in the Prussian Council of State from 1920. But in 1933 the National Socialists had removed him from all these offices. At the beginning of May 1945 the Americans reinstated him as mayor. But only a few months later, on October 6, 1945 Adenauer was dismissed without notice and ordered to leave the city by the British military governor of the Rhineland, Brigadier John Barraclough, on grounds of "incompetence and dereliction of duty." His dream of regaining his former political importance seemed shattered. Later Adenauer said that he was glad he had been dismissed because it was to that that he owed the office of Federal Chancellor. From the left: Adenauer, the President of the Rhine Province Hans Fuchs, and Barraclough.

Einer der stärksten Kontrahenten Adenauers auf seiten der Christdemokraten war zunächst der Vorsitzende der CDU in der sowjetischen Besatzungszone, Jakob Kaiser, hier auf einer Kundgebung vor dem Schöneberger Rathaus in Berlin im April 1946. Geprägt von der katholischen Soziallehre, forderte er einen »christlichen Sozialismus«, ein gesellschaftspolitisches System zwischen Sozialismus und Kapitalismus. Deutschlandpolitisch wies er seinem Vaterland die Funktion einer »Brücke zwischen Ost und West« zu. Nachdem er im Dezember 1947 von den sowjetischen Besatzungsbehörden abgesetzt worden war, war diesen Konzepten der Boden entzogen.

At first one of Adenauer's strongest rivals within the Christian Democrats was Jakob Kaiser, CDU party chairman in the Soviet zone of occupation, seen here at a rally outside the Schöneberg town hall in Berlin in April 1946. Kaiser, whose thinking had been stamped by Catholic social doctrines, called for a "christian socialism," a socio-political system between socialism and capitalism. As to the political position of Germany he saw the role of his fatherland as that of a "bridge between east and west." After he was removed from his post by the Soviet occupation authorities in December 1947, there was no longer any support for these concepts.

Die Machthaber in der sowjetischen Besatzungszone begnügten sich nicht damit, unliebsame Politiker abzusetzen. Ihnen ging es darum, die neu- oder wiedergegründeten Parteien zu beherrschen. Bei der Vergabe der Parteilizenzen verlangte die Sowjetische Militäradministration in Deutschland (SMAD) im Sommer 1945 daher die verbindliche Anerkennung des »Blocks antifaschistisch-demokratischer Parteien«. Am 21./22.4.1946 erzwang sie die Verschmelzung der Kommunistischen Partei Deutschlands (KPD) und der Sozialdemokratischen Partei Deutschlands (SPD) zur Sozialistischen Einheitspartei Deutschlands (SED). Der symbolische Händedruck zwischen den Parteiführern Wilhelm Pieck (KPD, links) und Otto Grotewohl in der Staatsoper in Berlin besiegelte nicht nur das Schicksal der SPD in Ostdeutschland. Sie blockierte auch den Aufbau eines pluralistischen Parteiensystems. Während die Männer der zweiten Reihe jubeln, beobachtete der starke Mann der KPD und spätere Staats- und Parteichef, Walter Ulbricht, die Szene mit vielsagendem Blick.

The rulers in the Soviet zone of occupation were not content with removing troublesome politicians from their posts. Their aim was to control the newly founded or re-founded parties. In summer 1945 therefore, when issuing party licenses the Soviet Military Administration in Germany (SMAD) demanded the binding recognition of the "block of antifascist-democratic parties." On April 21/22, 1946 it compelled the SPD to merge with the German Communist Party (KPD) to form the Socialist Unity Party (SED). The symbolic handshake between party leaders Wilhelm Pieck (KPD, on the left) and Otto Grotewohl in the Berlin State Opera house not only set the seal on the fate of the SPD in East Germany. It also prevented the creation of a pluralistic party system. While the men in the second row applaud, the KPD strongman and later head of state and party, Walter Ulbricht, looks on with a meaningful expression.

(rechts) Nach vollbrachter Tat hielt Ulbricht die neue Flagge der SED stolz in die Höhe.

(right) After the deed was done Ulbricht proudly held up the new SED flag.

(links) Der Widerstand der Demokraten gegen die sowjetisch gesteuerte Machtübernahme der SED in Berlin erlebte bei den Wahlen zur Stadtverordnetenkammer am 20.10.1946 einen großen Erfolg. Die SPD erzielte mit 48,7% der Stimmen einen grandiosen Sieg, die CDU zog mit 22,2% als zweitstärkste Fraktion ins Stadtparlament, die Liberaldemokratische Partei Deutschlands (LDP) verbuchte 9,3%. Die SED erlitt mit 19,8% der Stimmen eine schwere Niederlage. Ein zweites Mal wollte sie eine solche Blamage nicht erleben. Die ersten freien Wahlen in Großberlin sollten für Jahrzehnte auch die letzten sein.

(left) The democrats' resistance to the Soviet-led takeover of power by the SED in Berlin reaped a substantial success in the elections to the city parliament on October 20, 1946. The SPD won a splendid victory with 48.7% of the vote, the CDU, with 22.2%, entered the city parliament as the second strongest group, the Liberal Democratic Party (LDP) polled 9.3%. The SED, with 19.8% of the vote, suffered a heavy defeat. They determined not to be made such fools of a second time. The first free elections in Greater Berlin were also to be the last for decades.

In strikter Opposition zur Zwangsvereinigung verhielt sich die SPD in Westdeutschland mit ihrem Vorsitzenden Kurt Schumacher. Von Hannover aus, wo sich die Partei unter seiner Führung im Mai 1945 konstituiert hatte, kämpfte er für eine parlamentarische Demokratie auf der Grundlage einer sozialistischen Wirtschaftsordnung. Er betonte die nationale Einheit und folgte einer verstärkt antikommunistischen Linie, die sich auch gegen den Führungsanspruch der ostzonalen SPD richtete. Nach seiner Wahl zum Parteichef im Mai 1946 versuchte er in leidenschaftlichen Reden, wie hier am 20.6.1946 im Berliner Poststadion, seinen Anhängern seine politischen Überzeugungen nahezubringen und die Gefahren der kommunistischen Unterwanderung vor Augen zu führen: »Auf, Sozialisten schließt die Reihen«.

The SPD in West Germany with its party chairman Kurt Schumacher were diametrically opposed to the forced merger. From Hanover, where the party had constituted itself under his leadership in May 1945, Schumacher campaigned for a parliamentary democracy on the basis of a socialist economic order. He emphasised national unity and took a rigorous anti-Communist line, thus rejecting any claim to leadership by the SPD in the eastern zone. After his election as party leader in May 1946 he attempted, in passionate speeches, here on June 20, 1946 at the Post Stadium in Berlin, to impress his own political convictions on his supporters and to open their eyes to the dangers of communist infiltration: the banner reads: "Arise Socialists and close ranks!"

(oben) Mit seiner Rede vom 5.6.1947 stellte der amerikanische Außenminister Marshall den europäischen Staaten ein Hilfsprogramm zur Stabilisierung der wirtschaftlichen Lage in Aussicht. Durch Kredite sollten die westeuropäischen Volkswirtschaften zu eigener Güterproduktion befähigt werden. Dabei war die Vergabe der Gelder an eine Bedingung geknüpft: die Zusammenarbeit der Empfänger. Zur Abwicklung des »European Recovery Program« (ERP) gründeten sechzehn Staaten am 16.4.1948 die »Organization of European Economic Cooperation«. Allein nach Westdeutschland flossen bis zum Ende der Marshallplan-Hilfe im Jahre 1952 1,5 Milliarden Dollar, unter anderem auch in den Bau von Wohnungen für die Flüchtlingshilfe wie hier in Neumünster.

(above) In his speech on June 5, 1947 American Secretary of State Marshall held out to the states of Europe the prospect of an aid program to stabilize economic conditions. Credits were to enable the economies of western Europe to produce goods for themselves. A condition was attached to this provision of funds: that the recipients should cooperate with one another. In order to implement the "European Recovery Program" (ERP) sixteen states founded the "Organization for European Economic Cooperation" on April 16, 1948. By the time the Marshall Aid Plan came to an end in 1952, West Germany alone had received 1,5 billion dollars for, among other things, the construction of housing for refugees, as here in Neumünster.

(rechts) Eine Sonderhilfe aus ERP-Geldern wurde Berlin zuteil, um das Notprogramm an der Spree zu unterstützen.

(right) Special assistance was given to Berlin from ERP funds to support the emergency program in the city on the Spree.

Eine entscheidende Voraussetzung der vom Marshall-Plan anvisierten Sanierung der deutschen Wirtschaft war die Neuordnung der Währung. Ab November 1947 wurde das in den USA gedruckte neue Geld nach Deutschland transportiert und Mitte Juni 1948 unter größter Geheimhaltung von Frankfurt am Main zu den elf Landeszentralbanken der drei Westzonen gebracht. Gerüchte über den streng geheimen Tag »X« der Währungsreform führten zu einer großen Verunsicherung in der Bevölkerung. Wie hier in Berlin bildeten sich im Juni überall vor Sparkassen und Banken Schlangen besorgter Kunden.

A crucial prerequisite for putting the German economy back on its feet as envisaged in the Marshall Plan was a reform of the currency. The new money, which had been printed in the USA, was transported to Germany starting in November 1947 and was taken in mid-June 1948, under conditions of maximum secrecy, from Frankfurt am Main to the central banks of the eleven Länder of the three western zones. Rumors concerning the exact date of the currency reform, which was kept strictly secret, created great insecurity among the populace. In June lines of worried customers formed everywhere outside banks and savings banks, as here in Berlin.

Die Schaufenster der Einzelhandelsgeschäfte waren – hier in Berlin – prall mit Waren gefüllt, die man seit Kriegsbeginn nicht mehr gesehen hatte. Das System der Mangelverwaltung mit »Bezugsscheinen«, »Bergmanns-Punkten« und »Bezugsmarken« wurde zugunsten des »Frei-Verkaufs« abgeschafft, der Schwarzmarkt brach zusammen. Nur die Lebensmittelrationierung konnte erst im Frühjahr 1950 aufgehoben werden.

Retail shop windows – here in Berlin – were bursting with goods which had not been seen since the beginning of the war. The shortage management system of ration cards, "miner's points," and coupons was abolished and replaced by the free sale of goods. Only food rationing had to be retained until spring 1950.

Währungsreform / Currency Reform

Die Währungsreform vom 20.6.1948 zielte auf eine drastische Verminderung des Geldumlaufs. Private Verbindlichkeiten und alle Bank- und Sparguthaben wurden im Verhältnis 10:1 abgewertet. Als »Kopfgeld« erhielt jeder Einwohner der Westzonen vierzig D-Mark sofort und zwanzig D-Mark im August zum Kurs 1:1 ausgezahlt. Parallel dazu trat ein Gesetz über Leitsätze für die Bewirtschaftung und Preispolitik in Kraft, das Ludwig Erhard, der Direktor der Verwaltung für Wirtschaft im Vereinigten Wirtschaftsgebiet, ausgearbeitet hatte. Es leitete eine Liberalisierung des Marktes in Richtung der »Sozialen Marktwirtschaft« und das Ende der Preisbindungen ein. Da viele Händler ihre Produkte schon seit Tagen gehortet hatten, änderte sich mit der Einführung der neuen Preise auch schlagartig die Versorgungslage.

The aim of the currency reform of June 20, 1948 was a drastic reduction of the amount of money in circulation. Private liabilities and all bank and savings bank balances were devalued at a ratio of 10:1. Every inhabitant in the western zones received a gratuity of 40 Deutschmarks immediately and 20 Deutschmarks in August, paid out at a rate of 1:1. Parallel to this a law came into effect setting out basic principles for rationing and price policies drawn up by Ludwig Erhard, the director of economic administration in the United Economic Area. It inaugurated a liberalization of the market in the direction of the "social market economy" and the end of price controls. As many traders had been hoarding their wares for days beforehand the introduction of the new prices was accompanied by a sudden increase in supplies.

Berliner Luftbrücke

Drei Tage nach der Währungsreform in den drei westlichen Zonen zogen die Machthaber in der SBZ mit einer eigenen Geldumtauschaktion nach. Mangels neuer Banknoten mußten die alten Reichsmark-Scheine mit Coupons überklebt werden (»Tapetengeld«). Gleichzeitig verfügte die SMAD eine totale Blockade aller Land- und Wasserwege zu den Westsektoren Berlins, um die Umsetzung der Währungsreform im Westteil der Stadt zu verhindern. Damit brach die Versorgung mit Strom, Kohle und Lebensmitteln aus der Sowjetzone und dem Ostsektor zusammen. Für den amerikanischen Militärgouverneur General Clay wurde die Berlinblockade zum Wendepunkt seiner Deutschlandpolitik. Er entwickelte sich zur treibenden Kraft der sofort eingerichteten Luftbrücke, weil er davon ausging: »Wenn Berlin fällt, wird Westdeutschland fallen.« Nach einem generalstabsmäßig ausgearbeiteten Plan flogen die britische Royal Air Force und die amerikanischen Luftstreitkräfte ab dem 24.6.1948 von neun Flugplätzen nach Berlin. Sie begannen mit kleineren zweimotorigen Maschinen vom Typ Douglas C-47 und ersetzten sie bald durch größere C-54, die hier auf dem Rhein-Main-Flughafen in Frankfurt auf die Starterlaubnis warteten.

The Berlin Airlift

Three days after the currency reform in the three western zones, the rulers in the Soviet zone followed suit with a currency exchange operation of their own. In the absence of new bank notes the old Reichsmark notes were pasted over with coupons ("wallpaper money"). At the same time the SMAD ordered a total blockade of all land and water routes leading to the western sectors of Berlin, in order to prevent the currency reform from being implemented in the western part of the city. As a result the supply of electricity, coal, and food from the Soviet zone and the eastern sector collapsed. For the American military governor General Clay the Berlin blockade was a turning point in his policy towards Germany. He emerged as the driving force behind the airlift which was started immediately, because he proceeded from the assumption that "if Berlin falls, West Germany will fall." From June 24, 1948, following a plan worked out at general staff level, the British Royal Air Force and the American Air Force flew to Berlin from nine airports. They began with small twin-engine planes of the type Douglas C-47, but soon replaced them with larger C-54 planes, here waiting for clearance for takeoff at the Rhine-Main airport in Frankfurt.

Im Drei-Minuten-Takt transportierten die »Rosinenbomber«, wie der Berliner Volksmund die Flugzeuge nannte, etwa 10 Tonnen Lebensmittel, Kohle und Industriegüter. Auf dem Flugplatz Tegel, der innerhalb weniger Monate neu gebaut worden war, weil die bestehenden Landebahnen in Tempelhof und Gatow nicht ausreichten, verfolgten die Berliner Kinder die Landung der Versorgungsflugzeuge staunend und dankbar.

At three-minute intervals the »candy bombers,« as the planes were popularly known in Berlin, flew in around 10 tons of food, coal, and industrial commodities. At Tegel airport, which had been rebuilt in the space of a few months because the existing runways in Tempelhof and Gatow were inadequate, the children of Berlin, in amazement and gratitude, watched the supply planes landing.

(unten) Berlin ging aus der Blockade geteilt hervor. Der Berliner Magistrat war im Herbst 1948 durch einen kommunistischen Putsch vertrieben worden und fand ein neues Domizil im Westberliner Schöneberger Rathaus. Im Ostteil installierte die Besatzungsmacht einen eigenen Magistrat unter Friedrich Ebert. Die zweisprachigen Straßennamen, hier in der Nähe des Berliner Domes, ließen keinen Zweifel über die Machtverhältnisse in Ostberlin zu.

(below) Berlin itself emerged from the blockade a divided city. The freely elected municipal authority of Berlin had been driven out of its offices in the autumn of 1948 in a communist coup; it found a new domicile in the city hall of Schöneberg in West Berlin. In the eastern part the occupying power installed its own authority under Friedrich Ebert. The bilingual street names, here in the vicinity of the Berlin cathedral, left no doubt as to who held power in East Berlin.

(oben) Anführer und Seele des Widerstandes der Berliner gegen die Blockade wurde Ernst Reuter (SPD). Er war im Juni 1947 zum Oberbürgermeister von Berlin gewählt worden, doch die SMAD behinderte ihn an der Amtsausübung. Nachdem die Fraktionen der demokratischen Parteien in der Stadtverordnetenversammlung im Neuen Berliner Stadthaus in Ostberlin Anfang September 1948 gezwungen worden waren, fortan im Westteil der Stadt zusammenzutreten, rief Reuter am 9.9.1948 bei einer Ansprache vor der Ruine des Reichstags vor 300 000 Zuschauern die Welt beschwörend dazu auf, Berlin nicht preiszugeben: »Ihr Völker der Welt [...] Schaut auf diese Stadt [...] Völker der Welt, schaut auf Berlin!«

(above) The man who became the leader and the soul of the Berliners' resistance to the blockade was Ernst Reuter (SPD). He had been elected mayor in June 1947, but the SMAD made it difficult for him to carry out the functions of his office. After the democratic party groups in the city parliament in the New Berlin City Hall in East Berlin had been forced, at the beginning of September 1948, to assemble from that point on in the western part of the city, Reuter, addressing a crowd of 300,000 against the backdrop of the ruined Reichstag on September 9, 1948, implored the world not to abandon Berlin: "You nations of the world [...] look at this city [...], peoples of the world, look at Berlin!"

Am 4.5.1949 erzielten Unterhändler der USA und der Sowjetunion eine Vereinbarung über die Beendigung der Blockade. Seit dem 12.5. war Berlin wieder über den Landweg erreichbar. Jubelnd schickten die Berliner die ersten Interzonenbusse über die Autobahn nach Hannover ins Bundesgebiet.

On May 4, 1949 negotiators from the USA and the Soviet Union reached an agreement to end the blockade. From May 12 Berlin was once more accessible by land. The jubilant Berliners despatched the first inter-zone buses to the Federal Republic via the autobahn to Hanover.

Nicht weniger stolz feierten die Piloten das Ende der Blockade und den Sieg der Luftbrücke, hier auf dem Rhein-Main-Flughafen in Frankfurt. Mit 212 000 Flügen hatten sie 1,74 Millionen Tonnen Fracht befördert und damit das Überleben der 2,2 Millionen Westberliner in Freiheit gesichert. Die Kosten der »Operation Vittles« (Vittles für victuals, Lebensmittel) betrugen ca. 200 Millionen Dollar. Der Preis war hoch: 31 Amerikaner, 39 Engländer und acht Deutsche verloren bei dem Unternehmen ihr Leben.

The pilots celebrated the end of the blockade and the victory for the airlift no less proudly – here at the Rhine-Main airport in Frankfurt. In 212,000 flights they had transported 1.74 million tons of freight, thereby ensuring the survival in freedom of the 2.2 million inhabitants of West Berlin. "Operation Vittles" had cost around 200 million dollars. There was another high price to pay: 31 Americans, 39 Englishmen and eight Germans lost their lives during the operation.

(rechts) »Siehe, sie zogen zum Rheine, um dort den Ölzweig zu ringen«, dichtete Carlo Schmid mit Blick auf den Parlamentarischen Rat. Als Tagungsort hatten sich die Ministerpräsidenten Mitte August für Bonn entschieden. Sie kamen damit dem Wunsch der Politiker in der britischen Zone entgegen, Konferenzen über das Schicksal des entstehenden deutschen Staates nicht nur in der amerikanischen oder französischen Zone abzuhalten. Trotz enormer Anstrengungen konnte die »kleine Stadt am Rhein« den benötigten Raumbedarf in der kurzen Vorbereitungszeit nur teilweise decken. Wie die Hinweisschilder im Siebengebirge verdeutlichten, mußten die Parteien für ihre internen Beratungen auch in die Umgebung ausweichen.

(right) "Behold, they went to the Rhine, there to fashion the olive branch" wrote Carlo Schmid with the Parliamentary Council in mind. In mid-August, the minister presidents had decided on Bonn as the venue for their meetings. They thereby complied with the wish expressed by the politicians in the British zone that conferences concerning the fate of the emerging German state should not be held only in the American or French zone. Despite enormous efforts the "little town on the Rhine" was able to provide only part of the required accommodation at such short notice. For their internal deliberations the political parties were obliged, as can be seen from the signposts in the Siebengebirge, to find alternative venues in the surrounding area.

(gegenüber) Nach dem Scheitern der Moskauer Außenministerkonferenz einigten sich Amerikaner und Briten Ende Mai 1947 darauf, die Organe des Vereinigten Wirtschaftsgebietes (Bizone) in Frankfurt am Main organisatorisch zusammenzulegen. Als Lenkungsorgan der für Wirtschaft, Ernährung und Landwirtschaft, Finanzen, Post- und Fernmeldewesen und Verkehr bestehenden fünf »Verwaltungen« wurde ein Exekutivrat aus Vertretern der Länder eingerichtet. Daneben fungierte mit dem Wirtschaftsrat ein Parlament, das aus Delegierten der Landtage bestand. Im Februar/März 1948 erfolgte eine Umorganisation der Exekutivorgane. An der Spitze standen nunmehr ein Rat der Verwaltungschefs und ein Länderrat. Um den administrativen Charakter der Ressorts zu betonen, hießen die vom Wirtschaftsrat gewählten Leiter nicht Minister, sondern Direktoren und ihr Vorsitzender nicht Kanzler, sondern Oberdirektor. Von links: der Oberdirektor des Verwaltungsrates des Vereinigten Wirtschaftsgebietes, Hermann Pünder, sowie die Direktoren der Verwaltung für Wirtschaft, für Verkehr und für Finanzen, Ludwig Erhard, Edmund Frohne und Alfred Hartmann, im Jahre 1948.

(opposite) After the failure of the Moscow Conference of Foreign Ministers, the Americans and the British agreed, at the end of May 1947, to amalgamate the administrative bodies of the United Economic Area (the bizone) at the organizational level in Frankfurt am Main. An Executive Council consisting of representatives of the Länder was set up to act as a steering body for the five existing "administrations" responsible for the economy, food supplies and agriculture, finance, post and telecommunications, and transport. In addition there was the Economic Council which acted as a parliament, made up of delegates from the Landtage. In February/March 1948 the executive bodies were reorganized. At the top of the list were now a council of administrative heads and a Länder council. In order to emphasize the administrative nature of the departments, the heads, who were elected by the Economic Council, were not called Ministers but Directors and their chairman was not a Chancellor but a Director-in-Chief. From left to right: the Director-in-Chief of the Administrative Council of the United Economic Area, Hermann Pünder, with the Administrative Directors for the Economy, Transport, and Finance, Ludwig Erhard, Edmund Frohne, and Alfred Hartmann respectively, in 1948.

Am 1.7.1948 erhielten die westdeutschen Ministerpräsidenten im amerikanischen Hauptquartier, dem ehemaligen Verwaltungsgebäude des früheren Chemiekonzerns IG Farben in Frankfurt, aus den Händen der Militärgouverneure der drei Westzonen den Auftrag, eine verfassunggebende Nationalversammlung zwecks Ausarbeitung einer demokratischen Verfassung zu bilden. Im Dunst der Zigarren erkennt man schemenhaft von links die Regierungschefs von Nordrhein-Westfalen, Schleswig-Holstein und Niedersachsen, Karl Arnold, Hermann Lüdemann und Hinrich Kopf.

On July 1, 1948, at the American headquarters, the one-time administrative building of the former chemicals concern IG Farben in Frankfurt, the West German minister presidents were handed, by the military governors of the three western zones, documents instructing them to create a constituent national assembly for the purpose of drawing up a democratic constitution. In the haze of cigar smoke one can dimly make out, from left to right, the heads of government of North Rhine-Westphalia, Schleswig-Holstein and Lower Saxony, Karl Arnold, Hermann Lüdemann and Hinrich Kopf respectively.

(rechts) Im Parlamentarischen Rat wirkten auch vier Frauen: Friederike Nadig und Elisabeth Selbert, SPD-Abgeordnete aus Nordrhein-Westfalen bzw. Niedersachsen, Helene Weber, CDU-Delegierte aus Nordrhein-Westfalen, und Helene Wessel, Zentrumsparlamentarierin und erste Frau, die in Deutschland als Parteivorsitzende amtierte (von links). Die »Mütter« des Grundgesetzes beteiligten sich vor allem, aber keineswegs ausschließlich an den Beratungen zur Familienpolitik, wobei sie etwa in der Frage der Gleichbehandlung von ehelichen und unehelichen Kindern mitunter höchst kontroverse Positionen vertraten.

(right) The Parliamentary Council had four women members: (from left) Friederike Nadig and Elisabeth Selbert, SPD delegates from North Rhine-Westphalia and Lower Saxony respectively, Helene Weber, a CDU delegate from North Rhine-Westphalia, and Helene Wessel, a Center Party parliamentarian and the first woman in Germany to hold the office of party chairman. The "mothers" of the Basic Law were involved especially, but by no means exclusively, in deliberations concerning family policy, putting forward highly controversial views in some cases, for example in the matter of equal treatment for legitimate and illegitimate children.

Parlamentarischer Rat / Parliamentary Council

(gegenüber) Nach der Konstituierung im Museum König trat der Parlamentarische Rat am 1.9.1948 zur ersten Plenarsitzung in der Aula der Pädagogischen Akademie zusammen. Er bestand aus 65 von den elf Länderparlamenten gewählten Mitgliedern, je 27 von der CDU/CSU und der SPD, 5 von der FDP, je 2 von der DP, dem Zentrum und der KPD. Zu den ersten Aufgaben gehörte die Wahl der Vizepräsidenten Adolf Schönfelder (SPD) und Hermann Schäfer (FDP), bei der die Vertreter der KPD Max Reimann (1. Reihe links) und Hugo Paul (2. Reihe links) demonstrativ ihre Zustimmung verweigerten.

(opposite) After constituting itself in the König Museum the Parliamentary Council met for its first plenary session on September 1, 1948 in the auditorium of the Academy of Education. It was made up of 65 members elected by the eleven Land parliaments: 27 each from the CDU/CSU and the SPD, 5 from the FDP and two each from the DP, the Center Party, and the KPD. One of its first tasks was to elect the Vice-Presidents Adolf Schönfelder (SPD) and Hermann Schäfer (FDP), with the KPD delegates Max Reimann (front row, left) and Hugo Paul (second row, left) demonstratively withholding their agreement.

Zu den stärksten Persönlichkeiten des Parlamentarischen Rates gehörten der Vorsitzende der CDU in der britischen Zone, Konrad Adenauer (rechts), und Carlo Schmid (Mitte), der Justizminister von Württemberg-Hohenzollern, hier im September 1949 im Gespräch mit Kurt Schumacher, dem Vorsitzenden der SPD in den Westzonen. Da Schumacher krankheitsbedingt auf seine Mitwirkung verzichtet hatte, ebnete er Adenauer den Weg zum Präsidentenstuhl des Rates. Schmid, der als Fraktionsvorsitzender der SPD die Leitung im Hauptausschuß übernahm, bezeichnete diese Entscheidung später als »einen der verhängnisvollsten Fehler der SPD nach dem Krieg«, weil sie die Kanzlerschaft Adenauers vorprogrammiert habe. »Kurt und Konrad, diese beiden«, reimte Theodor Heuss unter Anspielung auf das Verhältnis zwischen Adenauer und Schumacher, »keiner konnte keinen leiden«. Und auch Schmid stand dem CDU-Vorsitzenden in diesen Monaten mit »Mißtrauen und Vorurteilen« gegenüber (Petra Weber).

Among the strongest personalities in the Parliamentary Council were the party chairman of the CDU in the British zone, Konrad Adenauer (right), and Carlo Schmid (center), the Minister of Justice of Württemberg-Hohenzollern, here in September 1949 in conversation with Kurt Schumacher, the party chairman of the SPD in the western zones. By declining to take part because of ill-health, Schumacher smoothed the way for Adenauer to become president of the Council. Schmid, who as leader of the SPD group chaired the main committee, later described this decision as "one of the SPD's most disastrous mistakes after the war," because it set the scene for Adenauer to become federal chancellor. "Kurt und Konrad, diese beiden, keiner konnte keinen leiden" – a bit of doggerel by Theodor Heuss alluding to the fact that Adenauer and Schumacher did not think a lot of each other. During these months Schmid also viewed the CDU party chairman with "mistrust and prejudice" (Petra Weber).

Mit 53 gegen 12 Stimmen (von der CSU, dem Zentrum, der DP und der KPD) stimmte das Plenum des Parlamentarischen Rates dem Grundgesetz am 8.5.1949 zu. Nachdem es von den Volksvertretungen der westdeutschen Länder mit Ausnahme Bayerns gebilligt worden war, durfte es Adenauer am 23.5.1949 in öffentlicher Sitzung verkünden. Neben ihm stehen Helene Weber (CDU), Hermann Schäfer, stellvertretender Vorsitzender des Landesverbandes der FDP von Hamburg, Adolf Schönfelder, ein erfahrener und respektierter Sozialdemokrat aus Hamburg, und Jean Stock, der Fraktionsvorsitzende der SPD im bayerischen Landtag (von links).

On May 8, 1949 the Parliamentary Council in plenary session passed the Basic Law by 53 votes to the 12 votes cast by the CSU, the Center Party, the DP, and the KPD. After it had been approved by the parliaments of the West German Länder with the exception of Bavaria, Adenauer was able to proclaim it at a public session on May 23, 1949. Standing beside him are (from left) Helene Weber (CDU); Hermann Schäfer, deputy chairman of the Hamburg FDP regional association; Adolf Schönfelder, an experienced and respected social democrat from Hamburg; and Jean Stock, the leader of the SPD group in the Bavarian Landtag.

Am 23.5.1949 wurde das Grundgesetz von den Abgeordneten, den Ministerpräsidenten und Präsidenten der elf Landtage in Anwesenheit der Vertreter der Militärregierungen und Abordnungen des Wirtschaftsrates der Bizone unterzeichnet. Die Bundesrepublik Deutschland gab sich mit ihm »für eine Übergangszeit eine neue Ordnung« und verpflichtete die Deutschen dazu, »in freier Selbstbestimmung die Einheit und Freiheit Deutschlands zu vollenden«. Nur die beiden Kommunisten Max Reimann und Heinz Renner verweigerten die Unterschrift. Das Bild zeigt den Parlamentarischen Rat vor der Zeremonie mit dem Grundgesetz auf dem Tisch nebst Stander in den Farben Schwarz-Rot-Gold. In der ersten Reihe saßen der Vorsitzende der FDP Theodor Heuss und links neben ihm der Berliner SPD-Abgeordnete Paul Löbe.

On May 23, 1949 the Basic Law was signed by the delegates, the minister presidents and presidents of the eleven Landtage in the presence of the representatives of the military governments and delegates from the Economic Council of the bizone. With the Basic Law the Federal Republic gave itself "a new order for a transitional period," committing the Germans "to accomplish the unity and liberty of Germany in free self-determination." Only the two communists Max Reimann and Heinz Renner refused to sign. The picture shows the Parliamentary Council before the ceremony, with the Basic Law on the table and a flag in the colors black, red, and gold. Sitting in the first row were the chairman of the FDP Theodor Heuss and next to him on the left Paul Löbe, the SPD delegate from Berlin.

1949–1957

Die Ära Adenauer
The Adenauer Era

Umgeben von schwarzen Glücksbringern und »weißen Mäusen«: Konrad Adenauer am 6.8.1953 im Bundestagswahlkampf in Regensburg.

Surrounded by black "bearers of good tidings" and "white mice": Konrad Adenauer in Regensburg on August 6, 1953 during the general election campaign.

Auftakt und Höhepunkt

»Im Anfang war Adenauer« (Arnulf Baring), so läßt sich der Beginn der Bundesrepublik kurz umreißen. Trotz seines hohen Alters, er war bereits 73 Jahre, sollte der erste Bundeskanzler die Geschicke der Bonner Republik vierzehn Jahre lang maßgeblich bestimmen. Dieser Erfolg war keineswegs vorprogrammiert.

Die innere Situation der soeben aus der Taufe gehobenen Republik war überaus labil. Verarmung und Entwurzelung, Wohnungsnot und Arbeitslosigkeit vieler Deutscher bildeten für die Regierung eine bedrückende Hypothek. Im Parlament sah sie sich einem durch eine Vielzahl von Regional- und Splittergruppen gekennzeichneten Parteiensystem gegenüber, das ungute Erinnerungen an die Weimarer Republik aufkommen ließ.

Nach außen fehlte dem jungen Staat nicht nur jegliches Ansehen, sondern auch ein hohes Maß an Souveränität. Seine beschränkte Entscheidungsfreiheit fand im Besatzungsstatut der drei Alliierten Hohen Kommissare vom 10.4.1949 ihren sichtbarsten Ausdruck. Darin wiesen sie sich außer der Zuständigkeit in einer Reihe von »Vorbehaltungsgebieten« auch in einer Generalklausel das Recht zu, »auf Weisung ihrer Regierungen die Ausübung der vollen Gewalt ganz oder teilweise wieder zu übernehmen«. Die Hauptaufgabe bestand für die Bundesregierung folglich darin, den Menschen eine Perspektive zu geben und dem Staat die Souveränität zu gewinnen. Ohne die Innen-, Wirtschafts- und Sozialpolitik vernachlässigen zu wollen, sah Adenauer die Außen- und Deutschlandpolitik als Kernstück seiner Arbeit an. Geprägt vom »Alpdruck Potsdam«, d.h. dem alliierten Übereinkommen auf Kosten Deutschlands, zielte er auf eine unauflösliche Bindung der Bundesrepublik mit dem Westen, da die »nationale Einsamkeit« seines Erachtens in »weltpolitische Verlassenheit« umschlagen konnte. Mißtrauisch gegenüber der politischen Labilität seines eigenen Volkes, setzte er auf die möglichst rasche Aufnahme als »gleichberechtigtes und gleichverpflichtetes Mitglied in die europäische Föderation«. Um der von der Sowjetunion ausgehenden Gefahr zu begegnen, plädierte er darüber hinaus für eine enge Verbindung zu den USA.

Wenngleich an eine Wiedervereinigung in Freiheit seiner Ansicht nach vorerst nicht zu denken war und die Einheit Deutschlands hinter Freiheit und Frieden zurückzutreten hatte, war sie für ihn keineswegs abgeschrieben. Vielmehr trachtete der Kanzler danach, die »deutsche Frage« »durch atlantische Bindung und ›europäischen Nationalismus‹« (Hans-Peter Schwarz) zu beantworten.

Trotz einiger Gemeinsamkeiten im entschiedenen Antikommunismus und der prinzipiellen Hinwendung zum Westen stieß diese Konzeption in der Opposition auf heftige Gegenwehr. Neben grundlegenden gesellschaftspolitischen Differenzen zeichnete dafür namentlich die unterschiedliche Beurteilung der deutschen Handlungsspielräume durch die beiden führenden Politiker in Bonn, Adenauer und Schumacher, verantwortlich. Im Gegensatz zum Kanzler strebte der SPD-Vorsitzende im »Dreiklang von Sozialismus, Demokratie und Nation« (Waldemar Besson) ein einiges, sozialistisches Deutschland als gleichberechtigtes Mitglied einer sozialistischen Föderation europäischer Staaten an, wobei die Westbindung die Vereinigung des geteilten Deutschland unter keinen Umständen behindern durfte.

Beginning and Climax

"In the beginning there was Adenauer" (Arnulf Baring); the beginning of the Federal Republic can be outlined in these words. Despite his great age – he was already 73 – the first Federal Chancellor was to exercise a decisive influence on the fortunes of the Federal Republic. This achievement was by no means a foregone conclusion.

The internal situation of the newly launched republic was extremely unstable. The loss of their roots, the poverty, inadequate housing and unemployment of many Germans constituted a severe burden for the government. In parliament it was confronted with a party system characterized by a large number of regional and splinter groups, awakening uneasy memories of the Weimar Republic.

To the outside world the young state not only had no standing whatsoever, it also to a great extent lacked sovereignty. Its restricted freedom of decision-making found its most visible expression in the Occupation Statute promulgated by the three Allied high commissioners on April 10, 1949. In it, in addition to authority in a number of "reserved areas," they allotted to themselves in a general clause, the right "on the instructions of their governments to resume, wholly or in part, the exercise of full powers." As a result the principal task facing the federal government was to give people some hope for the future and to obtain sovereignty for the state. Without wishing to neglect domestic, economic, and social policy Adenauer saw foreign policy and *Deutschlandpolitik* i.e. policy regarding the future of Germany, as his main responsibility. Haunted by the "Potsdam nightmare" of an agreement between the Allies at Germany's expense, he aimed to bind the Federal Republic inseparably to the West, it being his view that "national isolation" could turn into "international abandonment." Mistrusting the political instability of his own people he set his sights on Germany's acceptance, as quickly as possible, as a "member of the European federation with equal rights and equal obligations." On top of this he pleaded for close ties with the USA to counter the danger emanating from the Soviet Union.

Even though in his opinion there was for the time being no prospect of reunification in freedom, and German unity had to take second place to freedom and peace, he did not by any means write it off entirely. On the contrary the Chancellor sought a solution to the "German question" "through transatlantic ties and 'European nationalism.'" (Hans-Peter Schwarz)

Despite some common ground in decided anti-communism and a basic orientation towards the West, this conception encountered fierce resistance on the part of the political opposition. Apart from fundamental differences with regards to social policy the blame for this lay in particular with differing assessments of Germany's scope for independent action by the two leading politicians in Bonn, Adenauer and Schumacher. In contrast to the Chancellor, the SPD party chairman's goal was a single, socialist Germany as a member, with equal rights, of a socialist federation of European states, in the "triad of socialism, democracy, and nation" (Waldemar Besson); western integration, he believed, must on no account be allowed to prevent the unification of divided Germany. Even though, as a result of Schumacher's often brusquely worded nationalism, the Allies

Vertraute und Weggefährten Adenauers: Herbert Blankenhorn (rechts),
Hans Globke (links hinten) und Eugen Gerstenmaier.

Close friends and companions of Adenauer: Herbert Blankenhorn (right),
Hans Globke (left, at the back), and Eugen Gerstenmaier.

Auch wenn Adenauer den Alliierten wegen des von Schumacher
häufig schroff formulierten Nationalismus als der verläßlichere
deutsche Partner galt, waren diese keineswegs bereit, seinen
Forderungen nach einer möglichst raschen Ablösung des Besatzungsstatuts oder gar einer Wiederbewaffnung Westdeutschlands im
europäischen Rahmen widerspruchslos zu folgen. Erst im Mai 1952
kam es nicht zuletzt unter dem Druck des Kalten Krieges zum
Abschluß eines Vertragspaketes, das die Beziehungen zwischen der
Bundesrepublik Deutschland und den Westmächten auf eine neue
Basis stellte.

Während die SPD die Abkommen rundweg ablehnte, weil sie
ihrer Meinung nach keine Gleichberechtigung brachten und den
Weg zur Wiedervereinigung verbauten, fand Adenauers Politik im
Volk breite Zustimmung. Nachdem die »Gründungskrise« der
Bundesrepublik (Hans Günter Hockerts) aufgrund außenpoliti-
scher Erfolge und sozialpolitischer Maßnahmen überwunden
worden war und die soziale Marktwirtschaft ab 1951/52 einen
anhaltenden Aufschwung initiiert hatte, errang die Union bei den
Bundestagswahlen 1953 einen eindrucksvollen Sieg. Mit der
Erfolgsbilanz entwickelte sich die Akzeptanz der Bevölkerung
gegenüber der liberal-demokratischen Ordnung weiter und begün-
stigte die innere Stabilisierung. Parteipolitisch setzte ein durch die
5%-Klausel auf Bundesebene geförderter »Konsolidierungs- und
Konzentrationsprozeß« (Rudolf Morsey) ein, welcher der Union in
der Mitte und auf dem rechten politischen Flügel zusätzliche
Unterstützung brachte. Dank der von Adenauer gegenüber dem
Ausland gewonnenen Statur und seiner Autorität in Partei und
Kabinett konnte man den Eindruck gewinnen, die Bundesrepublik sei auf dem Wege zu einer »Kanzlerdemokratie« (Karl
Dietrich Bracher).

regarded Adenauer as the more reliable German partner, they were
by no means prepared to comply meekly when he demanded that
the Occupation Statute should be lifted as quickly as possible or
even that West Germany should be rearmed within a European
framework. It was not until May 1952 that a package deal was
concluded, not least under the pressure of the Cold War, putting the
relationships between the Federal Republic and the western powers
on a new footing.

Whereas the SPD rejected the agreements out of hand because
in their opinion they denied Germany equal rights and destroyed
any prospect of reunification, a large proportion of the general
public agreed with Adenauer's policy. Now that the "foundation
crisis" of the Federal Republic (Hans Günter Hockerts) had been
weathered by virtue of successes in foreign policy and socio-
political measures, and the social market economy had brought
about a sustained economic boom from 1951-1952 onwards, the
CDU won an impressive victory in the general election of 1953. In
line with this record of success, assent to the liberal democratic
order continued to grow among the populace and was conducive to
internal stabilization. In party politics a "process of consolidation
and concentration" (Rudolf Morsey) began, helped at federal level
by the 5% clause, bringing the CDU additional center and
right-wing support. Thanks to the stature which Adenauer had
acquired in the eyes of the outside world and his authority within
his party and the cabinet it was possible to have the impression that
the Federal Republic was on the way to becoming a "chancellor
democracy" (Karl Dietrich Bracher).

The failure of the European Defense Community in August
1954 was a harsh blow for Adenauer. It seemed as if his policy of
western integration had been built on sand. Both the abolition of
the Occupation Statute and the rearmament of the Federal Republic
were jeopardized. The clouds lifted after a few weeks. At the end of
October the western powers agreed on a viable alternative solution

Aufbau eines demokratischen Schulsystems: Mathematikunterricht für
ABC-Schützen in der neuen Münsterschule in Bonn 1954.

Building up a democratic school system: a mathematics lesson for school
beginners in the new cathedral school in Bonn in 1954.

Das Scheitern der Europäischen Verteidigungsgemeinschaft im August 1954 versetzte Adenauer einen herben Schlag. Seine Politik der Westbindung schien auf Sand gebaut. Sowohl die Aufhebung des Besatzungsstatuts als auch die Wiederbewaffnung der Bundesrepublik gerieten in Gefahr. Nach wenigen Wochen lichteten sich die Wolken. Ende Oktober vereinbarten die Westmächte eine tragfähige Ersatzlösung, die Anfang Mai 1955 in Kraft trat. Die Bundesrepublik betrachtete sich als »souverän«, blieb aber in hohem Maße von den Gezeiten der Weltpolitik abhängig.

Etwaige Hoffnungen auf eine aktive Wiedervereinigungspolitik mußten schon bald begraben werden. Denn die ehemaligen Besatzungsmächte interessierten sich weniger für die »deutsche Frage« als für Entspannung und Abrüstung. Die »Magnettheorie«, wonach die Bundesrepublik unwiderstehliche Anziehungskraft auf die Deutschen jenseits der Demarkationslinie ausüben würde, verlor an Überzeugungskraft. Da das Ziel der staatlichen Einheit in immer weitere Ferne rückte, entwickelte sich in der Bonner Republik ein widersprüchliches Selbstverständnis. Ein eigenständiges westdeutsches Staats- und Identitätsbewußtsein fehlte, zumal die Europa-Idee keinen Ersatz bildete.

Aufgrund »schwerer Planungsfehler« (Hans-Peter Schwarz) geriet auch der Aufbau der Bundeswehr in eine tiefe Krise. Durch die in der Bevölkerung heftig umstrittenen Umrüstungspläne der NATO, die auf eine Stärkung der Atomwaffen ausgerichtet waren, erfuhr sie zusätzliche Brisanz. Allein in der Europapolitik konnte die Bundesregierung mit der Gründung der Europäischen Wirtschafts- und Atomgemeinschaft (EWG und EURATOM) einen großen Erfolg verbuchen. Dennoch gewann die Union bei den Wahlen zum Dritten Bundestag im September 1957 die absolute Mehrheit der abgegebenen Stimmen – ein Triumph, den keine Partei seither hat wiederholen können.

Wirtschaftlicher Aufbau und innenpolitische Festigung

Die fünfziger Jahre gelten in der Bundesrepublik gemeinhin als die des »Wirtschaftswunders«, das als Glanzleistung der von Ludwig Erhard initiierten sozialen Marktwirtschaft betrachtet wird. Allzuleicht wird dabei vergessen, wie schwer dieser Erfolg erkämpft werden mußte. Der innerdeutsche Streit um die Wirtschaftsform war mit der Weichenstellung durch den Marshallplan und die Währungsreform noch nicht beendet. Mit den im Winter 1949/50 rapide steigenden Arbeitslosenzahlen – von 8,8% im September 1949 auf 13,5% im Februar 1950 – geriet die soziale Marktwirtschaft vielmehr unter heftigen Beschuß, weil sie eine konservative Finanzpolitik betrieb und auf kurzfristige Erleichterungen zugunsten einer mittel- und langfristigen Stärkung des Produktionsapparates verzichtete. Der Engpaß in der Kohleproduktion zwang die Bundesrepublik zu hohen Importen, was zu einem beängstigenden Zahlungsbilanzdefizit führte.

Erst der weltweite Aufschwung nach dem Ausbruch des Koreakrieges im Juni 1950 leitete die Wende ein. Für den beträchtlichen Wachstumsschub in der deutschen Wirtschaft zeichnete ein ganzes Bündel von Faktoren verantwortlich: Die von den USA verfochtene liberale Wirtschaftspolitik trug zum Abbau der Handelshemmnisse

which came into effect at the beginning of May 1955. The Federal Republic regarded itself as "sovereign" but remained to a large degree dependent on the vicissitudes of international politics.

Any hope of an active reunification policy soon had to be buried since the former occupying powers were less interested in the "German question" than in détente and disarmament. The "magnet theory," according to which the Federal Republic would hold an irresistible attraction for the Germans on the other side of the line of demarcation, became less convincing. With the goal of national unity becoming ever more distant, a contradictory self-perception developed in the Federal Republic. There was no sense of identity as an independent West German state, but at the same time the idea of Europe did not provide a substitute.

Because of "grave errors of planning" (Hans-Peter Schwarz) the establishment of the German armed forces also went through a profound crisis, which became even more explosive as a result of NATO plans, which were highly controversial among the populace as they provided for the increased deployment of atomic weapons. It was only in European policy that the federal government was able

Frauen am Fließband: Schneiderei von Herrenanzügen im Kölner Konfektionsunternehmen Bierbaum und Proenen 1954.

Women on the production line: a tailor's workshop producing men's suits at the Cologne clothing company of Bierbaum & Proenen in 1954.

to register a major success with the founding of the European Economic Community and the European Atomic Energy Community (EEC and Euratom). Even so, the CDU polled an absolute majority of the votes cast in the elections to the third federal parliament in September 1957 – a triumph which no party has since been able to repeat.

Economic Construction and Domestic Stabilization

In the Federal Republic the fifties are generally thought of as the years of the "economic miracle," which is regarded as the outstanding achievement of the "social market economy" introduced by

im westeuropäisch-atlantischen Raum bei. Da die westlichen Konkurrenten ihre Industrieproduktion auf den Rüstungsbereich umstellen mußten, konnte die deutsche Wirtschaft in die freiwerdenden zivilen Sektoren der Weltmärkte eindringen. Als hilfreich erwiesen sich nun sogar die ökonomisch sinnlosen Demontagen von Industrieanlagen nach dem Krieg, da jetzt der Aufbau modernster Produktionsstätten die deutsche Wettbewerbsfähigkeit förderte. Das große Potential qualifizierter, leistungswilliger Arbeitskräfte erlaubte es, die enorme Nachfrage zu stillen, wobei die Kooperationsbereitschaft von Gewerkschaften und Arbeitgebern den notwendigen Rahmen schuf. Seit Mitte 1951 zeichnete sich ein kontinuierlicher Aufwärtstrend in der westdeutschen Wirtschaft ab, der von gravierenden Verschiebungen zwischen den Sektoren begleitet wurde. Ab 1952/53 kamen dessen Früchte auch breiteren Schichten der Arbeitnehmerschaft zugute. Zum Motor der Expansion avancierten die Chemieindustrie, der Maschinenbau, die Automobilindustrie und die Elektroindustrie. Demgegenüber besaß die Landwirtschaft nur mäßigen Anteil am »Wirtschaftswunder«.

Die Bundesregierung nutzte die volkswirtschaftliche Blüte, um dem Sozialstaatsprinzip des Grundgesetzes gemäß auf sozialpolitischem Feld tätig zu werden. Nach der Überwindung der unmittelbaren materiellen Not widmete sie sich mit Vorrang der Versorgung der Kriegsopfer, der Beseitigung der Wohnungsnot und der Eingliederung der Heimatlosen. Neben dem Lastenausgleich für die Vertriebenen bzw. Flüchtlinge und dem Wohnungsbau gehörten die von allen großen Parteien geforderte Mitbestimmung sowie der Wiederaufbau einer umfassenden Sozial- und Rentenversicherung zu den Eckpfeilern ihrer Sozialpolitik. Gemeinsam mit dem »Wirtschaftswunder« trug sie maßgeblich zur inneren Stabilität der jungen Bonner Republik bei. Das Ergebnis der Bundestagswahlen vom September 1957 zeigte höchst eindrucksvoll, wie die Wähler die Prioritäten setzten. Sie folgten der von den Christdemokraten ausgegebenen Parole »Keine Experimente«, weil diese ihrem Sicherheitsstreben am besten entsprach. Adenauer stand im Zenit seiner politischen Macht.

Außenpolitik im Zeichen der Westbindung

Westbindung, Amerikaorientierung, Gleichberechtigung, Mitwirkung am Zusammenschluß Europas, so lauteten Adenauers außenpolitische Leitvorstellungen zu Beginn seiner Kanzlerschaft. In historischer Perspektive kamen sie einer »außenpolitischen Revolution« (Klaus Hildebrand) gleich. Ein Kernelement seiner Konzeption war die Aussöhnung mit Frankreich. Trotz seines ehrlichen Bemühens um Vertrauen und gewisser Konzessionen an das französische Sicherheitsbedürfnis konnte Adenauer nicht verhindern, daß das Verhältnis zum westlichen Nachbarn starken Spannungen ausgesetzt war. Aus der Sackgasse wurde es erst durch den Plan des französischen Außenministers Robert Schuman vom 9.5.1950 zur Integration der westeuropäischen Montanindustrie befreit. Nach harten Verhandlungen gründeten die Bundesrepublik Deutschland, Frankreich, Italien und die Benelux-Staaten im April 1951 die »Europäische Gemeinschaft für Kohle und Stahl« (EGKS). Die Grundstoffe der Kriegsindustrie sollten nun als Basis einer Friedensordnung dienen.

Spiegelbild des Wirtschaftsaufschwungs: Frauen- und Modezeitschriften an einem Zeitungskiosk in Bonn 1955.

A reflection of the economic boom: women's and fashion magazines at a newspaper kiosk in Bonn in 1955.

Ludwig Erhard. It is all too easy to forget what an effort this success required. The argument inside Germany over the form that the economy should take did not cease once the Marshall Plan and the currency reform had determined the direction of development. On the contrary, with the unemployment figures rising steeply in the winter of 1949-1950 – from 8.8% in September 1949 to 13.5% in February 1950 – the social market economy came under severe attack for its adoption of conservative financial policies whereby short-term relief was sacrificed for the sake of medium- and long-term strengthening of the productive sector of the economy. The shortfall in coal production obliged the Federal Republic to import large quantities, leading to a worrying deficit.

Not until the worldwide upswing following the outbreak of the Korean War in June 1950 did things begin to change. A whole series of factors was responsible for the substantial increase in the rate of growth of the German economy: the liberal economic policies pursued by the USA contributed to the removal of trade barriers in the west European-Atlantic area. Because their western competitors were obliged to shift their industrial production to the armaments sector, civilian sectors of world markets opened up which the

Mit dem Beitritt zur EGKS und der gleichzeitigen Aufnahme in den Europarat legte die Bundesrepublik wichtige Schritte auf dem Weg zur Eingliederung in die Gemeinschaft der westlichen Demokratien zurück. Die Phase des Mißtrauens war aber noch keineswegs beendet. Dies zeigte nicht zuletzt das Problem des deutschen Wehrbeitrags. Als der Ruf nach einer deutschen Aufrüstung im Zuge des Koreakrieges lauter wurde, legte Adenauer Ende August 1950 ein Angebot zur Aufstellung deutscher Truppen im Rahmen einer westeuropäischen Armee vor. Im Gegensatz zu seiner Parteibasis konnte sich auch Schumacher mit einem deutschen Wehrbeitrag durchaus anfreunden. Die von ihm aufgestellten Grundbedingungen – »Gleichberechtigung, Schicksalsgemeinschaft, Vorwärtsverteidigung« (Rudolf Hrbek) – gingen jedoch weit über die Vorstellungen Adenauers hinaus. Um die drohende nationale deutsche Bewaffnung zu verhindern, präsentierte Frankreich daraufhin das Projekt einer europäischen Armee mit deutschen Einheiten. Im Frühjahr 1951 nahm die Sechsergemeinschaft Verhandlungen über die bald so genannte Europäische Verteidigungsgemeinschaft (EVG) auf. Wenige Monate später begannen zwischen der Bundesrepublik und den Westmächten Beratungen über die Ablösung des Besatzungsstatuts.

Um einen Erfolg zu vereiteln, lockte die Sowjetunion im März 1952 mit einem Friedensvertrag und der Vereinigung eines neutralen Gesamtdeutschland. Die Westmächte lehnten das Angebot ab. Adenauer schloß sich dem vorbehaltlos an, weil er im Gegensatz zu Politikern der SPD und FDP, aber auch der eigenen Partei eine Prüfung der Offerte für fatal hielt. Mit der Unterzeichnung des

1 000 Kilometer bis zur verlorenen Heimat: Heimkehrer in Westdeutschland 1955 vor einer Landkarte „Mitteleuropas".

1,000 kilometers to the lost homeland: repatriated prisoners of war in front of a map of "Central Europe" in West Germany in 1955.

German economy was able to penetrate. Even the economically senseless postwar dismantling of industrial plants now proved to be a help, as the construction of the most modern production facilities helped to make Germany competitive. The availability of a large pool of qualified labor with a will to work enabled the huge demand to be met, with the cooperativeness of trade unions and employers creating the necessary framework.

From the middle of 1951 there was a continuous upward trend in the West German economy, with attendant shifts in the balance between sectors, which had grave consequences. From 1952-53 the fruits of the upward trend spread to broader sections of the working population. The expansion was led by the chemical industry, engineering and the automobile and electrical goods industries. Agriculture, by contrast, enjoyed only a modest share of the "economic miracle." The federal government took advantage of the economic boom to take steps in the field of social policy in accordance with the principle enshrined in the Basic Law of a "social" (that is to say socially responsible) state. Now that actual material hardship was a thing of the past, priority was given to caring for the victims of war, eliminating the housing shortage and resettling those people who had lost their homelands. Along with the "equalization of burdens" (i.e. financial compensation for losses suffered by the refugees and expellees) and construction of dwellings, the cornerstones of the government's social policy were industrial democracy ("codetermination"), which was demanded by all the major parties, and the restoration of a comprehensive social security and pensions system. Together with the "economic miracle" this policy contributed decisively to the domestic stability of the young Bonn republic. The result of the federal general election in September 1957 provided a most impressive demonstration of the voters' priorities. They went along with the CDU slogan of "no experiments" because it chimed in most closely with their desire for security. Adenauer was at the zenith of his political power.

Foreign Policy and the Aim of Western Integration

Western integration, orientation towards America, equal rights, contribution to European union – these were Adenauer's guiding concepts with regards to foreign policy at the outset of his chancellorship. Seen in a historical perspective they were tantamount to a "revolution in foreign policy" (Klaus Hildebrand). A central element in his conception was reconciliation with France. But despite his sincere efforts to gain the trust of the French and notwithstanding certain concessions to their need for security, Adenauer was unable to prevent the relationship with Germany's western neighbor from being exposed to severe strain. That relationship was only freed from this impasse by the plan for the integration of the west European coal and steel industries put forward by the French Foreign Minister Robert Schuman on May 9, 1950. In April 1951, after tough negotiations, the Federal Republic of Germany, France, Italy, and the Benelux states founded the European Coal and Steel Community (ECSC), for decades the essential materials of the war industry, were now to provide the basis for a peaceful order of things.

»Vertrages über die Beziehungen zwischen der Bundesrepublik Deutschland und den Drei Mächten« (Generalvertrag) und des »Vertrages über die Gründung der Europäischen Verteidigungsgemeinschaft« (EVG) Ende Mai 1952 in Bonn bzw. Paris wurden die auswärtigen Beziehungen Westdeutschlands auf eine völlig neue Basis gestellt. Der Abschluß des Luxemburger Wiedergutmachungsabkommens mit Israel und Vertretern der Jewish Claims Conference Mitte September verlieh der jungen Republik zusätzliche internationale Reputation.

Angetrieben von seiner Furcht vor einer Einigung der Großen Vier über die »deutsche Frage«, drängte Adenauer auf eine möglichst rasche Ratifizierung des Vertragswerkes. Zwar stimmte der Bundestag am 19.3.1953 den Dokumenten zu – trotz des entschiedenen Widerstandes der SPD und wachsender Mißstimmung weiter Bevölkerungskreise, die von der nach dem Tode Stalins Anfang März 1953 einsetzenden Entspannungseuphorie noch geschürt wurde. Da eine Entscheidung der französischen

Bundestagswahlkampf 1957: Bundesaußenminister Heinrich von Brentano als deutschlandpolitisches Gewissen der CDU.

The 1957 general election campaign: Foreign Minister Heinrich von Bretano as the conscience of the CDU with regard to the division of Germany.

By entering the ECSC and at the same time becoming a member of the Council of Europe, the Federal Republic took important steps on the path towards integration into the community of western democracies. But the phase of mistrust was by no means over. This was seen not least in the problem of Germany's contribution to defense.

At the end of August 1950, with the call for German rearmament becoming louder as a result of the Korean War, Adenauer offered to provide German troops within the framework of a West European army. Schumacher was also perfectly happy – unlike his party at grass roots level – with the idea of a German defense contribution. But the fundamental conditions which he laid down – "equal rights, a common destiny, forward defense" (Rudolf Hrbek) – went far beyond Adenauer's ideas. In order to avert the threat of a German national army, France thereupon put forward the project for a European army with German units. In the spring of 1951 the Community of Six opened negotiations concerning what soon came to be called the European Defense Community (EDC). A few months later consultations began between the Federal Republic and the western powers regarding the lifting of the Occupation Statute.

In order to frustrate this intention, the Soviet Union in March 1952 held out the enticing prospect of a peace treaty and the unification of a neutral Germany in its entirety. The western powers turned the offer down. Adenauer went along with this unreservedly because, unlike politicians in the SPD and FDP (but also in his own party) he believed that it would be fatal to put the offer to the test.

With the signing of the "Treaty concerning the relations between the Federal Republic of Germany and the Three Powers" (General Treaty) and of the "Treaty concerning the foundation of the European Defense Community (EDC)" at the end of May 1952 in Bonn and Paris respectively, West Germany's foreign relations were put on an entirely new footing. The young republic was given additional international respectability by the conclusion in mid-September of the Luxembourg Agreement on reparations with Israel and representatives of the Jewish Claims Conference.

Driven by his fear of an agreement between the Big Four concerning the "German question," Adenauer pressed for the treaties to be ratified as quickly as possible. The federal parliament did approve the documents on March 19, 1953, notwithstanding the determined opposition of the SPD and growing discord among large sections of the populace, which was magnified by the euphoric mood of détente that had set in following Stalin's death at the beginning of March 1953. But because the French National Assembly was slow to reach a decision Adenauer sought contact with the new American leadership. As regards the general atmosphere, his aim during his visit in April 1953 was to give expression to his feeling of gratitude towards the American people. On the political level it was "to ensure once and for all that east and west should not settle their differences at Germany's expense" (Herbert Blankenhorn). The Chancellor scored a great success by reaching broad agreement with President Eisenhower and Secretary of State Dulles in the assessment of the international situation. Even so he did not feel at all sure of his western partners.

The fact that despite the brutal suppression by Soviet troops of the rising in the GDR in mid-June the western powers were prepared to confer with the Soviet Union regarding the "German

Wettbewerbsfähigkeit durch zunehmende Automatisierung: moderne Achsmontagehalle bei Daimler-Benz im Mai 1956.

Competitiveness through increased automation: a modern axle assembly shop at Daimler Benz in May 1956.

Nationalversammlung aber auf sich warten ließ, suchte Adenauer den Kontakt zur neuen amerikanischen Führung.

Atmosphärisch ging es ihm bei seinem Besuch im April 1953 darum, das Gefühl der Dankbarkeit dem amerikanischen Volk gegenüber zum Ausdruck zu bringen; politisch zielte er darauf ab, »ein für allemal sicherzustellen, daß ein Ausgleich zwischen Ost und West nicht auf Kosten Deutschlands erfolgte« (Herbert Blankenhorn).

Die breite Übereinstimmung mit Präsident Eisenhower und Außenminister Dulles in der Beurteilung der Weltlage durfte der Bundeskanzler als großen Erfolg verbuchen. Dennoch fühlte Konrad Adenauer sich der westlichen Partner keineswegs sicher.

Daß die Westmächte sich trotz der brutalen Niederschlagung des Aufstandes in der DDR Mitte Juni durch sowjetische Truppen bereit fanden, mit der Sowjetunion über die deutsche Frage zu konferieren, verursachte bei Adenauer tiefe Beklemmung. Um so größer war seine Erleichterung, als die nach Berlin einberufene Außenministerkonferenz der Vier Mächte Mitte Februar 1954 ergebnislos scheiterte.

Seine Hoffnung, nun sei in Frankreich der Weg zur Ratifizierung des EVG-Vertrages frei, erwies sich als trügerisch. Am 30.8.1954 lehnte die Pariser Nationalversammlung die parlamentarische Behandlung definitiv ab. Damit war nicht nur der 1952 beschlossenen deutschen Wiederbewaffnung im europäischen Rahmen, sondern auch der Aufhebung des Besatzungsstatuts der Boden entzogen. Adenauer bewertete die Entscheidung Frankreichs als Katastrophe für Europa und für die deutsche Außenpolitik. Nachdem er kurzfristige Rücktrittsabsichten verworfen hatte,

question" caused Adenauer profound anxiety. His relief was all the greater when the Four-Power Conference of Foreign Ministers convened in Berlin broke down in mid-February 1954 without deciding anything.

His hope that the way would now be clear for the EDC treaty to be ratified in France proved illusory. On August 30, 1954 the National Assembly in Paris categorically refused to let the matter be put before parliament. This removed the basis not only for German rearmament within a European framework as decided on in 1952 but also for the lifting of the Occupation Statute.

Adenauer considered France's decision to be a disaster for Europe and for German foreign policy. After briefly considering but rejecting the possibility of resigning, he set to work with the Allies to pick up the pieces. Dulles in particular, who in mid-September strengthened the Chancellor's hand in Bonn during a trip to Europe, proved to be a reliable partner.

The western powers did indeed manage to find a viable alternative solution within a few weeks. At the Paris Conferences of October 19-23, 1954 the Occupation Statute was lifted and the Federal Republic was accepted as a member of NATO and of the newly created Western European Union (WEU). Furthermore the French Prime Minister Pierre Mendès-France and Adenauer agreed, in extremely difficult negotiations, on the "Europeanization" of the Saar, which was to be subject to a plebiscite.

Dynamischer Anstieg der Auto-Mobilität in der Bundesrepublik: Straßenverkehr vor dem Bonner Bahnhof im Juli 1956.

The rapid increase in auto-mobility in the Federal Republic: traffic in front of the railway station in Bonn in July 1956.

machte er sich mit den Verbündeten ans Werk, den Scherbenhaufen wegzuräumen. Insbesondere Dulles, der ihm auf einer Europareise Mitte September in Bonn den Rücken stärkte, erwies sich als zuverlässiger Partner.

Tatsächlich gelang es den Westmächten innerhalb weniger Wochen, eine tragfähige Ersatzlösung zu finden. Auf den Pariser Konferenzen vom 19. bis 23.10.1954 wurde das Besatzungsstatut aufgehoben und die Bundesrepublik in die NATO und die neugeschaffene Westeuropäische Union (WEU) aufgenommen. In äußerst schwierigen Verhandlungen einigten sich der französische Ministerpräsident Pierre Mendès-France und Adenauer außerdem auf eine »Europäisierung« der Saar, die einer Volksabstimmung unterworfen werden sollte.

Souveräne »Großmacht«-Politik und europäische Integration

Am 5.5.1955 traten die Pariser Verträge in Kraft. »Die Bundesrepublik Deutschland ist souverän«, frohlockte der Kanzler mit bezeichnender Übertreibung.

Sollte Konrad Adenauer jedoch gehofft haben, sich nunmehr mit Unterstützung der Bündnispartner dem Ziel der staatlichen Einheit zu nähern, so wurde er schon nach kurzer Zeit eines Besseren belehrt.

Bekämpfung der Wohnungsnot: Zimmerleute beim Hausbau in Berlin gegenüber der Gedächtniskirche im Juli 1958.

Combatting the housing shortage: carpenters working on house construction in Berlin near the Gedächtniskirche in July 1958.

Premiere für Adenauer und NATO-Botschafter Blankenhorn: erste Sitzung in der Atlantischen Allianz mit deutscher Beteiligung am 9.5.1955.

Debut for Adenauer and the ambassador to NATO, Blankenhorn: the first meeting of the Atlantic Alliance with Germany taking part, on May 9, 1955.

Sovereign "Great Power" Politics and European Integration

On May 5, 1955 the Paris Treaties came into effect. "The Federal Republic of Germany is sovereign" the chancellor exulted, with characteristic exaggeration. If he had hoped now, with the support of his partners in the alliance, to advance towards the goal of a unified state, he was soon disillusioned. None of the former occupying powers was prepared to give the Germans real help in this task. They committed themselves instead to the incipient détente in east-west relationships. The Soviet Union insisted on the two-states theory according to which two sovereign German states existed, each with a different social order, and turned down all proposals by western powers to combine reunification with a European security system. After the Geneva summit in July 1955, which was seen as a "watershed in world politics" (Hans-Peter Schwarz), the German question was pushed more and more into the background by disarmament negotiations and the quest for disengagement of the power blocs. Suspiciously observing the West's contacts with the East, Adenauer therefore did not hesitate for long when in the summer an invitation by the Soviet leadership to go to Moscow gave him the chance to assess for himself the extent of the Soviets' willingness to negotiate, and to make the western allies aware of the opportunities which existed for Germany. But he too failed to persuade the Soviet Union to back down. Nevertheless, during his

Keine der ehemaligen Besatzungsmächte war bereit, den Deutschen bei dieser Aufgabe wirklich zu helfen. Statt dessen verschrieben sie sich der im Ost-West-Verhältnis aufbrechenden Entspannung. Die Sowjetunion versteifte sich auf die Zwei-Staaten-Theorie, nach der zwei souveräne deutsche Staaten mit unterschiedlicher Gesellschaftsordnung bestanden, und wies alle Vorschläge der Westmächte zurück, die Wiedervereinigung mit einem Europäischen Sicherheitssystem zu verbinden. Nach der Genfer Gipfelkonferenz vom Juli 1955, die wie eine »weltpolitische Wasserscheide« (Hans-Peter Schwarz) wirkte, wurde die »deutsche Frage« mehr und mehr von Abrüstungsverhandlungen und dem Streben nach einem Auseinanderrücken der Machtblöcke (»Disengagement«) in den Hintergrund gedrängt.

Die westlichen Kontakte nach Osten argwöhnisch beobachtend, zögerte Adenauer deshalb nicht lange, als sich ihm im Sommer mit der Einladung der sowjetischen Führung nach Moskau die Möglichkeit bot, die sowjetische Verhandlungsbereitschaft persönlich auszuloten und den westlichen Verbündeten die deutschen Manövrierräume vor Augen zu führen. Aber auch ihm gelang es nicht, die Sowjetunion zum Einlenken zu bewegen. Dennoch willigte er bei seiner Visite im September 1955 gegen den heftigen Widerstand engster Berater in die Aufnahme diplomatischer Beziehungen ein, um damit die Freilassung der letzten Kriegsgefangenen zu erkaufen.

Parallel zu seiner Tuchfühlung mit Moskau suchte Adenauer die Nähe zu Paris. Angesichts unverkennbarer Anzeichen einer Renationalisierung der internationalen Beziehungen hoffte er darauf, der europäischen Integration neuen Auftrieb zu geben. Die Verständigung mit Frankreich war ihm so wichtig, daß er im Herbst sogar aktiv in den Wahlkampf an der Saar eingriff und nachdrücklich ein Ja zum Saar-Statut empfahl. Doch die Saarbevölkerung votierte am 23.10.1955 mehrheitlich gegen das Abkommen. Der befürchtete Rückschlag in den deutsch-französischen Beziehungen blieb indes aus. Beide Regierungen hielten an der gegenseitigen Verständigung fest.

Da Adenauer Europa als »das notwendige Sprungbrett« ansah, »um überhaupt wieder in die Außenpolitik zu kommen«, akzeptierte er die nun in Angriff genommene europäische Wirtschafts- und Atomgemeinschaft selbst um den Preis von Sonderrechten für die Franzosen. Damit geriet er in einen Konflikt mit Bundeswirtschaftsminister Ludwig Erhard, der die EWG als »volkswirtschaftlichen Unsinn« attackierte. Doch Konrad Adenauer hielt an seinem Kurs fest.

Als sich im Herbst im Zuge der Suez-Krise eine weitere Annäherung zwischen den USA und der Sowjetunion abzeichnete, reiste er gar persönlich nach Paris, um dem französischen Ministerpräsidenten Guy Mollet zur Seite zu stehen. Beflügelt von der Ende Oktober im Luxemburger Abkommen erzielten Beilegung des Saarproblems und getragen von dem gemeinsamen Willen, die EWG-Beratungen zum Erfolg zu führen, legten die beiden Regierungschefs den Grundstein für den Durchbruch der stagnierenden Verhandlungen.

Am 25.3.1957 unterzeichneten die Bundesrepublik Deutschland, Frankreich, Italien und die Benelux-Staaten auf dem Hügel des Kapitols in Rom die Gründungsakte zur Europäischen Wirtschafts- und Atomgemeinschaft.

visit in September 1955 he agreed, against the fierce resistance of his closest advisors, to establish diplomatic relationships as the price to be paid for the release of the last remaining prisoners-of-war.

Parallel to his face-to-face contacts with Moscow Adenauer sought a rapprochement with Paris. Faced with unmistakable signs of a renationalization of international relations he hoped to give fresh impetus to European integration. It was so important for him

Vor der Presse betont heiter: der sowjetische Ministerpräsident Nikolaj A. Bulganin und Adenauer am 10.9.1955 in Moskau.

Emphatically cheerful in front of the press: the Soviet Prime Minister Nikolay A. Bulganin and Adenauer in Moskow on May 10, 1955.

to reach an understanding with France that he even intervened actively in the election campaign in the Saarland in the autumn, emphatically recommending a vote of "Yes" to the Saar Statute. However, on October 23, 1955 the majority of the people of the Saarland voted against the agreement.

However, the setback which he had feared in Franco-German relationships did not come about. The two governments held fast to their mutual understanding. Since Adenauer regarded Europe as "the necessary springboard for getting back into foreign policy at all," he accepted the European Economic and Atomic Energy Communities on which work now began, even at the price of special rights for the French. This brought him into conflict with Erhard, the Federal Economics Minister, who attacked the EEC as "economic nonsense." But Adenauer was not to be deflected. In the autumn, when a further rapprochement between the USA and the Soviet Union became apparent as a result of the Suez crisis, he even went to Paris in person in order to give support to the French Prime Minister Guy Mollet. Spurred on by the settlement of the Saar problem which had been achieved in the Luxembourg Agreement at the end of October, and sustained by their shared desire to make the EEC deliberations succeed, the two heads of government laid the basis for a breakthrough in the stagnating negotiations. On March 25, 1957 on Capitol Hill in Rome the Federal Republic of Germany, France, Italy, and the Benelux states signed the act of foundation of the European Economic and Atomic Energy Communities.

Gründungsväter / Founding Fathers

Theodor Heuss, der am 12.9.1949 gewählte erste Bundespräsident, verband auf einzigartige Weise Politik und Geist. Seine Vielseitigkeit als Schriftsteller, Gelehrter und liberales Staatsoberhaupt ließ ihn als Vorbild in vorbildloser Zeit zu einem untypischen Exemplar des deutschen Politikers werden. Heuss setzte auf »metapolitische« Wirkungen, um das »Paraphengespinst« der Bundespräsidentschaft mit Leben zu füllen. Gewiß mehr als ein »politischer Nonvaleur« (Johannes Gross), wenngleich er gewisse Möglichkeiten des Amtes ungenutzt ließ: Theodor Heuss im Jahre 1952.

Kurt Schumacher, Vorsitzender der SPD und Oppositionsführer im Deutschen Bundestag, war »ein schwieriger Deutscher« (Peter Merseburger). Nach 1945 trat der in Konzentrationslagern gequälte Mann als erster deutscher Politiker mit einem gesamtdeutschen und europäischen Konzept auf. Schumacher verstand sich als deutscher Patriot und internationaler Sozialist. »Entweder«, so formulierte er sein Credo, »die neue deutsche Demokratie wird sozialistisch sein oder gar nicht sein. Und entweder ist der Sozialismus demokratisch oder er ist kein Sozialismus.« Kurt Schumacher wenige Monate vor seinem Tod im August 1952.

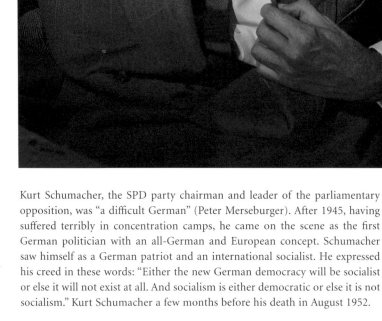

Theodor Heuss, the first Federal President, elected on September 12, 1949, uniquely combined the politician and the intellectual. His versatility as a writer, scholar and liberal head of state made him a paragon in an age without paragons, an untypical example of a German politician. Heuss aimed at exerting a "metapolitical" influence in order to give substance to the office of the Federal President. Certainly more than a "political nonentity" (Johannes Gross) even though he did not take advantage of certain opportunities offered by his office. Theodor Heuss in 1952.

Kurt Schumacher, the SPD party chairman and leader of the parliamentary opposition, was "a difficult German" (Peter Merseburger). After 1945, having suffered terribly in concentration camps, he came on the scene as the first German politician with an all-German and European concept. Schumacher saw himself as a German patriot and an international socialist. He expressed his creed in these words: "Either the new German democracy will be socialist or else it will not exist at all. And socialism is either democratic or else it is not socialism." Kurt Schumacher a few months before his death in August 1952.

Konrad Adenauer, der erste Bundeskanzler, hinterließ in der Geschichte Westdeutschlands tiefe Spuren. Seine Politik wurde zunächst von der Überzeugung geleitet, daß die Bundesrepublik einstweilen bloß »Objekt und weiter nichts« sei. Als Lehre aus der Vergangenheit und Maxime für die Zukunft verschrieb er den Deutschen eine feste Verankerung in der westlichen Welt. Die staatliche Einheit konnte Deutschland seiner Meinung nach nur in einem geeinten Europa erreichen. Konrad Adenauer, der »Wundergreis« (SebastianHaffner), 1952.

Konrad Adenauer, the first Federal Chancellor, made a profound mark on the history of West Germany. At first his policies were dominated by the conviction that for the time being the Federal Republic was merely a "passive object and nothing else." As a lesson to be learned from the past and a maxim for the future he ordained that Germany should be securely anchored in the western world. In his opinion Germany could only achieve national unity in a united Europe. Konrad Adenauer, the "aged prodigy" (Sebastian Haffner), in 1952.

Aus bitterer Erfahrung mit den Machtbefugnissen des Staatsoberhauptes in der Weimarer Republik beschränkte das Grundgesetz die Kompetenzen des Bundespräsidenten vornehmlich auf repräsentative Funktionen. Die Richtlinien der Politik bestimmt demgegenüber der Bundeskanzler. Die Dienstkarosse von Heuss vor seinem ersten Amtssitz, einem ehemaligen Erholungsheim der Reichsbahn auf der Viktorshöhe bei Bad Godesberg, und das Dienstfahrrad des Bundeskanzleramtes geben die wahren Machtverhältnisse in Bonn höchst unzureichend wieder.

From bitter experience with the powers of the head of state in the Weimar Republic, the Basic Law restricted the responsibilities of the Federal President principally to the role of a figurehead. The guidelines of policy, on the other hand, are determined by the Federal Chancellor. Heuss's official limousine in front of his first official residence, a former railwaymen's convalescent home on the Viktorshöhe outside Bad Godesberg, and the official bicycle of the federal chancellery are an inadequate reflection of the actual distribution of power in Bonn.

Theodor Heuss

Nach der Ratifikation des Vertrages über die Europäische Verteidigungsgemeinschaft (EVG) im März und der gewonnenen Bundestagswahl im September 1953 waren die dunklen Wolken zwischen den beiden ersten Männern im Staate verflogen. Bevor es Adenauer beruhigt in den Urlaub zog, verabschiedete er sich am 17.9.1953 in der Villa Hammerschmidt von Heuss.

After the ratification of the European Defense Community (EDC) Treaty in March and victory in the federal election in September 1953 the dark clouds between the two leading men in the state lifted. Before a relieved Adenauer went off on vacation, he said goodbye to Heuss in the Villa Hammerschmidt on September 17, 1953.

War Heuss ein geistreicher »Homme de lettres«, so war Adenauer der »Patriarch«. Seit sie sich im Herbst 1948 im Parlamentarischen Rat kennengelernt hatten, gewannen sie zunehmend Vertrauen und Respekt. Dennoch blieb ihr Verhältnis nicht spannungsfrei. Auf dem Empfang zu Adenauers 76. Geburtstag am 5.1.1952 ließen sie sich von den Enkeln des Kanzlers in ihrer Unterhaltung nicht stören.

If Heuss was a sophisticated "man of letters," then Adenauer was the "patriarch. "Following their first meeting in the Parliamentary Council in autumn 1948 they came increasingly to trust and respect each other. Even so their relationship did not remain free of tension. At the reception to mark Adenauer's 76th birthday on January 5, 1952 they did not let Adenauer's grandchildren disturb their conversation.

(unten) Im Rückblick auf die Glanzlosigkeit der Weimarer Republik versuchte Heuss, der Bonner Demokratie Stil und Würde zu verleihen. Seinen Sinn für kulturpolitische Symbolik bewies er 1951 mit der Stiftung des Bundesverdienstkreuzes und 1952 mit der Wiederbelebung des Ordens »Pour le mérite« für Wissenschaft und Künste. Zu neuen Ordensmitgliedern gehörte auch der Pädagoge und Philosoph Theodor Litt, der sein Ehrenzeichen freudig präsentierte.

(below) Looking back on the drabness of the Weimar Republic, Heuss tried to give style and dignity to the Bonn democracy. He demonstrated his sense of cultural symbolism when he founded the Bundesverdienstkreuz (federal cross of merit) in 1951 and in 1952 with the revival of the order "pour le mérite" for science and the arts. One of the new members of the order was the educationist and philosopher Theodor Litt, who took great pleasure in exhibiting his medal.

(oben) Wenngleich er von ihm zunächst einen Mangel an Überparteilichkeit erwartete, war für Kurt Schumacher nach der verlorenen Wahl zum Bundespräsidenten im September 1949 klar, daß die SPD Theodor Heuss so »ästimieren« werde, als hätte sie für ihn gestimmt. Da Heuss Schumacher stets mit hohem menschlichem Respekt begegnete, fiel es ihnen auf dem Bundespresseball in Bad Neuenahr am 17.11.1951 nicht schwer, gemeinsam genüßlich eine Zigarre zu rauchen.

(above) Even though Kurt Schumacher at first expected a lack of political neutrality from Heuss, it became clear to him after losing the federal presidential election in September 1949 that the SPD would hold Theodor Heuss in as high esteem as they would if they had voted for him. Since Heuss always showed Schumacher great respect as a man, they had no difficulty in enjoying a cigar together at the press ball in Bad Neuenahr on November 17, 1951.

Sehr freundschaftliche Beziehungen unterhielt Heuss zum Theologen und Missionsarzt Albert Schweitzer, seitdem er 1908 von ihm getraut worden war. Obwohl das Ordenskapitel Schweitzer bereits 1954 aufgenommen hatte, behielt sich Heuss vor, ihm den Orden am 11.11.1955 selbst zu überreichen.

Heuss kept up a very amicable relationship with the theologian and missionary doctor Albert Schweitzer, who had officiated at his wedding in 1908. Although the chapter of the order had already admitted Schweitzer in 1954, Heuss reserved for himself the presentation of the medal in person on November 11, 1955.

Eine besondere Aufgabe sah Heuss in der Förderung kultureller und wissenschaftlicher Einrichtungen. Dabei zielte er vor allem darauf, um »good will für den Staat« zu werben. Überdies bereitete ihm der Umgang mit der gelehrten und künstlerischen Welt auch großes Vergnügen. Mit zahlreichen Persönlichkeiten aus Kunst und Theater verbanden ihn freundschaftliche Beziehungen. Am 10.3.1955 empfing Heuss den Kulturkreis im Bundesverband der Deutschen Industrie in Bonn. Mit dem Schriftsteller Carl Zuckmayer und Carlo Schmid entsponn sich ein ernstes Gespräch.

Heuss made it his particular concern to give assistance to cultural and academic institutions. His aim was above all to seek "good will for the state." Moreover, it gave him great pleasure to mingle with scholars and artists. He was on friendly terms with numerous personalities from the world of art and the theater. On March 10, 1955 Heuss received the cultural circle of the federal association of German industry in Bonn. A serious conversation got under way with Carl Zuckmayer and Carlo Schmid.

Wenngleich er sich bisweilen darüber beschwerte, »Repräsentationsonkel« oder »Staatssklave im Frack« zu sein, begrüßte Heuss den integrierenden Charakter seines Amtes. Bei einer Reise nach Berlin zur Besichtigung verschiedener Bundesbehörden begutachtete er am 26.4.1958 auch die Instandsetzungsarbeiten am Reichstagsgebäude. Anschließend ließ er sich mit den Bauarbeitern ablichten.

Even if he complained now and again about being a "ceremonial old buffer" or a "frock-coated slave of the state." Heuss welcomed the social integration that his office served. On a trip to Berlin to visit various federal authorities he also took stock of work on the restoration of the Reichstag building on April 26, 1958. Afterwards he had himself photographed with the building workers.

Konrad Adenauer

(rechts) Am 21.11.1949 konnte Adenauer vom Museum König ins Palais Schaumburg, seinen neuen Dienstsitz, umziehen. Der klassizistische Bau, in dem der Kanzler Mitte Januar 1958 eine Rundfunk- und Fernsehansprache vorbereitete, war 1858 am Rheinufer errichtet worden. Seinen Namen gab ihm Fürst Schaumburg-Lippe, einer der Besitzer.

(right) On November 21, 1949 Adenauer was able to move from the König Museum to the Palais Schaumburg, his new official residence. The classical building, where the Chancellor prepared a radio and television address in mid-January 1958, had been built in 1858 beside the Rhine. It took its name from Prince Schaumburg-Lippe, one of its owners.

(links oben) Nach dem Tod seiner zweiten Frau Gussie 1948 - die erste, Emma, war 1916 verstorben - fühlte sich Adenauer sehr einsam. Allein die Schar seiner sieben Kinder bildete für ihn ein lebendiges Refugium. Kurz nach seiner Wahl zum Kanzler genoß er am 20.9.1949 in seinem Haus in Rhöndorf den Nachmittagskaffee mit dem Benjamin der Familie, Georg, und Tochter Lotte, die ihn während seiner Kanzlerschaft gewissermaßen als First Lady wiederholt auf Auslandsreisen begleiten sollte.

(links) Adenauer war kein Mann einsamer Dekrete, wenngleich er sich mitunter wie hier 1951 auch Rat in seiner Hausbibliothek in Rhöndorf holte. Beschlüsse resultierten vielmehr aus einem »komplizierten Integrationsprozeß« (Rudolf Morsey) der Entscheidungszentren und einer intensiven Abstimmung mit seinem Apparat. Ein »Schottensystem« (Arnulf Baring) streng voneinander geschiedener Dienststellen erlaubte es ihm, die Fäden in der Hand zu behalten.

(left above) After the death of his second wife Gussie in 1948 – his first wife Emma had died in 1916 – Adenauer was a very lonely man. But his large family of seven children provided him with a lively refuge. On September 20, 1949, shortly after his election as Federal Chancellor, he was enjoying afternoon coffee in his house in Rhöndorf with Georg, the baby of the family, and his daughter Lotte, who, as First Lady so to speak, was to accompany him repeatedly on trips abroad during his period in office.

(left) Adenauer was not a man to govern in solitude, even if he did consult his personal library in Rhöndorf now and then, as seen here in 1951. On the contrary, decisions emerged from a "complicated process of integration" (Rudolf Morsey) of the decision-making centers and intensive coordination of views with his staff. A "partition system" (Arnulf Baring) of departments that were kept strictly separate from one another enabled him to hold the reins.

1949–1957

Adenauers Alter, seine politische Erfahrung und sein Geschick im Umgang mit Personen und Institutionen verliehen ihm bald große Autorität im Kabinett, gegenüber den Koalitionsparteien und innerhalb seiner eigenen Fraktion. Der Vorrang des ihm unterstellten Bundeskanzleramts vor der Kollegialentscheidung des Kabinetts verhalf dem alten »Fuchs« zumindest in der Außenpolitik zu einem großen Handlungsspielraum. Die Polarität zwischen ihm und dem »Löwen« Kurt Schumacher (Peter Merseburger) prägte die junge Republik.

Adenauer's age, his political experience, and his skill in dealing with people and institutions soon gave him great authority in the cabinet, vis-à-vis the coalition parties and within his own parliamentary group. The primacy of the Federal Chancellery, of which he was the head, over the cabinet with its collective decision-making helped to give the old "fox" great freedom of action, at least in foreign affairs. The dichotomy between him and the "lion" Kurt Schumacher (Peter Merseburger) set its stamp on the young republic.

Nach der gewonnenen Bundestagswahl setzte Adenauer die Bildung einer Koalition aus CDU/CSU, FDP und DP durch. Am 15.9.1949 stellte sich das Kabinett den Fotografen. Untere Reihe von links: Bundesminister für Arbeit Anton Storch (CDU), Bundesminister für Wirtschaft Ludwig Erhard (CDU), Bundeskanzler Konrad Adenauer (CDU), Vizekanzler und Bundesminister für den Marshall-Plan Franz Blücher (FDP), Bundesminister für Gesamtdeutsche Fragen Jakob Kaiser (CDU), Bundesminister der Justiz Thomas Dehler (FDP), Bundesminister für Angelegenheiten der Vertriebenen Hans Lukaschek (CDU); zweite Reihe von links: Bundesminister für Ernährung, Landwirtschaft und Forsten Wilhelm Niklas (CSU), verdeckt Bundesminister für Wohnungsbau Eberhard Wildermuth (FDP); obere Reihe von links: Bundesminister für Angelegenheiten des Bundesrats Heinrich Hellwege (DP), Bundesminister für Angelegenheiten des Fernmeldewesens Hans Schuberth (CSU), Bundesminister des Innern Gustav Heinemann (CDU), Bundesminister der Finanzen Fritz Schäffer (CSU), Bundesminister für Verkehr Hans-Christoph Seebohm (DP).

After winning the parliamentary elections Adenauer succeeded in forming a coalition of the CDU/CSU, FDP, and DP. On September 15, 1949 the cabinet posed for photographers. Bottom row from left to right: Labor Minister Anton Storch (CDU), Economics Minister Ludwig Erhard (CDU), Federal Chancellor Konrad Adenauer (CDU), Vice Chancellor and minister for the Marshall Plan Franz Blücher (FDP), Minister for All-German Questions Jakob Kaiser (CDU), Minister of Justice Thomas Dehler (FDP), Minister for Expellee Matters Hans Lukaschek (CDU); second row from left to right: Minister of Food, Agriculture and Forestry Wilhelm Niklas (CSU), (concealed) Minister of Housing Eberhard Wildermuth (FDP); top row from left to right: Minister for Bundesrat Matters Heinrich Hellwege (DP), Minister of Posts and Telecommunications Hans Schuberth (CSU), Minister of the Interior Gustav Heinemann (CDU), Minister of Finance Fritz Schäffer (CSU), Minister of Transport Hans-Christoph Seebohm (DP).

ANSCHRIFTEN DER BUNDESMINISTERIEN

①	BUNDESKANZLER		
②	STELLV. BUNDESKANZLER UND ANGELEGENHEITEN DES MARSHALLPLANES	KOBLENZER STRASSE 150·160 LINIE 1 UND 5	→
	BUNDESMINISTERIEN		
③	INNERES		
③	JUSTIZ	RHEINDORFER STRASSE 198	←
③	ARBEIT	LINIE 1	
③	ANGELEGENHEITEN DER VERTRIEBENEN		
④	FINANZEN		
④	WIRTSCHAFT		
④	LANDWIRTSCHAFT UND ERNÄHRUNG	RHEINDORFER STRASSE 196 LINIE 1	←
④	WOHNUNGSBAU		
④	POST		
⑤	VERKEHR	ENDENICHER ALLEE 60 LINIE 3	→
⑥	GESAMTDEUTSCHE FRAGEN	BOTTLERPLATZ 3 300 m	→
⑦	...EGENHEITEN ...NDESRATES	... STRASSE 120	

LAGE... ...R EINZELNEN BUNDESMI...

Am 3.11.1949 ernannte der Deutsche Bundestag Bonn zur vorläufigen Bundeshauptstadt. Damit hatte sich Adenauer gegen die von der SPD befürwortete Wahl Frankfurts durchgesetzt. Beim Bonner Studentenkabarett »Wintergärtchen« bedankte er sich mit 300 DM für das beständige Singen ihres Liedes »Bonn, Bonn nur du allein«. Die Unterbringung der auf die ganze Stadt verteilten Ministerien verlief relativ problemlos. Nach ihrer Ankunft auf dem Bonner Bahnhof mußten sich die Abgeordneten und Ministerialbeamten erst einmal auf der gegenüber stehenden Anschriftentafel orientieren.

On November 3, 1949 the federal German parliament declared Bonn to be the provisional federal capital. Adenauer had got his way on this question against Frankfurt as advocated by the SPD. At the "Little Winter Garden" student cabaret in Bonn he gave 300 DM to thank them for continually singing their song "Bonn, Bonn, only you alone." Finding accommodation for the ministries, which were dispersed over the entire town, was relatively unproblematic. After arriving at Bonn railway station the members of the parliament and ministerial officials had to begin by taking their bearings from the list of addresses opposite the station.

(oben) Am 21.9.1949 trat das Bundeskabinett im Museum König zu seiner 3. Sitzung zusammen. Einziger Tagesordnungspunkt: der Wechselkurs der DM. Trotz heftiger Gegenwehr sah sich die Bundesregierung schließlich unter dem Druck der Alliierten Hohen Kommission gezwungen, die Währung stärker abzuwerten als gewünscht. Die Gesichter verraten den Ernst der Lage. Von links: Hellwege, Heinemann, verdeckt Dehler, Wildermuth, Blücher, Adenauer, verdeckt Kaiser, Niklas, Erhard und Lukaschek.

(links) Mit dem Inkrafttreten des Besatzungsstatuts am 12.9.1949 übernahm die Alliierte Hohe Kommission auf dem Petersberg bei Bonn die oberste Gewalt über Deutschland. Wie hartnäckig Adenauer die Gleichberechtigung der Bundesrepublik gegenüber dem Westen anstrebte, verdeutlichte er am 21.9.1949 bei der Vorstellung seines Kabinetts. Die Hohen Kommissare erwarteten ihn auf einem Teppich. Adenauer wurde ein Platz auf dem Parkett zugewiesen; dies verstand er als Diskriminierung und stellte sich demonstrativ auf eine Ecke des Teppichs. Von links: Schäffer, Dehler, Kaiser, Adenauer und Blücher.

(above) On September 21, 1949 the federal cabinet assembled in the König Museum for its third meeting. The only item on the agenda was the exchange rate of the Deutschmark. Under pressure from the Allied High Commission, the federal government finally found itself compelled, despite fierce resistance, to devalue the currency to a greater extent than it wished. The faces reveal the gravity of the situation. From left to right: Hellwege, Heinemann, (concealed) Dehler, Wildermuth, Blücher, Adenauer; (concealed) Kaiser, Niklas, Erhard, and Lukaschek.

(left) When the Occupation Statute came into force on September 12, 1949 the Allied High Commission on the Petersberg outside Bonn assumed supreme authority over Germany. When he presented his cabinet on September 21, 1949 Adenauer showed clearly how tenaciously he strove for equal rights for the Federal Republic vis-à-vis the West. The High Commissioners were awaiting him standing on a carpet. Adenauer was allocated a place on the parquet floor; he considered this to be discrimination and went and stood demonstratively on a corner of the carpet. From left to right: Schäffer, Dehler, Kaiser, Adenauer, and Blücher.

Kurt Schumacher führte die Sozialdemokratie hart und leidenschaftlich. Mit seinen eruptiven, schneidend vorgetragenen Bekenntnissen zur Wiedervereinigung Deutschlands eckte er im In- und Ausland häufig an. In vielfältiger Hinsicht unersetzliche Stütze war ihm seine Sekretärin, die spätere Bundestagspräsidentin Annemarie Renger. Am 2.12.1949 trafen sie sich im Bundeshaus mit dem stellvertretenden SPD-Vorsitzenden Erich Ollenhauer. Obwohl dieser »Biedermann und Patriot« (Brigitte Seebacher-Brandt) wie das Gegenteil Schumachers wirkte, trat er 1952 seine Nachfolge an.

Kurt Schumacher was a tough and passionate leader of the Social Democrats. The cutting outbursts with which he expressed his commitment to German reunification frequently gave offence, both at home and abroad. His secretary Annemarie Renger, later President of the Federal Parliament, gave him crucial support in many respects. On December 2, 1949 they met the deputy party chairman Erich Ollenhauer in the federal parliament building. Although this "petit bourgeois and patriot" (Brigitte Seebacher-Brandt) seemed to be the very opposite of Schumacher, he succeeded him as leader in 1952.

Flüchtlingsschicksale / The Fate of the Refugees

Die Integration der Vertriebenen und Flüchtlinge darf als eine der großen gesellschaftlichen Leistungen der Bundesrepublik Deutschland nach dem Zweiten Weltkrieg angesehen werden. Um jene zu entschädigen, die millionenfach durch Krieg, Vertreibung und Enteignungen in Ost- und Mitteldeutschland ihr Hab und Gut verloren hatten, verabschiedete der Bundestag im Mai 1952 das Lastenausgleichsgesetz. Diese »wohl größte Vermögensabgabe in der Geschichte der Bundesrepublik« (Rudolf Morsey) belegte alle Vermögen, die am Stichtag der Währungsreform 5000 DM überstiegen, mit einer Abgabe von 50 Prozent. Sie ermöglichte damit Aufbaudarlehen für Ausgebombte, Siedlungshilfe für Flüchtlinge und Investitionshilfen für Existenzgründungen.

The integration of expellees and refugees after the Second World War may be regarded as one of the greatest social achievements of the German Federal Republic. In order to compensate those millions of people from eastern and central Germany who had lost their property through war, expulsion, and expropriation, the federal parliament in May 1952 passed the "Equalization of Burdens" law. This, "probably the greatest levy on wealth in the history of the Federal Republic" (Rudolf Morsey) imposed a levy of 50% on all assets exceeding 5,000 DM owned on the day of the currency reform. This made it possible to provide reconstruction loans for people who had been bombed out of their homes, resettlement aid for refugees, and investment grants for setting up small businesses.

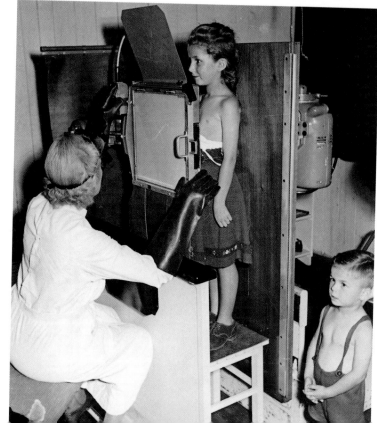

In den fünfziger Jahren schuf die Bundesrepublik noch zwei weitere sozial-politische Integrationsklammern: Im Oktober 1950 verabschiedete der Bundestag das Bundesversorgungsgesetz, das Leistungen für Kriegsopfer bereitstellte. Mitte Januar 1957 billigte das Parlament eine Neuregelung des seit Bismarcks Zeiten unveränderten Rentenrechts. Dank der »dynamischen« Rente stiegen die Rentenauszahlungen, hier am 28.12.1957 im Hauptpostamt Bonn, jährlich entsprechend der allgemeinen Einkommensentwicklung an.

In the fifties the Federal Republic created two more means of socio-political integration: in October 1950 parliament passed the Federal Law on Pensions to War Victims, which provided benefits for people who had suffered in the war. In mid-January 1957 parliament approved a revision of pensions legislation, which had been unchanged since Bismarck's day. Thanks to indexation, pensions, being paid out here on December 28, 1957 at the main post office in Bonn, rose annually in line with the general rise in incomes.

(gegenüber) Die seltenen Momente des Glücks und der Besinnung wie bei einer Goldenen Hochzeit konnten über die Notlage der Bewohner im Vertriebenenlager bei Eckernförde 1952 nicht hinwegtäuschen.
Glücklich in Sicherheit ließen die Kinder im Flüchtlingslager Uelzen 1952 auch die medizinische Vorsorge über sich ergehen.
Primitiv und schäbig waren die Flüchtlingsbaracken ausgestattet. Die Kochstelle mußte mit Holz befeuert werden, Schränke galten als Luxus.

(opposite) Rare moments of happiness and remembrance such as a golden wedding anniversary could not conceal the hardship suffered by the occupants of the expellee camp outside Eckernförde in 1952.
Happy and safe, the children in the Uelzen refugee camp in 1952 undergoing a medical check-up.
Facilities in the refugee huts were primitive and dingy. The cooking stove had to be fuelled with wood, cupboards were considered a luxury.

Wirtschaftswunder / Economic Miracle

Angesichts der Zerstörungen im Zweiten Welt-krieg und des Flüchtlingsstromes gehörte die Bekämpfung der Wohnungsnot zu den drängendsten sozialpolitischen Aufgaben der Republik. Nachdem die Bundesregierung sich zunächst auf die Förderung des Massen-wohnungsbaus konzentriert hatte, ermöglichte sie seit 1951 den Erwerb von Eigentumswoh-nungen. Mit dem im Juni 1956 verkündeten Zweiten Wohnungsbaugesetz förderte sie auch den Bau von Eigenheimen. Bis 1960 wurden mehr als fünf Millionen neue Wohnungen errichtet. Bau einer Wohnsiedlung bei Wiesbaden 1956.

Faced with the devastation of the Second World War and the influx of refugees, the need to com-bat the housing shortage constituted one of the most urgent tasks for the Republic in the sphere of social welfare. At first the federal government concentrated on promoting the construction of large-scale apartment blocks, but from 1951 onwards people were enabled to buy apartments for owner-occupation. With the second Housing Law announced in June 1956 the government also encouraged people to build their own homes. By 1960 more than five million new dwellings had been built. At right, a housing estate under construction outside Wiesbaden in 1956.

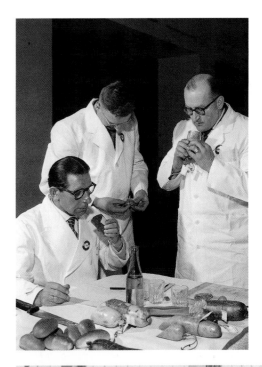

(rechts) Nach der abebbenden »Freßwelle« zu Beginn der fünfziger Jahre stieg bei den Verbrauchern das Qualitätsbewußtsein. Leistungsprüfungen kontrollierten die Güteklassen und förderten den Wettbewerb. Mit ihrem Gütesiegel »Made in Germany« entwickelte sich die Bundesrepublik zu einem international vertrauenswürdigen Handelspartner. Mit kritischem Blick und feiner Nase prüften Tester am 30.3.1955 auf dem Frankfurter Messegelände Fleisch- und Feinkosterzeugnisse.

(right) After the "great pig-out" had abated in the early 1950s consumers became more quality-conscious. Quality control and classification were introduced and led to increased competition. With its stamp of quality "Made in Germany" the Federal Republic evolved into an internationally trustworthy trading partner. Testers with a critical eye and a sharp nose checking meat and delicatessen products at the Frankfurt trade fair on March 30, 1955.

Der Produktname 4711 leitete sich von der Hausnummer des Produzenten in der Kölner Glockengasse ab. Sie stammte aus einer Zeit, als die Häuser noch durchnummeriert worden waren. In den sechziger Jahren avancierte das Eau de Cologne gar zu einem Gastgeschenk für ausländische Staatsoberhäupter. Bei einem Besuch in der Bundesrepublik im Juni 1962 wurde der Präsident der westafrikanischen Republik Mali, Modibo Keita, mit einer Flasche 4711 beglückt.

The brand-name 4711 was derived from the manufacturer's house number in the Glockengasse in Cologne. It dates from the time when all the houses in the city were still numbered continuously. In the sixties eau de cologne even attained the prestige of being presented as a gift to visiting heads of state from abroad. On a visit to the Federal Republic in June 1962 Modibo Keita, the President of the west african Republic of Mali, was delighted with a bottle of 4711.

Nachdem die »Trümmerfrauen« Mitte der vierziger Jahre Ansätze zur Emanzipation gezeigt hatten, knüpfte das Frauenbild in den fünfziger Jahren wieder am überlieferten Rollenverständnis an. Zurückdrehen ließ sich das Rad der Zeit aber nicht. Der Appell an die Rückbesinnung auf ihre 'eigentliche' Bestimmung war bei den meisten Frauen vergeblich. Sie beteiligten sich aktiv am Erwerbsleben wie hier bei der Verpackung des Duftwassers 4711 der Firma Ferdinand Mühlens.

Whereas the "rubble women" of the mid-forties had demonstrated the first signs of emancipation, in the 1950s the image of women harked back to the traditional conception of a woman's role. But the clock could not be turned back. Appealing to women to recall their "real" vocation was in vain as far as most of them were concerned. They played an active part as breadwinners, seen here packaging 4711 toilet water for the firm of Ferdinand Mühlens.

(links) Der Erfolg der »Sozialen Marktwirtschaft« war keineswegs vorgezeichnet. Erst der »Korea-Boom« leitete 1951/52 den Aufschwung ein. Als Hauptindikator galt die Automobilindustrie. Während 1949 355 000 Personenkraftwagen zugelassen waren, fuhren 1957 2,4 Millionen auf Deutschlands Straßen. Kein anderes Auto symbolisiert diesen Aufstieg so wie der VW-Käfer. 1947 war die Produktion des beschlagnahmten Werkes in Wolfsburg auf primitiven Montagestraßen wieder angelaufen. Anfang Dezember 1961 hatte die Zahl der produzierten Volkswagen bereits 5 Millionen erreicht.

(left) The success of the "social market economy" was by no means a foregone conclusion. The upswing did not set in until the "Korea boom" of 1951/52. The automobile industry was regarded as the main economic indicator. Whereas in 1949 355,000 cars were registered, by 1957 there were 2.4 million on Germany's roads. No other car symbolizes this rise like the Volkswagen "beetle." In 1947 production had recommenced on crude assembly lines at the confiscated plant in Wolfsburg. By the beginning of December 1961 the number of Volkswagen cars manufactured had reached five million.

(oben) Um sich im Kampf mit der in- und ausländischen Konkurrenz zu behaupten, steigerte Daimler-Benz in Stuttgart im Laufe der fünfziger Jahre den Grad der Automatisierung und weitete die Produktpalette auf dem Sportwagenmarkt aus. Politur eines Mercedes Sportcoupés 1956.

(above) During the 1950s Daimler-Benz of Stuttgart, in order to hold their own against their competitors at home and abroad, increased automation and extended their range of products to the sports car market. A Mercedes sports coupé getting a final polish in 1956.

Imponierende Zahlen konnte auch der Anfang der fünfziger Jahre erst allmählich von den Verbotsbestimmungen der Alliierten befreite Schiffsbau vorweisen. Bereits 1952 war das Produktionsniveau der Vorkriegszeit, 1960 der Vorkriegsstand der Handelstonnage erreicht. Doppelten Anlaß zur Freude bot der Stapellauf der »Zion« auf der »Deutschen Werft« in Hamburg am 19.7.1955: ein Sinnbild für die wachsende Produktivität dieses Industriezweigs wie für die deutsch-israelische Verständigung.

(gegenüber) Andere Firmen steuerten ihren Part zur positiven Bilanz bei. Dazu zählte auch die Adam Opel AG, die 1946 mit einem Opel-Blitz ihre Produktion wieder aufgenommen hatte und später mit Modellen wie dem Rekord große Erfolge erzielte. Endmontage von Achsen und Karosserie im Opel-Werk Rüsselsheim am 16.8.1960.

Impressive figures were also achieved by the shipbuilding industry, where the terms of the Allied ban had only gradually been lifted in the early fifties. It had regained the prewar level of production by 1952 and the prewar commercial tonnage by 1960. The launching of the "Zion" at the "Deutsche Werft" in Hamburg on July 19, 1955 was a twofold source of satisfaction, symbolizing as it did both the increased productivity of this industry and the rapprochement between Germany and Israel.

(opposite) Other companies contributed their share to the positive balance sheet. These included the firm of Adam Opel, which had resumed production in 1946 with an "Opel Blitz," and later achieved great success with models such as the "Rekord." The final assembly of axles and bodywork at the Opel works in Rüsselsheim on August 16, 1960.

(rechts) In der Plakatwerbung präsentierte sich die CDU im Bundestagswahlkampf 1957 als Garant für äußere Sicherheit und forderte das Volk dazu auf, wachsam zu bleiben. Sie vergaß aber auch nicht, das »hohe C« ihres Programms z.B. in der Familienpolitik anzustimmen.

(right) In their 1957 campaign posters, the CDU presented itself as the guarantor of external security. But it didn't forget to stress its "top C" program, for example with regard to family policy. The posters read: "Remain vigilant! CDU"; "Father and mother are voting for me."

(links) Noch im Frühjahr 1957 war nach den Umfragen der Meinungsforschungsinstitute zur Bundestagswahl ein Kopf-an-Kopf-Rennen von CDU/CSU und SPD zu erwarten. Dann aber zeichnete sich ein grandioser Erfolg der Union ab. Mit 50,2% erreichte sie am 15.9.1957 die absolute Mehrheit, während die SPD sich auf 31,8% verbesserte und die FDP auf 7,7% zurückging. In München traten neben der SPD und der noch jungen CSU zahlreiche kleinere Formationen von der FDP über BHE und DP bis zu BdD, DG oder der Bayernpartei an.

(left) According to opinion polls in the spring of 1957 the CDU/CSU and the SPD were still expected to be neck and neck in the elections. But what emerged was a spectacular CDU success. On September 15, 1957 they won an absolute majority with 50.2% of the vote, while the SPD improved its share of the vote to 31.8% and the FDP dropped to 7.7%. In Munich along with the SPD and the still young CSU, numerous smaller groupings appeared, ranging from the FDP via the BHE (Bund der Heimatvertriebenen und Entrechteten: "association of those who have been driven out of their homelands and deprived of their rights") and the DP (Deutsche Partei: "German Party") to the BdD (Bund der Deutschen: "Association of Germans"), DG (Deutsche Gemeinschaft; "German Community") and the "Bavarian Party."

Um die Erfolge und Leistungen der Bundesrepublik ins rechte Licht zu rücken und die Demokratie zu fördern, schickte die Bundesregierung Ende 1956 einen Ausstellungszug durchs Land, der kurz vor der Wahl auf ein Abstellgleis gebracht wurde.

At the end of 1956, in order to give due prominence to the successes and achievements of the Federal Republic and to promote democracy, the government despatched an exhibition train up and down the country, which was shunted into a siding shortly before the election. The words on the side of the train read: "Germany is in good standing again."

Die Union setzte im Wahlkampf in erster Linie auf den Kanzler, der auf zahlreichen Wahlreisen – hier im August 1957 im Saarland – unermüdlich und mit bisweilen provisorischen Mitteln seine Botschaft verkündete.

In the election campaign the CDU put its main emphasis on the Chancellor, who on numerous campaign junkets – here in August 1957 in the Saarland – proclaimed his message tirelessly, sometimes with improvised technical aids.

Westbindung / Western Ties

(unten) Angesichts wachsender Kriegsfurcht nach dem Ausbruch des Koreakrieges im Juni 1950 verständigten sich die Westmächte darauf, die Bundesrepublik in die Verteidigung des Westens einzubinden und den Kriegszustand mit ihr zu beenden. Am 23.9.1950 unterrichteten die Alliierten Hohen Kommissare den Bundeskanzler über diese Entscheidungen. Anschließend stellten sie sich den Fotografen. Von links: John McCloy (USA), Ludwig Erhard, Ivone Kirkpatrick (Großbritannien), Konrad Adenauer und André François-Poncet (Frankreich).

(below) Faced with growing fear of war after the outbreak of the Korean War in June 1950, the western powers agreed to integrate the Federal Republic into the defense of the west and to end the state of war with it. The Allied High Commissioners informed the Federal Chancellor of these decisions on September 23, 1950. Afterwards they posed for the photographers. From left to right: John McCloy (USA), Ludwig Erhard, Ivone Kirkpatrick (Great Britain), Konrad Adenauer and André François-Poncet (France).

(rechts) Herzstück der Europapolitik war für Adenauer die Verständigung mit Frankreich. Doch die Schatten der »Erbfeindschaft« waren noch zu lang, als daß Frankreich dem ehemaligen Kriegsgegner die Rückkehr in die europäische Gemeinschaft gleichsam problemlos zubilligen mochte. Gesten des guten Willens, wie die Reise des französischen Außenministers Robert Schuman Mitte Januar 1950 nach Bonn, reichten nicht aus, um die Wunden der Vergangenheit zu schließen. Der freundschaftliche Händedruck mit Adenauer täuschte darüber hinweg, daß der Besuch im Fiasko endete.

(right) The central core of Adenauer's European policy was rapprochement with France. But "hereditary enmity" still cast too long a shadow for France to be willing to approve unproblematically, so to speak, the return of its former wartime enemy to the community of Europe. Goodwill gestures such as the visit by the French Foreign Minister Robert Schuman to Bonn in mid-January 1950 were not enough to heal the wounds of the past. The friendly handshake with Adenauer concealed the fact that the visit ended in a fiasco.

Mitte April 1951 versammelten sich die Außenminister der Sechsergemeinschaft in Paris, um feierlich den Vertrag über die Montanunion zu schließen. Adenauer maß der Reise eine ganz besondere Bedeutung zu, handelte es sich dabei doch – abgesehen vom Aufenthalt Hitlers – um den ersten Besuch eines deutschen Regierungschefs in der französischen Hauptstadt seit Jahrzehnten. Die Fahrt an die Seine blieb Adenauer stets in guter Erinnerung, nicht nur weil der französische Hohe Kommissar François-Poncet ihm die bisher unbekannte Weltstadt als Reiseführer zeigte.

In mid-April 1951 the foreign ministers of the Community of Six assembled in Paris for the ceremonial conclusion of the ECSC Treaty. Adenauer set very special store by this trip, for – apart from the time Hitler spent there – it was the first visit to the French capital by a German head of government for decades. Adenauer always kept happy memories of the journey to the Seine, not only because the French High Commissioner François-Poncet took him on a guided tour of the metropolis which had until then been unknown to him.

(links) Unvergeßlich wurde der Aufenthalt für Adenauer in Paris auch deshalb, weil er auf der Rückfahrt in seinem Koffer ein kostbares Gut transportierte: Eine junge Studentin hatte ihm nämlich kurz vor der Abreise als Geste der Versöhnung mit den Deutschen das »Croix de Guerre«, das ihrem Vater im Ersten Weltkrieg verliehen worden war, zukommen lassen.

(left) Adenauer's visit to Paris was also unforgettable because on the return journey he carried a precious possession in his suitcase: shortly before his departure a young student, as a gesture of reconciliation with the Germans, had sent him the *Croix de Guerre* which her father had been awarded in the First World War.

Mit strahlendem Lächeln und freundlichem Händeschütteln verkündeten die Außenminister Großbritanniens, der Bundesrepublik, der USA und Frankreichs, Anthony Eden, Konrad Adenauer, Dean Acheson und Robert Schuman, am 26.5.1952 in Bonn das Ende der Verhandlungen über die Ablösung des Besatzungsstatuts. Anschließend begaben sie sich in den Bundesratssaal, um das Ergebnis ihres harten Ringens, den »General-« oder Deutschlandvertrag, zu besiegeln. »Nicht ohne Beklemmung schaut die Welt auf diesen Vertragsabschluß. [...] Die Wunden bluten noch.« (Heinrich Krone)

On May 26, 1952 in Bonn the foreign ministers of Britain, the Federal Republic, the USA, and France: Anthony Eden, Konrad Adenauer, Dean Acheson and Robert Schuman respectively, with smiles and friendly handshakes, announced the conclusion of negotiations for the lifting of the Occupation Statute. Afterwards they proceeded to the chamber of the Bundesrat to set the seal on the outcome of their hard struggle: the "General Treaty" or "Germany Treaty." "Not without trepidation does the world look on the conclusion of this treaty. [...] The wounds are still bleeding." (Heinrich Krone)

Bei der Zeremonie zur Unterzeichnung des Generalvertrags wurde Konrad Adenauer am 26.5.1952 vom Chef des Protokolls, Hans Herwarth von Bittenfeld (links), assistiert. Die ausländischen Repräsentanten am Tisch verfolgten die Szene eher mit Desinteresse: Von links: der Leiter der französischen EVG-Delegation Hervé Alphand und Walter Hallstein. Tags darauf begab sich die Ministerriege nach Paris, um den Vertrag über die Gründung der EVG zu signieren.

At the ceremony of the signing of the General Treaty on May 26, 1952, Konrad Adenauer was assisted by the Chief of Protocol Hans Herwarth von Bittenfeld (left). If anything, the representatives from other countries at the table followed the proceedings with a lack of interest: from left to right, the leader of the French EDC delegation Hervé Alphand and Walter Hallstein. On the following day the ministerial team proceeded to Paris to sign the EDC foundation treaty.

Obwohl Adenauer eine rasche parlamentarische Absegnung der Westverträge wünschte, zogen sich die Prozeduren monatelang hin. Für die Opposition galt das Urteil Schumachers: »Wer diesem Generalvertrag zustimmt, hört auf, ein Deutscher zu sein«. Als am 19.3.1953 die Stunde der Wahrheit im Bundestag anbrach, herrschte auf der Regierungsbank große Anspannung. Nach der Stimmenauszählung wich sie der Genugtuung über den Sieg. In der ersten Reihe von rechts: der stellvertretende Vorsitzende der CDU/CSU-Fraktion, Franz Josef Strauß, Adenauer, Hallstein, Dehler und der Pressesprecher des Auswärtigen Amtes, Günter Diehl.

Although Adenauer wanted parliament to give a speedy blessing to the Western treaties, the procedure dragged on for months. The opposition's standpoint was expressed in Schumacher's verdict: "Anyone who agrees to this General Treaty ceases to be a German." When on March 19, 1953 the moment of truth came in the federal parliament, there was great tension on the government front bench. After the votes had been counted it gave way to the satisfaction of victory. In the front row from right to left: the deputy chairman of the parliamentary CDU/CSU group Franz Josef Strauß, Adenauer, Hallstein, Dehler, and the foreign office press spokesman Günter Diehl.

Noch heikler als die Beziehungen zu den Westmächten gestaltete sich das Verhältnis der Bundesrepublik zu Israel. Für Adenauer stand die moralische Verpflichtung der Wiedergutmachung am jüdischen Volk außer Frage. Am 10.9.1952 vereinbarte er mit dem israelischen Ministerpräsidenten Moshe Sharett im Rathaus zu Luxemburg, Israel innerhalb von 12–14 Jahren drei Milliarden DM zu überweisen. Weitere 450 Millionen DM erhielt die Jewish Claims Conference. Nicht wenige Israelis lehnten die Zahlungen als »Blutgeld« ab. Entsprechend frostig verlief das Treffen der Regierungschefs.

Even more sensitive than its relations with the western powers was the developing relationship of the Federal Republic to Israel. For Adenauer the moral obligation to make restitution to the Jewish people was unquestionable. In the town hall in Luxembourg on September 10, 1952, he agreed, with the Israeli Prime Minister Moshe Sharett, to pay Israel 3 billion DM within 12–14 years. The Jewish Claims Conference received a further 450 million DM. Not a few Israelis condemned the payments as "blood money." The meeting between the heads of government was accordingly a frosty one.

Mit der gewonnenen Bundestagsabstimmung über die West-
verträge im Rücken brach Adenauer Anfang April 1953 zu seinem
ersten Besuch in die USA auf. In den Gesprächen mit dem neuen
Präsidenten Dwight D. Eisenhower und Außenminister John
Foster Dulles gelang es ihm, die Spannungen der zurückliegenden
Wochen zu glätten. Vor der Presse im Statler Hotel in Washington
bot sich ein Bild der Eintracht und Heiterkeit: Oben, von links:
Konrad Adenauer, Mrs. Janet Avery Dulles, Lotte Adenauer, John
Foster Dulles.

With victory in the parliamentary vote on the Western treaties
under his belt, Adenauer set off at the beginning of April 1953 on
his first visit to the USA. In conversations with the new President
Dwight D. Eisenhower and Secretary of State John Foster Dulles
he succeeded in smoothing over the tensions of the preceding
weeks. In the Statler Hotel in Washington the press was presented
with an image of harmony and gaiety: above, from left to right,
Konrad Adenauer, Mrs Janet Avery Dulles, Lotte Adenauer, John
Foster Dulles.

Der fast zweiwöchige Aufenthalt in den USA entwickelte sich zu
einer »nicht abreißenden Kette von Besuchen, Konferenzen,
Empfängen und Reden« (Paul Weymar). Adenauer besichtigte
neben Washington auch San Francisco, New York und Boston. Am
13.4.1953 landete er mit einer Sondermaschine auf dem Midway-
Flughafen in Chicago, wo er von Richard Daley, Vorsitzender der
Demokratischen Partei im Verwaltungsbezirk Cook, Geschäfts-
leuten und Honoratioren der Stadt begrüßt wurde.

The stay in the USA, which lasted for almost a fortnight, developed
into an "unbroken succession of visits, conferences, receptions, and
speeches" (Paul Weymar). In addition to Washington D.C.,
Adenauer also visited San Francisco, New York, and Boston. On
April 13, 1953 he landed by special plane at Midway airport in
Chicago, where he was welcomed by Richard Daley, chair of the
Democratic Party in Cook Country, businessmen, and city notables.

Beharrlich kämpfte der französische Außenminister Georges Bidault gegen eine übernationale Föderation und für eine »Gemeinschaft souveräner Staaten«. Adenauer konnte ihn bei einem Treffen am 10.8.1953 im Bonner Bundeskanzleramt nicht umstimmen. Nach den Besprechungen begaben sie sich ans Rheinufer, wo einige hundert »Renault«-Arbeiter ihnen vom Dampfer »Frieden« aus zuwinkten. Von links: Bidault, Adenauer, Heinrich von Brentano, der Vorsitzende der CDU/CSU-Fraktion im Deutschen Bundestag, Frau Bidault und Hallstein.

The French Foreign Minister Georges Bidault set himself tenaciously against any supra-national federation and advocated a "community of sovereign states." Adenauer could not persuade him to change his mind when they met on August 10, 1953 in the Federal Chancellery in Bonn. After their discussions they went down to the bank of the Rhine where a few hundred Renault workers waved to them from the steamship "Frieden" ("Peace"). From left to right: Bidault, Adenauer, Heinrich von Brentano, the chairman of the CDU/CSU parliamentary group, Mme Bidault, and Hallstein.

Obwohl von Frankreich 1950 initiiert, stieß die EVG seit 1952 gerade dort auf wachsende Ablehnung. Um den Widerstand aufzuweichen, plante man nun die Gründung einer Europäischen Politischen Gemeinschaft (EPG). In der Jugend fand diese Idee begeisterte Anhänger. Als die Außenminister der Montanunion am 7.8.1953 in Baden-Baden nach einer Kompromißlinie suchten, wurden sie von jugendlichen Demonstranten ermahnt, den Zeitpunkt zur europäischen Einigung nicht zu verpassen.

Although the EDC was initiated by France in 1950, it was there in particular that it encountered growing rejection from 1952 onwards. In order to weaken resistance it was planned to create a European Political Community (EPC). This idea found enthusiastic supporters among the young. On August 7, 1953 in Baden-Baden, when the ECSC foreign ministers were trying to find a compromise, they were admonished by youthful demonstrators not to miss the moment for European unity. The demonstrators' placards read: "It's the eleventh hour. Europe" and "We choose freedom."

Seit der Gründung der DDR im Oktober 1949 hatte die weitgehend bürgerlich-demokratische Verfassung eine stete Aushöhlung erlitten. Unter der Führung der SED wurde die Staatsform mehr und mehr dem Modell der Sowjetunion angeglichen. Zur Durchsetzung ihres unbedingten Führungsanspruchs definierte sich die SED 1950 als »Partei neuen Typs«, die dem »demokratischen Zentralismus« verpflichtet war und sich den Dogmen von Marx, Engels, Lenin und Stalin unterwarf. Begleitet von straff organisierten Aufmärschen der Partei und paramilitärischer Einheiten verschrieb sich die SED auf der Zweiten Parteikonferenz vom 9.-12.7.1952 dem »Aufbau des Sozialismus«. Damit nahm sie offiziell Abschied von der 1949 festgesetzten Strategie einer demokratischen Politik.

Since the foundation of the GDR in October 1949 its largely bourgeois-democratic constitution had been steadily eroded. Under the leadership of the SED the state increasingly took on a form modelled on that of the Soviet Union. In order to impose its unconditional claim to leadership the SED defined itself in 1950 as a "new type of party" committed to "democratic centralism" and governed by the dogmas of Marx, Engels, Lenin, and Stalin. At the second party conference from July 9-12, 1952, to the accompaniment of tightly organized parades by the party and paramilitary units, the SED committed itself to the "building of socialism." It thereby officially abandoned the democratic political strategy that had been laid down in 1949.

(rechts) Im Juli 1952 zerschlug die Regierung der DDR die bestehenden Länder und richtete eine neue territoriale Gliederung ein. Kurz darauf erließ sie eine Verordnung über eine »besondere Ordnung an der Demarkationslinie«. Dadurch wurde der bisher mögliche kleine Grenzverkehr – wie hier an der Zonengrenze bei Großburschla – behindert.

Erschwert wurde durch das neue Grenzregime auch der von der Bundesrepublik scharf beobachtete Warenschmuggel in Richtung Osten.

(right) In July 1952 the government of the GDR broke up the existing Länder and created a new territorial structure. Shortly afterwards it issued a decree concerning "special arrangements at the line of demarcation." This prevented such minimal cross-border traffic as had been possible hitherto – here at the zonal boundary near Grossburschla.

New procedures at the border also made it difficult to smuggle goods into the East – an activity on which the Federal Republic also kept a sharp watch.

Parallel zur politischen und ökonomischen Transformation änderte die SED seit 1949 auch das Schul- und Bildungswesen in der DDR. Die Jugendlichen, so lautete ihr Ziel seit 1952, sollten als »entwickelte Persönlichkeiten« bereit sein, den Sozialismus aufzubauen. Schulbücher und Lehrpläne hatten sich an marxistisch-leninistischen Inhalten zu orientieren. Die einzige ursprünglich überparteiliche Jugendorganisation »Freie Deutsche Jugend« (FDJ) entwickelte sich unter ihrem Vorsitzenden Erich Honecker nunmehr zur Kaderreserve der SED.

Parallel to the political and economic transformation the SED made changes to the school and education system in the GDR from 1949 onwards. From 1952 their goal was for young people, as "developed personalities," to be prepared to build socialism. School books and curricula had to be Marxist-Leninist in content. Under its chairman Erich Honecker the only youth organization that had originally been a non-party association, the "Freie Deutsche Jugend" (FDJ, Free German Youth), developed from now on into an SED reserve cadre. The slogan reads "Many Ones and Twos (i.e. high marks) shall be our thank you to the government and the party of the working class."

Um angesichts des wenig erfreulichen Konsumvergleichs zwischen Ost und West die Zweifel an den Fähigkeiten der Planwirtschaft nicht grassieren zu lassen, erweckte die SED die im 19. Jahrhundert entstandenen Interessengemeinschaften der Verbraucher, die Konsumgenossenschaften (KO), wieder zum Leben. Daneben gab es die 1948 gegründete staatliche Handelsorganisation HO, in denen kontingentierte Waren frei verkauft wurden.

To prevent doubt becoming rife regarding the efficiency of the planned economy in view of the discouraging comparison between East and West in terms of consumption, the SED revived the consumers' organizations (KO's), the cooperatives that had come into being in the nineteenth century. In addition there was the state retail organization (HO) created in 1948, in which apportioned goods could be bought without ration cards.

Im Selbstverständnis ihrer politischen Führung bildeten die DDR und Ostberlin den demokratischen Teil Deutschlands. Mit großen Hinweistafeln, die in der »Hauptstadt der DDR« Anfang und Ende des »Demokratischen Sektors« markierten, versuchte die SED das Bewußtsein der eigenen Bevölkerung zu schärfen.

As their political leaders saw the matter, the GDR and East Berlin constituted the democratic part of Germany. In the "capital of the GDR," the SED tried to sharpen the awareness of their own populace by means of large billboards indicating the beginning and end of the "democratic sector."

Ein wichtiges Objekt im Propagandakampf der DDR war die Jugend der Bundesrepublik. Vom 27.-30.5.1950 veranstaltete die FDJ in Ostberlin ein Deutschlandtreffen, das sich an junge Menschen in Ost und West wandte. Die Staatsführung warb bei den 500 000 Teilnehmern für den Kampf gegen die angeblichen Kriegsabsichten der sogenannten »Imperialisten« im Westen. »Wer ein richtiger Jungpionier ist, ist auch ein Held im Kampf für den Frieden«, hieß es in der Eröffnungsansprache des Präsidenten der DDR, Wilhelm Pieck. Die Bundesregierung sah das Treffen als Aufmarsch irregeleiteter Jugendlicher.

An important target of the GDR's propaganda effort was the youth of the Federal Republic. From May 27-30, 1950 the FDJ organized a "German meeting" in East Berlin aimed at young people in both East and West. The country's leaders tried to enlist the support of the 500,000 participants for the struggle against the alleged warlike intentions of the so-called "imperialists" in the West. In his opening address Wilhelm Pieck, the President of the GDR said: "Anyone who is a proper young pioneer is also a hero in the struggle for peace." The federal government saw the meeting as a parade of misled young people. The words on the photograph read: "German boys and girls, the capital of Germany awaits you."

Volksaufstand in der DDR / The People's uprising in the GDR

Infolge der verstärkten Sowjetisierung kam es in der DDR Anfang 1953 zu schweren Produktionseinbußen, einer Ernährungskrise und steigenden Flüchtlingszahlen. Anfang Juni verkündete die Führung auf Druck aus Moskau einen »Neuen Kurs«, der eine bessere Konsumgüterversorgung, die Einstellung des Kampfes gegen die Kirchen und einen veränderten Umgangsstil gegenüber der Bevölkerung vorsah. Da sie aber an der geplanten zehnprozentigen Normerhöhung für Arbeiter festhielt, formierte sich am 16.6.1953 auf der Stalinallee in Ostberlin ein Demonstrationszug von Bauarbeitern. Er wirkte wie ein Fanal.

At the beginning of 1953 increased Sovietization in the GDR led to severe drops in production, a food supply crisis, and rising numbers of refugees. At the beginning of June the leaders, under pressure from Moscow, announced a "New Line" which was to entail better provision of consumer goods, an end to the campaign against the churches, and a change of manner in dealing with the populace. But because they held fast to the planned 10% increase in work quotas, a procession of demonstrating building workers formed in the Stalinallee in East Berlin on June 16, 1953. It acted as a signal.

1949–1957

In Berlin marschierten Ostberliner mit schwarz-rot-goldenen Fahnen durchs Brandenburger Tor. In den nächsten Tagen kam es auch an anderen Orten der DDR zu weiteren Kundgebungen, deren Zielsetzung von der Rücknahme der Normerhöhung auf den Rücktritt der Regierung sowie freie Wahlen umschlug.

In Berlin, East Berliners with flags in black, red, and gold marched through the Brandenburg Gate. In the days which followed there were also demonstrations in other places in the GDR at which the demand for the quota increase to be cancelled turned into the demand for the resignation of the government and for free elections.

Mit dem brutalen Einsatz sowjetischer Truppen, hier auf der Potsdamer Straße in Ostberlin, nahm der Aufstand am 17.6.1953 ein jähes Ende.

The uprising came to an abrupt end on June 17, 1953 with the brutal use of Soviet troops, here on the Potsdamer Straße in East Berlin.

Am Ende blieb den Demonstranten nicht nur in Ostberlin die Kapitulation und Flucht vor den heranrollenden Panzern. Über 100 Menschen kostete der »Rückfall der Russen in ein System der nackten Gewaltanwendung« (Walter Hallstein) das Leben.

In the end the demonstrators, in East Berlin and elsewhere, could only surrrender or flee from the approaching tanks. The "relapse of the Russians into a system based on the use of naked force" (Walter Hallstein) cost the lives of over 100 people.

(gegenüber) In ihrer Wut und Ohnmacht brannten die Aufständischen Grenzmarkierungen, Informationszentren und Zeitungsstände nieder.

(opposite) In their rage and helplessness the protesters burned down border signs, information centers, and newspaper kiosks.

Eine wichtige Stütze für die Politik der Bundesregierung stellten die Katholische und in Teilen auch die Protestantische Kirche dar, die in den ersten Jahren des Wiederaufbaus noch starken Zuspruch in der Gesellschaft fanden. In der Endphase des Wahlkampfes suchte Adenauer Unterstützung auch dort, wo die Partei des »hohen C« ohnehin Zustimmung erwarten durfte: bei den Nonnen auf Schloß Erbach im Odenwald.

Important support for the policies of the federal government came from the Catholic, and in some respects also from the Protestant church. In the early years of reconstruction the churches still had a large following among the people. In the final phase of the election campaign Adenauer canvased support even in places where the "top C" party could expect support anyway: with the nuns at Schloss Erbach in the Odenwald.

Der Sieg der deutschen Fußballnationalmannschaft bei der Weltmeisterschaft im Juli 1954 verschaffte dem besetzten Land internationale Anerkennung. Die Truppe um Kapitän Fritz Walter stieg zu nationalen Helden auf. Menschliche Schwächen wurden gern übersehen. Der Equipe sollte am 26.7.1954 von Bundespräsident Heuss im Berliner Olympiastadion vor 85 000 Zuschauern das silberne Lorbeerblatt überreicht werden. Walter zog es aus Flugangst vor, mit dem Auto anzureisen. Als er seine Mannschaftskameraden vom Flughafen abholte, wurde ihm sinnigerweise ein Flugzeug geschenkt.

The victory of the German national football team in the World Cup in July 1954 brought international recognition to the occupied country. The team captained by Fritz Walter became national heroes. Human weaknesses were willingly overlooked. The squad was to be presented with the silver laurel leaf by Federal President Heuss on July 26, 1954 in the Olympic Stadium in Berlin in front of 85,000 spectators. Walter was afraid of flying and preferred to make the journey by car. When he went to meet his fellow players at the airport, he was appropriately presented with an airplane.

Auf dem Weg zur Souveränität / On the Road to Sovereignty

Um das Problem des deutschen Wehrbeitrags zu lösen, empfahl der französische Ministerpräsident Pierre Mendès-France die Aufnahme der Bundesrepublik in den Brüsseler Vertrag von 1948. Einen Beitritt zur NATO lehnte er ab, konnte sich aber auf der vom 28.9.-3.10.1954 dauernden Londoner Konferenz der EVG-Staaten, Großbritanniens, Kanadas und der USA nicht durchsetzen. Der Unterschrift Adenauers unter die Schlußakte schaute er entsprechend mürrisch zu. Von links: die Außenminister Joseph Bech (Luxemburg), Gaetano Martino (Italien), Eden (Großbritannien), Adenauer, Mendès-France, Lester Pearson (Kanada).

In order to solve the problem of the German contribution to defense, the French Prime Minister Pierre Mendès-France recommended that the Federal Republic should be brought into the Brussels Treaty of 1948. He rejected the idea of German membership of NATO, but at the London conference of EDC states, Britain, Canada, and the USA, which lasted from September 28 to October 3, 1954 he failed to get his way. He was accordingly bad-tempered as he watched Adenauer sign the final act. From left to right: Foreign Ministers Joseph Bech (Luxembourg), Gaetano Martino (Italy), Eden (Britain), Adenauer, Mendès-France, Lester Pearson (Canada).

Je stärker die Einsicht in die Notwendigkeit der deutschen Wiederbewaffnung wuchs, desto mehr nahm in Frankreich die Bereitschaft ab, als Preis die Opferung seiner Handlungsfreiheit in der EVG zu zahlen. Am 30.8.1954 lehnte die Nationalversammlung es ab, den EVG-Vertrag zur Ratifikation zuzulassen. Dieser »Anschlag gegen Europa« wurde nicht nur in Bonn als »schwarzer Tag« empfunden (Heinrich Krone). Mit einem Blitzbesuch stellte sich Außenminister Dulles dem bedrängten Bundeskanzler demonstrativ zur Seite. Adenauer begrüßte ihn am 16.9.1954 als »Engel des Himmels«.

The stronger the realization of the necessity of German rearmament became, the less willing France became to pay the price of sacrificing its freedom of action in the EDC. On August 30, 1954 the National Assembly refused to let the EDC Treaty be presented for ratification. Not only in Bonn was this "attack on Europe" felt to be a "black day" (Heinrich Krone). In a lightning visit Secretary of State Dulles lent demonstrative support to the beleaguered Chancellor. Adenauer welcomed him on September 16, 1954 as an "angel from heaven."

(gegenüber) In vier verschiedenen Konferenzen gelang es dem Westen Mitte Oktober in Paris, die Londoner Beschlüsse zu besiegeln. Am 23.10.1954 billigten die Delegationen im Palais de Chaillot die sog. Pariser Verträge. Gebannt verfolgten die Außenminister die Unterzeichnung durch Pierre Mendès-France, von links: Hans-Christian Hansen (Dänemark), Stephan Stephanopoulos (Griechenland), Kristin Gudmundsson (Island), Bech, Martino, Johan Willem Beyen (Niederlande), Halvard Lange (Norwegen), Paulo Cunha (Portugal), Mehmet Fuat Köprülü (Türkei), Eden und Dulles.

(opposite) In Paris in mid-October the West succeeded, in four different conferences, in setting the seal on the London decisions. On October 23, 1954 in the Palais de Chaillot the delegations approved the so-called Paris Treaties. As if spellbound, all the Foreign Ministers' eyes were on Pierre Mendès-France as he signed: from left, to right: Hans-Christian Hansen (Denmark), Stephan Stephanopoulos (Greece), Kristin Gudmundsson (Iceland), Bech, Martino, Johan Willem Beyen (Netherlands), Halvard Lange (Norway), Paulo Cunha (Portugal), Mehmet Fuat Köprülü (Turkey), Eden, and Dulles.

Um das Ratifikationsverfahren der Pariser Verträge in der Nationalversammlung zu erleichtern, regte Mendès-France im Dezember 1954 die Wiederaufnahme von Ost-West-Verhandlungen an. Solange die Verträge nicht unter Dach und Fach gebracht waren, wollte Adenauer davon nichts wissen. Es wirkte fast wie eine politische Demonstration, als er auf seinem 79. Geburtstag am 5.1.1955 den Pressefotografen in Bonn ein Buch mit dem Titel »Über die Dummheit« entgegenhielt.

In order to make it easier for the Paris Treaties to be ratified in the National Assembly, Mendès-France suggested in December 1954 that East-West negotiations should be resumed. Adenauer would not hear of this as long as the treaties were not entirely safe. It was almost like a political demonstration when on his 79th birthday on January 5, 1955 he held up a book with the title "On Stupidity" for the press photographers in Bonn to see.

Am 14.1.1955 trafen Adenauer und Mendès-France in Baden-Baden zusammen. Trotz freundlicher Atmosphäre kam es in der Frage neuer Ost-West-Verhandlungen zu keiner Annäherung. Allein im Bereich der wirtschaftlichen Zusammenarbeit erzielten sie handfeste Ergebnisse. Beim Fototermin rang sich denn auch nur Walter Hallstein ein Lächeln ab, während Mendès-France den Ausführungen Adenauers eher skeptisch folgte.

On January 14, 1955 Adenauer and Mendès-France met in Baden-Baden. Despite a friendly atmosphere there was no rapprochement in the matter of East-West negotiations. Only in the sphere of economic cooperation did they achieve solid results. Hence when they posed for the photographers it was only Walter Hallstein who managed to smile, while Mendès-France attended to what Adenauer was saying.

Am 5.5.1955 unterzeichneten die Hohen Kommissare der drei Westmächte eine Proklamation über die Aufhebung des Besatzungsstatuts. Anschließend übergaben sie Bundespräsident Heuss ihre Beglaubigungsschreiben als neuernannte Botschafter. François-Poncet sollte sich seines neuen Amtes nicht allzu lang erfreuen. Schon im Oktober 1955 kehrte er nach Paris zurück. Am 29.9.1955 gab Adenauer ihm zu Ehren einen Abschiedsempfang im Palais Schaumburg. Stolz trug François-Poncet das Großkreuz des Verdienstordens der Bundesrepublik Deutschland, das Heuss ihm verliehen hatte.

On May 5, 1955 the High Commissioners of the three western powers signed a proclamation lifting the Occupation Statute. They then handed Federal President Heuss their letters of accreditation as newly appointed ambassadors. François-Poncet was not to enjoy his new office for very long. He returned to Paris in October 1955. On September 29, 1955 Adenauer gave a farewell reception in his honor in the Palais Schaumburg. François-Poncet proudly wore the Grand Cross of the Order of Merit of the Federal Republic of Germany which Heuss had awarded him.

Nach der Ratifizierung durch die beteiligten Staaten konnten die Pariser Verträge in Kraft treten. Am 20.4.1955 hinterlegte der amerikanische Hohe Kommissar James B. Conant in einem feierlichen Akt die Ratifikationsurkunden für das Protokoll über die Beendigung des Besatzungsregimes und den Truppenvertrag. Seine Kollegen aus Frankreich und Großbritannien, André François-Poncet und Frederik Hoyer Millar, sollten es ihm zwei Wochen später nachtun. Gedankenversunken betrachtete Adenauer den Moment der Unterzeichnung durch Conant (links) und den Leiter der Rechtsabteilung im Auswärtigen Amt, Hans Berger.

After ratification by the countries involved the Paris Treaties were put into effect. On April 20, 1955 the American High Commissioner James B. Conant, in a solemn act, deposited the documents of ratification of the protocol for the ending of the occupation régime and the armed forces treaty. His opposite numbers in France and Britain, André François-Poncet and Frederik Hoyer Millar respectively were to follow suit two weeks later. Lost in thought, Adenauer contemplated the moment when Conant (left) and Hans Berger, the Head of the Foreign Office Legal Department, signed their names.

Der neue Status der Bundesrepublik belebte natürlich auch ihre Beziehungen zur Außenwelt. Staatsvisiten ausländischer gekrönter oder ungekrönter Häupter spiegelten die gewonnene Reputation sinnfällig wider. Den Auftakt hatte der äthiopische Kaiser Haile Selassie I. bereits vom 8.-14.11.1954 gemacht, hier nach seiner Ankunft im Zug vor Kaldenkirchen. In Düsseldorf beeindruckte er durch eine rührende Geste der Menschlichkeit, als er einer blinden Straßenzeitungsfrau sämtliche Blätter abkaufte, obwohl er sie gar nicht lesen konnte.

The new status of the Federal Republic naturally also gave a boost to its relations with the outside world. State visits by crowned or uncrowned heads from abroad were an appropriate reflection of the respectability which Germany had achieved. The Ethiopian Emperor Haile Selassie I, here after his arrival in the train outside Kaldenkirchen, had set the ball rolling on November 8-14, 1954. In Düsseldorf he made an impression with a touching gesture of humanity when he bought all the news-papers from a blind woman who was selling them in the street, although he was quite unable to read them.

Den Klerikern des Kölner Domes bot Kaiser Haile Selassie bei seiner Stippvisite in ihrem Gotteshaus am 10.11.1954 offenbar einen sehr exotischen Anblick. Von links: Weihbischof Wilhelm Stockums, Domkapitular Prälat Albert Lenné, Domkapitular Prälat Ludwig Lieser.

To the churchmen of Cologne cathedral, Emperor Haile Selassie, on his flying visit to their house of God on November 10, 1954, was evidently a very exotic sight to see. From left to right: Suffragan Bishop Wilhelm Stockums, Canon Prelate Albert Lenné, Canon Prelate Ludwig Lieser.

(gegenüber) Nach zehnjährigem Besatzungsregime wurde die Bundesrepublik souverän. Das deutsche Schiff kam »aus der Küstenschiffahrt hinaus auf die hohe See« (Herbert Blankenhorn). Aus diesem Anlaß wurde im Garten des Palais Schaumburg im Beisein von Adenauer die Bundesflagge gehißt.

(opposite) After ten years of the occupation régime the Federal Republic became a sovereign state. The German ship of state "left coastal waters for the high seas." (Herbert Blankenhorn) To mark the occasion the federal flag was hoisted in the garden of the Palais Schaumburg in Adenauer's presence.

Vom 23.2. bis 5.3.1955 weilte der iranische Kaiser Mohammed Reza Schah Pahlevi in der Bundesrepublik. Besonders herzlich begrüßte die Bevölkerung Kaiserin Soraya, war die als Schönheit geltende Frau doch in Berlin geboren. Auf dem Bild ist das iranische Kaiserpaar bei einem Abendempfang in der Godesberger Redoute zu sehen.

The Iranian Emperor Mohammed Reza Shah Pahlevi visited the Federal Republic from February 23 to March 5, 1955. The people gave a particularly warm welcome to Empress Soraya, a woman well known for her beauty, who had been born in Berlin. The Iranian imperial couple at an evening reception at the "Redoute" in Bad Godesberg.

Zu den »profiliertesten Führungspersönlichkeiten« (Konrad Adenauer) der jungen asiatischen Staaten gehörte der indische Ministerpräsident Jawaharlal Nehru, der im Juli 1956 in die Bundesrepublik kam. Auf einer Rheinschiffahrt, zu der Adenauer Nehru, seine Tochter Indira Gandhi und ihre beiden Söhne am 15.7.1956 eingeladen hatte, kamen sich die Staatsmänner näher. Führende Köpfe der Regierung bzw. der CDU dienten als Reisebegleiter. Von links: von Brentano, Gerstenmaier, Blücher; verdeckt: Erhard.

One of the "most high-profile leading personalities" (Konrad Adenauer) of the young Asian states was the Indian Prime Minister Jawaharlal Nehru, who came to the Federal Republic in July 1956. The two statesmen got to know each other better during a boat trip on the Rhine on July 15, 1956 to which Adenauer had invited Nehru, his daughter Indira Gandhi and her two sons. Leading lights in the government and the CDU acted as escorts. From left to right: von Brentano, Gerstenmaier, Blücher, (concealed) Erhard.

Elf Jahre nach der Potsdamer Konferenz betrat der britische Staatsmann Winston Churchill erstmals wieder deutschen Boden. In Anerkennung seiner Verdienste um die Einigung Europas verlieh ihm die Stadt Aachen am 10.5.1956 den internationalen Karlspreis. Für Teile der deutschen Vertriebenen war diese Ehrung nur schwer erträglich, da sie Churchill für den Verlust der Heimat verantwortlich machten. Ihr Aufruf zur Demonstration blieb weithin ungehört. Erleichtert über die ausgebliebenen Zwischenfälle, gab Adenauer Churchill am Tag darauf einen Empfang im Palais Schaumburg. Anschließend begleitete der Kanzler ihn als vollendeter Gastgeber bis zur abfahrbereiten Staatskarosse.

Eleven years after the Potsdam Conference the British statesman Winston Churchill stepped onto German soil once again. In recognition of his contribution to European unity, the city of Aachen on May 10, 1956 awarded him the international Charlemagne prize. For some German expellees this honoring of Churchill was difficult to accept as they held him responsible for the loss of their homelands. Their call for a protest demonstration remained largely unheard. Relieved that no incidents had occurred, Adenauer gave a reception for Churchill on the following day at the Palais Schaumburg. Afterwards the Chancellor, the perfect host, accompanied him to the state limousine which stood ready to depart.

(rechts) Daß auch eine Republik Glanz verbreiten kann, zeigte sich beim Staatsbesuch von König Paul I. und Königin Friederike von Griechenland, einer Enkelin des letzten deutschen Kaisers Wilhelm II. Daß darüber nicht die dunklen Seiten des deutsch-griechischen Verhältnisses in Vergessenheit gerieten, zeigten Heuss und Paul I. bei einem Diner am 17.9.1956 in Schloß Brühl, als sie daran erinnerten, daß sich beide Völker noch wenige Jahre zuvor in feindlichen Kriegslagern gegenübergestanden hatten.

(right) That a republic can also radiate brilliance could be seen during the state visit of King Paul I and Queen Friederike of Greece, a granddaughter of the last German emperor, Wilhelm II. This did not mean that the dark areas in German-Greek relations were forgotten, as Heuss and Paul I showed at a dinner at Schloß Brühl on September 17, 1956 when they recalled that only a few years earlier the two nations had confronted each other as wartime enemies.

Im Rahmen der Aktion »Kinder-Luftbrücke« wurden im Sommer 1955 rund 1800 Kinder mit amerikanischen Militärmaschinen vom Flughafen Berlin-Tempelhof zu Ferieneltern in die Bundesrepublik geflogen. Nach dem Start am 6.7.1955 wurde es so manchem fröhlichen Kinderherz doch ziemlich mulmig.

In operation "Children's Airlift" in the summer of 1955, around 1,800 children were flown by American military aircraft from Berlin Tempelhof airport to "vacation fosterparents" in the Federal Republic. After takeoff on July 6, 1955 there were quite a few happy children who began to get butterflies in their tummies.

Heimkehrerschicksale / Fateful Homecoming

Seit Gründung der Bundesrepublik trafen die Transporte mit deutschen Kriegs- und Zivilgefangenen aus der Sowjetunion nur noch selten ein. Jene, die aus dem Westen Deutschlands stammten, wurden zunächst in das Grenzdurchgangslager Friedland geleitet. Von dort aus ging die Reise dann in die Heimatorte, mitunter mit Fern-D-Zügen, die – obwohl der kleine Bahnhof eigentlich kein Halteort war – stoppten, um die Heimkehrer zu ihren Familien zu bringen.

After the founding of the Federal Republic it was only seldom that batches of German prisoners of war and civilian prisoners arrived from the Soviet Union. Those who came from western Germany were at first directed to the border crossing camp at Friedland. From there they continued their journey to their hometowns, sometimes on fast through trains which stopped at the little station, although it was not actually a stopping point, in order to take the returnees home to their families.

Am Ende des Zweiten Weltkriegs befanden sich mehr als 8 Millionen Deutsche als Kriegsgefangene im Gewahrsam der Siegermächte. Fast zehn Jahre später wurden noch immer 1,2 Millionen Wehrmachtsangehörige im Osten vermißt. Sie aufzuspüren oder ihr Schicksal zu klären, war die Aufgabe des Suchdienstes des Deutschen Roten Kreuzes. Meist endeten die Recherchen mit einer traurigen Mitteilung für die Angehörigen. 1 Million deutsche Soldaten erklärte der Suchdienst, der in den Heimkehrerlagern wie hier in Friedland bei Göttingen Meldestellen einrichtete, für tot.

At the end of the Second World War more than 8 million Germans were prisoners of war in the custody of the victorious powers. Almost ten years later 1.2 million servicemen were still missing in the east. To track them down or to clarify their fate was the task of the German Red Cross missing persons service. Enquiries usually ended with sad news for the men's families. A million German soldiers were declared dead by the missing persons service, which set up registration points in the camps for repatriated prisoners, here in Friedland near Göttingen.

Nach der Entlassungsaktion des Winters 1953/54 begab sich Adenauer am 2.1.1954 nach Friedland, um die Neuankömmlinge willkommen zu heißen. Gebannt, aber auch in sich versunken, lauschten sie seinen Worten. Adenauer versprach, alles zu tun, um die Eingliederung in die neuen Lebensverhältnisse zu erleichtern. Mit neuer Hoffnung verabschiedeten die Heimkehrer den Kanzler – seinem eigenen Empfinden nach – »geradezu triumphal«.

After the prisoner of war discharge operation in the winter of 1953/54 Adenauer went to Friedland on January 2, 1954 to welcome the new arrivals. They were engrossed by his words, though at the same time self-absorbed.

Adenauer promised to do everything he could to ease their integration into their new life and circumstances. With fresh hope, the returnees took their leave of the Chancellor in a "positively triumphant" atmosphere, as he himself felt.

Nach hitzigen ersten Verhandlungsrunden änderte sich die Atmosphäre bei Adenauers historischem Besuch in Moskau vom 8.-14.9.1955 erst bei einem Gespräch in der ehemaligen Datscha des russischen Dichters Maxim Gorki. Vor der Presse zeigten sich der sowjetische Ministerpräsident Nikolaj A. Bulganin und Adenauer am 10.9. betont heiter. Mit breitem Lächeln neben dem Kanzler der Generalsekretär der KPdSU, Nikita Chruschtschow, und der Stellvertretende Ministerpräsident Michail G. Perwuchin. Hinten von links: Dolmetscher Professor Maximilian Braun, Staatssekretär Walter Hallstein, der Vorsitzende des Auswärtigen Ausschusses des Deutschen Bundestages, Kurt Georg Kiesinger, und Herbert Blankenhorn.

During Adenauer's historic visit to Moscow from September 8-14, 1955, after heated opening rounds of negotiations it was only during a conversation in the former dacha of the Russian writer Maxim Gorki that the atmosphere changed. Posing for the press on September 10, the Soviet Prime Minister Nikolay A. Bulganin and Adenauer presented an emphatically cheerful appearance. Standing next to the Chancellor with a broad smile is the General Secretary of the Communist Party of the Soviet Union, Nikita Khrushchev, and the Deputy Prime Minister Mikhail G. Pervuchin. At the back, from left to right: the interpretor Professor Maximilian Braun, State Secretary Walter Hallstein, the Chairman of the Foreign Affairs Committee of the German parliament, Kurt Georg Kiesinger, and Herbert Blankenhorn.

Ohne greifbare Ergebnisse in der Frage der deutschen Einheit stimmte Adenauer in Moskau der Aufnahme diplomatischer Beziehungen mit der Sowjetunion zu. Als er am 15.9.1955 auf dem Flughafen Köln-Wahn das Ergebnis seiner Visite bekanntgab, sah man seinen Begleitern an, wie schwer sie daran zu tragen hatten. Zu den heftigsten Kritikern zählte von Brentano (links neben Adenauer), der sich anschickte, »Außenminister der Wiedervereinigungspolitik« zu werden (Daniel Kosthorst). Nicht weniger ernst wirkten Carlo Schmid, Hallstein, Kiesinger, Blücher, Storch und Bundesinnenminister Gerhard Schröder.

In Moscow, without any tangible results on the question of German unification, Adenauer agreed to establish diplomatic relationships with the Soviet Union. When he announced the results of his visit at Cologne-Wahn airport on September 15, 1955, the faces of those accompanying him showed how difficult it was for them to accept this. One of the fiercest critics was von Brentano (on the left next to Adenauer) who was shaping up to become the "foreign minister of reunification policy" (Daniel Kosthorst). Carlo Schmid, Hallstein, Kiesinger, Blücher, Storch, and federal minister of the Interior Gerhard Schröder made an equally grave impression.

Das Gros seiner Landsleute bewertete die Freilassung der letzten deutschen Kriegsgefangenen aus der Sowjetunion als die größte politische Leistung Adenauers. Als im Oktober 1955 die letzten Rußlandheimkehrer eintrafen – 9626 von 98229 namentlich bekannten Kriegsgefangenen und 20000 von 30000 Zivilinternierten – schnellte die Popularitätskurve des Kanzlers hoch.

The majority of his compatriots regarded the release of the last German prisoners of war from the Soviet Union as Adenauer's greatest political achievement. When the last returnees arrived back home from Russia in October 1955 – 9,626 of the 98,229 prisoners of war known by name and 20,000 out of 30,000 civilian internees – Adenauer's popularity soared.

(gegenüber) Im Gegensatz zur Rückführung der Kriegsgefangenen, welche die Sowjetunion loyal zu den gemachten Vereinbarungen abwickelte, lief die Freilassung der Zivilinternierten nur schleppend an. Auch nach Jahren hatte sich das Grenzdurchgangslager Friedland nicht überlebt. Mit kostenlosen Filmvorführungen – hier Mitte Februar 1958 – versuchte die Leitung, die »Lagerinsassen« vom tristen Alltag abzulenken.

(opposite) In contrast to the repatriation of prisoners of war, which the Soviet Union faithfully implemented in accordance with the agreement reached, the release of civilian internees was sluggish. Even years later the border crossing camp at Friedland had not outlived its purpose. With free movie showings – here in mid-February 1958 – the camp administration tried to take the minds of the camp inmates off the drabness of their everyday lives.

(oben) Sehnsüchtig wurden die Freigelassenen von ihren Familien in Friedland erwartet. Während einige Frauen und Mütter voll Dankbarkeit ihre Väter und Brüder in Empfang nahmen, brachte die Ankunft der Transporte für andere eine bittere Enttäuschung. Ihr Wunsch auf Nachricht über das Schicksal noch vermißter Kriegsteilnehmer blieb unerfüllt.

(above) The released prisoners were longingly awaited for by their families in Friedland. While some wives and mothers gratefully welcomed their loved ones, the arrival of the former prisoners brought bitter disappointment for others. Their desire for news of the fate of servicemen who were still missing remained unfulfilled.

Wiederbewaffnung / Rearmament

Mit den Pariser Verträgen vom Oktober 1954 war der Bundesrepublik das Recht zugebilligt worden, nationale Streitkräfte unter dem Dach der NATO aufzustellen. Der Aufbau einer ganzen Armee aus dem Nichts bedeutete eine ungeheure Aufgabe. Es fehlte an Kasernen, an Soldaten, an Material. Auf der Grundlage des Freiwilligen-Gesetzes vom 23.7.1955 meldeten sich bis zum 1.8.1955 mehr als 150000 Männer. Einen Tag nach dem Jahreswechsel traten die ersten 1000 Soldaten in der rheinischen Garnisonsstadt Andernach ihren Dienst an.

In the Paris Treaties of October 1954 the right of the Federal Republic to set up its own national armed forces under the umbrella of NATO had been approved. To build up a whole army from scratch was an immense task. There was a shortage of barracks, of soldiers, of materials. By August 1, 1955 more than 150,000 men had volunteered, in accordance with the Volunteers Act of July 23 of that year. On New Years Day, the first 1,000 soldiers commenced their duties in the garrison town of Andernach on the Rhine.

Am 20.1.1956 stattete Adenauer den fünf Lehrkompanien in Andernach einen Besuch ab. Der Nebel über dem Rhein und die mausgrauen Uniformen der Soldaten verdüsterten die Szene. Ernst schritt der Kanzler mit dem Bundesminister der Verteidigung Theodor Blank und den »frisch vergoldeten Generalen« (Gerd Schmückle) Hans Speidel, Adolf Heusinger und Helmut Laegeler eine Ehrenformation ab.

On January 20, 1956 Adenauer paid a visit to the five training companies in Andernach. The mist over the Rhine and the soldiers' mouse-gray uniforms created a gloomy scene. The Chancellor gravely inspected a parade of honor with Federal Defense Minister Theodor Blank and "freshly gilded generals" (Gerd Schmückle) one of whom was the Chairman of the Military Command Council at the Federal Ministry of Defense, Lieutenant General Adolf Heusinger.

Nur langsam ließ sich die Malaise im Aufbau der Bundeswehr beheben. Nach monatelangen Auseinandersetzungen sprach sich der Bundestag im Sommer 1956 gegen eine Berufsarmee aus. Am 21.7.1956 wurde das Gesetz über die allgemeine Wehrpflicht verkündet. Seine Gegner warfen der Regierung vor, sich nun zur »Politik der Stärke« aufzuschwingen. In der Bevölkerung wich die noch im Frühjahr vorhandene Akzeptanz einer breiten Ablehnung. Mit öffentlichen Demonstrationen – wie hier auf dem Bonner Marktplatz – wurde Adenauer aufgefordert, zu verhandeln statt zu schießen.

Bad feeling regarding the build-up of federal armed forces could only be overcome gradually. In the summer of 1956, after arguments lasting for months, the federal parliament came out in favor of conscription. On July 21, 1956 a law was announced making military service obligatory. Its opponents accused the government of aspiring to a "policy of strength." The popular support which had still existed in spring gave way to widespread opposition. At public demonstrations – here on the market square in Bonn – Adenauer was called on to "negotiate, not shoot." The slogan in the background reads: No army ever again.

In einer Ansprache vor den auf dem Kasernengelände angetretenen Offizieren und Mannschaften verheimlichte Adenauer nicht, wie wichtig der Tag für ihn war. Erst die Armee, so schrieb er den Zuhörern ins Stammbuch, würde der Bundesrepublik die Souveränität bringen.

Addressing officers and other ranks lined up on the parade ground, Adenauer made no secret of how important a day it was for him. He impressed on his listeners that only the army would give the Federal Republic its sovereignty.

Nachdem die Saarbevölkerung sich im Oktober 1955 gegen eine Europäisierung ausgesprochen hatte, verhandelten die Bundesrepublik und Frankreich über die Modalitäten einer Eingliederung der Saar in das Bundesgebiet. Ende Oktober 1956 wurde das Ziel im Luxemburger Saar-Abkommen um den Preis erheblicher deutscher wirtschaftlicher Zugeständnisse erreicht. Am 1.1.1957 fand die »Kleine Wiedervereinigung« statt. In Saarbrücken begannen die Feierlichkeiten mit einer kurzen Gedenkstunde im Hof des Regierungsgebäudes und dem Hissen der deutschen Fahne.

After the people of the Saarland had voted against Europeanization in October 1955, the Federal Republic and France negotiated over ways and means to incorporate the Saarland into the territory of the Federal Republic. At the end of October 1956 the goal was reached in the Luxembourg Saar Agreement, at the price of considerable economic concessions on Germany's part. On January 1, 1957 the "Little Reunification" took place. In Saarbrücken the solemn occasion began with a brief ceremony of commemoration in the courtyard of the government building as the German flag was hoisted.

Nach dem Scheitern der EVG im Sommer 1954 kam es von seiten Frankreichs und Belgiens zu Bemühungen um eine Wiederbelebung der europäischen Integration (»relance européenne«). Das angestrebte Ziel eines europäischen Marktes führte in der Bundesrepublik zwischen Erhard, von Brentano und Adenauer zu einem heftigen Richtungsstreit über die deutsche Europapolitik. Der joviale Schulterschlag des Bundeswirtschaftsministers vom 5.2.1953 täuschte über die tiefen Gräben, die sich zwischen ihm und dem Kanzler auftaten, hinweg.

After the failure of the EDC in the summer of 1954, there were efforts by France and Belgium to give a fresh boost to European integration ("relance européenne.") Their goal of a European common market sparked off a vehement argument in the Federal Republic between Erhard, von Brentano, and Adenauer over the direction to be taken by Germany's European policy. The jovial pat on the shoulder by the Federal Economics Minister – on February 5, 1953 – concealed the deep rifts which were opening up between him and the Chancellor.

Als am 25.3.1957 die feierliche Unterzeichnung der Römischen Verträge auf dem Kapitol begann, lag den Delegationen nur ein Packen weißen Papiers vor. Denn die Originaldokumente waren noch nicht fertig. Am Konferenztisch die Bevollmächtigten der sechs Unterzeichnerstaaten, von links: Paul-Henri Spaak und Jean-Charles Snoy et d'Oppuers (Belgien), Christian Pineau und Maurice Faure (Frankreich), Konrad Adenauer und Walter Hallstein (Bundesrepublik), Antonio Segni und Gaetano Martino (Italien), Joseph Bech (Luxemburg), Joseph Luns und Johannes Linthorst Homan (Niederlande).

When the solemn signing of the Treaty of Rome began at the Capitol on March 25, 1957, all that the delegates had in front of them was a stack of white paper. For the actual documents were not yet ready. The representatives of the six signatory states at the conference table, from left to right: Paul-Henri Spaak and Jean-Charles Snoy et d'Oppuers (Belgium), Christian Pineau and Maurice Faure (France), Konrad Adenauer and Walter Hallstein (Federal Republic), Antonio Segni and Gaetano Martino (Italy), Joseph Bech (Luxembourg), Joseph Luns and Johannes Linthorst Homan (Netherlands).

1957–1963

Umschwung und Ausklang
Change of Course and End of an Era

Botschafter des neuen, demokratischen Deutschland: Bundespräsident
Heuss auf Staatsvisite in den USA im Juni 1958.

Ambassador for the new democratic Germany: President Heuss during a
state visit to the USA in June 1958.

Mit ihrem fulminanten Wahlsieg vom September 1957 standen Adenauer und die CDU auf dem Höhepunkt ihrer Macht. Die Freude über die Bestätigung durch die Wähler ließ den Kanzler jedoch nicht vergessen, daß der Erfolg ein hohes Maß an Verantwortung bedeutete. »Wir sind noch kein fertiges Land«, diktierte er seiner Partei ins Stammbuch. »Ganz Europa ist noch nicht in Ordnung. Alles das kommt noch auf uns zu.«

Schon die Kabinettsbildung führte ihm vor Augen, wie schwer das Regieren mit einer absoluten parlamentarischen Mehrheit sein konnte. Erst Ende Oktober stand seine Koalition aus Vertretern der CDU, der gestärkten bayerischen CSU und der niedersächsischen DP fest. In der Innenpolitik verschrieb sich die neue Regierung vor allem der Fortführung der Sozialreform. Sie zielte auf eine breite Streuung des Privateigentums, weitete die marktwirtschaftlichen Grundsätze in der Wohnungswirtschaft aus und leitete Unterstützungsmaßnahmen zur Förderung der strukturell benachteiligten Landwirtschaft ein. Die seit 1958 wieder anziehende Konjunktur erleichterte es, den Forderungen der Interessengruppen nachzugeben. Weitsichtige Beobachter wie Ludwig Erhard warnten aber bereits vor den Grenzen der »Gefälligkeitspolitik« (Hans-Peter Schwarz).

Konturen einer Wohlstandsgesellschaft mit ihren charakteristischen Konsummustern zeichneten sich ab. Zugleich ließ das politische System nach der Dynamik der Anfangsjahre Symptome der Unbeweglichkeit erkennen. Je länger die Ära Adenauer dauerte, desto lähmender wirkte sich der Zwang zur Kompromißfindung auf die Reformfähigkeit der Bundesregierung aus. Zunehmend lauter wurden die Stimmen jener, die den Alten Herrn aus Rhöndorf als hemmendes Element empfanden. Mehr und mehr büßte Adenauer seine lange Zeit unumschränkte Führungsrolle ein.

Sein schwindendes Prestige trug mit dazu bei, daß der Kanzler eine »eigenartig sprunghafte, unklare und in sich nicht sehr stimmige Außenpolitik« (Hans-Peter Schwarz) betrieb. Das hing auch mit den bereits vorhandenen bzw. neu auftauchenden Gefahren in den internationalen Beziehungen zusammen. Die »deutsche Frage« verlor ihre zentrale Bedeutung in der Weltpolitik. Die Weltmächte beschäftigten sich im Zeichen der eigenen nuklearen Hochrüstung mit Fragen der Entspannung und Abrüstung. Um sich aus der Abhängigkeit von der westlichen Vormacht zu lösen, strebte die Bundesregierung in Zusammenarbeit mit Frankreich den Aufbau gemeinsamer Kernwaffen an und willigte in die Aufstellung von Atomraketen der NATO auf deutschem Boden ein. Da an eine »Wiedervereinigung in Freiheit« vorläufig nicht zu denken war, entwickelte Adenauer im Frühjahr 1958 deutschlandpolitische Initiativen, die vor allem auf eine Verbesserung der Lebensumstände im östlichen Teil Deutschlands abzielten. Doch die Sowjetunion ging auf seine Vorstellungen nicht ein. Vielmehr löste sie mit der im November 1958 ausbrechenden Berlinkrise eine neue Eiszeit zwischen Ost und West aus. Obwohl es dem Kreml nicht gelang, Westberlin in eine entmilitarisierte Stadt zu verwandeln, machte sich bei Adenauer Argwohn über die Verläßlichkeit der Partner breit. Allein der seit Juni 1958 amtierende starke Mann Frankreichs, Charles de Gaulle, schien ihm eine verläßliche Stütze, wenngleich ihre Ansichten in zentralen Fragen der Außenpolitik wie der europäischen Integration oder dem Verhältnis zur NATO keineswegs deckungsgleich waren.

After their spectacular election victory in September 1957 Adenauer and the CDU were at the peak of their power. However, in his delight that the electors had confirmed their support for him the Chancellor was still very much aware that his success entailed a high degree of responsibility. "We are not yet a fully-fledged country" he impressed on his party. "The whole of Europe is not yet in order. All that still lies before us."

Even forming a cabinet made him realize how difficult it could be to govern with an absolute majority in parliament. It was not until the end of October that his cabinet coalition of representatives of the CDU, the Bavarian CSU – support for which had increased – and the DP from Lower Saxony was finalized. In domestic policy the new government committed itself above all to continue social reform. It aimed at a wide distribution of private property, extended the principles of the market economy in the housing market and introduced measures to aid the structurally disadvantaged agricultural sector. The economy began to pick up again in 1958, making it easier to yield to the demands of pressure groups. But farsighted observers such as Ludwig Erhard were already warning of the limits of the "politics of accommodation" (Hans-Peter Schwarz). The outlines of an affluent society with its characteristic patterns of consumption were beginning to be discernible. At the same time the political system, after the dynamism of the early years, showed symptoms of stagnation. The longer the Adenauer era lasted, the more paralyzing became the effect of enforced compromise on the government's capacity for reform. The voices of those who perceived the old man from Rhöndorf as an obstruction grew ever louder. Adenauer increasingly forfeited the leading role which had for so long known no limit.

His dwindling prestige was one factor which contributed to the Chancellor's pursuit of a "curiously volatile, confused, and not very consistent foreign policy" (Hans-Peter Schwarz). This was also connected with both existing and newly emerging dangers in international relations. The "German question" lost its central importance in world politics. The world powers, while themselves stockpiling nuclear arms, turned their attention to détente and disarmament issues. In order to break free of dependence on the leading western power, the government strove to build up joint nuclear weapons in collaboration with France and consented to the deployment of NATO atomic missiles on German soil. Since there could for the time being be no question of "reunification in freedom," Adenauer in the spring of 1958 launched initiatives in "German policy" aimed above all at improving conditions for people living in the eastern part of Germany. But the Soviet Union did not respond to his ideas. On the contrary, it triggered off a new ice age between east and west with the Berlin crisis which broke out in November 1958. Although the Kremlin did not succeed in turning West Berlin into a demilitarized city, Adenauer became very suspicious of the reliability of his partners. Only the strong man of France, Charles de Gaulle, who had been in office since June 1958, seemed to offer reliable support, even though their views on central issues of foreign policy, European integration, and their relations with NATO did not by any means coincide.

Because the General strengthened the Chancellor's hand in his conflict with Moscow and expressed support for a continental European union, Adenauer agreed to a deal: support for France's

»Lieber drei Bundestagswahlen hintereinander als eine Kabinettsbildung«, seufzte Adenauer nach den Querelen über die neue Regierungszusammensetzung. Erst am 29.10.1957, sechs Wochen nach der Wahl, konnte er Heuss seine Ministerriege vorstellen. 1. Reihe von links: Bundesminister des Auswärtigen Heinrich von Brentano, Bundeskanzler Konrad Adenauer, Bundespräsident Theodor Heuss, Bundesminister des Innern Gerhard Schröder; 2. Reihe von links: Bundesminister für Vertriebene, Flüchtlinge und Kriegsgeschädigte Theodor Oberländer, Bundesminister für das Post- und Fernmeldewesen Richard Stücklen, Bundesminister für Ernährung, Landwirtschaft und Forsten Heinrich Lübke, Bundesminister für Wirtschaft Ludwig Erhard, Bundesminister der Justiz Fritz Schäffer, Bundesminister der Finanzen Franz Etzel; 3. Reihe von links: Bundesminister für Atomkernenergie und Wasserwirtschaft Siegfried Balke, Bundesminister für Gesamtdeutsche Fragen Ernst Lemmer, Bundesminister der Verteidigung Franz Josef Strauß, Bundesminister für Verkehr Hans-Christoph Seebohm; 4. Reihe von links: Bundesminister für Wohnungsbau Paul Lücke, Bundesminister für wirtschaftlichen Besitz des Bundes Hermann Lindrath, Bundesminister für Arbeit Theodor Blank, Bundesminister für Familien- und Jugendfragen Franz Josef Wuermeling.

"I'd rather have three general elections one after the other than form a cabinet," Adenauer sighed after all the arguments over the composition of the new government. It was not until October 29, 1957, six weeks after the election, that he was able to present his ministerial team to Heuss. Front row, from left to right: Foreign Minister Heinrich von Brentano, Chancellor Konrad Adenauer, President Theodor Heuss, Minister of the Interior Gerhard Schröder; second row, from left to right: Minister for Expellees, Refugees and the War-Disabled Theodor Oberländer, Minister of Posts and Telecommunications Richard Stücklen, Minister of Food, Agriculture, and Forestries Heinrich Lübke, Economics Minister Ludwig Erhard, Minister of Justice Fritz Schäffer, Minister of Finance Franz Etzel; third row, from left to right: Minister of Nuclear Energy and Water Supply Siegfried Balke, Minister for All-German Affairs Ernst Lemmer, Minister of Defense Franz-Josef Strauß, Minister of Transport Hans-Christoph Seebohm; fourth row, from left to right: Minister of Housing Paul Lücke, Minister for Federal Economic Property Hermann Lindrath, Minister of Labor Theodor Blank, Minister of Family and Youth Questions Franz Josef Wuermeling.

(gegenüber) Eine tragende Säule der Bundesregierung war Ludwig Erhard, die überaus populäre »gepolsterte Verkörperung des Wirtschaftswunders« (Ernst Richert). Die Glücksverheißung seines 1957 erschienenen Buches »Wohlstand für Alle« ließ sich zwar nicht vollständig umsetzen. Die Bilanz konnte sich dennoch sehen lassen: Der Index des Bruttosozialprodukts stieg zwischen 1950 und 1960 von 100 auf 215; das reale Bruttosozialprodukt erhöhte sich von 206,8 Milliarden 1958 auf 268,6 Milliarden im Jahr 1961; die Arbeitslosenquote sank 1961 auf 1%.

(opposite) Ludwig Erhard, the extremely popular "well-padded embodiment of the economic miracle" (Ernst Richert), was an essential pillar of the government. The promise of good fortune held out in his book "Wohlstand für Alle" ("Prosperity through Competition"), published in 1957, could not, it is true, be entirely fulfilled. Nevertheless the balance-sheet was impressive: between 1950 and 1960 the gross national product index rose from 100 to 215; real GNP rose from 206,800 million in 1958 to 268,600 million in 1961; unemployment dropped to 1% in 1961.

(rechts) Für die Arbeitnehmer schlug sich das »Wirtschaftswunder« zunächst im Ausbau des Systems der sozialen Sicherung und der Einführung von Mitbestimmungsrechten nieder. Seit Mitte der fünfziger Jahre kamen sie auch in den Genuß von Arbeitszeitverkürzungen. Lag die durchschnittliche Wochenarbeitszeit der Industriearbeiter nach 1950 bei etwa 48 Stunden, setzte 1956 ein gleitender Übergang zur Vierzigstunden- und Fünftagewoche ein, der innerhalb weniger Jahre abgeschlossen wurde.

(right) For working people, the "economic miracle" consisted to begin with in an expansion of social security provision and the introduction of codetermination rights. From the mid-fifties they also had the benefit of reduced working hours. Whereas after 1950 an industrial worker worked on average around 48 hours per week, a progressive transition to a 40-hour, five-day week began in 1956 and was completed within a few years.

(links) Als Gehilfen, mitunter auch als Initiatoren des wirtschaftlichen Aufstiegs wirkten die Unternehmer. Nur wenigen gelang freilich der Weg aus dem Nichts zum Millionär.

(left) Entrepreneurs acted as helpers, sometimes as initiators of the economic boom, but only a few succeeded in working their way up from nothing to become millionaires.

(links) »Auffälligster Gradmesser der Modernisierung« (Adolf M. Birke) war der rasante Zuwachs an Kraftfahrzeugen. Von 1957-1961 stieg die Zahl von 2,36 auf 4,84 Millionen. Zu Beginn der Motorisierung erfreuten sich vor allem kleine und kleinste Autos wie der VW-Käfer, das Goggomobil oder die BMW-Isetta größter Beliebtheit. Später überwogen PS-stärkere Mittelklassewagen. Ein Blick vom Rathausturm in München auf den Marienplatz zeigte Ende August 1953 die Anfänge der mobilen Gesellschaft.

(left) "The most conspicuous indicator of modernization" (Adolf M. Birke) was the meteoric rise in the number of automobiles. From 1957-1961 the number increased from 2.36 million to 4.84 milllion. At the beginning of this increase in automobile ownership the most popular models were small and very small cars such as the Volkswagen "Beetle," the "Goggomobil" or the BMW Isetta. Later, higher mid-sized cars became more predominant. Looking down from the tower of the Town Hall in Munich onto the Marienplatz at the end of August 1953 one could see the beginnings of the mobile society.

(gegenüber) Das seit dem Krieg kaum veränderte Straßennetz war dem Ansturm der Kraftfahrzeuge kaum gewachsen. Zunehmende Staus und eine steigende Zahl von Verkehrstoten zwangen die Politik, dem Straßenbau stärkere Aufmerksamkeit zu schenken. In den sechziger Jahren flossen die Finanzmittel vor allem in die Erweiterung des Autobahnnetzes. Bestehende Strecken wie die Autobahn Hannover-Köln waren indes schon früher, links im Juni 1957, modernisiert worden.

(opposite) The highway system, which had hardly changed since the war, was insufficent for the onslaught of automobiles. Increasing traffic jams and the rising number of deaths on the roads forced the politicians to pay more attention to highway construction. In the sixties resources went primarily into the expansion of the autobahn network. Existing superhighways such as that between Hanover and Cologne had however already been modernized, as seen at left in June 1957.

Trotz abnehmender Arbeitszeiten hielt sich die Bereitschaft der Männer zur Mitarbeit im Haushalt in eng gesteckten Grenzen. Ein Schürze tragender, abwaschender Hausmann paßte mit dem noch immer weit verbreiteten Selbstverständnis, das ihnen die Rolle als Ernährer der Familie zuwies, nicht überein.

Despite the reduced work hours, the willingness on the part of men to lend a hand in the household remained limited. The image of an apron-clad houseman doing the dishes simply did not fit into the widely accepted role of the family's provider.

1960 begann der Abbau der Wohnungszwangswirtschaft. In der Ausstattung gab es bei Möbeln und Gebrauchskunst neben der modernen und der dem »Zeitgeist« folgenden schwungvollen Linie eine ungebrochene Kontinuität alter Geschmacksvorstellungen. Die Ansprüche an Wohnungsgröße und Zahl der Zimmer waren zunächst noch sehr gering. Nicht selten dienten Wohnräume auch als Schlafgemächer. Ein separates Badezimmer galt noch als großer Luxus.

Housing control began to be phased out in 1960. In matters of decor, as well as the bold modern style which followed the "spirit of the times" in furniture and decorative artwork, there was also an unbroken continuity of older tastes and ideas. To begin with people were very undemanding with regards to living space and number of rooms. Living rooms were not infrequently doubled as bedrooms. A separate bathroom was still considered a great luxury.

135

Relativ gering fiel in den Anfangsjahren des Fernsehens der Anteil der reinen Unterhaltungssendungen aus. Im Vordergrund des Publikumsinteresses standen neben aktuellen und religiösen Sendungen politische Programme. Eine gewisse Bürgernähe boten Gesprächsrunden zwischen Journalisten und Politikern wie hier mit Bundestagspräsident Eugen Gerstenmaier. Im Kontrast zur Nüchternheit des Studios wurde die Urform der Talkshow durch hochprozentigen Alkohol aufgelockert.

In the early years of television the proportion of programs devoted purely to entertainment was relatively small. What viewers were most interested in were political programs, along with current affairs and religious broadcasts. Panel discussions between politicians and journalists, here with the Federal President Eugen Gerstenmaier, did something to make politicians less remote from the general public. In contrast to the soberness of the studio, high-proof liquor gave a more relaxed atmosphere to this prototype of the talkshow.

Nachdem das Fernsehen am 25.12.1952 seinen täglichen Dienst aufgenommen hatte, ließen sich immer mehr Bundesbürger von den »Flimmerkisten« verzaubern. Waren Anfang 1955 noch keine 100000 Fernsehteilnehmer registriert, so standen 1963 bereits 8000000 Empfänger in deutschen Wohnzimmern. Einen gewissen Ruhm erlangte die kleine Schar jener junger Damen, die den Zuschauern den Programmablauf schilderte. Zu ihnen gehörte auch Victoria Voncampe, hier am 3.11.1953 im kargen Fernsehstudio in Köln.

After the introduction of a daily television service from December 25, 1952, more and more citizens of the Federal Republic came under the spell of the "goggle-box." Whereas there were fewer than 100,000 registered television viewers at the beginning of 1955, by 1963 there were 8,000,000 sets in Germany's living rooms. A certain fame was achieved by that small group of young ladies who informed the viewers about the schedule of programs. One of them was Victoria Voncampe, here on November 3, 1953 in the spartan TV studio in Cologne.

Mag das heutige Urteil über die Filme der fünfziger Jahre auch häufig negativ ausfallen, so war der Zuspruch an den Kinokassen vor allem bei Heimat-, aber auch Kriegsfilmen durchaus positiv. Einen Hauch von internationalem Glamour bot die Verleihung des Preises der deutschen Filmkritik am 13.2.1959 in Berlin. Von links: James Stewart, der den Preis – eine von Ewald Mataré geschaffene Muschel mit Perle – stellvertretend für Danny Kaye entgegennahm, Joseph Offenbach, Hanne Wieder, Gert Fröbe, Fablito Calvo in Vertretung für Ladislao Vajdas, Johanna von Koczian und O.W. Fischer.

Although today one often encounters a low opinion of the films of the fifties, box-office returns were high, above all for those sentimental films with a regional setting known in German as *Heimatfilme*, but also for war films. A breath of cosmopolitan glamour was provided by the award of the German Film Critics' Prize on February 13, 1959 in Berlin. From left to right: James Stewart, who accepted the prize – a seashell with a pearl, created by Ewald Mataré – on behalf of Danny Kaye, Josef Offenbach, Hanne Wieder, Gert Fröbe, Fablito Calvo (standing in for Ladislao Vajdas), Johanna von Koczian and O.W.Fischer.

Schatten der Vergangenheit / The Dark Past

Am 20.9.1959 in der Anwesenheit Adenauers feierlich eingeweiht, wurde die Synagoge in Köln in der Weihnachtsnacht 1959 das Ziel von Hakenkreuzschmierereien. Eine Reihe von Nachahmungstaten führte zu weltweiter Empörung. Das Schreckgespenst des Antisemitismus trieb über Wochen sein Unwesen.

The synagogue in Cologne, which had been solemnly consecrated in Adenauer's presence on September 20, 1959, was daubed with swastikas during the night of Christmas 1959. This act was imitated in a number of other places and caused worldwide outrage. The specter of anti-Semitism went about its evil mischief for weeks.

Das Verfahren gegen den ehemaligen SS-Obersturmbannführer Adolf Eichmann in Jerusalem 1961 erregte in der Weltöffentlichkeit großes Aufsehen. Im Mai 1960 vom israelischen Geheimdienst aus Argentinien entführt, entpuppte sich Eichmann im Prozeß als krimineller Kleinbürger mit großem Organisationstalent. Der Verbrechen gegen das jüdische Volk und gegen die Menschheit sowie des Kriegsverbrechens für schuldig befunden, wurde er am 1.6.1962 hingerichtet.

In 1961 the trial of Adolf Eichmann in Jerusalem caused a great public stir the world over. Kidnapped by the Israeli secret service in Argentina in May 1960, Eichmann emerged during the trial as a petit bourgeois criminal with a great talent for organization. After being found guilty of crimes against the Jewish people and against humanity, and of war crimes, he was executed on June 1, 1962.

(gegenüber) Auf Schadensbegrenzung erpicht, sagte Adenauer bei seiner international beachteten Unterredung mit Ben Gurion am 14.3.1960 im Waldorf-Astoria-Hotel in New York eine großangelegte deutsche Beteiligung an der Entwicklung Israels zu – auch nach Ablauf des Wiedergutmachungsabkommens aus dem Jahre 1952. Außerdem billigte er eine kurz zuvor zwischen Strauß und israelischen Beauftragten verabredete Lieferung von U-Booten und Fernlenkgeschossen.

(opposite) Anxious to limit the damage, Adenauer, in his talk with Ben Gurion in the Waldorf Astoria Hotel in New York on March 14, 1960, which aroused international interest, promised a large-scale German contribution to Israel's development, even after the 1952 agreement on restitution expired. Moreover, he gave his approval for the supply of submarines and guided missiles which had been agreed shortly before between Strauß and Israeli representatives.

Am 1.7.1959 trat die Dritte Bundesversammlung zusammen, um einen Nachfolger für den scheidenden Bundespräsidenten Heuss zu küren. Im Zweiten Wahlgang setzte sich der Christdemokrat Heinrich Lübke mit 526 Stimmen gegenüber dem Sozialdemokraten Carlo Schmid (386) und dem Liberalen Max Becker (99) durch. In der Presse galt das neue Staatsoberhaupt wegen der von Adenauer verursachten Präsidentschaftskrise als »Lübkenbüßer« (»Der Spiegel«). Am 16.9.1959 verabschiedete Lübke seinen Amtsvorgänger auf dem Bonner Hauptbahnhof mit militärischen Ehren.

On July 1, 1959 the Federal Assembly convened for the third time to elect a successor to Heuss, the outgoing President. In the second ballot Heinrich Lübke (CDU) received 526 votes, defeating Carlo Schmid (SPD, 386 votes) and Max Becker (FDP, 99 votes). Because of the presidency crisis caused by Adenauer, the press gave the new head of state the nickname "Lübkenbüßer." (Der Spiegel), (Lückenbüßer: stopgap) On September 16, 1959 Lübke bade farewell to his predecessor in office with military honors at the main railway station in Bonn.

In der Presse wurde der Wechsel vom rhetorisch brillanten Bildungsbürger Heuss zum Agrarökonomen Lübke bissig als Abkehr vom »Humanismus zum Humus« (»Der Spiegel«) gedeutet. Am 8.1.1960 empfing Lübke das Bundeskabinett zum Neujahrsfest in der Villa Hammerschmidt. Von links: Erhard, von Brentano, Schröder, Etzel, Schwarz, Strauß, Adenauer im Vordergrund, Seebohm.

In the press the changeover from Heuss, with educated middle-class background and blend of rhetorical brilliance and, to Lübke, the agricultural economist, was waspishly described as a move " from humanism to humus." (*Der Spiegel*) On January 8, 1960 Lübke received the cabinet to celebrate the new year in the Villa Hammerschmidt. From left to right: Erhard, von Brentano, Schröder, Etzel, Schwarz, Strauß, Adenauer in the foreground, Seebohm.

Angesichts eines rapiden Ansehensverlusts ihres Vorsitzenden warb die CDU im Wahlkampf 1961 mit dem Slogan »Adenauer, Erhard und die Mannschaft«. Der Kanzler reiste unermüdlich durch die Lande, um sich als »Friedenskanzler« zu profilieren. Auf seiner Wahlkampfreise nach Kiel ahnte er am 11.8.1961 noch nicht, welch harte Bewährungsprobe ihm wenige Tage später mit der Krise in Berlin auferlegt werden sollte.

In the 1961 election campaign, faced with their party chairman's rapid loss of prestige, the CDU adopted the slogan "Adenauer, Erhard and the team." The Chancellor travelled tirelessly through the country presenting a distinctive image of himself as the "Chancellor of peace." During his campaign visit to Kiel on August 11, 1961 he had no idea how severe a test he would have to face a few days later in the shape of the Berlin crisis.

Die SPD schickte mit Willy Brandt den Regierenden Bürgermeister von Berlin ins Rennen um die Kanzlerschaft. Nicht nur das junge, dynamische Aussehen des »deutschen Kennedy« wirkte auf viele Wähler anziehend. Auch in programmatischer Hinsicht konnte seine Partei seit dem Godesberger Programm und der »Flurbereinigung« (Willy Brandt) des außenpolitischen Kurses gegenüber der CDU an Boden gewinnen.

The SPD put forward Willy Brandt, the governing mayor of (West) Berlin, as their candidate for the Chancellorship. Not only were many voters attracted by the dynamic, youthful appearance of the "German Kennedy"; his party was also able to gain ground from the CDU with its program, following the Godesberg Program and the "redrawing of the map" (Willy Brandt) with regards to foreign policy.

143

Adenauers politische Mißgriffe verstärkten in der Bevölkerung den Eindruck, er sei als Krisenmanager überfordert. Der Kanzler nutzte wegen der auf dem Land lastenden Kriegsfurcht das Sicherheitsbedürfnis der Deutschen und warnte – wie hier am 8.9.1961 in Wachtberg-Vilip bei Bonn – mit erhobenem Zeigefinger davor, Deutschland nicht »aufs Spiel« zu setzen. Am Ende verlor die Union zwar die absolute Mehrheit, blieb aber am 17.9.1961 mit 45,3% der Stimmen stärkste Kraft. Die SPD verzeichnete einen bedeutenden Zuwachs auf 36,2%; sensationell war das Anwachsen der FDP auf 12,2%.

Adenauer's political blunders strengthened the impression among the populace he was not up to the task of crisis management. With the country haunted by fear of war, the Chancellor recognized the Germans' need for security – here in Wachtberg-Vilip near Bonn on September 8, 1961, wagging his finger to warn against putting Germany "at risk." In the end, on September 17, 1961 the CDU, with 45.3% of the vote, lost its absolute majority but remained the strongest party in parliament. The SPD's share of the vote increased substantially to 36.2%. The FDP caused a sensation by increasing its share of the vote to 12.2%.

Der Bau der Berliner Mauer brachte die Wahl-
kampfstrategie der CDU gehörig durcheinander.
Während Brandt seine Wahlkampfauftritte vorerst
absagte, hielt Adenauer an seinen Terminen fest. Er
spitzte die innenpolitische Auseinandersetzung
sogar noch zu und verstieg sich zu einer persönlichen Diffamierung seines Kontrahenten. Nach
der herabsetzenden Anspielung auf Brandts
Emigration und dessen uneheliche Geburt
(»Brandt alias Frahm«) durfte sich Adenauer
nicht wundern, daß ihre Begegnung am 22.8.1961
eisig ablief.

The building of the Berlin Wall wreaked havoc in
the CDU's election strategy. Whereas Brandt cancelled his campaign appearances for the time
being, Adenauer kept to his schedule. He even
sharpened the terms of the domestic policy debate and did not stop short of personal defama-
tion of his rival. After his slighting allusion to the
fact that Brandt had left Germany during the
Third Reich and that he was an illegitimate child
("Brandt alias Frahm"), Adenauer had no cause to
be surprised that their meeting on August 22, 1961
was an icy one.

Schweren Schaden nahm Adenauers Reputation im
Zuge der sog. »Spiegel-Affäre«. Am 10.10.1962
bezeichnete das Magazin die Bundesrepublik in
einem aufsehenerregenden Artikel, der nach
Ansicht des Verteidigungsministeriums geheime
Informationen enthielt, als »Bedingt abwehr-
bereit«. Minister Strauß initiierte daraufhin die
Verhaftung des Verfassers Conrad Ahlers sowie des
Herausgebers Rudolf Augstein. In der Fragestunde
des Bundestages am 7.11. zur Rede gestellt, leug-
nete er jegliche Beteiligung. Adenauer stellte sich
hinter seinen Minister und sprach von einem
»Abgrund von Landesverrat«. Mit versteinertem
Blick nahm er die Intervention von Innenminister
Höcherl zur Kenntnis.

Adenauer's standing was badly damaged by the so-
called "Spiegel affair." On October 10, 1962 the news
magazine, in a sensational article which in the opinion of the Ministry of Defense contained classified
information, described the Federal Republic as
"only partially able to defend itself." The Defense
Minister Strauß thereupon took steps to have the
author of the article, Conrad Ahlers and the editor,
Rudolf Augstein arrested. When called to account
during questioning in parliament on November 7,
he denied any involvement. Adenauer stood by his
minister and spoke of an "abyss of treason." With a
stony look he took note of the intervention by
Minister of the Interior Höcherl.

Atombewaffnung der Bundeswehr / Atomic Armament of the Military

In Anbetracht der zunehmend drängenden Forderungen nach einem atomaren Mitspracherecht der Partner beschlossen die Regierungschefs der 15 Mitgliedstaaten mit dem Generalsekretär der NATO Mitte Dezember 1957 in Paris die Übertragung von Mittelstreckenraketen auf den Oberbefehlshaber der Alliierten Streitkräfte in Zentraleuropa. Von links: Achille H. van Acker, John G. Diefenbaker, Hans C. Hansen, Félix Gaillard, Konrad Adenauer, Konstantin Karamanlis, Adone Zoli, Hermann Jonasson, Paul-Henri Spaak, Joseph Bech, Joseph Luns, Einar Gerhardsen, Marcello Caetano, Adnan Menderes, Harold M. Macmillan, Dwight D. Eisenhower.

Faced with the increasingly insistent demands that the partners should have a say in atomic matters, the heads of government of the 15 member states of NATO together with the Secretary General decided in mid-December 1957 in Paris to transfer responsibility for medium-range missiles to the Commander-in-Chief of the Allied armed forces in Central Europe. From left to right: Achille H. van Acker, John G. Diefenbaker, Hans C. Hansen, Félix Gaillard, Konrad Adenauer, Konstantin Karamanlis, Adone Zoli, Hermann Jonasson, Paul-Henri Spaak, Joseph Bech, Joseph Luns, Einar Gerhardsen, Marcello Caetano, Adnan Menderes, Harold M. Macmillan, Dwight D. Eisenhower.

(oben) Mitte der fünfziger Jahre zeichnete sich ein Wandel der amerikanischen Sicherheitsstrategie ab. Sie wies den europäischen Verbündeten die Aufgabe zu, die konventionelle Verteidigung zu übernehmen, während die USA für den atomaren Schutzschild sorgen sollten. Da die Bundesrepublik und Frankreich eine solche Zurücksetzung nicht akzeptierten, strebten sie gemeinsam den Besitz von Kernwaffen an. Zu den energischsten Fürsprechern dieser Kooperation zählte auf der deutschen Seite neben Adenauer Verteidigungsminister Strauß, hier bei einer Herbstübung der Bundeswehr in der Lüneburger Heide.

(above) In the mid-fifties a new American security strategy began to emerge, which gave America's European allies responsibility for conventional defense while the USA was to provide the protective shield of nuclear weapons. Because it was unacceptable to the Federal Republic and France to be downgraded in this way, they joined forces in a bid to acquire nuclear weapons. In addition to Adenauer, one of the most vigorous advocates of this cooperation on the German side was Defense Minister Strauß, here at a fall army exercise on the Lüneburg Heath.

Wenige Wochen nach der Atomdebatte des Bundestags paraphierte Strauß mit seinen Kollegen aus Frankreich und Italien ein Abkommen über die Produktion von Kernwaffen. Aus Verärgerung über die Aussetzung dieses Dokuments durch den neuen französischen Regierungschef Charles de Gaulle im Sommer 1958 entschied sich Strauß bei der Anschaffung von Kampfflugzeugen nicht für die ursprünglich von ihm gewünschte französische »Mirage«, sondern für den amerikanischen »Starfighter«. Anfang 1960 führte er Adenauer die Maschine mit einem Album vor.

A few weeks after the parliamentary debate on atomic armaments Strauß and his opposite numbers from France and Italy initialled an agreement for the manufacture of nuclear weapons. Annoyed at the refusal by the new French head of government Charles de Gaulle to endorse this document in summer 1958, Strauß, when deciding what bomber planes to purchase, came out in favor not of the French "Mirage" that he had originally wanted but of the American "Starfighter." At the beginning of 1960 he demonstrated the plane to Adenauer with the aid of a photo album.

»Atomare Waffen, wenn es zu keiner Abrüstung kommt, oder nicht«, war die zentrale Frage, und die Abgeordneten des Bundestags beantworteten sie teils mit Sachlichkeit, teils mit »tollste[r] Hetze« (Heinrich Krone). Die Opposition attackierte die Nuklearpolitik der Regierung mit großer Schärfe, forderte Abrüstungsverhandlungen und legte einen Gesetzentwurf über eine Volksbefragung zur atomaren Ausrüstung der Bundeswehr vor. Der Kanzler hingegen warnte in seiner Rede am 20.3.1958 mit vielsagender Gestik vor dem Zerfall der NATO, wenn die Bundesrepublik sich der Umrüstung verweigere. Gegen die Stimmen der SPD und bei Enthaltung der FDP votierte das Parlament am Ende sowohl für die allgemeine Abrüstung als auch für die Ausrüstung der deutschen Streitkräfte mit Atomwaffen.

"Atomic weapons – failing disarmament – or not": that was the central question, and some members of parliament answered it with calm objectivity, others with the "wildest aggressiveness." (Heinrich Krone) The opposition attacked the government's nuclear policy in extremely harsh terms, demanded disarmament negotiations and submitted a draft bill for a referendum on atomic armaments for the armed forces. The Chancellor on the other hand, in his speech on March 20, 1958, warned, with eloquent gestures, that NATO would disintegrate if the Federal Republic refused to accept atomic armaments. With the SPD voting against and the FDP abstaining, parliament in the end voted both for general disarmament and for the equipment of the German armed forces with atomic weapons.

(gegenüber) Gegen die Ankündigung der Stationierung atomarer Trägersysteme erhob sich in der deutschen Öffentlichkeit leidenschaftlicher Protest. Politiker, Gewerkschafter, Wissenschaftler und evangelische Theologen verlangten den Verzicht auf Kernwaffen. Demgegenüber verteidigte die Bundesregierung uneingeschränkt die nuklearpolitischen Planungen der Allianz. Die Ausgangspositionen waren unversöhnlich. So war es nicht verwunderlich, daß die parlamentarische Auseinandersetzung über die Atombewaffnung Ende März 1958 zu den härtesten in der Ära Adenauer zählte.

(opposite) The German public protested passionately at the announcement that atomic carrier systems were to be stationed in their country. Politicians, trade unionists, scientists, and protestant theologians demanded the renunciation of nuclear weapons. The government on the other hand unreservedly defended NATO's nuclear policy and planning. The basic positions were irreconcilable. It was thus not surprising that the parliamentary debate on atomic armaments at the end of March 1958 was one of the most acrimonious of the Adenauer era.

Am 27.1.1958 verlangte der sowjetische Ministerpräsident Nikita Chruschtschow von den Westmächten den Abzug ihrer Truppen aus West-Berlin und dessen Umwandlung in eine »Freie Stadt« innerhalb von sechs Monaten. Im Januar 1959 regte er die Einberufung einer Konferenz zwecks Abschluß eines Friedensvertrages mit den zwei neutralisierten, demilitarisierten deutschen Staaten an. Um den Forderungen Nachdruck zu verleihen, verschärfte die DDR ihre Grenzkontrollen, hier auf der Avus vor Dreilinden.

On November 27, 1958 the Soviet Prime Minister Nikita Khrushchev demanded that the western powers withdraw their troops from West Berlin and that it be transformed into a "Free City" within six months. In January 1959 he suggested that a conference should be convened with the aim of concluding a peace treaty with the two neutralized, demilitarized German states. In order to give emphasis to his demands the GDR tightened their border controls, as here on the "Avus" (a high-speed stretch of highway near Berlin) outside Dreilinden.

THE NEXT
MILES
WILL BE IN THE
IET ZONE
NOT STOP

WESTBERLIN MUSS EINE FREIE ENTMILITARISIERTE STADT WERDEN !

Nach monatelangen Diskussionen über den Sinn eines neuen Dialogs zwischen Ost und West trafen sich die Staats- und Regierungschefs der Vier Mächte Mitte Mai 1960 in Paris. Aber noch ehe die Gespräche begonnen hatten, provozierte Chruschtschow den Abbruch der Konferenz. Anfang Juni stellte er die Forderung auf, die Verhandlungen in sechs bis acht Monaten wiederaufzunehmen. Mit Transparenten wie im Ostberliner Stadtteil Köpenick versuchte er seinem Ziel, Westberlin in eine »Freie Stadt« zu verwandeln, Nachdruck zu verschaffen.

After discussions lasting for months about the point of a fresh dialogue between East and West, the political leaders of the four powers met in Paris in mid-May 1960. But even before the talks had begun, Khrushchev engineered the collapse of the conference. At the beginning of June he put forward the demand that negotiations should be resumed in six to eight months. With banners such as the one seen here in the district of Köpenick in East Berlin he attempted to underline his goal of transforming West Berlin into a "free city." The slogan reads: West Berlin must become a free demilitarized city.

Das von Chruschtschow verursachte Scheitern der Pariser Gipfelkonferenz befreite Adenauer im Sommer 1960 für kurze Zeit von seinen größten Befürchtungen. »Wir haben nochmals fies Jlück gehabt!«, lautete sein prägnanter Kommentar. In gelöster Stimmung zeigte er sich am 28.6.1960 mit Tochter Lotte bei einem Empfang zu Ehren des argentinischen Präsidenten Arturo Frondizi. Die außenpolitischen Gefahren sah er aber keineswegs gebannt. Auch in Zukunft galt es mit einer zwischen Drohung und Verführung schwankenden Politik Moskaus zu rechnen.

In the summer of 1960 the failure of the Paris summit brought about by Khrushchev freed Adenauer for a short time from his worst fears. "We've been damned lucky again" was his terse comment. On June 28, 1960, with his daughter Lotte, he appeared to be in a relaxed mood at a reception in honor of the Argentinian President Arturo Frondizi. He did not, however, think that the dangers in foreign affairs were in any way permanently averted. In future he would still have to be prepared for Moscow's policy to vacillate between threats and bribes.

Um die prekäre Sicherheitslage der Bundesrepublik an der Schnittstelle zwischen den Blöcken zu verbessern, setzte die Bundesregierung auf den Ausbau der NATO zur vierten Nuklearmacht. Denn damit bot sich die Möglichkeit, den nichtnuklearen Status der Bundesrepublik auf Dauer zu revidieren. Namentlich Bundesverteidigungsminister Strauß, hier im Gespräch mit Bundestagspräsident Gerstenmaier bei einem Empfang am 29.6.1960 im Hotel Petersberg, war von der Überzeugung durchdrungen, daß eine Nation ohne Atomwaffen eine »entmannte Nation« sei.

In order to improve the precarious security position of the Federal Republic at the interface between the power blocs, the government backed the expansion of NATO to become the fourth nuclear power. For this held out the possibility of amending the non-nuclear status of the Federal Republic indefinitely. Defense Minister Strauß in particular, here in conversation with the President of the Bundestag Gerstenmaier at a reception on June 29, 1960 in the Petersberg Hotel, was utterly convinced that a nation without atomic weapons was an "emasculated" nation.

Der Auftritt des amerikanischen Präsidenten John F. Kennedy im Januar 1961 auf der Bühne der Weltpolitik wurde von Adenauer alles andere als freudig begrüßt. Kennedy galt nicht unbedingt als deutschlandfreundlich; er hatte auch mehrfach offen zugegeben, daß er Adenauers Außenpolitik als zu unflexibel betrachtete. Ihre erste Begegnung am 12.4.1961 in Washington verlief nach der herzlichen Begrüßung durch die Amerikaner, die Adenauer bei strahlendem Sonnenschein im Cabriolet genoß, reserviert und sachlich.

The appearance of the American President John F. Kennedy on the stage of world politics in January 1961 was anything but welcome to Adenauer. Kennedy was not thought to be entirely sympathetic to Germany and he had frankly admitted a number of times that he considered Adenauer's foreign policy to be too inflexible. Their first meeting in Washington on April 12, 1961, after a cordial welcome by the Americans, which Adenauer enjoyed in an convertible coupé in bright sunlight, was reserved and matter-of-fact.

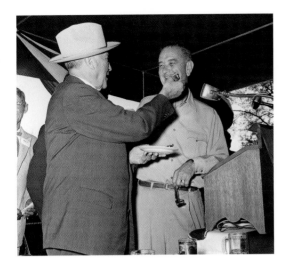

Angenehmer als die politischen Gespräche am Potomac gestaltete sich der zweitägige Aufenthalt Adenauers auf der Ranch von Vizepräsident Lyndon B. Johnson in Texas. Zur Begrüßung veranstaltete der Gastgeber ein Barbecue, auf dem ein Mädchenchor Volkslieder in deutscher Sprache wie »Du, du liegst mir im Herzen« sang. Ausgelassen ließ sich der Vizepräsident gar vom Kanzler füttern. Gewiß hätte Adenauer es gern gesehen, wenn auch Kennedy ihm aus der Hand »gegessen« hätte.

Adenauer's two-day visit to Vice President Lyndon B. Johnson's Texas ranch was a more enjoyable experience than the political talks in Washington. The host gave a barbecue to welcome him at which a girls' choir sang folk songs in German such as "Du, du liegst mir am Herzen." ("You are close to my heart") The Vice President, in a lighthearted mood, even let the Chancellor feed him. Adenauer would surely have been glad to see Kennedy also "eating out of his hand."

»Krieg - nein. Wachsende Spannungen - wahrscheinlich«, so lautete die unheilschwangere Prognose Heinrich Krones für das Jahr 1961. Vor allem die Lage an der Spree bot in Anbetracht des wachsenden Flüchtlingsstroms aus der DDR und aus Ostberlin Anlaß zu Sorge. Immer mehr Menschen wandten der Propaganda, die den sicheren Sieg des Sozialismus gegenüber dem Klassenfeind proklamierte, angewidert den Rücken zu. Die martialische Maiparade am Tag der Arbeit in Ostberlin ließ jedoch erahnen, daß die politische Führung das Feld nicht kampflos räumen würde.

"War – no. Growing tension – probably" was Heinrich Krone's ominous forecast for 1961. The situation in Berlin gave particular cause for concern in view of the growing flood of refugees from the GDR and East Berlin. More and more people were turning their backs in disgust on the propaganda which proclaimed the certain victory of socialism over the class enemy. The martial parade on Labor Day, May 1, in East Berlin, however, suggested that the political leaders would not accept defeat without a struggle. The slogan reads: For victory.

In den frühen Morgenstunden des 13.8.1961 begann, gesichert von schwerbewaffneten Volkspolizisten, in der Zimmerstraße die Errichtung von Betonpfählen und Stacheldraht durch Pioniereinheiten. Einige Tage später setzte der eigentliche Bau der Mauer als Teil eines festen Sperrsystems ein.
(rechts) In den auf Ostberliner Gebiet direkt an der Sektorengrenze gelegenen Häusern wurden – wie hier an der Bernauer Straße im Bezirk Wedding - die Fenster und Türen in Richtung Westen zugemauert.

In the early hours of the morning of August 13, 1961 pioneer units, guarded by heavily armed people's police, began to put up concrete posts and barbed wire in the Zimmerstraße. A few days later work began on the actual building of the Wall as part of a permanent barrier.
(right) In the houses situated on East Berlin territory at the actual sector boundary doors and windows facing west were bricked up – here on the Bernauer Straße in the Wedding district.

Berliner Mauerbau

Zur Verhinderung der »Republikflucht« hatten die Behörden der DDR seit Anfang der fünfziger Jahre entlang der Demarkationslinie umfangreiche Sperranlagen errichtet. Planungen über eine befestigte Grenze gegenüber Westberlin wurden zwar eingeleitet, aber nicht umgesetzt. So blieb den Gegnern des Regimes die Möglichkeit, über Ostberlin in den Westen zu fliehen. Seit Juni 1961 nahm der Exodus dramatische Formen an. Die Existenz der DDR stand auf dem Spiel. Schon Ende März 1961 hatte Ulbricht für eine Stacheldrahtbarriere längs der Sektorengrenze quer durch die Stadt plädiert, war damit aber bei den Regierungen des Ostblocks auf Widerspruch gestoßen. Dennoch ließ ihn die massenhafte Flucht nicht ruhen. Mitte Juni fiel dann in einem Interview seine verräterische Bemerkung: »Niemand hat die Absicht, eine Mauer zu errichten.« Als sich im Juli 30 000 DDR-Bewohner »zu einer Abstimmung mit den Füßen« entschieden, billigten die Mitgliedstaaten des Warschauer Paktes dem SED-Regime Anfang August aus Furcht vor einer kriegerischen Eskalation die völlige Abriegelung des Ostsektors zu.

The Building of the Berlin Wall

To prevent what they termed "flight from the Republic," i.e. emigration without official permission, since the early fifties the GDR authorities had set up extensive barriers along the line of demarcation. Plans for securing the border with West Berlin were drawn up but not implemented. Thus opponents of the régime still had the possibility of fleeing to the West via East Berlin. From June 1961 the exodus swelled to dramatic proportions. The existence of the GDR was at stake. At the end of March 1961 Ulbricht had already argued in favor of a barbed-wire barrier to cut right across the city along the sector boundary, but the governments of the eastern bloc states had refused to agree to this. But the mass exodus gave him no respite. Then, in an interview in mid-June, he let slip the giveaway remark: "Nobody has the intention of building a wall." When in July 30,000 inhabitants of the GDR decided to "vote with their feet," the member states of the Warsaw Pact, fearing that the situation could escalate into war, gave the SED régime their approval at the beginning of August for the eastern sector to be completely sealed off.

Ähnlich wie die amerikanischen Soldaten, die sich hinter Sandsäcken verbarrikadierten, gingen die Westmächte politisch »in Deckung«. »US-Präsident Kennedy schweigt ... Macmillan geht auf die Jagd ... und Adenauer schimpft auf Brandt«, titelte die »Bildzeitung«. Für viele Deutsche, die die Hoffnung auf die Aufhebung der staatlichen Teilung nicht aufgegeben hatten, brach »die Stunde der großen Desillusion« (Heinrich Krone) an.

Like the American soldiers barricading themselves in behind sandbags, the western powers "took cover," politically speaking. "US President Kennedy is silent ... Macmillan goes hunting ... and Adenauer abuses Brandt" was the front page news in the *Bildzeitung*. For many Germans who had not given up hope that the division of Germany would be lifted, the moment of truth, the "hour of great disillusionment" (Heinrich Krone) had come.

Erschüttert über die »leere Bühne«, die die Westmächte nach dem Aufzug des Vorhangs im »deutschen Theater« boten, brach Willy Brandt seine Wahlkampfreise ab und eilte nach Berlin. Am 19.8.1961 begrüßte er auf einer Großkundgebung vor dem Schöneberger Rathaus den von Kennedy entsandten legendären »Vater der Luftbrücke« General Lucius D. Clay und Bundesaußenminister von Brentano. Einen Mitflug Adenauers von Bonn nach Berlin hatten die Amerikaner abgelehnt.

Deeply shocked by the "empty stage" which the western powers presented when the curtain went up in the "German theater," Willy Brandt broke off his campaign tour and hastened to Berlin. At a big rally outside the Schöneberg Town Hall on August 19, 1961 he welcomed General Lucius D. Clay, the legendary "father of the airlift," who had been dispatched by Kennedy, and Foreign Minister von Brentano. The Americans had turned down a suggestion that Adenauer should join the flight from Bonn to Berlin.

Um ein Stück verlorenes Vertrauen in seine Politik zurückzugewinnen und der aufgewühlten Atmosphäre in Westberlin gegenzuwirken, veranlaßte Kennedy nach der Ankunft von Clay und dem mitgereisten Vizepräsidenten Johnson die Verstärkung der US-Truppen in Westberlin um 1 500 Soldaten. Die Bevölkerung begrüßte die Kampfgruppe mit Jubel und Erleichterung.

In order to restore some degree of lost confidence in his policies and to counteract the turbulent atmosphere in West Berlin, Kennedy, after the arrival of Clay accompanied by Vice President Johnson, had US troops in West Berlin reinforced by 1,500 men. The people welcomed the task force with jubilation and relief.

(links) Nachdem Johnson die amerikanische Sicherheitsgarantie für die West-
sektoren am 19.8.1961 bekräftigt hatte, ließ Clay am 20.8. Panzer am Check-
point Charlie auffahren. Doch trotz dieser kämpferischen Gesten ging es dem
Westen vor allem darum, Ruhe und Ordnung an der Grenze zu bewahren.
Am 25.10.1961 bezogen amerikanische Panzer an der Sektorengrenze in der
Friedrichstraße Posten.

(left) After Johnson had confirmed the American security guarantee for the
western sector on August 19, 1961, Clay had tanks drawn up at Checkpoint
Charlie on August 20. But despite these bellicose gestures the West was concerned above all to preserve calm and order at the frontier.
On October 25, 1961 American tanks took up positions in the Friedrichstraße
at the sector boundary.

Aus Furcht vor Aktionen der wütenden Bevölkerung zögerte Adenauer eine Fahrt nach Berlin lange hinaus. Erst am 22.8.1961, 9 Tage nach dem Bau der Mauer, reiste er an die Spree. Unter starkem Polizeischutz besichtigte er die Absperrungen entlang der Sektorengrenze. Links neben ihm der Bundesminister für Gesamtdeutsche Fragen Lemmer (mit Zigarre) und der Vorsitzende der CSU-Landesgruppe im Deutschen Bundestag Höcherl.

Fearing how the helpless and enraged populace might act, Adenauer hesitated for a long time before going to Berlin. It was not until August 22, 1961, nine days after the building of the Wall that he went there. Under heavy police guard he went to look at the barriers along the sector boundary. Next to him on the left is the Minister for All-German Affairs Lemmer (with cigar) and the chairman of the CSU regional parliamentary group Höcherl.

1957–1963

(oben) Zynisch proklamierten die Machthaber der DDR die Parole: »Für gute Beziehungen zwischen Westberlin und der DDR«.
(gegenüber) Mit dem Ausbau der Absperranlagen – hier am Brandenburger Tor – sollte sich die Lage in Berlin allmählich beruhigen.

(above) The GDR rulers cynically proclaimed the slogan: "For good relations between West Berlin and the GDR."
(opposite) The situation in Berlin gradually became calmer as the barrier was extended – here at the Brandenburg Gate.

Für den Verkehr zwischen den Stadthälften blieben zunächst dreizehn Übergänge geöffnet. Um den erwarteten Besucherstrom zu kanalisieren, errichtete die DDR am 23.8.1961 Passierscheinbüros auf Westberliner S-Bahnhöfen. Die Alliierte Kommandantur wies diese Maßnahme als Anmaßung von Hoheitsrechten umgehend zurück. Im Gegenzug verwehrte die SED den Bewohnern Westberlins das Betreten des Ostsektors. Den Freunden und Angehörigen über Hunderte von Metern zuzuwinken, wie hier an der Bernauer Straße in Berlin-Wedding, blieb für viele die einzige Möglichkeit eines persönlichen Kontakts.

At first, thirteen crossing points were kept open for travel between the two halves of the city. On August 23, 1961, in order to control the expected influx of visitors, the GDR set up offices for the issue of visitors' passes at stations of the Berlin city railway in West Berlin. At Allied headquarters this measure was immediately rejected as an arrogation of sovereign rights. The SED countered by refusing to allow inhabitants of West Berlin to enter the eastern sector. For many people, waving to friends and relatives at a distance of several hundred yards – as seen here at the Bernauer Straße in Berlin-Wedding – was the only remaining opportunity for personal contact.

1957–1963

Zahlreiche Deutsche bezahlten ihre Sehnsucht nach Freiheit mit dem Leben. Nach den Ermittlungen der »Zentralen Erfassungsstelle Salzgitter« starben bei Fluchtversuchen aus der DDR von 1949 bis 1989 insgesamt 899 Menschen, davon 255 an der Grenze um Westberlin. Zu ihnen zählte auch der achtzehnjährige Peter Fechter. Durch einen Schuß von Grenzbeamten schwer getroffen, blieb er am 17.8.1962 eine Stunde ohne jede Hilfe und verblutete im Niemandsland zwischen Mauer und Stacheldraht, bevor DDR-Soldaten ihn abtransportierten.

Numerous Germans paid for their longing for freedom with their lives. Between 1949 and 1989, according to statistics compiled by the Central Registry in Salzgitter, a total of 899 people died while trying to escape from the GDR, 255 of them at the boundary surrounding West Berlin. One of them was the 18-year-old Peter Fechter. After being severely wounded by a shot fired by border guards on August 17, 1962 he was left for an hour without any help and bled to death in the no-man's-land between the Wall and the barbed wire before being taken away by GDR soldiers.

Trotz des perfiden Schießbefehls konnten sich die Menschen in Berlin mit der »versteinerte[n] Absage an die Menschlichkeit« (Richard von Weizsäcker) nie abfinden. Am 22.8.1961 suchte ein Angehöriger der Nationalen Volksarmee sein Heil in der Flucht.

Despite the vile "shoot-to-kill" order, the people of Berlin could never come to terms with the "stony denial of humanity." (Richard von Weizsäcker) On August 22, 1961 a member of the National People's Army sought his salvation in flight.

Seit 1964 »verfeinerte« die DDR den sog. »friedensstiftenden« »antifaschistischen Schutzwall«. Ein immer ausgefeilteres Absperrsystem funktionierte die »moderne Grenze« – wie hier am Potsdamer Platz – allmählich zum Todesstreifen um.

From 1964 on the GDR added "refinements" to the so-called "peacemaking" "anti-fascist protective wall." An ever more sophisticated system of barriers gradually converted the "modern boundary" – here at the Potsdamer Platz – into a death trap.

Als Zeichen der Solidarität und Verbundenheit schnürten etliche Westberliner am 13.8.1962, dem ersten Jahrestag des Mauerbaus, ein Päckchen für Freunde und Bekannte in Ostberlin.

On August 13, 1962, the first anniversary of the building of the Wall, quite a few West Berliners made up parcels for friends and acquaintances in East Berlin as a token of solidarity and attachment.

1957–1963

Als demonstratives Zeichen ihres Willens zur Verteidigung der Stadt führten die Westmächte am 25.4.1964 in Westberlin den Tag der Alliierten Streitkräfte ein und hielten erstmals seit dem Kriegsende wieder eine gemeinsame Militärparade ab.

On April 25, 1964, in order to demonstrate their determination to defend the city, the western powers introduced Allied Armed Forces Day in West Berlin and organized a joint military parade for the first time since the end of the war.

Nach dem Bau der Berliner Mauer erlebte der Kanzler auf Abruf in seiner Amtszeit nur noch wenige Momente so unbeschwerter Freude wie beim Gratulationsdefilee zu seinem 86. Geburtstag am 5.1.1962 im Palais Schaumburg. Wenige Tage nach diesen glücklichen Stunden erlitt er einen ersten Herzinfarkt; nach der Genesung plagte ihn die Furcht vor der Untreue der USA.

For the Chancellor "on notice," after the building of the Berlin Wall and during what remained of his term in office, there were only a few occasions of such unalloyed pleasure as the "march past" of his family, who lined up in the Palais Schaumburg to give him their best wishes on his 86th birthday on January 5, 1962. Only a few days after those happy hours he suffered his first heart attack; after he had recovered he was plagued by fears of American disloyality.

Einsam in der Macht, gab Adenauer im Sommer 1962 die langjährig gültige Linie deutscher Außenpolitik zugunsten einer »ziemlich ungeschützten Option für einen deutsch-französischen Zweibund« (Hans-Peter Schwarz) auf. Nicht Senilität, sondern Angst beherrschte ihn vor der Schutzlosigkeit als nuklearer Habenichts, den einzig wahren Bundesgenossen zu verlieren, vor der von ihm niemals ganz ausgeschlossenen französisch-russischen Allianz!

Lonely in his power, in summer 1962 Adenauer abandoned the foreign policy stance to which he had adhered for many years, in favor of the "rather vulnerable option of a Franco-German dual alliance." (Hans-Peter Schwarz) It was not senility but fear that governed the actions of him of being left unprotected as a nuclear have-not, of losing his one true ally, of an alliance between France and Russia that he never wholly ruled out in his mind.

Deutsch-Französische Versöhnung / Franco-German Reconciliation

Deutsche und Franzosen müßten Brüder werden, meinte der französische Staatspräsident Ende Juni 1962. Daher zelebrierte er den Besuch des Bundeskanzlers im Juli als eine »große Demonstration deutsch-französischer Versöhnung« (Hans-Peter Schwarz). Nach der Ankunft Adenauers begleitete de Gaulle ihn am 2.7.1962 im offenen Wagen mit der Republikanischen Garde durch fahnengeschmückte Straßen zu seinem Quartier. Einen Teil der Route wurden sie von der Kavallerie eskortiert. Die Uhrzeit der Fahrt war bewußt so ausgewählt worden, daß sie die Aufmerksamkeit der Pariser Bevölkerung erregen mußte.

Germans and Frenchmen should become brothers, said the French President at the end of June 1962. He therefore celebrated the Chancellor's visit in July as a "great demonstration of Franco-German reconciliation." (Hans-Peter Schwarz) After Adenauer's arrival on July 2, 1962 de Gaulle accompanied him to his quarters along with the Republican Guard in a convertible car through streets hung with flags. For part of the route they were escorted by the cavalry. The ride was deliberately timed so that it would be bound to attract the attention of the people of Paris.

Am 8.7.1962, dem letzten Tag seiner »Tour de France«, standen für Adenauer und de Gaulle gleich zwei Höhepunkte auf dem Programm: Auf dem Truppenübungsplatz Mourmelon in der Champagne, Ort zahlreicher blutiger Schlachten beider Völker, nahmen sie eine deutsch-französische Militärparade ab. Anschließend begaben sie sich sinnigerweise direkt zum Hochamt in die Kathedrale des nahen Reims. Vor dem Gotteshaus nahm Erzbischof Marty die beiden Staatsmänner in Empfang.

On July 8, 1962, the last day of his "Tour de France," not one but two high points were scheduled for Adenauer and de Gaulle: at the Mourmelon military training ground in the Champagne region, the scene of numerous bloody battles between the two peoples, they inspected a Franco-German military parade. Afterwards, appropriately, they went straight to High Mass at Reims Cathedral nearby. Archbishop Marty received the two statesmen in front of the house of God.

Ein Bild, das um die Welt ging: De Gaulle und Adenauer vor zwei mit rotem Samt bezogenen Gebetsstühlen am 8.7.1962 in der Kathedrale von Reims. Mit dem feierlichen Tedeum in der alten Krönungsstätte zahlreicher fränkischer Könige wurde ein Akt von historischer Bedeutung vollzogen. Nicht allen gefiel der »französisch-deutsche ›Flirt‹« (Raymond Poidevin).

A picture that went round the world: de Gaulle and Adenauer standing in front of two prayer seats covered in red velvet on July 8, 1962 in Reims Cathedral. With the solemn Te deum in the ancient church where so many Franconian kings had been crowned, an act of historic importance was performed. Not everyone was happy with the "Franco-German 'flirtation'." (Raymond Poidevin)

Wenige Wochen nach der Frankreichreise des Bundeskanzlers putzte sich Deutschland heraus, um den Staatspräsidenten willkommen zu heißen. In ihren politischen Gesprächen erzielten Adenauer und de Gaulle ein Einverständnis über die Konzertierung der Außen-, Verteidigungs- und Entwicklungspolitik sowie eine enge Kooperation auf dem Feld der Erziehungspolitik.

A few weeks after the Chancellor's trip to France, Germany put on its Sunday best to welcome the French President. In their political talks Adenauer and de Gaulle agreed on a concerted foreign, defense and development policy, along with close cooperation in the field of education policy.

In seinen zahlreichen Ansprachen an das Volk kämpfte de Gaulle »um die Seele der Deutschen« (Hans von Herwarth). Er träufelte Balsam in ihre Wunden, sprach in verständlichen Worten anerkennend über ihre Geschichte, Leistungen, auch Opfer und gab ihnen damit ein Stück Selbstbewußtsein zurück. Ihre Dankbarkeit und Ehrerbietung zeigte sich in höchst unterschiedlicher Form.

In his numerous addresses to the people de Gaulle strove to win "the soul of the Germans." (Hans von Herwarth) He poured balm on their wounds, speaking to them in language they could understand, acknowledging their history and achievements, and also their sacrifices, thereby restoring some of their self-respect. They showed their gratitude and respect in a great variety of ways.

(rechts) Auf dem Bonner Marktplatz zog de Gaulle am 5.9.1962 10000 Zuhörer mit pathetischen Ausrufen an »das große deutsche Volk« in den Bann. Mit einem Bad in der Menge setzte er sich über sämtliche Sicherheitsvorkehrungen hinweg.

(right) On the Market Square in Bonn on September 5, 1962, de Gaulle captivated his 10,000 listeners with rhetorical pronouncements about the "great German people." He plunged into the crowd, security precautions.

Am 6.9.1962, dem dritten Tag der »Tour d'Allemagne«, ging es für de Gaulle mit dem Schiff rheinabwärts nach Düsseldorf. Obwohl es bei der Ankunft in Strömen goß, verlangte er bei der Fahrt von der Anlegestelle in die Stadt, daß das Verdeck seines Cabriolets geöffnet würde, damit die wartende Menge ihn sehen könne. Als er bei Ministerpräsident Meyers völlig durchnäßt ankam, bat er ihn, sich umziehen zu dürfen: »So bin ich kein schöner Anblick«.

On September 6, 1962, the third day of the "Tour d'Allemagne," de Gaulle went down the Rhine to Düsseldorf by ship. Although it was pouring with rain when he arrived, he asked for the roof of his convertible to be opened during the ride from the mooring point into the city, so that the waiting crowds could see him. When he was met by Minister President Meyers he was drenched, and began by asking if he could change his clothes: "I'm not very nice to look at like this."

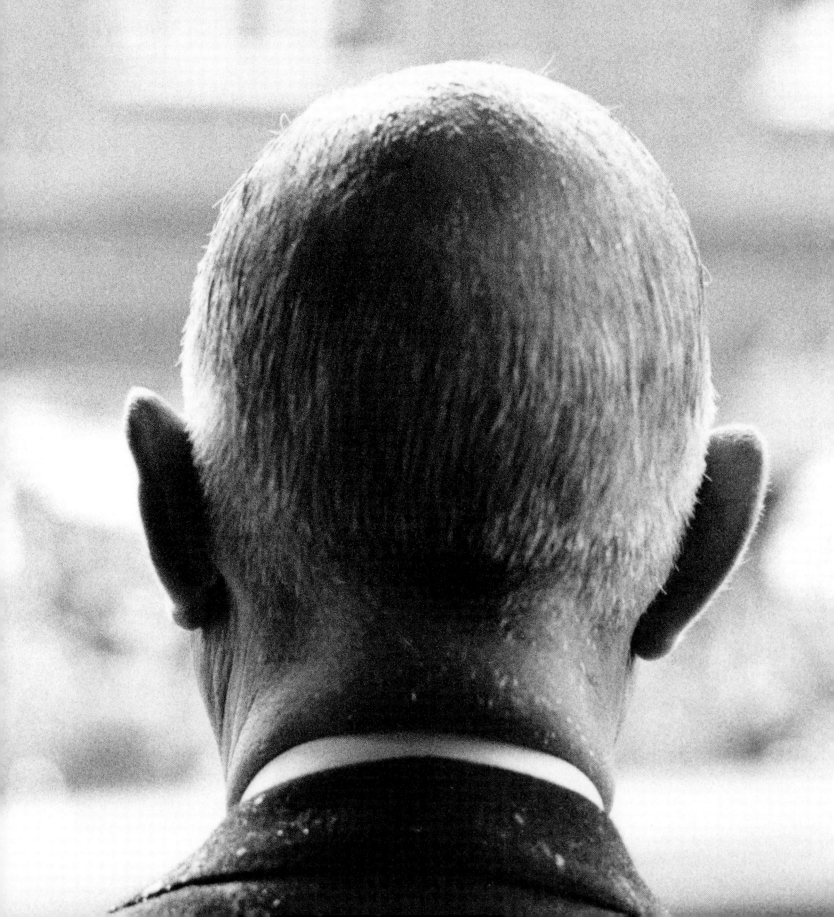

Seinen Auftritt vor den Stahlkochern der Thyssen-Hütte in Duisburg-Hamborn am 6.9.1962 verstand de Gaulle als eine Verneigung vor der werktätigen Bevölkerung. Sie wirkte um so symbolkräftiger, als sie in jenem Teil Deutschlands stattfand, der in der Geschichte der Nachbarn besonders umkämpft gewesen war – dem Ruhrgebiet.

His appearance before the steel workers of the Thyssen plant in Duisburg-Hamborn on September 6, 1962 was conceived by de Gaulle as an act of homage to the working populace. Its symbolic effect was all the greater because it took place in that part of Germany which had been a particular bone of contention in the history of its neighbors: the Ruhr region.

Am 22.1.1963 signierten Adenauer und de Gaulle im Salon Murat des Pariser Elysée-Palastes einen Vertrag über die deutsch-französische Zusammenarbeit, der politische Konsultationen beider Regierungen und eine verstärkte Zusammenarbeit in der Außen- und Verteidigungspolitik sowie in Erziehungs- und Jugendfragen vorsah. Nach der Unterzeichnung beglückwünschten sie sich mit einer »Accolade«. »Übervoll ist mein Herz und dankbar mein Gemüt«, meinte der General tief bewegt. Der Kanzler zog es vor, dem nichts hinzuzufügen.

On January 22, 1963 in the Salon Murat of the Elysée Palace in Paris Adenauer and de Gaulle signed a Franco-German Cooperation Treaty providing for political consultation between the two governments and increased cooperation in foreign and defense policy as well as education and youth issues. After signing, they congratulated each other with a ceremonial embrace. With deep emotion the General said: "My heart is full to overflowing and my spirit is full of thanks." The Chancellor preferred not to add anything.

Kein Besuch eines ausländischen Staatsgastes machte der Bundesregierung in der Ära Adenauer so viel Arbeit wie der des amerikanischen Präsidenten Ende Juni 1963, keiner kostete »so viel Nerven« (Horst Osterheld). Am 23.6.1963 wurde Kennedy von Adenauer mit militärischen Ehren auf dem Flughafen Köln-Bonn begrüßt. Anschließend begab man sich zum Hochamt in den Kölner Dom.

No state visit from abroad during the Adenauer era caused as much work for the government as that of the American President at the end of June 1963, none was "so hard on the nerves." (Horst Osterheld) On June 23, 1963 Kennedy was welcomed by Adenauer with military honors at Köln-Bonn airport. Afterwards they went to High Mass in Cologne Cathedral.

Wo immer Kennedy während seines viertägigen Aufenthaltes auftauchte, schlug ihm, wie hier am 23.6.1963 vor 20000 Menschen auf dem Bonner Marktplatz, eine Welle der Begeisterung entgegen. Sein Charme, seine Jugend und die Kombination von Idealismus und Macht gaben seinem Auftreten das »Flair des Außergewöhnlichen, des Triumphalen« (Horst Osterheld).

Wherever Kennedy appeared during his four-day visit he was met with a surge of enthusiasm, here on June 23, 1963 addressing 20,000 people on the Market Square in Bonn. His charm, his youth, and the combination of idealism and power gave his appearances an "aura of the exceptional, the triumphal." (Horst Osterheld)

Manchen Passagen seiner Rede vor dem Schöneberger Rathaus gab Kennedy einen starken antikommunistischen Zungenschlag. Mit den von ihm sonst bevorzugten moderaten Tönen waren sie nur schwer in Einklang zu bringen. Offenbar ließ er sich von den Gefühlen leiten, die ihn kurz zuvor beim Anblick des mit rotem Tuch verhangenen Brandenburger Tores und einer mit scharfen Vorwürfen versehenen Schrifttafel erfüllt hatten.

Kennedy gave a strong anti-Communist slant to some parts of his speech in front of the Schöneberg Town Hall, very much out of keeping with the moderate language which he generally preferred. He was evidently swayed by the emotions which had assailed him shortly beforehand when he saw the Brandenburg Gate draped in red and the placard printed with strong reproachement.

(gegenüber) Nachdem Kennedy sein Programm in Bonn, Wiesbaden und Frankfurt am Main absolviert hatte, flog er am 26.6.1963 nach Westberlin, in die geteilte Stadt. Nach der Landung fuhr er gemeinsam mit Adenauer und Brandt im offenen Wagen durch die von enthusiastischen Menschen gesäumten Straßen. Eine riesige Motorradeskorte geleitete die Fahrzeugkolonne.

(opposite) On June 26, 1963 after completing his schedule in Bonn, Wiesbaden, and Frankfurt am Main, Kennedy flew to West Berlin, to the divided city. After landing he drove, together with Adenauer and Brandt, in a convertible through streets lined with enthusiastic people. A huge motorcycle escort accompanied the convoy.

Am 26.6.1963 bekräftigte Kennedy in einer Ansprache vor dem Rathaus Schöneberg in Anwesenheit von Adenauer und Brandt das amerikanische Engagement für Berlin: »Alle freien Menschen, wo immer sie leben mögen, sind Bürger dieser Stadt Westberlin, und deshalb bin ich als freier Mann stolz darauf sagen zu können: Ich bin ein Berliner!«

On June 26, 1963 speaking in front of the Schöneberg Town Hall in the presence of Adenauer and Brandt, Kennedy confirmed America's commitment to Berlin: "All free men, wherever they may live, are citizens of Berlin. And therefore, as a free man, I take pride in the words 'ich bin ein Berliner'."

Manch kritischer Zuhörer fand Kennedys Worte mitunter zu pathetisch, zu schmeichelhaft und damit zuwenig glaubwürdig. Die Öffentlichkeit reagierte hingegen auf die Emotionalität seiner Worte mit Dankbarkeit. Gerade unter Jugendlichen, wie denen, die ihm am 26.6.1963 vor dem Rathaus Schöneberg zujubelten, galt der Präsident als Hoffnungsträger. Wenige Monate später machte das Attentat von Dallas ihre Wünsche zunichte.

Not a few critical listeners found Kennedy's words in some places too histrionic, too flattering and hence lacking in credibility. The public in contrast responded gratefully to the emotional tone of his words. Young people in particular, such as those who welcomed him jubilantly on June 26, 1963 in front of the Schöneberg Town Hall, saw the President as someone on whom they could pin their hopes. His assassination in Dallas only a few months later put an end to that.

Für einige weibliche Zuschauer in Berlin war die Aufregung beim Anblick des strahlenden Helden John F. Kennedy offenbar zu groß.

For a few female spectators in Berlin the excitement of seeing John F. Kennedy, their knight in shining armor, was evidently too great.

Kennedys Ausstrahlung wirkte nicht zuletzt auf die Damenwelt faszinierend. Sie lag ihm in Köln, hier bei seiner Anfahrt zum Dom, ebenso verzückt zu Füßen wie etwa in Bonn vor dem Rathaus oder in Frankfurt auf dem Römer.

The magnetism of Kennedy's personality evoked a powerful response from women. They succumbed totally to his charm, here on his arrival at Cologne Cathedral no less than before the Town Hall in Bonn or on the Römer in Frankfurt.

Über 100 000 Zuschauer wurden Zeuge, als Adenauer am 12.10.1963 auf dem Truppenübungsplatz Wunstorf bei Hannover mit Bundesverteidigungsminister Kai-Uwe von Hassel und General Foertsch eine Feldparade abnahm. Zur Freude des »Erzzivilisten« Adenauer (Hans-Peter Schwarz) präsentierte die Bundeswehr Panzer, Düsenjäger und die neuen Honest-John-Raketen.

Over 100,000 spectators witnessed Adenauer taking the salute at a field parade on October 12, 1963 at the Wunstorf drill ground near Hanover together with Defense Minister Kai-Uwe von Hassel and General Foertsch. To the delight of Adenauer the "arch-civilian" (Hans-Peter Schwarz) the army displayed tanks, jet fighters, and the new Honest John missiles.

(gegenüber) Alle wußten um den historischen Rang der Stunde, als am 15.10.1963 Adenauer von seinem Platz auf der Regierungsbank der Laudatio des Bundestagspräsidenten in der Abschiedssitzung des Parlaments lauschte. Denn Adenauer war in hundert Jahren sturmbewegter deutscher Geschichte der einzige, der nach so langer Regierungszeit »unbesiegt und im Frieden« zurücktrat. Nicht nur deshalb schloß Gerstenmaier seine Rede mit den Worten: »Konrad Adenauer hat sich um das Vaterland verdient gemacht.«

(opposite) Everybody was aware of the historic importance of the moment on October 15, 1963 as Adenauer listened from his seat on the government front bench to the eulogy delivered by the President of the Bundestag during the final meeting of parliament. For in a hundred tempestuous years of German history Adenauer was the only leader to resign "undefeated and in peace" after such a lengthy period in office. Gerstenmaier concluded his speech – not only for that reason – with the words: "Konrad Adenauer has rendered outstanding services to the Fatherland."

(rechts) Von vielen sehnsüchtig erwartet, endete am 15.10.1963 die »Ära Adenauer«. An der Spitze der Bundesregierung erfolgte die Wachablösung. Mitsamt seinem Kabinett erhielt Adenauer von Bundespräsident Lübke die Entlassungsurkunde. Von links: Lübke, Adenauer, Erhard, Schröder und Höcherl.

(right) The end of the Adenauer era, longingly awaited by many, came on October 15, 1963. At the apex of the government there was a changing of the guard. Adenauer, along with his cabinet, was handed his certificate of discharge by President Lübke. From left to right: Lübke, Adenauer, Erhard, Schröder, and Höcherl.

1963–1966

Von Erhard zur Großen Koalition
From Erhard to the Grand Coalition

»Volkskanzler« mit Charisma, aber ohne Autorität: Ludwig Erhard am 29.8.1966 auf dem Flug nach Norwegen.

"Chancellor of the people" with charisma but without authority: Ludwig Erhard during a flight to Norway on August 29, 1966.

Die Kanzlerschaft Erhards

Die Wahl Ludwig Erhards zum Bundeskanzler am 16.10.1963 erfolgte in einer Zeit internationaler Umbrüche und innenpolitischer Veränderungen. Die beiden Supermächte näherten sich in einer Weise an, die kritische Beobachter wie Konrad Adenauer an »Kott-Freunde« erinnerte, wobei »kott« im Rheinland soviel wie »böse« bedeutet. Unterhalb des sowjetisch-amerikanischen »Duopols« bildete sich eine neue Staatengesellschaft mit multipolarem Charakter heraus. Aus Bonner Sicht war diese Entwicklung mit einer Reihe von Gefahren und Unwägbarkeiten verbunden. Dem Status quo in Zentraleuropa drohte die Zementierung, was für die Bundesrepublik sowohl deutschland- als auch sicherheitspolitisch unangenehme Konsequenzen aufwarf. Da sie keine nationale Identität besaß, mußte sie bestrebt sein, diese »durch die Wiedervereinigung zu gewinnen und ihr in einem vereinigten Europa neue Gestalt zu verleihen« (Klaus Hildebrand).

Mit der Relativierung des Ost-West-Konfliktes nahm bei den Verbündeten aber das ohnehin geringe Interesse an der Aufhebung der deutschen Teilung weiter ab. Da der Kontinent gleichzeitig von einer Renaissance des alten Nationalstaatsdenkens erfaßt wurde, breitete sich in der Bundesrepublik eine »Krise der Wiedervereinigungsidee« (Karl-Dietrich Bracher) aus. Parallel dazu lockerten die in den Vietnamkrieg verstrickten Vereinigten Staaten von Amerika ihre Verteidigungsgarantie für Europa und lösten unter den Deutschen damit das Gefühl schwindender Sicherheit aus. Großen Herausforderungen sah sich Ludwig Erhard auch in der Innen-, Gesellschafts- und Wirtschaftspolitik ausgesetzt.

Bei der Bewältigung der vor ihm liegenden Aufgaben gedachte sich der Bundeskanzler in doppelter Weise von den Strategien seines Vorgängers abzuheben. Zum einen erblickte Erhard im Gegensatz zu Adenauer nicht in der Politik, sondern in der Wirtschaft das »Schicksal« der Staaten. Zum anderen bedurfte es zur Durchsetzung der nationalen Interessen seiner Meinung nach nicht der Macht, sondern »der Stärke und Kraft«. Überzeugt vom Erfolg der Sozialen Marktwirtschaft, sah er die Lösung der Weltprobleme in der Verwirklichung eines von Protektionismus befreiten Welthandels und einer offenen internationalen Gesellschaft. »Freiheit, Sicherheit und Wohlstand für alle Bürger«, so lauteten die Ziele in Erhards Regierungserklärung vom 18.10.1963, mit der er sich einer »Politik der Mitte und der Verständigung« verschrieb. Der Schwerpunkt seiner programmatischen Aussagen lag eindeutig auf der Innenpolitik. Der Kanzler kündigte eine »Sozialpolitik aus einem Guß« an. Er versprach Konzepte für eine mehrjährige Haushaltsplanung, plädierte für eine Priorität der Gemeinschaftsaufgaben vor den Interessen der Verbände und betonte die Bedeutung von Bildung und Forschung.

Auf außenpolitischem Terrain bemühte er sich darum, ein Bild bruchloser Kontinuität zum Kurs Adenauers zu zeichnen. Erhard bekannte sich zur Sicherheitspartnerschaft mit den USA und bezeichnete Frankreich als unentbehrlichen Verbündeten für die deutsche Europapolitik. Er unterstrich das Ziel der Wiedervereinigung Deutschlands in Freiheit und verpflichtete sich nachdrücklich dazu, die europäische Integration voranzutreiben.

Der Kanzler wußte sehr wohl, daß seine Pläne auch und gerade in den eigenen Reihen kritisch beobachtet wurden.

Erhard's Chancellorship

Ludwig Erhard was elected as Federal Chancellor on October 16, 1963, at a time of international upheavals and national change. There was a rapprochement between the two superpowers which to critical observers such as Konrad Adenauer seemed like a friendship based as much on aversion as on liking. (The dialect expression Adenauer used, "Kott-Freunde," suggests the kind of friends who might just as well be enemies.) Beneath the Soviet-American " duopoly" a new association of states was evolving which was characterized by "multipolarity." From the Federal Republic's point of view this development entailed a number of dangers and imponderables. There was the threat of the status quo in central Europe becoming permanent, with consequences for the Federal Republic as regards both its security policy and its policy towards East Germany. Lacking any national identity it had to strive to "achieve [an identity] by means of reunification and to give it a new shape within a united Europe" (Klaus Hildebrand). But now that the East-West conflict had lost its absolute quality, the Allies' interest in German reunification, which had always been weak, declined still further. As the continent was at the same time experiencing a resurgence of the idea of the nation state, a "crisis for the idea of reunification" (Karl-Dietrich Bracher) spread in the Federal Republic. Parallel to this development, the US, which was embroiled in the Vietnam War, was scaling down its commitment to the defense of Europe, thereby giving the Germans a feeling of dwindling security. Erhard also faced great challenges in domestic, social and economic policy. In tackling the tasks facing him the Chancellor intended to depart in two ways from his predecessor's strategy. On the one hand Erhard, in contrast to Adenauer, saw the "destiny" of states as determined not by politics but by economics. On the other hand the assertion of national interests necessitated, in his opinion, not power but "strength and vigor." Convinced of the success of the social market economy, he believed that the world's problems could be solved if his ideal of world trade liberated from protectionism were put into practice within an open international society.

"Freedom, security and affluence for all members of society," these were the objectives defined by Erhard in his inaugural speech on October 18, 1963. He intended to pursue a "policy of the center and of mutual understanding." As he set out his program, his main emphasis was unequivocally on domestic policy. The Chancellor announced a "unified social policy." He promised to provide a framework for budgetary planning over a number of years, argued in favor of giving priority to communal tasks rather than vested interests, and stressed the importance of education and research.

As regards foreign affairs, he was at pains to convey a conception of seamless continuity with Adenauer's policies. Erhard expressed his commitment to the security partnership with the US and described France as an indispensable ally for Germany's European policy. He underlined the goal of German reunification in freedom and emphatically promised to promote European integration. The Chancellor was well aware that his plans met with criticism within his own ranks – indeed especially there – as well as outside. The polarization in the final phase of the Adenauer era by no means came to an end when Erhard took up office. From the outset the new head of government came up against very grave doubts as to

Janusgesicht der Modernisierung: Emanzipation und Manipulation im Großraumbüro der Bundesbesoldungsstelle Mehlem 1963.

The Janus face of modernization: emancipation and manipulation in the open-plan office of the federal Paymaster's Office in Mehlem 1963.

den Neuordnung der Montanindustrie zu begegnen, stellte sich an der Ruhr 1966 eine zunehmende Radikalisierung ein. Bei den Landtagswahlen in Nordrhein-Westfalen bezog die CDU im Juli eine schwere Niederlage. Nur knapp verfehlte die SPD die absolute Mehrheit.

Als die Konjunktur im Herbst regelrecht einbrach, stiegen die Arbeitslosenzahlen; die Währungsreserven schmolzen. Im Haushaltsentwurf für das Jahr 1967 klaffte eine Deckungslücke von vier Milliarden DM. Die ökonomische Misere weitete sich zu einer Regierungskrise aus, da die FDP die von der Union als allerletztes Mittel ins Auge gefaßte Steuererhöhung strikt verwarf und den Kabinettstisch Ende Oktober verließ. Am 10.11.1966 beschloß die Unionsfraktion, den Ministerpräsidenten von Baden-Württemberg Kurt Georg Kiesinger zum Nachfolger Erhards zu nominieren. In den folgenden Wochen verhandelten führende Unionspolitiker mit Vertretern der SPD über die Bildung einer neuen Mehrheit.

Deutschlandpolitik in Bewegung

In ihrem Bemühen um Verständigung schenkten die USA und die Sowjetunion dem Problem der deutschen Teilung zunehmend weniger Aufmerksamkeit. Erhard wollte sich damit nicht abfinden. Voll guten Willens, aber ohne Fortune in der Außenpolitik verlangte er immer wieder, die Entspannung von Fortschritten bei der Wiedervereinigung abhängig zu machen. Damit bezog er Positionen, die Adenauer in seinen letzten Amtsjahren als Regierungschef bereits aufgegeben hatte. Auch Außenminister Schröder setzte auf eine vorsichtige Lockerung der bisherigen Ost- und Deutschlandpolitik.

Tatsächlich rückte der Ostblock aufgrund seiner wirtschaftlichen Interessen von der Haltung des Alles oder Nichts ab. Doch nach dem Sturz Chruschtschows im Oktober 1964 blockierte die

brought him not trust but mockery. In 1966 the government's refusal to avert the threatened loss of livelihood for many miners by means of a drastic reorganization of the coal and steel sector led to increased radicalism in the Ruhr. At the regional elections in North Rhine-Westphalia in July the CDU suffered a heavy defeat. The SPD only just failed to gain an absolute majority. When the economy slumped in the autumn, the unemployment figures rose and currency reserves dwindled. In the draft budget for 1967 there was a yawning deficit of 4,000 million DM. The parlous state of the economy triggered a government crisis when the FDP rejected out of hand the increases in taxation which the CDU was considering as a last resort, and withdrew from the cabinet at the end of October. On November 10, 1966 the CDU parliamentary group decided to nominate Kurt Georg Kiesinger, the Minister President of Baden-Württemberg, as Erhard's successor. In the weeks that followed leading CDU politicians negotiated with SPD representatives regarding the creation of a new majority alliance.

Policy Developments With Regard to the Divided Country

In their attempts to come to an understanding with each other, the US and the Soviet Union paid less and less attention to the problem of the division of Germany. Erhard was unwilling to accept this. Full of good intentions but hapless in foreign affairs, he demanded again and again that detènte should be made conditional on progress towards reunification. In so doing he took up a position which Adenauer had already abandoned during his last years in office as head of government. Foreign Minister Schröder was also in favor of a cautious relaxation of the policies that had been followed hitherto with regard to East Germany and the eastern bloc states.

The eastern bloc, prompted by economic interests, was in fact moving away from its all-or-nothing stance. But after Khrushchev's fall in October 1964 the Soviet Union blocked any further normalization of relations between its satellite states and the Federal Republic. Schröder's ideas were controversial within the CDU since they appeared to put the existing legal position in question. The FDP and, above all, the SPD adopted a more positive attitude towards the jettisoning of old dogmas concerning the divison of Germany. However, the Social Democrats with their motto of "change through rapprochement" (Egon Bahr) concentrated their attention less on the states of east central Europe than on the GDR. In order to foster a change of heart there, the SPD argued for a cooperative attitude towards the SED in order to improve conditions for the inhabitants of the GDR. This "policy of small steps" began with an agreement on the issue of frontier-crossing permits, signed in December 1963 between the government of the GDR and the Berlin Senate and further agreements were reached during the following years. But since the Federal Republic upheld its basic principles with regard to relations with the GDR, the GDR had lost interest in such agreements by 1966. The breakthrough which had been hoped for the GDR had not been achieved.

Franz Josef Strauß, and also, in certain respects, Konrad Adenauer, developed a conception which started from quite different assumptions from those of the "policy of making life easier

Sowjetunion eine weitergehende Normalisierung des Verhältnisses ihrer Satellitenstaaten zur Bundesrepublik. Schröders Vorstellungen waren in der Union nicht unumstritten, da sie bisherige Rechtsstandpunkte in Frage zu stellen schienen. Wesentlich positiver standen die FDP und vor allem die SPD dem Aufbrechen alter deutschlandpolitischer Dogmen gegenüber. Mit ihrer Parole vom »Wandel durch Annäherung« (Egon Bahr) konzentrierten sich die Sozialdemokraten indes weniger auf die Staaten Ostmitteleuropas denn auf die DDR. Um sie zu einer inneren Wandlung zu bewegen, plädierte die SPD dafür, der SED entgegenzukommen und den Bürgern der DDR Erleichterungen zu verschaffen.

Den Auftakt dieser Politik der »kleinen Schritte« bildete das im Dezember 1963 unterzeichnete »Passierscheinabkommen« zwischen der Regierung der DDR und dem Senat von Berlin, dem in den nächsten Jahren weitere Übereinkommen folgen sollten. Da die Bundesrepublik ihre zentralen deutschlandpolitischen Grundsätze aber aufrechterhielt, verlor die DDR 1966 ihr Interesse an den Vereinbarungen. Der erhoffte Durchbruch auf dem internationalen Parkett war ihr nicht gelungen.

Von ganz anderen Voraussetzungen als die »Politik der menschlichen Erleichterungen« ging eine von Franz Josef Strauß, in gewisser Hinsicht auch von Konrad Adenauer entfaltete Konzeption aus. Sie zielte auf ein von den USA emanzipiertes Europa, das auch den sowjetischen Satellitenstaaten Heimstatt geben sollte. In ihm mochte Deutschland seine staatliche Einheit wiedergewinnen, aber keine nationale Restauration erlangen, da das nationalstaatliche Denken insgesamt aufgehoben sein würde. Erhard betrachtete eine solche »Europäisierung der deutschen Frage« als »indiskutabel«, weil sie die Vereinigten Staaten zu »Garanten minderen Rechts und Ranges« degradierte. Dies glaubte er sich um so weniger erlauben zu können, als der Druck der Sowjetunion nicht nachließ und ihr Bemühen um eine internationale Aufwertung der DDR sich mit dem schwierigen Verhältnis der Bundesrepublik zu Israel verschränkte.

Auftakt zur »Politik der kleinen Schritte«: Einreise nach Ost-Berlin im Zuge des ersten »Passierscheinabkommens« am 4.1.1964.

The beginning of the "policy of small steps": entering East Berlin on January 4, 1964, following the first Visitors' Permit Agreement (Passierscheinabkommen).

for people." The goal here was a Europe that would be emancipated from the US, which would also provide a home for the Soviet satellite states. In this Europe Germany might regain its unity as a state, but without any national restoration, since the whole idea of nation states would have been transcended.

Erhard regarded such a "Europeanization of the German issue" as "out of the question" because it demoted the US to the status of "a low-level guarantor." He felt that he could not afford to do this, the more so as the Soviet Union kept up the pressure, its attempts to raise the international standing of the GDR becoming entangled with the difficult relations of the Federal Republic with Israel.

Notwithstanding the 1952 agreement on reparations to Israel and the secret supply of weapons to Tel Aviv which began in the late fifties, the two states were still a long way away from normal relations. The Federal Republic had hitherto refused to establish diplomatic relations, which the Israelis would certainly have welcomed, fearing that the Arab world might counter any such move by recognizing the GDR. The situation became even more complicated in mid-1964 when the US urged the Federal Republic to pass on American tanks that were no longer in service to Israel, thereby provoking protest from Egypt. At the end of January 1965, encouraged by substantial economic and military aid from the Soviet Union, President Gamal Abdel Nasser invited Ulbricht, the chairman of the GDR Council of State, to pay a goodwill visit. The federal government interpreted this as an attack on their "claim to sole representation" of Germany and threatened to take counter-measures. Instead, after Ulbricht had been welcomed with all the honors due to a head of state, the federal cabinet decided on March 7, 1965 to establish diplomatic relations with Israel. The reaction of the Arab states came hot on its heels: they broke off almost all contacts with the Federal Republic, without, however, officially recognizing the GDR.

Nevertheless the Middle East debacle provided the clearest possible proof that the standing of the GDR in the world of international politics had changed. In order, therefore, to comply with the desire of the world powers for détente, but also in order to reinforce its crumbling integration into the West, the federal government resolved to "loosen up" (Ludwig Erhard) its policy towards eastern Europe. On March 25, 1966 it presented to numerous countries a "note on disarmament and the safeguarding of peace" which had the backing of all political parties. But since this initiative did not involve giving up either the goal of reunification or the claim to sole representation, it led only to a very limited dialogue with the Warsaw Pact states. As a result the idea increasingly gained ground in the Federal Republic that the policy of détente towards the East must gradually be separated from the policy towards the GDR and that the goal of reunification must take second place to that of improving the situation of people living in the GDR.

European Policy at a Standstill

With regard to European policy as well as to policy towards the GDR, Erhard's term of office must be regarded as a transitional phase. In contrast to his predecessor his objective was not an "Inner Europe" driven by a Franco-German powerhouse; his conception was rather one of a "Europe of free and equal peoples" to include all

Trotz des Wiedergutmachungsabkommens von 1952 und der Ende der fünfziger Jahre aufgenommenen geheimen Waffenlieferungen an Tel Aviv waren beide Staaten von einem normalen Verhältnis noch weit entfernt. Die Aufnahme diplomatischer Beziehungen, von israelischer Seite durchaus gewünscht, hatte die Bundesregierung bisher abgelehnt, da sie im Gegenzug die Anerkennung der DDR durch die arabische Welt befürchtete.

Die Lage verkomplizierte sich, als die USA die Bundesrepublik Mitte 1964 zur Abgabe ausrangierter amerikanischer Panzer an Israel drängten und damit den Protest Ägyptens herausforderten. Von beträchtlicher Wirtschafts- und Militärhilfe der Sowjetunion ermuntert, lud Präsident Gamal Abd el Nasser Ende Januar 1965 den Staatsratsvorsitzenden der DDR Ulbricht zu einem Freundschaftsbesuch ein. Die Bundesregierung faßte dies als Angriff auf ihren Alleinvertretungsanspruch auf und drohte mit Gegenmaßnahmen. Nachdem Ulbricht mit allen Ehren eines Staatsoberhauptes empfangen worden war, beschloß das Bundeskabinett am 7.3.1965, nun doch diplomatische Beziehungen zu Israel aufzunehmen. Die Reaktion der arabischen Staaten folgte auf dem Fuße. Sie brachen fast alle ihre Kontakte zur Bundesrepublik ab, ohne offiziell die DDR anzuerkennen. Dennoch dokumentierte das Nahost-Debakel in aller Deutlichkeit den gewandelten Stellenwert der DDR in der internationalen Staatenwelt. Um dem Verlangen der Weltmächte nach Entspannung zu entsprechen, aber auch der brüchiger gewordenen Westintegration neuen Halt zu geben, entschloß sich die Bundesregierung daher zu einer »Auflockerung« ihrer Ostpolitik (Ludwig Erhard). Am 25.3.1966 richtete sie an zahlreiche Länder eine von allen Parteien mitgetragene »Note zur Abrüstung und Sicherung des Friedens«. Da die Initiative aber vom Ziel der Wiedervereinigung und dem Alleinvertretungsanspruch nicht abrückte, kam es nur zu einem sehr beschränkten Dialog mit den Staaten des Warschauer Paktes. Mehr und mehr gewann deshalb in der Bundesrepublik die Auffassung an Boden, man müsse die Ost- und Entspannungspolitik allmählich von der Deutschlandpolitik abkoppeln und das Ziel der Wiedervereinigung hinter das der Verbesserung der Lebenssituation in der DDR zurücktreten lassen.

Europapolitik im Stillstand

Wie in der Deutschlandpolitik muß die Regierungszeit Erhards auch in der Europapolitik als Phase des Übergangs gelten. Im Gegensatz zu seinem Vorgänger ging es ihm nicht um ein vom deutsch-französischen Motor angetriebenes Kleineuropa; ihm schwebte vielmehr ein »Europa der Freien und der Gleichen« vor, das alle Demokratien des Kontinents einbezog und in engster Verbindung zur atlantischen Welt stand. Adenauers Mißtrauen gegenüber den USA teilte Erhard nicht. Die Amerikaner blieben für ihn Dreh- und Angelpunkt seiner Außenpolitik, Garant der deutschen Sicherheit und Hüter eines freien Welthandels. Während de Gaulle ihm stets fremd blieb, fand er Präsident Johnson, der nach der Ermordung Kennedys im November 1963 ins Weiße Haus einzog, besonders sympathisch.

Freilich war sich der Bundeskanzler bewußt, daß er auf den französischen Staatspräsidenten angewiesen war, um die europäische Einigung voranzubringen. Es gelang ihm in den ersten

the continental democracies, with the closest relationship with the Atlantic world. Erhard did not share Adenauer's distrust of the US. The Americans were always the center of his foreign policy, the guarantors of German security and the guardians of free world trade. Whereas de Gaulle was always a stranger to him, he found President Johnson, who entered the White House after the assassination of President Kennedy in November 1963, particularly congenial. The Chancellor was of course well aware that he was dependent on the French President for the furtherance of European unity. He also managed during his first few months in office to establish a more relaxed relationship with the General. But Erhard soon became entangled in agricultural price policy, and the limits set by de Gaulle's conception of Europe. His tactics were aimed at buying France's political support for his project of political integration by means of one-sided concessions in the agricultural issue, which was of vital concern to the French. But the profound rift between his "Europe of free and equal peoples" and de Gaulle's plan for a "European Europe" free from American interference, made it unlikely that they would reach agreement.

As a result combat broke out in the CDU between "Atlanticists" and "Gaullists" concerning the direction to be taken in German foreign policy. In particular the former Chancellor and the "Adenauer wing" (Hans-Peter Schwarz) which formed around him put pressure on Erhard. When de Gaulle came to Bonn for routine consultations in early July 1964 they urged the Chancellor get in line with de Gaulle's policies. But Erhard refused. At the end of 1964 he gave way on the agricultural issue and presented his EEC partners with proposals concerning political union. His hope that he could now expect cooperation from France proved illusory. In June 1965 de Gaulle recalled his EEC representative, in order to put an end to any supra-national integration. For the federal government, France's "empty seat policy" was untimely, coming as it did when

Wahlen werden nicht mit braven Kindern gewonnen: Kundgebung Erhards vor der Landtagswahlniederlage in Nordrhein-Westfalen im Juli 1966.

Elections are not won with well-behaved children: rally in support of Erhard before defeat at the regional elections in North Rhine-Westphalia in July 1966.

Monaten seiner Amtszeit, sein Verhältnis zum General zu entkrampfen. Doch bald verfing sich Erhard im Netz der Agrarpreispolitik und in den von de Gaulles Europakonzeption gesteckten Grenzen. Seine Taktik zielte darauf ab, durch einseitige Zugeständnisse in der Frankreich vital interessierenden Agrarfrage dessen Unterstützung für sein Projekt der politischen Integration zu ›erkaufen‹. Allein, die tiefe Kluft zwischen seinem »Europa der Freien und der Gleichen« und de Gaulles Plan von einem von amerikanischer Bevormundung freien »europäischen Europa« ließ eine Einigung als wenig wahrscheinlich erscheinen.

In der CDU brach infolgedessen ein Kampf zwischen »Atlantikern« und »Gaullisten« über den Kurs der deutschen Außenpolitik aus. Insbesondere der Altbundeskanzler und der sich um ihn ausbildende »Adenauer-Flügel« (Hans-Peter Schwarz) setzten Erhard hart zu. Als de Gaulle Anfang Juli 1964 zu routinemäßigen Konsultationen nach Bonn kam, drängten sie den Kanzler dazu, auf dessen Politik einzuschwenken. Erhard aber sperrte sich. Ende 1964 lenkte er in der Agrarfrage ein und übermittelte den EWG-Partnern eine Initiative zur Politischen Union. Seine Hoffnung, nunmehr Anspruch auf ein Entgegenkommen Frankreichs zu haben, trog. Im Juni 1965 rief de Gaulle seinen Vertreter bei der EWG zurück, um der supranationalen Integration den Garaus zu machen. Frankreichs »Politik des leeren Stuhls« kam in der heißen Phase des Bundestagswahlkampfes ungelegen. Adenauer sah den Verantwortlichen des Desasters im Kanzleramt. Nach dem Ende Januar 1966 beigelegten Streit der EWG-Staaten gab er keine Ruhe, zumal die Krise zwischen Bonn und Paris nun auf die westliche Verteidigungsallianz übergriff. Im Februar kündigte de Gaulle den Austritt aus der militärischen Organisation der NATO an. Gleichzeitig – und für die Sicherheit der Bundesrepublik noch bedenklicher – konkretisierten sich die Anzeichen, daß die USA ein atomares Einverständnis mit der Sowjetunion selbst um den Preis einer Erosion des Bündnisses mit Europa suchten.

Wie wenig sich Erhard auf seinen »Freund« Johnson verlassen konnte, zeigte sich im Herbst im Zuge des Streits über die »Offset-Abkommen«. Die Bundesrepublik war verpflichtet, die Dollar-Ausgaben der in Deutschland stationierten US-Truppen durch Rüstungskäufe in den USA auszugleichen. Aufgrund der angespannten Haushaltslage war sie damit in erheblichen Rückstand geraten. Gegen den Rat seiner Mitarbeiter brach der Kanzler Ende September nach Washington auf, um einen Zahlungsaufschub zu erbitten. Doch Johnson, wegen des immer stärkeren Engagements in Vietnam innenpolitisch bedrängt, drohte sogar mit dem Abzug amerikanischer Truppen. Nach dieser Brüskierung wurde offen über Erhards Ablösung diskutiert. Als die FDP die Koalition über die Haushaltsfrage platzen ließ, verlor er in seiner Partei jegliche Unterstützung. In seinem ostensiblen Missionsbewußtsein hatte der Kanzler geglaubt, die Pflege der Freundschaft zu den USA mit einer guten Nachbarschaft zu Frankreich verknüpfen zu können. Tatsächlich aber war das Verhältnis zu beiden Bündnispartnern angespannt, wenn nicht zerrüttet. Als die Bundesrepublik in die Gefahr der Isolierung geriet, entzog der Bundestag dem Regierungschef das Vertrauen. Am 30.11.1966 reichte Erhard sein Rücktrittsgesuch ein. Wie Adenauer war es auch ihm nicht gelungen, die Gesetze der internationalen wie innerparteilichen Machtpolitik auszuschalten.

Bitte um Unterstützung der USA in Vietnam: Justizminister Robert Kennedy mit Bundespräsident Lübke am 25.6.1964 in Bonn.

Request for support for the US in Vietnam: Attorney General Robert Kennedy with President Lübke in Bonn on June 25, 1964.

the election campaign was heating up. Adenauer blamed the Chancellor for the disaster. Even after the disagreement among the EEC states had been settled at the end of January 1966, he gave Erhard no peace, particularly now that the crisis between Bonn and Paris also began to affect the western defense alliance. In February de Gaulle announced France's withdrawal from the military organization of NATO. At the same time – and even more worryingly as regards the security of the Federal Republic – there were now tangible indications that the US was seeking an understanding with the Soviet Union with regard to atomic armaments, even at the price of a deteriorating alliance with Europe. How little Erhard could rely on his "friend" Johnson could be seen in the autumn during the dispute over the "offset agreement." The Federal Republic was obliged to offset the dollars spent by the US troops stationed in Germany by purchasing armaments from the US. Due to budgetary difficulties it was considerably in arrears with these purchases. Against the explicit advice of his colleagues, the Chancellor set off in late September to Washington in order to ask for an extension. But Johnson, who was under pressure at home because of increasing commitment in Vietnam, even threatened to withdraw some of the American troops.

After this snub there was open discussion of replacing Erhard in Bonn. When the FDP brought the coalition to an end over the budget issue he lost his support even within his own party. The Chancellor had believed that he could cultivate both a friendship with the US and good neighborly relations with France. But in fact relations with both these allies were under strain, if not in ruins. When the Federal Republic found itself in danger of becoming isolated, parliament withdrew its confidence from the head of government. On November 30, 1966 Erhard submitted his resignation. Like Adenauer, he too had failed to disenable the laws of international and internal party power politics.

Bei der Wahl Ludwig Erhards zum zweiten deutschen Bundeskanzler stimmten am 16.10.1963 279 Abgeordnete für den Kandidaten der CDU/CSU, 180 gegen ihn. 24 Parlamentarier aus den Koalitionsfraktionen enthielten sich der Stimme. Mochte Erhards Aufstieg in der deutschen Öffentlichkeit auch auf breite Zustimmung stoßen, so hatte er die Herzen seiner Parteifreunde noch nicht alle erreicht. Als er am 18.11.1963 im Palais Schaumburg einen Presseempfang gab, sah der neue Hausherr in skeptische Gesichter.

On October 16, 1963, when the CDU/CSU candidate Ludwig Erhard was elected as the second German Chancellor, 279 members of parliament voted for him, 180 against. 24 members from the coalition party groups abstained. Although Erhard's success was broadly welcomed by the German public, he had not yet won the hearts of all his fellow party members. When he gave a reception for the press in the Palais Schaumburg on November 18, 1963, the new master of the house saw sceptical faces before him.

Kanzlerwechsel / Changing of the Chancellors

Die Zusammenarbeit zwischen den beiden führenden Persönlichkeiten in der Bundesrepublik gestaltete sich alles andere als reibungslos. Wegen seiner »tiefsitzenden Aversion« gegen die Freien Demokraten (Rudolf Morsey) war Lübke ein ausgesprochener Befürworter einer Koalition aus Christ- und Sozialdemokraten, die seiner Meinung nach am besten von Gerstenmaier geführt werden sollte. Auch persönlich fand er zu Erhard keinen Zugang. Dies hielt den Bundeskanzler am 14.10.1965, dem 71. Geburtstag des Bundespräsidenten, natürlich nicht ab, auf dessen Wohl anzustoßen.

Cooperation between the two leading personalities of the Federal Republic proved to be anything but smooth. Because of his "profound aversion" (Rudolf Morsey) to the Free Democrats Heinrich Lübke was an emphatic supporter of a CDU/SPD coalition, for which in his opinion Gerstenmaier would be the best leader. Nor did he manage to be on easy terms with Ludwig Erhard on a personal level. This did not of course deter the Chancellor from drinking to the President's health on the latter's 71st birthday on October 14, 1965.

Die Zusammensetzung des ersten Kabinetts Erhard unterschied sich von der letzten Regierung Adenauer nur in wenigen Positionen. Die wichtigste Veränderung betraf das Ministerium für gesamtdeutsche Fragen, das der FDP-Vorsitzende und Vizekanzler Erich Mende (rechts) übernahm. Eugen Gerstenmaier (Mitte), der die Kanzlerschaft Erhards gefördert hatte, blieb auf seinem Posten als Bundestagspräsident. Auf dem Abschiedsempfang für Konrad Adenauer am 11.10.1963 besprachen sie letzte Einzelheiten.

The composition of Erhard's first cabinet differed from that of Adenauer's last government only with regards to a few posts. The most important change was at the Ministry for All-German Affairs, which was taken over by the FDP party chairman and Deputy Chancellor Erich Mende (right). Eugen Gerstenmaier (center), who had helped to make Erhard Chancellor, retained his post as President of the Bundestag. At Konrad Adenauer's farewell reception on October 11, 1963 they discussed the final details.

In Kontrast zu seinem barocken Äußeren stand Erhards Vorliebe für strenge Formen. Auch deshalb dürfte er froh gewesen sein, das gediegene Arbeitszimmer im Bundeswirtschaftsministerium verlassen zu dürfen. Kurz nach seinem Umzug ins Palais Schaumburg ließ er sich 1964 vom Architekten Sepp Ruf ein neues Arbeits- und Wohnhaus errichten. Von seinen Kritikern wurde der nicht unumstrittene »Kanzler-Bungalow« als »Ludwigslust« apostrophiert.

Erhard's ample figure was in contrast to his liking for austere design. This was probably a further reason why he was glad to be able to leave his conventionally tasteful study in the Economics Ministry. After moving into the Palais Schaumburg he had a new house built in 1964 by the architect Sepp Ruf, a house in which he both lived and worked. Critics gave the not uncontroversial "Chancellor's bungalow" the name of "Ludwig's Folly."

Nicht nur auf Auslandsreisen wie am 4.5.1964 im Sonderzug nach Luxemburg verließ sich Erhard auf einen kleinen Kreis enger Mitarbeiter, die »Brigade Erhard«. Dazu zählten insbesondere sein Persönlicher Referent Dankmar Seibt (rechts) und der Bundesminister für besondere Aufgaben, seit Juni 1964 auch Chef des Bundeskanzleramtes, Ludger Westrick (links am Tisch). Sehr kritisch stand dem Kanzler hingegen der Leiter des Außenpolitischen Büros im Bundeskanzleramt, Horst Osterheld, gegenüber.

It was not only on journeys abroad, for example in the special train to Luxembourg on May 4, 1964, that Erhard relied on a small group of close colleagues, the "Erhard Squad." They included in particular his personal adviser Dankmar Seibt (right) and the Special Task Minister and, from June 1964, Head of Chancellery Ludger Westrick (left at the table). The Head of the Foreign Affairs Office at the Chancellery Horst Osterheld, in contrast, was highly critical of the Chancellor.

»Erhard ist ein Träumer«, wetterte Adenauer über seinen Nachfolger, von dem ihn nicht nur das Politikverständnis trennte: hier der politisch denkende, gewiefte Machtpolitiker, dort der auf die Gesetze des freien Marktes setzende Nationalökonom, der Macht als »öde«, »brutal« und »dumm« brandmarkte. Die Einweihung des »Kanzler-Bungalows« bot ihnen neuen Zündstoff. Mochte er Erhard auch am 12.11.1964 ruhig zuhören, behagte dem Alten Herrn aus Rhöndorf die Funktionalität, Sachlichkeit und Kälte des sehr modern gehaltenen Gebäudes doch ganz und gar nicht.

"Erhard is a dreamer" was Adenauer's furious verdict on his successor, who was alien to him not only because of his conception of politics: on the one hand the crafty power politician and political thinker, on the other the political economist with his faith in the laws of the free market, who castigated power as "dreary," "brutal," and "stupid." The opening ceremony at the "Chancellor's bungalow" added fuel to the flames. Even though he listened calmly to Erhard on November 12, 1964, the "old gentleman" from Rhöndorf was not at all at ease with the functionalism, practicality, and bareness of the ultra-modern building.

Bot die Staatskarosse, mit der sich Lübke am 10.1.1964 zum Neujahrsempfang für das Diplomatische Corps in die Godesberger Redoute chauffieren ließ, auch für ihn kein »Objekt der Begierde«, so übte er sein Amt doch nicht ohne Standesbewußtsein aus.

Even though the official limousine in which Lübke was driven to the New Year reception for the diplomatic corps at the "Redoute" in Bad Godesberg on January 10, 1964 was for him not an "object of desire," he nevertheless conducted himself in office with a due awareness of his position.

1963–1966

Heinrich Lübke

In seiner sachlichen Art und »menschlichen Redlichkeit« (Theodor Heuss) verstand es Lübke, hier am 3.10.1963 im Staatsfrack und von Gattin Wilhelmine begleitet, manches zu bewirken. Er führte das Staatsamt »treu und redlich, aber ohne Glanz« (Carlo Schmid). Lübke fehlten die zwingend notwendigen rhetorischen Gaben. Sein sauerländischer Eigensinn, sein »missionarischer Eifer« (Rudolf Morsey) und seine sprachlichen Pannen fügten seinem Ansehen in der Öffentlichkeit vor allem in der zweiten Amtsperiode nach 1965 schweren Schaden zu.

With his businesslike manner and "human sincerity" (Theodor Heuss), Lübke, here on October 3, 1963 in formal tailcoat and accompanied by his wife Wilhelmine, was not ineffective. He performed his duties "loyally and sincerely, but without brilliance." (Carlo Schmid) Lübke lacked the indispensable gift for public speaking. The stubbornness which had its roots in his Westphalian background, his "missionary zeal" (Rudolf Morsey) and his linguistic blunders seriously damaged his public standing, especially during his second term of office after 1965.

(gegenüber) »Liebenswürdig, kultiviert und polyglott« (François Seydoux), sprachgewandt und resolut, konnte Wilhelmine Lübke, die Gattin des Bundespräsidenten, manche Schwäche ihres Mannes ausgleichen. Obwohl sie fast zehn Jahre älter als er war – was sie vor der Öffentlichkeit zu verheimlichen suchte –, begleitete sie ihn auf fast allen Auslandsreisen. Daß sich das Ehepaar auch bei offiziellen Veranstaltungen mit Kosenamen ansprach und »Minken« ihren Mann gelegentlich mit der Aufforderung »Heini, wir gehen zu Bett!« vom Staatsbankett zog (»Der Spiegel«), registrierte mancher Beobachter allerdings mit Naserümpfen. Am 29.6.1960 verabschiedeten sie den argentinischen Präsidenten Frondizi auf dem Bonner Hauptbahnhof.

(opposite) "Amiable, cultivated, and multilingual" (François Seydoux), resolute and articulate, Wilhelmine Lübke, the President's wife, was able to compensate for some of her husband's deficiencies. Although she was almost ten years older than him – which she tried to keep secret from the public – she accompanied him on almost all his journeys abroad. However, the fact that the couple addressed each other by their pet names even at official events, and "Minken" occasionally removed her husband from a state banquet with the words "Heini, we're going to bed!" (Der Spiegel), was noted by some observers with disapproval. On June 26, 1960 they said farewell to the Argentinian President Frondizi at the main railway station in Bonn.

Neben dem Bemühen um die Integration der Bundeswehr in den Staat und dem Pochen auf die Wiedervereinigung gehört der Einsatz für die Entwicklungshilfe zu den wesentlichen Leistungen Lübkes. Seine Stegreifreden wie hier am 16.1.1962 in Maneah in Guinea trafen indes nicht immer den richtigen Ton. Daß er Präsident Sékou Touré die Lieferung von Eisenbahnwaggons in Aussicht stellte, wurde in Bonn nicht unbedingt freudig begrüßt. Um die Folgekosten der Staatsbesuche des Bundespräsidenten zu begrenzen, schickte die Bundesregierung fortan einen Vertreter des Ministeriums für wirtschaftliche Zusammenarbeit als »Aufpasser« mit.

Along with his efforts to make the army an integral part of the state and his insistence on the goal of reunification, Lübke's basic achievements included his support for aid to developing countries. However, in unscripted speeches, here on January 16, 1962 in Maneah in Guinea, he did not always strike the right note. The fact that he promised President Sékou Touré to supply railway freight cars did not meet with unalloyed approval in Bonn. From then on, in order to curb the expenses arising from the President's state visits, the government sent along a representative of the Ministry for Economic Cooperation as a "minder."

Ein besonderes Anliegen war Lübke das Recht auf Heimat. Die Oder-Neiße-Linie blieb für ihn daher stets inakzeptabel. Um das deutsch-polnische Verhältnis zu entkrampfen und die Grenze durchlässiger zu machen, regte er die Schaffung eines doppelten – nationalen und europäischen – Staatsbürgerrechts an. Diese Idee trug Lübke unter anderem auch Königin Elisabeth II. von England und Prinz Philip im Mai 1965 vor, allerdings nicht beim Staatsempfang am 18.5.1965 auf Schloß Brühl, sondern während einer Teestunde in der Villa Hammerschmidt. Rechts neben ihm der Chef des Protokolls des Auswärtigen Amtes Ehrenfried von Holleben.

A special concern of Lübke was the right to a homeland. Hence the Oder-Neiße Line was always unacceptable to him. In order to make German-Polish relations more relaxed and the frontier easier to cross, he suggested the creation of dual – i.e. national and European – civil rights. Lübke proposed this idea to, among others, Queen Elizabeth II of England and Prince Philip in May 1965, not, however, at the state reception on May 18, 1965 at Schloß Brühl, but while taking tea in the Villa Hammerschmidt. Next to him on the right is the Foreign Office Chief of Protocol Ehrenfried von Holleben.

Jubel und Begeisterung begleiteten Elisabeth II. und Prinz Philip bei ihrem triumphalen Staatsbesuch in der Bundesrepublik vom 18.-28.5.1965. Nur den Soldaten der britischen Rheinarmee in Sennelager bei Paderborn verwehrte das militärische Zeremoniell am 26.5.1965 die stürmische Begrüßung ihrer Monarchin.

Elizabeth II and Prince Philip were given an enthusiastic and jubilant welcome on their triumphal state visit to the Federal Republic from May 18-28, 1965. Only the troops of the British Army of the Rhine at Sennelager near Paderborn were prevented by military formality from giving a tempestuous welcome to their sovereign on May 26, 1965.

Der Volkskanzler / The people's Chancellor

Seinen 68. Geburtstag beging Erhard am 4.2.1965 bewußt als Arbeitstag. Nur eine Begrüßung durch die Mitarbeiter und ein Ständchen der Enkelkinder ließ er zu. Die Zeit war freilich auch nicht nach Feiern. Insbesondere die Konjunkturprobleme bereiteten Erhard Kopfzerbrechen. Wenige Tage nach seinem Ehrentag überraschte er die Öffentlichkeit mit der Formel von der »Formierten Gesellschaft«, die die Übermacht der Interessenverbände zurückdrängen sollte. Zur Bewältigung dringlicher »Gemeinschaftsaufgaben« schlug Erhard ein »Deutsches Gemeinschaftswerk« vor.

Erhard chose to spend his 68th birthday on February 4, 1965 working. Only congratulations from his staff and a serenade by his grandchildren were permitted. Indeed, it was no time to celebrate. Economic problems in particular were giving Erhard a headache. A few days after his birthday he surprised the public with his notion of the "aligned society," which was to curb the predominance of pressure groups. Erhard proposed a "German community program" to solve urgent "communal tasks."

Im Wahlkampf 1965 baute Erhard erneut auf seine wiederholt bewiesene Fähigkeit, den Bundesbürgern Vertrauen einzuflößen. In zwölf mehrtägigen Wahlkampfreisen trat der Bundeskanzler in nahezu 300 Orten auf, hier im August 1965; in der Wagenmitte Max Schulze-Vorberg. Zu einer scharfen Auseinandersetzung kam es, als Erhard sich Anfang Juli mit den Schriftstellern Rolf Hochhuth und Günter Grass anlegte, die seinen Herausforderer Willy Brandt unterstützten und seine Marktwirtschaft angriffen: »Da hört der Dichter auf, da fängt der ganz kleine Pinscher an.«

In the 1965 election Erhard again relied on his ability, repeatedly proven, to inspire public confidence. In twelve campaign tours, each lasting several days, the Chancellor (here in August 1965, with Max Schulze-Vorberg in the center of the car) made appearances in almost 300 places. There was an acrimonious exchange at the beginning of July when Erhard got into an argument with the writers Rolf Hochhuth and Günter Grass, who supported his rival Willy Brandt and attacked his market economics: "That's where the writer ends and the pipsqueak begins."

Kaum weniger hart als die politischen Gegner setzten Erhard, hier im August 1965 an der Küste, seine Parteifreunde zu. Führende Unionspolitiker traten ungeniert für eine Große Koalition ein, weil sie wußten, daß Erhard dafür nicht zu haben war.

Erhard – here at the coast in August 1965 – came under scarcely less pressure from his fellow party members than from his political adversaries. Leading CDU politicians unabashedly expressed their support for a Grand Coalition, knowing that Erhard could not be won over for it.

Ebensoviel Grund zum Jubel wie auf der Wahlkundgebung in Lippstadt am 22.8.1965 hatte Erhard am 19.9.1965, dem Tag der Bundestagswahl. Er errang für die CDU/CSU 47,6% der Stimmen. Die SPD erreichte 39,3%, die FDP fiel auf 9,5% ab. Erhards Erfolg erwies sich indes als »Pyrrhussieg« (Rolf Lahr). Zu augenscheinlich waren die Divergenzen innerhalb der Union über grundlegende politische Fragen.

On election day September 19, 1965 Erhard had as much reason to rejoice as he had had at the election meeting in Lippstadt on August 22, 1965. He won 47.6% of the vote for the CDU/CSU. The SPD polled 39.3%, the FDP dropped to 9.5%. However, Erhard's success proved to be a "Pyrrhic victory" (Rolf Lahr). Differences of opinion within the CDU on fundamental political issues had become too obvious.

Mit Geschick und Entschlossenheit wehrten die Freien Demokraten in den Koalitionsverhandlungen im Oktober 1965 die Attacken der Union gegen ihren Parteivorsitzenden Mende ab. Nachdem Bundestagsvizepräsident Thomas Dehler offen die Koalitionsfrage gestellt hatte, gab Erhard nach und überließ Mende das Bundesministerium für gesamtdeutsche Fragen. Gut lachen hatte auch Walter Scheel, hier mit Dehler und Mende am Rande der FDP-Fraktionssitzung im Berliner Reichstag am 18.1.1966, der das seit 1961 geführte Bundesministerium für wirtschaftliche Zusammenarbeit behalten durfte.

During the coalition negotiations in October 1965 the Free Democrats defended their party chairman Erich Mende with skill and determination against attacks by the CDU. After Thomas Dehler, the Deputy President of the Bundestag, had brought the coalition issue out into the open, Erhard backed down and gave Mende the Ministry for All-German Affairs. Walter Scheel, seen here with Dehler and Mende on the sidelines of the meeting of the FDP parliamentary group in the Reichstag building in Berlin on January 18, 1966, also had good reason to be cheerful, having been allowed to keep the Ministry for Economic Cooperation of which he had been the head since 1961.

Die wachsenden Strukturschwierigkeiten des Bergbaus ließen Erhard nicht ungerührt. Anfang April 1965 unternahm er eine Informationsfahrt ins Ruhrgebiet und besichtigte ein Steinkohlebergwerk. Mit einem »Teufkübel« fuhr er in Begleitung des nordrhein-westfälischen Ministerpräsidenten Franz Meyers (rechts) in die Schachtanlage. Seine Appelle zur Mobilität und Flexibilität wurden von den Bergarbeitern ignoriert. Am 26.9.1966 demonstrierten 60000 dieser lange Zeit umworbenen, heimatverbundenen »Aristokraten« der Region (Klaus Hildebrand) in Bonn für den Erhalt ihrer Arbeitsplätze.

The growing structural problems in the mining industry did not leave Erhard unmoved. In early April 1965 he went on a fact-finding tour of the Ruhr and visited a coal mine. He went down into the pit in a miners' bucket, accompanied by Franz Meyers, the Minister President of North Rhine-Westphalia (right). His appeals for mobility and flexibility were ignored by the miners. On September 26, 1966, 60,000 of these "aristocrats" (Klaus Hildebrand) of the region, with deep roots in their native soil, who had been courted by politicians for so long, demonstrated in Bonn for the preservation of their jobs.

Guten Tag!
Wenn Du heute aufpaßt,
haben wir einen Unfall weniger
Denke daran!

Wenngleich die Zuwachsrate des Bruttosozialprodukts auch 1966 noch 2,9% betrug und die Arbeitslosigkeit bei 0,6% lag, machte sich in der Bundesrepublik Mißstimmung breit. Von lenkenden Eingriffen in den Wirtschaftsprozeß wollte Erhard, am 7.3.1966 in den Hamburger Howaldswerken, aber nichts wissen.

Even though in 1966 the gross national product was still growing at a rate of 2.9% and unemployment stood at 0.6%, discord was spreading in the Federal Republic. But Erhard, here at the Howald works in Hamburg on March 7, 1966, refused to consider intervening in order to steer the workings of the economy.

Folgen der Teilung Deutschlands / After Germany's Division

Mit seiner »Politik der Bewegung« hielt Bundesaußenminister Schröder, hier am 1.3.1964 mit Bundeskanzler Erhard und dem amtierenden Vorsitzenden der CDU/CSU-Fraktion Rainer Barzel auf dem Bonner Bahnhof, an der Nichtanerkennung der Oder-Neiße-Linie fest. Er versuchte aber, mit den osteuropäischen Staaten unterhalb der Ebene offizieller diplomatischer Beziehungen auf wirtschaftspolitischem Gebiet in Kontakt zu kommen.

With his "policy of movement" Foreign Minister Schröder held fast to the non-recognition of the Oder-Neiße Line; he is seen here on March 1, 1964 with Chancellor Erhard and the then chairman of the CDU/CSU parliamentary group Rainer Barzel at the railway station in Bonn. But in matters of economic policy he did attempt to establish contacts with the states of eastern Europe below the level of official diplomatic relations.

In ihrem Bemühen um eine nukleare Teilhabe im Rahmen der NATO brachte die Bundesrepublik der von den USA 1962 angeregten multilateralen Nuklearstreitmacht großes Interesse entgegen. Um den eigenen Statusvorteil als Atommacht gegenüber den Deutschen nicht zu verlieren, entwickelte Großbritannien eine atlantische Variante dieser MLF. Bei einem Besuch in Bonn versuchte Premierminister Harold Wilson, hier mit Erhard in der Residenz des britischen Botschafters am 8.3.1965, die Bundesregierung für sein Konzept zu gewinnen. Letztlich wurden beide Projekte nicht realisiert.

In its attempts to become a nuclear partner within NATO the Federal Republic showed great interest in the multilateral nuclear strike force proposed by the USA in 1962. In order not to forfeit its own superior status as an atomic power vis-à-vis the Germans, Britain developed an Atlantic variant of this MLF. On a visit to Bonn, Prime Minister Harold Wilson – here with Erhard at the British Ambassador's residence on March 8, 1965 – tried to win over the federal government for his idea. In the end neither of the two projects became a reality.

1963–1966

Mit Billigung des Bundesministers für gesamtdeutsche Fragen und des Regierenden Bürgermeisters von Berlin unterzeichneten der Senat von Westberlin und die Regierung der DDR am 17.12.1963 ein Protokoll über die Ausgabe von Passierscheinen. Die Regelung erlaubte den Westberlinern, vom 19.12.1963 bis 5.1.1964 zu Verwandtenbesuchen in den Ostsektor der Stadt zu fahren. Am Tag vor dem Inkrafttreten wurden z. B. in der Riesengebirgsschule im Bezirk Schöneberg die Anträge entgegengenommen.

On December 17, 1963, with the approval of the Minister for All-German Affairs and the governing mayor of Berlin, the West Berlin Senate and the government of the GDR signed a protocol relating to the issuing of frontier-crossing permits. The agreement allowed inhabitants of West Berlin to travel to the eastern sector of the city between December 19, 1963 and January 5, 1964, in order to visit relatives. Applications were accepted on the day before the agreement came into force at the Riesengebirge School in the district of Schöneberg.

Am ersten Ausgabetag der Passierscheine, dem 19.12.1963, bildeten sich vor den zwölf Verteilstellen, hier in der Schillerstraße im Bezirk Tiergarten, lange Warteschlangen. Innerhalb der Bundesregierung war das Abkommen nicht unumstritten. Neben Erhard erhob vor allem Außenminister Schröder Bedenken. Er befürchtete eine Aufwertung der DDR. Sein Ziel war es aber, Ostberlin mit der Errichtung von Handelsvertretungen in Warschau, Bukarest, Budapest und Sofia zu isolieren.

On the first day on which frontier-crossing permits were issued, December 19, 1963, long lines formed at the twelve issuing points, here in the Schillerstraße in the Tiergarten district. The agreement caused controversy within the federal government. Along with Erhard, Foreign Minister Schröder in particular had doubts. He feared that it would improve the standing of the GDR, whereas his aim was to isolate East Berlin by setting up trade missions in Warsaw, Bucharest, Budapest, and Sofia.

Mit der Passierscheinregelung öffnete sich im Winter 1963/64 für 1,2 Millionen Westberliner erstmals nach dem Bau der Mauer wieder der Ostteil der Stadt. Entsprechend groß war die Freude über das Wiedersehen.
Auch zahlreiche Bundesbürger nutzten die Chance, um nach Ostberlin einzureisen. Vor dem Übergang Heinrich-Heine-Straße wartete am 23.12.1963 eine lange Kraftfahrzeugkarawane.

In the winter of 1963/64, for the first time since the building of the Wall, the frontier-crossing permit agreement opened the eastern part of the city for 1.2 million inhabitants of West Berlin. The joy of short reunion was great.
Numerous citizens also took advantage of the chance to travel to East Berlin. A long line of motor vehicles waits at the Heinrich-Heine-Straße crossing point on December 23, 1963.

(rechts) Geradezu entgeistert begegneten sich am 21.12.1963 Polizisten aus Westberlin und ein Mitglied der Nationalen Volksarmee der DDR am Sektorenübergang Oberbaumbrücke, der für Fußgänger reserviert war.

(right) Policemen from West Berlin and a border guard from the GDR National People's Army were positively dumbfounded when, on December 21, 1963, they came face to face at the Oberbaumbrücke sector crossing, which was reserved for pedestrians.

214

Mit der steigenden Wirtschaftskraft wuchs das Ansehen der DDR in der Dritten Welt. Sie trat allmählich aus dem Satellitendasein heraus, ohne sich freilich von der Sowjetunion zu entfernen. Seit an Seit begingen die militärischen und politischen Führungen am 8.5.1965 den 20. Jahrestag der Kapitulation des Deutschen Reiches. Auf der Tribüne in der Mitte Erich Honecker (Sekretär des Zentralkomitees der SED für Sicherheit), Alexej Kossygin (Vorsitzender des sowjetischen Ministerrates) und Walter Ulbricht (Vorsitzender des Staatsrates der DDR).

With its growing economic power the GDR's prestige in the Third World grew also. It gradually emerged from its satellite existence, without, however, loosening its ties with the Soviet Union. On May 8, 1965 the military and political leaders of the two countries celebrated the twentieth anniversary of the surrender of the German Reich side by side. On the rostrum in the center Erich Honecker (Secretary for Security of the SED Central Committee), Aleksey Kosygin (Chairman of the Soviet Council of Ministers) and Walter Ulbricht (Chairman of the GDR Council of State).

(links) Mit einer Militärparade feierte die DDR am 8.5.1965 den Sieg über den Nationalsozialismus.

(left) On May 8, 1965 the GDR celebrated the victory over National Socialism with a military parade.

(gegenüber) Am Rande der Heerschau bereiteten sich Soldaten der Nationalen Volksarmee am 8.5.1965 in ihren Gardeuniformen für den Auftritt vor.

(opposite) On the sidelines of the military parade soldiers from the National People's Army in their Guards uniforms prepare for their public appearance on May 8, 1965.

Außenpolitische Orientierungsschwäche

Neben Tunesien und Libyen gehörte Marokko zu den Staaten der arabischen Liga, die die Aufnahme diplomatischer Beziehungen zwischen der Bundesrepublik und Israel im Mai 1965 nicht mit der Abberufung ihrer Diplomaten aus Bonn quittierten. König Hassan II. bemühte sich um eine deutsch-arabische Wiederannäherung und hoffte auf substantielle deutsche Entwicklungshilfe. Im Rahmen einer Afrikareise, die ihn vom 12.-16.3.1966 auch nach Marokko führte, traf Bundespräsident Lübke mit dem König zusammen und unterstrich die Bereitschaft zu dauerhafter Unterstützung.

Along with Tunisia and Libya, Morocco belonged to the member states of the Arab League which did not react to the establishment of diplomatic relations between the Federal Republic and Israel in May 1965 by recalling their diplomats from Bonn. King Hassan II tried to bring about a fresh German-Arab rapprochement, hoping for substantial development aid from Germany. During a trip to Africa which included a visit to Morocco from March 12-16, 1966, President Lübke met the King and stressed Germany's willingness to give long-term support.

The Weakness in Foreign Policy Orientation

In einer »Friedensnote« vom 25.3.1966 bot die Bundesrepublik allen Ländern, mit denen sie Beziehungen unterhielt, sowie den Ostblockstaaten außer der DDR den Austausch von Gewaltverzichtserklärungen an. Die Anregung dazu hatte der Staatssekretär des Auswärtigen Amtes Karl Carstens, hier mit Erhard bei einer Zugfahrt 1964, nach Gesprächen in der Sowjetunion im September 1965 gegeben. Der Erfolg der »Friedensnote« blieb sehr bescheiden. Hoffnungen auf Fortschritte bei der Aufhebung der deutschen Teilung erwiesen sich als illusorisch. Carstens schien die Zeit der Wiedervereinigungspolitik »vorbei« zu sein.

In the "peace note" of March 25, 1966 the Federal Republic offered to exchange declarations renouncing the use of force with all those countries with which it maintained relations, along with the eastern bloc states with the exception of the GDR. This had been suggested in September 1965 by Karl Carstens, State Secretary at the Foreign Office – here traveling by train with Erhard in 1964 – after talks in the Soviet Union. The "peace note" had only a very modest success. Hopes of progress in reunifying Germany proved illusory. It seemed to Carstens that the era of reunification policy was "over."

Obwohl Frankreich für Erhard keineswegs der wichtigste Partner war, führte ihn sein erster Auslandsbesuch Ende November 1963 bewußt nach Paris. Dem Ziel, »durch neue Aktivität in der politischen Formierung Europas Fortschritte zu erreichen«, sollte der deutsch-französische Vertrag nutzbar gemacht werden. Seine Gespräche mit Staatspräsident de Gaulle, hier am 21.11.1963 im Elysée-Palast, verliefen besser als erwartet. Wenngleich die Herzlichkeit des Verhältnisses zwischen de Gaulle und Adenauer fehlte, fanden beide Staatsmänner zu einem konstruktiven Dialog.

Although for Erhard France was by no means the most important partner, it was to Paris that he chose to make his first trip abroad in late November 1963. His intention was to make the Franco-German Treaty serve the end of "achieving progress by means of fresh activity in the political shaping of Europe." His talks with President de Gaulle, here on November 21, 1963 in the Elysée Palace, went better than expected. Even though the cordiality of the relationship between de Gaulle and Adenauer was lacking, the two statesmen succeeded in conducting a constructive dialogue.

Das Halbjahrstreffen im Rahmen des Elysée-Vertrags, zu dem die Spitze der Bundesregierung am 13.2.1964 aufbrach, entwickelte sich zu einem ermutigenden Beleg für die Qualität der deutsch-französischen Beziehungen. Die atmosphärischen Verbesserungen konnten allerdings nicht über die tiefgreifenden Meinungsverschiedenheiten in zentralen Fragen der Außenpolitik hinwegtäuschen. Von rechts: Bundesaußenminister Schröder, Bundeskanzler Erhard, Bundesverteidigungsminister von Hassel, Bundesminister für wirtschaftliche Zusammenarbeit Scheel und Staatssekretär Carstens.

The six-monthly meeting provided for by the Franco-German Cooperation Treaty, to which the leading members of the federal government set off on February 13, 1964, provided encouraging evidence of the quality of Franco-German relations. The improved atmosphere could not, however, conceal the profound differences of opinion on crucial foreign policy issues. From the right: Foreign Minister Schröder, Chancellor Erhard, Defense Minister von Hassel, Minister for Economic Cooperation Scheel, and State Secretary Carstens.

Ein »glückliches Europa«, so meinte Erhard im Sommer 1964, sei erst dann erreicht, »wenn auch die kleineren Länder ihren vollen Anteil haben, wenn die Spaltung in Europa beendet sein wird und wenn wirklich ein Europa der Gleichen und der Freien verwirklicht sein wird«. In den Niederlanden, denen er vom 1.-3.3.1964 seinen Antrittsbesuch abstattete, durfte er sich des Beifalls sicher sein. Am letzten Tag des Aufenthaltes wurden Erhard und Schröder von Prinz Bernhard auf Schloß Soestdijk empfangen.

A "happy Europe," thus Erhard gave his opinion in summer 1964, would only be achieved "when the smaller countries also have their full share, when the division of Europe is ended and when a Europe of free and equal peoples has actually become a reality." In the Netherlands, to which he made his inaugural visit from March 1-3, 1964, he could be sure of applause. On the last day of the visit Erhard and Schröder were received by Prince Bernhard at Soestdijk Palace.

»Ich gehe nicht leichten Herzens«, hatte Adenauer beim Abschied aus dem Kanzleramt erklärt. Wer glaubte, der 87jährige Herr werde sich aufs Altenteil zurückziehen, sah sich getäuscht. Zwar frönte er auch zukünftig seiner Lieblingsurlaubsbeschäftigung, dem Boccia-Spiel in Cadenabbia am Comer See, hier im Sommer 1958. Er trat aber keineswegs in den politischen Ruhestand, entwickelte sich vielmehr zu einem scharfen Widersacher der Außenpolitik Ludwig Erhards. Anfang Juli 1964 forderte er ihn dazu auf, endlich gemeinsam mit de Gaulle die politische Einigung Europas anzugehen.

"I do not go gladly," Adenauer had declared on giving up the office of Chancellor. Anyone who thought that at 87 he would retire from public life, was deceived. He did continue to indulge in his favorite vacation activity, playing "Boccia" in Cadenabbia on Lake Como, here in summer 1958. Politically speaking he did not by any means retire, but instead became a fierce opponent of Erhard's foreign policies. At the beginning of July 1964 he called on Erhard to join with de Gaulle at last to tackle the political unification of Europe.

Ob Erhard auf der »Zugfahrt der deutschen Europapolitik« noch die Richtung angeben sollte, wurde in der Union seit dem Sommer 1964 immer heftiger in Frage gestellt. Gern hätten ihn seine Kritiker aufs Abstellgleis, zumindest in die »zweite Klasse«, abgeschoben. Daß der Kanzler auf seiner Fahrt nach Luxemburg am 4.5.1964 im zweiten Wagen Platz nahm, symbolisierte indes keineswegs seine Kapitulation.

Whether Erhard should continue to determine the direction of the "railway journey of German European policy" was increasingly called into question within the CDU from summer 1964 onwards. His critics would dearly have liked to shunt him into a siding, or at least to put him in a "second-class" carriage. However, the fact that on his journey to Luxembourg on May 4, 1964 the Chancellor had a seat in the second carriage was not by any means a symbol of his surrender.

»Die Zeit des Zögerns und des Ablenkungsmanövers ist vorbei«, soll de Gaulle nach Presseberichten bei seinem Besuch in Bonn am 3./4.7.1964 gedroht haben. Doch Erhard lehnte die ihm angebotene Mitwirkung an einem deutsch-französischen Zusammenschluß als Kern einer späteren europäischen Föderation entschieden ab, weil er die übrigen EWG-Staaten nicht düpieren wollte. Auch den Köder einer Beteiligung an der französischen »Force de frappe« ließ er unbeachtet liegen, da seiner Meinung nach nur der amerikanische Schutzschirm Sicherheit bot. Adenauer empfand Erhards Verhalten als »Skandal«.

"The time for hesitation and for creating diversions is past," de Gaulle was reported by the press as having threatened during his visit to Bonn on July 3-4, 1964. But Erhard decisively turned down the invitation to collaborate in a Franco-German union as the core of a later European federation because he was unwilling to deceive the other EEC states. Nor did he rise to the bait of collaboration in the French strike force, because in his opinion only the American umbrella offered security. Adenauer regarded Erhard's behavior as "scandalous."

»Der Präsident verehrt mich, und ich verehre ihn«, meinte Erhard vor seiner Abreise nach Washington am 24.9.1966. Daraus politische Folgerungen abzuleiten, war fatal. Seit seinem ersten Besuch bei Johnson im Dezember 1963, hier bei einem Barbecue zu Ehren Erhards am 29.12.1963 in Stonewall, einem Nachbarort der Ranch Johnsons in Texas, hatten sich die Zeiten dramatisch geändert. Wenngleich sich Erhard wie damals immer noch als der treueste Verbündete der USA verstand, kam Johnson ihm nicht einen Fußbreit entgegen. Damit trug er nicht unerheblich zum Sturz des Kanzlers bei.

"The President has great respect for me, and I have great respect for him," Erhard said before leaving for Washington on September 24, 1966. To draw political inferences from this was a fatal mistake. Times had changed dramatically since he first visited Johnson in December 1963 – here at a barbecue in Erhard's honor on December 29, 1963 in Stonewall, the neighborhood of Johnson's Texas ranch. Even though Erhard still regarded himself, as he had then, as the Americans' most loyal ally, Johnson would not budge an inch. He thereby helped to a not inconsiderable degree bring about the Chancellor's fall.

»Ob nun eine Föderation oder eine Konföderation entsteht oder welche Rechtsform es immer sein mag: Handeln, Anfangen ist die Hauptsache«, lautete Adenauers europapolitische Devise an seinem Lebensabend. Im April 1966 erholte er sich von seinen Sorgen um Europa am Comer See und stand dem Maler Oskar Kokoschka drei Wochen lang Modell. Am 19.4.1966 präsentierten sie in ausgelassener Stimmung das Ergebnis: mit schielendem Blick, grünem Schnurrbart, roter Nase und flacher Stirn. Im Bild links Gerstenmaier, der die Weichheit des Bildes wenig realitätsnah fand.

"Whether a federation or a confederation comes about, or whatever the legal form may be: the main thing is to act, to make a start." That was Adenauer's maxim for European policy towards the end of his life. In April 1966, recovering from his worries about Europe at Lake Como, he sat for three weeks for the painter Oskar Kokoschka. On April 19, 1966, in a lighthearted mood, they exhibited the result: cross-eyed, with a green moustache, a red nose and a flat forehead. On the left of the picture Gerstenmaier, who did not find the softness of the painting very realistic.

Der Streit über den unausgeglichenen Bundesetat besiegelte das Schicksal der Regierung Erhard. Am 26.10.1966 stimmten drei der vier liberalen Bundesminister Steuererhöhungen zu. Einen Tag später trat Scheel aus Protest zurück. Da die Fraktion auf seiner Seite stand, folgten die FDP-Kabinettskollegen seinem Beispiel. Am 28.10.1966 erhielten sie von Lübke ihre Entlassungsurkunde. Von links Ewald Bucher (Bundesminister für Wohnungswesen, Städtebau und Raumordnung), Erich Mende (Bundesminister für gesamtdeutsche Fragen), Walter Scheel (Bundesminister für wirtschaftliche Zusammenarbeit) und Rolf Dahlgrün (Bundesminister der Finanzen).

The dispute over the failure to balance the budget set the seal on the fate of the Erhard government. On October 26, 1966 three of the four Liberal ministers voted for tax increases. A day later Scheel resigned in protest. Since he had the FDP parliamentary group on his side, his FDP cabinet colleagues followed his example. On October 28, 1966 they received their certificates of termination of office from Lübke. From left to right: Ewald Bucher (Minister of Housing, Town, and Regional Planning), Erich Mende (Minister for All-German Affairs), Walter Scheel (Minister for Economic Cooperation), and Rolf Dahlgrün (Minister of Finance).

»Und wenn das Wunder ausbleibt, weg mit ihm« (Sebastian Haffner), hieß die Devise der Union gegenüber ihrem glücklosen Parteivorsitzenden und Bundeskanzler im Herbst 1966. Zermürbt und verbittert über die fehlende »Fairneß und Noblesse« nahm Erhard am 30.11.1966 Abschied aus dem Kanzleramt. Adenauer jubilierte: »Hauptsache, et is einer wech!«

"Unless there is a miracle, he will have to go" (Sebastian Haffner): that was the CDU's motto in the autumn of 1966 where their hapless party chairman and Chancellor were concerned. Worn out and embittered at being treated so "unfairly and ignobly," Erhard left the Chancellery on November 30, 1966. Adenauer was jubilant: "The main thing is, he's gone!"

Kurt Georg Kiesinger

(gegenüber) Seit dem 27.10.1966 amtierte Erhard nur noch als »Geister-Kanzler« (*Der Spiegel*). Am 1.12.1966 wählte der Bundestag Kurt Georg Kiesinger mit 340 gegen 109 Stimmen bei 23 Enthaltungen zum Bundeskanzler. Seine Nominierung verdankte er vornehmlich der Unterstützung durch die CSU und der Selbstblockade seiner Gegenkandidaten Rainer Barzel und Gerhard Schröder. Im Mai 1967 übernahm Kiesinger von seinem Vorgänger, dem er hier im Park des Bundeskanzleramtes die Leviten zu lesen scheint, auch noch das Amt des Parteivorsitzenden der CDU.

(opposite) After October 27, 1966 Erhard held office only as a "ghost Chancellor." (*Der Spiegel*) On December 1, 1966 parliament elected Kurt Georg Kiesinger as Chancellor by 340 votes to 109 with 23 abstentions. He owed his appointment principally to the support of the CSU and the fact that the rival candidates Rainer Barzel and Gerhard Schröder ruled themselves out. In May 1967 Kiesinger also took over the post of CDU party chairman from his predecessor, whom he seems here to be raking over the coals in the Chancellery grounds.

Mit seiner breiten Bildung und Offenheit für die Welt des Geistes war Kiesinger, hier am 15.10.1968 auf dem Bundespresseball, eine Ausnahmeerscheinung auf der Bonner Politikbühne. Der ihm zugeschriebene Ausdruck »König Silberzunge« wurde ihm gleichwohl nicht gerecht, denn Kiesinger war weit mehr als ein Schönredner. Gewiß ein Grandseigneur, besaß er neben aller Liebenswürdigkeit und Eleganz auch Machtbewußtsein und Durchsetzungsvermögen.

With his breadth of education and openness to the world of the intellect Kiesinger, here at the press ball on October 15, 1968, was an unusual phenomenon on the political scene in Bonn. He was said to have coined the nickname of "King Silvertongue" himself, but even so it did not do him justice, for Kiesinger was far more than a smooth talker. For all his aristocratic manner, his charm and elegance, he nonetheless had a sense of power and the ability to get his way.

Nach der Begrüßung durch eine Ehrenformation zog mit Kiesinger am 1.12.1966 ein Kanzler des Ausgleichs ins Palais Schaumburg ein. Versuche aus der Publizistik, diesen »Politiker zwischen den Zeiten« (Rolf Zundel) unter Hinweis auf seine NSDAP-Mitgliedschaft zu diskreditieren, blieben ohne Fundament in der Sache.

When on December 1, 1966 Kiesinger entered the Palais Schaumburg after being welcomed with a guard of honor, it was as a Chancellor who believed in conciliation. Attempts by the media to discredit this "politician who bridged the eras" (Rolf Zundel) by pointing to his National Socialist party membership lacked any real basis.

Säulen der großen Koalition / The Pillars of the Grand Coalition

(unten) Kiesinger und Wehner, die eigentlichen »Gründungsväter« und tragenden Säulen der Großen Koalition, hatten am Abend des 1.12.1966 allen Grund zur Freude. Kernelement ihres Bündnisses war die gemeinsame Absicht zu einer aktiveren Ostpolitik. Allerdings gab es dabei eine fundamentale Differenz: Kiesinger setzte auf eine Verbesserung des Verhältnisses zu Moskau, um langfristig den Weg für eine Lösung der Deutschen Frage zu bereiten; Wehner lag daran, mit den Machthabern in Ostberlin kurzfristig Vereinbarungen abzuschließen, die ein weiteres Auseinanderleben der Menschen in Ost- und Westdeutschland verhindern sollten.

Kiesinger and Wehner, the real "founding fathers" and supporting pillars of the Grand Coalition, had every reason to be happy on the evening of December 1, 1966. The central core of their alliance was their shared intention to pursue a more active policy towards eastern Europe. There was however a fundamental difference between them: Kiesinger's strategy was to improve relations with Moscow in order to pave the way in the long term for a solution of the German question; Wehner's concern was to conclude agreements with East Berlin in the short term which would prevent the inhabitants of East and West Germany from growing further apart.

(gegenüber) Zum Auftakt der Regierungsarbeit hieß Kiesinger am 7.12.1966 Außenminister Willy Brandt zur ersten Kabinettssitzung willkommen. Im Hintergrund beobachtete Staatssekretär Karl Carstens die Szene, der kurz darauf vom Auswärtigen Amt ins Bundesverteidigungsministerium wechselte und Anfang 1968 zum Chef des Bundeskanzleramtes aufstieg. Der Händedruck zwischen dem Kanzler und seinem Vize leitete »ein neues Kapitel der politischen Geschichte der Bundesrepublik« ein (Helmut Schmidt).

(opposite) Kiesinger began the work of government on December 7, 1966 by welcoming Foreign Minister Willy Brandt to the first meeting of the cabinet. In the background State Secretary Karl Carstens observed the scene; shortly afterwards he moved from the Foreign Office to the Ministry of Defense and was promoted to Head of Chancellery early in 1968. The handshake between the Chancellor and his Deputy inaugurated a "new chapter in the political history of the Federal Republic." (Helmut Schmidt)

Willy Brandt

(oben) Der Schein trügt. Brandt war
über den Einzug ins Auswärtige Amt
alles andere als begeistert. Weder der
Zeitpunkt noch die Umstände behag-
ten ihm. Auch die Große Koalition
gefiel ihm, wie er freimütig bekannn-
te, »keineswegs«.

(above) Appearances are deceptive.
Brandt was anything but enthusiastic
about taking over the Foreign Office.
Neither the time nor the circumstances
suited him. And as he candidly admitt-
ted, he was "by no means" happy with
the Grand Coalition.

Hauptthema der Mammutsitzung des Bundeskabinetts Anfang Juli 1967 war die Sanierung der Staatsfinanzen. Von links u.a.: Bundesminister für Wirtschaft Karl Schiller, Bundesminister der Justiz Gustav Heinemann (SPD), Bundesminister des Auswärtigen Willy Brandt, Bundeskanzler Kurt Georg Kiesinger, Bundesminister des Innern Paul Lücke (CDU), Bundesminister der Finanzen Franz Josef Strauß (CSU), Bundesminister für Ernährung, Landwirtschaft und Forsten Hermann Höcherl (CSU), Bundesminister der Verteidigung Gerhard Schröder (CDU), Bundesminister für Gesundheitswesen Käte Strobel (SPD), Bundesminister für den wirtschaftlichen Besitz des Bundes Kurt Schmücker (CDU), Bundesminister für Familie und Jugend Bruno Heck (CDU), Bundesminister für gesamtdeutsche Fragen Herbert Wehner (SPD), Bundesminister für Wohnungswesen und Städtebau Lauritz Lauritzen (SPD), Bundesminister für Verkehr Georg Leber (SPD), Bundesminister für Arbeit und Sozialordnung Hans Katzer (CDU).

The main topic at the mammoth cabinet meeting in early July 1967 was how to put state finances back on an even keel. From left to right, among others: Economics Minister Karl Schiller, Minister of Justice Gustav Heinemann (SPD), Foreign Minister Willy Brandt, Chancellor Kurt Georg Kiesinger, Minister of the Interior Paul Lücke (CDU), Finance Minister Franz Josef Strauß (CSU), Minister of Food, Agriculture, and Forestries Hermann Höcherl (CSU), Minister of Defense Gerhard Schröder (CDU), Minister of Health Käte Strobel (SPD), Minister for Federal Economic Property Kurt Schmücker (CDU), Minister for Youth and Family Affairs Bruno Heck (CDU), Minister for All-German Affairs Herbert Wehner (SPD), Minister of Housing, Town, and Regional Planning Lauritz Lauritzen (SPD), Minister of Transport Georg Leber (SPD), Minister of Labor and Social Affairs Hans Katzer (CDU).

Anläßlich des 64. Geburtstags des Kanzlers trafen sich enge Mitarbeiter und Weggefährten am 6.4.1968 zu einem Umtrunk im Kanzleramt. Von links: Staatssekretär Günter Diehl, der Chef des Presse- und Informationsamtes der Bundesregierung, Staatssekretär Karl Carstens, der Chef des Bundeskanzleramtes, Konrad Kraske, der CDU-Bundesgeschäftsführer, Conrad Ahlers, der Stellvertretende Leiter des Presse- und Informationsamtes der Bundesregierung, Horst Osterheld, der Leiter des Außenpolitischen Büros im Kanzleramt, Arthur Rathke, Sprecher des CDU-Bundesvorstandes, Gerhard Schröder und Herbert Wehner.

Close colleagues and companions of the Chancellor met at the Chancellery to drink to his health on the occasion of his 64th birthday on April 6, 1968. From left to right: State Secretary Günter Diehl, head of the government press and information office, State Secretary Karl Carstens, Head of Chancellery, Konrad Kraske, CDU party manager, Conrad Ahlers, deputy head of the government press and information office, Horst Osterheld, head of the foreign affairs office at the Chancellery, Arthur Rathke, CDU executive committee spokesman, Gerhard Schröder and Herbert Wehner.

(unten) Daß die alten Wunden vergangener innenpolitischer Fehden vernarbt waren, demonstrierten der Herausgeber des Nachrichtenmagazins »Der Spiegel« Rudolf Augstein und Gerhard Schröder am 4.11.1966 auf dem Bundespresseball in der Bonner Beethovenhalle.

(below) That the old wounds of bygone domestic policy feuds had healed was demonstrated by Rudolf Augstein, the editor of the news magazine *Der Spiegel*, and Gerhard Schröder at the press ball in the Beethovenhalle in Bonn on November 4, 1966.

(gegenüber) Im Laufe der Koalitionsverhandlungen hatte Brandt Interesse am Forschungsministerium angemeldet, weil er glaubte, daß der Vorsitz der SPD und die Vizekanzlerschaft sich mit der Übernahme eines größeren Ressorts nicht vereinbaren ließen. Helmut Schmidt, hier bei einem Empfang zu Ehren des Präsidenten der EWG-Kommission Walter Hallstein am 19.10.1967 in der Godesberger Redoute, gehörte zu jenen Genossen, die ihm diese Idee ausredeten und darauf bestanden, daß der Parteivorsitzende auch das höchste Ministeramt bekleiden müsse.

(opposite) In the course of the coalition negotiations Brandt had indicated his interest in the Ministry of Research and Technology, because he thought that the SPD chairmanship and the Deputy Chancellorship could not be combined with one of the larger ministries. Helmut Schmidt, here at a reception in honor of the President of the EEC Commmission Walter Hallstein on October 19, 1967 in the "Redoute" in Bad Godesberg, was one of the colleagues who talked him out of this idea, insisting that the party chairman must also occupy the highest ministerial office.

Auf eine erfolgreiche Amtszeit prosteten sich am 1.12.1966 Bundesminister der Justiz Gustav Heinemann, Bundesminister für Angelegenheiten des Bundesrates Carlo Schmid, Bundesminister für Wirtschaft Karl Schiller und die Vorzeigedame im ansonsten ausschließlich aus Männern bestehenden Kabinett, Käte Strobel, zu. Aus ihren Gesichtern sprach nicht eben Begeisterung über den politischen Aufstieg. Vor allem Schmid, der sich als eine Art »Minister des Äußern im Innern« betrachtete, hatte sein neues Amt nur wider Willen und auf verstärkte Bitten der Parteispitze angenommen.

Minister of Justice Gustav Heinemann, Minister for *Bundesrat* Affairs Carlo Schmid, Economics Minister Karl Schiller, and the token woman in a cabinet which otherwise consisted exclusively of men, Käte Strobel, raising their glasses to drink to a successful term of office on December 1, 1966. Their faces did not exactly suggest enthusiasm at their political promotion. Schmid in particular, who regarded himself as a kind of "domestic Foreign Minister," had accepted his new office only reluctantly and at the urgent request of the party leaders.

(gegenüber) Seit der Bildung der Großen Koalition hatte sich Konrad Adenauer, das »politische Urgestein« der Bundesrepublik Deutschland (Herbert Wehner), aus der Tagespolitik weitgehend zurückgezogen. Er hatte diese Regierung begrüßt und schöpfte Hoffnung, daß die politischen Probleme der Republik behoben werden könnten.

(opposite) After the formation of the Grand Coalition Konrad Adenauer, the "immutable political bedrock" of the Federal Republic (Herbert Wehner) had to a large extent withdrawn from day-to-day political life. He had welcomed this government, which led him to hope that the Republic's political problems might be solved.

Am 5.1.1967 gab das Präsidium der CDU anläßlich des 91. Geburtstages von Adenauer einen Empfang, an dem neben dem Altbundeskanzler auch die Hoffnungsträger der Partei teilnahmen, hier der rheinlandpfälzische Landesvorsitzende der CDU, Helmut Kohl.

On January 5, 1967 the CDU executive committee gave a reception to mark Adenauer's 91st birthday at which the former Chancellor was joined by rising stars of the party: here Helmut Kohl, the regional chairman of the CDU in Rhineland-Palatinate.

Seit einem Herzinfarkt Ende März 1967 lief Adenauers Lebensuhr rasch ab. Seine letzten Tage verbrachte er meist ohne Bewußtsein in seinem Wohnhaus in Rhöndorf. Am 19.4.1967 verkündeten die mit Kamerateleskopen und Radioempfängern vor seinem Heim wartenden Journalisten die Nachricht von seinem Tode .

Following a heart attack at the end of March 1967 time was rapidly running out for Adenauer. He spent his last days for the most part lying unconscious in his house in Rhöndorf. On April 19, 1967 journalists who had been waiting outside his home with their telescopic lenses and radio receivers announced the news of his death.

Nach dem Pontifikalrequiem von Kardinal Frings wurde der Katafalk zum Rheinufer getragen, von wo ihn ein Schnellboot der Bundesmarine zur Beisetzung nach Rhöndorf brachte. Weitere Schiffe und zwölf Starfighter der Luftwaffe gaben ihnen Geleit. Einen imposanteren Trauerzug hatte der Strom in seiner Geschichte wohl nie gesehen. Vierhundert Millionen Fernsehzuschauer verfolgten in aller Welt das Geschehen.

After the Pontifical Requiem celebrated by Cardinal Frings, the catafalque was taken to the bank of the Rhine; from there it was conveyed by a Federal Navy speedboat to Rhöndorf for burial. It was escorted by more ships and 12 German Air Force Starfighters. The river had probably never in its entire history witnessed a more impressive funeral procession. Four hundred million people all over the world watched the event on television.

Daß die schon legendäre Gründerpersönlichkeit Israels David Ben Gurion am 24.4.1967 zur Trauerfeier für Adenauer anreiste, zeigte eindrucksvoll das Verdienst des Verstorbenen für die Wiederherstellung des deutschen Ansehens. Am Tage nach der Beisetzung empfing Kiesinger ihn im Palais Schaumburg.

The fact that the legendary founder of the state of Israel, David Ben Gurion, attended Adenauer's funeral, arriving on April 24, 1967, provided an impressive demonstration of how much the deceased had contributed to restoring Germany's standing. Kiesinger received him in the Palais Schaumburg on the day after the funeral.

(gegenüber) Das Konzept für die Beisetzung des ersten deutschen Bundeskanzlers hatte sein früherer Staatssekretär Hans Globke nach dem Vorbild des Staatsbegräbnisses von Winston Churchill entwickelt. Am 22.4.1967 wurde Adenauer im Großen Kabinettssaal des Palais Schaumburg aufgebahrt, tags darauf in den Hohen Dom zu Köln überführt. Zur Trauerfeier am 25.4. trafen Delegationen aus 54 Staaten, von 14 internationalen und 4 kirchlichen Organisationen in Adenauers Geburtsstadt ein, u.a. Präsident Johnson, Staatspräsident de Gaulle und Premierminister Wilson.

(opposite) The arrangements for the funeral of the first German Federal Chancellor had been worked out by his former State Secretary Hans Globke following the example of the state funeral of Winston Churchill. Adenauer lay in state in the Great Cabinet Hall of the Palais Schaumburg on April 22, 1967, and was taken on the following day to Cologne Cathedral. The funeral ceremony in his native city on April 25 was attended by representatives of 54 countries, 14 international and four ecclesiastical organizations; they included President Johnson, President de Gaulle, and Prime Minister Wilson.

»Plisch und Plum« nannte der Volksmund die Bundesminister der Finanzen und für Wirtschaft, Franz Josef Strauß und Karl Schiller, hier am 5.9.1968 bei einer Pressekonferenz in Bonn. Ebenso einträchtig wie erfolgreich versuchten sie, Wirtschaftswachstum und Finanzstabilität miteinander zu verknüpfen. Die schnelle Überwindung der Rezession gelang nicht zuletzt mit Hilfe einer durchgreifenden Reform des wirtschaftspolitischen Instrumentariums. Gesetzgeberischen Ausdruck fand dies im Gesetz zur Förderung der Stabilität und des Wachstums in der Wirtschaft vom 10.5.1967, der »Magna Charta« der Großen Koalition (Hans-Hermann Hartwich).

"Plisch and Plum" were the comic character names by which the Finance and Economics Ministers, Franz Josef Strauß and Karl Schiller, here at a press conference in Bonn on September 5, 1968, were popularly known. They succeeded in their shared goal of combining economic growth with financial stability. That the recession was speedily overcome was due not least to a thorough reform of the instruments of economic policy. On the legislative level this took the form of the Economic Stability and Growth Promotion Act of May 10, 1967, the "Magna Carta" of the Grand Coalition (Hans-Hermann Hartwich).

Sparmaßnahmen und Einnahmeverbesserungen senkten das Haushaltsdefizit. Investitionsanreize förderten Inlandsnachfrage und Außenhandel. Der wachsende Wohlstand in der Bundesrepublik, der sich etwa im Buffet anläßlich des Staatsbesuchs des birmanischen Generals Ne Win am 17.10.1968 widerspiegelte, wurde im Ausland durchaus kritisch beobachtet. Chauvinistisch angehauchte Presseberichte »Jetzt sind die Deutschen Nummer 1 in Europa« (»Bildzeitung«) trugen zur Beunruhigung der Nachbarn bei.

Savings measures and increased revenue reduced the budget deficit. Investment inducements boosted domestic demand and foreign trade. Foreign observers cast a highly critical eye on the increasing affluence in the Federal Republic, reflected, for example, in the buffet on October 17, 1968 to mark the state visit by the Burmese General Ne Win. Press reports tinged with chauvinism such as "The Germans are now No. 1 in Europe" (*Bildzeitung*) concerned Germany's neighbors.

»Die Germanen drückten ihren Brustkorb wieder heraus«, kommentierte der französische Botschafter François Seydoux die Stimmung in der Bundesrepublik. Gewiß, niemand neidete den Deutschen die Freude über hohe staatliche Auszeichnungen wie das Verdienstkreuz am Bande. Daß die Bundesrepublik sich aber im Winter 1968 einer Aufwertung der DM widersetzte und sich auf ihre staatlichen Interessen zurückzog, verursachte bei den Partnern großes Mißvergnügen.

"The Teutons are swelling with pride once more": thus the French ambassador François Seydoux commented on the mood in the Federal Republic. Of course, nobody begrudged the Germans their delight at being awarded outstanding decorations such as the Cross of Merit with Ribbon. But their partners were extremely displeased when in the winter of 1968 the Federal Republic insisted on safeguarding its national interests and refused to revalue the Deutschmark.

Der Staatsbesuch des Schah Reza Pahlevi mit Kaiserin Farah Diba in der Bundesrepublik vom 27.5.-4.6.1967 markierte in der Entwicklung der Studentenbewegung einen tiefen Einschnitt. Während die Regenbogenpresse und die Gefolgsleute dem Paar am 27.5. vor dem Hotel Petersberg bei Bonn einen begeisterten Empfang bereiteten, prangerten Studentenverbände die Folterpraktiken des persischen Regimes an.

The state visit to the Federal Republic by Reza Shah Pahlevi with Empress Farah Diba from May 27 to June 4, 1967 marked a decisive turning point in the evolution of the student movement. Whilst the couple were welcomed enthusiastically by the tabloid press and their own supporters outside the Petersberg Hotel in Bonn on May 27, student associations denounced the use of torture by the Persian régime.

1966–1969

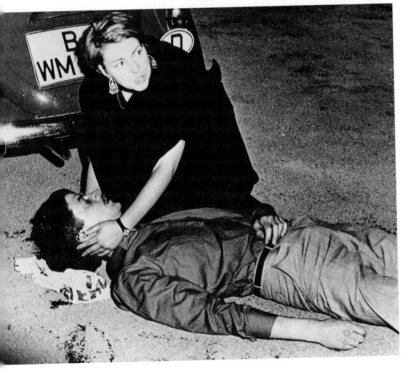

Als die Monarchen am 2.6.1967 in der Berliner Oper Mozart hörten, tobte draußen eine Straßenschlacht, in der der Student Benno Ohnesorg versehentlich durch einen Polizisten getötet wurde. Die Hilfe der Passantin Friederike Hausmann kam zu spät. In einem Autokorso wurde der Leichnam Ohnesorgs am 8.6.1967 von Berlin nach Hannover überführt. Die Beerdigung am folgenden Tag leitete in gewissem Sinne die »Geburtsstunde« (Klaus Hildebrand) der Außerparlamentarischen Opposition (APO) ein.

While the royal couple were listening to Mozart in the Berlin Opera on June 2, 1967, violent street fighting was taking place outside, in the course of which the student Benno Ohnesorg was accidentally killed by a policeman. Help from passerby Friederike Hausmann came too late. A procession of motor vehicles accompanied Ohnesorg's body from Berlin to Hanover on June 8, 1967. His funeral on the following day "brought about the birth" (Klaus Hildebrand), in a certain sense, of the extra-parliamentary opposition (APO).

Am ersten Tag des Prozesses gegen Teufel protestierten etwa 1000 Personen am 27.11.1967 vor dem Gericht Moabit. Angeführt von Rudi Dutschke, durchbrach die Menge die Absperrung.

On November 27, 1967, the first day of Teufel's trial, about 1000 people protested outside the courthouse in Moabit. Led by Rudi Dutschke, the crowd broke through the police cordon.

Zum Inbegriff »politischer Clownerie« und »sexueller Enthemmung« (»Der Spiegel«) wurde die Ende 1966 begründete »Kommune I« in Berlin, zu deren Mitgliedern neben Fritz Teufel auch der Psychologiestudent Rainer Langhans und seine Freundin Uschi Obermaier gehörten.

The members of "Commune I," which was founded in Berlin in late 1966, included, as well as Fritz Teufel, psychology student Rainer Langhans and his girlfriend Uschi Obermaier. It became a byword for "political clowning" and the "shedding of sexual inhibitions" ("Der Spiegel").

Gefesselt von den Theorien ihrer geistigen Väter, steigerte sich unter den Studenten das Verlangen nach Demokratisierung der Hochschulen und Abschaffung der Ordinarien-Universität zur Forderung nach Veränderung aller Lebensbereiche, ja zur Zerschlagung des liberalen Staates als vermeintlichem Interessenverwalter des Kapitals. Zum Hauptagitator, »SDS-Ideologen« (Karl Carstens) und Studentenführer stieg der 1961 aus der DDR nach West-Berlin gekommene Soziologiestudent Rudi Dutschke auf. Im Juli 1967 hatte er sich in Anwesenheit seines Verteidigers Horst Mahler vor dem Landgericht Moabit zu verantworten.

Captivated by the theories of their intellectual mentors, the students desired to bring democracy into higher education and to abolish the dominance of university professors. This desire escalated into the demand for change in all areas of life, indeed for the destruction of the liberal state as the custodian, as they saw it, of capitalist interests. Rudi Dutschke, a sociology student who had moved to West Berlin from the GDR in 1961, emerged as the principal agitator, "SDS ideologist" (Karl Carstens) and student leader. In July 1967 he was called to account before the district court in Moabit; his defense lawyer Horst Mahler was present.

Zu den extrovertiertesten Vertretern der Studentenrevolte gehörte der Publizistikstudent Fritz Teufel. Im August 1967 aus der Haft entlassen, veranstalteten seine Anhänger auf dem Kurfürstendamm ein Happening unter dem Motto: »Man muß den Teufel feiern, solange er los ist«. Wenige Monate später hatte Teufel wegen Landfriedensbruch erneut vor dem Landgericht Moabit zu erscheinen; an seiner Seite abermals Rechtsanwalt Mahler.

One of the most extroverted representatives of the student revolt was Fritz Teufel, a student of journalism and media studies. When Teufel (whose name means "Devil") was released from prison in August 1967 his followers staged a "happening" on the Kurfürstendamm with the motto: "When all hell's let loose, we have to celebrate the devil." A few months later Teufel was again summoned to appear before the district court in Moabit, charged with a breach of the peace; his lawyer Mahler was once again at his side.

Besondere Dynamik gewann die Studentenrevolte in den Demonstrationen gegen die amerikanische Kriegführung in Vietnam. Namentlich Dutschke organisierte zahlreiche Veranstaltungen gegen den Militäreinsatz der USA in Fernost, hier am 18.2.1968 auf dem internationalen Vietnam-Kongreß im Auditorium Maximum der Technischen Universität Berlin.

The student revolt took on a particular dynamism in the demonstrations against the war being waged by the Americans in Vietnam. Dutschke in particular organized numerous protests against US military operations in the Far East, here at the international Vietnam congress in the main lecture hall of the Technical University of Berlin on February 18, 1968.

Der Mordanschlag auf Dutschke, von dem die Zeitungen am 11.4.1968 in riesigen Lettern berichteten, bereitete der revolutionären Karriere dieser »einzigen einigermaßen charismatischen Leitfigur« der APO (Michael Salewski) ein jähes Ende.

The attempted murder of Dutschke, which was reported by the newspapers in huge letters on April 11, 1968, brought the revolutionary career of "the only leading figure in the APO with a certain degree of charisma" (Michael Salewski) to an abrupt end.

Nach dem Attentat auf Dutschke kam es im April 1968 zu den schwersten Straßenunruhen, die die Bundesrepublik bisher gesehen hatte. Wie hier vor dem Schöneberger Rathaus in Berlin lieferten sich Sympathisanten des APO-Führers mit der Polizei vielerorts harte Gefechte.

The attempt on Dutschke's life in April 1968 was followed by the most severe rioting that had ever been seen in the Federal Republic. There were violent clashes, as seen here outside the Town Hall in Schöneberg, Berlin, between police and those who were in sympathy with the APO leader.

1966–1969

In weiten Teilen der Bevölkerung stießen die Jugendlichen mit ihren »sit-ins«, »go-ins«, »teach-ins« als neue Formen des Massenprotestes auf offene Ablehnung. Nicht wenige Bundesbürger fühlten sich in ihrem Ruhebedürfnis massiv gestört. In Berlin protestierten am 21.8.1968 Tausende gegen den SDS und seinen Radikalismus.

The young people with their sit-ins, go-ins, and teach-ins as new forms of mass protest encountered unconcealed hostility in large parts of the populace. Not a few members of the public felt that their need for peace and quiet was being drastically infringed. On August 21, 1968 thousands of people in Berlin protested against the SDS and its radical behavior.

Notstandsgesetze

Neben dem Vietnamkrieg der USA boten die Pläne der Bundesregierung zur Verabschiedung einer Notstandsgesetzgebung der APO einen zweiten Anknüpfungspunkt zum Protest. Die seit 1958 währende Diskussion war bisher ohne durchgreifenden Erfolg verlaufen. Widerstand kam vor allem von den Gewerkschaften, die sich auch nicht von dem Argument bekehren ließen, die Bundesrepublik gewinne ein Stück Souveränität. Erst als die Große Koalition sich darauf verständigte, die parlamentarische Kontrolle der Exekutive im Fall des Notstands nicht auszusetzen, nahm der DGB von dem angedrohten Generalstreik Abstand. Dennoch erfüllte viele Bundesbürger die dumpfe Angst, das »Machtkartell« der beiden großen Parteien ziele auf die Ausschaltung demokratischer Grundrechte, galt doch das Fehlen einer starken parlamentarischen Opposition bereits als Zeichen des »Zerfalls der Demokratie« (Karl Jaspers).

Emergency Laws

Along with America's Vietnam War, the government's plans to put emergency laws on the statute book gave the APO a second target for its protests. Discussions which had been going on since 1958 had not as yet produced any positive results. Resistance came especially from the trade unions who were not persuaded by the argument that there would be a gain in sovereignty for the Federal Republic. Only when the Grand Coalition agreed that even in cases of emergency the government's accountability to parliament would continue did the DGB (German Federation of Trade Unions) withdraw its threat of a general strike. Nevertheless many members of the public felt a vague fear that the "power monopoly" of the two major parties was aiming to suspend basic democratic rights, particularly as the absence of any effective parliamentary opposition was already being seen as a symptom of the "decline of democracy" (Karl Jaspers).

Den Höhepunkt der Protestveranstaltungen gegen die Notstandsgesetzgebung bildete ein vom Kuratorium »Notstand der Demokratie« und der »Kampagne für Demokatie und Abrüstung« am 11.5.1968 organisierter Sternmarsch auf Bonn.

Protest against the emergency laws reached its peak in the marches organized by the "Emergency for Democracy" committee and the "Campaign for Democracy and Disarmament," which converged on Bonn on May 11, 1968.

(gegenüber) Trotz der öffentlichen Proteste verabschiedete der Bundestag am 30.5.1968 die »einfachen« Notstandsgesetze und die Notstandsverfassung. 384 Abgeordnete stimmten mit Ja, 100 mit Nein. Mit diesen Grundgesetzänderungen, die am 28.6.1968 in Kraft traten, wurden die seit 1955 gültigen Vorbehaltsrechte der Alliierten abgelöst und genaue gesetzliche Regelungen für den Verteidigungsfall und andere Krisensituationen geschaffen. Von der Regierungsbank verfolgten etliche Minister die Debatte, von rechts: Kiesinger, Brandt, Innenminister Benda, Justizminister Heinemann.

(opposite) On May 30, 1968, despite public protest, parliament passed "simple" emergency laws and emergency constitution. 384 members voted in favor, 100 voted against. With these changes to Basic Law, which came into effect on June 28, 1968, the special rights reserved to themselves by the Allies since 1955 fell into abeyance and precise legal provisions were established to apply in the event of a military attack and other crisis situations. From the government bench there were quite a few ministers who followed the debate. From right: Kiesinger, Brandt, Interior Minister Benda, and Justice Minister Heinemann.

Ungeachtet der mindestens 30000 Teilnehmer gelang den Organisatoren nicht der Durchbruch zu einer Volksbewegung. Die Spruchbänder der Demonstranten stempelten die Bundesregierung zu Scharfmachern, doch das breite Publikum schloß sich dieser Meinung nicht an.

Although at least 30,000 people took part, the organizers did not succeed in founding a people's movement. The demonstrators' banners branded the government as trouble-makers, but the broad general public did not share this opinion.

(oben) Als Sprecher gegen die Notstandsgesetze trat am 11.5.1968 auch Heinrich Böll auf.

(links) Wenig überzeugend wirkte der von ehemaligen KZ-Häftlingen am 11.5.1968 angeführte Vergleich zwischen der Bundesregierung und dem Hitler-Regime.

(above) Heinrich Böll, here on May 11, 1968, also spoke out against the emergency laws.

(left) The comparison made by former concentration camp inmates between the government and the Hitler régime, on May 11, 1968, was not very convincing.

500.000 Westberliner kamen zu uns.
Wir haben sie als Gäste empfangen.

Wer aber die Grenze verletzt,
wer den Frieden antastet,
muß die Folgen tragen!

(links) In der Frage der Wahlrechtsreform lehnten starke Kräfte in der SPD den Gedanken an eine Änderung, der die FDP zum Opfer fallen würde, ab. Nach einem letzten Meinungsaustausch in der Fraktion, hier am 5.3.1968 im Berliner Reichstags-gebäude, vertagten die Sozialdemokraten das Thema bis auf weiteres. Neben der Deutschland- und Ostpolitik bot den Genossen damit auch die Rechtspolitik eine Basis für eine Annäherung an die Liberalen. Von links: Herbert Wehner, Carlo Schmid, Alex Möller und Helmut Schmidt.

(left) With regards to reform of electoral law, there were influential forces within the SPD which reject-ed the idea of a change of which the FDP would be the victim. After a final exchange of views in the parliamentary group, here on March 5, 1968 in the Reichstag building in Berlin, the Social Democrats postponed the issue indefinitely. Thus, in addition to policy towards East Germany and eastern Europe, legislation policy also provided a basis for the SPD to seek a rapprochement with the Liberals. From left to right: Herbert Wehner, Carlo Schmid, Alex Möller, and Helmut Schmidt.

Deutschlandpolitik in Bewegung / Germany's Politics in Action

(gegenüber) »Gräben überwinden und nicht vertiefen«, »einen Anfang finden«, lautete Kiesingers Motto gegenüber den Machthabern der DDR, deren militante Propaganda, wie hier Anfang 1966 an der Berliner Mauer, nicht gerade ermutigend wirkte. Sowohl er als auch Wehner strebten mit der DDR einen Vertrag »zur Regelung der innerdeutschen Beziehungen für eine Übergangszeit« an. Bis zur Wiedervereinigung wollte der Kanzler der DDR eine »befristete Geschäftsfähigkeit« (Günter Diehl) einräumen.

(opposite) "To bridge gaps, not to widen them," "to make a beginning": these were Kiesinger's mottos with regards to the rulers of the GDR, whose militant propaganda, as seen here at the Berlin Wall early in 1966, was not exactly encouraging. Both he and Wehner strove for a treaty with the GDR "regulating inter-German relations for a transitional period." Pending reunification the Chancellor was willing to concede "temporary competence" (Günter Diehl) to the GDR.

Mitte April 1967 unterbreitete der Kanzler einen Katalog von konkreten Möglichkeiten zur »Erleichterung des täglichen Lebens für die Menschen in beiden Teilen Deutschlands«. Dabei dachte er auch an die Vereinfachung des Reiseverkehrs, der an hohen Festtagen – wie hier zu Ostern 1967 – immer wieder zu langen Wartezeiten führte. Später signalisierte er gar die Bereitschaft zu einer persönlichen Begegnung mit Ministerpräsident Stoph.

In mid-April 1967 the Chancellor presented a list of specific ways of "making daily life easier for people in both parts of Germany." What he had in mind included simplifying travel, which on public holidays – here at Easter 1967 – repeatedly led to long lines of waiting cars. He later even signalled his willingness to meet Prime Minister Stoph in person.

Auf einer zehntägigen Asienreise gewann Kiesinger, hier am 22.11.1967 in Begleitung seines Staatssekretärs Freiherr zu Guttenberg im Swedagon-Pagado in Rangun, den Eindruck, daß eine Aufgabe der dogmatischen Handhabung der »Hallstein-Doktrin« keine Anerkennungswelle durch die Staaten der Dritten Welt nach sich zöge. Über erste Ansätze eines neuen Dialogs mit dem Warschauer Pakt sollte die Bundesregierung wegen der Differenzen innerhalb der Koalition über die Frage der Anerkennung des Status quo in Europa nicht hinausgelangen.

On a ten-day tour of Asia, Kiesinger – seen here in Swedagon-Pagado, Rangoon on November 22, 1967, accompanied by his State Secretary Freiherr zu Guttenberg – formed the impression that to abandon the dogmatic application of the "Hallstein Doctrine" would not lead to widespread recognition of the GDR by third-world countries. But because of differences of opinion within the coalition regarding the question of recognition of the status quo in Europe, the government did not progress beyond the preliminary stages of a new dialogue with the Warsaw Pact countries.

Wie er in einer großen Rede im Juni 1967 formuliert hatte, betrachtete Kiesinger ein wiedervereinigtes Deutschland als eine »kritische Größenordnung«: »Es ist zu groß, um in der Balance der Kräfte keine Rolle zu spielen, und zu klein, um die Kräfte um sich herum selbst im Gleichgewicht zu halten.« Folglich war es für ihn ein Gebot staatsmännischer Klugheit, auch in Indien, das er am 22.11.1967 verließ, etwaige Ängste vor einem geeinten Deutschland zu beruhigen.

As he put it in a major speech in June 1967, Kiesinger regarded a reunified Germany as a "critical mass": "too large not to affect the balance of forces, and too small to maintain the balance of surrounding forces itself." Diplomatic prudence consequently required him, in his view, to assuage any country's possible fears of a united Germany – including India, which he left on November 22, 1967.

Am 3.2.1968 wurde Kiesinger im Vatikan von Papst Paul VI. zu einer Privataudienz empfangen. Dabei bekräftigte der Heilige Vater seine Zustimmung zu dem Wunsch des deutschen Volkes, seine legitimen Ziele mit friedlichen Mitteln zu erreichen.

On February 3, 1968 Kiesinger was given a private audience by Pope Paul VI in the Vatican. On that occasion the Holy Father confirmed his approval of the German people's desire to achieve their legitimate goals by peaceful means.

Anfang April 1969 konferierte Bundesaußenminister Brandt mit seinen Kollegen aus Frankreich, Großbritannien und den USA in Washington über die Deutsche Frage. Sie vereinbarten die Ausarbeitung von Vorschlägen zwecks Verbesserung der Kontakte zwischen beiden Teilen Deutschlands und der Verbindungen zu Berlin. Ein Abstecher nach New York brachte ihn am 9.4.1969 ins Watergate-Hotel, das Präsident Nixon 1974 zum Verhängnis werden sollte.

In early April 1969 in Washington Foreign Minister Brandt conferred with his opposite numbers from France, Britain, and the USA regarding the German question. They agreed to work out proposals for improving contacts between the two parts of Germany and links with Berlin. On April 9, 1969 a detour to New York took him to the Watergate Hotel, which was to be of fatal importance for President Nixon in 1974.

Schon in den fünfziger Jahren gehörte Kiesinger im Bundestag zu den außenpolitischen Glanzlichtern. Auch nach seiner Wahl zum Bundeskanzler betrieb er die Außenpolitik in den ihm gesteckten Grenzen mit Leidenschaft. Zahlreiche Auslandsreisen boten ihm das entsprechende Terrain. Am 23.10.1967 brachte ihn ein Hubschrauber des Bundesgrenzschutzes vom Park des Kanzlerbungalows zum Flughafen Köln-Wahn zwecks Weiterflug nach London.

Even in the fifties Kiesinger was one of the foreign policy stars in parliament. After his election as Chancellor his passionate involvement in foreign policy continued within the limits to which he was subject. Numerous visits abroad provided appropriate opportunities. On October 23, 1967 a Federal Border Guards helicopter took him from the grounds of the Chancellor's bungalow to Cologne-Wahn airport to fly on to London.

Im Zentrum seiner Westpolitik stand bei Kiesinger die Absicht, eine Option zugunsten der USA oder Frankreichs zu vermeiden. Nach dem Tiefpunkt, den die Beziehungen zu Paris in den Jahren der Regierung Erhard erreicht hatten, ging es ihm darum, das deutsch-französische Verhältnis zu aktivieren, um gemeinsam auf die Herstellung einer gesamteuropäischen Friedensordnung hinzuarbeiten. Bei seinen Gesprächen mit Staatspräsident de Gaulle am 13./14.1.1967 in Paris betonte der Kanzler seinen Willen, das in der Vergangenheit »Versäumte nachzuholen«.

At the heart of Kiesinger's western policy was his determination to avoid having to choose between Paris and Washington. After the low reached by relations with Paris in the years of the Erhard government he was concerned to activate Franco-German relations in order to work together towards establishing a framework for peace throughout Europe. In his talks with President de Gaulle in Paris on January 13-14, 1967, the Chancellor stressed his desire to "make up for past omissions."

Aufgrund der verfassungsmäßig andersartigen Machtverteilung besaß Kiesinger in der französischen Regierung im Grunde keinen gleichrangigen Gesprächspartner. Während de Gaulle als Staatspräsident über dem Kanzler stand, besaß Premierminister Pompidou, hier mit Kiesinger Mitte Januar 1967, aufgrund der Vorbehaltsrechte des Staatsoberhauptes nur eng begrenzte Möglichkeiten, in die Exekution der Außen- und Verteidigungspolitik einzugreifen.

Because of the different constitutional distribution of powers, Kiesinger basically had no opposite number of equal rank in the French government to hold talks with. De Gaulle, as President, ranked above the Chancellor, whereas because of the rights reserved to the head of state, Prime Minister Pompidou – here with Kiesinger in mid-January 1967 – had only very limited influence with regards to the implementation of foreign and defense policy.

Am Rande der Trauerfeierlichkeiten zu Ehren Konrad Adenauers versuchte Bundespräsident Lübke zusammenzubringen, was nicht zusammengehörte. Seine gutgemeinte Geste, die Hände des amerikanischen und des französischen Präsidenten bei einem Empfang der Staats- und Regierungschefs in der Godesberger Redoute am 25.4.1967 zusammenzufügen, geriet zur Peinlichkeit. Johnson und de Gaulle mochten ihr Unbehagen nicht verbergen. Nur Lübkes Frau Wilhelmine schien begeistert: »Jetzt hast Du auch diese beiden versöhnt«, lautete ihr am Rhein kolportierter Kommentar.

On the sidelines of Konrad Adenauer's funeral ceremony, President Lübke tried to join together what did not belong together. His well-meant gesture of joining the hands of the American and the French President at a reception for the political leaders at the "Redoute" in Bad Godesberg on April 25, 1967 created an embarrassing moment. Johnson and de Gaulle did not conceal their unease. Only Lübke's wife Wilhelmine seemed enthusiastic: her comment: "Now you have reconciled these two as well," was gossiped about on the Rhine.

(links) Eindringlich warnte Johnson am 16.8.1967 vor einer Kettenreaktion im Falle deutscher Truppenreduzierungen, die die NATO demontiere. Kiesinger versuchte ihn mit dem Hinweis zu beruhigen, daß eine nennenswerte Kürzung nicht vorgesehen sei. Er machte aber keinen Hehl daraus, daß er sich amerikanischem Druck nicht beugen werde.

(left) On August 16, 1967 Johnson emphatically warned that German troop reductions would produce a chain reaction leading to the collapse of NATO. Kiesinger tried to placate him by pointing out that no cuts worth mentioning were envisaged. But he made no secret of the fact that he would not yield to American pressure.

Auch der Presse blieb die gedrückte Stimmung zwischen den USA und der Bundesrepublik nicht verborgen, als Kiesinger zu seinem ersten offiziellen Besuch vom 14.-17.8.1967 nach Washington kam. Die Entscheidung des Bundeskabinetts über eine Reduzierung des Verteidigungshaushaltes, die Frage der Devisenausgleichszahlungen für die in der Bundesrepublik stationierten amerikanischen Soldaten und das Verhältnis zu Frankreich boten seiner Unterredung mit Präsident Johnson am 16.8.1967 im Park des Weißen Hauses reichlich Stoff für kontroverse Diskussionen.

The press did not fail to note the downbeat mood between the USA and the Federal Republic when Kiesinger went to Washington on his first official visit from August 14-17, 1967. The cabinet decision to reduce the defense budget, the question of compensatory currency payments in respect of the American troops stationed in the Federal Republic, and relations with France – all these provided a wealth of controversial subject matters for his talk with President Johnson in the grounds of the White House on August 16, 1967.

Insgesamt gelang es Kiesinger, hier am 15.8.1967 in Damenbegleitung, die von Journalisten so genannte »Konsultationslücke« zwischen beiden Regierungen zu schließen. Während Adenauer stets wie ein »Eisberg« und Erhard wie ein »Gummilöwe« gewirkt habe, sei es Kiesinger mit Freundlichkeit und Humor gelungen, die schwierigen Klippen zu umschiffen (»Washington Post«).

All in all Kiesinger – here in female company on August 15, 1967 – succeeded in closing the "consultation gap," as journalists called it, between the two governments. The *Washington Post* reported that whereas Adenauer had always been like an "iceberg" and Erhard like a "rubber lion," Kiesinger had succeeded, with humor and amicability, in navigating the difficult waters.

Das deutsch-britische Regierungstreffen vom 23.-25.10.1967 in London stand ganz im Zeichen des erneuten Antrags der Briten auf EG-Beitritt. Das abermalige Veto de Gaulles brachte Kiesinger in eine prekäre Lage. Auf seiner Pressekonferenz am 23.10.1967 ließ er, rechts neben ihm Staatssekretär Karl-Günther von Hase, keinen Zweifel an seiner Absicht, das Gesuch zu unterstützen. Nicht zuletzt aufgrund seiner vorzüglichen Sprachkenntnisse gelang es ihm, sich als Mann des Ausgleichs und als überzeugter Europäer zu präsentieren.

The meeting between the German and British governments in London from October 23-25, 1967 was entirely dominated by Britain's renewed application for EC membership. When de Gaulle again vetoed the application, Kiesinger found himself in a precarious position. At his press conference on October 23, 1967 – here with State Secretary Karl-Günther von Hase standing next to him on the right – he had left no doubt that he intended to support the application. Thanks not least to his fluent command of languages he succeeded in presenting himself as a man of conciliation and a convinced European.

(gegenüber) Kiesinger, hier am 24.10.1967 in der Deutschen Botschaft in London, wußte nur zu gut, daß es den Briten letztlich um das gleiche ging wie den Franzosen: um die Vormacht in Europa. »Willy, Du mußt uns hereinholen, damit wir die Führung übernehmen können«, sollte der britische Außenminister George Brown seinen deutschen Kollegen Willy Brandt wenig später beschwören. Kiesinger lehnte de Gaulles harte Haltung ab, ließ sich aber auch nicht in eine Frontstellung gegen Frankreich locken.

(opposite) Kiesinger, here at the German Embassy in London on October 24, 1967, knew only too well that the British ultimately wanted the same thing as the French: to be supreme in Europe. "Willy, you must get us in, so we can take the lead," the British Foreign Secretary George Brown was to beseech his German opposite number Willy Brandt shortly afterwards. Kiesinger rejected de Gaulle's hard line but did not let himself be lured into adopting a confrontational stance towards France.

Die Niederschlagung des unter Alexander Dubcek in der Tschechoslowakei im Frühjahr 1968 eingeschlagenen Reformkurses durch Truppen des Warschauer Paktes am 21.8.1968 verurteilte Kiesinger nach Rücksprache mit allen drei Bundestagsfraktionen als klare Verletzung der Souveränität der CSSR und als Einmischung in deren innere Angelegenheiten. Am selben Tag empfing er den Botschafter der UdSSR, Zarapkin, der eine Erklärung seiner Regierung vorlas. Kiesinger lauschte dem Diplomaten mit sichtlichem Mißvergnügen.

The suppression by Warsaw Pact troops on August 21, 1968 of the reform policies adopted in Czechoslovakia under Alexander Dubcek in the spring of 1968 was condemned by Kiesinger, after consulting with all the parliamentary party groups, as a clear violation of Czechoslovakia's sovereignty and as interference in its internal affairs. On the same day he received the Soviet ambassador, Zarapkin, who read out a statement by his government. Kiesinger listened to the diplomat with visible displeasure.

Obwohl das gewaltsame Ende der Demokratisierungsbewegung in der CSSR der Verständigung zwischen Ost und West im Sommer 1968 einen schweren Schlag versetzte, kehrten die Supermächte nach einer Schamfrist auf den alten Kurs zurück. Der im Januar 1969 ins Weiße Haus einziehende amerikanische Präsident Richard M. Nixon gab der Entspannungspolitik neue Kontur, indem er eine Strategie des globalen Gleichgewichts lancierte. Bei einem Arbeitsbesuch in Berlin bekräftigte er am 26./27.2.1969 die Verantwortung der USA für die Freiheit der Stadt und wurde dafür von der Bevölkerung begeistert gefeiert.

Although the violent end to the democracy movement in Czechoslovakia dealt a severe blow to East-West relations in summer 1968, the superpowers reverted to their former policies as soon as a decent interval had elapsed. The American President Richard M. Nixon, who entered the White House in January 1969 gave a new thrust to détente by lauching a strategy of global balance. On February 26-27, 1969, during a working visit to Berlin, he confirmed America's responsibility for the freedom of the city, for which he was enthusiastically cheered by the people.

Am Ende seiner Amtszeit konnte Kiesinger, hier mit seinem Enkelkind »Fröschle«, Anfang April 1969 in Washington anläßlich der Trauerfeierlichkeiten für den früheren amerikanischen Präsidenten Eisenhower, wortgewandt, aber ein wenig wehmütig resümieren: »Ich bin 1966 Kanzler geworden nicht durch einen Wahlsieg, sondern in einer Krise meiner Partei. Und nun verliere ich meine Kanzlerschaft nicht durch eine Krise meiner Partei, sondern nach einem Wahlsieg.«

When his term of office came to an end Kiesinger – here with his granddaughter "Froggy" on a visit to Washington in early April 1969 to attend the funeral of former US President Eisenhower – was able to give this eloquent but slightly melancholy summing-up: "I became Chancellor in 1966 not by winning an election but during a crisis in my party. And now I lose the office of Chancellor not because of a crisis in my party but after an electoral victory."

1969–1974

Die Regierung Brandt/Scheel
The Brandt/Scheel Government

Willy Brandt in der Jacke eines Park Rangers während seines USA-Besuchs
im April 1970.

Willy Brandt in a park ranger's jacket during his visit to the USA in April 1970.

Die Wahl Willy Brandts zum Bundeskanzler markiert eine tiefe Zäsur in der Geschichte der Bundesrepublik Deutschland. Im Wechsel der Regierungsverantwortung stellte die Nachkriegsdemokratie ihre Funktionsfähigkeit unter Beweis. Zum ersten Mal seit 1949, übernahm ein Sozialdemokrat das wichtigste politische Amt. Erst damit, so meinten viele Zeitgenossen, war das Ende der Ära Adenauer wirklich besiegelt. Eine Zeit hoffnungsvoller und längst überfälliger Veränderungen schien angebrochen. Unverbrauchte, jüngere Köpfe sollten das Land regieren. Eine neue, in den Zielsetzungen anspruchsvollere und in den Methoden beweglichere Politik versprach einen grundlegenden »Wandel der Republik«.

Der Machtwechsel

Dieser Regierungswechsel im Herbst 1969 war nicht einfach die schlichte Folge einer Bundestagswahl. Er hatte sich seit längerem vorbereitet. Schon die Bundespräsidentenwahl im März erwies sich als wichtiges Signal und erste Weichenstellung für die neue, sozialliberale Koalition. Am Anfang stand jedoch die Neuorientierung der FDP. Mit dem im Januar 1968 vollzogenen Wechsel im Parteivorsitz von Erich Mende zu Walter Scheel wurde der Wandel von einer eher national-liberalen Partei zu einer nunmehr eher linksliberalen Reformpartei auch nach außen sichtbar. Die FDP stand jetzt wie die SPD für einen Neuansatz in der Deutschland- und Ostpolitik und profilierte sich auch in der Innenpolitik als Partei der Veränderungen. Die gemeinsame Wahl des SPD-Kandidaten Gustav Heinemann zum Bundespräsidenten am 5.3.1969 wurde zur erfolgreichen Generalprobe sozial-liberaler Zusammenarbeit auf Bundesebene. »Ein Stück Machtwechsel«, nannte Heinemann selbst seine Wahl. Die fehlenden weiteren Stücke fügten Walter Scheel und Willy Brandt nach der Bundestagswahl vom 28.9.1969 rasch zusammen.

Neue Ostpolitik

Das Schwergewicht der Regierungsarbeit lag von Anfang an im Bereich der Deutschland- und Ostpolitik. Hier setzte der Bundeskanzler schon am 28.10.1969 in seiner Regierungserklärung vor dem Bundestag deutliche Akzente. Erstmals tauchte das Wort »Wiedervereinigung« nicht mehr auf. Aber vor allem die Formulierung, daß »zwei Staaten in Deutschland« existierten, die für einander zwar »nicht Ausland« sein könnten, aber »über ein geregeltes Nebeneinander zu einem Miteinander« finden sollten, wurde als Sensation empfunden. Damit kündigte sich ein Abschied vom westdeutschen Alleinvertretungsanspruch und von der Hallstein-Doktrin unüberhörbar an. Mit der Bereitschaft zum Abschluß verbindlicher Gewaltverzichtsabkommen mit den mittel- und osteuropäischen Nachbarn knüpfte Brandt an die Politik der Regierungen Erhard und Kiesinger an. Er ging jedoch wesentlich über sie hinaus, indem er ausdrücklich auch die DDR zu den Adressaten dieses Angebots zählte.

Die neue Bundesregierung traf allerdings für ihre vielbeachtete »Entspannungspolitik« auf sehr viel günstigere internationale Voraussetzungen als ihre Vorgänger. Seit dem Amtsantritt des

---

Willy Brandt's election as Federal Chancellor marked a radical break with the past in the history of the German Federal Republic. This changeover to a new governing party proved that German post-war democracy was fully viable. For the first time since 1949, indeed since 1930, a Social Democrat took over the highest political office in Germany. Only this, so many contemporaries thought, brought the Adenauer era truly to an end. An era of hope and long overdue change seemed to be dawning. Younger, fresher minds were to govern the country. A new policy, with more ambitious goals and more flexible methods, promised a fundamental "change in the Republic."

Change of Power

The change of government in the autumn of 1969 was not just the simple consequence of a general election. It had been in preparation for some time quite. The presidential election in March of that year had clearly shown which way the wind was blowing and had set the scene for the new social-liberal coalition.

It was preceded, however, by a change of direction on the part of the FDP. The change of party chairman from Erich Mende to Walter Scheel in January 1968 demonstrated to the outside world the change from a more national-liberal party to a left-liberal party of reform. Like the SPD, the FDP now stood for a new approach in "*Deutschlandpolitik*" and "*Ostpolitik*" while also presenting the image of a party of change in domestic affairs. When Liberals and Social Democrats joined forces to elect the SPD candidate Gustav Heinemann as Federal President on March 5, 1969, it was a successful dress rehearsal for their cooperation at federal level. Heinemann himself described his election as "part of a change at the top." The other, missing parts were swiftly assembled by Walter Scheel and Willy Brandt after the general election on September 28, 1969.

The New "*Ostpolitik*"

The central task facing the government lay from the outset in the sphere of "*Deutschlandpolitik*" and "*Ostpolitik*". Here the Chancellor made his priorities very clear as early as October 28, 1969 in his inaugural speech before parliament. For the first time, the word "reunification" did not occur. What was particularly sensational was his use of the phrase "two states in Germany," which, he said, existed, which could not be "foreign countries" to each other, but which ought to find a way "via a regulated existence 'alongside each other' to an existence 'with each other.'" Brandt thereby unmistakably indicated that the West German claim to sole representation and the Bonn government's "Hallstein Doctrine" were to be abandoned. With his readiness to enter into binding nonaggression agreements with the neighboring states of Central and Eastern Europe Brandt took up and continued the policies of the Erhard and Kiesinger governments. However, he went substantially beyond them in explicitly including the GDR among the countries to whom his offer was addressed.

The new government, of course, encountered much more favorable international conditions for its policy of détente, which

Bundespräsident Gustav Heinemann gratuliert dem neuen Bundeskanzler Willy Brandt anläßlich der Überreichung der Ernennungsurkunde am 21.10. 1969. Jetzt war die Anspannung der letzten Stunden von Brandt abgefallen. Bis zur Bekanntgabe des Abstimmungsergebnisses im Bundestag hatte er noch gezweifelt, ob die für seine Wahl erforderliche Mehrheit tatsächlich zustandekommen werde.

President Gustav Heinemann congratulates the new Chancellor Willy Brandt after presenting him with his certificate of appointment on October 21, 1969. Brandt no longer shows signs of the strain of the past few hours. Right up until the result of the parliamentary vote was announced he had doubted whether the necessary majority would be achieved for him to be elected.

Die neue Regierung wird besichtigt: Nach der Übergabe der Ernennungsurkunden durch Bundespräsident Heinemann posiert das neue Kabinett am 22.10.1969 vor der Villa Hammerschmidt. Erste Reihe von links: Justizminister Gerhard Jahn (SPD), Familienministerin Käte Strobel (SPD), Bundespräsident Gustav Heinemann, Bundeskanzler Willy Brandt (SPD), Außenminister Walter Scheel (FDP), Wirtschaftsminister Karl Schiller (SPD), Verkehrsminister Georg Leber (SPD); zweite Reihe: Verteidigungsminister Helmut Schmidt (SPD), Finanzminister Alex Möller (SPD), Minister für Wirtschaftliche Zusammenarbeit Erhard Eppler (SPD), Innenminister Hans-Dietrich Genscher (FDP), Arbeitsminister Walter Arendt (SPD); dritte Reihe: Minister für Innerdeutsche Beziehungen Egon Franke (SPD), Wohnungsbauminister Lauritz Lauritzen (SPD), Bildungsminister Hans Leussink (parteilos), Minister für besondere Aufgaben und Chef des Bundeskanzleramtes Horst Ehmke (SPD), Landwirtschaftsminister Josef Ertl (FDP).

The new government on parade. After the certificates of appointment were presented by President Heinemann, the new cabinet posed outside the Villa Hammerschmidt on October 22, 1969. Front row, from left to right: Minister of Justice Gerhard Jahn (SPD), Family Minister Käte Strobel (SPD), President Gustav Heinemann, Chancellor Willy Brandt (SPD), Foreign Minister Walter Scheel (FDP), Economics Minister Karl Schiller (SPD), Transport Minister Georg Leber (SPD); second row: Defense Minister Helmut Schmidt (SPD), Finance Minister Alex Möller (SPD), Minister for Economic Cooperation Erhard Eppler (SPD), Minister of the Interior Hans-Dietrich Genscher (FDP), Minister of Labor Walter Arendt (SPD); third row: Minister for Inter-German Relations Egon Franke (SPD), Minister of Housing Lauritz Lauritzen (SPD), Minister of Education Hans Leussink (independent), Minister without Portfolio and Head of Chancellery Horst Ehmke (SPD), Minister of Agriculture Josef Ertl (FDP).

Von Gegnern kommentierte Wahl-
werbung der NPD im Bundestagswahlkampf 1969. Die NPD hatte
sich nach Erfolgen bei den Landtagswahlen in Hessen, Bayern, Niedersachsen, Bremen und Baden-
Württemberg gute Chancen auf den
Einzug in den Bundestag ausgerechnet. Sie erreichte jedoch nur 4,3% der
Stimmen und verschwand nach 1970
auch in den Ländern rasch wieder von
der politischen Bühne.

An NPD election poster from the 1969
campaign, with a comment from the
party's opponents. After successes in
regional elections in Hesse, Bavaria,
Lower Saxony, Bremen and Baden-
Württemberg the NPD reckoned that
it had a prospect of entering parliament. However, it polled only 4.3% of
the vote and in the *Länder* also it
rapidly disappeared again from the
political arena after 1970. The paste-
over slogan reads: One Adolf was one
too many!

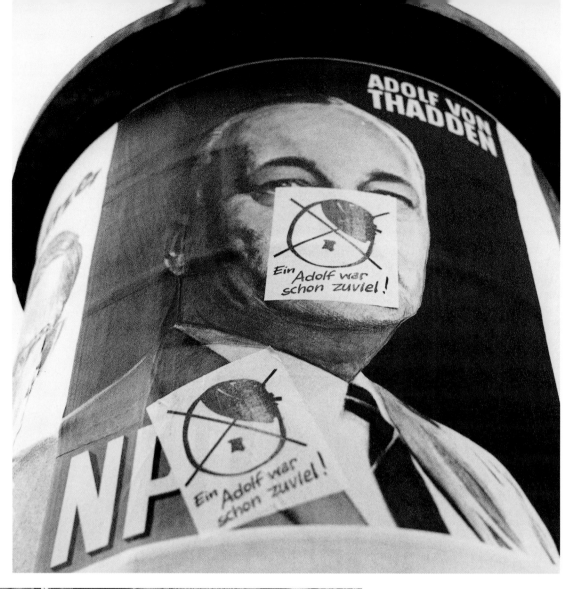

Die Fraktionsvorsitzenden Rainer
Barzel (CDU/CSU), Wolfgang Misch-
nick (FDP) und Helmut Schmidt
(SPD) am 28. 9. 1969 in der Wahlson-
dersendung von ARD und ZDF. Im
Hintergrund der Leiter des ARD-
Studios in Bonn und spätere Inten-
dant des WDR, Friedrich Nowottny.
Noch herrscht über den Wahlausgang
keine Klarheit.

Party whips Rainer Barzel (CDU/
CSU), Wolfgang Mischnick (FDP),
and Helmut Schmidt (SPD) on
September 28, 1969 in the special
election broadcast put out by the
public channels ARD and ZDF. In the
background the chief of the ARD
studio in Bonn and later Director
of WDR (West German Radio),
Friedrich Nowottny. The outcome of
the election is still uncertain.

Wahlentscheidung 1969 / Election Results 1969

Das Ergebnis der Bundestagswahl des Jahres 1969 war denkbar knapp. Die ersten Hochrechnungen hatten zunächst sogar eine absolute Mehrheit für die CDU/CSU vorhergesagt. Als die Fraktionsvorsitzenden der im Bundestag vertretenen Parteien am Wahlabend vor den Fernsehkameras saßen, war die künftige Regierungsbildung noch völlig offen. Absehbar war dagegen bereits, daß der gefürchtete Einzug der NPD in den Bundestag nicht stattfinden würde. Die rechtsradikale Partei unter ihrem Vorsitzenden Adolf von Thadden scheiterte an der Fünf-Prozent-Hürde. Doch der eigentliche Verlierer der Wahl wurde, obwohl seine Partei die absolute Mehrheit nur knapp verfehlt hatte, der bisherige Bundeskanzler Kurt-Georg Kiesinger. Die CDU/CSU glaubte sich um den Sieg betrogen und fand nur schwer in die ungewohnte Rolle der Opposition.

The 1969 general election was an extremely close-run one. Early projections had at first even predicted an absolute majority for the CDU/CSU. As the party whips of the parties that were represented in parliament sat in front of television cameras on the evening of election day, the composition of the future government was still completely open. On the other hand it could already be foreseen that the NPD would not enter parliament as had been feared. This radical right-wing party under its chairman Adolf von Thadden failed to clear the 5% hurdle. But the real loser in the election, although his party had only narrowly failed to achieve an absolute majority, was the previous Chancellor Kurt-Georg Kiesinger. The CDU/CSU felt that it had been cheated of victory and found it difficult to adapt to the unaccustomed role of an opposition party.

Der amtierende Bundeskanzler wird in der Wahlnacht von Journalisten umringt. Kurt-Georg Kiesinger hielt zunächst noch eine CDU/CSU-FDP-Koalition für möglich und bat den für seine guten Verbindungen zu den Liberalen bekannten rheinland-pfälzischen Ministerpräsidenten Helmut Kohl (rechts im Bild), Kontakt mit der FDP aufzunehmen. Doch es war zu spät. Willy Brandt und Walter Scheel waren sich längst einig: Sie wollten zusammen die erste sozial-liberale Koalition auf Bundesebene etablieren.

The incumbent Federal Chancellor surrounded by journalists on election night. At first Kurt-Georg Kiesinger thought that a CDU/CSU-FDP coalition was possible and asked Helmut Kohl, the Minister President of Rheinland-Palatinate (on the right in the picture), who was well known for his excellent connections with the Liberals, to make contact with the FDP. But it was too late. Willy Brandt and Walter Scheel had long since reached an agreement: together they intended to form the first social-liberal coalition at federal level.

Gustav Heinemann

»Ich liebe keine Staaten, ich liebe meine Frau, fertig!« Diese Äußerung Gustav Heinemanns kennzeichnet treffend das politische Selbstverständnis des dritten Bundespräsidenten der Bundesrepublik Deutschland. Der ehemalige Essener Bergwerksdirektor und Oberbürgermeister Heinemann, ein bekennender Christ und Pazifist, war 1950 wegen seiner Ablehnung der deutschen Wiederbewaffnung als Adenauers Innenminister zurückgetreten und hatte erst 1957 zur SPD gefunden. Als Justizminister hatte er nach dem Attentat auf Rudi Dutschke auf dem Höhepunkt der Osterunruhen in einer eindrucksvollen Rede am 14.4.1968 versöhnliche und vermittelnde Worte gefunden und so maßgeblich zur Deeskalation beigetragen. Als Bundespräsident verkörperte er mit seiner geradlinigen, unpathetischen Amtsführung einen neuen Stil der westdeutschen Demokratie. Das glänzende Gepränge staatlicher Repräsentation blieb ihm zeitlebens fremd. Dennoch verschaffte ihm seine hohe moralische Autorität Respekt im In- und Ausland. Nach außen bemühte sich der Präsident um Versöhnung mit den Staaten, in denen die Erinnerung an die nationalsozialistische Herrschaft besonders lebendig war. Im Innern suchte er die mit der Studentenbewegung entstandenen Brüche der westdeutschen Gesellschaft zu entschärfen. Gemeinsam mit seiner Frau Hilda widmete er sich darüber hinaus besonders den benachteiligten Minderheiten in Deutschland.

"I don't love any nation, I love my wife, period." These words by Gustav Heinemann aptly indicate the political self-image of the third President of the Federal Republic of Germany. Heinemann, a former coal mine director and mayor of the city in Essen, an avowed Christian and pacifist, had resigned as Adenauer's Minister of the Interior in 1950 because of his opposition to German rearmament. He did not join the SPD until 1957. As Minister of Justice, in an impressive speech on April 14, 1968, at the height of the Easter unrest following the attempted assassination of Rudi Dutschke, he had found words of mediation and conciliation and had thereby made a decisive contribution towards de-escalating the conflict. As Federal President he embodied a new style in West German democracy with his straightforward and unpretentious performance of his official duties. The pomp and splendor of state ceremonies remained alien to him throughout his life. Even so his high moral authority earned him respect both at home and abroad. Vis-à-vis the outside world the President worked for reconciliation with the countries where memories of National Socialist rule were particularly strong. At home he tried to heal the rifts in West German society which had opened up as a result of the student movement. Over and above this he devoted himself particularly, along with his wife Hilda, to disadvantaged minorities in Germany.

(oben) Das Ehepaar Heinemann am 11.5.1970 während der Japanreise vom 7. bis 17.5.1970. Beide versuchten auch auf Staatsbesuchen so oft wie möglich dem großen Trubel zu entfliehen.

(rechts) Eine Bootspartie während der Visite in Schweden vom 23. bis 26.6.1970. Die förmliche Kleidung verrät allerdings, daß dem Bundespräsidenten keine lange Pause von den repräsentativen Verpflichtungen vergönnt war.

(gegenüber) Wie Adenauer tankte auch Gustav Heinemann gelegentlich neue Kraft für den politischen Alltag in einem Liegestuhl – hier in seiner Wohnung im Bonner Regierungsviertel.

(above) The Heinemanns on May 11, 1970 during their trip to Japan May 7-17, 1970. Even when on state visits they both tried to escape as often as possible from the hustle and bustle.

(right) A boat trip during the state visit to Sweden June 23-26, 1970. However, their formal dress reveals that the President were not allowed any lengthy respite from their ceremonial duties.

(opposite) Gustav Heinemann, like Adenauer, occasionally gathered new strength for daily politics while lounging in his recliner. Shown here in his apartment in Bonn's government district.

Während seines Staatsbesuches in Norwegen vom 9. bis 12.9.1970 besichtigt das Präsidentenpaar das Heimatfrontmuseum in Oslo und läßt sich erläutern, mit welchen Waffen das Land den Soldaten der deutschen Wehrmacht bei ihrem Überfall entgegenzutreten suchte.

During his state visit to Norway, from September 9-12, 1970, the President and his wife visit the Home Front Museum in Oslo and listen to an explanation of the weapons with which the country attempted to resist the invading soldiers of the German army.

Der Bundespräsident schreitet während seines Staatsbesuches in Belgien vom 26. bis 29.3.1974 zusammen mit Prinz Albert und einer unbekannten jungen Dame die auf dem Großen Platz in Antwerpen angetretene Ehrenkompanie ab.

During his state visit to Belgium from March 26-29, 1974 the President inspects the guard of honor on the "Grote Markt," the main city square in Antwerp, together with Prince Albert and an unidentified young lady.

Walter Scheel überbringt am 18.12.1969 seine Glückwünsche zum 56. Geburtstag von Willy Brandt. In der Mitte Verteidigungsminister Helmut Schmidt, der ursprünglich kein Freund einer sozialliberalen Koalition gewesen war. Im Hintergrund der spätere Bildungsminister Klaus von Dohnanyi.

Walter Scheel congratulating Willy Brandt on his 56th birthday on December 18, 1969. In the center Defense Minister Helmut Schmidt, who was originally not well-disposed towards a social-liberal coalition. In the background the later Minister of Education Klaus von Dohnanyi.

Die Väter der sozialliberalen Koalition: Willy Brandt und Walter Scheel am 14.1.1970 im Palais Schaumburg, dem Sitz des Bundeskanzleramtes bis 1976. Der Außenminister hatte es in der Anfangsphase der Koalition schwer, sich öffentlich in Szene zu setzen. Die entscheidenden ostpolitischen Verhandlungen sollten im Kanzleramt koordiniert und vom Staatssekretär Egon Bahr geführt werden. Der gute Kontakt zwischen Brandt und Scheel bildete jedoch eine tragfähige Basis und ließ tiefgreifende Verstimmungen nicht aufkommen.

The fathers of the social-liberal coalition: Willy Brandt and Walter Scheel on January 14, 1970 in the Palais Schaumburg, where the Chancellery was housed until 1976. In the initial phase of the coalition it was difficult for the Foreign Minister to create a role for himself. The decisive negotiations with the East European countries were to be coordinated in the Chancellery, and conducted by State Secretary Egon Bahr. But the friendly rapport between Brandt and Scheel provided a solid basis for cooperation, so that no far-reaching discord arose.

Hauptdarsteller / Protagonists

Der Familienvater: Walter Scheel mit seiner Frau Mildred und Tochter Cornelia, die zur Einschulung eine große Wundertüte geschenkt bekommt.

The family man: Walter Scheel with his wife Mildred and daughter Cornelia, who is given the customary bag of surprises on her first day at school.

Der »Kanzlermacher«: Der FDP-Vorsitzende Walter Scheel spielte beim Regierungswechsel des Jahres 1969 eine Schlüsselrolle. Schon vor der Bundestagswahl hatte er sich auf eine Koalition mit der SPD festgelegt und das Verhandlungsangebot Willy Brandts noch in der Wahlnacht angenommen. 1972 bedurfte es dagegen keines »Kanzlermachers« mehr. Als Scheel während des Bundesparteitags der FDP vom 22. bis 25.10.1972 in Freiburg den »Spiegel« las, zeichnete sich ein eindeutiges Ergebnis ab. »Genosse Trend« bescherte am 19.11.1972 dem amtierenden Bundeskanzler einen überwältigenden Wahlsieg.

The "Chancellor-maker": FDP party chairman Walter Scheel played a key part in the change of government in 1969. He had already decided on a coalition with the SPD before the general election, and even before election day was over he had accepted Willy Brandt's offer to negotiate. In contrast, in 1972 there was no longer any need for a "Chancellor-maker." When Scheel was seen reading *Der Spiegel* during the FDP federal party conference in Freiburg from October 22-25, 1972, the implication was unmistakeable. On November 19, 1972 the voters followed the trend and re-elected the incumbent Chancellor by an overwhelming majority.

Der Architekt der »Neuen Ostpolitik«: Bereits 1963 hatte Bahr, damals noch Berliner Pressechef unter dem Regierenden Bürgermeister Brandt, in Abstimmung mit diesem sein deutschlandpolitisches Konzept eines »Wandels durch Annäherung« öffentlich vorgetragen. 1966 zog er mit dem nunmehrigen Außenminister Brandt ins Auswärtige Amt und konnte seine Vorstellungen als Leiter des Planungsstabs konkretisieren. Im Oktober 1969 wurde Bahr Staatssekretär im Bundeskanzleramt, 1972 Bundesminister für besondere Aufgaben. In diesen Funktionen führte er die entscheidenden Verhandlungen, an deren Ende die Verträge mit Moskau, Warschau und Ostberlin standen.

The architect of the "New *Ostpolitik*": as early as 1963 Bahr, who at the time was still chief press officer in Berlin under Brandt, the governing mayor, had, with the latter's agreement, put forward in public his concept of "change through rapprochement" as a policy for divided Germany. In 1966 he joined the Foreign Office with Brandt, who by then was Foreign Minister, and as head of his planning staff was able to give concrete form to his ideas. In October 1969 Bahr became State Secretary at the Chancellery and in 1972 Minister without Portfolio. In these capacities he conducted the decisive negotiations which culminated in the Treaties with Moscow, Warsaw and East Berlin.

Als »Hans Dampf in allen Gassen« machte sich Horst Ehmke auf der Bonner Bühne rasch einen Namen. Der neue Chef des Bundeskanzleramtes, erstmals in der Geschichte der Bundesrepublik zugleich als Bundesminister für besondere Aufgaben am Kabinettstisch präsent, war unermüdlich bemüht, seine Behörde zur beherrschenden Schaltzentrale der Macht auszubauen. Er stieß dabei auf wenig Gegenliebe bei seinen Kabinettskollegen, die Einmischungen in ihre Ressorts nicht widerspruchslos hinnehmen mochten. Das Kanzleramt wurde in der Ära Brandt erneut, wie schon zu Konrad Adenauers Zeiten, zum entscheidenden Zentrum der Regierungsarbeit.

Horst Ehmke quickly made a name for himself in the Bonn arena as someone with a finger in every pie. The new Head of Chancellery, the first in the history of the Federal Republic to be at the same time a Minister without Portfolio with a seat in the cabinet, labored unremittingly to build up the Chancellery into a central powerhouse. This did not however greatly endear him to his fellow cabinet members, who were not disposed to accept without demur any interference in the business of their ministries. Even so, in the Brandt era the Chancellery once again became, as it had been in Konrad Adenauer's days, the fundamental center of the government's work.

Der »Zuchtmeister« / The "Hard Taskmaster"

Herbert Wehner hatte seit den fünfziger Jahren alles darangesetzt, die SPD in die Regierung zu bringen. Dennoch war er 1969 zunächst keineswegs begeistert von dem Regierungsbündnis mit der FDP, weil ihm die Liberalen zu unberechenbar schienen. Er übernahm den Vorsitz der SPD-Bundestagsfraktion, die er bis 1983 mit eiserner Hand führte. Sein Verhältnis zum neuen Bundeskanzler blieb kühl. Der mürrische, durch seine kommunistische Vergangenheit tragisch gezeichnete Moralist hielt den Publikumsliebling Brandt für einen leichtlebigen, letztlich führungsunfähigen Mann, dem er sich nur aus selbstloser Parteitreue unterordnete.

Since the fifties Herbert Wehner had done everything he could to make the SPD a party of government. Nevertheless in 1969 he was not at all enthusiastic at first about the government alliance with the FDP, who seemed to him to be too unpredictable. He took on the job of party whip, ruling with an iron hand until 1983. His relationship with the new Chancellor remained cool. Wehner, a morose moralist on whom his communist past had left its mark, regarded Brandt, the darling of the public, as a self-indulgent man who ultimately lacked the capacity for leadership and whose authority he accepted only out of selfless loyalty to the party.

Ein »Jahrhundert-Wahlergebnis«: Der SPD-Fraktionsvorsitzende kommentiert am Abend des 19.11.1972 den Sieg seiner Partei bei den Bundestagswahlen. Rechts im Bild der Bonner ARD-Korrespondent Ernst Dieter Lueg, den Wehner auch einmal boshaft als Herrn »Lüg« ansprach.

The "election result of the century": the SPD party whip on the evening of November 19, 1972, commenting on his party's general election victory. On the right in the photo the ARD Bonn correspondent Ernst Dieter Lueg, whom Wehner on one occasion spitefully addressed as "Herr Lüg" (Lüg = lie, falsehood.)

Herbert Wehner am 7.5.1974, einen Tag nach dem Rücktritt Willy Brandts, beim Verlassen des Palais Schaumburg in Bonn. Daß Wehner ihm nicht so entschlossen und vorbehaltlos wie Walter Scheel seine Rückendeckung signalisiert hatte, trug maßgeblich zu Willy Brandts Entschluß bei, als Bundeskanzler zurückzutreten.

Herbert Wehner on May 7, 1974, leaving the Palais Schaumburg in Bonn on the day after Willy Brandt's resignation. The fact that Wehner had not indicated his support as resolutely and unreservedly as Scheel had done, contributed decisively to Willy Brandt's decision to resign as Chancellor.

(gegenüber) Wehner und Brandt auf dem außerordentlichen Parteitag der SPD am 12./13.10.1972 in Dortmund. Die tiefe Distanz zwischen diesen beiden so unterschiedlichen sozialdemokratischen Schlüsselpersonen ließ sich selten verhüllen.

(opposite) Wehner and Brandt at the SPD extraordinary party conference in Dortmund on October 12-13, 1972. The gulf separating these two central but so widely differing Social Democrat figures could seldom be concealed.

Günter Grass (zweiter von links) im Kreis von Journalisten um Willy Brandt auf dem Rückflug aus Israel am 11.6.1973; hinter dem Bundeskanzler der seit Dezember 1972 amtierende Regierungssprecher und spätere erste Botschafter der Bundesrepublik bei der UNO, Rüdiger von Wechmar.

Günter Grass (second from the left) with a group of journalists gathered around Willy Brandt on his return flight from Israel on June 11, 1973. Behind the Chancellor is Rüdiger von Wechmar, who had held the post of government spokesman since December 1972 and was later to be the first West German ambassador to the UN.

Heinrich Böll mit Gustav Heinemann und dessen Frau Hilda anläßlich eines Empfangs des Bundespräsidenten für die Mitglieder des Internationalen Schriftsteller-Verbandes (PEN) am 10.11.1972 im Schloß Bellevue in Berlin.

Heinrich Böll with Gustav Heinemann and his wife Hilda at a reception given by the Federal President for members of International PEN in Schloß Bellevue in Berlin on November 10, 1972.

Willy Brandt begrüßt die TV-Showmaster Hans-Joachim Kulenkampff und Peter Frankenfeld am 20.6.1973 anläßlich des Sommerfestes im Bundeskanzleramt. Beide unterstützten nachdrücklich seine Ostpolitik.

TV entertainers Hans-Joachim Kulenkampff and Peter Frankenfeld being welcomed by Willy Brandt at a summer party in the Chancellery on June 20, 1973. Both of them emphatically supported his *Ostpolitik*.

Schlagerstar Roy Black überreicht dem Bundespräsidenten am 5.12.1973 einen Scheck mit dem Erlös einer Wohlfahrts-Schallplatte zugunsten der Hilda-Heinemann-Stiftung. Rechts im Bild der spätere Fernsehmoderator Frank Elstner.

Pop star Roy Black donating a check to the Hilda Heinemann Foundation with the proceeds of a record, on December 5, 1973. On the right of the picture Frank Elstner, who was later to become a TV presenter.

Udo Jürgens singt für das Ehepaar Brandt während des Kanzlerfestes am 27.6. 1970 im Garten des Palais Schaumburg.

Udo Jürgens singing for Brandt and his wife at a party given by the Chancellor in the garden of the Palais Schaumburg on June 27, 1970.

Vom Kniefall in Warschau führt eine direkte Linie zum 11.12.1971. An diesem Tag wurde Willy Brandt in der Aula der Universität von Oslo als viertem Deutschen nach Ludwig Quidde, Gustav Stresemann und Carl von Ossietzky der Friedensnobelpreis verliehen. Mit dieser Auszeichnung wurde sein Engagement für Ausgleich und Verständigung über alle Blockgrenzen hinweg honoriert. Das Bild zeigt die Überreichung der Urkunde durch die Vorsitzende des Nobelpreiskomitees, Aase Lionaes.

There was a direct link between Brandt's kneeling at the memorial in Warsaw and the event that took place on December 11, 1971 in the Great Hall of Oslo University: Willy Brandt was the fourth German, after Ludwig Quidde, Gustav Stresemann, and Carl von Ossietzky, to be awarded the Nobel Peace Prize. The award honored his commitment to conciliation and rapprochement across all bloc frontiers. The photo shows the document being presented by the chairperson of the Nobel Prize Committee, Aase Lionaes.

Dieses Bild ging um die Welt. Es wurde zum Symbol der »Neuen Ostpolitik« der Bundesrepublik Deutschland. Willy Brandt hat die Szene am Morgen des 7.12.1970 vor dem Ehrenmal für die Opfer des Aufstands im Warschauer Ghetto rückblickend so beschrieben: »Ich hatte nichts geplant, aber Schloß Wilanow, wo ich untergebracht war, in dem Gefühl verlassen, die Besonderheit des Gedenkens am Ghetto-Monument zum Ausdruck bringen zu müssen. Am Abgrund der deutschen Geschichte und unter der Last der Millionen Ermordeten tat ich, was Menschen tun, wenn die Sprache versagt.«

This picture went round the world, becoming a symbol for West Germany's "New *Ostpolitik*." Looking back on this scene from the morning of December 7, 1970 before the memorial to the victims of the Warsaw ghetto rising, Willy Brandt described it in these words: "I had not planned anything but had left Schloß Wilanow, where I was staying, feeling that I had to find a way of expressing the special nature of an act of remembrance at the ghetto memorial. Before the abyss of German history and beneath the burden of the millions who were murdered, I did what people do when words fail them."

Kontaktaufnahme mit der DDR / Making Contact with the GDR

(gegenüber) »Als ich mich zurückgezogen hatte«, erinnerte sich der Bundeskanzler später, »tönte es in Sprechchören: 'Willy Brandt ans Fenster!' Dem folgte ich nicht gleich, dann aber doch, um mit der Gestik der Hände um Zurückhaltung zu bitten. Ich war bewegt und ahnte, daß es ein Volk mit mir war. Wie stark mußte das Gefühl der Zusammengehörigkeit sein, das sich auf diese Weise entlud!«

(opposite) The Chancellor later recalled: "After I had gone back into my room people began to chant: 'Willy Brandt to the window!' I did not comply immediately, but then I did so, in order to ask them, by means of gestures with my hands, for restraint. I was moved and I had the feeling that they and I were one people. How powerful the sense of belonging together must have been for them to give vent to it in this way!"

Begrüßung des Bundeskanzlers durch den Ministerpräsidenten der DDR, Willi Stoph, am 19.3.1970 auf dem Erfurter Hauptbahnhof. Zum ersten Mal seit der Gründung der Bundesrepublik und der DDR im Jahr 1949 reichen sich die Regierungschefs beider Teile Deutschlands die Hände. Die Bedeutung des Augenblicks spiegelt sich ebenso in den Gesichtern wider wie die wechselseitige Anspannung.

The Federal Chancellor being welcomed by the Prime Minister of the GDR Willi Stoph at the main railway station in Erfurt on March 19, 1970. The heads of government of the two parts of Germany shook hands for the first time since the foundation of the Federal Republic and the GDR in 1949. The faces reflect both the significance of the moment and the effort being made on both sides.

Trotz der Absperrungsmaßnahmen von Volkspolizei und Staatssicherheit versammelte sich am 19.3.1970 in Erfurt eine Menschenmenge auf dem Platz zwischen dem Hauptbahnhof und dem Hotel »Erfurter Hof«, in dem der Gast aus der Bundesrepublik residierte.

Although the area had been cordoned off by People's Police and state security, a crowd gathered in Erfurt on March 19, 1970 on the square between the main station and the "Erfurter Hof" hotel, where the visitor from the Federal Republic was staying.

Abfahrt aus Erfurt: Willy Brandt, der Bundesminister für innerdeutsche Beziehungen Egon Franke und der Parlamentarische Staatssekretär im Bundesinnenministerium Wolfram Dorn am Fenster des Sonderzugs des Bundeskanzlers.

Departure from Erfurt: Willy Brandt, the Minister for Inter-German Relations Egon Franke and the parliamentary State Secretary at the Ministry of the Interior Wolfram Dorn at the window of the Chancellor's special train.

Die Erfurter Gespräche blieben ergebnislos. Der Leiter der DDR-Delegation, Willi Stoph, verlangte schlicht die sofortige völkerrechtliche Anerkennung der DDR, den Austausch von Botschaftern und die gleichberechtigte Aufnahme in die UNO. Dem konnte Bundeskanzler Brandt nicht zustimmen. Einigkeit wurde nur darüber erzielt, das Gespräch bei einem weiteren Treffen fortzusetzen.

The Erfurt talks did not lead to any results. The leader of the GDR delegation, Willi Stoph, made a pure and simple demand: immediate recognition of the GDR in accordance with international law, by means of an exchange of ambassadors and membership of the UN on equal terms. Chancellor Brandt could not agree to this. The only agreement that was reached was to continue talks at a further meeting.

Auch das zweite Treffen auf deutsch-deutscher Regierungsebene, diesmal am 21.5.1970 in Kassel, brachte keinen Durchbruch. Auf dem Bahnsteig des Hauptbahnhofes verabschieden Bundeskanzler Brandt, Staatssekretär Dorn und der hessische Ministerpräsident Osswald die Gäste aus der DDR. Aus dem Abteilfenster beugen sich Außenminister Winzer und Ministerpräsident Stoph.

Nor did the second meeting at German-German government level, this time in Kassel on May 21, 1970, lead to a breakthrough. On the platform at the main railway station Chancellor Brandt, State Secretary Dorn, and Osswald, the Minister President of Hesse, take their leave of the visitors from the GDR. Foreign Minister Winzer and Prime Minister Stoph leaning out of the compartment window.

Die Ostverträge / The Eastern Treaties

Feierliche Unterzeichnung des Moskauer Vertrags durch Bundeskanzler Brandt und den sowjetischen Ministerpräsidenten Kossygin am 12.8.1970 im Katharinensaal des Kreml. Am Tisch links Bundesaußenminister Scheel, rechts der Außenminister der UdSSR, Gromyko; in der Mitte (stehend) der Generalsekretär der KPdSU, Leonid Breschnew.

The solemn signing of the Moscow Treaty by Chancellor Brandt and the Soviet Prime Minister Kosygin in the Catherine Hall of the Kremlin on August 12, 1970. At the table on the left Federal Foreign Minister Scheel, on the right USSR Foreign Minister Gromyko; in the center (standing) the General Secretary of the Soviet Communist Party, Leonid Brezhnev.

Austausch der Urkunden nach der Unterzeichnung des Warschauer Vertrags am 7.12.1970 im Palais des polnischen Ministerrats. Am Tisch (von links): Bundesaußenminister Scheel, Staatssekretär Bahr, Bundeskanzler Brandt, der Generalsekretär der polnischen KP, Wladyslaw Gomulka, der polnische Ministerpräsident Josef Cyrankiewicz und sein Außenminister, Stefan Jedrychowski. Im Hintergrund hinter Egon Bahr der Publizist Henri Nannen.

The exchange of documents after the signing of the Warsaw Treaty on December 7, 1970 in the Palace of the Polish Council of Ministers. At the table (from left to right) Federal Foreign Minister Scheel, State Secretary Bahr, Chancellor Brandt, the General Secretary of the Polish Communist Party Wladyslaw Gomulka, the Polish Prime Minister Jozef Cyrankiewicz and his Foreign Minister Stefan Jedrychowski. In the background behind Egon Bahr, the publicist Henri Nannen.

Unterzeichnung des Vier-Mächte-Abkommens über Berlin zwischen den Siegermächten des Zweiten Weltkriegs (Frankreich, Großbritannien, USA und UdSSR) am 3.9.1971 im Gebäude des ehemaligen Alliierten Kontrollrats in Berlin-Schöneberg. Die deutschen Regierungen und der Senat von Berlin waren nur indirekt an den Gesprächen beteiligt.

The signing of the Four-Power Accord on Berlin between the victors of the Second World War (France, Britain, USA and USSR) in the building which formerly housed the Allied Control Council in Berlin-Schöneberg, on September 3, 1971. The German governments and the Berlin Senate were only indirectly involved in the talks.

Staatssekretär Egon Bahr und der Staatssekretär beim Ministerrat der DDR, Michael Kohl, tauschen die Urkunden nach der Unterzeichnung des Transitabkommens am 17.12.1971 in Bonn. Das Abkommen ergänzte als fester Bestandteil das Vier-Mächte-Abkommen.

State Secretary Egon Bahr and the State Secretary at the GDR Council of Ministers, Michael Kohl, exchanging documents after the signing of the Transit Agreement in Bonn on December 17, 1971. The Agreement complemented the Four-Power Accord, of which it was a permanent component.

(oben) Staatssekretär Egon Bahr wird am 21.12.1972 von Staatssekretär Michael Kohl am Ostberliner Flughafen Schönefeld zur Unterzeichnung des Grundlagen-Vertrags abgeholt.

(unten) Nach der Paraphierung des Grundlagen-Vertrags zwischen der Bundesrepublik und der DDR am 8.11.1972 in Bonn: Die Staatssekretäre Egon Bahr, Bundeskanzleramt, und Michael Kohl, Ministerrat der DDR, werden von Journalisten umringt.

(above) State Secretary Egon Bahr being met at the Schönefeld airport in East Berlin by State Secretary Michael Kohl on December 21, 1972 for the signing of the Basic Treaty.

(below) After the initialling of the Basic Treaty between the Federal Republic and the GDR in Bonn on November 8, 1972: State Secretaries Egon Bahr (Federal Chancellery) and Michael Kohl (GDR Council of Ministers) are surrounded by journalists.

Das Verhältnis der Bundesrepublik zur DDR blieb trotz der Verträge überaus schwierig. Die in der Folge von allen westlichen Staaten völkerrechtlich anerkannte DDR betonte mit gewachsenem Selbstbewußtsein ihre Eigenstaatlichkeit und verschärfte zugleich ihre Abgrenzung von der Bundesrepublik.

Despite the Treaties, relations between the Federal Republic and the GDR remained extremely difficult. The GDR was subsequently recognized in accordance with international law by all the western states, and emphasized its sovereignty with increased self-confidence while at the same time reinforcing its separateness from the Federal Republic.

Gleichzeitige Aufnahme der Bundesrepublik und der DDR in die UNO: Generalsekretär Kurt Waldheim hält am 18.9.1973 anläßlich des feierlichen Fahnenaufzugs vor dem UNO-Gebäude in New York eine kurze Ansprache.

The Federal Republic and the GDR became members of the UN at the same time: Secretary-General Kurt Waldheim making a short speech to mark the solemn hoisting of the flags outside the UN building in New York on September 18, 1973.

Erste Rede an die Welt – Bundesaußenminister Scheel erklärt am 19.9. 1973 vor der UNO-Generalversammlung in New York: »Sie werden uns immer dort finden, wo es um die internationale Zusammenarbeit geht, um die Bewahrung des Friedens und um die Rechte des Menschen. Wenn wir etwas aus eigener bitterer Erfahrung gelernt haben, so ist es dies: Der Mensch ist das Maß aller Dinge.«

The first speech to the world – addressing the UN General Assembly in New York on September 19, 1973 Foreign Minister Scheel declares: "You will always find us wherever it is a matter of international cooperation, of the preservation of peace and of human rights. If we have learned anything from our own bitter experience, it is this: man is the measure of all things."

Von Anfang an richtete die sozial-liberale Koalition ihre Bemühungen auch auf die europäische Einigung. Schon bei der EG-Gipfelkonferenz am 1./2.12.1969 in Den Haag plädierte Willy Brandt offen für die Erweiterung der Gemeinschaft, die drei Jahre später mit dem Beitritt Dänemarks, Großbritanniens und Irlands Wirklichkeit wurde. Damit war freilich auch der einstweilige Abschied vom Traum eines »europäischen Bundesstaats« vollzogen. Als die am 19./20.10.1972 in Paris versammelten Staats- und Regierungschefs beschlossen, bis 1980 eine »Europäische Union« zu schaffen, war dies bereits kein realistisches Ziel mehr.

From the outset the social-liberal coalition also directed its efforts towards European union. At the EC summit in The Hague on December 1-2, 1969 Willy Brandt was already arguing openly for an expansion of the Community, which came about three years later with the accession of Denmark, Britain and Ireland. But this also, of course, meant giving up the dream of a "Federal European state" for the time being. When the political leaders who had assembled in Paris on October 19-20, 1972 resolved to create a "European Union" by 1980, this had already ceased to be a realistic goal.

Die Basis jeder europäischen Politik war und blieb die von Willy Brandt treffend als »entente élémentaire« bezeichnete deutsch-französische Freundschaft. Mit dem französischen Staatspräsidenten George Pompidou – hier am 22.6.1973 mit Ministerpräsident Pierre Messmer im Bundeskanzleramt in Bonn – war die Zusammenarbeit erheblich einfacher als mit dessen Vorgänger Charles de Gaulle, auch wenn es vor allem über den Umgang mit den USA weiterhin Differenzen gab.

The fixed basis of all European policy was Franco-German friendship, aptly described by Willy Brandt as "entente élémentaire." Cooperation with French President Georges Pompidou – here on June 22, 1973 with Prime Minister Pierre Messmer at the Chancellery in Bonn – was considerably easier than with his predecessor Charles de Gaulle, even if differences of opinion persisted, particularly as regards dealings with the USA.

Internationale Beziehungen / International Relations

»Unsere Ostpolitik hatte im Westen zu beginnen«, so hat Willy Brandt in seinen »Erinnerungen« treffend die entscheidende Voraussetzung seiner Verständigungspolitik mit dem Osten beschrieben. Neben der »Neuen Ostpolitik« bildete daher die Vertiefung des deutsch-französischen Verhältnisses, der europäischen Zusammenarbeit und der Beziehungen mit den USA einen zweiten Schwerpunkt der Außenpolitik der sozial-liberalen Koalition. So gelang es, die deutschen Interessen in den entspannungspolitischen Trend der Weltpolitik einzufügen und damit westliches Mißtrauen gegenüber neuen deutschen Sonderwegen im Keim zu ersticken. Durch die Anerkennung der machtpolitischen Realitäten in Europa gewann die Bundesrepublik als »Staat unter Staaten« neue Selbständigkeit und erweiterte ihren Spielraum. Sie mußte jedoch der DDR denselben Vorteil zugestehen.

"Our *Ostpolitik* had to begin in the West." That is how Willy Brandt, in his *Memoirs*, aptly defined the essential precondition of his policy of seeking mutual understanding with the East. Hence in addition to the "New *Ostpolitik*," the consolidation of Franco-German relations, of European cooperation and of relations with the USA were also of central importance in the foreign policy of the social-liberal coalition. This made it possible for German interests to be accommodated within the general trend towards détente in world politics, thereby nipping in the bud the distrust of the West regarding the possibility that Germany might go new ways of its own. By acknowledging the realities of European power politics, the Federal Republic, as "one state among others," acquired a new independence and increased scope for action. It was, however, compelled to concede the same advantage to the GDR.

Schon am 27.10.1969, einen Tag vor seiner Regierungserklärung, hatte Willy Brandt seinem britischen Amtskollegen Harold Wilson zugesagt, sich für die Aufnahme Großbritanniens in die Europäische Gemeinschaft einzusetzen. Die Briten dankten es ihm. Bei seiner ersten Englandreise im März 1970 – hier beim Besuch in Downing Street No. 10 – wurde dem Bundeskanzler die seltene Ehre zuteil, vor beiden Häusern des Parlaments sprechen zu dürfen.

On October 27, 1969, the day before his inaugural speech in parliament, Willy Brandt had already promised his British opposite number Harold Wilson that he would support Britain's accession to the European Community. The British were grateful to him. On his first trip to England in March 1970 – here on a visit to 10 Downing St. – the Chancellor had the rare honor of being allowed to address both Houses of Parliament.

(gegenüber) Begrüßung des deutschen Bundeskanzlers am 27.9.1973 in Chicago: Einen Vergleich mit seinem berühmten Vorgänger, Reichskanzler Otto von Bismarck, hätte Willy Brandt wohl schon wegen dessen konservativer Innenpolitik abgelehnt. In der Außenpolitik ließen sich gleichwohl Bezüge finden, auch wenn Brandt am 18.1.1971 zum 100. Jahrestag der Gründung des Deutschen Reiches zu Recht feststellte: »Die Lösung von vor 100 Jahren entsprach den damaligen Einsichten und Möglichkeiten. Die weltpolitische Situation heute verlangt neue Formen des politischen Zusammenlebens und Zusammenwirkens der Deutschen, die heute in zwei scharf abgesetzten und nicht vermischten Gesellschaftsformen leben.«

(opposite) The German Chancellor is welcomed to Chicago on September 27, 1973: the conservative domestic policies of his illustrious predecessor, Imperial Chancellor Otto von Bismarck, would presumably have been sufficient reason for Brandt to reject any comparison. Points of contact could nonetheless be found in foreign policy, even if Brandt on the centenary of the founding of the German Reich on January 18, 1971 rightly observed: "The solution adopted a hundred years ago was in keeping with the level of understanding and the opportunities of the age. Today the international political situation demands new forms of political coexistence and cooperation on the part of the Germans, who now inhabit two quite distinct and separate forms of society."

USA-Reise vom 27. bis 29.12.1971: Bundeskanzler Brandt und der amerikanische Präsident Richard Nixon treffen in Key Biscayne ein. Die USA begrüßten den deutschen Beitrag zur Entspannung, zeigten sich jedoch auch besorgt, daß die »Neue Ostpolitik« auf lange Sicht zu einer Abkehr der Bundesrepublik von ihrer Westorientierung und zu einer neuen Sonderrolle Deutschlands zwischen Ost und West führen könnte.

Trip to the US from December 27-29, 1971: Chancellor Brandt and American President Richard Nixon arriving at Key Biscayne. The USA welcomed the German contribution to détente but also expressed concern that the "New Ostpolitik" might in the long term mean that the Federal Republic would abandon its western orientation in favor of a special position for Germany between East and West.

(unten) Nachdenkliche Konzentration vor dem Auftritt: Der Bundeskanzler vor Beginn der überaus populären und wichtigen Interviewsendung »Issues and Answers« des amerikanischen Fernsehens am 16.6.1971 in Washington.

(below) Thoughtful concentration before a TV appearance: the Chancellor before the beginning of an interview in the very popular and important American television program "Issues and Answers" in Washington on June 16, 1971.

Brandt selbst kam in den Vereinigten Staaten sehr gut an, hatte seit seiner Zeit als Regierender Bürgermeister der bedrohten Teilstadt Berlin eine ausgemacht gute Presse. Zu seiner Popularität trug bei, daß er sich bei seinen zahlreichen Besuchen gerne wie hier in Aspen (1973) mit Cowboyhut ausstaffieren ließ und so seine Verbundenheit mit den Amerikanern auch optisch geschickt zum Ausdruck brachte.

Brandt himself was very well received in the USA, having had very good press since his days as governing mayor of the threatened half-city of West Berlin. He owed his popularity on his numerous visits in part to the fact that he liked to have himself kitted out with a ten-gallon hat – here in Aspen (1973), thus skillfully giving visual expression to his affinity with the Americans.

Der Sicherheitsberater Nixons und spätere amerikanische Außenminister Henry Kissinger befürwortete zwar prinzipiell die neue deutsche Ostpolitik und einen Interessenausgleich zwischen den Blöcken, fürchtete aber gelegentlich, von Brandt und insbesondere Egon Bahr überspielt und übergangen zu werden. 1973 entwickelte er das Konzept einer neuen »Atlantik-Charta« zur Zusammenarbeit zwischen den USA und Westeuropa. Nach der Bereinigung der Beziehungen mit der UdSSR und der Volksrepublik China sowie dem Ende des Vietnam-Kriegs sollte die Europäische Gemeinschaft in die von den USA angeführte Atlantische Allianz eingefügt werden. Bundeskanzler Brandt, der sich persönlich stark für eine Partnerschaft Europas mit den USA engagierte, geriet damit zunehmend zwischen neu aufbrechende französisch-amerikanische Gegensätze.

In principle Henry Kissinger, Nixon's security adviser and later American Secretary of State, supported the new German *Ostpolitik* and a reconciliation of interests between the power blocs, but he occasionally feared being out-maneuvered and bypassed by Brandt and especially Bahr. In 1973 he developed the concept of a new "Atlantic Charter" for cooperation between the USA and Western Europe. Now that relations with the USSR and the People's Republic of China had been settled and the war in Vietnam appeared to be over, the European Community was to be integrated into the Atlantic Alliance led by the USA. Chancellor Brandt, with his strong personal committment to partnership between Europe and the USA, consequently found himself increasingly embroiled in the conflict which resurfaced between France and the USA.

(gegenüber) Der Staatsbesuch des sowjetischen Parteiführers vom 18. bis 22.5.1973 in der Bundesrepublik sollte die deutsch-sowjetischen Beziehungen weiter vertiefen. Leonid Breschnew lag vor allem an einem Ausbau der wirtschaftlichen Zusammenarbeit, für die er großartige Perspektiven ausmalte. Einen Schwerpunkt der Gespräche – wie hier im Bonner Bundeskanzleramt – bildete jedoch das Problem der Anwendung des Vier-Mächte-Abkommens über Berlin, für das die Bundesregierung ein Entgegenkommen der UdSSR erhofft hatte. Diese Erwartung erfüllte sich nicht.

(opposite) The state visit of the Soviet party leader to the Federal Republic from May 18-22, 1973 was intended to bring about further consolidation of relations between Germany and the USSR. Leonid Brezhnev desired increased economic cooperation above all, and held out splendid prospects for it. However, one of the main topics of the talks – here at the Chancellery in Bonn – was the problem of the implementation of the Four-Power Berlin Accord, where the government had hoped for cooperation on the part of the USSR. This expectation was not fulfilled.

Mit dem Abschluß der Ostverträge entstand zwischen der Bundesrepublik und der UdSSR für kurze Zeit ein eigenständiges Nahverhältnis, ein »begrenzter Bilateralismus« (Willy Brandt), der sich auch in den engen persönlichen Beziehungen zwischen Bundeskanzler Brandt und Generalsekretär Breschnew spiegelte. Bei den Treffen vom 16. bis 18.9.1971 in Oreanda auf der Halbinsel Krim kam es zu mehreren Gesprächen unter vier Augen, so zum Beispiel während einer Bootsfahrt auf dem Schwarzen Meer. Die entscheidenden Differenzen blieben jedoch bestehen.

For a while the conclusion of the Eastern Treaties created an independent close relationship between the Federal Republic and the USSR, a "limited bilateralism" (Willy Brandt) which was also reflected in the close personal relationship between Chancellor Brandt and General Secretary Brezhnev. During their meetings from September 16-18, 1971 in Oreanda on the Crimean Peninsula they had several private conversations, for example during a boat trip on the Black Sea. However, the crucial differences of opinion between them remained.

Leonid Breschnew mit Rut und Willy Brandt am 18.5.1973 vor dem Kanzlerbungalow in Bonn. Das am nächsten Tage unterzeichnete Abkommen über die Intensivierung der wirtschaftlichen, kulturellen und technischen Zusammenarbeit sowie des bilateralen Luftverkehrs war zu diesem Zeitpunkt schon unterschriftsreif – insofern herrschte bei diesem Staatsbesuch trotz der Differenzen bezüglich Berlin eine aufgelockerte Atmosphäre.

Leonid Brezhnev with Rut and Willy Brandt on May 18, 1973 outside the Chancellor's bungalow in Bonn. The agreement which was signed the following day concerning the expansion of economic, cultural and technological cooperation along with bilateral air traffic, was at this point in time already ready for signing. To that extent there was, notwithstanding the differences of opinion with regard to Berlin, a relaxed atmosphere for this state visit.

(gegenüber) Als Brandt kurz vor seiner Abreise aus Israel am 11.6.1973 noch die Bergfestung von Massada, das Symbol jüdischen Selbstbehauptungswillens, besuchen wollte, wurde der Hubschrauber beim Aufsetzen von einer schweren Windbö erfaßt und drohte in den Abgrund zu stürzen. Nur mit knapper Not gelang es dem Piloten, die Katastrophe zu verhindern. Der Bundeskanzler meinte anschließend erleichtert: »Dies ist ein Land, wo man Wunder erwarten kann!«

(opposite) When, shortly before his departure from Israel on June 11, 1973, Willy Brandt wanted to visit the mountaintop fortress at Masada, the symbol of Jewish national heroism, the helicopter was caught by a sharp gust of wind as it landed and threatened to plunge into the abyss. The pilot only just managed to prevent a disaster. The relieved Chancellor said afterwards: "This is a country where one can expect miracles."

Willy Brandt hielt sich vom 7. bis 11.6.1973 als erster Regierungschef der Bundesrepublik Deutschland zu einem offiziellen Besuch in Israel auf. Als die israelische Ministerpräsidentin Golda Meir am 7. Juni beim Abendessen in der Knesset ihren deutschen Gast mit einer Ansprache ehrte, blieben noch vier Monate, bis am 6. Oktober, dem jüdischen Feiertag »Jom Kippur«, der vierte Nahost-Krieg ausbrach. Der daraufhin von den arabischen Staaten verhängte Ölboykott hatte schwerwiegende Folgen für die Weltwirtschaft.

Willy Brandt was the first head of government of the Federal Republic to make an official visit to Israel, where he stayed from June 7-11, 1973. When the Israeli Prime Minister Golda Meir made a speech in honor of her German guest at dinner in the Knesset on June 7, there were four months to go before the fourth Middle East war broke out on October 6, 1973, the Jewish religious festival of Yom Kippur. The Arab states thereupon imposed an oil embargo, with grave consequences for the world economy.

Die Bundesrepublik war im Nahen Osten stets um eine »Politik der Ausgewogenheit« bemüht. Nach dem »Jom-Kippur-Krieg« des Jahres 1973, der ohne eindeutigen Sieger endete, ergaben sich neue Chancen für eine friedliche Regelung des seit Jahrzehnten schwelenden Konflikts. Eine Schlüsselrolle spielte der ägyptische Staatspräsident Anwar El Sadat, hier mit Bundeskanzler Brandt am 21.4.1974 in seiner Residenz in Giza. Sadat trat im arabischen Lager für Verhandlungen mit Israel ein und ebnete den Weg zu dem 1975 unter amerikanischer Vermittlung zustande gekommenen Sinai-Vertrag, der erstmals einen Gewaltverzicht der Kriegsgegner festlegte. 1981 wurde er wegen seiner Ausgleichspolitik von Fundamentalisten ermordet.

In the Middle East the Federal Republic always aimed at a "policy of even-handedness." After the Yom Kippur war in 1973, which ended without a clear victory for either side, there were fresh prospects of a peaceful settlement of the conflict that had been smouldering for decades. A key part was played by the Egyptian President Anwar el Sadat, here with Chancellor Brandt on April 21, 1974 at his residence in Giza. Within the Arab camp Sadat supported negotiations with Israel and smoothed the way to the Sinai Treaty, brokered by the Americans and concluded in 1975, in which both sides for the first time renounced the use of force. In 1981 he was murdered by fundamentalists because of his policy of conciliation.

Die Bergarbeiter der westdeutschen Kohlereviere an Saar, Rhein und Ruhr gehörten zu den treuesten Anhängern der SPD. Auch sie profitierten von den sozialpolitischen Reformen der Regierung Brandt. Doch die schwerwiegende Strukturkrise in diesem Wirtschaftszweig stand schon am Horizont, als der Bundeskanzler am 4.12.1973 in Saarbrücken bzw. am 1.3.1974 in Duisburg mit den Kumpels sprach.

Miners from the Saar, Rhine and Ruhr coalfields in West Germany were among the most loyal supporters of the SPD. They too benefited from the social reforms of the Brandt government. But the serious structural crisis in this industry was already looming as the Chancellor talked with colliers in Saarbrücken on December 4, 1973 and in Duisburg on March 1, 1974.

Wirtschaft und Gesellschaft / Economy and Society

Die Liste der Reformvorhaben der sozial-liberalen Koalition betraf fast alle Bereiche des gesellschaftlichen Lebens. Gerade im Bereich der Sozialpolitik, wo die Verbesserungen breiten Bevölkerungsschichten zugute kommen sollten, entstanden daraus erhebliche finanzielle Belastungen für Staat und Wirtschaft. Für die Arbeitnehmer, für deren Sorgen sich ein sozialdemokratischer Kanzler besonders verantwortlich fühlen mußte, brachten vor allem die Lohnfortzahlung im Krankheitsfall, die verstärkte Förderung der Vermögensbildung und die Reform des Betriebsverfassungsgesetzes eindeutige Zugewinne. Zugleich wuchsen die Erwartungen auf stetige Lohnsteigerungen, dauerhafte Vollbeschäftigung und Sicherheit der Arbeitsplätze. Doch eine »Kanzler-Garantie für die Hochkonjunktur«, wie man in Wirtschaftskreisen spöttelte, konnte es nicht geben. Der Ölschock des Jahres 1973 konfrontierte das Land mit den harten Fakten der ökonomischen Realität. Die Begrenztheit ökonomischer Ressourcen und Möglichkeiten wurde erstmals schmerzlich spürbar.

The social-liberal coalition's list of reform projects affected almost every area of social life. In the field of social policy in particular, where improvements were intended to benefit large sections of the population, this entailed considerable financial burdens on the state and the economy. Working people, for whose concerns a Social Democrat Chancellor was bound to feel especially responsible, reaped clear benefits, above all the continued payment of wages during sickness, the expansion of wealth-creation schemes for workers and the reform of the *Betriebsverfassungsgesetz*, the law relating to industrial democracy. At the same time there were rising expectations of continued wage increases, permanent full employment and job security. But there could be no such thing as a "Chancellor-guaranteed boom" as it was mockingly put by those involved in the economy. The oil shock of 1973 forced the country to face up to the hard facts of economic reality. For the first time, the limits of economic resources and opportunities became painfully apparent.

Bundeskanzler Brandt empfängt am 27.8.1973 führende Vertreter der deutschen Wirtschaft zu einem Spitzengespräch auf Gut Neuhof bei Frankfurt. Links neben Willy Brandt sitzt Detlev Karsten Rohwedder, damals Staatssekretär im Bundeswirtschaftsministerium, der 1991 von RAF-Terroristen ermordet werden sollte.

Chancellor Brandt met leading representatives of the German business world on August 27, 1973 for summit talks at Gut Neuhof near Frankfurt. Detlev Karsten Rohwedder on the left next to Brandt, at that time state secretary at economics ministry, 1991 assassinated by RAF-terrorists.

Bundeskanzler Brandt am 8.4.1974 auf einer Betriebsversammlung in Helmstedt. Brandt war ein eindrucksvoller Redner, der ganz unterschiedliche Zuhörerkreise in seinen Bann zu schlagen verstand.

Chancellor Brandt on April 8, 1974 at a plant meeting in Helmstedt. Brandt was an impressive speaker who knew how to captivate different groups of listeners.

Gastarbeiter / Foreign Workers

Nachdem Anfang Dezember 1970 die Zahl der in der Bundesrepublik lebenden Gastarbeiter die Zwei-Millionen-Grenze überschritten hatte, wurde am 23.11.1973 ein Anwerbestopp für ausländische Arbeitnehmer verhängt. Seit dem Ende der fünfziger Jahre waren in den Zeiten der Hochkonjunktur Menschen aus ganz Europa als Arbeitskräfte für die deutsche Wirtschaft angeworben worden. Ihre Teilnahme am wirtschaftlichen und öffentlichen Leben gehört seitdem zum Alltag der Republik.

At the beginning of December 1970 the number of immigrant workers living in the Federal Republic rose above the two million threshold, and on November 23, 1973 the recruitment of foreign workers was halted by the government. Since the late fifties workers from all over Europe had been recruited for German industry during periods of economic boom. Since then their involvement in economic and public life has been part of the everyday reality of the Federal Republic.

21.12.1971: Gastarbeiter warten auf dem Kölner Hauptbahnhof auf ihre Abreise zum Weihnachtsbesuch in der Heimat.

On December 21, 1971 foreign workers at the main railway station in Cologne, on their way home to spend Christmas in their homelands.

Eines der umstrittensten Reformvorhaben der sozial-liberalen Koalition war die Neuregelung des § 218 des Strafgesetzbuchs. Mit der am 26.4. 1974 im Bundestag verabschiedeten Fristenlösung sollte eine Abtreibung innerhalb der ersten drei Monate einer Schwangerschaft straffrei bleiben. Dieser Beschluß kam gegen die Stimmen der CDU/CSU-Opposition und gegen heftigen öffentlichen Protest zustande, in den sich auch die Kirchen einreihten. An einer solchen Protestkundgebung in Bonn beteiligten sich am 29.9.1973 auch katholische Bischöfe – links der Erzbischof von München, Julius Döpfner, rechts der Kölner Erzbischof Joseph Höffner, daneben der Paderborner Weihbischof Degenhardt.

One of the most controversial reform projects of the social-liberal coalition was the revision of Paragraph 218 of the Penal Code by the introduction of the so-called *Fristenlösung*, which was approved by parliament on April 26, 1974, legalizing abortion within the first three months of pregnancy. This decision was taken against the votes of the CDU/CSU opposition and despite vehement public protest in which the churches also joined. For example, Catholic bishops also took part in one such protest demonstration in Bonn on September 29, 1973: on the left the Archbishop of Munich Julius Döpfner, on the right the Archbishop of Cologne Joseph Höffner, next to him Suffragan Bishop Degenhardt of Paderborn.

Frauen demonstrieren am 9.1.1975 für eine stärkere Berücksichtigung ihrer Interessen. Sechs Wochen darauf verwarf das Bundesverfassungsgericht in Karlsruhe die Fristenlösung. Erst am 18.5.1976 kam es mit der Einführung der Indikationsregelung zu einer dauerhaften Reform des § 218.

Women demonstrating on January 9, 1975, demanding that their interests should be taken more into account. Six weeks later the Federal Constitutional Court in Karlsruhe threw out the new legislation. It was not until May 18, 1976 that Paragraph 218 was permanently revised when the "indication ruling" was introduced, legalizing termination of pregnancy on medical or social grounds. The slogans read, from left to right: "We demand the development of contraception methods that pose no danger to health," "Women! Together we are strong," Women in parliament (with statistics), "Down with unequal pay for equal work," "In the home we're the tops, but outside we're second-class citizens."

Leere Autobahnen – wie hier am 2. 12.1973 auf einem Teilstück zwischen Köln und Bonn – symbolisieren die Auswirkungen des Ölboykotts der arabischen Staaten für die Industrienationen. Durch die am 19.11.1973 verordneten Sonntagsfahrverbote bekam auch der einfache Bundesbürger die Folgen von Ölschock und Weltwirtschaftskrise unmittelbar zu spüren.

Empty highways – on December 2, 1973 on part of the autobahn between Cologne and Bonn – symbolize the effects of the Arab oil embargo on the industrialized nations. The ban on Sunday driving, announced on November 19, 1973, made the ordinary German citizen directly aware of the consequences of the oil shock and the international economic crisis.

Triumph des Siegers / The Winner's Triumph

(links) Sieger unter sich: Parteifreunde umringen gratulierend und mit lang anhaltendem Beifall und Jubel den sichtlich bewegten Willy Brandt im Bundestag nach dem Scheitern des gegen ihn gerichteten Mißtrauensvotums der CDU/CSU-Opposition vom 27.4.1972.

(left) The winners among themselves: in parliament on April 27, 1972, fellow party members applauding and cheering, at length, a visibly moved Willy Brandt on the failure of the CDU/CSU Opposition's attempt to unseat him by means of a constructive vote of no confidence.

(gegnüber) Der Verlierer und der Sieger: Nach dem Scheitern des Mißtrauensvotums gratuliert Oppositionsführer Barzel am Nachmittag des 27.4.1972 Bundeskanzler Brandt. Die versteinerten Züge des Kanzlers spiegeln die Anspannung und Härte der Auseinandersetzung. Auf der Regierungsbank macht sich dagegen Erleichterung und auch ein wenig Schadenfreude über den unerwarteten Ausgang der Abstimmung breit. Aufmerksam wird außerdem beobachtet, in welcher Haltung Rainer Barzel, dem Willi Weyer von der FDP während der Stimmenauszählung in einem Nebenraum des Plenarsaals schon zum gelungenen Machtwechsel gratuliert hatte, die für ihn überraschende Niederlage aufnimmt.

(opposite) The loser and the winner: after the failure of the constructive vote of no confidence, Barzel, the Leader of the Opposition, congratulating Chancellor Brandt on the afternoon of April 27, 1972. The Chancellor's stony expression reflects the tension and acrimony of the conflict. On the government benches, on the other hand, relief is felt, along with a little malicious pleasure at the unexpected outcome of the vote. Furthermore, they attentively observe the dignified bearing with which Rainer Barzel reacted to the surprising defeat. While the votes were still being counted, he had been congratulated by Willi Weyer of the FDP, in a room adjoining the plenary chamber, on the successful change of power.

Das peinliche Nachspiel: Der CDU-Bundestagsabgeordnete Julius Steiner (links) und der Parlamentarische Geschäftsführer der SPD-Fraktion, Karl Wienand (rechts), werden am 5.9.1973 im Untersuchungsausschuß des Bundestages befragt. Der Ausschuß versuchte von Juni 1973 bis März 1974 zu klären, ob Wienand als enger Vertrauter Herbert Wehners in dessen Auftrag den CDU-Abgeordneten mit Geld zur Stimmenthaltung beim Mißtrauensvotum vom 27.4.1972 bewogen hatte und ob überhaupt Bestechung beim verblüffenden Ausgang der Abstimmung im Spiel gewesen war. Auch wenn damals der Vorwurf nicht erhärtet werden konnte, schadete die schmutzige Affäre dem moralischen Ansehen der Regierung Brandt erheblich.

The embarrassing epilogue: member of parliament Julius Steiner (CDU) (on the left) and SPD party whip, Karl Wienand (on the right) being questioned in the parliamentary committee of enquiry on September 5, 1973. From June 1973 to March 1974 the committee tried to establish whether Wienand, as a close confidant of Herbert Wehner and on his behalf, had persuaded the CDU member to abstain in the constructive vote of no confidence on April 27, 1972, and whether bribery had played any part in the astonishing outcome of the vote. Even though the accusation could not be substantiated at the time, the grubby affair did considerable damage to the standing of the Brandt government.

Ein großer Sieg / A Big Victory

Die innerparteiliche Stellung von Oppositionsführer Rainer Barzel war schon nach dem gescheiterten Mißtrauensvotum stark geschwächt. Nach der verheerenden Niederlage bei der Bundestagswahl vom 19.11.1972 wurde in der Union der Ruf nach einer personellen und inhaltlichen Erneuerung immer lauter. Dem Abschied vom Fraktionsvorsitz folgte auf dem Bundesparteitag am 12.6.1973 in Bonn der Wechsel im Amt des Parteivorsitzenden, auf dessen Stuhl der rheinland-pfälzische Ministerpräsident Helmut Kohl Platz nahm, noch ehe das Namensschild ausgetauscht war.

The Opposition Leader Rainer Barzel's position within his party had already been severely weakened following the failure of the constructive vote of no confidence. After the devastating defeat at the general election on November 19, 1972 voices were increasingly heard in the CDU calling for a renewal on both personnel and policy-making. Barzel first lost the position of Chief Whip, then, at the party conference on June 12, 1973 in Bonn, that of party chairman. The Minister President of Rhineland Palatinate, Helmut Kohl, took Barzel's place even before the nameplate had been changed.

Nach dem Verlust der parlamentarischen Mehrheit sollten der sozial-liberalen Regierung vorgezogene Bundestagswahlen zu einer neuen Machtbasis verhelfen. Im Mittelpunkt des kurzen und harten Wahlkampfs standen Politik wie Person des Bundeskanzlers. Willy Brandt – hier bei einer Wahlkampfveranstaltung am 9.11.1972 in Münster – war am Wahlabend des 19.11.1972 der unumstrittene Sieger der »Willy-Wahl«.

After losing its parliamentary majority the social-liberal government hoped to create a new power base by bringing forward the next general election. At the center of the short and tough election campaign were the personality and policies of the Chancellor; and Willy Brandt – here at an election meeting in Münster on November 9, 1972 – was the undisputed victor in the "Willy-Wahl" ("Willy's election") on November 19, 1972.

(unten) Als Willy Brandt, Walter Scheel und Horst Ehmke nach Bekanntgabe der Hochrechnungen am Abend des 19.11.1972 der wartenden Menge freudig zuwinkten, hatten 45,8% der Deutschen der Partei des Bundeskanzlers ihre Stimme gegeben. Die SPD war damit erstmals stärkste Partei im Bundestag geworden und verfügte jetzt gemeinsam mit der ebenfalls gestärkten FDP über eine komfortable Mehrheit. Die Wahlbeteiligung lag bei 91,1% und war damit so hoch wie nie zuvor bei freien Wahlen in Deutschland.

(below) When Willy Brandt, Walter Scheel and Horst Ehmke were waving joyfully to the waiting crowd after the projections had been announced on the evening of election day, November 19, 1972, 45.8% of Germans had voted for the Chancellor's party. Thus for the first time the SPD had now become the strongest party in parliament. The FDP had likewise increased its share of the vote, and together they had a comfortable majority. The turnout was 91.1%, higher than ever before in free elections in Germany.

(links) Nach ihrem großen Wahlsieg konnte die SPD erstmals, den parlamentarischen Gepflogenheiten entsprechend, das Amt des Bundestagspräsidenten besetzen. Hier gratuliert Herbert Wehner der soeben gewählten Annemarie Renger, die von 1972 bis1976 als erste Sozialdemokratin und erste Frau dieses zweithöchste Staatsamt bekleiden sollte.

(left) After their great electoral victory, the President of the Bundestag, in accordance with parliamentary practice, came from the ranks of the SPD for the first time. Herbert Wehner is seen congratulating Annemarie Renger, who had just been elected and who from 1972 to 1976 was to be the first Social Democrat and the first woman to occupy the second-highest office of state.

Willy Brandt – Porträts einer Ära / Willy Brandt – Portraits of an Era

Willy Brandt war eine der prägenden Persönlichkeiten deutscher Politik in der zweiten Hälfte des Zwanzigsten Jahrhunderts. Mit seinem Amtsantritt als erster sozialdemokratischer Kanzler der Bundesrepublik wurde ein neues Kapitel der Nachkriegsgeschichte aufgeschlagen. Schon die Tatsache, daß er, der uneheliche Sohn einer Lübecker Verkäuferin, der 1933 aus Deutschland emigriert war, im Oktober 1969 Regierungschef werden konnte, symbolisierte den Wandel. Für die Nachwelt ist sein Name untrennbar mit der »Neuen Ostpolitik« verknüpft, deren Auswirkungen zu den Voraussetzungen der Wiederherstellung der deutschen Einheit im Jahr 1990 gehören. Als Mensch hat Willy Brandt im In- und Ausland die Glaubwürdigkeit deutscher Politik verkörpert. Die Kraft, diesem hohen Anspruch gerecht zu werden, fiel ihm nicht einfach zu. Der eher Zögerliche, zu Selbstzweifeln Neigende hat sie sich immer wieder abringen müssen.

Willy Brandt was one of the personalities who had a decisive influence on German politics in the second half of the twentieth century. When he took office as the first Social Democrat Chancellor of the Federal Republic, a new chapter in postwar history began. The mere fact that Brandt, the illegitimate son of a salesgirl from Lübeck, who had gone into exile from Germany in 1933, was able to become head of government in October 1969, symbolized a fundamental change. His name is inseparably linked with the "New *Ostpolitik*", the effects of which helped to make possible the restoration of German unity in 1990. On a human level Willy Brandt embodied, both at home and abroad, the credibility of German politics. The strength to do justice to this lofty responsibility did not come to him automatically. He was, if anything, a hesitant man, a man of self-doubt rather than certainties, who had to struggle constantly to achieve that strength.

Das Idol: Der amerikanische Pop-Art-Künstler Andy Warhol bei den fotografischen Vorarbeiten für sein Porträt von Willy Brandt. Auch wenn die Pose mit Zigarettenspitze »gestellt« wirkt: Brandt verstand es in späteren Jahren immer eindrucksvoller, als Weltmann und Grandseigneur aufzutreten.

The idol: the American exponent of Pop Art, Andy Warhol, taking photographs in preparation for his portrait of Willy Brandt. Even if the pose seems contrived, down to the cigarette holder, Brandt in later years knew how to present himself impressively as a *grand seigneur* and a man of the world.

1969–1974

(rechts) Geradezu jungenhaft konnte sich der Kanzler im vertrauten Kreis geben. Herzhaft und gern lachte er über einen guten Witz. Im Sommer 1973, als diese Aufnahme entstand, gab es für ihn politisch allerdings bereits seltener Anlaß zu solcher Ausgelassenheit.

(unten rechts) Als Zuschauer bei den Olympischen Sommerspielen in München am 30.8.1972. Wirklich zerzaust vom Wind der Geschichte wurde Brandt allerdings erst in der zweiten Hälfte seiner Kanzlerschaft, als ihm nach der Bundestagswahl vom November 1972 die Zügel der Regierungsgeschäfte mehr und mehr entglitten.

(unten links) Willy Brandt wurde dank seiner charismatischen Qualitäten von vielen seiner Anhänger als eine »Lichtgestalt« betrachtet. Doch der Kanzler empfand den Glanz, in den die erwartungsvolle Verehrung der Massen ihn tauchte, stets auch als Bürde .

(right) Among his close friends the Chancellor was sometimes positively boyish. He liked to laugh heartily at a good joke. But by the summer of 1973, when this picture was taken, he had fewer occasions in political life for such light-heartedness.

(below right) As a spectator at the Summer Olympics in Munich on August 30, 1972. It was, however, only in the second half of his Chancellorship that Brandt was really dishevelled by the wind of history, when, after the election of November 1972, the reins of government increasingly slipped from his grasp.

(below left) Thanks to his charismatic qualities Willy Brandt was regarded by many of his supporters as a kind of shining light. But the Chancellor always also felt burdened by the glamor with which the masses invested him, with their veneration and their expectations.

Willy Brandt wurde eine besondere Wirkung auf Frauen nachgesagt, weshalb ihn manche politische Weggefährten beneideten. Als ihm Rómulo Betancourt, der langjährige Staatspräsident Venezuelas, bei einer Visite gestand, er bewundere ihn als Staatsmann – aber noch mehr als Mann, war der Bundeskanzler geschmeichelt. Fest steht, daß die Frauen zu seinen treuesten Wählern zählten.

Willy Brandt was said to have a special impact on women. Some of his political comrades envied him this. When Romulo Betancourt, the long-standing President of Venezuela, once confessed to him during a visit that he admired him as a statesman but even more so as a man, the Chancellor was flattered. What is certain is that women were among his most loyal voters.

1969–1974

(oben) Abendempfang im Weißen Haus in Washington, 10.4.1970. Von links nach rechts und allesamt trotz großer Roben entspannt und fröhlich: Rut Brandt, Pat Nixon, Pearl Bailey, Willy Brandt.
(rechts) Das Ehepaar Rut und Willy Brandt. Bedeutende musikalische Erfolge sind – anders als bei Walter Scheel – im Falle des Kanzlers Brandt nicht belegt.
(gegenüber) Die israelische Schlagersängerin Esther Ofarim im Gespräch mit Willy Brandt am 28.11.1969 auf dem Bundespresseball in der Bonner Beethovenhalle. Auch hier wird nicht der Gedankenaustausch über musikalische Themen im Vordergrund gestanden haben.

(above) An evening reception at the White House in Washington on April 10, 1970. From left to right: Rut Brandt, Pat Nixon, Pearl Bailey, Willy Brandt – all of them relaxed and cheerful despite their highly formal dress.
(right) Willy Brandt and his wife Rut. There is no evidence of any significant musical successes in Brandt's case – unlike the case of Walter Scheel.
(opposite) The Israeli pop singer Esther Ofarim in conversation with Willy Brandt at the press ball in the Beethovenhalle in Bonn on November 28, 1969. Here too we may safely assume that the exchange of views on musical topics did not occupy a very prominent place in their conversation.

Der Sturz / The Fall

Am 24.4.1974 wurde der als Agent des DDR-Geheimdienstes enttarnte Persönliche Referent des Bundeskanzlers, Günter Guillaume, in seiner Wohnung verhaftet. Am 6.5.1974 übernahm Willy Brandt die politische Verantwortung für den Fall und erklärte seinen Rücktritt. Doch die Affäre war nur der Anlaß, nicht die Ursache des Rücktritts. Der Bundeskanzler, und mit ihm seine Partei, waren schon seit längerer Zeit in die Defensive geraten. Der Stimmungswandel hatte bei den Wahlen zur Hamburger Bürgerschaft am 3.3.1974 zu erdrutschartigen Verlusten der SPD geführt. Brandt war nicht mehr fähig, den drohenden Machtverfall aufzuhalten. Er selbst hat dazu später geschrieben: »Die Schwierigkeiten in und mit der Regierung hatten seit Jahresbeginn '73 zugenommen und meine Position, gewiß auch mein Durchhaltevermögen geschwächt... In der physischen und psychischen Verfassung späterer Jahre wäre ich nicht zurückgetreten, sondern hätte da aufgeräumt, wo aufzuräumen war.«

On April 24, 1974 Günter Guillaume, the Chancellor's personal adviser, was unmasked as an agent of the GDR secret service and was arrested at his home. On May 6, 1974 Willy Brandt accepted political responsibility for the matter and announced his resignation. But the affair merely triggered off the resignation, it was not its real cause. The Chancellor, and his party with him, had been on the defensive for some considerable time. The change of mood had led to landslide losses for the SPD in the elections to the Hamburg City Parliament on March 3, 1974. Brandt was no longer able to stave off the imminent loss of power. He himself later wrote: "The difficulties in and with the government had increased since the beginning of 1973 and my position was weakened as was also undoubtedly my stamina... Had I been in the same physical and psychological shape as in later years I would not have resigned but would have sorted things out where they needed sorting out."

(gegenüber) Günter Guillaume, der 1956 als Perspektivagent und »Schläfer« (er sollte so lange unauffällig bleiben, bis er in eine wichtige Position aufgerückt war) vom DDR-Geheimdienst in den Westen geschickt worden und ein Jahr später in die hessische SPD eingetreten war, wurde zwei Jahre nach seiner Einstellung im Kanzleramt 1972 Referent im Persönlichen Büro des Bundeskanzlers. Rasch verstand er es, das Vertrauen Willy Brandts zu gewinnen und sich als dessen Faktotum und Helfer bei den alltäglichen politischen und privaten Verpflichtungen wie hier während einer Weinprobe unentbehrlich zu machen.

(opposite) Günter Guillaume had been sent to the West by the GDR secret service in 1956 as a long-term agent and "sleeper" (he was under instructions to remain inconspicuous until he had advanced to an important position). A year later he had joined the SPD in Hesse, and two years after being appointed to the Chancellery in 1972 he had been made an adviser in the Chancellor's personal office. He quickly managed to gain Brandt's confidence and to make himself indispensable as his factotum and aide in his day-to-day political and private commitments, as seen here at a wine-tasting.

Das Ehepaar Brandt beim Sonntagsspaziergang am 25. 11. 1973 auf dem Venusberg bei Bonn. Im Hintergrund der später als Agent des DDR-Geheimdienstes verhaftete Persönliche Referent des Bundeskanzlers, Guillaume.

Brandt and his wife on their Sunday walk on the Venusberg near Bonn on November 25, 1973. In the background the Chancellor's personal adviser Günter Guillaume, who was later arrested as an agent of the GDR secret service.

(gegenüber) Bonn, 20.9.1974: Der SPD-Vorsitzende und frühere Bundeskanzler Brandt wird vom Parlamentarischen Untersuchungsausschuß des Bundestags zur Affäre Guillaume vernommen. Daß die andere Seite ausgerechnet ihn, der sich wie kein zweiter Kanzler für eine Verständigung und einen Ausgleich mit den Staaten des Warschauer Paktes eingesetzt hatte, über Jahre hinweg durch einen Verräter und Spitzel ausspionieren ließ, hat Willy Brandt mit verständlicher Verbitterung registriert.

(opposite) Bonn, September 20, 1974: the SPD party chairman and former Chancellor Brandt giving evidence concerning the Guillaume affair before the parliamentary committee of enquiry. That the other side had used a traitor and secret agent to spy on him over a period of years, him of all people, who had worked as had no other Chancellor for mutual understanding and conciliation with the Warsaw Pact states – Brandt reacted to this with understandable bitterness.

Günter Guillaume wurde 1975 zu 13 Jahren Haft wegen schweren Landesverrats verurteilt und 1981 in die DDR entlassen. Von seinem höchsten Vorgesetzten, Staatssicherheitsminister Erich Mielke, wurde Guillaume 1987 als »Brandt-Stifter« gefeiert. Er selbst wollte sich jedoch eher als »Friedensstifter« sehen.

Günter Guillaume was sentenced in 1975 to 13 years imprisonment for high treason and released to the GDR in 1981. Guillaume's ultimate superior Erich Mielke, the Minister for State Security, honored Guillaume in 1987 as a "Brandt-Stifter" (Brand(t)stifter = fire raiser, fire maker). For his own part, however, he preferred to see himself as a "peace-maker."

1974–1982

Die Regierung Schmidt/Genscher
The Schmidt/Genscher Government

Trotz aller hanseatischen Distanz offen für die Sorgen anderer: Helmut
Schmidt im Gespräch mit polnischen Werft-Arbeitern am 24.11.1977 in
Gdingen.
Sympathetic towards other peoples worries notwithstanding his patrician
aloofness: Helmut Schmidt in conversation with Polish shipyard workers on
November 24, 1977 in Gdingen.

Als der bisherige Finanzminister Helmut Schmidt am 16.5.1974 das Amt des Bundeskanzlers übernahm, hatte die Ölkrise des Vorjahres die politische und ökonomische Situation der Bundesrepublik tiefgreifend verändert. Die westdeutsche Wirtschaft stand vor enormen Herausforderungen. Die »Grenzen des Wachstums« zeichneten sich ab.

Für viele Anhänger der sozial-liberalen Reformpolitik wirkte der Kanzlerwechsel wie eine Ernüchterung. Der pragmatische, auf Rationalität und Effizienz bedachte neue Chef im Bundeskanzleramt ließ für manchen den mitreißenden Schwung und die weltanschaulichen Visionen seines Vorgängers Brandt vermissen. Doch der neue, eher nüchterne Regierungsstil entsprach durchaus den veränderten Anforderungen. In Helmut Schmidts Amtszeit fiel die schwierige Aufgabe, die Ökonomie des Wirtschaftswunderlandes den veränderten weltwirtschaftlichen Rahmenbedingungen anzupassen. Schmidt löste die heikle Aufgabe, die Bundesrepublik so glimpflich wie möglich durch die Gefahren der globalen Wirtschaftskrise zu führen und auf diesem Weg die vor ihm begonnenen Reformprojekte auf ein finanzierbares Maß zu reduzieren. Eine wirklich nachhaltige Eindämmung der wachsenden Staatsverschuldung mißlang allerdings. Außenpolitisch glückte ihm die weitere Profilierung der Bundesrepublik als europäische Mittelmacht. Er selbst wurde zum angesehenen Partner der Staats- und Regierungschefs in West und Ost.

Alltag und Bewährung

Angesichts der ökonomischen Turbulenzen forderte der neue Kanzler schon in seiner ersten Regierungserklärung am 17.5.1974 eine »Besinnung auf das Mögliche« und verschwieg dabei nicht die unausweichlichen Folgen für die Reformen. Gleichwohl konnten in den Anfangsjahren seiner gemeinsam mit Außenminister Hans-Dietrich Genscher geführten sozial-liberalen Regierung einige der seit längerem diskutierten Reformvorhaben abgeschlossen werden. So erfolgte 1975 die Herabsetzung des Volljährigkeitsalters auf 18 Jahre. Im Jahr darauf wurden das Hochschulrahmengesetz, die endgültige Neuregelung des § 218 und die paritätische Mitbestimmung für Arbeitnehmer in Großbetrieben verabschiedet. 1977 schließlich kam es zur Reform des Ehe- und Familienrechts.

Doch die wirtschaftlichen Krisenerscheinungen rückten zunehmend in den Vordergrund. Der Prozeß wirtschaftlicher Konzentration beschleunigte sich, mittelständische Unternehmen hatten immer häufiger das Nachsehen. Zugleich verschlechterte sich die Leistungsbilanz der Bundesrepublik und wies 1979 erstmals seit Mitte der sechziger Jahre ein Defizit auf. Alle Faktoren zusammen führten zu einem dramatischen Abbau von Arbeitsplätzen und zu einer Erhöhung der Arbeitslosenzahl, die 1975 erstmals seit den frühen fünfziger Jahren wieder die Millionenmarke überschritt und bis Ende 1982 auf über zwei Millionen kletterte.

Die Bundesregierung versuchte zunächst, den Schwierigkeiten mit Hilfe von Konjunkturprogrammen sowie durch eine Anhebung der Sozialleistungen zu begegnen, um die Inlandsnachfrage zu stärken. Angesichts der negativen Rahmenbedingungen der Weltwirtschaft war diesen Bemühungen aber keine durchschlagende Wirkung beschieden. Im Gegenteil – zur Finanzierung der

When Helmut Schmidt, who had hitherto been Finance Minister, took over the office of Federal Chancellor on May 16, 1974, the oil crisis of the previous year had profoundly altered the political and economic situation of the Federal Republic. The West German economy faced enormous challenges. The "limits of growth" began to be discernible.

Many supporters of the social-liberal reform policies were brought back down to earth by the change of Chancellor. The new Chancellor's pragmatism, his emphasis on rationality and efficiency seemed to some to lack the exhilarating energy and ideological vision of his predecessor Brandt. But the new, more sober style of government was precisely what was needed to meet the new demands. The difficult process, in the country of the economic miracle, of adapting the economy to the changed conditions in the world outside, fell within Helmut Schmidt's period in office. Schmidt solved the tricky problem of how to steer the Federal Republic through the perils of the global economic crisis with as little damage as possible, and, in so doing, to cut back the reform projects which had been introduced before his time to financially feasible proportions. He did not, however, succeed in permanently curbing the growth of government debt. But he did succeed, in foreign affairs, by giving the Federal Republic the image of a medium-grade European power. He himself became a respected partner of the political leaders in the East and West.

Day-to-Day Business and Challenges to be Met

Faced with economic turmoil, the new Chancellor was already calling on his listeners, in his inaugural government statement on May 17, 1974, to "reflect on what was feasible"; he made no secret of the inescapable consequences of this for the reforms. Even so, in the early years of his social-liberal government in harness with his Foreign Minister Hans-Dietrich Genscher it proved possible to complete some of the long-standing reform projects. Thus in 1975 the age of legal majority was lowered to 18. In the following year legislation providing guidelines for the reform of higher education was passed, and the final revision of Paragraph 218 became law, as did co-determination on the basis of parity of representation for workers in large industrial enterprises. Finally in 1977 the reform of matrimonial and family law was approved by parliament.

But the symptoms of economic crisis came increasingly to dominate the situation. Production costs rose as a result of increases in the prices of energy and raw materials, causing massive cutbacks in investment and the intensification of attempts to make industrial production more efficient. High interest rates led to increasing numbers of bankruptcies. The process of economic concentration was accelerated, with medium-sized firms suffering more and more frequently as a result. At the same time the Federal Republic's balance of payments deteriorated and in 1979 showed a deficit for the first time since the mid-sixties. All these factors combined to bring about a dramatic loss of jobs and rise in the number of unemployed, which in 1975 went above a million for the first time since the early fifties and had risen to over two million by the end of 1982.

The government tried at first to cope with these difficulties with the help of measures to boost the economy and increases in social

RAUCHEN NICHT GESTATTET

Der »Genußmensch«: Über lange Jahre hinweg konnte Helmut Schmidt den Freuden des Tabakgenusses nur schwer widerstehen – selbst wenn es wie hier nicht mit den Vorschriften in Einklang zu bringen war.

The "hedonist": for many years Schmidt had great difficulty resisting the pleasure of tobacco smoking – even when as here it was against regulations.

Der Jongleur: Der Balanceakt, den der Kanzler am 25.6.1982 beim Sommerfest im Garten des Palais Schaumburg vorführte, gelang ihm zur selben Zeit im politischen Koalitionsalltag mit der FDP und vor allem auch mit seiner eigenen Partei immer weniger.

The juggler: the balancing act performed by the Chancellor at the summer fête in the garden of the Palais Schaumburg on June 25, 1982 was something at which in the day-to-day political business of the coalition he was becoming less and less successful as regards both the FDP and, especially, his own party.

Der Staatsmann: Bundeskanzler Helmut Schmidt, mittlerweile über den Regierungsstrapazen ergraut und mit einem Herzschrittmacher versehen, aber noch entspannt und zuversichtlich im Versailler Schloßpark während der Konferenz der Staats- und Regierungschefs der sieben führenden Industrienationen vom 5.bis 6.6.1982.

The statesman: Chancellor Helmut Schmidt, his hair by now turned grey with the strain of government and with a pacemaker, but still relaxed and confident, in the grounds of the Palace of Versailles during the conference of the political leaders of the Group of Seven, the leading industrial nations of the world, on June 5-6, 1982.

Das Ehepaar Schmidt besichtigt während des Aufenthalts in Spanien vom 7. bis 9.1.1979 das Museo del Prado in Madrid. Wie die meisten Besucher dieser berühmten Gemäldesammlung sind auch der Bundeskanzler und seine Frau von der »nackten Maya« des spanischen Malers Francisco de Goya fasziniert.

Schmidt and his wife visiting the Prado in Madrid during their trip to Spain January 7-9, 1979. Like most visitors to this famous collection of paintings the Chancellor and his wife were fascinated by the Spanish painter Francisco de Goya's "Naked Maja."

Ähnlich faszinierend muß auf Helmut Schmidt und seine Kabinettskollegen der furiose Tanz des allerdings bekleideten »Funkenmariechen« auf dem Kabinettstisch im Kanzleramt am 25.2.1976 gewirkt haben. Die strahlenden Gesichter (von links) von Hans-Dietrich Genscher, Helmut Schmidt, Manfred Schüler, Marie Schlei und Klaus Bölling sind gut zu erkennen.

The whirling dance of the "Funkenmariechen" (a traditional Rhineland carnival figure) on the cabinet table in the Chancellery on February 25, 1976 must have had a fascinating effect on Helmut Schmidt and his cabinet colleagues. The beaming faces (from left to right) of Hans-Dietrich Genscher, Helmut Schmidt, Manfred Schüler, Marie Schlei and Klaus Bölling are easily recognizable.

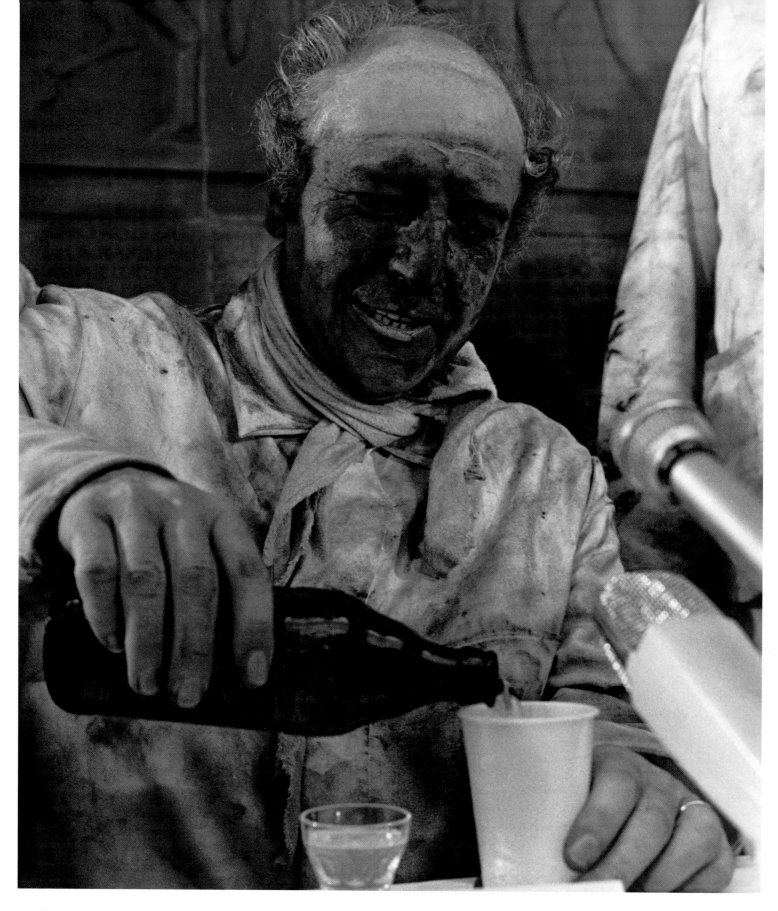

Bundespräsident Scheel gelang es, in allen Kreisen der deutschen Gesellschaft Anerkennung zu finden. Mit der Kraft der öffentlichen Rede und seinem jovialen Auftreten – hier am 19.3.1975 bei einer Zechenbesichtigung in Castrop-Rauxel – erreichte er eine bemerkenswerte Popularität. Bis heute unvergessen ist auch sein Beitrag zur Pflege der Volksmusik, den er mit der Schallplatteneinspielung des Liedes »Hoch auf dem gelben Wagen« krönte.

Federal President Scheel gained the respect of all social groups in Germany. With his forcefulness as a public speaker and his jovial manner – here on March 19, 1975 during a visit to a coal mine in Castrop-Rauxel – he achieved remarkable popularity. People also remember to this day his contribution to folk music, which reached its high point with his recording of the song "Hoch auf dem gelben Wagen."

Die Bundespräsidenten / The Federal Presidents

Walter Scheel, der am 15.5.1974 gewählte vierte Bundespräsident der Bundesrepublik Deutschland, erschien vielen wie ein Gegenbild zu seinem gelegentlich spröde und distanziert wirkenden Vorgänger Gustav Heinemann. Er betonte die Repräsentationsaufgaben seines Amtes und nutzte sie ausdrücklich, um im In- und Ausland das Bewußtsein für die gewachsene Bedeutung und Verantwortung des demokratischen Deutschland zu schärfen. Zugleich bemühte er sich um die Integration der Gesellschaft und suchte den unmittelbaren Kontakt mit der Bevölkerung. Sein am 23.5.1979 gewählter Nachfolger Karl Carstens setzte diese Amtsführung fort. Obwohl er der CDU angehörte und zeitweilig sogar Fraktionsvorsitzender der Opposition im Bundestag gewesen war, pflegte er spannungsfreie Beziehungen zur sozialliberalen Regierung. Sein persönliches Verhältnis zu Bundeskanzler Schmidt war sogar besser als das seines Vorgängers Scheel.

Walter Scheel, the fourth President of the Federal Republic of Germany, elected on May 15, 1974, seemed to many to be the complete opposite of his predecessor Gustav Heinemann, who at times seemed aloof and distant. He made much of the ceremonial duties of his office and used them expressly to create an increased awareness, both at home and abroad, of the increased significance and responsibility of democratic Germany. At the same time he worked for social integration and sought direct contact with the people. His successor Karl Carstens, elected on May 23, 1979 conducted himself in office in a similar manner. Although he belonged to the CDU and had indeed at one time been the opposition party whip, his relationship with the social-liberal government was free from stress. He was indeed personally on better terms with Chancellor Schmidt than his predecessor Scheel had been.

Karl Carstens verkörperte in der Öffentlichkeit in besonderem Maß die Würde des Präsidentenamts. Er verband jedoch damit eine unverstellte menschliche Wärme. Das erklärt die Selbstverständlichkeit, mit der er am 11.10.1980 einem seiner Berliner Patenkinder – für das siebente Kind in einer deutschen Familie übernimmt der Bundespräsident traditionell die Patenschaft – anläßlich einer Einladung im Schloß Bellevue für das Erinnerungsfoto Modell saß.

For the general public Karl Carstens embodied the dignity of the office of President to a particularly high degree. At the same time he also had genuine human warmth. Thus it was a matter of course for him to pose for a souvenir photograph on October 11, 1980 for one of his godchildren in Berlin, whom he had invited to Schloß Bellevue. In German families the Federal President is traditionally godfather to the seventh child.

Das »Markenzeichen« der Amtszeit des fünften Bundespräsidenten der Bundesrepublik waren seine Wanderungen, die ihn in alle Teile des Landes führten. Ausgehend von Hohwacht in Schleswig-Holstein legten Karl Carstens und seine Frau Veronica zwischen 1979 und 1981 in 44 Tagesetappen insgesamt rund 1130 Kilometer zurück. Oft wurden die prominenten Gäste aus Bonn – so wie hier auf ihrer 17. Etappe am 10.10.1981 in Bayern – von Landes- und Ortspolitikern sowie vielen weiteren Wanderfreunden begleitet.

Hiking around the entire country was the "trademark" of the fifth Federal President's term of office. Between 1979 and 1981, starting from Hohwacht in Schleswig-Holstein, Karl Carstens and his wife Veronica walked a total of about 1,130 kilometers in 44 daily stages. The distinguished visitors from Bonn were often accompanied by local and regional politicians along with many other fellow hikers, as here in Bavaria on their 17th day's walk on October 10, 1981.

CDU/CSU–Opposition

Der CDU/CSU-Opposition gelang seit Mitte der siebziger Jahre eine umfassende programmatische Erneuerung. Für die Außenpolitik zeigte sich dies in der Hinnahme der Ostverträge, für die Innenpolitik vor allem in der Besinnung auf die »Neue soziale Frage«. Zugleich brachen allerdings zwischen den Schwesterparteien Gegensätze auf über die richtige Strategie für eine Rückkehr an die Macht. Die CDU setzte unter ihrem Vorsitzenden Kohl auf einen Bruch der sozialliberalen Koalition und auf ein Zusammengehen mit der FDP. Dagegen votierte der CSU-Vorsitzende Strauß für einen klaren Konfrontationskurs gegenüber beiden Regierungsparteien. Nach den Bundestagswahlen des Jahres 1976, die trotz des Gewinns von 48,6 Prozent der Stimmen keinen Erfolg brachten, drohte zeitweilig sogar die Spaltung der Union. Die Machtfrage zwischen Kohl und Strauß wurde schließlich 1980 durch die Bundestagswahl entschieden, bei der der CSU-Vorsitzende als Kanzlerkandidat der Union eine herbe Niederlage einstecken mußte.

From the mid-seventies onwards the CDU/CSU opposition succeeded in carrying out a comprehensive revision of its program. This was to be seen in foreign affairs in the acceptance of the Eastern Treaties, and in domestic politics above all in the response to the "new social question." At the same time, however, differences of opinion appeared between the sister parties regarding the correct strategy for a return to power. The CDU under its chairman Kohl saw its best hope in a breach in the social-liberal coalition and an alliance with the FDP. The CSU chairman Strauß, in contrast, favored a clear policy of confrontation with both government parties. After the 1976 general election, which the CDU/CSU lost despite winning 48.6% of the vote, there was for a time even the threat of a split between CDU and CSU. The power struggle between Kohl and Strauß was finally decided in the 1980 general election at which the CSU chairman stood as CDU/CSU candidate for the Chancellorship and suffered a heavy defeat.

(gegenüber) Am 19.11.1976 verkündeten der CSU-Vorsitzende Strauß (links) und der Chef der CSU-Landesgruppe in Bonn, Friedrich Zimmermann (rechts), nach einer Klausurtagung der Bundestagsabgeordneten im bayerischen Wildbad Kreuth die Auflösung der Fraktionsgemeinschaft mit der CDU. Erst die Drohung der Christdemokraten, in diesem Fall auch selbst eigenständig in Bayern auf Stimmenfang zu gehen, veranlaßte die CSU-Spitze zum Rückzug. Mitte Dezember einigte man sich auf die Fortsetzung der Fraktionsgemeinschaft.

(opposite) On November 19, 1976, following a meeting behind closed doors of the CSU members of the federal parliament in the Bavarian health spa of Wildbad Kreuth, the CSU party chairman Strauß (left) and the leader of the regional CSU group in Bonn, Friedrich Zimmermann (right), announced that the CSU would no longer form a joint parliamentary group with the CDU. Only when the CDU threatened that in that case they would in their turn field candidates independently in Bavaria did the CSU leaders back down. In mid-December it was agreed that the two parties would continue to form a joint group in parliament.

(links) Der Ministerpräsident von Rheinland-Pfalz – hier mit dem damaligen Leiter der Landesvertretung in Bonn, Roman Herzog – setzte früh auf ein Auseinanderbrechen der sozialliberalen Koalition. Mit Helmut Kohl errangen die Unionsparteien 1976 bei den Bundestagswahlen das zweitbeste Ergebnis ihrer Geschichte. Doch der Streit mit der CSU hätte den CDU-Vorsitzenden bald darauf beinahe den Posten des Oppositionsführers gekostet. Durch seinen Verzicht auf die Kanzlerkandidatur zugunsten des Rivalen Franz Josef Strauß rettete er 1980 die Einheit der Union und wahrte seine eigene Chance auf eine spätere Regierungsübernahme.

(left) The Minister President of Rhineland-Palatinate – here with Roman Herzog, who at that time headed the representation of the Land to the Federation – saw at an early stage a chance for the opposition in the collapse of the social-liberal coalition. With Helmut Kohl the CDU/CSU achieved the second-best result in its history at the 1976 general election. But shortly afterwards the dispute with the CSU almost cost the CDU chairman his position as leader of the opposition. By standing down in 1980 as candidate for the Chancellorship in favor of his rival Franz Josef Strauß, Kohl salvaged the unity of the CDU/CSU while preserving his own future prospects of taking over the reins of government at a later date.

(gegenüber) Nach der auch für ihn als hartgesottenen politischen Kämpfer bitteren Wahlniederlage wußte Strauß, daß er seine bundespolitischen Ambitionen aufgeben mußte. Er konzentrierte sich fortan auf die Machtposition des bayerischen Ministerpräsidenten und nahm von München aus immer wieder Einfluß auf die Bonner Entwicklungen.

(opposite) After what even for such a hardboiled political fighter was a bitter electoral defeat, Strauß knew that he had to abandon his political ambitions at federal level. From then on he concentrated on his powerful position as Minister President of Bavaria, and from his base in Munich repeatedly influenced developments in Bonn.

Mit der Kanzlerkandidatur für die Bundestagswahl 1980 erfüllte sich für Franz Josef Strauß ein Lebenstraum, um dessen Verwirklichung er zäh und unerbittlich gekämpft hatte. Doch die Siegeszuversicht, die er – hier mit dem früheren Oppositionsführer Rainer Barzel bei einer Wahlkampfveranstaltung in Essen – zur Schau stellte, erfüllte sich nicht. Der ganz auf die Kandidaten Strauß und Schmidt zugeschnittene Wahlkampf, der zu einem der härtesten in der Geschichte der Bundesrepublik wurde, glich einem Duell der Giganten. Am Ende stand eine deutliche Niederlage der CDU/CSU, die mit 44,5 Prozent der Stimmen gegenüber dem Wahlergebnis von 1976 4,1 Prozent einbüßte.

In standing as a candidate for the Chancellorship in the 1980 general election Franz Josef Strauß fulfilled the dream of a lifetime, for which he had struggled relentlessly and tenaciously. But the victory of which he was confident – here with former opposition leader Rainer Barzel at an election meeting in Essen – did not materialize. The election campaign, which was focused entirely on the Chancellor candidates Strauß and Schmidt and was one of the toughest in the history of the Federal Republic, was a battle of giants. It ended in a clear defeat for the CDU/CSU, who polled 44.5% of the vote, a loss of 4.1% as against their showing in the 1976 election.

1 Million DM Belohnung
Dringend gesuchte Terroristen

Albrecht, Susanne
1.3.51
1,76 groß, besondere Merkmale:
wulstige Lippen, Sommersprossen

Krabbe, Friederike
31.5.50
1,72 groß

von Dyck, Elisabeth
11.10.50
1,68 groß

Maier-Witt, Silke
21.1.50
1,71 groß

Mohnhaupt, Brigitte Margret Ida
24.6.49
1,60 groß, besonderes Merkmal:
kurzsichtig, benötigt beim Autofahren
und bei Dunkelheit eine Brille

Plambeck, Juliane
16.7.52
1,70 groß

Viett, Inge
12.1.44
1,55 groß, besondere Merkmale:
1 cm lange Narbe am rechten Zeigefinger, kurze X-Beine

Speitel, Angelika
12.2.52
1,64 groß, besonderes Merkmal:
obere Schneidezähne stehen
auffallend auseinander

Sternebeck, Sigrid
19.6.49
1,69 groß

Klar, Christian
20.5.52
1,82 groß, besonderes Merkmal:
deutlich sichtbarer Adamsapfel

Schulz, Adelheid
31.3.55
1,62 groß, besonderes Merkmal:
auf der rechten Wange 2 Muttermale

Heißler, Rolf Gerhard
3.6.48
1,75 groß, besondere Merkmale:
erbsengroße Warze (Muttermal)
neben dem linken Mundwinkel, unterhalb des rechten Ohrläppchens und
am rechten Nasenwinkel ebenfalls
Muttermal

Wagner, Rolf Klemens
30.8.44
1,75 groß, besonderes Merkmal:
Brillenträger, am linken Unterkiefer
etwa 3 cm lange Narbe

Stoll, Willy Peter
12.6.50
1,73 groß, besonderes Merkmal:
deutlich sichtbarer Adamsapfel

Lang, Jörg
14.3.40
1,70 groß

Neu in die Fahndung aufgenommen sind:

Helbing, Monika Brigitte
16.11.53
1,70 groß

Friedrich, Baptist-Ralf
30.11.46
1,81 groß, besonderes Merkmal:
an linker Stirn- und Wangenseite
linsengroße Hautverfärbungen

Hofmann, Sieglinde
14.3.45
1,57 groß

Wisniewski, Stefan
8.4.53
1,85 groß

Boock, Peter
3.9.51
1,72 groß

Für Hinweise, die zur Ergreifung einer der gesuchten Personen führen, sind je **50 000 DM** (insgesamt 1 Million DM) Belohnung ausgesetzt, die unter Ausschluß des
Rechtsweges zuerkannt und verteilt werden. Sie sind nicht für Personen bestimmt, zu deren Berufspflichten die Verfolgung strafbarer Handlungen gehört.

Vorsicht Schußwaffen !

Herbst des Terrorismus / Autumn of Terrorism

Nach der Verhaftung der Führungsclique der »Rote-Armee-Fraktion« (RAF) im Sommer 1972 schien der deutsche Terrorismus zunächst besiegt. Doch schon 1974 trat eine zweite Generation von Terroristen mit der Ermordung des Berliner Kammergerichtspräsidenten Günter von Drenkmann hervor. 1975 wurde von der mit der RAF konkurrierenden »Bewegung 2. Juni« der Berliner CDU-Vorsitzende Peter Lorenz entführt und kurz darauf von einem »RAF-Kommando« die deutsche Botschaft in Stockholm überfallen. Zwei Diplomaten kamen dabei ums Leben. Den Höhepunkt erreichte der Terror zwei Jahre darauf mit den Morden an Siegfried Buback, Jürgen Ponto und Hanns Martin Schleyer. Die Entführung des Arbeitgeberpräsidenten und der Lufthansa-Maschine »Landshut« hielt die Bundesrepublik im Herbst 1977 sieben Wochen lang in Atem.

After the gang-leaders of the Red Army Faction (RAF) had been arrested in the summer of 1972 it seemed at first that German terrorism had been defeated. But by 1974 a second generation of terrorists had emerged with the assassination of Günter von Drenkmann, President of the Supreme Court in Berlin. In 1975 the party chairman of the CDU in Berlin, Peter Lorenz, was kidnapped by the "June 2nd movement," which was in competition with the RAF, and shortly afterwards the German Embassy in Stockholm was raided by an "RAF squad" in an attack in which two diplomats lost their lives. Terrorism reached its peak two years later when Siegfried Buback, Jürgen Ponto and Hanns Martin Schleyer were assassinated. In the autumn of 1977 the kidnapping of the president of the employers' federation, followed by the hijacking of the Lufthansa aircraft "Landshut," kept the Germans on tenterhooks for seven weeks.

Siegfried Buback, Generalbundesanwalt seit 1974, am 7.4.1977 in Karlsruhe auf dem Weg zum Bundesgerichtshof von einem RAF-Kommando ermordet. Mit ihm fanden der Fahrer seines Dienstwagens und wenige Tage später ein bei dem Attentat schwer verletzter Sicherheitsbeamter den Tod.

Hanns Martin Schleyer, Präsident der Bundesvereinigung der deutschen Arbeitgeberverbände und des Bundesverbands der Deutschen Industrie. Am 5.9.1977 wurden in Köln-Braunsfeld sein Fahrer sowie seine drei Sicherheitsbeamten ermordet und er selbst von Mitgliedern der RAF entführt. Am 19.10.1977 wurde Schleyer ermordet im Kofferraum eines Autos in Mühlhausen/Elsaß gefunden.

Jürgen Ponto, Vorstandssprecher der Dresdner Bank AG, am 30.7.1977 in seinem Wohnhaus in Oberursel/Taunus bei einem gescheiterten Entführungsversuch durch eine Terrorgruppe der RAF erschossen.

Siegfried Buback, Public Prosecutor General since 1974, assassinated by an RAF squad in Karlsruhe on April 7, 1977 while on his way to the Federal Court of Justice. The driver of his official car also lost his life, and a bodyguard who was severely injured in the attack died a few days later.

Hanns Martin Schleyer, president of the Confederation of German Employers' Associations and of the Federation of German Industries. His driver and three bodyguards were ambushed and murdered on September 5, 1977. He himself was kidnapped by members of the RAF and was found murdered in the boot of his car in Mühlhausen (Alsace) on October 19, 1977.

Jürgen Ponto, spokesman for the Management Board of the Dresden Bank, shot at his home in Oberursel (Taunus) on July 30, 1977 during an abortive kidnap attempt by an RAF terrorist group.

Lagebesprechung im Kanzlerbungalow mit Außenminister Genscher, dem FDP-Fraktionsvorsitzenden Mischnick sowie dem rheinland-pfälzischen Ministerpräsidenten und CDU-Vorsitzenden Kohl anläßlich der Entführung des Berliner CDU-Politikers Peter Lorenz am 27.2.1975 durch ein Terrorkommando der »Bewegung 2. Juni«. Dem Krisenstab gehörten der Bundeskanzler, die Führungen der im Bundestag vertretenen Parteien und die Regierungschefs der Länder an. Während der Schleyer-Entführung im Herbst 1977 tagte dieses Gremium, in dem Regierung und Opposition einmütig handelten, ein- bis zweimal wöchentlich. Daneben traf sich Bundeskanzler Schmidt täglich in der sogenannten »Kleinen Lage« zum Gespräch mit ausgewählten Regierungsmitgliedern sowie dem Generalbundesanwalt und dem Präsidenten des Bundeskriminalamtes.

Foreign Minister Genscher, FDP parliamentary group leader Mischnik and Kohl, Minister President of Rhineland-Palatinate and CDU party chairman discuss the situation in the Chancellor's bungalow following the kidnapping of the Berlin CDU politician Peter Lorenz on February 27, 1975 by a terrorist squad from the "2nd June movement." The crisis action committee included the Chancellor, the leaders of the parliamentary parties and the heads of government of the *Länder*. Following the Schleyer kidnapping in autumn 1977 this group, in which government and opposition acted in full agreement, met once or twice a week. In addition Schmidt met selected members of the government as well as the Public Prosecutor General and the president of the Federal Criminal Police Office, for daily talks in a smaller group.

Der Staatsminister im Bundeskanzleramt Hans-Jürgen Wischnewski trug wegen seiner guten Beziehungen zu den arabischen Staaten den Spitznamen »Ben Wisch«. Er leitete die Verhandlungen mit den Behörden in der somalischen Hauptstadt Mogadischu, auf deren Flugplatz die entführte Lufthansa-Maschine »Landshut« seit dem 17.10.1977 stand. Noch am selben Tag begannen die Vorbereitungen zur Erstürmung der Boeing 737, deren Modell Wischnewski hier in den Händen hält.

Hans-Jürgen Wischnewski, Minister of State at the Federal Chancellery, was nicknamed "Ben Wisch" on account of his good relations with the Arab states. He led the negotiations with the authorities in the Somalian capital Mogadishu where the hijacked Lufthansa aircraft "Landshut" had been standing at the airport since October 17, 1977. On that very same day preparations began for the storming of the Boeing 737, a model of which Wischnewski is holding here.

Die GSG 9, eine 1973 gegründete Spezialeinheit des Bundesgrenzschutzes, befreite in der Nacht des 17./18.10.1977 die 86 Passagiere und 4 Besatzungsmitglieder des Lufthansa-Flugzeugs, das vier Tage zuvor auf dem Weg von Mallorca nach Frankfurt entführt worden war. Am 20.10. dankte Bundeskanzler Helmut Schmidt der nach Bonn zurückgekehrten Truppe und ihrem Kommandeur Ulrich Wegener für den erfolgreichen Einsatz, bei dem alle Geiseln mit Ausnahme des Kapitäns der »Landshut« unversehrt blieben: Jürgen Schumann war vom Anführer der palästinensischen Terroristen in einer grausamen Demonstration ihrer Entschlossenheit am 16.10. erschossen worden.

In the night of October 17-18, 1977 the GSG 9, a special unit of the federal border guards set up in 1973, rescued the 86 passengers and four crew members of the Lufthansa aircraft, which had been hijacked four days previously while on route from Majorca to Frankfurt. On October 20 Chancellor Helmut Schmidt thanked the unit, for their successful mission, during which all the hostages had been rescued unharmed except for the captain of the "Landshut": Jürgen Schumann had been shot dead by the ringleader of the Palestinian terrorists on October 16 in a savage demonstration of their determination.

(gegenüber) Am 19.10.1977 erhielt Bundeskanzler Schmidt die Nachricht, daß Hanns Martin Schleyer kaltblütig ermordet worden war. Wenig später, am 25.10., saß der Kanzler beim Trauergottesdienst für den Ermordeten neben Frau Schleyer. Was ihn in diesen Tagen bewegte, hat er in seiner Regierungserklärung zu den Ereignissen selbst formuliert: »Wer weiß, daß er so oder so, trotz allen Bemühens, mit Versäumnis und Schuld belastet sein wird, wie immer er handelt, der wird von sich selbst nicht sagen wollen, er habe alles getan und alles sei richtig gewesen... Wohl aber wird er sagen dürfen: Dieses und dieses haben wir entschieden, jenes und jenes haben wir aus diesen oder jenen Gründen unterlassen. Alles dies haben wir zu verantworten.«

(opposite) On October 19, 1977 Chancellor Schmidt received the news that Hanns Martin Schleyer had been murdered in cold blood. Shortly after, on October 25 the Chancellor sat next to Mrs. Schleyer at the funeral service for the victim. In his government statement concerning these events he put into words what he had thought and felt during those days: "Anyone who knows that either way, whatever he does, despite all his efforts, he will bear the burden of guilt and failure, will not wish to claim that he did everything possible and that everything he did was right. But what he can say is: this is what we decided to do, and this is what we decided not to do for this and this reason. For all this we bear the responsibility."

Die Angehörigen der Terroropfer hatten unter dem irrwitzigen Kampf der selbsternannten Weltverbesserer am meisten zu leiden. Keine Form der menschlichen Anteilnahme vermochte die Sinnlosigkeit des Geschehens aufzuheben. Diese Erfahrung mag die Witwe von Siegfried Buback bewegt haben, als sie, begleitet von Bundespräsident Scheel, am 13.4.1977 nach dem Staatsakt in Karlsruhe den Blick zum Himmel hob.

The families of the terrorists' victims suffered most from the insane battle waged by the self-appointed world improvers. No manifestation of human sympathy could count in the balance against the senselessness of these events. Maybe this was what made Siegfried Buback's widow raise her eyes to heaven after the state funeral in Karlsruhe on April 13, 1977, at which she was escorted by Federal President Scheel.

Innerdeutsche Beziehungen / The two Germanies

Die innerdeutschen Beziehungen bewegten sich im Spannungsfeld zwischen Normalisierung und fortdauernder Anomalität. Im Mai 1974 nahmen die Ständigen Vertretungen der DDR und der Bundesrepublik in Bonn bzw. Ostberlin ihre Arbeit auf. Erster Vertreter der Bundesrepublik wurde der vormalige Staatssekretär im Bundeskanzleramt, Günter Gaus – hier am 20.5.1975 im Interview mit dem Leiter des Ostberliner ARD-Studios, Lothar Loewe. Wie verkrampft das Verhältnis zwischen beiden Teilen Deutschlands dennoch blieb, zeigte sich nicht zuletzt im Dezember 1976, als Loewe wegen seiner angeblich negativen Berichterstattung aus der DDR ausgewiesen wurde.

Relations between the two parts of Germany oscillated between the two poles of normalization and continuing abnormality. In May 1974 the Permanent Representatives of the GDR and the Federal Republic took up their posts in Bonn and East Berlin respectively. The first representative of the Federal Republic was Günter Gaus, formerly state secretary at the Chancellery – here on May 20, 1975 being interviewed by Lothar Loewe, the head of the ARD studio in East Berlin. However, Loewe's expulsion from the GDR in December 1976 on the grounds of alleged negative reporting showed as clearly as anything how strained the relationship between the two parts of Germany remained.

Trotz der bestehenden Verträge versuchte die DDR wiederholt, den innerdeutschen Reiseverkehr durch die Erhöhung des Mindestumtauschs oder auch durch direkte Behinderungen einzuschränken. Nach Anhebung des Pflichtumtauschs auf 25 DM pro Tag gingen im Oktober 1980 die Anträge auf Passierscheine für einen Besuch im Ostteil der Stadt Berlin in den Westberliner Ausgabestellen um 60 Prozent gegenüber dem Vorjahr zurück.

Despite existing agreements the GDR repeatedly attempted to restrict travel between the two parts of Germany by raising the minimum amount of currency to be exchanged by visitors from the West as well as by direct obstruction. In October 1980, after the exchange minimum had been increased to DM 25 per day, applications for permits to visit East Berlin dropped by 60% against the previous year.

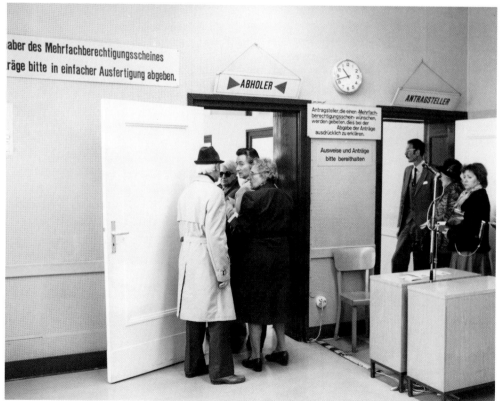

Eine Aufnahme wie diese war in den siebziger und achtziger Jahren kaum vorstellbar. Die Anlagen der Grenzübergangsstellen galten als militärisches Sperrgebiet. DDR-Bürger bekamen sie erst 1990 zu Gesicht, als auch dieses Foto entstand.

A photo such as this was most unimaginable in the seventies and eighties. The areas around border crossing points were treated as a military prohibited zone and were off limits. Citizens of the GDR did not get to see them until 1990, when this photo was taken.

Grenzübergang Heinrich-Heine-Straße in Berlin. Der innerdeutsche Verkehr verlief weitgehend einseitig. Während Bundesbürger und Westberliner inzwischen relativ leicht in den anderen Teil des Landes reisen konnten, war für die arbeitende Bevölkerung der DDR eine Reise in die Bundesrepublik allenfalls in dringenden Familienangelegenheiten denkbar. Selbst diese Möglichkeit wurde von den Ostberliner Behörden Ende der siebziger Jahre immer seltener gewährt.

The border crossing point in the Heinrich Heine Straße in Berlin. Travel between the two parts of Germany was to a large extent in one direction only. Whereas it was relatively easy by then for citizens of the Federal Republic and of West Berlin to travel to the other part of Germany, a journey to the Federal Republic for working people in the GDR was something that could be considered only for the most urgent of family matters. By the end of the seventies even this opportunity was being granted more and more rarely by the East Berlin authorities.

1974–1982

Einen Höhepunkt der Abgrenzungsbemühungen des SED-Regimes bildete die Zwangsausbürgerung des Liedermachers Wolf Biermann – hier am 19.11. 1976 in Köln bei einer gemeinsamen Pressekonferenz mit den Schriftstellern Heinrich Böll und Günter Wallraff. Dieses Vorgehen sprach den Verpflichtungen der KSZE-Schlußakte von Helsinki Hohn, entlarvte die Arroganz der SED-Machthaber und wurde zu einem Meilenstein für die in der DDR wachsende Oppositionsbewegung der achtziger Jahre.

The attempts by the SED régime to assert the separate identity of the GDR reached a peak when the writer and singer Wolf Biermann – here on November 19, 1976 at a joint press conference with the writers Heinrich Böll and Günter Wallraff in Cologne – was stripped of his GDR citzenship. This measure made a mockery of the commitments undertaken in the CSCE Final Act in Helsinki, exposed the arrogance of the SED rulers and became a milestone for the growing opposition movement of the eighties in the GDR.

Geradezu gespenstisch war die Atmosphäre im mecklenburgischen Güstrow, das Bundeskanzler Schmidt und der Staatsratsvorsitzende der DDR Honecker am 13.12.1981 besuchten. Hunderte von uniformierten und zivilen Sicherheitskräften versetzten das Städtchen in den Belagerungszustand. Unbescholtene Bürger waren zuvor als »negative Elemente« in Polizeigewahrsam genommen worden, nur ausgesuchte Kader durften sich überhaupt in der Nähe der prominenten Besucher blicken lassen. Ein zweites »Erfurt«, als die Jubelrufe der DDR-Bevölkerung für den damaligen Bundeskanzler Brandt um die Welt gingen, sollte unter allen Umständen verhindert werden.

The atmosphere in Güstrow in Mecklenburg was positively eerie when Chancellor Schmidt and Honecker, the President of the GDR State Council, paid a visit there on December 13, 1981. Hundreds of uniformed and plainclothes security police created a state of siege in the little town. Respectable citizens had previously been taken into police custody as "negative elements," only groups of selected party members were allowed anywhere near the distinguished visitors. A repetition of "Erfurt," when the cheers of the GDR populace for the then Chancellor Brandt went around the world, was to be prevented at any cost.

Das Bild der Spaziergänger am Werbellinsee versprach mehr als die deutsch-deutsche Begegnung vom 11. bis 13.12.1981 hielt. Die Gespräche zwischen Helmut Schmidt und Erich Honecker blieben ohne besonderes Ergebnis. Allein die Tatsache ihres Stattfindens machte in Anbetracht der erkalteten Ost-West-Beziehungen ihre politische Bedeutung aus.

The picture of the men walking by the Lake Werbellin seemed to promise more than was in fact achieved at the intra-German meeting from December 11-13, 1981. The talks between Helmut Schmidt and Erich Honecker did not produce any particular results. Given the coldness in East-West relations, their political significance lay solely in the fact that they took place at all.

Verabschiedung in Güstrow: Erich Honecker reichte dem Bundeskanzler vor der Abfahrt des Sonderzugs ein Bonbon. Sehr viel mehr hatte Helmut Schmidt nach diesem Besuch auch nicht in der Hand. Neben ihm im Abteilfenster der Bundesminister für innerdeutsche Beziehungen Egon Franke.

Farewells in Güstrow: before the special train departed Erich Honecker gave the Chancellor a sweet. Helmut Schmidt had very little more to show for this visit. Next to him at the compartment window is Egon Franke, Minister for Intra-German Relations.

Verabschiedung des Europäischen Währungssystems am 5.12.1978 durch den Europäischen Rat in Brüssel. Von links: der französische Außenminister François-Poncet, Staatspräsident Giscard d'Estaing, Bundeskanzler Schmidt als amtierender Ratspräsident, Außenminister Genscher. Damit war ein erster Schritt in Richtung auf eine gemeinsame europäische Währung gemacht.

The European Council in Brussels approved the European Monetary System on December 5, 1978. From left to right: the French Foreign Minister François-Poncet, President Giscard d'Estaing, Chancellor Schmidt (who was President of the Council at the time), Foreign Minister Genscher. This was a first step in the direction of a common European currency.

Kanzlerspuren – Mantel und Prinz-Heinrich-Mütze des Bundeskanzlers, abgelegt vor den deutsch-französischen Gipfelgesprächen am 3. und 4. Februar 1977 in Paris.

Traces of the Chancellor: the Chancellor's overcoat and Prince Heinrich cap which he took off before the Franco-German summit talks in Paris on February 3-4, 1977.

Gipfelkontakte / Summit Contacts

Bundeskanzler Helmut Schmidt und US-Präsident Gerald Ford am 5./6.12.1974 auf dem Balkon des Weißen Hauses in Washington. Seit der »Atlantischen Deklaration« vom 26.6.1974, mit der die zeitweiligen Kontroversen zwischen den USA und den westeuropäischen Staaten bereinigt worden waren, konnten auch die deutsch-amerikanischen Beziehungen als ungetrübt gelten. Doch mit dem Wiederaufleben der Spannungen zwischen den Supermächten ergaben sich bald neue Meinungsverschiedenheiten.

Chancellor Helmut Schmidt and United States President Gerald Ford on the balcony of the White House in Washington on December 5-6, 1974. Following the "Atlantic Declaration" of June 26, 1974 which settled the temporary disputes between the US and the states of western Europe, relations between Germany and America could be described as untroubled. But tensions between the superpowers soon revived, bringing fresh differences of opinion.

Die während des Deutschland-Besuches vor Präsident Carter angetretenen Truppen ahnten von den schweren Verstimmungen auf höchster Ebene naturgemäß nichts.

The troops that were drawn up before President Carter during his visit to Germany naturally had no idea of the high degree of bad feeling at the top level.

In der Amtszeit des amerikanischen Präsidenten Jimmy Carter erreichten die Beziehungen zwischen der Bundesrepublik und den USA einen Tiefpunkt. Während Carter – wie Helmut Schmidt es sah – mit seiner Menschenrechtskampagne gegen die UdSSR die Aussichten auf einen Abschluß des Abrüstungsabkommens SALT II verdüsterte, suchte er der Bundesrepublik die Verantwortung für die Einführung der umstrittenen Neutronenwaffe zuzuschieben, deren Produktion er am Ende jedoch selbst verhinderte. Beim Deutschlandbesuch Carters vom 13. bis 15.7.1978, als das Bild entstand, war die Vertrauensbasis zwischen beiden Politikern bereits gestört. Carter verzieh es dem Bundeskanzler nicht, daß dieser ihn wiederholt im Kreise der Regierungschefs durch barsche Belehrungen brüskiert hatte.

During President Jimmy Carter's term in office relations between the Federal Republic and the US reached a new low. As Helmut Schmidt saw the matter, Carter, while placing obstacles in the way of concluding the SALT II disarmament agreement with his human rights campaign against the USSR, was trying at the same time to make the Federal Republic responsible for the introduction of the controversial neutron weapon, the production of which, however, he himself ultimately prevented. By the time Carter visited Germany, from July 13-15, 1978, when this picture was taken, the basis of trust between the two politicians was already impaired. Carter did not forgive the Chancellor for repeatedly correcting him in a peremptory fashion in the presence of other heads of government.

Das Ehepaar Ronald und Nancy Reagan (Mitte) begrüßt Hannelore und Helmut Schmidt am 21.5.1981 zu einem abendlichen Bankett im Weißen Haus in Washington. Die Beziehungen des Bundeskanzlers zum neuen amerikanischen Präsidenten standen ganz im Zeichen der wiederaufgebrochenen Ost-West-Konfrontation. Reagans ideologischer Feldzug gegen die UdSSR als »Reich des Bösen« kollidierte mit dem Bemühen Schmidts, den Dialog mit den Sowjets fortzuführen. Andererseits weckte der interne deutsche Streit um die Nachrüstung, die der Bundeskanzler selbst gefordert hatte, amerikanische Zweifel an der Bündnistreue der Bundesrepublik. Dies galt umso mehr, als weite Teile von Schmidts eigener Partei den Kanzler in diesem zentralen Punkt im Stich zu lassen drohten.

Ronald Reagan and his wife Nancy (center) welcoming Hannelore and Helmut Schmidt to an evening banquet at the White House in Washington on May 21, 1981. Relations between the Chancellor and the new American President were entirely dominated by the confrontation between East and West that had erupted once again. Reagan's ideological campaign against the USSR as the "evil empire" came into collision with Schmidt's efforts to keep up a dialogue with the Russians. For the Americans, on the other hand, the internal German dispute over updated weaponry, which the Chancellor had himself demanded, cast doubt on the Federal Republic's loyalty to the Alliance. This was all the more so as large sections of Schmidt's own party were threatening to desert the Chancellor on this central issue.

Spiegelbilder einer schwierigen Partnerschaft. Nur eine Woche nach ihrem Amtsantritt führte Bundeskanzler Schmidt am 10./11.5.1979 in London erste Gespräche mit der neuen britischen Premierministerin. Margaret Thatcher, bald als »Iron Lady« bekannt, machte sich in Europa mit der kompromißlosen Verfechtung nationaler Interessen einen Namen. Den Kampf um die Verringerung des britischen EU-Beitrags eröffnete sie zur Verblüffung ihrer Kollegen Ende November 1979 in Dublin mit den Worten: »I want my money back, and I want it now!«

Reflections of a difficult partnership. Chancellor Schmidt had his first talks with the new British Prime Minister in London on May 10-11, 1979 only a week after she took office. Margaret Thatcher, soon to be known as the Iron Lady, made a name for herself in Europe with her uncompromising assertion of national interests. In Dublin in late November 1979 she amazed her fellow politicians when she began her campaign to have Britain's contribution to the EC reduced with the words: "I want my money back, and I want it now!"

Staatsbesuch des Königs Kahlid von Saudi-Arabien vom 16. bis 19.6.1980 in der Bundesrepublik. Die ernsten Gesichter, insbesondere das von Bundeswirtschaftsminister Otto Graf Lambsdorff (rechts außen), vermitteln einen Eindruck von den düsteren Aussichten, die in dieser Zeit der Weltkonjunktur und damit auch der Wirtschaftsentwicklung der Bundesrepublik durch die zweite Ölpreisexplosion drohten.

State visit to the Federal Republic by King Khalid of Saudi Arabia from June 16-19, 1980. The grave faces, especially that of Federal Economics Minister Otto Graf Lambsdorff (far right), conveyed an impression of the gloomy prospects facing the world economy and hence also threatening the economic development of the Federal Republic in the wake of the second oil price explosion.

Das gewachsene Gewicht der Bundesrepublik auf dem internationalen Parkett zeigte sich auch in der Zahl der Besuche ausländischer Staatsmänner und der Auslandsreisen des Bundeskanzlers. 36 offizielle Staatsbesuche und ungezählte Arbeitstreffen führten in den Jahren 1974 bis 1982 Repräsentanten aus aller Welt in das Land. 1978 war Bonn erstmals Tagungsort eines Weltwirtschaftsgipfels. Helmut Schmidt bereiste als erster deutscher Bundeskanzler alle Kontinente. Allein 14mal hielt er sich zu offiziellen Anlässen in den USA auf, 22 Reisen führten ihn nach Frankreich.

The increased weight of the Federal Republic on the international stage could also be seen from the number of visits by foreign statesmen and of the Chancellor's trips abroad. During the years 1974-1982, 36 official state visits and innumerable working meetings brought emissaries from all over the world to Germany. In 1978 Bonn was for the first time the venue for a world economic summit. Helmut Schmidt was the first German Chancellor to travel to all the continents of the world. He made no fewer than 14 official visits to the US and 22 visits to France.

Der israelische Ministerpräsident Jitzhak Rabin (links) mit Regierungssprecher Klaus Bölling am 11.7.1975 vor der Bundespressekonferenz in Bonn. Bölling verstand es meisterhaft – gestützt auf ein enges Vertrauensverhältnis zum Bundeskanzler –, diese Pressekonferenzen zu zelebrieren und dabei den wißbegierigen Journalisten wertvolle Informationen weiterzureichen, ohne allzuviel preiszugeben. Diese Mischung scheint es auch Rabin angetan zu haben.

The Israeli Prime Minister Yitzhak Rabin (left) with government spokesman Klaus Bölling on July 11, 1975 before the press conference in Bonn. Bölling, a close confidant of the Chancellor's, was a master at stage-managing these press conferences, passing on important information to clamoring journalists without giving away any great secrets. This combination seems also to have appealed to Rabin.

Bundeskanzler Helmut Schmidt empfängt am 21.11.1974 in seinem Arbeitszimmer in Bonn den schwedischen Ministerpräsidenten Olof Palme. Schweden hatte unter anderem durch seinen mit Willy Brandt eng befreundeten Botschafter Sven Backlund die »Neue Ostpolitik« der sozialliberalen Koalition auf vielen diskreten Wegen nachhaltig unterstützt. Die Beziehung zwischen den beiden sozialdemokratischen Regierungschefs stand in dieser Tradition.

Chancellor Helmut Schmidt receiving the Swedish Prime Minister Olof Palme in his study in Bonn on November 21, 1974. Sweden had in many discreet ways given sustained support to the "New Ostpolitik" of the social-liberal coalition, among them via its ambassador Sven Backlund, who was a close friend of Willy Brandt. The two Social Democrat heads of government followed in their wake as regards their own relations.

(gegenüber) Ein Höhepunkt des Jahres 1980 war der Besuch von Papst Johannes Paul II. – hier das »Papamobil« vor dem Kölner Dom – vom 15. bis 19.11.1980 in der Bundesrepublik.

(opposite) A high point of 1980 was the visit to the Federal Republic by Pope John Paul II from November 15-19. The "Popemobile" is seen here in front of Cologne Cathedral.

Erstmals trafen sich vom 15. bis 17.11.1975 auf Schloß Rambouillet bei Paris die Staats- und Regierungschefs der USA, Frankreichs, Großbritanniens, der Bundesrepublik, Italiens und Japans, um ihre gemeinsamen Anstrengungen zur Bekämpfung der Weltwirtschaftskrise abzustimmen. Von links: der amerikanische Präsident Gerald Ford, der französische Staatspräsident Valéry Giscard d'Estaing und Bundeskanzler Helmut Schmidt. Die beiden letzteren hatten auf die Institutionalisierung solcher Gipfeltreffen in der Erkenntnis gedrängt, daß nichts in der internationalen Politik so wertvoll und unersetzlich ist wie der persönliche Kontakt und Meinungsaustausch der verantwortlichen Regierungschefs.

From November 15-17, 1975 the political leaders of the US, France, Britain, the Federal Republic, Italy and Japan met for the first time at Rambouillet Castle outside Paris in order to coordinate their joint efforts to combat the world economic crisis. From left to right: American President Gerald Ford, French President Valéry Giscard d'Estaing and Chancellor Helmut Schmidt. The two last-named had pressed for summit meetings of this kind to be insitutionalized, realizing that in international politics nothing is as valuable, indeed indispensable as personal contact and exchange of views between responsible heads of government.

Protestbewegungen / Protest movements

Zu der bis dahin größten Demonstration in der Geschichte der Bundesrepublik versammelten sich am 10.10.1981 250 000 Anhänger der Friedensbewegung auf der Hofgartenwiese in Bonn. Daß ein Teil dieser Friedensbewegung durch kommunistische Gruppen unterwandert und mit Finanzmitteln aus der DDR subventioniert worden war, wurde erst nach Öffnung der Archive der Staatssicherheit bekannt. Diese Mittel für subversive Propaganda waren aus Sicht der SED gut angelegt, denn die Unterstützung, die die zunehmend auch antiamerikanische Tendenzen aufweisende Kampagne gegen die Nachrüstung aus den Reihen der SPD erhielt, bedeutete für die Regierung Schmidt/Genscher eine immer bedrohlichere Zerreißprobe.

250,000 suppporters of the peace movement assembled on the "Hofgartenwiese" in Bonn on October 10, 1981 for what was the largest demonstration hitherto in the history of the Federal Republic. Only after the archives of the State Security were opened up did it become known that sections of this peace movement had been infiltrated by communist groups and subsidised with funds from the GDR. From the point of view of the SED these funds for subversive propaganda were a good investment: the support from the ranks of the SPD for the campaign against the deployment of new weapons, which was also taking on an increasingly anti-American slant, confronted the Schmidt/Genscher goverment with a growing threat and a crucial test of mettl.

»Bald kommt das 'Aus' für Schmidt und Strauss«: Dieser Slogan auf dem Transparent der »Grünen« bei einer Kundgebung am 14.10.1979 in Bonn symbolisiert eine Tiefenströmung der Ende der siebziger Jahre zunehmenden Massendemonstrationen. Die Proteste richteten sich nicht allein gegen einzelne politische Entscheidungen, sondern drückten zugleich ein grundsätzliches Mißtrauen gegen die Parteiendemokratie und ihre Repräsentanten aus. Die Bonner Politik schien im Widerstreit wirtschaftlicher Zwänge, parteipolitischer Interessen und parlamentarischer Verfahrensregeln nicht mehr hinreichend fähig, einen gesellschaftlichen Konsens herzustellen. In einer Zeit großer Herausforderungen, die vielerorts Ängste hervorriefen, verbreitete sich ein Gefühl der Lähmung und Ohnmacht.

"Schmidt and Strauß will soon be out": this slogan on the banner of the "Greens" at a rally in Bonn on October 14, 1979 reveals an undercurrent in the mass demonstrations which took place with increasing frequency in the late seventies. The protests were not only against particular political decisions but were at the same time the expression of a fundamental distrust of democratic party politics and those involved in them. In the clash of economic necessity, party political interests and the rules of parliamentary procedure, politics as practised in Bonn no longer seemed sufficiently capable of creating a social consensus. At a time when great challenges created widespread anxiety, a feeling of paralysis and powerlessness took hold.

Anläßlich der Gipfelkonferenz der NATO-Staaten am 10.6.1982 in Bonn, in deren Umfeld der amerikanische Präsident Ronald Reagan die Bundesrepublik und West-Berlin besuchte, kam es zu einem neuen Höhepunkt der Massendemonstrationen. Am 6.6.1982 nahmen in Bonn etwa 100 000 Menschen an einer von der CDU-Opposition unterstützten Kundgebung für die Atlantische Allianz und für die deutsch-amerikanische Freundschaft teil.

During the NATO summit conference in Bonn on June 10, 1982, as an offshoot of which American President Ronald Reagan visited the Federal Republic and West Berlin, mass demonstrations reached a new high point. On June 6, 1982 about 100,000 people took part in a rally in Bonn, supported by the CDU opposition, in favor of the Atlantic Alliance and German-American friendship.

Besetztes Haus in Berlin-Kreuzberg, Mai 1981. Das illegale Bewohnen leerstehender Gebäude stellte die Behörden in vielen westdeutschen Großstädten vor schwierige Probleme. Polizeiliche Zwangsräumungen führten meist zu schweren Auseinandersetzungen. Doch auch die Versuche, zwischen Hausbesitzern und Hausbesetzern Nutzungsverträge zu vermitteln, waren problematisch, da sie die sogenannten »Instandbesetzungen« nachträglich legalisierten.

A house in Berlin-Kreuzberg occupied by squatters in May 1981. Illegal occupation of empty buildings created difficult problems for local authorities in many West German cities. Evictions by the police usually led to severe clashes. But attempts to negotiate utilization agreements between house owners and squatters (who claimed to have carried out necessary repairs) also raised problems since they retrospectively legalized the occupancy.

Die Räumung eines besetzten Hauses wie hier im September 1981 in der Berliner Winderfeldtstraße erforderte ein umfangreiches Polizeiaufgebot und führte bisweilen zu bürgerkriegsähnlichen Konfrontationen.

Evicting squatters, as here in Winderfeldtstraße in Berlin in September 1981 required a substantial police contingent and sometimes led to clashes that smacked of civil war.

Am 10.6.1982 demonstrierten Anhänger der Friedensbewegung – unter ihnen Soldaten der Bundeswehr sowie der ehemalige Bundeswehrgeneral Gert Bastian, der Künstler Joseph Beuys und der »Grünen«-Politiker Lukas Beckmann – in Bonn gegen die Nachrüstung.

On June 10, 1982 supporters of the peace movement demonstrated in Bonn against the updating of NATO's nuclear capability; they included soldiers from the Federal German armed forces and the former general Gert Bastian, the artist Joseph Beuys and the "Green" politician Lukas Beckmann.

Am 11.6.1982 kam es während des Besuchs von US-Präsident Reagan in West-Berlin zu schweren Krawallen. Die Friedensbewegung wurde mittlerweile von Gewalttätern mißbraucht, die nichts anderes bewegte als die Abneigung gegen den Staat als solchen.

On June 11, 1982 during US President Reagan's visit to West Berlin there was serious rioting. The peace movement was by then being misused by violent elements who were motivated merely by hostility to the state as such.

Endzeitstimmung / Apocalyptic mood

Zielbestimmung nach dem Wahlsieg: Bundeskanzler Helmut Schmidt und Bundesaußenminister Hans-Dietrich Genscher am Abend des 5.10.1980 nach der Bekanntgabe der ersten Hochrechnungen zur Bundestagswahl. Hinter ihnen freuen sich die Begründer der sozialliberalen Koalition, Willy Brandt und Walter Scheel.

Setting their sights after the election victory: Chancellor Helmut Schmidt and Foreign Minister Hans-Dietrich Genscher on the evening of election day, October 5, 1980, after the first projections had been announced. Behind them the founders of the social-liberal coalition, Willy Brandt and Walter Scheel, show their delight.

Als Bundeskanzler Schmidt, Außenminister Genscher und Innenminister Baum am 14.1.1982 im Bundestag der Antwort des Oppositionsführers Helmut Kohl auf eine Regierungserklärung des Kanzlers lauschten, war das verschlechterte Koalitionsklima bereits an ihren Gesichtern abzulesen.

As Chancellor Schmidt, Foreign Minister Genscher and Minister of the Interior Baum listened to the opposition leader Helmut Kohl's reply, in parliament on January 14, 1982, to a government statement by the Chancellor, the deteriorating mood of the coalition was already written on their faces.

Hauptstreitpunkt zwischen den Koalitionspartnern war angesichts der neuen ökonomischen Krisenzeichen am Ende der Regierung Schmidt/Genscher die Wirtschafts- und Finanzpolitik. Vor allem Bundeswirtschaftsminister Otto Graf Lambsdorff verlangte eine Kehrtwende zur Beschneidung der Sozialleistungen und zur Entlastung der Unternehmen. Zugleich geriet er selbst in den Strudel der sogenannten Parteispenden-Affäre, die die Glaubwürdigkeit der Bonner Politik in der Öffentlichkeit beeinträchtigte und schwerwiegende Rückwirkungen auf die sozialliberale Koalition hatte.

The main bone of contention between the coalition partners, faced with renewed signs of economic crisis at the tail end of the Schmidt/Genscher government, was economic and financial policy. It was above all Economics Minister Otto Graf Lambsdorff who demanded a radical change of policy with cuts in social security benefits and easing of the burdens on businesses. At the time he himself became involved in the turmoil of the party donations scandal which damaged the government's credibility among the general public and had grave consequences for the social-liberal coalition.

Auch die sogenannte »Troika« der SPD-Führung – Bundeskanzler Schmidt, der Parteivorsitzende Brandt und der Fraktionsvorsitzende Wehner in der Sitzung am 13.9.1982 – funktionierte am Ende der sozialliberalen Ära nicht mehr. Brandt und der linke Parteiflügel der SPD waren immer weniger bereit, dem unpopulären Kurs des Kanzlers in der Sicherheits- und Wirtschaftspolitik zu folgen. Einschnitte in das soziale Netz zur Sanierung der Staatsfinanzen lehnte eine Mehrheit in der SPD ebenso ab wie die Stationierung neuer westlicher Mittelstreckenraketen im Gefolge des NATO-Doppelbeschlusses. Die Kräfte des 76jährigen »Fuhrmanns« Wehner reichten nicht aus, um Schmidt den Rücken freizuhalten und die SPD-Fraktion auf Kanzlerkurs zu zwingen.

By the end of the social-liberal era, the so-called SPD leadership "troika" – Chancellor Schmidt, party chairman Brandt and party whip Wehner, here at a meeting of the parliamentary party on September 13, 1982 – was no longer viable. Brandt and the left wing of the SPD were less willing to follow the Chancellor's unpopular line in security and economic policy. A majority in the SPD were opposed to cuts in social security benefits in order to put government finances in order, and to the stationing of new western medium-range missiles following the NATO dual-track resolution. The 76 year-old "coachman" Wehner no longer had sufficient energy to cover Schmidt's back and compel the SPD parliamentary group to follow the Chancellor's line.

(gegenüber) Am 5.2.1982 gelang es dem Bundeskanzler zum letzten Mal, die Koalitionsparteien mit einer Vertrauensfrage im Bundestag geschlossen hinter sich zu sammeln. Als der SPD-Fraktionsvorsitzende Wehner gratulierte, hatten alle 269 Abgeordneten der Regierungsfraktionen für Schmidts Verbleiben im Amt gestimmt. Doch die Spannungen waren längst zu stark, als daß sie mit solchen Schachzügen dauerhaft hätten beseitigt werden können.

(opposite) On February 5, 1982 the Chancellor succeeded for the last time in uniting the coalition parties behind him when he asked for a parliamentary vote of confidence. The SPD party whip Wehner is seen congratulating him after all 269 members of the government parliamentary groups had voted for Schmidt's continuation in office. But tensions had for a long time been too severe to be permanently removed by such maneuvers.

Der Tag des Abschieds: Nachdem am 17.9.1982 die vier FDP-Minister im Kabinett Schmidt zurückgetreten waren, einigten sich die Führungen von FDP und CDU/CSU, die verbliebene SPD-Minderhetsregierung abzulösen und Oppositionsführer Helmut Kohl zum neuen Bundeskanzler zu wählen. Hildegard Hamm-Brücher, die unmittelbar nach dem Mißtrauensvotum am 1.10.1982 dem SPD-Fraktionsvorsitzenden Wehner ihr Bedauern ausdrückte, war für eine Fortsetzung der sozialliberalen Koalition eingetreten.

Departure day. After the resignation of the four FDP ministers in Schmidt's cabinet on September 17, 1982, the FDP and CDU/CSU leaders agreed to take over from the remaining SPD minority government and to elect the opposition leader Helmut Kohl to be the new Chancellor. Hildegard Hamm-Brücher, who immediately after the vote of no confidence on October 1, 1982 expressed her regret to SPD party whip Herbert Wehner, had also supported the continuation of the social-liberal coalition.

Unter den Augen der Welt . . . der bitterste Augenblick: Helmut Schmidt am 1.10.1982 während der Bekanntgabe des Ergebnisses des konstruktiven Mißtrauensvotums. Neben ihm auf der Regierungsbank der Bundesminister für innerdeutsche Beziehungen und zuletzt auch Stellvertreter des Bundeskanzlers, Egon Franke.

As the world watched . . . the bitterest moment: Helmut Schmidt on October 1, 1982 as the result of the constructive vote of no confidence is announced. Next to him on the government front bench is Egon Franke, Minister for Intra-German Relations and by the end also Deputy Chancellor.

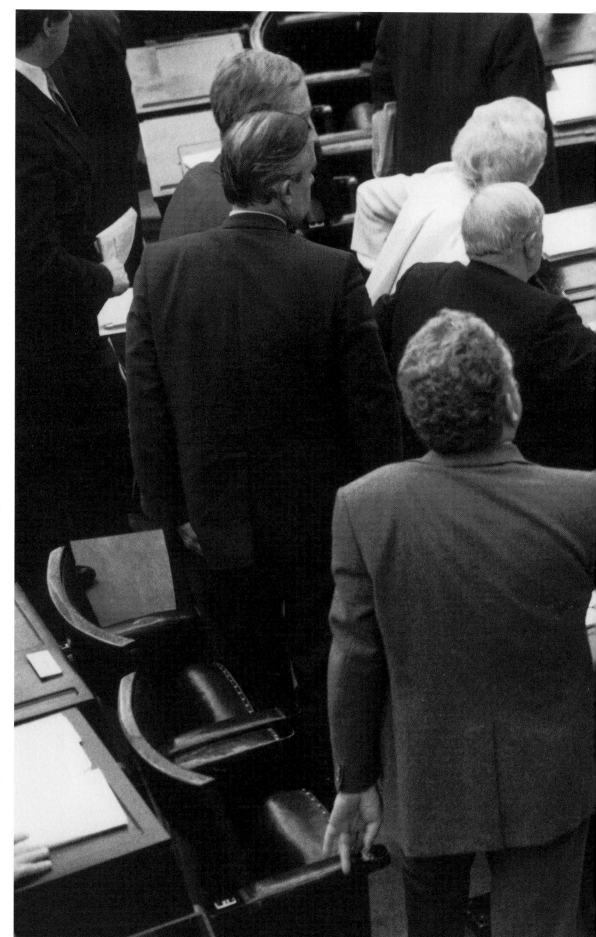

Der Lotse geht von Bord: Helmut Schmidt verläßt am 1.10.1982 nach seiner Abwahl den Plenarsaal des Bundestages in Bonn. Am Abend des folgenden Tages beobachtete Marion Gräfin Dönhoff seine Ankunft auf dem Flughafen seiner Heimatstadt Hamburg: »Er stieg langsam und schweigend die Treppe herunter. Niemand begleitete ihn. Ich dachte an viele glanzvolle Auftritte in Frankreich und Amerika, an entscheidende Verhandlungen in Polen und der Sowjetunion – und nun ein einsamer Mann auf diesem dunklen Platz. Das war nun wirklich das Ende einer großen politischen Karriere.«

The pilot leaves the ship: Helmut Schmidt leaving the plenary chamber of the federal parliament in Bonn on October 1, 1982 after being voted out of office. On the evening of the following day Countess Marion Dönhoff watched him arrive at the airport of his native city of Hamburg: "He walked down the steps slowly, without a word. Nobody accompanied him. I thought of his many brilliant visits to France and America, of decisive negotiations in Poland and the Soviet Union – and now a lonely man in this dark spot. It really was the end of a great political career."

1982–1989

Die christlich-liberale Koalition bis zur Einheit
The Christian Liberal Coalition until unification

Benediktiner-Mönche bei Bundeskanzler Helmut Kohl am 12.9.1983 im
Kanzleramt in Bonn.

Benedictine monks with Chancellor Helmut Kohl at the Chancellery in Bonn
on September 12, 1983.

Als Helmut Kohl, der CDU-Partei- und Fraktionsvorsitzende, am 1.10.1982 zum neuen Bundeskanzler ernannt wurde, war er mit 52 Jahren der jüngste Regierungschef in der westdeutschen Nachkriegsgeschichte. Mit ihm trat, wie sein Vorgänger Helmut Schmidt bei der Amtsübergabe zu Recht betonte, zum ersten Mal ein Vertreter jener Generation an die Spitze der Bundesregierung, die den Zweiten Weltkrieg nur noch im Kindesalter erlebt hatte. Der Erfahrungshorizont dieser Generation war von der Entwicklung der Bundesrepublik geprägt, die nun ihrerseits mehr und mehr als eigenständige Epoche der deutschen Geschichte betrachtet wurde.

Deutlichstes Symptom des damit einhergehenden Bewußtseinswandels war die intensive Auseinandersetzung mit der Vergangenheit, die in den achtziger Jahren anläßlich der verschiedenen Gedenkveranstaltungen öffentlich ausgetragen wurde. Die Diskussion 1984 um den deutschen Widerstand gegen das Hitler-Regime, die Rede von Bundespräsident Richard von Weizsäcker zum vierzigsten Jahrestag des Kriegsendes am 8.5.1985 und der sogenannte »Historikerstreit« im Jahr 1986 mobilisierten die Öffentlichkeit und bewiesen, daß keine Verdrängung oder Tabuisierung der NS-Zeit stattfand, sondern ein differenzierter Umgang mit der nationalsozialistischen Hypothek möglich wurde. Demgegenüber standen 1989 die Feierlichkeiten zum 40. Geburtstag der Bundesrepublik betont im Zeichen der neuen, demokratisch und westlich orientierten Traditionslinie deutscher Geschichte.

Die Bundesrepublik Deutschland erhielt so in den achtziger Jahren nun auch im Bewußtsein ihrer Bürger jenen Status der Normalität, den sie wirtschaftlich und politisch seit den sechziger bzw. siebziger Jahren längst erreicht hatte. Daß diese Normalisierung ausgerechnet zu einem Zeitpunkt abgeschlossen wurde, als die Grundlagen des bipolaren Staatssystems vor ihrem Zusammenbruch standen, war seinerzeit nicht erkennbar.

Der Regierungswechsel

Die »Wende« im Herbst 1982 kam nicht völlig überraschend. Schon im Frühjahr des Jahres hatten die Landtags- bzw. Bürgerschaftswahlen in Niedersachsen und Hamburg den Wandel angezeigt. Die SPD hatte – selbst in der Heimatstadt des populären Bundeskanzlers Helmut Schmidt – dramatische Verluste, die CDU dagegen sensationelle Gewinne verbucht. Vor allem aber war die FDP bei beiden Wahlgängen von der jeweiligen Formation der »Grünen« überrundet und in Hamburg sogar aus dem Parlament geworfen worden. Es wurde immer deutlicher, daß das Bündnis mit der SPD mittlerweile für die FDP die Existenzfrage heraufbeschwor und bei einer weiteren Fixierung auf diesen Partner der politische Untergang drohte. Für die im September bevorstehenden Landtagswahlen in Hessen legten sich die Freien Demokraten daher im Juni 1982 erstmals auf eine Koalitionsaussage zugunsten der CDU fest.

Vor diesem Hintergrund hielten sich den ganzen Sommer Gerüchte über einen unmittelbar bevorstehenden Bruch des sozialliberalen Regierungsbündnisses. Offenbar suchten beide Koalitionspartner nur noch den geeigneten Anlaß für die Beendigung ihrer Zusammenarbeit. Dieser wurde Anfang September mit dem sogenannten »Lambsdorff-Papier« gefunden, in dem der Bundeswirtschaftsminister zur Sanierung der Staatsfinanzen eine vollständige

When Helmut Kohl, CDU party chairman and leader of the parliamentary party, was elected as the new Federal Chancellor on October 1, 1982, he was, at 52, the youngest head of government in postwar West German history. As his predecessor Helmut Schmidt rightly emphasized when handing over the reins of office, Kohl was the first head of government to belong to the generation that had experienced the Second World War only as children. The experiences and perceptions of that generation were bound up with the evolution of the Federal Republic, which in its turn was now increasingly regarded as a separate period of German history.

The clearest symptom of the change in awareness that went along with this process was the intensive debate about the past, which in the eighties was conducted in public in connection with various memorial events. The discussion in 1984 concerning the German resistance to the Hitler régime, the speech made by President Richard von Weizsäcker on May 8, 1985 to mark the 40th anniversary of the end of the war, and the so-called *Historikerstreit* (conflict among the historians) in 1986 – these activated the general public and proved that there was no consensus for continuing to repress the National Socialist era and to make it a taboo subject, but that it was possible to deal with the burden of the National Socialist legacy in a discriminating fashion. On the other hand, the ceremonies in 1989 marking the 40th anniversary of the founding of the Federal Republic were emphatically oriented towards Germany's new, democratic, West-oriented historical tradition.

Thus in the eighties, the Federal Republic of Germany achieved in the minds of its citizens that status of normality which it had long since achieved in the economic and political spheres in the sixties and seventies respectively. There was no way of knowing then that by the time this normalization process was complete, the basis for the bipolar existence of two states was shortly to collapse.

The Change of Government

The "change" in autumn 1982 did not come as a complete surprise. Back in the spring of that year the regional elections in Lower Saxony and the elections to the City Parliament in Hamburg had indicated that a change was in the air. Even in popular Chancellor Helmut Schmidt's native city the SPD suffered severe losses, whilst the CDU achieved sensational gains. But it was the FDP above all which in both elections was outstripped by the local grouping of the Greens, and in Hamburg was even thrown out of the City Parliament. It was becoming increasingly clear that by now the alliance with the SPD was putting the very existence of the FDP at risk, that it was threatened with political ruin if it remained attached to this partner. In June 1982, therefore, with regional elections due in Hesse in September, the FDP committed itself for the first time to a coalition with the CDU.

Against this background, rumors of an imminent collapse of the social-liberal government alliance circulated throughout the summer. It was evident that both coalition partners were merely looking for an appropriate pretext for terminating their cooperation. They found it in early September in the so-called "Lambsdorff Paper," in which the Economics Minister proposed a complete change of course in economic and finance policy in order to put government finances

einer perspektivlosen Konfrontationspolitik überging. Die Bundesrepublik wurde im Sommer 1984 mit einer »Revanchismus«-Kampagne überzogen, die DDR mit demonstrativen Manövern sowjetischer Streitkräfte und dem Verbot des geplanten Besuchs von Erich Honecker in Bonn zur Linientreue gezwungen.

Dementsprechend blieb die Politik der Regierung Kohl/Genscher gegenüber der UdSSR in den ersten Jahren zwangsläufig zurückhaltend. Mit der Fortführung der umfangreichen Wirtschaftskontakte setzte sie freilich, trotz amerikanischer Vorbehalte, auf diesem Feld ein Zeichen der Kontinuität.

Auch nach dem Amtsantritt des neuen sowjetischen Parteichefs Michail Gorbatschow im März 1985 gestalteten sich die Beziehungen zunächst noch schwierig. Der neue Kremlchef richtete seine Außenpolitik erst einmal auf die USA aus, die ihrerseits mit der militärtechnologischen Vision des Raketenabwehrsystems SDI (Strategic Defense Initiative) einen neuen Rüstungsschub vorbereiteten, dem sich die Bundesrepublik schon aus bündnispolitischen Gründen schwerlich entziehen konnte.

Die Bundesregierung konzentrierte daher ihre Aktivitäten einstweilen auf die Westpolitik. Innerhalb kürzester Zeit gelang es Bundeskanzler Kohl, persönliche Vertrauensbeziehungen zu den führenden Repräsentanten der Partnerstaaten herzustellen, die sich besonders im Fall des französischen Staatspräsidenten François Mitterrand wiederholt in symbolischen Gesten der Freundschaft niederschlugen. Zugleich setzte die Bonner Regierung ihre Bemühungen um die Einigung Europas fort. Unter ihrer Präsidentschaft wurde auf der Stuttgarter Ratstagung Mitte Juni 1983 eine »Feierliche Deklaration zur Europäischen Union« verabschiedet. Im Februar 1986 folgte die Unterzeichnung der »Einheitlichen Europäischen Akte« (EEA). Mit diesem Vertragswerk, das die Schaffung eines europäischen Binnenmarktes bis Ende 1992 vorsah, gewann der Zusammenschluß Westeuropas eine neue Dimension, die auch in Osteuropa, namentlich in der UdSSR, ihren Eindruck nicht verfehlte.

Allmählich zeigte sich auch, daß mit dem Führungswechsel in Moskau eine entscheidende weltpolitische Weichenstellung vollzogen worden war. Michail Gorbatschows Politik der »Offenheit« (glasnost) und »Umgestaltung« (perestroika), die der östlichen Weltmacht durch innere Reformen zu neuer Kraft verhelfen sollte, eröffnete bis dahin kaum für möglich gehaltene Chancen für das Ost-West-Verhältnis. Das zeigte sich zuerst bei den Abrüstungsbemühungen. Am 8.12.1987 konnte in Washington mit der »doppelten Null-Lösung« im Bereich der Mittelstreckenraketen ein Abrüstungsabkommen unterzeichnet werden, das erstmals die tatsächliche Vernichtung von Waffen beinhaltete. Im selben Zeitraum verringerte die UdSSR ihr weltpolitisches Engagement und leitete 1988 den Rückzug aus Afghanistan ein, dessen Besetzung acht Jahre zuvor die »neue Eiszeit« zwischen den Supermächten mit verursacht hatte.

Das veränderte Klima wirkte rasch auf die Bundesrepublik zurück. Nun wurde der mehrfach verschobene Besuch des DDR-Staatsratsvorsitzenden Erich Honecker möglich. Diese Visite im September 1987 markierte eine Zäsur für die deutsch-deutschen Beziehungen. Einerseits stellte der reibungslose protokollarische Ablauf die inzwischen entstandene Normalität zwischen beiden Staaten unter Beweis. Andererseits erreichte Bundeskanzler

In the early years, accordingly, the relations of the Kohl/ Genscher government with the USSR remained aloof out of necessity. However, by perpetuating its wide range of economic contacts it struck a blow for continuity in this area, despite American reservations. Even after the new Soviet party leader Mikhail Gorbachev took office in March 1985, relations remained strained at first. As regards foreign policy, the new chief in the Kremlin initially focussed his attention on America, which for its part was projecting a new phase of armaments development, with the military-technological vision of its SDI (Strategic Defense Initiative) missile-defense system and the "Star Wars" program – a development in which, for reasons of Alliance policy alone, it was difficult for the Federal Republic not to become involved.

For the time being therefore the federal government concentrated its activities on political relations with the West. Within a very short time Chancellor Kohl succeeded in gaining the confidence of the leading representatives of the partner states, which, particularly in the case of the French President François Mitterrand, took the form of repeated symbolic gestures of friendship. At the same time the Bonn government continued to work for European unity. At the meeting of the European Council in Stuttgart in mid-June 1983, during Mitterrand's presidency, a "Solemn Declaration on European

Freies Schußfeld: Die DDR ließ am 28.1.1985 die Versöhnungskirche an der Bernauer Straße in Ost-Berlin sprengen.

An unobstructed field of fire: on January 28, 1985 the GDR blew up the "Versöhnungskirche" (Church of Atonement) at "Bernauer Straße" in East Berlin.

Sommer der Annäherung: Michail Gorbatschow und Richard von Weizsäcker während des abendlichen Empfangs am 13.6.1989 auf Schloß Brühl bei Bonn.

A summer of approachement: Mikhail Gorbachev and Richard von Weizsäcker during the evening reception at Brühl Castle near Bonn on June 13, 1989.

Helmut Kohl eine weitere Ausdehnung der Reisemöglichkeiten für DDR-Bürger und bekräftigte gegenüber dem Staatsratsvorsitzenden und Generalsekretär des ZK der SED unverblümt sein Festhalten am Ziel der Einheit Deutschlands. Zugleich demonstrierten die Umstände des Honecker-Besuchs glaubwürdig, daß die Bundesregierung dieses Ziel ausschließlich mit friedlichen diplomatischen Mitteln verfolgte.

Diese Tatsache wurde um so wichtiger, je mehr die Reformpolitik Gorbatschows die Staaten des Ostblocks erfaßte und damit Auswirkungen auf die Situation in Deutschland immer wahrscheinlicher werden ließ. Im Juni 1989 bestätigte der sowjetische Parteichef in der gemeinsamen Abschlußerklärung am Ende seines Besuches in der Bundesrepublik erstmals uneingeschränkt das Selbstbestimmungsrecht der Völker. Einen Monat darauf verwarf er ausdrücklich die sogenannte »Breschnew-Doktrin«, die seit dem Prager Frühling von 1968 jedes aus dem sozialistischen Lager ausscherende Land mit militärischen Gegenmaßnahmen der sowjetischen Hegemonialmacht bedroht hatte. Zur selben Zeit brachen sich, während die DDR-Führung sich noch den rasanten Veränderungen im sowjetischen Machtbereich entgegenzustemmen suchte, historische Umwälzungen Bahn, die in Polen zu freien Wahlen und in Ungarn zur Öffnung des »Eisernen Vorhangs« an der Grenze zu Österreich führten. Nun geriet auch die DDR – unter dem doppelten Druck der eigenen Bürger, die für ihre Freiheit in Scharen aus dem Land liefen oder im Land selbst massenhaft auf die Straßen gingen – ins Wanken. Während des Besuchs von Bundeskanzler Kohl in Polen fiel am 9.11.1989 die Mauer in Berlin. Eine Epochenwende zeichnete sich ab.

Union" was approved. This was followed in February 1986 by the signing of the "Single European Act" (SEA). With this Treaty which provided for the creation of a single European market by the end of 1992, the western European Union took on a new dimension, which did not fail to also make an impression in eastern Europe, especially in the USSR.

It also gradually became apparent that the change of leadership in Moscow entailed a distinct new course in international politics. Mikhail Gorbachev's policy of "openness" (*glasnost*) and "restructuring" (*perestroika*), intended to reinvigorate the eastern world power by means of internal reforms, opened up opportunities for East-West relations that until then had scarcely been thought possible. This first became evident in efforts to bring about disarmament. The "double zero solution" in the area of medium range missiles made it possible for a disarmament agreement to be signed, in Washington on December 8, 1987, which for the first time concerned the actual destruction of weapons. During the same period the USSR reduced its involvement in world affairs and in 1988 began to withdraw from Afghanistan, where its invasion eight years previously had been one of the causes of the "new Ice Age" between the superpowers.

The changed climate quickly made its effects felt in the Federal Republic. The visit by the Chairman of the GDR State Council Erich Honecker, which had been postponed several times, now became possible. This visit in September 1987 marked a decisive turning point in relations between the two Germanies. On the one hand the smooth running of the diplomatic formalities gave proof of the normal relations which now existed between the two countries. On the other hand Chancellor Kohl achieved a further increase in the opportunities for people in the GDR to travel, and in talks with the Chairman of the State Council and General Secretary of the SED Central Committee frankly reaffirmed that he still held fast to the goal of German unity. At the same time, the circumstances of Honecker's visit convincingly demonstrated that the Federal government was pursuing this goal exclusively by peaceful, diplomatic means.

This fact became all the more important, the more Gorbachev's reform policies spread to the states of the eastern bloc, making it increasingly probable that they would also affect the situation in Germany. In June 1989, in the joint final declaration at the end of his visit to the Federal Republic, the Soviet party leader for the first time unreservedly confirmed the right of national self-determination. A month later he explicitly rejected the so-called "Brezhnev doctrine," which since the Prague Spring of 1968 had threatened that any country in the socialist camp which broke ranks would face military reprisals by the Soviet hegemony.

At the same time, while the GDR leaders were trying to stem the tidal wave of change in the Soviet sphere of influence, historic upheavals broke out, leading to free elections in Poland and to the opening of the Iron Curtain in Hungary at its frontier with Austria. Now the GDR also began to totter under the dual pressure from its own citizens, who were either leaving the country in droves to gain their freedom or else flocking onto the streets in vast numbers in the country itself. The Berlin Wall came down on November 9, 1989, while Chancellor Kohl was visiting Poland. A new era was beginning.

»Der Bundestag wolle beschließen: Der Deutsche Bundestag spricht Bundeskanzler Helmut Schmidt das Mißtrauen aus und wählt als seinen Nachfolger den Abgeordneten Dr. Helmut Kohl zum Bundeskanzler der Bundesrepublik Deutschland. Der Bundespräsident wird ersucht, Bundeskanzler Helmut Schmidt zu entlassen«. 256 Abgeordnete stimmten am Nachmittag des 1.10.1982 für diesen gemeinsamen Antrag der Fraktionen der CDU/CSU und der FDP. Damit war Helmut Kohl zum Bundeskanzler gewählt. Unter den ersten Gratulanten waren von der FDP der Parteivorsitzende Hans-Dietrich Genscher und der Fraktionsvorsitzende Wolfgang Mischnick. Zwischen Kohl und Genscher war die neue Koalition zuvor verabredet und vorbereitet worden.

"It is moved that: the German Bundestag express its lack of confidence in Federal Chancellor Helmut Schmidt and elect as his successor the member Dr. Helmut Kohl as Chancellor of the Federal Republic of Germany. The Federal President be requested to dismiss Chancellor Helmut Schmidt." On the afternoon of October 1, 1982, 256 members voted in favor of this motion tabled jointly by the CDU/CSU and FDP parliamentary groups. Helmut Kohl was thereby elected Federal Chancellor. The first members to congratulate him were the FDP party chairman Hans-Dietrich Genscher and party whip Wolfgang Mischnik. The new coalition had been agreed and prepared before by Kohl and Genscher.

Auch der scheidende Bundeskanzler Helmut Schmidt gratulierte nach dem konstruktiven Mißtrauensvotum am 1.10.1982 seinem Nachfolger Helmut Kohl. Im Hintergrund applaudieren die CDU-Abgeordneten Philipp Jenninger (links), künftig Staatsminister im Bundeskanzleramt, und Manfred Wörner, der drei Tage darauf zum Bundesminister der Verteidigung ernannt werden sollte.

The departing Chancellor Helmut Schmidt also congratulated his successor Helmut Kohl following the constructive vote of no confidence on October 1, 1982. In the background CDU members Philipp Jenninger (left), the future Minister of State at the Chancellery, and Manfred Wörner, who was to be appointed as Defense Minister three days later.

Dank nach oben: Helmut Kohl und seine Familie nach der Kanzlerwahl, links Ehefrau Hannelore, rechts die beiden Söhne Walter und Peter.

Giving thanks: Helmut Kohl and his family after his election as Chancellor, on the left his wife Hannelore, on the right their two sons Walter and Peter.

Amtsübergabe im Bundeskanzleramt am 4.10. 1982. Beim anschließenden Gang vor die Presse fand Helmut Kohl noble Worte der Anerkennung für die Verdienste seines Vorgängers: »Wo immer man politisch stehen mag, und bei aller Kritik und Auseinandersetzung auch zwischen uns beiden in diesen Jahren bis in die letzten Tage hinein, will ich Ihnen hier ausdrücklich meinen Respekt und meine Hochachtung für diese Leistung, für diese patriotische Leistung für unser Vaterland bezeugen.«

The handing over of office in the Chancellery on October 4, 1982. Facing the press afterwards, Helmut Kohl found generous words of acknowledgement for what his predecessor had achieved: "Wherever one may stand politically, and notwithstanding all the criticism and argument also between the two of us during these years right down to the last few days, I wish here explicitly to put on record my respect and esteem for this achievement, for this patriotic achievement for our fatherland."

(gegenüber) Der neugewählte Bundeskanzler erhielt unmittelbar nach seiner Wahl von Bundespräsident Carstens die Ernennungsurkunde und wurde noch am selben Tag im Bundestag vereidigt. Jahre später hat Helmut Kohl bekannt, er habe in diesem Moment sehr intensiv die besondere Verantwortung empfunden, die das hohe Amt dem Bundeskanzler auferlege.

(opposite) Immediately after being elected, the new Chancellor received his certificate of appointment from President Carstens and was sworn in that same day in parliament. Years later Helmut Kohl confessed that at that moment he had a very strong sense of the special responsibility placed on the Chancellor by his high office.

Wahlkampf 1983: Die Spitzenkandidaten der CDU/CSU und der SPD stellen sich am 3.3.1983 im Fernsehen den Wählern. Hans-Jochen Vogel (rechts), langjähriger erfolgreicher Oberbürgermeister von München, 1974 bis 1981 Bundesminister der Justiz und seit Juni 1981 Oppositionsführer im Berliner Abgeordnetenhaus, war nach dem Verzicht von Helmut Schmidt zum Kanzlerkandidaten der SPD aufgestiegen. Dem brillianten Organisator fehlte jedoch die publikumswirksame Ausstrahlung seines Vorgängers. Er leitete bis 1991 die Bundestagsfraktion der SPD und formte sie zu einer schlagkräftigen Opposition. 1987 übernahm er zusätzlich das Amt des SPD-Parteivorsitzenden.

The 1983 general election campaign: the CDU/CSU and SPD front-runners presenting themselves to the voters on television on March 3, 1983. Hans-Jochen Vogel (right), successful mayor of Munich for many years, Minister of Justice 1974-1981 and leader of the Opposition in the Berlin parliament since June 1981, had risen to become the SPD chancellor candidate after Helmut Schmidt stepped down. He was a brilliant organizer, but he lacked the charisma of his predecessor. He led the SPD parliamentary group until 1991 and shaped it into a strong and effective Oppposition. In 1987 he also took on the post of SPD party chairman.

Rita Süssmuth wurde im September 1985 Nachfolgerin von Heiner Geißler im Ministerium, das seit dem 6.6.1986 zusätzliche Aufgaben für Jugend, Familie, Frauen und Gesundheit erhielt. Die Gleichstellung der Frauen machte die Ministerin auch als Vorsitzende der Frauen-Union in der CDU zu ihrem besonderen Anliegen. 1988 übernahm sie mit dem Amt der Bundestags-präsidentin das zweithöchste Staatsamt.
(links) Für einen guten Zweck konnte Rita Süssmuth auch aus ihrer seriösen Rolle fallen – hier verkleidete sie sich im Mai 1986 in Köln während einer Wohl-tätigkeitsveranstaltung des Zirkus Roncalli als Clown.

In September 1985 Rita Süssmuth succeeded Heiner Geißler at the Ministry, which from June 6, 1986 was given additional responsibilities of Youth, Family Affairs, Women and Health. The Minister, who also chaired the CDU women's group, made equality for women her particular concern. In 1988 she became President of the Bundestag, thereby assuming the second-highest office of state in the Federal Republic.
(left) Rita Süssmuth was quite capable of stepping out of her serious role in a good cause – here she is dressed up as a clown at a charity event organized by the Roncalli circus in Cologne in May 1986.

Wolfgang Schäuble, seit 1981 Parlamentarischer Geschäftsführer der CDU/CSU-Fraktion im Bundestag, wurde am 15.11.1984 als Bundesminister für besondere Aufgaben neuer Chef des Bundeskanzleramtes. In dieser Funktion formte er die Behörde zu einem effizienten Instrument zur Umsetzung der in den Spitzengesprächen beim Kanzler getroffenen Entscheidungen auf der Ebene der Regierungsverwaltung.

On November 15, 1984 Wolfgang Schäuble, who had been parliamentary manager of the CDU/CSU group since 1981, became a Minister without Portfolio and the new Head of Chancellery. In this capacity he shaped the Chancellery into an efficient instrument for implementing, on the administrative level, decisions taken in top-level talks with the Chancellor.

Heiner Geißler, Generalsekretär der CDU von 1977 bis 1989, übernahm 1982 das Bundesministerium für Jugend, Familie und Gesundheit. Geißler hatte wesentlichen Anteil an der programmatischen Erneuerung der CDU in den siebziger Jahren gehabt. Er war bemüht, das eigenständige Profil der Union auch nach der Regierungsübernahme zu erhalten. Ende der achtziger Jahre entstanden daraus zunehmend Spannungen mit Helmut Kohl, der als Bundeskanzler und Parteivorsitzender die uneingeschränkte Loyalität seines Generalsekretärs verlangte.

Heiner Geißler, CDU General Secretary from 1977 to 1989, took over the Ministry of Youth, Family Affairs, Women and Health in 1982. Geißler had played a substantial part in the renewal of the CDU program in the seventies. He was concerned that even after taking over the reins of government the CDU should preserve its own special image. In the late eighties this gave rise to increasing tension between him and Helmut Kohl, who as Chancellor and party chairman demanded unconditional loyalty from his General Secretary.

1982–1989

Der neue Bundeskanzler war, anders als sein sozialdemokratischer Vorgänger, nicht nur Regierungschef, sondern zugleich auch Vorsitzender der größten Koalitionspartei. In der souveränen Beherrschung des CDU-Parteiapparates lag lange Zeit ein wesentliches Fundament seiner Macht. Als Helmut Kohl im Juli 1977 in seinem traditionellen österreichischen Urlaubsort St. Gilgen am Wolfgangsee Erholung suchte, hatte er sich diese Machtbasis erst wenige Wochen zuvor erneut sichern können. Am 7.3.1977 war er mit großer Mehrheit in seinem Amt bestätigt worden. Er sollte es weitere 21 Jahre lang ausüben.

The new Chancellor, unlike his Social Democrat predecessor, was not only head of government but also at the same time the chairman of the largest coalition party. For a long time his power was firmly rooted in his sovereign control of the CDU party machine. When Helmut Kohl sought relaxation during his traditional vacation in St. Gilgen on Lake Wolfgang in Austria in July 1977, he had been given renewed assurance of this power base only a few weeks previously. On March 7, 1977 he was confirmed in his post by a large majority. He was to hold it for another 21 years.

Szenen einer »Männerfreundschaft«: Im Juli 1984 beendeten Helmut Kohl und Franz Josef Strauß demonstrativ ihre langjährige Fehde. Zu einer gemeinsamen Wanderung in der Nähe des oberbayrischen Tegernsees luden sie einen Fotografen ein, der die vertrauten Gespräche, den freundschaftlichen Umgang und die gemeinsame Freude an einer deftigen Mahlzeit für die Öffentlichkeit dokumentierte. Strauß war aber weiterhin der Auffassung, daß er selbst die Aufgaben in Bonn besser würde meistern können als der Mann aus Oggersheim. Allerdings unterschätzte er die Ausdauer und das Durchsetzungsvermögen Kohls – wie so viele.

Scenes from a "men's friendship": in July 1984 Helmut Kohl and Franz Josef Strauß demonstratively ended their long-standing feud. They invited a photographer to accompany the two of them on a ramble in the vicinity of Lake Tegern in Upper Bavaria and record for the public their friendly conversations, their amicable manner and their shared pleasure in a satisfying meal. But Strauß remained on the opinion that he himself would be better able to cope with the political demands of Bonn than the man from Oggersheim. However, he underestimated Kohl's stamina and ability to get his way – as so many people did.

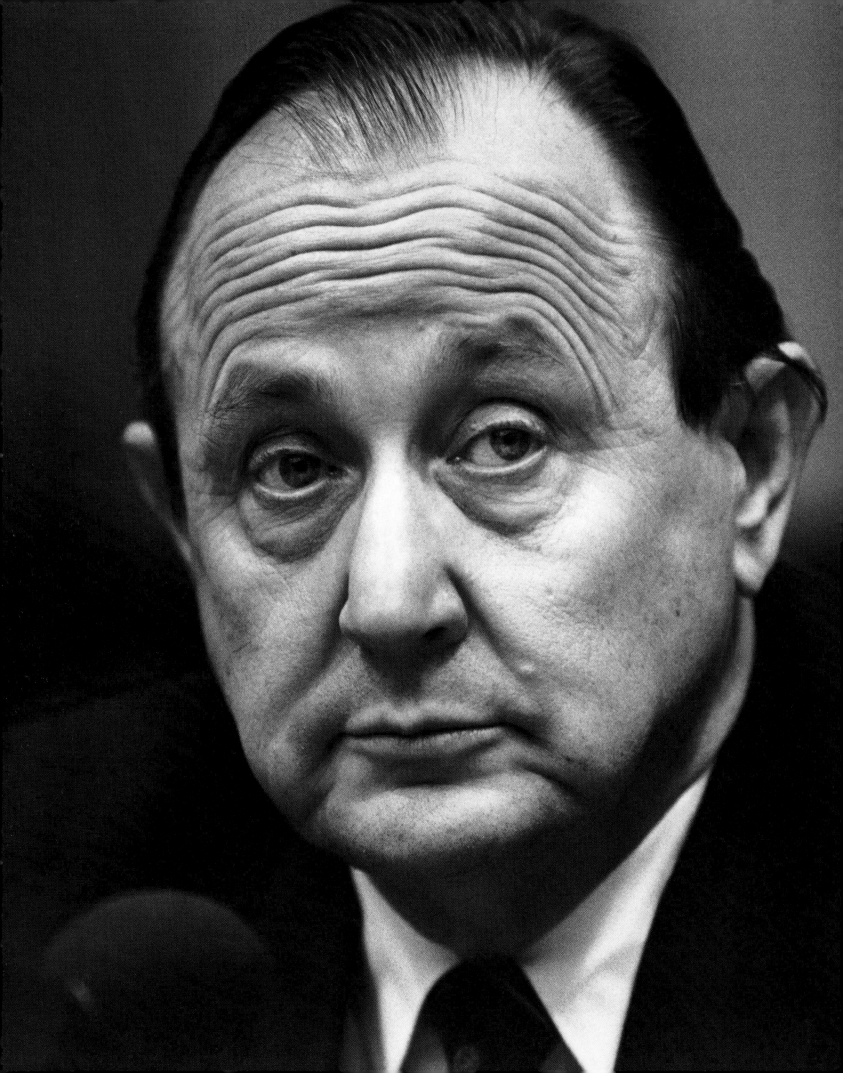

(gegenüber) Hans-Dietrich Genscher ging bei der »Wende« des Jahres 1982 ein hohes Risiko ein. Es gab einflußreiche Kräfte in der FDP, die den Koalitionswechsel ablehnten und einen Rücktritt ihres Parteivorsitzenden forderten. Doch die »Sphinx«, wie Genscher wegen seiner manchmal verklausulierten Stellungnahmen genannt wurde, setzte sich durch. In der neuen Regierung übernahm er wiederum die Leitung des Auswärtigen Amts und verkörperte damit deutlich sichtbar die Kontinuität deutscher Außenpolitik. Als Genscher 1992 zurücktrat, war er einer der längstgedienten Außenminister der Welt.

(opposite) Hans-Dietrich Genscher took a great risk during the "sea change" in 1982. There were influential forces in the FDP who were against a change in the coalition and who demanded the resignation of their party chairman. But the "sphinx," as Genscher was called because of the complex qualifications with which he sometimes hedged his statements, got his way. In the new government he again took on the post of Foreign Minister, thereby clearly and visibly embodying the continuity of German foreign policy. When Genscher resigned in 1992 he was one of the longest-serving Foreign Ministers in the world.

Zur hohen Schule der Diplomatie gehört das Vermögen, Gesprächspartner für die eigene Person und Sache einzunehmen. Daß Hans-Dietrich Genscher über diese Fähigkeit in großem Maß verfügte, illustrieren diese Bilder aus dem Oktober 1991. Zwar ist nicht bekannt, welche Anekdote der Außenminister den um ihn versammelten amerikanischen Senatoren erzählte, aber deren Gesichter bürgen für den hohen Unterhaltungswert des Vortrags.

Part of the art of diplomacy is the ability to win over one's partners in discussion for oneself and one's cause. That Hans-Dietrich Genscher possessed this ability to a high degree is illustrated by these photos taken in 1991. It is not known what anecdote the Foreign Minister was telling the American senators gathered around him, but their faces are proof of how entertaining it was to listen to him.

Nach dem Scheitern der Verhandlungen über den Abbau der sowjetischen Mittelstreckenraketen kam es im Herbst 1983 zu verstärkten Protesten der Friedensbewegung. Eine besondere Demonstrationsform waren Sitzblokkaden oder Menschenketten. So wurde am 15.10.1983 in West-Berlin die amerikanische Andrews-Kaserne im Stadtteil Lichterfelde von 5000 Demonstranten umstellt.

(links) Eine andere Form des Protests gegen die Nachrüstung bestand in der Schaffung von »atomwaffenfreien Zonen«. Während der Bundestag über die Nachrüstung debattierte, taten die »Grünen« – hier die Abgeordnete Christa Nickels – ihre Ablehnung auf symbolische Weise kund.

In autumn 1983, following the failure of negotiations concerning the dismantling of Soviet medium range missiles, there were increased protests by the peace movement. A particularly preferred form of demonstration was to seal off military installations temporarily by means of sit-down blockades or human chains. Thus on October 15, 1983 the American Andrews barracks in the Lichterfelde district of West Berlin was surrounded by 5,000 demonstrators.

(left) Another form of protest against force modernization was the creation of "nuclear weapons-free zones." While parliament was debating modernization, the "Greens" – here the member Christa Nickels – likewise proclaimed their rejection in this symbolic manner.

Während im Plenarsaal des Bundestages die Abgeordneten um ihre Entscheidung rangen, demonstrierten im November 1983 rund um das Regierungsviertel in Bonn Anhänger der Friedensbewegung gegen die Nachrüstung. Die Abriegelung durch Polizei und Bundesgrenzschutz verhinderte das Eindringen der Demonstranten in die »Bannmeile«, die das Parlament vor öffentlichen Protestkundgebungen jeglicher Art schützt.

In November 1983, while in the main chamber of parliament members were struggling to come to a decision, supporters of the peace movement surrounding the government area in Bonn were demonstrating against the deployment of more and new nuclear weapons. Police and border guards cordoned off the area to prevent the demonstrators from entering the "statutory mile," the inviolable area which safeguards parliament from expressions of public protest of any kind.

Vom 2. bis 7.11.1987 statteten der britische Thronfolger Prinz Charles und seine Frau Prinzessin Diana der Bundesrepublik ihren ersten offiziellen Besuch ab. Nach dem Empfang in Bonn – hier der Bundespräsident und die Princess of Wales beim Abendessen am 2.11.1987 in der Bad Godesberger Redoute im charmanten Gespräch – brachen sie zu einer fünftägigen Rundreise auf.

The British heir to the throne Prince Charles and his wife Princess Diana paid their first official visit to the Federal Republic from November 2-7, 1987. After the reception in Bonn they set off on a five-day round trip. The President and the Princess of Wales are seen here conversing charmingly over dinner on November 2, 1987 at the Redoute in Bad Godesberg.

Der Moment für einen freundschaftlich-würdigen Toast: Königin Elizabeth II. und Bundespräsident Richard von Weizsäcker beim Staatsbankett zu Ehren der britischen Königin am 19.10.1992 in Bonn. Das feierliche Abendessen fand anläßlich des dritten Staatsbesuchs der Queen in der Bundesrepublik Deutschland statt.

The moment for a dignified and friendly toast: Queen Elizabeth II and President Richard von Weizsäcker at a state banquet in honor of the British Queen in Bonn on October 19, 1992. The ceremonial dinner was given during the third state visit by the Queen to the Federal Republic.

Gruppenbild mit einem gekröntem und einem gewählten Staatsoberhaupt. Richard und Marianne von Weizsäcker im Kreis der niederländischen Königsfamilie anläßlich des Staatsbesuchs des Bundespräsidenten vom 30.5. bis 1.6.1985 in den Niederlanden. Links Königin Juliane, rechts ihre Tochter, Königin Beatrix der Niederlande.

Group portrait with one crowned and one elected head of state. Richard and Marianne von Weizsäcker surrounded by the Dutch royal family during the President's state visit to the Netherlands from May 30 to June 1, 1985. On the left Queen Juliana, on the right her daughter Queen Beatrix of the Netherlands.

Nur ganz selten wurde der Bundespräsident so im Regen stehen gelassen wie hier während des Staatsbesuches des Präsidenten von Costa Rica, Rafael Angel Calderon Fournier, am 25.1.1993 in Bonn vor der Villa Hammerschmidt.

Only very rarely was the President left standing in the rain as here during the state visit by the President of Costa Rica, Rafael Angel Calderon Fournier, outside the Villa Hammerschmidt in Bonn on January 25, 1993.

(gegenüber) Der Ministerpräsident des Landes Schleswig-Holstein, Uwe Barschel, im Februar 1983. Viereinhalb Jahre später, am 2.10.1987 trat der CDU-Politiker von diesem Amt zurück, nachdem sich Presseberichte über unsaubere Machenschaften eines seiner Mitarbeiter gegen den SPD-Oppositionsführer Björn Engholm bestätigt hatten. Noch 14 Tage zuvor hatte Barschel auf einer Pressekonferenz sein Ehrenwort gegeben, daß alle Vorwürfe »erstunken und erlogen« seien. Am 10.10.1987 wurde er in einem Genfer Hotel tot aufgefunden. Die genauen Umstände und Hintergründe seines Todes blieben ungeklärt.

(opposite) The Minister President of the *Land* of Schleswig-Holstein, CDU politician Uwe Barschel, in February 1983. Four and a half years later, on October 2, 1987, he resigned from this office, after press reports of underhanded machinations by a member of his staff against the leader of the SPD Opposition Björn Engholm had been confirmed. Only a fortnight earlier Barschel had given his word of honor at a press conference that all the accusations were "a filthy pack of lies." On October 10, 1987 he was found dead in a hotel in Geneva. The precise circumstances and background of his death were never established.

Johannes Rau, seit 1978 Ministerpräsident von Nordrhein-Westfalen, war einer der beliebtesten Landesväter der Bundesrepublik. Doch als Kanzlerkandidat der SPD verlor er am 25.1.1987 die Bundestagswahl. Die CDU/CSU unter Bundeskanzler Kohl konnte trotz des zweitschlechtesten Ergebnisses seit 1949 gemeinsam mit der FDP erneut die Regierung bilden. Rau blieb Regierungschef in Düsseldorf und erwarb mit seiner ausgeprägten Verbindlichkeit Respekt und Ansehen in allen Teilen der Bevölkerung.

Johannes Rau, Minister President of North Rhine-Westphalia since 1978, was one of the most popular regional leaders in the Federal Republic. But as the SPD chancellor candidate he lost the general election on January 25, 1987. Despite its second-worst showing since 1949, the CDU/CSU under Chancellor Kohl was again able to form a joint government with the FDP. Rau remained the head of government in Düsseldorf and won respect and prestige in all sections of the common people with the marked courtesy of his manner.

Die Barschel-Affäre begann im Vorfeld der Landtagswahl in Schleswig-Holstein am 13.9.1987. Nach dem Rücktritt des Wahlsiegers Barschel wurden am 8.5.1988 Neuwahlen durchgeführt, bei denen die SPD die absolute Mehrheit der Stimmen errang. Der neue Ministerpräsident Björn Engholm wurde 1992 sogar Bundesvorsitzender der SPD. Er trat jedoch ein Jahr darauf von allen Ämtern zurück, nachdem bekanntgeworden war, daß er 1987 über die verdeckten Aktivitäten gegen ihn sehr viel früher informiert war, als er im Untersuchungsausschuß des schleswig-holsteinischen Landtags zunächst behauptet hatte.

The Barschel affair began in the run-up to the regional elections in Schleswig-Holstein on September 13, 1987. Barschel won the election, but after he had resigned fresh elections were held on May 8, 1988 at which the SPD polled an absolute majority of the votes. The new Minister President Björn Engholm even became the SPD federal party chairman in 1992. But a year later he resigned from all his posts after it was revealed that in 1987 he had been informed of the covert activities against him very much earlier than he had initially stated when giving evidence before the investigative committee of the regional government of Schleswig-Holstein.

Deutschland, Europa und die Welt / Germany, Europe and the World

Helmut Kohl besaß eine besondere Gabe, unverkrampft auf Menschen zuzugehen. Nach der Regierungsübernahme im Oktober 1982 entwickelte er innerhalb kürzester Zeit persönliche Beziehungen zu den wichtigsten Repräsentanten der westlichen Welt. Sein Vertrauensverhältnis mit dem amerikanischen Präsidenten Ronald Reagan trug maßgeblich dazu bei, die in den USA entstandenen Zweifel an der Bündnistreue der Deutschen zu zerstreuen. Auch mit dem französischen Staatspräsidenten François Mitterrand entstand rasch ein freundschaftlicher Umgang. Mit zunehmender Dauer seiner Amtszeit wurde Helmut Kohl zum allseits geachteten und repektierten Vermittler im schwierigen diplomatischen Geschäft.

Helmut Kohl had a special gift for dealing with people in a relaxed manner. Within a very short time after taking over government in October 1982 he developed personal relationships with the most important representatives of the western world. The relationship of trust between him and the American President Ronald Reagan was a major factor in dispelling the doubts that had arisen in the US regarding Germany's loyalty to the Alliance. Friendly relations were also quickly established with the French President François Mitterrand. As his term in office progressed, Helmut Kohl came to enjoy universal esteem and respect as a mediator in the difficult business of diplomacy.

»First Ladies first«: Hannelore Kohl (links) und Nancy Reagan begeben sich am 14.11.1982, begleitet von sanfter Klaviermusik, zum feierlichen Dinner. Im Hintergrund die Ehegatten, Präsident Ronald Reagan (links) und Bundeskanzler Helmut Kohl. Das Abendessen fand aus Anlaß des Antrittsbesuchs des Bundeskanzlers in Washington statt.

"First Ladies first": Hannelore Kohl (left) and Nancy Reagan going in to a ceremonial dinner, to the accompaniment of soft piano music, on November 14, 1982. In the background their husbands, President Ronald Reagan (left) and Chancellor Helmut Kohl. The dinner was given to mark the Chancellor's inaugural visit to Washington.

»Mister Gorbatschow, öffnen Sie dieses Tor!« Dieser visionäre Appell, den der amerikanische Präsident Ronald Reagan am 12.6.1987 am Brandenburger Tor in seiner Rede zur 750-Jahr-Feier der Stadt Berlin aussprach, wurde berühmt. Zweieinhalb Jahre vor dem überraschenden Fall der Mauer hielten ihn viele allerdings für inhaltsleere Propaganda.

"Mr. Gorbachev, tear down this wall!" This visionary appeal by the American President Ronald Reagan in his speech at the Brandenburg Gate on June 12, 1987 during the celebrations marking 750 years of the city of Berlin, became famous. However, two and a half years before the unforeseen fall of the Berlin Wall, many regarded it as empty propaganda.

Bundeskanzler Helmut Kohl, General a.D. Johannes Steinhoff, Präsident Ronald Reagan und General a.D. Matthew B. Ridgway am 5.5.1985 auf dem Ehrenfriedhof Kolmeshöh in Bitburg. Die Kranzniederlegung sollte ein Höhepunkt des Staatsbesuchs des amerikanischen Präsidenten sein. Doch die Versöhnungsgeste geriet zum öffentlichen Streitfall, weil auf dem Friedhof auch Angehörige der Waffen-SS begraben waren.

Chancellor Helmut Kohl, General Johannes Steinhoff (retd), President Ronald Reagan and General Matthew B. Ridgway (retd) at the Kolmeshöh military cemetery in Bitburg on May 5, 1985. The laying of wreaths was intended as a high point in the American President's state visit. But the gesture of reconciliation gave rise to public controversy because members of the *Waffen-SS* were also buried in the same cemetery.

Auch mit dem neuen amerikanischen Präsidenten George Bush, der im Januar 1989 als bisheriger Vizepräsident die Nachfolge von Ronald Reagan antrat, knüpfte Bundeskanzler Helmut Kohl rasch persönlichen Kontakt. Die Freundschaft zwischen Kohl und Bush – hier anläßlich des Präsidentenbesuchs am 30./31.5.1989 in der Bundesrepublik – wurde zum Fundament der vorbehaltslosen amerikanischen Unterstützung bei der deutschen Wiedervereinigung im Jahr 1990.

Chancellor Kohl also quickly established personal contact with the new American President George Bush, the previous Vice President who succeeded Ronald Reagan in January 1989. The friendship between Kohl and Bush – here during the President's visit to the Federal Republic on May 30/31, 1989 – laid the basis for the unconditional American support for German reunification in 1990.

Helmut Kohl und François Mitterrand besaßen beide ein ausgeprägtes Gespür für die Bedeutung der Geschichte im Leben der Völker. Sie teilten ferner den Glauben an die tiefe Wirkungskraft symbolischer Gesten. Beides mag sie bewegt haben, als sie sich am 22.9.1984 – 70 Jahre nach den blutigen Schlachten des Ersten Weltkriegs – in Verdun über den Gräbern der 500 000 dort gefallenen Soldaten die Hände reichten. Welch hohe Bedeutung der Bundeskanzler den deutsch-französischen Beziehungen von Anfang an beimaß, belegt die Tatsache, daß er bereits in den ersten zehn Wochen seiner Amtszeit viermal mit dem französischen Staatschef zusammengetroffen war.

Helmut Kohl and François Mitterrand both had a keen sense of the importance of history in the life of nations. They also shared a belief in the profound effect of symbolic gestures. Both may have been in their minds in Verdun on September 22, 1984 when – 70 years after the bloody battles of the first world war – they clasped hands at the graves of the 500,000 soldiers who were killed there. The great importance which the Chancellor attached from the outset to Franco-German relations can be seen from the fact that during his first ten weeks in office he had four meetings with the French head of state.

Wenn sie auf ihr Kabinett herabblickte, habe sich die britische Premierministerin Thatcher gefühlt wie eine Tigerin, umgeben von lauter Hamstern, erinnerte sich einer ihrer Minister. Die »Eiserne Lady« verfocht die Interessen ihres Landes aber auch an anderen Fronten mit Angriffslust und stählerner Härte. Auch Helmut Kohl geriet ins Fadenkreuz ihrer Kritik.

Looking down at her cabinet, the British Prime Minister Mrs. Thatcher felt like a tigress surrounded by hamsters, one of her ministers recalled. But on other fronts also, the "Iron Lady" defended her country's interests aggressively and with steely determination. Sometimes she even had Helmut Kohl in her critical sights.

Nachdem am 17.2.1986 die »Einheitliche Europäische Akte« unterzeichnet worden war, die die Vollendung des gemeinsamen Binnenmarktes bis Ende 1992 vorsah, stand als nächster Schritt eine Neuregelung der Finanzen auf der Tagesordnung der Europäischen Gemeinschaft. Erst im Februar 1988 gelang auf einem Sondergipfel des Europäischen Rats in Brüssel die Lösung. Mit dem sogenannten Eigenmittelbeschluß erhielt die Gemeinschaft zusätzliche Einnahmen gemäß den Bruttosozialprodukten der einzelnen Mitgliedstaaten. Bundeskanzler Helmut Kohl und EG-Kommissionspräsident Jacques Delors (rechts) zeigten sich mit diesem Resultat zufrieden.

After the signing, on February 17, 1986, of the Single European Act, which envisaged the completion of the single European market by the end of 1992, financial reform was the next item on the European Community agenda. A solution was only found in February 1988, at a special summit meeting of the European Council in Brussels. The so-called "own-resources resolution" gave the Community extra revenue calculated according to the gross national product of individual member states. Chancellor Helmut Kohl and the President of the EC Commission Jacques Delors (right) showed that they were satisfied with this outcome.

Am 3.5.1983 empfingen Helmut und Hannelore Kohl (außen) im Bonner Bundeskanzleramt den spanischen Ministerpräsidenten Felipe Gonzáles und seine Frau Carmen Romero de Gonzáles. Der neue spanische Regierungschef nutzte seine erste Auslandsreise, um für einen raschen Beitritt Spaniens zur Europäischen Gemeinschaft zu werben. Die Bundesregierung unterstützte diesen Wunsch. Zum 1.1.1986 wurden Spanien und Portugal in die damit zwölf Staaten umfassende Gemeinschaft aufgenommen.

On May 3, 1983 Helmut and Hannelore Kohl (far right and far left respectively) received the Spanish Prime Minister Felipe Gonzáles and his wife Carmen Romero de Gonzáles at the Chancellery in Bonn. The new Spanish head of government took advantage of his first trip abroad to canvass support for Spain's speedy entry into the European Community. The federal government supported this wish. Spain and Portugal joined the Community, which was thereby enlarged to twelve states, with effect from January 1, 1986.

(gegenüber) Die feste Verankerung im Nordatlantischen Verteidigungsbündnis gehört zu den außenpolitischen Fundamenten der Bundesrepublik Deutschland seit Konrad Adenauer. Beim Gruppenfoto zur Gipfelkonferenz, die aus Anlaß des 40-jährigen Bestehens der NATO vom 29.-30.5.1989 in Brüssel stattfand, hatte offenbar auch der deutsche Bundeskanzler (links) bereits einen festen Platz. Seine Kollegen aus den Niederlanden und Spanien, Lubbers und Gonzáles (Mitte), wiesen ihn mit unmißverständlicher Geste ein.

(opposite) Since Konrad Adenauer's day it has been one of the fundamental elements of the Federal Republic's foreign policy that it remains firmly anchored in the North Atlantic defense alliance. In the group photo taken at the summit conference which was held in Brussels on May 29/30, 1989 to mark 40 years of NATO's existence, it is plain that the German Chancellor (left) already had his own place too. His opposite numbers from the Netherlands and Spain, Lubbers and Gonzáles (center), indicated where this was with unmistakable gestures.

Vom 26. bis 29.1.1986 hielt sich der israelische Premierminister Shimon Peres in der Bundesrepublik auf. Am Tag nach seiner Ankunft gedachte er im ehemaligen Konzentrationslager Bergen-Belsen bei Hannover der 30 000 dort ermordeten Juden.

The Israeli Prime Minister Shimon Peres visited the Federal Republic from January 26-29, 1986. On the day after his arrival he went to the former concentration camp at Bergen-Belsen near Hanover to honor the memory of the 30,000 Jews who were murdered there.

Die Pflege der deutsch-israelischen Beziehungen war ein besonderes Anliegen aller Bundesregierungen. Die Israel-Reise im Januar 1984 – im Bild Helmut Kohl während seiner Ansprache anläßlich der Verleihung der Ehrendoktorwürde der Universität Tel Aviv – war nicht ganz frei von Mißtönen. Vor allem des Kanzlers Wort von der »Gnade der späten Geburt«, mit dem er die Perspektive der jüngeren, zur NS-Zeit noch minderjährigen Deutschen auf den Holocaust hatte umschreiben wollen, rief Mißverständnisse hervor.

Every federal government has been particularly concerned to cultivate relations between Germany and Israel. The visit to Israel in January 1984 – the photo shows Helmut Kohl making a speech after being awarded an honorary doctorate of the University of Tel Aviv – was not entirely free of discord. Misunderstanding arose in particular from the Chancellor's use of the phrase "the mercy of having been born later," which he had meant as a paraphrase for the perspective on the holocaust of the younger generation of Germans who were children under the Nazis.

Die Glienicker Brücke in Berlin war seit den sechziger Jahren Schauplatz west-östlicher Austauschaktionen der Geheimdienste. Am 11.2.1986 wurden an dieser Stelle fünf in den USA und der Bundesrepublik inhaftierte Ostagenten gegen drei westliche Spione und den sowjetischen Regimekritiker Anatolij Schtscharanskij ausgetauscht, der vom Bonner US-Botschafter Richard Burt unmittelbar darauf nach Frankfurt am Main zum Weiterflug in die USA geleitet wurde.

Since the sixties the Glienicke bridge in Berlin had been the scene of exchanges by the secret services of East and West. Here, on February 11, 1986, five East German agents who had been imprisoned in the US and the Federal Republic were exchanged for three western spies and the Soviet dissident Anatoly Shcharansky, who was immediately taken by the US ambassador in Bonn, Richard Burt, to Frankfurt am Main from where he flew to the US.

Der Empfang des DDR-Staatsratsvorsitzenden am 7.9.1987 gehörte zu den schwierigsten Aufgaben der Bonner Diplomatie. Der Besuch Honeckers war erklärtermaßen ein Arbeitsbesuch, der jedoch im protokollarischen Ablauf einem Staatsbesuch ähnelte. Darauf verwies auch das offizielle Begrüßungszeremoniell vor dem Bundeskanzleramt. Für Erich Honecker war es ein stolzer, für Helmut Kohl ein bitterer Moment. Für beide aber war es, wie die Szene zeigt, ein Moment höchster Anspannung.

The reception of the Chairman of the GDR Council of State on September 7, 1987 was one of the most difficult tasks ever for West German diplomacy. Honecker's visit was purportedly a working visit, but one which as far as diplomatic formalities were concerned, resembled a state visit. This was to be seen in the official welcoming ceremony in front of the Chancellery. For Erich Honecker it was a proud moment, for Helmut Kohl a bitter one. But, as the picture shows, it was an extremely tense moment for both men.

»Diese Teilung ist widernatürlich«, erklärte Bundeskanzler Helmut Kohl zur Lage Deutschlands, als er am 24. 10. 1988 beim feierlichen Empfang im Kreml das Wort an seinen Gastgeber Michail Gorbatschow richtete. Es war der erste offizielle Besuch des Kanzlers vom 24. bis 27. 10. 1988 in Moskau, bei dem u.a. deutsch-sowjetische Abkommen über Zusammenarbeit auf den Gebieten des Umweltschutzes und der Erforschung des Weltraums unterzeichnet wurden.

Addressing his host Mikhail Gorbachev at the ceremonial reception in the Kremlin on October 24, 1988, Helmut Kohl spoke of the state of the German nation and declared: "This division goes against nature." The occasion was the first official visit by the Chancellor to Moscow, from October 24-27, 1988, during which, inter alia, German-Soviet agreements were signed concerning cooperation in the fields of environmental protection and space research.

Der Besuch des sowjetischen Staats- und Parteichefs Michail Gorbatschow und seiner Frau vom 12. bis 15.6.1989 brachte einen Durchbruch in den deutsch-sowjetischen Beziehungen. Nach außen wurde dies in der überwältigenden Herzlichkeit sichtbar, mit der die Deutschen den Generalsekretär begrüßten. Tausende verfolgten am 14.6. die Szene auf der Treppe vor dem Rathaus. Gegenüber Helmut Kohl gestand Gorbatschow später, »auf dem Bonner Marktplatz habe er sich gefühlt wie auf dem Roten Platz in Moskau!« Der Kanzler selbst vertraute seinen Mitarbeitern an, er habe in diesen Tagen, besonders bei einem langen, sehr offenen nächtlichen Gespräch an den Ufern des Rheins, »den Schlüssel zum Herzen Gorbatschows« gefunden.

The visit to the Federal Republic by the Soviet state and party leader Mikhail Gorbachev and his wife from June 12-15, 1989 brought a breakthrough in German-Soviet relations. This was outwardly visible in the overwhelming cordiality with which the Germans welcomed the General Secretary. On the market square in Bonn on June 14, thousands watched the scene on the steps outside the town hall. Gorbachev later confessed to Helmut Kohl: "On the market square in Bonn I felt just like I do in Red Square in Moscow!" The Chancellor himself confided to his colleagues that he "had found the key to Gorbachev's heart" during these days, especially during a long, very frank nocturnal conversation on the banks of the Rhine.

Unterzeichnung der »Gemeinsamen Erklärung« am 13.6.1989 im Bonner Bundeskanzleramt. Die wichtigste Passage lautete: »Bauelemente des Europas des Friedens und der Zusammenarbeit müssen sein: Die uneingeschränkte Achtung der Integrität und der Sicherheit jedes Staates. Jeder hat das Recht, das eigene politische und soziale System frei zu wählen. Die uneingeschränkte Achtung der Grundsätze und Normen des Völkerrechts, insbesondere Achtung des Selbstbestimmungsrechts der Völker«. Damit war für die Staaten des Ostblocks die Möglichkeit einer freiheitlichen Entwicklung eröffnet, die am Ende auch die DDR erfaßte.

The signing of the "joint declaration" in the Chancellery in Bonn on June 13, 1989. The most important passage reads: "The building blocks for a Europe of peace and cooperation must be: unconditional respect for the integrity and the security of every state. Each one has the right freely to choose its own political and social system. Unconditional respect for the principles and norms of international law, in particular respect for the right of national self-determination." For the eastern bloc states this opened up the possibility of developing in freedom, which in the end also took hold of the GDR.

Vom 9. bis 14.11.1989 war Bundeskanzler Helmut Kohl zu einem Besuch in Polen eingeladen. Einen Höhepunkt bildete der gemeinsame Gottesdienst mit dem ersten frei gewählten polnischen Ministerpräsidenten Tadeusz Mazowiecki (links) am 12.11.1989 im schlesischen Kreisau, wo sich während des Zweiten Weltkriegs der Widerstandskreis um Helmuth James Graf von Moltke getroffen hatte. Der Termin hatte verschoben werden müssen, weil Kohl seinen Aufenthalt in Polen für zwei Tage unterbrach, nachdem ihn am Abend seiner Ankunft die Nachricht von der Öffnung der Mauer in Berlin erreicht hatte.

Chancellor Helmut Kohl had been invited to visit Poland from November 9-14, 1989. A high point of the visit came when he attended a church service together with the first freely elected Polish Prime Minister, Tadeusz Mazowiecki (left), on November 12, 1989 in Kreisau in Silesian, where the resistance circle around Count Helmuth James von Moltke had met during the second world war. It had been necessary to postpone the event because Kohl broke off his visit for two days after receiving, on the evening of his arrival, the news that the Berlin Wall had been opened.

Der Fall der Mauer weckte in Polen alte Ängste vor einem übermächtigen und nationalistischen Deutschland. Die polnische Regierung wollte die Reise nach Kreisau am 12.11.1989 am liebsten absagen. Kohl bekannte später: »Für mich war dies einer der ganz wichtigen Punkte auf dem Besuchsprogramm. Kreisau ist ein herausragendes Symbol für das andere, für das bessere Deutschland auch imdunkelsten Abschnitt unserer Geschichte... Das Gut des Grafen Moltke – so wünschte ich es mir – sollte eine deutsch-polnische Begegnungsstätte werden, getragen vom Geist der Versöhnung.« Tatsächlich entstand auf dem Gelände eine internationale Jugendbegegnungsstätte.

In Poland, the opening of the Berlin Wall awakened old fears of an all-powerful, nationalistic Germany. The Polish government would have preferred to cancel the trip to Kreisau on November 12, 1989. Kohl later admitted: "For me this was one of the really important items scheduled for the visit. Kreisau is a towering symbol of the other, better Germany, even during the darkest period of our history...Count Moltke's estate – this was what I wanted – was to become a place for Germans and Poles to meet in a spirit of reconciliation." An international meeting place for young people was indeed created in the grounds of the estate – the old manor can still be seen in the background.

Zum Abschluß seines Aufenthaltes in Polen besuchte der Bundeskanzler am 13.11.1989 Auschwitz. Er wurde begleitet vom Vorsitzenden des Zentralrates der Juden in Deutschland Heinz Galinski, der den Holocaust überlebt und zahlreiche Angehörige in den Vernichtungslagern verloren hatte, sowie vom Warschauer Oberrabbiner Menachem Joskowicz – beide rechts im Bild, im Hintergrund Regierungssprecher Hans Klein. In das Buch des Gedenkens schreib Kohl, daß die Mahnung von Auschwitz nie vergessen werden dürfe und fuhr fort: "Hier geloben wir erneut, alles zu tun, damit das Leben, die Würde, das Recht und die Freiheit jedes Menschen, gleich zu welchem Gott er sich bekennt, welchem Volk er angehört und welcher Abstammung er ist, auf dieser Erde unverletzt bleibe".

The Chancellor concluded his stay in Poland by visiting Auschwitz on November 13, 1989. He was accompanied by the Chairman of the Central Council of Jews in Germany, Heinz Galinski, who had survived the holocaust but had lost numerous relatives in the death camps, along with the Chief Rabbi of Warsaw Menachem Joskowicz – both on the right in the photo; in the background government spokesman Hans Klein. Kohl wrote in the visitors' book that the memory of Auschwitz must be preserved forever, and continued: "Here we vow once more to do everything to ensure that the life, dignity, rights and freedom of all human beings, regardless of what God they worship, what nation they belong to and of what extraction they are, remain inviolable on this earth."

1989–1990

Friedliche Revolution und Wiedervereinigung
Peaceful Revolution and Reunification of Germany

Viele hatten es eilig: Mit Klebestreifen machte dieser Fahrer aus seinem
DDR-»Trabi« noch vor der Vereinigung einen Wagen der Bundesrepublik.

A lot of people were in a hurry: this driver used sticky tape to turn his GDR
"Trabi" into a car of the federal republic before unification.

Am 9.11.1989 fiel die Mauer in Berlin. Damit zerbrach das Fundament der Deutschen Demokratischen Republik, die 40 Jahre zuvor als erster deutscher »Arbeiter- und Bauernstaat« gegründet worden war. Ihre Urheber waren die sowjetische Besatzungsmacht und deutsche Kommunisten gewesen, die ihren Herrschaftsbereich mit rücksichtslosem Fanatismus dem sozialistischen Experiment unterworfen hatten.

Annähernd drei Millionen Menschen – ein Sechstel der Gesamt-bevölkerung – waren deswegen bis 1961 aus dem Land geflüchtet. Die Dagebliebenen hatten trotz allem auf ein besseres Leben in der Heimat gehofft, manche auch ehrlich an den Erfolg des Sozialismus geglaubt.

Eine dauerhafte Sicherung ihrer Herrschaft erreichten die Machthaber erst durch den Gewaltakt des Mauerbaus. Sowohl die eigenen Bürger als auch die westdeutschen und europäischen Nach-barn begannen jetzt, sich mit der Deutschen Demokratischen Republik abzufinden und einzurichten. In den siebziger Jahren erlangte sie schließlich eine Stabilität, die ihr nach außen zu inter-nationaler Anerkennung verhalf und auch im Inneren eine gewisse Identifikation der Bevölkerung erzeugte.

Doch gerade die innere Akzeptanz blieb stets gefährdet. Un-erfüllte Entfaltungs- und Konsumwünsche sowie der stets präsente Vergleich mit der in vielerlei Hinsicht erfolgreicheren Bundes-republik Deutschland sorgten dafür, daß die in breiten Schichten weiterhin vorherrschende Distanz und Skepsis gegenüber dem System und seinen Funktionären nie vollständig überwunden wer-den konnten.

Auch wenn das Regime die Lebensqualität gegenüber den fünfziger Jahren spürbar zu steigern vermochte und in der Ära Honecker sich etwas größere Frei- und Spielräume besonders im kulturellen Bereich auftaten, nahm die Zahl aktiver Kritiker nicht ab, sondern eher zu.

Die fortwährenden Menschenrechtsverletzungen, der Mangel an Freizügigkeit, die fehlende Rede- und Meinungsfreiheit wurden ebenso thematisiert wie der ökonomische und ökologische Raub-bau. Der Partei- und Staatsapparat begegnete dieser Kritik mit einer Perfektionierung des Überwachungsapparates und weiterhin mit Unterdrückungsmaßnahmen, die von Berufsverboten und physischer wie psychischer Folter über Haft bis zur Ausweisung reichten, ohne allerdings die Regimegegner wirklich dauerhaft mundtot machen zu können.

So war das Fundament der Diktatur der Sozialistischen Einheitspartei längst brüchig, ehe deren greise Repräsentanten es richtig wahrnahmen und ehe die Massenproteste es zum Einsturz brachten.

Die meisten Westdeutschen wurden von dieser Entwicklung überrascht. Zu lange hatte die Teilung ihr Weltbild geprägt. Mittlerweile erschien sie vielen geradezu als Grundvoraussetzung für den Frieden in Europa. Zwar hatte man den Umbruch in Polen seit 1980 mit Sympathie verfolgt und die wachsende Zahl der Über-siedler aus der DDR bis hin zur Fluchtbewegung des Sommers 1989 mit Genugtuung registriert. Doch daß tatsächlich die Existenz der Deutschen Demokratischen Republik auf dem Spiel stand und ihr Untergang nahe war, konnten sich bis zuletzt nur wenige vorstellen.

On November 9, 1989 the Berlin Wall came down. This shattered the foundations of the German Democratic Republic, which had been founded 40 years prior as the first German "Workers' and Peasants' State." It had been the creation of the Soviet occupying power and German Communists who, with ruthless fanaticism, had subjected the territory under their jurisdiction to the socialist experiment. As a result, approximately three million people – one sixth of the entire population – had fled from the country by 1961. The people who stayed behind had hoped, in spite of everything, for a better life in their homeland; some had sincerely believed that socialism would succeed.

It was only by the brutal act of building the Wall that the rulers were able to ensure the long-term impregnability of their authority. Both their own citizens and their West German and European neighbors now began to accept the existence of the GDR and to come to terms with it. It eventually took on, in the seventies, a stability which, as far as the outside world was concerned, helped it to achieve international recognition. On the home front, identification with the state was engendered to a certain extent.

But it was precisely this acceptance by its own citizens that remained continually at risk. Unsatisfied desires as regards consumption and self-realization, and the ever-present comparison with the Federal Republic, which was in many respects more successful, ensured that a critical reserve and scepticism towards the system and its functionaries would continue to prevail in large sections of the populace, and it was never completely overcome.

Even though the régime did succeed in perceptibly raising the quality of life in comparison with the fifties, and greater areas of freedom and self-fulfillment were opened up in the Honecker era, particularly in the sphere of culture, the number of critical voices increased rather than decreased.

The continual infringement of human rights, the lack of freedom of movement, freedom of speech and the free expression of opinion became topics of discussion, as did the economic and ecological overexploitation of the country's resources. The party and state machinery reacted to these criticisms by perfecting its system of surveillance and continuing its repressive measures. These ranged from withdrawal of the right to work to physical and psychological torture to imprisonment and expulsion from the country. However, it proved impossible to silence the opponents of the régime perma-nently.

Hence the foundations of the SED dictatorship had begun to crumble long before its aged figureheads perceived it, and before mass protest destroyed those foundations.

This development took most West Germans by surprise. The division had for too long been written into their view of the world. By then it had actually come to appear to many as the basic precondition of peace in Europe. The radical changes in Poland since 1980 had been followed with sympathetic interest, and the growing number of people leaving the GDR, culminating in the mass exodus of the summer of 1989, had been noted with satisfaction. But right up to the end only a few people were able to imagine that the very existence of the GDR was at stake, that it was threatened with destruction.

Die friedliche Revolution in der DDR

Die Ursachen der Umwälzungen im Ostblock waren vielfältig. Jeder der Mitgliedstaaten besaß eine eigene Geschichte der enttäuschten Hoffnungen und des frustrierten Engagements seiner Bürger, des Aufbegehrens gegen die Diktatur und der Unterdrückung durch die jeweiligen Sicherheitsapparate. Eine gemeinsame Zäsur bildete jedoch Mitte der achtziger Jahre die Einleitung der Reformpolitik durch Michail Gorbatschow. Erstmals konnten sich all jene, die Veränderungen einforderten, auf die ideologische und militärische Vormacht des Sowjetimperiums selbst stützen. Überraschend sahen sich die Regime der Satellitenstaaten einer verkehrten Frontstellung gegenüber.

Die Reaktionen auf diese neue Lage waren wiederum unterschiedlich. Während in Polen und Ungarn, wo der gesellschaftliche Druck auf Veränderungen schon vorher eingesetzt hatte, die Reformkräfte zusätzlichen Auftrieb erhielten, reagierten die Machthaber in der CSSR und in der DDR mit Ignoranz und verstärkter Abschottung. Vor allem im ostdeutschen Musterland des Sozialismus wurde Gorbatschows Politik als unerwünschte Gefährdung des kommunistischen Fortschritts betrachtet. Unverhohlen distanzierte sich die DDR-Führung vom politischen Kurs jenes Staates, dessen militärischer und politischer Absicherung sie ihre ungeteilte Macht und ihren staatlichen Machtbereich verdankte, und applaudierte demonstrativ, als die chinesische Regierung im Juni 1989 die studentische Opposition blutig unterdrückte.

Die durchlässige Grenze: DDR-Soldaten und Volkspolizisten am 11.11.1989 vor dem neuen Grenzübergang Schlesische Straße/Puschkinallee in Berlin.

The border is no longer impassible: GDR soldiers and people's police on November 11, 1989 at the new Schlesische Straße/Puschkinallee border crossing in Berlin.

The Peaceful Revolution in the GDR

There were a number of different reasons for the upheavals in the eastern bloc. Each of the member states had its own history of disappointed hopes and frustrated involvement on the part of its citizens, of rebellion against dictatorship and of suppression by the country's security services. They shared, however, the break in continuity constituted by the reform policies inaugurated by Mikhail Gorbachev in the mid-eighties. For the first time, all those who were demanding change could back up their demands by pointing to the dominant ideological and military power in the Soviet Empire itself. To their surprise, the régimes of the satellite states found themselves facing reversed battle lines.

Reactions to this new situation also varied however. In Poland and Hungary, where social pressure for change had begun much earlier, the forces of reform were given an additional boost, whereas the rulers in Czechoslovakia and the GDR reacted by refusing to recognize the situation and barricading themselves in even more resolutely. In East Germany in particular – the model socialist country – Gorbachev's policies were regarded as an unwanted threat to the progress of communism. The GDR leaders made no bones about dissociating themelves from the political line being taken in the state to whose military and political umbrella they owed their own unrestricted power and state authority. They demonstratively applauded the Chinese government's bloody suppression of student opposition in June 1989.

This rigid stance, intended to secure power, in fact helped to bring about the collapse of that power. With the destruction of their

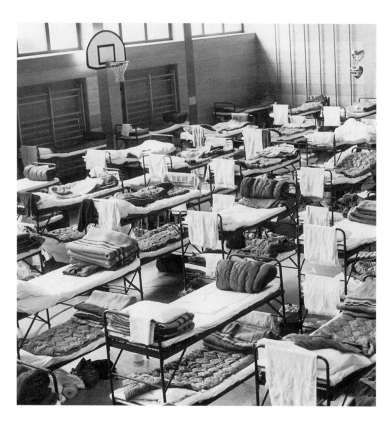

Als Behelfsunterkünfte für die Flüchtlinge der DDR wurden – wie hier in Passau – auch Turnhallen als provisorische Schlafsäle eingerichtet.

Improvised accommodation for the refugees of the GDR included the use of gymnasiums as temporary dormitories, as here in Passau.

Diese auf starre Machtsicherung ausgerichtete Haltung beförderte ungewollt den Machtverfall. Mit der Zerstörung der Hoffnungen auf innere Reformen setzte in der Bevölkerung der DDR ein entscheidender Bewußtseinswandel ein. Zum Gefühl der wirtschaftlichen Ausweglosigkeit, der geistigen und politischen Entmündigung sowie des Eingesperrtseins im eigenen Land trat nun der Verlust jeder Aussicht auf eine bessere Zukunft. Gerade die jüngere Generation, die mit den vermeintlichen Früchten des sozialistischen Aufbaus großgezogen worden war, sah in der DDR jetzt keine Perspektive mehr.

Das äußerte sich zunächst in der drastischen Zunahme der Ausreiseanträge in die Bundesrepublik. Von 1984 bis 1988 kehrten jährlich durchschnittlich 30 000 bis 40 000 Bürger der DDR den Rücken. Im Jahr 1989 explodierten die Zahlen. In den zehn Monaten bis zum Fall der Mauer hatten bereits etwa 225 000 Menschen die DDR verlassen – das erinnerte bedrohlich an die Zeiten vor dem Mauerbau. Dieser Massenexodus wurde möglich, weil Ungarn im Juni 1989 zunächst die Grenzsperren nach Österreich abbaute und ab September auch die Grenzkontrollen aufhob. War es zunächst Hunderten von DDR-Bürgern gelungen, ihre Übersiedlung durch die Besetzung der Bonner Vertretungen in Budapest, Prag, Warschau und Ost-Berlin zu erzwingen, so nutzten nun Zehntausende von Urlaubern aus der DDR die Gelegenheit zur Flucht über die offene ungarisch-österreichische Grenze. Anfang November 1989 wurde sogar die legale Ausreise über die CSSR möglich.

Zugleich setzte in der DDR selbst eine Massenbewegung gegen die von alledem scheinbar unbeeindruckte Staatsführung ein. Das bis dahin von den SED-Funktionären und der Staatssicherheit für beherrschbar gehaltene Protestpotential, das in erster Linie von lokalen, oft kirchlich geprägten Umwelt- und Friedensinitiativen getragen worden war, fand nun wachsende Unterstützung in der breiten Bevölkerung. Durch die Gründung überregionaler politischer Vereinigungen beschleunigte sich eine allgemeine Politisierung und gipfelte im Herbst 1989 in landesweiten Demonstrationen. Alle Versuche, die betont friedlichen Kundgebungen durch brutale Polizeieinsätze zu unterbinden, blieben erfolglos. Bereits am 9.10.1989 erreichte der wöchentliche Protestzug nach dem traditionellen Friedensgebet in der Leipziger Nikolaikirche mit 70 000 Teilnehmern eine Dimension, die eine Diffamierung als staatsfeindliche Minderheitenaktion und eine Zerschlagung mit polizeilichen Mitteln nicht mehr zuließ. Doch vor dem angedrohten Militäreinsatz schreckten die Verantwortlichen zurück, zumal die UdSSR signalisiert hatte, daß ihre vor Ort stationierten Truppen diesmal, anders als 1953, keine Unterstützung leisten und die sowjetischen Panzer in den Kasernen bleiben würden. Damit war, nur zwei Tage nach den pompösen Feierlichkeiten zum 40. Jahrestag der DDR, die Ohnmacht ihrer Führung offenkundig geworden und gleichzeitig bereits die Existenz des gesamten Staates in Frage gestellt. Von nun an gingen in vielen Städten des Landes Hunderttausende auf die Straßen und forderten mit wachsendem Selbstbewußtsein die Abdankung der Machthaber sowie Demokratie und Reisefreiheit, bald aber auch die Vereinigung mit dem anderen, dem westlichen Teilstaat der seit 1949 getrennten deutschen Nation.

Mit halbherzigen Zugeständnissen lief der verunsicherte Staatsapparat den Ereignissen hinterher. Am 18.10.1989 wurde der

hopes of internal reforms, a decisive shift of awareness began among the people of the GDR.

To the feeling of economic hopelessness, of having no intellectual or political voice of their own, and of being imprisoned in their own country, there was now added the loss of any prospect of a better future. Precisely the younger generation, which had been nurtured with the supposed fruits of the building of socialism, now no longer saw any future for themselves in the GDR.

At first this feeling found expression in the drastic increase in applications for permission to leave the country for the Federal Republic. Between 1984 and 1988 an average of thirty to forty thousand people a year turned their backs on the GDR. In 1989 the numbers rocketed. In the ten months before the Wall came down,

Die Mauer fällt: Am 12.11.1989 strömen Westberliner auf dem Potsdamer Platz in den Ostteil der Stadt.

The wall comes down: on November 12, 1989 West Berliners on the Potsdamer Platz flocking to the eastern part of the city.

225,000 people had already left the GDR. This was dangerously reminiscent of the period before the Wall was built. The mass exodus was possible because Hungary first dismantled the barriers at the border with Austria in June 1989, and then, from September, also put an end to border checks. Whereas to start with, hundreds of people from the GDR had succeeded in compelling the authorities to allow them to emigrate to the Federal Republic by occupying its embassies or missions in Budapest, Prague, Warsaw and East Berlin, tens of thousands of vacationers from the GDR now took advantage

Besuchs von Staatspräsident Mitterrand in Ost-Berlin deutlich sichtbar geworden waren, wandelte sich das Bild mit Beginn des neuen Jahres grundlegend. Anfang Januar 1990 sicherte sich Bundeskanzler Helmut Kohl die Unterstützung des französischen Staatspräsidenten Mitterrand für eine mit der europäischen Einigung gekoppelte deutsche Vereinigung. Kurz darauf bot die sowjetische Bitte um Lebensmittelhilfe Gelegenheit, auch der östlichen Hegemonialmacht die langfristigen Vorteile einer guten Nachbarschaft mit einem wiedervereinigten Deutschland aufzuzeigen. Vor allem aber wurde der beschleunigte Niedergang der DDR zum Argument für die Notwendigkeit raschen Handelns. Zugleich bewies der Ausgang der Volkskammerwahlen Mitte März 1990 aller Welt, daß eine eindrucksvolle Mehrheit der DDR-Bürger nachdrücklich für die deutsche Wiedervereinigung optierte. Sollte das seit Jahrzehnten vom Westen propagierte Selbstbestimmungsrecht der Völker nicht zur leeren Propagandaformel verkommen, das westliche Bündnis darüber schweren Schaden nehmen und nicht zuletzt auch an Glaubwürdigkeit einbüßen, mußte man den Deutschen ihre Wiedervereinigung zugestehen.

Im engen Zusammenwirken mit der amerikanischen Diplomatie erreichte die Bundesregierung innerhalb weniger Monate die allseitige Zustimmung zum Einigungsprozeß. Bereits am 10.2.1990 erhielt Bundeskanzler Kohl in Moskau das prinzipielle Einverständnis des sowjetischen Staatschefs Gorbatschow. Drei Tage später einigten sich in Ottawa die Außenminister der beiden deutschen Staaten und der Vier Mächte auf Verhandlungen nach der Formel »Zwei plus Vier«, die sowohl Vier-Mächte-Beschlüsse ohne deutsche Beteiligung als auch eine Mitsprache Dritter – im schlimmsten Fall sämtlicher früherer Kriegsgegner Deutschlands – ausschloß.

Das schwierigste Problem stellte die Bündniszugehörigkeit des wiedervereinigten Deutschlands dar. Vor allem für die USA war die

Feinabstimmung – die Außenminister Genscher und Baker während der »Zwei plus Vier«-Gespräche in Ost-Berlin am 21.6.1990.

Fine tuning: foreign ministers Genscher and Baker during the "two plus four" talks in East Berlin on June 21, 1990.

relations with a reunified Germany. But it was above all the increasingly rapid collapse of the GDR which convinced those concerned of the need to act quickly.

At the same time the outcome of the Volkskammer elections in mid-March 1990 had proved to the whole world that an impressive majority of the citizens of the GDR emphatically opted for German reunification. If the right of national self-determination that had been put about by the West for decades was not to degenerate into an empty propaganda slogan, entailing severe damage and, not least, loss of credibility for the western alliance, then the Germans' right to their reunification had to be conceded.

Thus within a few months the federal government, in close cooperation with American diplomats, achieved all-around approval for the process of unification. As early as February 10, 1990 in Moscow, Chancellor Kohl was informed of the Soviet leader Gorbachev's agreement in principle. Three days later in Ottawa the foreign ministers of the two German states and the Four Powers agreed to hold negotiations under the "two plus four" formula, which would rule out on the one hand four-power decisions without German involvement, and on the other the involvement of third parties – in the worst case scenario all Germany's former wartime enemies.

The most difficult problem concerned the reunified Germany's membership of the Alliance. For the US above all, full German membership of NATO was an essential condition. At Camp David at the end of February 1990 Chancellor Kohl and President Bush laid it down as a goal that this condition should be met, and this was eventually wrested from the Soviet leaders by a concerted effort. In April the federal government indicated to the USSR that it was prepared to put relations on a completely new footing, and confirmed this intention shortly afterwards by approving credit running to billions of Deutschmarks. At the end of May Gorbachev for the first time indicated to the US government his fundamental consent for a united Germany to enter freely into whatever alliance it chose.

But it was only after the NATO summit conference in London in early July 1990, which by revising its previous defense strategy resolved to end hostile relations with the Warsaw Pact, that Helmut Kohl was able to achieve a final breakthrough in his famous talks with Gorbachev in Moscow and the Caucasus on July 10 and 11, 1990. Mikhail Gorbachev made huge concessions: by giving up the GDR he relinquished the Soviet sphere of influence which extended into the middle of Europe, thereby reversing the consequences of the "Great Patriotic War."

A further difficulty in the international negotiations was likewise bound up with the aftermath of the second world war: the question of Germany's eastern frontier. The Polish government, supported by London and Paris as well as Moscow, demanded that the existing border be confirmed by treaty before reunification. Nor was there at any time any doubt in Bonn as to the finality of the Oder-Neiße border. Chancellor Kohl, however, bearing in mind unwanted reactions at home and proceeding cautiously with an eye to possible Polish demands for reparations, took the view, which accorded with international law, that only a parliament of the whole of Germany could give the necessary guarantees. Here too it proved possible, with energetic support from Washington, to find a solution.

vollgültige deutsche Mitgliedschaft in der NATO eine entscheidende Bedingung. Ihre Erfüllung wurde Ende Februar 1990 zwischen Bundeskanzler Kohl und Präsident Bush in Camp David als Ziel festgelegt und schließlich mit vereinten Kräften der sowjetischen Führung abgerungen. Im April äußerte die Bundesregierung der UdSSR die Bereitschaft zu einer völlig neuen Qualität der Beziehungen und bestätigte diese Absicht kurz darauf mit der Zusage eines Milliardenkredits. Ende Mai signalisierte Gorbatschow der US-Regierung erstmals seine grundsätzliche Zustimmung zu einer freien Bündniswahl Gesamtdeutschlands. Doch erst nach der NATO-Gipfelkonferenz Anfang Juli in London, die mit der Revision der bisherigen Verteidigungsstrategie das Ende der Gegnerschaft mit dem Warschauer Pakt beschloß, konnte Helmut Kohl am 10. und 11.7.1990 bei seinen berühmt gewordenen Gesprächen mit Gorbatschow in Moskau und im Kaukasus den endgültigen Durchbruch erzielen. Die Zugeständnisse von Michail Gorbatschow waren immens – er gab mit der DDR die bis in die Mitte Europas hineinreichende sowjetische Einflußsphäre frei, machte damit das wichtigste Ergebnis des »Großen Vaterländischen Krieges« rückgängig.

Eine weitere Schwierigkeit bei den internationalen Verhandlungen hing gleichfalls mit den Folgen des Zweiten Weltkrieges zusammen – die Frage der Ostgrenze Deutschlands. Die polnische Regierung verlangte eine vertragliche Festlegung der bestehenden Grenzziehung noch vor der Wiedervereinigung und fand dafür Unterstützung sowohl in London und Paris als auch in Moskau. An der Endgültigkeit der Oder-Neiße-Grenze bestand auch in Bonn zu keinem Zeitpunkt irgendein Zweifel. Bundeskanzler Helmut Kohl vertrat jedoch aus Rücksicht auf unerwünschte Reaktionen im Innern und aus Vorsicht gegenüber eventuellen polnischen Reparationsforderungen den völkerrechtlich korrektenStandpunkt, daß nur ein gesamtdeutsches Parlament die nötigen Garantien geben könne. Auch hier gelang es mit tatkräftiger Unterstützung aus Washington, eine Lösung zu finden.

Am Ende der Verhandlungen stand der sogenannte »Zwei-plus-Vier-Vertrag« vom 12.9.1990. Er ermöglichte die mit dem deutsch-deutschen Einigungsvertrag vereinbarte Wiedervereinigung im Rahmen der Europäischen Gemeinschaft und der NATO. Die Vier Mächte gaben ihre bisherigen Vorbehaltsrechte auf. Sie übertrugen die volle Souveränität auf das vereinigte Deutschland, das sich seinerseits zur Wahrung des Friedens verpflichtete, die Begrenzung seiner militärischen Stärke zusagte und auf den Besitz atomarer, biologischer und chemischer Waffen verzichtete. Polen erhielt die Bestätigung seiner Westgrenze, deren endgültige Besiegelung einem besonderen deutsch-polnischen Vertrag vorbehalten wurde. Die UdSSR übernahm die Verpflichtung, ihre in Ostdeutschland stationierten Truppen bis Ende 1994 abzuziehen und sicherte sich dafür weitreichende finanzielle Überbrückungshilfen.

Nachdem auch die 35 Staaten der Konferenz über Sicherheit und Zusammenarbeit in Europa (KSZE) die Vereinbarungen offiziell bestätigt hatten, wurde am 3.10.1990 mit dem Beitritt der DDR zur Bundesrepublik Deutschland die Wiedervereinigung vollzogen. 45 Jahre nach dem Ende des Zweiten Weltkriegs wurde ein geeintes Deutschland Teil einer neuen gesamteuropäischen Staatenordnung, die sowohl die Strukturen der Nachkriegszeit als auch die der Vorkriegszeit überwand und die Chance auf eine neue Zukunft erschloß.

Der Tag der deutschen Einheit: Am 3.10.1990 wird um 0.00 Uhr vor dem Reichtagsgebäude die schwarz-rot-goldene Bundesflagge gehißt.

The day of German unity: at 0.00 on October 3, 1990 the black-red-gold federal flag is hoisted outside the Reichstag building.

In the end the negotiations produced the so-called "Two-plus-Four Treaty" of September 12, 1990. It made possible the reunification within the framework of the European Community and NATO that had been agreed in the German-German unification treaty. The four powers relinquished their previously reserved rights. They transferred full sovereignty to the united Germany, which for its part undertook to preserve peace and to limit its military strength, and renounced the possession of atomic, biological and chemical weapons. Poland was given an assurance that its western boundary would remain unchanged, final confirmation being reserved for a special Polish-German treaty. The USSR undertook to withdraw its troops stationed in East Germany by the end of 1994, for which it secured substantial tide-over aid.

After the 35 states of the Conference on Security and Cooperation in Europe (CSCE) had also officially confirmed the agreements, reunification came about with the accession of the GDR to the Federal Republic on October 3, 1990. 45 years after the end of the second world war a unified Germany became part of a new political order for the whole of Europe which left behind the structures of both the postwar and the prewar eras, and opened up the prospect of a new future.

Im Sommer 1989 erreichte die innerdeutsche Ost-West-Wanderung eine neue Dimension. Mit dem Abbau der Grenzanlagen zu Österreich im Juni hatte die Regierung in Budapest das entscheidende Signal gesetzt: Der Eiserne Vorhang begann sich zu heben. Zu Zehntausenden nutzten schon bald DDR-Bürger ihre Urlaubsreisen nach Ungarn, in die Tschechoslowakei und Polen zur Flucht. Zunächst suchten sie ihre Ausreise über die Besetzung der Botschaften der Bundesrepublik zu erzwingen. Als Ungarn am 11.9.1989 die Grenze nach Österreich für Deutsche aus der DDR öffnete, strömten allein in drei Tagen 15 000 Flüchtlinge in Richtung Westen. Bis Ende Oktober flüchteten über 50 000 Menschen über Ungarn und Österreich in die Bundesrepublik. Insgesamt kamen im Jahr 1989 225 000 Deutsche aus dem Osten in den Westen Deutschlands.

In summer 1989 the migration from East to West Germany took on a new dimension. By removing the installations at the border with Austria in June, the government in Budapest had sent a decisive signal: the Iron Curtain was beginning to be lifted. Before long tens of thousands of GDR citizens were taking advantage of their vacation trips to Hungary, Czechoslovakia and Poland to flee from the GDR. At first they tried to compel the authorities to allow them to leave by occupying the embassies of the Federal Republic. When, on September 11, 1989, Hungary opened its border with Austria for Germans from the GDR, a flood of 15,000 refugees left in a mere three days, heading for the West. By the end of October over 50,000 people had fled to the Federal Republic via Hungary and Austria. In 1989 a total of 225,000 Germans left the eastern part of Germany for the western part.

Mitte Juli 1989 suchten die ersten DDR-Bürger Zuflucht in den diplomatischen Vertretungen der Bundesrepublik in Budapest, Prag und Ost-Berlin, wenig später dann auch in Warschau. Da das SED-Regime sich anfänglich jeder Lösung des Problems verweigerte, mußten die Gebäude bald wegen Überfüllung geschlossen werden. Die hygienischen Verhältnisse wurden zunehmend unhaltbar, wie der Blick auf das Gelände der Prager Botschaft zeigt. Vom Balkon des Palais Lobkowicz verkündete Außenminister Hans-Dietrich Genscher am Abend des 30.9.1989 die Ausreisegenehmigung der DDR-Behörden. Seine Rede ging im Jubel der 6000 Zuhörer unter.

In mid-July 1989 the first people from the GDR sought refuge in the embassies or missions of the Federal Republic in Budapest, Prague and East Berlin, and a little later in Warsaw also. Since the SED régime at first rejected all solutions to the problem, the buildings soon became overcrowded and had to be closed. Conditions with regard to hygiene became increasingly intolerable, as can be seen here in the grounds of the embassy in Prague. It was from the balcony of the Palais Lobkowitz that Foreign Minister Hans-Dietrich Genscher announced, on the evening of September 30, 1989, that the GDR authorities had given their approval for those concerned to leave the country. His words were drowned by the cheers of the 6,000 listeners.

Massenflucht / Mass exodus

In zwei Wellen durften am 1. bzw. 4. Oktober 1989 die Prager Botschaftsflüchtlinge mit insgesamt acht Sonderzügen in die Bundesrepublik ausreisen. Bei der Durchfahrt durch die DDR kam es zu Tumulten, weil weitere Ausreisewillige auf die Züge zu springen versuchten. In Dresden wurde der von der Polizei abgesperrte Hauptbahnhof von Demonstranten regelrecht belagert. Glückliche Szenen gab es dagegen bei der Ankunft der Züge in der bayerischen Grenzstadt Hof. Mit großer Herzlichkeit wurden die Flüchtlinge aus der DDR von ihren deutschen Landsleuten begrüßt.

The people who had taken refuge at the embassy in Prague were allowed to leave for the Federal Republic in two waves, on October 1 and 4, 1989, in a total of eight special trains. As they passed through the GDR there was turmoil as others who wished to leave tried to jump onto the trains. In Dresden, the main station, which had been cordoned off by the police, came under a veritable siege by demonstrators. There were happy scenes, on the other hand, when the trains arrived at the Bavarian border town of Hof. The refugees from the GDR were given a very warm welcome by their fellow-Germans.

Die Sonderzüge aus Prag trafen am 5.10.1989 in Hof ein. Für 8000 DDR-Bürger war damit der Traum von einem Leben im Westen Wirklichkeit geworden. Sie schämten sich ihrer Freudentränen nicht. Viele hatten lange auf diesen Moment gewartet und in der DDR Benachteiligungen bis hin zum Verlust der Existenzgrundlagen hingenommen. Die zumeist jüngeren Flüchtlinge ließen Eltern, Freunde und Arbeitskollegen in der alten Heimat zurück und mußten damit rechnen, sie für Jahre nicht wiederzusehen.

The special trains from Prague arrived at Hof on October 5, 1989. For 8,000 people from the GDR the dream of a life in the West had come true. They were not ashamed to shed tears of joy. Many of them had waited a long time for this moment, having faced discrimination in the GDR to the point of forfeiting their livelihood. The refugees, most of whom were relatively young, left their parents, friends and colleagues behind in their former homeland and had to reckon with the possibility that they would not see them again for years.

Am 6.11.1989 fordern auf der bis dahin machtvollsten Demonstration in Leipzig Hunderttausende die Abdankung der SED und freie Wahlen – einen Tag später tritt die Regierung der DDR zurück.

During a most spectacular demonstration in Leipzig on November 11, 1989 hundretthousands East Germans demanded that the SED, the official party, resign and grant free elections. One day later the government stepped down.

Nachdem sich die Demonstranten anfänglich aus Vorsicht vor Übergriffen der Polizei auf Sprechchöre beschränkt hatten, führten sie ab Oktober 1989 zusätzlich vielgestaltige Transparente mit. Ein Teilnehmer des Leipziger Protestzugs vom 6.11. erinnerte mit seinem Schild an den Prager Frühling des Jahres 1968, als Panzer des Warschauer Paktes die Reformhoffnungen in der Tschechoslowakei blutig niedergewalzt hatten. Daß 1989 die sowjetischen Truppen in den Kasernen blieben, war eine wesentliche Voraussetzung für den Erfolg der »friedlichen Revolution« in der DDR.

To begin with, in order not to provoke police interference, the demonstrators confined themselves to shouting slogans. But from October 1989 they also carried a variety of banners. One protest marcher in Leipzig on November 6 carried a placard with a reminder of the Prague Spring of 1968, when hopes for reform in Czechoslovakia were brutally crushed by Warsaw Pact tanks. The fact that in 1989 Soviet troops remained in their barracks was an essential precondition for the success of the "peaceful revolution" in the GDR.

Massenprotest / Mass protest

Leipzig, 6.11.1989. Auf dem Karl-Marx-Platz – heute wieder Augustusplatz – demonstrieren annähernd 500 000 Menschen für Freiheit und Demokratie vor dem Ende der fünfziger Jahre erbauten Gebäude der Leipziger Oper und dem 1981 fertiggestellten Konzerthaus des berühmten Gewandhausorchesters, dessen Kapellmeister Kurt Masur vier Wochen zuvor zusammen mit anderen öffentlich zur Gewaltlosigkeit aufgerufen und damit maßgeblich zum friedlichen Verlauf der entscheidenden Montagsdemonstration vom 9. Oktober beigetragen hatte.

Leipzig, November 6, 1989. In Karl Marx Square – today once again the Augustus Square – close to 500,000 people demonstrated for freedom and democracy in front of the Leipzig opera house, built in the late fifties, and the concert hall of the famous Gewandhaus orchestra, completed in 1981, whose conductor Kurt Masur had four weeks previously made a public appeal, along with others, for there to be no violence, thereby decisively contributing to the peaceful outcome of the crucial Monday demonstration on October 9.

Während im Herbst 1989 Zehntausende der DDR den Rücken kehrten, gingen im Land selbst Hundertausende auf die Straßen und forderten Demokratie, Reisefreiheit und die Ablösung des reformunfähigen SED-Regimes. Der Durchbruch zur Massenbewegung gelang am 9.10.1989 in Leipzig, als nach dem traditionellen Montagsgebet in der Nikolaikirche 70 000 friedliche Demonstranten auf den Straßenring um die Innenstadt strömten. Nur ein Militäreinsatz hätte die Massen auseinanderjagen können. Doch zu dem befürchteten Blutbad kam es nicht. Von nun an schwollen die Protestzüge Woche für Woche an. Am 16.10.1989 demonstrierten 120 000, am 23.10. 250 000 und am 30.10. bereits 300 000 Menschen in der »Heldenstadt«. Auch in vielen anderen Städten fanden die Bürger den Mut zum offenen Protest. Die DDR-Führung mußte ohnmächtig zusehen, wie eine friedliche Revolution ihre Herrschaft zu untergraben begann.

While tens of thousands were turning their backs on the GDR in autumn 1989, in the country itself, hundreds of thousands took to the streets demanding democracy, freedom to travel and since it was incapable of reform, the removal of the SED régime. The explosion into a mass movement came in Leipzig on October 9, 1989, when following the traditional Monday prayer in the Nikolaikirche 70,000 peaceful demonstrators poured onto the ring road around the city center. The crowd could only have been dispersed by bringing in troops. But the dreaded bloodbath did not happen. From then on the protest marches increased week by week. On October 16, 1989 there were 120,000 demonstrators, on October 23 there were 250,000 and by October 30 the number had reached 300,000 in the "city of heroes." In many other cities, too, people found the courage to protest openly. The GDR leaders had to look on helplessly as a peaceful revolution began to undermine their rule.

(gegenüber) Die entscheidenden Akteure der »friedlichen Revolution« in der DDR waren die Demonstranten. Nach vierzig Jahren der Bevormundung übernahm schließlich tatsächlich das Volk die Macht, die es angeblich schon seit dem Sieg des Sozialismus innegehabt hatte. Einfache Bürger – darunter viele, die sich bislang unauffällig und unpolitisch mit und in der DDR arrangiert hatten – fanden jetzt den Mut zum offenen Protest. Ihr Gewaltverzicht, der im Symbol der Kerze seinen sichtbaren Ausdruck fand, wurde ihre stärkste Waffe, weil er den Gewaltigen des Staates die Waffen aus den Händen schlug.

(oppposite) The crucial protagonists in the "peaceful revolution" in the GDR were the demonstrators. Finally a forty years of being treated like children, the common people did indeed take the power which they had supposedly held since the victory of socialism. Ordinary members of the public, including many who until then had learned to live with and in the GDR, keeping out of politics and not drawing attention to themselves, now found the courage to protest openly. Their renunciation of violence, visibly expressed in the symbol of the candle, became their strongest weapon, because it disarmed the mighty state leaders.

Am 4.11.1989 versammelten sich in Berlin über eine halbe Million Menschen zur größten nichtstaatlichen Kundgebung in der Geschichte der DDR. Neben Intellektuellen und Künstlern traten auch als reformfreudig geltende SED-Funktionäre an die Mikrofone. Doch ihre Worte gingen in den wütenden Pfiffen der Zuhörer unter. Die Regierenden hatten jede Glaubwürdigkeit verspielt. Auf einem der Transparente wurde der neue Staatschef Egon Krenz als scheinheilig verkleideter Rotkäppchen-Wolf karikiert. Demgegenüber lautete die selbstbewußte Parole der Massen: »Wir sind das Volk«.

On November 4, 1989 over half a million people gathered in Berlin for the biggest non-state rally in the history of the GDR. Along with intellectuals and artists, some SED party officials who were thought to be in favor of reform also stepped up to the microphone. But their words were drowned by the listeners' furious catcalls. The rulers had forfeited all credibility. On one of the banners the new political leader Egon Krenz was caricatured as a hypocritical Little Red Riding Hood wolf in disguise. Opposite that banner was the crowd's self-confident slogan: "We are the people."

Hinter der Mauer sicherte am 10.11. 1989 noch eine Postenkette von Volkspolizisten und Grenzsoldaten der DDR das Brandenburger Tor. Eine unkontrollierte Überquerung durch die euphorischen Menschenmassen sollte verhindert werden.

Behind the Wall the Brandenburg Gate was still guarded by a cordon of people's police and border guards on November 10, 1989. The aim was to prevent the euphoric crowds from crossing unchecked.

In der Nacht des 9.11.1989 glich West-Berlin einem Volksfest. Seit dem Mauerbau im August 1961 hatten viele Ostberliner davon geträumt, einmal auf dem Kurfürstendamm zu spazieren. Plötzlich war es möglich. Jubelnd begrüßten sich die Bewohner der 28 Jahre lang geteilten Stadt. Auch völlig Fremde fielen sich um den Hals. Vielerorts spielten sich unbeschreibliche Freudenszenen ab.

In the night of November 9, 1989 West Berlin was like one great street party. Since the building of the Wall in August 1961, many East Berliners had dreamed of walking along the Kurfürstendamm one day. Suddenly it was possible. The inhabitants of the city that had been divided for 28 years greeted one another jubilantly. Total strangers embraced each other. Everywhere there were indescribable scenes of rejoicing.

Am 9.11.1989 gegen 19 Uhr verlas Günter Schabowski, Sekretär des Zentralkomitees der SED, auf einer live im staatlichen Fernsehen und Rundfunk übertragenen Pressekonferenz den Beschluß der DDR-Regierung, daß Genehmigungen für Westreisen »kurzfristig« und »ohne Vorliegen von Voraussetzungen« erteilt würden. Er übersah jedoch den Schlußsatz, daß diese Regelung erst am folgenden Tag veröffentlicht werden sollte, und erklärte statt dessen auf Nachfrage, sie gelte »sofort, unverzüglich«. Augenblicklich machten sich Tausende von DDR-Bürgern auf den Weg zu den Grenzübergängen in Berlin. Die überforderten Posten standen dem Ansturm hilflos gegenüber. Gegen 21.30 Uhr überquerten die ersten Ostberliner die Grenze, zwei Stunden später waren es Zehntausende, die nach West-Berlin drängten. Ein Freudentaumel ergriff die Stadt. Die Mauer war gefallen.

On November 9, 1989 at around 7:00 p.m. hours, at a press conference which was broadcast live on state radio and television, Günter Schabowski, Secretary of the SED Central Committee, read out the GDR government's decision that permits for travel to the West would be issued "on short notice" and "with no conditions attached." However, he overlooked the final sentence, viz. that this ruling was not to be published until the following day, and declared instead, when asked, that it applied "at once, without delay." Instantly, thousands of GDR inhabitants set off for the border crossing points in Berlin. Faced with this crowd the guards were helpless. At around 9:30 p.m. hours the first East Berliners crossed the border, two hours later there were tens of thousands surging through to West Berlin. The city was jubilent. The Wall had come down.

Am späten Nachmittag des 10.11.1989 versammelten sich 20 000 Berliner vor dem Schöneberger Rathaus. An der Kundgebung nahmen auch (von links) der SPD-Ehrenvorsitzende Willy Brandt, der Regierende Bürgermeister Walter Momper, Bundeskanzler Helmut Kohl sowie der Partei- und Fraktionsvorsitzende der SPD Hans-Jochen Vogel teil. Bei dieser Gelegenheit sprach der ehemalige Bundeskanzler Brandt den entscheidenden Satz, der ihn zu einer der Symbolfiguren des Einigungsprozesses machte: »Jetzt wächst zusammen, was zusammen gehört!«. Das durch Chaoten massiv gestörte Absingen der Nationalhymne mißriet allerdings zur Kakophonie.

In the late afternoon of November 10, 1989, 20,000 Berliners gathered outside the Schöneberg Town Hall. The rally was also attended by (from left to right) the honorary chairman of the SPD, Willy Brandt, the governing mayor Walter Momper, Chancellor Helmut Kohl and SPD party chairman and leader of the parliamentary party Hans-Jochen Vogel. It was here that the former Chancellor Brandt spoke the decisive words which made him into one of the symbols of the unification process: "Now, what belongs together is growing together!" However, the singing of the national anthem was severely disrupted by anarchistic troublemakers and degenerated into cacophony.

Die Bürger der DDR ließen sich von den strengen Blicken der Grenzsoldaten nicht länger beeindrucken. Unbekümmert freuten sie sich – hier am 11.11.1989 an der Oberbaumbrücke in Berlin-Kreuzberg – daß die Mauer endlich durchlässig geworden war.

The citizens of the GDR were no longer impressed by the stern looks of the border guards. They took an unabashed delight – here at the Oberbaum bridge in Berlin-Kreuzberg on November 11, 1989 – in the fact that at last it was possible to pass through the Wall.

Die Grenzposten der DDR wurden vom Fall der Mauer völlig überrascht. Seit 1961 hatte die Grenze als »antifaschistischer Schutzwall« und ihre Bewachung als ehrenvoller »Friedensdienst« gegolten. Jetzt sollte das alles plötzlich nicht mehr wahr sein. Auch die am 12.11.1989 beim neugeschaffenen Übergang am Potsdamer Platz postierten Grenzbeamten fühlten sich in ihrer neuen Rolle noch nicht recht wohl. Statt des Wachdienstes bestand ihre Aufgabe plötzlich in der raschen Ausgabe von Sichtvermerken für die Ausreise von DDR-Bürgern. Formulare und Stempel hielten sie in eigens dafür vorgesehenen Umhängetaschen bereit.

The GDR border guards were taken completely by surprise when the Wall came down. Since 1961 the Wall had been regarded as an "anti-Fascist protective barrier" and guarding it had been considered as an honorable "peace duty." Now they were suddenly told that all this was no longer true. The border officials on duty at the newly created crossing at Potsdam Square on November 12, 1989 were also still uncomfortable in their new role. Suddenly, instead of guard duty their job now was the speedy issue of exit visas to inhabitants of the GDR. Forms and stamps were kept in document cases specially provided for that purpose.

Nach dem 9.11.1989 hatten die Ordnungshüter auf beiden Seiten der Mauer plötzlich eine gemeinsame Aufgabe. Seite an Seite sorgten ein West-Berliner Polizeibeamter (links) und ein Angehöriger der DDR-Grenztruppen für einen reibungslosen Fußgängerverkehr am Potsdamer Platz.

After November 9, 1989 the guardians of the law on both sides of the Wall suddenly had a common task. Side by side a West Berlin policeman (left) and a GDR border guard ensured the smooth movement of pedestrians on Potsdam Square.

Nicht nur in Berlin nutzten die Bürger der DDR in Scharen die unverhoffte Chance zu einer Spritztour in den Westen. Auch an der innerdeutschen Grenze – hier am Übergang Helmstedt/Marienborn – bildeten sich lange Schlangen mit »Trabis« und »Wartburgs«. Am Wochenende vom 10. bis 12.11. 1989 kamen insgesamt 3 Millionen Besucher aus der DDR nach West-Berlin und in die Bundesrepublik. Auf westlicher Seite säumten zur Begrüßung Hunderte die Straßen.

Not only in Berlin did the inhabitants of the GDR take advantage in droves of the unexpected chance to take a trip by car to the West. Long lines of "Trabants" and "Wartburgs" also formed at the internal German border – here at the Helmstedt/Marienborn crossing. During the weekend of November 10-12, 1989 a total of 3 million visitors from the GDR went to West Berlin and the Federal Republic. On the western side hundreds of people lined the streets to welcome them.

Am 14.3.1990 kamen in Leipzig 300 000 Menschen zusammen, um zum Abschluß des Wahlkampfs zur ersten freien Volkskammerwahl Helmut Kohl zu hören. Auf demselben Platz zwischen Oper und Gewandhaus, auf dem sie im Herbst 1989 gegen die Machthaber der DDR demonstriert hatten, jubelten sie nun mit schwarz-rot-goldenen Fahnen dem Bundeskanzler der Bundesrepublik Deutschland zu. Aus der Demonstrationsbewegung für die Freiheit war eine Massenbewegung für die Einheit geworden.

In Leipzig 300,000 people gathered on March 14, 1990 to listen to Helmut Kohl at the end of the election campaign for the first free elections to the Volkskammer. At the same place between the opera and the Gewandhaus where they had demonstrated against the GDR rulers in autumn 1989, now, carrying black, red and gold flags, they cheered the Chancellor of the Federal Republic of Germany. The movement which had demonstrated for freedom had become a mass movement for national unity.

Bei der abschließenden Pressekonferenz von Ministerpräsident Modrow (links) und Bundeskanzler Kohl am 13.2.1990 in Bonn war an den Gesichtern abzulesen, daß die Regierungsgespräche nicht ohne Spannungen verlaufen waren.

At the final press conference given by Prime Minister Modrow (left) and Chancellor Kohl in Bonn on February 13, 1990, their faces showed that the government talks had not been free of tension.

Die CDU erhielt bei den Volkskammerwahlen am 18.3.1990 fast 41 Prozent der Stimmen und errang zusammen mit ihren in der »Allianz für Deutschland« vereinten Partnerparteien einen spektakulären Sieg. Am Wahlabend gaben der zukünftige Ministerpräsident Lothar de Maizière (links) und der Generalsekretär der DDR-CDU Martin Kirchner (Mitte) dem Korrespondenten des westdeutschen Fernsehens Fritz Pleitgen ein erstes Interview.

At the elections to the Volkskammer on March 18, 1990, the CDU polled almost 41% of the vote and, with the parties that had joined forces with them in the "Alliance for Germany," won a spectacular victory. On the evening of election day the future Prime Minister Lothar de Maizière (left) and the General Secretary of the GDR-CDU Martin Kirchner (center) gave their first interview to West German television reporter Fritz Pleitgen.

Auf dem Weg zur Einheit / On the Way to internal Unity

Zu Beginn des Jahres 1990 beschleunigte sich der Niedergang der DDR dramatisch. Unter diesem Eindruck beschloß der von der Regierung und Vertretern der Bürgerbewegung gebildete »Runde Tisch«, den ursprünglich für Anfang Mai 1990 vorgesehenen Termin der ersten freien Volkskammerwahl vorzuverlegen. Als Hans Modrow Mitte Februar zum zweiten Mal mit Helmut Kohl zusammenkam, war er ein Ministerpräsident auf Abruf. Die Bundesregierung verschloß sich seiner Bitte, die DDR mit einer Soforthilfe in zweistelliger Milliardenhöhe zu unterstützen. Bundeskanzler Kohl setzte auf das Votum der Bürger, von deren Wunsch nach Wiedervereinigung er seit seinem Besuch in Dresden überzeugt war. Tatsächlich errangen am 18.3.1990 jene Parteien eine deutliche Mehrheit, die für einen raschen Beitritt der DDR zur Bundesrepublik Deutschland eintraten.

Early in 1990 the collapse of the GDR was dramatically accelerated. The effect of this was to lead the "Round Table," made up of the government and representatives of the civil rights movement, to bring forward the date for the first free elections to the Volkskammer, which were originally scheduled for early May 1990. When in mid-February Hans Modrow had his second meeting with Helmut Kohl, he was a prime minister under notice to quit. The Federal government turned a deaf ear to his plea for support for the GDR in the shape of an immediate grant running into tens of thousands of million Deutschmarks. Chancellor Kohl relied on the votes of the people of the GDR who, as he had been convinced since his visit to Dresden, wanted reunification. And indeed, the parties which supported the speedy accession of the GDR to the Federal Republic won a clear majority on March 18, 1990.

Der eigentliche Gewinner der Wahlen in der DDR war Helmut Kohl. Er erreichte bei seinen Wahlkampfauftritten – hier am 14.3.1990 in Leipzig – fast eine Million DDR-Bürger. Der Bundeskanzler hatte die Stimmung in Ostdeutschland besser erfaßt als viele andere und den Wunsch der Bevölkerung nach Wiedervereinigung von Anfang an ernstgenommen. Das Vertrauen, das ihm hier entgegengebracht wurde, war schier grenzenlos. Doch in den übergroßen Hoffnungen lag auch der Keim späterer Enttäuschungen.

The real winner in the GDR elections was Helmut Kohl. He reached almost a million people in the GDR through his election appearances – here in Leipzig on March 14, 1990. The Chancellor had grasped the mood in East Germany better than many others had, and had from the outset taken seriously the people's desire for reunification. The confidence they had in him was absolutely boundless. But their exaggerated hopes also contained the germ of later disappointments.

Die Diskussion um den Umtausch-kurs bei der Währungsunion trieb viele DDR-Bürger im Frühjahr 1990 erneut auf die Straßen. Auf diese Weise unterstrichen am 5.3. auch Demonstranten im Berliner Lust-garten entschlossen ihre Forderung, bei der Umstellung des Geldes für jede mühsam erarbeitete oder ersparte DDR-Mark eine volle D-Mark zu erhalten.

In the spring of 1990 the arguments about the exchange rate for monetary union brought many people in GDR out onto the streets once more. In this way demonstrators in the Lustgarten square in Berlin on March 5 resolute-ly underlined their demand that when the currency was changed they should be given a whole Deutschmark for every GDR Mark which they had labo-riously earned or saved.

Am 1.7.1990 war es soweit. Noch ein-mal standen die Bürger der DDR Schlange: dieses Mal jedoch nicht für seltene Konsumgüter, sondern für das neue Geld. Zuvor waren innerhalb weniger Tage 27,5 Milliarden DM aus der Bundesrepublik in die DDR ge-schafft worden, 600 Tonnen in Mün-zen und 460 Tonnen in Banknoten. Der größte Geldtransport in der deutschen Geschichte machte es mög-lich, daß auch die Wartenden in der Puschkinstraße in Schwerin pünktlich bedient werden konnten.

On July 1, 1990 the time had come. People in the GDR were lining up again, but this time not for scarce consumer goods but for the new money. Prior to this, in the space of a few days, 27,5 billion DM had been transported to the GDR from the Federal Republic, 600 tons of coins and 460 tons of banknotes. The lar-gest movement of money in German history enabled people waiting on Pushkin Street in Schwerin to be attended to without delay.

Währungsunion / Monetary Union

Angesichts des drohenden Zusammenbruchs der DDR-Wirtschaft und der fortdauernden Abwanderung in Richtung Bundesrepublik bot die Bundesregierung der DDR bereits im Februar 1990 eine rasche Wirtschafts- und Währungsunion an. Der ökonomisch riskante und unter Experten durchaus umstrittene Vorschlag führte sofort zu einem Rückgang der Übersiedlerzahlen und beeinflußte nachhaltig das Wahlverhalten bei der Volkskammerwahl. Nach dem Amtsantritt der neuen Regierung begannen unverzüglich die Vorbereitungen, bei denen sich die Festlegung des »richtigen« Umtauschkurses als das schwierigste Problem erwies. Die Währungsumstellung erfolgte schließlich am 1.7.1990 zu einem Kurs von eins zu eins für Einkommen, Renten und Mieten. Alle anderen Verbindlichkeiten wurden im Verhältnis zwei Mark Ost zu einer D-Mark verrechnet. Begrenzte Ausnahmen galten für private Sparkonten. Damit entsprach der Umtauschmodus weitgehend den hohen Erwartungen der DDR-Bürger, nicht jedoch dem tatsächlichen Wert ihrer alten Währung. Gemessen daran hätte der Umtauschkurs vier Ostmark zu einer D-Mark betragen müssen.

Faced with the imminent collapse of the GDR economy and continued migration to the Federal Republic, the Federal government as early as February 1990 offered the GDR a speedy monetary and economic union. This proposal, which was risky in economic terms and the subject of considerable controversy among experts, immediately led to a drop in the numbers of people leaving the GDR and substantially affected the voters' behavior at the Volkskammer elections. After the new government had taken office preparations began without delay. Determining the "correct" exchange rate proved to be the most difficult problem. The currency changeover finally came about on July 1, 1990 at a rate of one to one for incomes, pensions and rents. All other liabilities were calculated at a rate of two East Marks to one Deutschmark, with limited exceptions for personal savings accounts. These exchange arrangements were to a large extent in keeping with the expectations of people in the GDR, but were out of line with the lower purchasing power of their old currency. If that had been the benchmark an exchange rate of four East Marks to one Deutschmark would have been more appropriate.

Lange war in der DDR die »Westmark« eine wertvolle Schattenwährung gewesen, für die alles zu kaufen war und auch mancher Handwerker Wunder wirkte. In den siebziger Jahren ließ die DDR-Führung sogar eigene »Intershops« für den Einkauf mit der D-Mark einrichten. Nach der Währungsunion konnte jeder über das begehrte Geld verfügen. Für die junge Berlinerin war es am 1. Juli 1990 jedoch noch sichtlich ungewohnt, es plötzlich wirklich in der Hand zu halten.

For a long time the "West Mark" had been a highly valued shadow currency in the GDR, with which one could buy anything and for which many a plumber or electrician worked miracles. In the seventies the GDR leaders even set up their own "Intershops" to sell goods for Deutschmarks. After monetary union everybody had the coveted currency. But the young woman in Berlin on July 1, 1990 was still visibly unaccustomed to actually holding it in her hand.

(oben) Ministerpräsident de Maizière, Bundeskanzler Kohl, DDR-Finanzminister Romberg und
Bundesfinanzminister Waigel stoßen am 18.5.1990
auf dem Balkon des Palais Schaumburg auf die
Schaffung der Währungs-, Wirtschafts- und Sozial-
union zwischen der Bundesrepublik und der DDR
an.
(links) Vertragsunterzeichnung im Bundeskanzleramt.

(above) Prime Minister de Maizière, Chancellor
Kohl, GDR Finance Minister Romberg and Federal
Finance Minister Waigel raise their glasses to the
signing of the Monetary Union Treaty, Economic
and Social Union between the Federal Republic of
Germany and the GDR, on the balcony of the Palais
Schaumburg in Bonn on May 18, 1990.
(left) Signing the Treaty at the Federal Chancellery.

Unterzeichnung des Vertrags über die Herstellung der Einheit Deutschlands am 31.8.1990 in Ostberlin. Links Bundesinnenminister Wolfgang Schäuble, rechts der Staatssekretär im Amt des Ministerpräsidenten der DDR, Günther Krause. In der Mitte: DDR-Ministerpräsident auf Abruf DDR-Ministerpräsident Lothar de Maizière, der bei aller Zufriedenheit über das Zustandekommen der deutschen Vereinigung wußte, daß seine Tage als Chef einer ostdeutschen Regierung gezählt waren.

The signing of the Treaty concerning the unification of Germany in East Berlin on August 31, 1990. On the left Federal Minister of the Interior Wolfgang Schäuble, on the right the State Secretary in the GDR prime minister's office Günter Krause. In the center: Lothar de Maizière, the GDR Prime Minister under notice, who for all his satisfaction at the unification of Germany knew that his days as head of an East German government were numbered.

Willy Brandt und Helmut Kohl im früheren Arbeitszimmer Konrad Adenauers im Bonner Palais Schaumburg. Die drei Namen stehen für jene Kanzler der Bundesrepublik, die die Voraussetzungen für die Wiedervereinigung Deutschlands schufen: Adenauer mit der Westbindung, Brandt mit den Ostverträgen und Kohl mit dem entschlossenen Zugriff auf die historische Chance. Zwischen Brandt und Kohl entstanden im Zuge des Einigungsprozesses fast freundschaftliche Bande. So fand der Streit um die Ostpolitik der siebziger Jahre ein versöhnliches Ende.

Willy Brandt and Helmut Kohl in Konrad Adenauer's former study in the Palais Schaumburg in Bonn. These were the three Chancellors of the Federal Republic who created the preconditions for the reunification of Germany: Adenauer, who integrated the Federal Republic into the West; Brandt, who concluded the Eastern Treaties; and Kohl who resolutely seized the historic opportunity. During the process of unification relations between Brandt and Kohl became almost friendly. Thus the disputes over the *Ostpolitik* of the seventies ended in reconciliation.

Ein weiterer Meilenstein auf dem Weg zur Einheit war das sowjetische Einverständnis mit der vollen Mitgliedschaft des vereinigten Deutschlands in der NATO. Nachdem der sowjetische Staatschef schon in Washington entsprechende Andeutungen gemacht und die NATO ihrerseits das Ende der Gegnerschaft mit dem Warschauer Pakt verkündet hatte, erklärte Michail Gorbatschow dem Bundeskanzler am 14.7.1990 in Moskau offen seine Zustimmung. Bei der gemeinsamen Wanderung im Kaukasus, wohin die Delegationen am folgenden Tag aufbrachen, herrschte daraufhin eine fröhliche, fast ausgelassene Stimmung.

A further milestone on the path to unity was Soviet agreement to full NATO membership of a unified Germany. The Soviet leader had already hinted as much in Washington, and NATO for its part had announced the end of hostile relations with the Warsaw Pact. Mikhail Gorbachev now gave the Federal Chancellor his open agreement in Moscow on July 14, 1990. Following this, there was a cheerful, almost exuberant mood during the ramble together in the Caucasus for which the delegations set off the following day.

Eine wichtige Voraussetzung für die sowjetische Unterstützung der Wiedervereinigung war die deutsche Bereitschaft, die Beziehungen mit der UdSSR auf eine völlig neue Grundlage zu stellen. Schon im April 1990 hatte Bundeskanzler Kohl der Sowjetregierung entsprechende Vereinbarungen mit dem vereinigten Deutschland angeboten. Am 9.11.1990 konnte in Bonn der deutsch-sowjetische Vertrag über gute Nachbarschaft, Partnerschaft und Zusammenarbeit unterzeichnet werden. Zwischen Helmut Kohl und Michail Gorbatschow war es, wie das Bild zeigt, inzwischen sogar zu einer persönlichen Freundschaft gekommen.

An important precondition of Soviet support for reunification was the Germans' willingness to put relations with the USSR on a completely new footing. Back in April 1990 Chancellor Kohl had offered the Soviet government appropriate agreements with the unified Germany. By November 9, 1990 they were able to sign, in Bonn, the German-Soviet Good Neighborliness, Partnership and Cooperation Agreement. By then, as the photo shows, a personal friendship had developed between Helmut Kohl and Mikhail Gorbachev.

Die europäischen Partner reagierten 1989 auf die plötzliche Rückkehr der deutschen Frage auf die Tagesordnung der Weltpolitik zunächst besorgt. Die Eintracht der Staats- und Regierungschefs auf dem Erinnerungsfoto zur EG-Gipfelkonferenz vom 8.-9.12.1989 in Straßburg täuschte. Er habe »niemals einen EG-Gipfel in so eisiger Atmosphäre miterlebt wie diesen«, erinnerte sich Helmut Kohl rückblickend.

Germany's European partners reacted apprehensively at first to the sudden return of the German question to the international political agenda in 1989. The harmony between the political leaders in the souvenir photo taken at the EC summit conference in Strasbourg on December 8/9, 1989 was deceptive. Helmut Kohl later recalled that he had "never experienced an EC summit in such an icy atmosphere as this one."

Auf dem Rückflug von Moskau am 11.2.1990 hatten Außenminister Hans-Dietrich Genscher und Bundeskanzler Helmut Kohl allen Anlaß zur Zufriedenheit. In den vorangegangenen Gesprächen mit der sowjetischen Regierung war ein Durchbruch für die Wiedervereinigung Deutschlands erzielt worden. Staats- und Parteichef Gorbatschow hatte unumwunden erklärt, »daß es zwischen der Sowjetunion, der Bundesrepublik und der DDR keine Meinungsverschiedenheiten über die Einheit gebe... Die Deutschen in der Bundesrepublik und in der DDR müßten es selbst wissen, welchen Weg sie gehen wollten.«

Foreign Minister Hans-Dietrich Genscher and Chancellor Helmut Kohl had every reason to be satisfied as they flew back from Moscow on February 11, 1990. In their talks with the Soviet government a breakthrough had been achieved as regards German reunification. State and party leader Gorbachev had frankly declared "that there are no differences of opinion between the Soviet Union, the Federal Republic and the GDR concerning unity... Germans in the Federal Republic and the GDR must know themselves which way they wish to go."

Mit Vorsicht und Zurückhaltung hatte anfänglich der französische Staatspräsident auf die Ereignisse in Deutschland reagiert. Als François Mitterrand nach den deutsch-französischen Konsultationsgesprächen am 26.4.1990 gemeinsam mit Helmut Kohl den Élysée-Palast verließ, waren freilich alle Unstimmigkeiten ausgeräumt. Auf amerikanisches Drängen hatte der Präsident schon einige Tage zuvor der Wiedervereinigung und Wiederherstellung der vollen Souveränität Deutschlands zugestimmt. Übereinstimmung bestand zwischen ihm und dem Bundeskanzler über die Notwendigkeit, den deutschen Einigungsprozeß untrennbar mit dem europäischen zu verknüpfen.

The French President's initial reaction to events in Germany had been cautious and reserved. But by the time François Mitterrand and Helmut Kohl left the Elysée Palace together on April 26, 1990 after the Franco-German consultative talks, all differences between them had been ironed out. At the urgent request of the Americans, the President had already given his agreement a few days previously to the reunification of Germany and the restoration of its full sovereignty. He and the Chancellor were agreed as to the necessity of inseparably linking the German and the European unification process.

(gegenüber) Die Amerikaner hielten Wort. Von Anfang an war der deutsche Einigungsprozeß in Washington mit Sympathie begleitet worden. Während die Europäer in Erinnerung an die unheilvolle Geschichte zunächst über eine mögliche Renaissance deutschen Großmachtstrebens beunruhigt gewesen waren, erkannten die Amerikaner in der Vereinigung Deutschlands eine Chance für die Zukunft. Die deutsch-amerikanische Freundschaft wurde zum wichtigsten Garanten für die außenpolitische Absicherung der Einheit.

(opposite) The Americans kept their promise. The German unification process had from the outset been looked upon with sympathy in Washington. While the Europeans, remembering Germany's disastrous history, had at first been worried by the idea of a possible resurgence of Germany's ambition to be a great power, the Americans recognised in German unification a chance for the future. The friendship between Germany and America became the most important guarantee that unification would not be jeopardized by foreign policy factors.

Herzliche Begrüßung am 24.2.1990 zwischen den Ehepaaren Kohl und Bush bei der Ankunft in Camp David. In der Abgeschiedenheit der Bergwelt von Maryland einigten sich der deutsche Bundeskanzler und der amerikanische Präsident auf eine gemeinsame Strategie für die Verhandlungen mit der UdSSR. Als Ziel wurde, worauf die USA entschiedenen Wert legten, die volle Mitgliedschaft auch des vereinigten Deutschlands in der NATO festgelegt. Dafür sagte Bush die uneingeschränkte amerikanische Unterstützung in den Zwei-plus-Vier-Gesprächen mit den Briten, Franzosen und Sowjets zu.

Warm greetings on February 24, 1990 between Kohl and Bush and their wives on arrival at Camp David. In the seclusion of the Maryland mountains the German Chancellor and the American President agreed to a joint strategy for negotiations with the USSR. The goal of full NATO membership for the united Germany was fixed – a point by which the US set decisive store. Bush promised full American support for this in the two-plus-four talks with the British, the French and the Russians.

Der »Zwei Plus Vier« -Vertrag / The "Two plus Four" -Treaty

Auftakt der Zwei-plus-Vier-Verhandlungen am 5.5. 1990 in Bonn. Nachdem die Grundsatzfragen der Wiedervereinigung Deutschlands in den Gipfelgesprächen geklärt worden waren, bestand die Aufgabe der Außenminister darin, die Details in eine abschließende Vertragsform zu bringen. Teilnehmer waren (von links) die Außenminister Markus Meckel (DDR), Hans-Dietrich Genscher (Bundesrepublik Deutschland), Eduard Schewardnadse (UdSSR), James Baker (USA), Roland Dumas (Frankreich) und Douglas Hurd (Großbritannien).

The opening of the two-plus-four negotiations in Bonn on May 5, 1990. Once the fundamental issues of German reunification had been clarified in the summit talks, the task facing the Foreign Ministers was to put the details into the final form of a treaty. Those taking part were (from left to right) Foreign Ministers Markus Meckel (GDR), Hans-Dietrich Genscher (Federal Republic), Eduard Shevardnadze (USSR), James Baker (USA), Roland Dumas (France) and Douglas Hurd (Britain).

Da der Zwei-Plus-Vier-Vertrag erst nach der Ratifizierung durch die Parlamente der Teilnehmerstaaten in Kraft treten konnte, erklärten die Vier Mächte am 1.10.1990 ihren vorzeitigen Verzicht auf alle Verantwortlichkeiten in Deutschland und Berlin. Damit erhielt Deutschland bereits am Tag seiner Vereinigung faktisch seine volle Souveränität. Symbolhaft war schon einige Monate zuvor, am 22.6.1990, im Beisein der Außenminister Frankreichs, Großbritanniens, der UdSSR und der USA der ehemalige Grenzübergang »Checkpoint Charlie« an der Friedrichstraße in Berlin demontiert worden.

As the Two-plus-Four Treaty could not come into effect until it had been ratified by the parliaments of the states involved, the four powers declared on October 1, 1990 that they relinquished all responsibilities in Germany and Berlin before the scheduled date. Thus Germany received its full sovereignty de facto on the day of its unification. A few months earlier, on June 22, 1990, "Checkpoint Charlie," the former border crossing on Friedrichstraße in Berlin, had been symbolically demolished in the presence of the Foreign Ministers of France, Britain, the USSR and the US.

(gegenüber) Besondere Verdienste im schwierigen Prozeß der deutschen Vereinigung erwarb sich der sowjetische Außenminister und spätere Präsident Georgiens, Eduard Schewardnadse, hier im Juni 1991 mit Außenminister Genscher, der ihn »meinen Freund« nannte. Nicht von ungefähr führte Genschers letzte Reise als Außenminister im Frühjahr 1992 zu Schewardnadse nach Tiflis. Es war Abschiedsbesuch und Danksagung zugleich.

(opposite) A special contribution was made to the difficult process of German unification by the Soviet Foreign Minister and later President of Georgia, Eduard Shevardnadze, here in June 1991 with Foreign Minister Genscher, who called him "my friend." It was no accident that Genscher's last journey as Foreign Minister in the spring of 1992 took him to Tbilisi to visit Shevardnadze. It was both a farewell visit and an expression of thanks.

Auf der Ehrentribüne vor dem Hauptportal des Reichstags waren am Tag der Einheit auch die führenden Repräsentanten Deutschlands vereint. Von links: der saarländische Ministerpräsident und Kanzlerkandidat der SPD Oskar Lafontaine, der SPD-Ehrenvorsitzende Willy Brandt, Außenminister Hans-Dietrich Genscher, Hannelore Kohl und Bundeskanzler Helmut Kohl, Bundespräsident Richard von Weizsäcker, der letzte Ministerpräsident der DDR Lothar de Maizière.

On the day of unity leading representatives of Germany were also united on the VIP rostrum in front of the main entrance to the Reichstag. From left to right: the Minister President of the Saarland and SPD chancellor candidate Oskar Lafontaine, the honorary party chairman of the SPD Willy Brandt, Foreign Minister Hans-Dietrich Genscher, Hannelore Kohl and Chancellor Helmut Kohl, Federal President Richard von Weizsäcker, the last prime minister of the GDR Lothar de Maizière.

Am 3.10.1990 vollzog sich mit dem Inkrafttreten des Einigungsvertrags die Wiedervereinigung Deutschlands. Aus diesem Anlaß fand vor dem Reichstag in Berlin ein Festakt statt. Seit hundert Jahren war das Gebäude Zeuge der wechselvollen deutschen Geschichte. Hier hatte das Parlament des Kaiserreichs getagt, hatte Philipp Scheidemann 1918 die Republik ausgerufen, hatte 1933 die erste deutsche Demokratie in den Flammen des Reichstagsbrandes ihr Ende gefunden, hatte die sowjetische Fahne 1945 das Ende des »Großdeutschen Reiches« besiegelt und hatte 1948 der Berliner Bürgermeister Ernst Reuter den Widerstand des freien Teils der Stadt gegen den Kommunismus beschworen. Jetzt wurde hier der Tag der Deutschen Einheit gefeiert.

Germany was reunified on October 3, 1990 when the Unification Treaty came into effect. The event was marked by a ceremony outside the Reichstag building in Berlin. For a hundred years the building had witnessed the vicissitudes of German history. It was here that the parliament of imperial Germany had met, Philipp Scheidemann had proclaimed the Republic in 1918, the first German democracy had perished in the flames of the Reichstag fire in 1933, the Soviet flag had signalled the end of "Greater Germany" in 1945, and Ernst Reuter, the Mayor of Berlin, had inspired the resistance of the free part of the city to communism in 1948. Now the day of German unity was celebrated here.

1990–1998

Vereintes Deutschland
Unified Germany

Demonstration für einen Umtauschkurs von 1:1 am 5.3.1990 im Ost-Berliner Lustgarten.

Demonstration in the pleasure gardens in East Berlin on March 5, 1990 calling for an exchange rate of 1 to 1.

Am 2.12.1990 fanden die ersten gesamtdeutschen Bundestagswahlen statt. 60,5 Millionen Wahlberechtigte waren aufgerufen, erstmals seit 1933 für ganz Deutschland ein freies Parlament zu wählen. Mit großer Mehrheit bestätigten sie die amtierende Koalition von CDU/CSU und FDP unter Bundeskanzler Helmut Kohl. Damit besaß Deutschland nach seiner staatlichen Wiedervereinigung nun auch wieder eine gemeinsame Volksvertretung und Regierung.

Doch der Prozeß der deutschen Vereinigung war damit noch nicht abgeschlossen. Das Zusammenwachsen des über 40 Jahre in zwei gegensätzliche Wirtschafts- und Gesellschaftsordnungen geteilten Landes begann erst. In den fünf neuen Ländern der Bundesrepublik – Brandenburg, Mecklenburg-Vorpommern, Sachsen, Sachsen-Anhalt und Thüringen – mußten in kürzester Zeit die politischen und wirtschaftlichen Strukturen neu geordnet oder überhaupt erst geschaffen werden. Die öffentliche Verwaltung, die Justiz sowie die Sozial- und Bildungssysteme waren umzustellen; Industrie, Handwerk und Landwirtschaft mußten – soweit möglich – marktwirtschaftlich organisiert, privatisiert und modernisiert werden; die Verkehrswege, die Post- und Telekommunikation sowie der Wohnungsbestand waren zu sanieren und auszubauen; komplizierte Eigentums- und Vermögensfragen verlangten nach rascher Klärung; darüber hinaus galt es, die erheblichen Umweltbelastungen zu beseitigen. Schließlich mußte auch der Versuch einer Aufarbeitung des unter der SED-Diktatur begangenen Unrechts in Angriff genommen werden.

Diese historisch einmalige Situation stellte die Bundesrepublik vor enorme Herausforderungen. An Vorarbeiten, Planungen und Konzepten fehlte es. Die Einheit kam für die allermeisten Westdeutschen gänzlich überraschend. Unter dem Eindruck der friedlichen Revolution in der DDR wuchs aber das Zusammengehörigkeitsgefühl rasch wieder. Nachhaltige Proteste gegen die mit dem Aufbau im Osten Deutschlands verbundenen finanziellen Belastungen, die entgegen ursprünglicher Annahmen und Ankündigungen alsbald für jeden Bürger spürbar wurden, blieben aus. Die Ostendeutschen meisterten die Umstellung auf eine völlig veränderte Lebenswelt. Gleichwohl ist festzuhalten, daß sich der Anpassungsprozeß in der früheren DDR unter sehr viel günstigeren Bedingungen vollziehen konnte als in den Nachbarländern des ehemaligen Ostblocks. Anders als diese war das vereinigte Deutschland von Anfang an Teil der durch NATO und Europäische Union garantierten westlichen Stabilitätszone und gehörte zu den wirtschaftlich und politisch stärksten Staaten der Welt.

Auf dem Weg zur inneren Einheit

Die Ausgangssituation des inneren Vereinigungsprozesses war schwierig. Das SED-Regime hatte die DDR bis zuletzt als zehntstärkste Wirtschaftsnation der Welt präsentiert. Selbst die noch unter der Regierung Modrow eingerichtete Treuhandanstalt, der die Verwaltung des gesamten industriellen und wirtschaftlichen Erbes der DDR übertragen wurde, schätzte dessen Verkaufswert anfänglich noch auf 800 bis 1000 Mrd. DM. Doch die Wahrheit sah anders aus. Staat und Wirtschaft der DDR waren hoch verschuldet. Allein die laufenden Zinsverpflichtungen überstiegen die Summe

The first all-German general election took place on December 2, 1990. The 60.5 million who were entitled to vote were called on to elect a free parliament for the whole of Germany for the first time since 1933. They confirmed by a large majority the existing CDU/CSU-FDP coalition led by Chancellor Helmut Kohl. Thus Germany, following its reunification as a single state, now also had a single parliament and a single government.

But this was not yet the end of the process of German unification. The process of "growing together" in a country that had been divided for over 40 years into two totally different economic and social orders, was only just beginning. In the Federal Republic's five new *Länder* – Brandenburg, Mecklenburg-Western Pomerania, Saxony, Saxony-Anhalt and Thuringia – the political and economic structures had to be reorganized or created from scratch within an extremely short time. Public administration, the judiciary, social welfare and the education system had to be reformed. Industry, the skilled trades and agriculture had to be organized, privatized and modernized as far as possible in line with the market economy. Highways, posts and telecommunications and the housing stock had to be refurbished and expanded. Complex questions relating to property and assets required speedy clarification. Furthermore, there was the job of repairing the substantial damage that had been inflicted on the environment. And finally an attempt had to be made to deal with the injustices that had been committed under the SED dictatorship.

This historically unique situation presented huge challenges to the Federal Republic. There were no preliminary studies, plans or theoretical models. The great majority of West Germans were taken completely by surprise by unification. But under the impact of the peaceful revolution in the GDR, the sense of belonging together quickly grew again. There was no sustained protest against the financial burdens entailed by reconstruction in eastern Germany, the effects of which, despite original assumptions and pronouncements to the contrary, every citizen soon began to feel. The East Germans cope with the changeover to a totally new way of life. Even so the fact should not be overlooked that the process of adjustment took place in the former GDR under very much more favorable conditions than in the neighboring countries of the former eastern bloc. Unlike these, the unified Germany was from the outset part of the western zone of stability guaranteed by NATO and the European Union, and was both economically and politically one of the strongest nations in the world.

On the Road to Internal Unity

The situation at the outset of the process of internal unification was a difficult one. The SED régime had to the end presented the GDR as being economically the tenth strongest nation in the world. Even the *Treuhand* (the state holding company established to privatize former state-owned enterprises) which was set up under the Modrow government and given the responsibility for administering the entire industrial and economic legacy of the GDR, at first estimated its sale value at 800-1000 billion Deutschmarks. But the reality was very different. The GDR state and its trade industry were heavily in debt. Current interest liabilities alone exceeded the GDR's

Am 4.10.1990 konstituierte sich der erste gesamtdeutsche Bundestag im Berliner Reichstagsgebäude. Außer den 663 westdeutschen nahmen an der Sitzung erstmals auch die 144 ostdeutschen Abgeordneten teil, die noch von der DDR-Volkskammer bestimmt worden waren. Bereits Anfang August war der Termin für die ersten gesamtdeutschen Parlamentswahlen im deutsch-deutschen Wahlvertrag auf den 2.12.1990 festgelegt worden. Die von CDU/CSU und FDP getragene Bundesregierung stellte sich zur Wiederwahl. Von links: Justizminister Hans Engelhard, Innenminister Wolfgang Schäuble, Außenminister Hans-Dietrich Genscher, Bundeskanzler Helmut Kohl.

The first all-German parliament constituted itself in the Reichstag building in Berlin on October 4, 1990. Along with the 663 West German members, the 144 East German members who had been delegated by the Volkskammer also attended the meeting for the first time. Back in early August, in the German-German Election Agreement, December 2, 1990 had been set as the date for the first all-German parliamentary elections. The CDU/CSU-FDP government presented itself for re-election. From left to right: Minister of Justice Hans Engelhard, Minister of the Interior Wolfgang Schäuble, Foreign Minister Hans-Dietrich Genscher, Chancellor Helmut Kohl.

Der Vereinigungsparteitag der SPD hatte Ende September 1990 fast einstimmig den saarländischen Ministerpräsidenten Oskar Lafontaine zum Kanzlerkandidaten für die Bundestagswahlen am 2.12. bestimmt. Der Herausforderer – hier am 4.10.1990 am Rednerpult des alten Plenarsaals im Berliner Reichstag – zeigte sich anders als beispielsweise Willy Brandt wenig angetan von der raschen deutschen Vereinigung und wies früh auf die damit verbundenen finanziellen Belastungen hin. Seine Warnungen trafen jedoch nicht die Stimmung der Wähler. Diese folgten der Auffassung der Bundesregierung, daß die einzigartige Gunst der Stunde genutzt werden müsse und dafür auch ein hoher Preis gerechtfertigt sei. Über die tatsächlichen »Kosten der Einheit« waren sich aber alle Beteiligten damals noch im unklaren.

The SPD unification party conference at the end of September 1990 had almost unanimously chosen Oskar Lafontaine, Minister President of the Saarland, as chancellor candidate for the parliamentary elections on December 2. Unlike Willy Brandt for example, the challenger – at the speaker's desk in the old plenary chamber of the Reichstag building in Berlin on October 4, 1990 – showed little enthusiasm for the rapid unification of Germany, and was quick to point out the financial burdens which it would entail. But his warnings were out of keeping with the mood of the voters. They went along with the government's view that the opportunity presented by this uniquely auspicious moment must be grasped and that a high price for doing so was justified. At that time none of those involved were as yet aware of the actual "cost of unity."

Erstmals seit 1933 wählten die Deutschen am 2.12.1990 in freier Abstimmung ein gemeinsames Parlament. Für die Bürger in Ostdeutschland war es zugleich die erste Bundestagswahl. Mit besonderer Aufmerksamkeit studierten sie, denen in den zurückliegenden vier Jahrzehnten lediglich Einheitslisten vorgelegt worden waren, die Wahlzettel.

On December 2, 1990 the Germans, in a free vote, elected a parliament for the whole country for the first time since 1933. For people in East Germany it was at the same time their first election for the Bundestag. For the past forty years they had been presented only with single lists. Now they paid particularly careful attention to the voting slips.

Auch die »Partei des Demokratischen Sozialismus« (PDS) nahm an den ersten gesamtdeutschen Wahlen teil. Sie war im Dezember 1989 aus der SED hervorgegangen. Auch nach dem Parteiausschluß ehemaliger Spitzenfunktionäre waren die meisten Mitglieder frühere SED-Kader. Unter der medienwirksamen Leitung ihres Parteivorsitzenden Gregor Gysi (Mitte) erreichte die Partei zwar insgesamt nur 2,4 Prozent der Wählerstimmen, konnte aber im gesondert berechneten Wahlgebiet Ost klar die Fünf-Prozent-Hürde überspringen und so in den neuen Bundestag einziehen. In den folgenden Wahlen etablierte sie sich in den fünf ostdeutschen Ländern als feste Größe im Parteienspektrum.

The "Party of Democratic Socialism" (PDS) also contested the first all-German elections. It had emerged in December 1989 from the SED, and even after former top party officials had been excluded, most of its members were former SED cadre members. Led by its telegenic party chairman Gregor Gysi (center), the party, although it won only 2.4% of the overall vote, easily cleared the 5% hurdle in the East, for which votes were counted separately, and was thus able to take up seats in parliament. In subsequent elections it established a secure place for itself in the party-political spectrum of the five eastern German *Länder*.

Mit insgesamt 54,8 Prozent errang die christlich-liberale Koalition 1990 die absolute Mehrheit im Bundestag. Am 18.1.1991 wurde das neue Kabinett ernannt. Erste Reihe von links: Ministerin für Frauen und Jugend Angela Merkel (CDU), Finanzminister Theo Waigel (CSU), Bundeskanzler Helmut Kohl (CDU), Bundespräsident Richard von Weizsäcker, Außenminister Hans-Dietrich Genscher (FDP), Wirtschaftsminister Jürgen W. Möllemann (FDP); zweite Reihe: Minister für besondere Aufgaben und Chef des Bundeskanzleramtes Rudolf Seiters (CDU), Arbeitsminister Norbert Blüm (CDU), Landwirtschaftsminister Ignaz Kiechle (CSU), Familienministerin Hannelore Rönsch (CDU), Bauministerin Imgard Adam-Schwaetzer (FDP); dritte Reihe: Verkehrsminister Günther Krause (CDU), Bildungsminister Rainer Ortleb (FDP), Umweltminister Klaus Töpfer (CDU), Postminister Christian Schwarz-Schilling (CDU), Gesundheitsministerin Gerda Hasselfeldt (CSU), Justizminister Klaus Kinkel (FDP), Innenminister Wolfgang Schäuble (CDU), Forschungsminister Heinz Riesenhuber (CDU), Minister für wirtschaftliche Zusammenarbeit Carl-Dieter Spranger (CSU) und Verteidigungsminister Gerhard Stoltenberg (CDU).

With a total of 54.8% of the vote the Christian-liberal coalition won an absolute parliamentary majority in 1990. The new cabinet was appointed on January 18, 1991. Front row from left to right: Minister for Women and Youth Angela Merkel (CDU), Finance Minister Theo Waigel (CSU), Chancellor Helmut Kohl (CDU), President Richard von Weizsäcker, Foreign Minister Hans-Dietrich Genscher (FDP), Economics Minister Jürgen W. Möllemann (FDP); second row: Minister without Portfolio and Head of Chancellery Rudolf Seiters (CDU), Minister of Labor Norbert Blüm (CDU), Minister of Agriculture Ignaz Kiechle (CSU), Family Minister Hannelore Rönsch (CDU), Minister of Construction Irmgard Adam-Schwaetzer (FDP); third row: Minister of Transport Günther Krause (CDU), Minister of Education Rainer Ortleb (FDP), Minister of the Environment Klaus Töpfer (CDU), Minister of Posts Christian Schwarz-Schilling (CDU), Minister of Health Gerda Hasselfeldt (CSU), Minister of Justice Klaus Kinkel (FDP), Minister of the Interior Wolfgang Schäuble (CDU), Minister of Research Heinz Riesenhuber (CDU), Minister for Economic Cooperation Carl-Dieter Spranger (CSU) and Defense Minister Gerhard Stoltenberg (CDU).

Die Deutschen gaben ihrer Abscheu vor den Gewalttätern in öffentlichen Kundgebungen Ausdruck. Am 14.11.1992 demonstrierten in Bonn über 100 000 Menschen unter dem Motto »Grundrechte verteidigen, Flüchtlinge schützen, Rassismus bekämpfen« gegen Ausländerfeindlichkeit.

The Germans gave vent in public rallies to their revulsion against the perpetrators of this violence. On November 14, 1992 over 100,000 people demonstrated in Bonn against xenophobia, under the motto: "defend basic rights, protect refugees, combat racism."

Mit Schrecken reagierten Deutschland und die Welt, als sich erstmals im September 1991 im sächsischen Hoyerswerda Rechtsradikale in brutalen Ausschreitungen gegen wehrlose Ausländer austobten. Diese Gespenster der Vergangenheit hatte man aufgrund des stets propagierten Antifaschismus in der DDR und des demokratischen Grundkonsenses in der Bundesrepublik für gebannt gehalten. Doch die Aktionen hörten nicht auf. Am 29.5.1993 kamen in dem hier abgebildeten Haus im nordrhein-westfälischen Solingen bei einem Brandanschlag fünf türkische Mädchen ums Leben.

Germany and the world were horrified in September 1991 when right-wing radicals went on the rampage for the first time in Hoyerswerda in Saxony, with acts of brutal violence against defenseless foreigners. These ghosts of the past were thought to have been laid, given the anti-fascism that had been constantly taught in the GDR and the fundamental democratic consensus in the Federal Republic. But the campaigns did not stop. On May 29, 1993 five Turkish girls died when the house shown here in Solingen in North Rhine-Westphalia was set on fire.

Nun gingen auch im Westen Deutschlands – hier im Februar 1993 in Düsseldorf – die Menschen mit Kerzen auf die Straßen, wie es während der friedlichen Revolution 1989 die Bürger in Ostdeutschland getan hatten. Doch nicht nur die Demonstranten zeigten, daß die Bundesrepublik kein fremdenfeindliches Land ist. Deutschland bot jährlich Hunderttausenden von Bedrängten aus aller Welt Schutz und rang sich nur schwer zu einer Neuregelung seiner Asyl-Gesetzgebung durch. Während des Krieges im ehemaligen Jugoslawien nahm es mehr Flüchtlinge auf als alle anderen europäischen Staaten zusammen.

Now it was the turn of people in western Germany to take to the streets carrying candles – here in Düsseldorf in February 1993 – as people in East Germany had done during the peaceful revolution in 1989. But it was not only the demonstrators who showed that Germany was not a country hostile to foreigners. Every year Germany offered refuge protection to hundreds of thousands of oppressed people from all over the world, and could only with difficulty bring itself to modify its laws relating to asylum-seekers. During the war in former Yugoslavia it admitted more refugees than all other European countries together.

Schlote wie diese bei Bitterfeld rauchten einst so sehr, daß die DDR mit einem jährlichen Ausstoß von 5 Millionen Tonnen Schwefeldioxid und 2,1 Millionen Tonnen Staub die höchste Luftbelastung in Europa aufwies. Durch die Sanierung oder Stillegung der Industrien konnte die ökologische Situation in Ostdeutschland entscheidend verbessert werden. Zugleich wurden jedoch ganze Landstriche dauerhaft entindustrialisiert. So waren beispielsweise 60 Prozent des Bitterfelder Chemie-Reviers so schwer mit Schadstoffen verseucht, daß sie für eine neue Bebauung nicht mehr in Frage kamen.

Factory chimneys such as these near Bitterfeld at one time gave out so much smoke that the GDR had the highest level of air pollution in Europe, with annual emission rates of 5 million tonnes of sulphur dioxide and 2.1 million tonnes of dust. A decisive improvement in the ecological situation in East Germany has been achieved by refurbishing some plants and closing down others. At the same time, however, whole regions have been permanently deindustrialized. Thus, for example, 60% of the Bitterfeld chemicals manufacturing area was so seriously contaminated with harmful substances that no new plants could be built there.

Die Braunkohle war der Hauptenergieträger der DDR. Riesige Bagger schufen endlose Mondlandschaften und bauten eine stark schwefelhaltige Kohle ab, die güterzugweise in Strom- und Heizkraftwerken verfeuert wurde. Nach der deutschen Wiedervereinigung wurden 29 solche Tagebaue stillgelegt. Durch Flutung und Wiederanstieg des Grundwassers entsteht aus den ehemaligen Braunkohlerevieren eine Seenlandschaft. »Eiserne Ungetüme« wie das im Mai 1993 in Spremberg aufgenommene Exemplar werden allenfalls als Industriedenkmale überleben.

Brown coal was the main source of energy in the GDR. Gigantic excavators left endless lunar landscapes behind them, extracting coal with a high sulphur content, one train load after another of which was used in power stations generating electricity and thermal power. After the reunification of Germany, 29 such opencast mines were closed down. The mines were flooded, the water table rose again, and thus the former brown coal mining areas were turned into lake districts. "Iron monsters" such as this one photographed in Spremberg in May 1993 will at best survive as industrial monuments.

Aufbau Ost / Reconstruction in the East

Die Ausgangslage für den marktwirtschaftlichen Neuanfang im Osten Deutschlands war denkbar schwierig. Die meisten Betriebe waren überschuldet, ihre Werkstätten hoffnungslos veraltet, die Produktion mit schweren Umweltrisiken belastet. Für viele kam eine Modernisierung nicht mehr in Betracht. Sie mußten stillgelegt und mit hohen Kosten demontiert werden. Andere Betriebe schafften zunächst den Übergang in die neue Zeit, konnten jedoch im harten Wettbewerb mit westlichen Produzenten und deren Verkaufsstrategien nicht dauerhaft bestehen. Manche wurden auch von ihren Konkurrenten im Westen übernommen, nur um sie – wie es bald umgangssprachlich hieß – »plattzumachen«. Viele westdeutsche und europäische Firmen retteten jedoch mit hohem Einsatz Zehntausende von Arbeitsplätzen, indem sie in den Aufbau modernster Produktionsanlagen investierten. Doch von einem selbsttragenden Wirtschaftsaufschwung blieb der Osten Deutschlands weit entfernt.

At the outset of the new beginning in the East with a market economy, conditions were as difficult as could be. Most businesses were heavily in debt, their equipment was hopelessly obsolete, production posed grave risks to the environment. For many of them modernization was out of the question. They had to be closed down and dismantled at great expense. Other businesses did initially manage the transition to the new era, but in the long term could not survive the tough competition from western manufacturers and their marketing strategies. Some were taken over by their western competitors, but only in order to "take them out," as the process soon became popularly known. However, many West German and European firms did go to considerable lengths to save tens of thousands of jobs by investing in the construction of highly modern production plants. But for a long time the eastern part of Germany was far from any self-sustaining economic boom.

Die 1990 gegründete Treuhandanstalt hatte die Aufgabe, das ihr übertragene wirtschaftliche Erbe der DDR zu verwalten, die geeigneten Betriebe zu sanieren und zu privatisieren sowie die nicht überlebensfähigen Produktionsanlagen stillzulegen. Als die Präsidentin der Treuhandanstalt Birgit Breuel zum Ende der Arbeit am 30.12.1994 symbolisch das Türschild ihres bisherigen Amtssitzes abmontierte, waren 15000 Unternehmen verkauft, 1,5 Millionen Arbeitsplatzgarantien und Investitionszusagen in Höhe von 211 Milliarden DM erreicht worden.

The task facing the "Treuhand", the privatization agency set up in 1990, was to administer the economic legacy of the GDR which it inherited, to put businesses back on their feet and privatize them where this was feasible, and to close down those that were clearly not viable. By December 30, 1994, when the task had been completed and the president of the "Treuhand", Birgit Breuel, symbolically removed the plate from the door of what had been her office, 15,000 enterprises had been sold, 1.5 million jobs were guaranteed and there was a commitment to investments totalling 211 thousand million DM.

Mai 1993: Arbeitsalltag im Ausbesserungswerk der Reichsbahn im thüringischen Meiningen. Für die meisten Beschäftigten der unrentablen Altindustrien der DDR bedeutete deren »Abwicklung« den Weg in die Arbeitslosigkeit. Bis 1992 ging die Zahl der industriellen Arbeitsplätze in Ostdeutschland von etwa 3,5 Millionen auf weniger als eine Million zurück. Die Zahlen lassen nur ahnen, welch bittere individuelle Schicksale mit diesem Einbruch verbunden waren.

May 1993: Daily working routine at the railway maintenance plant in Meiningen in Thuringia. For most of the people who worked in the loss-making traditional GDR industries, closing down plants meant that they became unemployed. By 1992 the number of jobs in industry in eastern Germany had fallen from c. 3.5 million to less than one million. The figures do no more than hint at what bitter individual misfortune this collapse entailed.

Roman Herzog

Roman Herzog am 17.12.1996 bei der Aufzeichnung der Weihnachtsansprache des Bundespräsidenten, die traditionell am 24.12. jedes Jahres in Rundfunk und Fernsehen der Bundesrepublik ausgestrahlt wird.

Roman Herzog on December 17, 1996 recording the presidential Christmas message which is traditionally broadcast each year on December 24 on German radio and television.

Bundespräsident Herzog trat sein Amt unter schwierigen Voraussetzungen an. Eigentlich sollte 1994, im vierten Jahr der deutschen Einheit, ein Kandidat aus Ostdeutschland zum Bundespräsidenten gewählt werden. Bundeskanzler Kohl hatte den sächsischen Innenminister Steffen Heitmann vorgeschlagen. Doch Heitmann mußte nach einer Medienkampagne wegen mißverständlicher Interviewaussagen aufgeben. So nominierte die CDU den bisherigen Präsidenten des Bundesverfassungsgerichts, der die Wahl am 23.5.1994 für sich entschied. Roman Herzog erwarb sich rasch über alle Landes- und Parteigrenzen hinweg großes Ansehen. Die selbstbewußte Selbstverständlichkeit seines Auftretens, das offene Worte mit bajuwarischem Humor vereint, verschaffte ihm breite Sympathien. Seine früh geäußerte Absicht, nur für eine Amtsperiode zur Verfügung zu stehen, wurde daher von vielen bedauert.

President Herzog took up office under difficult circumstances. In 1994, the fourth year of German unity, it had actually been intended that a candidate from eastern Germany should be elected as President. Chancellor Kohl had proposed the Minister of the Interior in Saxony, Steffen Heitmann. But following a media campaign Heitmann had to stand down because of statements made in interviews which were open to misunderstanding. The CDU therefore nominated the man who had until then been president of the Constitutional Court, who was successfully elected on May 23, 1994. Roman Herzog quickly achieved great prestige, transcending the boundaries of country and party. His self-confident, natural bearing, his blend of outspokenness and traditional Bavarian humor, made him widely liked. As a result, many people regretted his intention, which he announced at an early stage, of only serving for a single term of office.

Die Verhüllung des Reichstagsgebäudes in Berlin gehört zu den spektakulärsten Aktionen des amerikanischen Künstlerpaares Christo und Jean-Claude. Hunderttausende strömten im Sommer 1995 nach Berlin, um den »wrapped Reichstag« zu sehen, unter ihnen auch Bundespräsident Roman Herzog und seine Frau. Das Präsidentenehepaar durfte dem Gebäude am 1.7.1995 sogar im Beisein der Künstler aufs Dach steigen.

The "wrapping" of the Reichstag building in Berlin was one of the most spectacular performances of the two American artists Christo and Jean-Claude. In the summer of 1995 hundreds of thousands of people flocked to Berlin to see the "wrapped Reichstag," including President Roman Herzog and his wife. The presidential couple were even allowed to climb onto the roof of the building in the artists' presence, on July 1, 1995.

(unten) Ein »Bützchen« für den Präsidenten: In der »fünften Jahreszeit«, dem rheinischen Karneval, übernehmen bunt kostümierte Narren für »drei tolle Tage« die Macht in Stadt und Land. Unter ihnen sind traditionell die Corps der Stadtsoldaten, in deren Reihen auch weibliche Mitglieder mit den Waffen des »schwachen Geschlechts« Dienst tun. Am 23.2.1995 wurde mit roten Lippen auch Bundespräsident Roman Herzog entwaffnet.

(below) A "smack" for the President: In the "fifth season of the year," the Rhineland Carnival, revellers in colorful costumes rule for "three crazy days" in town and countryside. Among the traditional figures are "soldiers" from the "city guard," in whose ranks female members also render service with the weapons of the "weaker sex." On February 23, 1995 President Roman Herzog was also disarmed by a pair of red lips.

Erstmals seit 1969 tagte 1994 die Bundesversammlung wieder in Berlin, und erstmals seit 1949 wurde ein Bundespräsident für das ganze Deutschland gewählt. Nachdem Roman Herzog im dritten Wahlgang die absolute Mehrheit erhalten hatte, gratulierte ihm auch die Kandidatin der FDP, Hildegard Hamm-Brücher, die nach dem zweiten Wahlgang nicht mehr angetreten war. Am unteren Bildrand ist der gleichfalls unterlegene SPD-Kandidat, der Ministerpräsident des Landes Nordrhein-Westfalen Johannes Rau, zu erkennen.

In 1994 the Federal Convention met in Berlin again for the first time since 1969, and for the first time since 1949 a president for the whole of Germany was elected. After winning an absolute majority at the third ballot, Roman Herzog was congratulated by, among others, the FDP candidate Hildegard Hamm-Brücher, who had withdrawn after the second ballot. The SPD candidate Johannes Rau, the Minister President of North Rhine-Westphalia, who was likewise defeated, is visible at the lower edge of the photo.

Als einziger Minister des ersten Kabinetts von Helmut Kohl blieb Arbeitsminister Norbert Blüm (Mitte) mit dem Bundeskanzler bis zum Ende der Regierungszeit im Oktober 1998 im Amt. In den achtziger Jahren setzte er gegen große Widerstände eine Gesundheits- und Rentenreform durch, bis 1995 gelang ihm darüber hinaus die Einführung der Pflegeversicherung. Mit seinem Humor und Wortwitz gewann Blüm viele Sympathien. Anläßlich des Papstbesuchs in Berlin erlaubte er sich am 23.6.1996 sogar einen Spaß mit den versammelten deutschen Bischöfen der katholischen Kirche, die ihn als »scharzes Schaf« in ihrer Mitte begrüßten.

Minister of Labor Norbert Blüm (center) was the only minister from Helmut Kohl's first cabinet to remain in office along with the Chancellor until the latter's period of government came to an end in October 1998. In the eighties, against fierce resistance, he pushed through pension and health service reform, and by 1995 he had also succeeded in introducing compulsory "care insurance." Blüm was much liked for his humor and verbal wit. During the Pope's visit to Berlin on June 23, 1996 he even allowed himself some fun with the assembled German Catholic bishops, who greeted him as a "black sheep" in their midst.

Klaus Kinkel war lange Jahre engster Mitarbeiter von Hans-Dietrich Genscher im Bundesinnenministerium und von 1974 an im Auswärtigen Amt. 1991 wurde er erster Justizminister des vereinigten Deutschlands und übernahm im Mai 1992 nach dem Rücktritt Genschers dessen Nachfolge im Amt des Außenministers. Er war bestrebt, die Kontinuität deutscher Außenpolitik zu wahren. 1993 übernahm er zusätzlich das Amt des FDP-Parteivorsitzenden, das er jedoch zwei Jahre später nach Mißerfolgen der Partei bei verschiedenen Landtagswahlen wieder aufgab. Er blieb bis zum Regierungswechsel im Jahr 1998 Vizekanzler und Außenminister der Bundesrepublik.

Klaus Kinkel was for many years Hans-Dietrich Genscher's closest colleague at the Ministry of the Interior and, from 1974 onwards, at the Foreign Office. In 1991 he became the first Minister of Justice in the unified Germany and succeeded Genscher as Foreign Minister after the latter's resignation in May 1992. He was concerned to preserve the continuity of German foreign policy. In 1993 he also took over the office of FDP party chairman, which he relinquished, however, two years later after the party had done badly in various regional elections. He remained Deputy Chancellor and Foreign Minister until the change of government in 1998.

Theo Waigel, seit 1988 Nachfolger von Strauß im Parteivorsitz der CSU, wurde im April 1989 Bundesminister der Finanzen. Fast zehn Jahre überwachte er den Haushalt des Bundes und schuf die finanziellen Rahmenbedingungen für die deutsche Einheit. Zugleich engagierte er sich für die gemeinsame Währung der Europäischen Union und war maßgeblich an ihrer Namensgebung beteiligt. Das Bild zeigt ihn am 7.8.1998 bei der Prüfung der ersten Probeprägung einer Euro-Münze im Bayrischen Hauptmünzamt in München.

Der langjährige CSU-Generalsekretär und bayerische Innenminister Edmund Stoiber wurde im Mai 1993 Ministerpräsident von Bayern. Mit seinem ebenso effizienten wie volksverbundenen Regierungsstil verkörpert er seitdem das zwischen Tradition und Modernität vermittelnde Bild des Freistaats. Immer wieder nahm er, wie hier am 28.11.1997 im Bundesrat, in Bonn energisch Einfluß auf die Bundes- und Europapolitik.

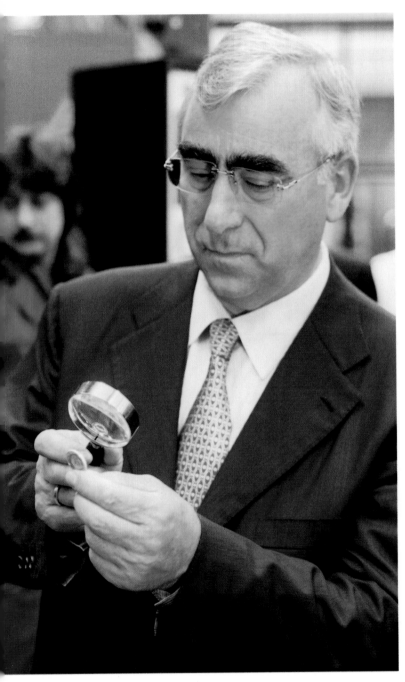

Theo Waigel, CSU party chairman since 1988, when he succeeded Strauß, became Finance Minister in April 1989. For almost ten years he kept a stern eye on the federal budget, and it was he who created the financial framework for German unity. At the same time he was involved in laying the foundations for a European Union common currency and played a decisive part in choosing a name for it. The photo shows him inspecting the first trial minting on August 7, 1998.

After being General Secretary of the CSU and Bavarian Minister of the Interior for many years, Edmund Stoiber became Minister President of Bavaria in May 1993. Since then, with his style of government combining efficiency and close contact with the people, he has embodied the image of the Free State of Bavaria with its harmonious blend of tradition and modernity. He has time and again exercised an energetic influence on federal German and European politics, as here in the *Bundesrat* in Bonn on November 28, 1997.

(gegenüber) Ein entscheidendes Element des Integrationskurses, den der SPD-Vorsitzende Lafontaine der Partei verordnete, war die Verschiebung jeder Diskussion um den Kanzlerkandidaten. Auch der Favorit, der niedersächsische Ministerpräsident Schröder, hielt sich daran, traf jedoch durch die Verknüpfung seiner Kandidatur mit seinem Abschneiden bei den Landtagswahlen vom 1. März 1998 eine Vorentscheidung. Sein eindeutiger Wahlsieg klärte die Situation. Tags darauf verkündeten zwei gut gelaunte Konkurrenten der Presse in Bonn, daß der SPD-Vorstand Gerhard Schröder als Spitzenkandidaten für die Bundestagswahl am 27. September 1998 nominiert habe.

(opposite) A decisive element in the pursuit of unity which the SPD party chairman Lafontaine prescribed for the party, was the postponement of any discussion of who was to be chancellor candidate. Even the favorite Schröder, the Minister President of Lower Saxony, kept to this policy, but made a preliminary decision by linking his candidacy to his showing in the regional elections on March 1, 1998. His clear victory at the election clarified the situation. On the following day two good-humored rivals announced to the press in Bonn that the SPD party executive had nominated Gerhard Schröder as front-runner for the general election on September 27, 1998.

Bundesparteitag der SPD vom 14. bis 17.11.1995 in Mannheim. Von links: der Partei- und Fraktionsvorsitzende Scharping, der nordrhein-westfälische Ministerpräsident Rau, der Ministerpräsident des Saarlandes Lafontaine, der stellvertretende Ministerpräsident von Baden-Württemberg Spöri und die schleswig-holsteinische Ministerpräsidentin Simonis. Nach der Niederlage bei den Bundestagswahlen 1994 entstanden in der SPD-Führung Konflikte über den zukünftigen Kurs. Überraschend kandidierte Oskar Lafontaine auf dem Parteitag für den Bundesvorsitz und wurde in einer Kampfabstimmung anstelle von Rudolf Scharping gewählt.

The SPD federal party conference in Mannheim from November 14-17, 1995. From left to right: party chairman and leader of the parliamentary party Rudolf Scharping, the Minister President of North Rhine-Westphalia Rau, the Minister President of the Saarland Lafontaine, the Deputy Minister President of Baden-Württemberg Spöri and the Minister President of Schleswig-Holstein Ms. Simonis. After the SPD's defeat at the 1994 general election conflicts arose in the leadership over future policy. At the party conference Oskar Lafontaine, surprisingly, ran for the post of party chairman; a ballot was held and he was elected in place of Scharping.

Bei der Bundestagswahl im Oktober 1994 gelang
der PDS erneut der Einzug ins Parlament. Zwar
verfehlte sie wieder die notwendigen 5 Prozent der
Stimmen, doch sie errang vier Direktmandate. Eines
davon gewann Gregor Gysi, der die PDS zu einer
normalen Bundestagspartei zu machen suchte. In
Ostdeutschland wurde die SED-Nachfolgepartei
tatsächlich als dritte Kraft koalitionsfähig und
trat mit der SPD in mehrere Landesregierungen
ein. Die Zusammenarbeit auf Bundesebene blieb
jedoch – wie hier am 5.2.1998 mit dem Grünen-
Abgeordneten Fischer – auf kollegiale Hilfe
beschränkt.

At the general election in October 1994 the PDS
again managed to win seats in parliament. It again
failed to poll the necessary 5% of the vote, but won
four direct mandates. One of these was won by
Gregor Gysi, who tried to make the PDS into a normal parliamentary party. In eastern Germany the
PDS, the successor party to the SED, did indeed
become the third strongest party and was thus able
to form coalitions with the SPD in several regional
governments. Cooperation at federal level, however,
was limited to being helpful to fellow members –
as here, with the Green member Joschka Fischer on
February 5, 1998.

Geschätzter Partner/ Esteemed Partner

London, 17.7.1991. Zum Fototermin anläßlich des 17. Weltwirtschaftsgipfels hatte das Protokoll vorgesehen, daß die Staatschefs gemeinsam mit Queen Elizabeth auf den Sesseln im Vordergrund Platz nähmen, während die Regierungschefs dahinter stehen sollten. Doch ein Stuhl blieb frei... So bat man den deutschen Bundeskanzler nach vorn. Helmut Kohl ließ sich nicht lange drängen. Zur sichtlichen Erheiterung der Kollegen setzte er sich ohne Zögern in die erste Reihe.

London, July 17, 1991. For the photo call at the 17th world economic summit it had been decided according to protocol that the heads of state should sit on the chairs in the front along with Queen Elizabeth, while the heads of government should stand behind them. But there was one chair vacant... and so the German Chancellor was asked to come to the front. Helmut Kohl was not coy. To the visible amusement of his opposite numbers he unhesitatingly went and sat in the front row.

Das wiedervereinigte Deutschland nimmt eine wichtige Stellung in der Welt ein. Erstmals in der jüngeren Geschichte hat das Land gute Beziehungen mit allen seinen Nachbarn. Seine Wirtschaftskraft macht es zum angesehenen Handelspartner, seine politische Bedeutung verleiht ihm diplomatisches Gewicht. Gleichberechtigt nimmt die Bundesrepublik an internationalen Organisationen teil und wirkt in enger Abstimmung mit ihren europäischen und atlantischen Verbündeten an allen Entscheidungen mit. Die verhängnisvolle Sonderrolle, die Deutschland seit der Reichsgründung im Jahr 1871 so oft gespielt hat, ist endgültig beendet.

The reunified Germany occupies an important position in the world. For the first time in recent history the country is on good terms with all its neighbors. Its economic power makes it a respected trading partner, its political significance gives it diplomatic weight. The Federal Republic is involved as an equal partner in the international organizations, contributing, in close collaboration with its European and Atlantic allies, to all decisions. The disastrous role so often played by Germany since the founding of the Reich in 1871, is now once and for all at an end.

Lyon, 28.6.1996. »Entspannungspolitik« während des 22. Weltwirtschaftsgipfels: Angesichts der hochsommerlichen Temperaturen genehmigten sich die Staats- und Regierungschefs eine gelockerte Kleiderordnung. Eine Ausnahme machte nur der deutsche Bundeskanzler Helmut Kohl (rechts). Von dort im Uhrzeigersinn: Staatspräsident Jacques Chirac (Frankreich), Premierminister John Major (Großbritannien), EU-Präsident Jacques Santer, Premierminister Jean Chrétien (Kanada), Präsident Bill Clinton (USA), Ministerpräsident Ryutaro Hashimoto (Japan) und Ministerpräsident Romano Prodi (Italien).

Lyons, June 28, 1996. "Détente politics" during the 22nd world economic summit: in view of the midsummer temperatures the political leaders opted for casual dress. The only exception was the German Chancellor Helmut Kohl (right). Clockwise from there: President Jacques Chirac (France), Prime Minister John Major (Britain), EU President Jacques Santer, Prime Minister Jean Chrétien (Canada), President Bill Clinton (US), Prime Minister Ryutaro Hashimoto (Japan) and Prime Minister Romano Prodi (Italy).

München, 8.7.1992. Zum Abschluß des 18. Weltwirtschaftsgipfels präsentierte sich der deutsche Bundeskanzler gemeinsam mit dem russischen und dem amerikanischen Präsidenten den Fotografen. Boris Jelzin (links) nahm – wenn auch noch nicht als reguläres Mitglied – zum ersten Mal, George Bush zum letzten Mal an dieser Konferenz teil. Das Foto spiegelt treffend die Position des wiedervereinigten Deutschland in Europa. Es verbindet Ost und West, doch sein Gesicht ist eindeutig nach Westen gewandt.

Munich, July 8, 1992. At the end of the 18th world economic summit the German Chancellor posed for the photographers along with the Russian and American Presidents. Boris Yeltsin (left) was taking part in this conference for the first time – though not as yet as a proper member – George Bush for the last time. The photo aptly reflects the position of a reunified Germany in Europe. It is a link between East and West, but its face is unequivocally turned towards the West.

Die Freundschaft der Völker lebt auch vom familiären Umgang ihrer Repräsentanten: Am 26.3.1993 stellte der amerikanische Präsident Bill Clinton dem deutschen Bundeskanzler im Weißen Haus in Washington seine Mutter vor.
(links) Deutsch-amerikanische Freundschaft: Bundeskanzler Helmut Kohl und US-Präsident Bill Clinton am 23.5.1996 bei einem Empfang vor dem Rathaus von Milwaukee, Wisconsin. Es herrscht, was alle Politiker lieben: Kräftiger Rückenwind.

Friendship between nations also thrives on family contacts between their representatives: American President Bill Clinton introduces his mother to the German Chancellor at the White House in Washington on March 26, 1993.
(left) German-American friendship: Chancellor Helmut Kohl and US President Bill Clinton on May 23, 1996 at a reception in front of the town hall in Milwaukee (Wisconsin, US). The weather is what all politicians like: a strong tailwind.

Verläßliche Freundschaften

Die von Konrad Adenauer eingeleitete Westbindung Deutschlands hat sich bewährt. Nur durch die enge Zusammenarbeit mit den mächtigen Verbündeten und Partnern im Westen gelang der Aufstieg der Bundesrepublik nach dem Zweiten Weltkrieg und die Wiederherstellung der deutschen Einheit nach über 40 Jahren der Teilung. Die in Jahrzehnten gewachsene Freundschaft mit den ehemaligen Kriegsgegnern bleibt das wichtigste Fundament der friedlichen Zukunft Deutschlands.

Reliable Friendships

Germany's ties with the West, inaugurated by Konrad Adenauer, have stood the test of time. The success of the Federal Republic after the second world war and the restoration of German unity after over 40 years of division were only made possible by close cooperation with its powerful western allies and partners. The friendship which has grown during these decades with its wartime enemies remains the most important foundation for Germany's peaceful future.

Die Berliner Luftbrücke stand am Beginn der Freundschaft zwischen den Deutschen und den westlichen Siegern, insbesondere den USA. Im Sommer 1998 feierte Berlin den 50. Jahrestag dieses historischen Ereignisses. Am 14.5.1998 nahmen auch US-Präsident Clinton, Bundeskanzler Kohl und der berühmte Candy-Pilot Halverson (rechts) an den Feierlichkeiten teil. Vor einem modernen Luftransporter präsentierte Berlins Regierender Bürgermeister Eberhard Diepgen das Jubiläumsbanner. Es zeigt die Abbildungen der Nationalflaggen der drei Westmächte und des Luftbrückendenkmals, von den Berlinern liebevoll-scherzhaft »Hungerkralle« genannt.

The friendship between the Germans and the western victors, especially the US, began with the Berlin airlift. Berlin celebrated the 50th anniversary of this historic event in summer 1998. US President Clinton, Chancellor Kohl and the famous candy pilot Halverson (right) attended the ceremony on May 14, 1998. Standing in front of a modern transport aircraft, the governing mayor of Berlin, Eberhard Diepgen, presented the anniversary banner. It has illustrations of the national flags of the three western powers and the airlift memorial, known by the Berliners with affectionate humor as the "hunger claw."

Die enge Zusammenarbeit zwischen Deutschland und Frankreich ist längst zu einer Konstante der europäischen Politik geworden. Personelle Veränderungen an der Staats- bzw. Regierungsspitze spielen kaum noch eine Rolle. So bestand auch zwischen Staatspräsident Jacques Chirac und Bundeskanzler Helmut Kohl – hier beim NATO-Gipfel Anfang Juli 1997 in Madrid – ein herzliches Einvernehmen.

Close cooperation between Germany and France has long since become a constant in European politics. Changes of heads of state or government scarcely affect the matter any more. Thus there was also a cordial rapport between President Jacques Chirac and Chancellor Helmut Kohl – here at the NATO summit in Madrid in early July 1997.

Bundeskanzler Helmut Kohl war der dienstälteste Regierungschef in Europa. Als er am 15.6.1998 bei der EU-Ratstagung im walisischen Cardiff mit Tony Blair (Mitte) scherzte, sprach er in seiner Amtszeit bereits mit dem dritten Premierminister Großbritanniens.

Chancellor Helmut Kohl was the senior head of government in Europe. When he joked with Tony Blair (center) at the meeting of the EU Council in Cardiff (Wales) on June 15, 1998, it was by then the third British Prime Minister with whom he had spoken while in office.

Deutsch-britische Freundschaft: Seit dem Rücktritt der »Eisernen Lady« Margaret Thatcher im November 1990 verbesserten sich auch die persönlichen Beziehungen der Regierungschefs Großbritanniens und der Bundesrepublik. Bei den deutsch-britischen Konsultationen am 27.4.1994 gab es offensichtlich sowohl für Premierminister John Major als auch für Bundeskanzler Helmut Kohl Grund zu regelrechter Ausgelassenheit.

German-British friendship. After the "Iron Lady" Margaret Thatcher had resigned in November 1990, the personal relationship between the heads of government of Britain and the Federal Republic also improved. At the German-British consultations on April 27, 1994 there were evidently grounds for both Prime Minister John Major and Chancellor Helmut Kohl to be in positively high spirits.

Nach der Auflösung der UdSSR im Dezember 1991 setzte die Bundesrepublik die gutnachbarlichen Beziehungen mit den Nachfolgestaaten der »Gemeinschaft Unabhängiger Staaten« (GUS) fort. Rasch war zwischen Bundeskanzler Kohl und dem russischen Präsidenten Jelzin das Eis gebrochen. Daß die beiden nicht lange im trüben fischten, zeigten auch die deutsch-russischen Gespräche vom 14. bis 16.12.1992, bei denen erneut erhebliche Finanzhilfen der Bundesrepublik für Rußland vereinbart wurden. Ob tatsächlich große Fische beim gemeinsamen winterlichen Angeln in der Nähe der Regierungsdatscha in Sawidowo gefangen werden konnten, ist nicht bekannt.

After the collapse of the USSR in December 1991 the Federal Republic continued to maintain good neighborly relations with its successor states in the "Commonwealth of Independent States" (CIS). The ice was quickly broken between Chancellor Kohl and the Russian President Yeltsin. That the two of them did not spend long fishing in troubled waters was evident in the German-Russian talks from December 14-16, 1992, at which further substantial financial aid for Russia from the Federal Republic was agreed. Whether similarly big fish were caught during a wintry joint fishing outing in the vicinity of the government dacha in Savidovo, is not known.

Am 31.8.1994 verabschiedeten Bundeskanzler Kohl und Präsident Jelzin in einer feierlichen Zeremonie in Berlin die russischen Truppen. Sie waren seit dem Zweiten Weltkrieg als sowjetische Streitkräfte im Gebiet der ehemaligen DDR stationiert gewesen. Jetzt verließen sie, vier Monate vor dem im »Zwei-plus-Vier-Vertrag« von 1990 festgelegten Termin, das Land. Der vorzeitige Abzug war im Dezember 1992 bei den deutsch-russischen Konsultationen in Moskau vereinbart worden.

On August 31, 1994, at ceremony in Berlin, Chancellor Kohl and President Yeltsin said goodbye to the Russian troops. They had been stationed as Soviet armed forces on the territory of the former GDR since the second world war. Now they were leaving the country, four months before the date laid down in the 1990 "Two-plus-Four Treaty." Their early departure had been agreed at the German-Russian consultations in December 1992.

(gegenüber) Der letzte russische Soldat verläßt deutschen Boden. Mit der Abfahrt des letzten Truppentransports am 1.9.1994 war der Abzug von insgesamt 380 000 Soldaten und 210 000 Zivilpersonen aus Rußland und den übrigen Nachfolgestaaten der UdSSR abgeschlossen.

(opposite) The last Russian soldier leaves German soil. The departure of the last batch of troops on September 1, 1994 completed the withdrawal of a total of 380,000 soldiers and 210,000 civilians from Russia and the other successor states of the USSR.

Deutschland besitzt nach seiner Wiedervereinigung eine gewachsene Verantwortung in der Welt. Es hat nach dem Wiedergewinn seiner vollen Souveränitätsrechte auch die damit verbundenen Pflichten übernommen. Dazu gehört nicht zuletzt die Mitwirkung an den Bemühungen der Vereinten Nationen zur Beilegung von Konflikten. Die Bundeswehr ist eine der weltweit modernsten Armeen. Sie hat in kurzer Zeit die Integration von Teilen der ehemaligen Nationalen Volksarmee der DDR sowie deren Abrüstung bewerkstelligt. Zugleich ist ihr der Aufbau der Verteidigungsstrukturen in Ostdeutschland und die eigene Umstellung auf die neue Lage nach dem Ende des Kalten Krieges gelungen. Seit dem Urteil des Bundesverfassungsgerichts vom 12.7.1994, das Einsätze der Bundeswehr nach Zustimmung des Bundestags auch außerhalb des NATO-Gebiets erlaubt, nehmen deutsche Soldaten gleichberechtigt an den Friedensmissionen der UNO teil.

Following its reunification Germany bears increased responsibility in the world. Having regained its full sovereignty it has also taken on the duties which that entails. These include, not least, participation in the efforts of the UN to resolve conflicts. The German army is one of the most modern in the entire world. It has managed in a short space of time to carry out the disarmament of the former GDR National People's Army and to absorb parts of that army. At the same time it has succeeded in building up defense structures in East Germany and in adapting to the new situation following the end of the Cold War. Since the ruling by the Federal Constitutional Court on July 12, 1994 allowing the German army to be deployed, with the prior approval of parliament, outside NATO territory, German troops have taken part on an equal footing in UN peace missions.

In weniger als fünf Jahren rüstete die Bundesrepublik gemäß ihren vertraglichen Verpflichtungen fast das gesamte Waffenpotential der ehemaligen Nationalen Volksarmee der DDR ab. So wurden rund 1,4 Millionen Handfeuerwaffen und 303 000 t Munition vernichtet, 134 000 Radfahrzeuge und 12 200 Panzerfahrzeuge aus dem Verkehr gezogen. Die letzten der 2 761 Kampfpanzer der NVA – hier ein Blick auf eine Halde im sächsischen Löbau – wurden am 23.5.1995 verschrottet. Die Kosten dieser einmaligen Waffenvernichtungsaktion betrugen insgesamt etwa 1,4 Milliarden DM.

In less than five years the Federal Republic, as obliged by treaty, dismantled almost the entire arsenal of the former GDR National People's Army. Around 1.4 million handguns and 303,000 tonnes of ammunition were destroyed, while 134,000 wheeled vehicles and 12,200 armored vehicles were withdrawn from use. The last of the 2,761 combat tanks of the National People's Army – here at a scrapheap in Löbau in Saxony – were broken up on May 23, 1995. The total cost of this unique weapons destruction program amounted to around 1.4 billion DM.

(gegenüber) Zu ihrer Verabschiedung aus Berlin wurden die amerikanischen, britischen und französischen Truppen am Abend des 8.9.1994 durch einen »Großen Zapfenstreich« geehrt. Daß dieses höchste militärische Zeremoniell der Bundeswehr auf dem Platz vor dem Brandenburger Tor stattfinden konnte, bezeugte eindrucksvoll die auf friedliche Weise zurückgewonnene volle Souveränität Deutschlands.

(opposite) To mark their withdrawal from Berlin, the American, British and French troops were honored with a Ceremonial Tattoo on the evening of September 8, 1994. The fact that this, the German army's highest military ceremony, could take place on the square in front of the Brandenburg Gate was impressive testimony to the full sovereignty which Germany had peacefully regained.

(gegenüber) Seit August 1992 leistete die Bundesrepublik humanitäre Hilfe zur Linderung der Hungersnot im afrikanischen Somalia. Auf dem Flughafen von Mogadischu, auf dem 15 Jahre zuvor die von Terroristen gekaperte Lufthansa-Maschine »Landshut« befreit wurde, entluden am 9.9.1992 somalische Arbeiter eine mit Hilfsgütern beladene Maschine der Bundeswehr.

(opposite) From August 1992 the Federal Republic provided humanitarian aid to alleviate starvation in Somalia in Africa. At Mogadishu airport, where 15 years previously the Lufthansa aircraft "Landshut" was liberated after being hijacked by terrorists, Somalian workers unload a German army aircraft carrying aid supplies on September 9, 1992.

Seit Dezember 1995 beteiligte sich die Bundesrepublik an der internationalen Friedenstruppe für Bosnien-Herzegowina. Die am 4.12.1997 in der Innenstadt von Sarajewo diensttuende Panzerbesatzung gehörte zu den 3000 deutschen Soldaten innerhalb des von 35 Staaten unter der Führung der NATO gebildeten SFOR-Kontingents.

From December 1995 the Federal Republic was involved in the international peace-keeping force in Bosnia-Herzegovina. The members of the tank crew on duty in the center of Sarajevo on December 4, 1997 were among the 3,000 German soldiers in the SFOR contingent provided by 35 states under NATO leadership.

Im Sommer 1997 ereignete sich mit dem »Jahrhundert-Hochwasser« an der Oder die bislang größte Naturkatastrophe im wiedervereinigten Deutschland. Zusammen mit anderen Hilfsorganisationen kämpfte die Bundeswehr mehrere Wochen mit rund 10000 Soldaten um den Erhalt der durchweichten Uferdämme. Wehrpflichtige aus allen Teilen des Landes füllten und verbauten gemeinsam Tag und Nacht Millionen von Sandsäcken. Auch Bundeskanzler Kohl sprach ihnen dafür seine Anerkennung aus. Am 27.7.1997 besuchte er mit dem Einsatzleiter, General von Kirchbach (Mitte), eine Einheit in Neuhardenberg.

In the summer of 1997 the "flood of the century" occurred on the Oder, united Germany's worst natural disaster until then. Together with other aid organizations, around 10,000 troops from the army struggled for several weeks to save the waterlogged riverbanks. Conscripts from all parts of the country worked together day and night filling and positioning millions of sandbags. Chancellor Kohl also expressed his gratitude to them. On July 27, 1997 he visited a unit in Neuhardenberg with the officer in charge of operations, General von Kirchbach (center).

Europäische Perspektiven / European Perspectives

Deutschlands Zukunft liegt in Europa, dieser Satz gilt mehr denn je. Die europäische Integration war eine der entscheidenden Voraussetzungen für die friedliche Wiedervereinigung, und sie bleibt die entscheidende Bedingung für Frieden und Wohlstand in Europa. Mit dem Vertrag von Maastricht gelang 1992 der Durchbruch zur Europäischen Union. Damit wird Europa zu einem einheitlichen Wirtschafts- und Währungsgebiet, das die amerikanische und asiatische Konkurrenz im weltwirtschaftlichen Wettbewerb nicht zu fürchten braucht. Zugleich werden die Europäer noch stärker als bisher ihre Gemeinsamkeiten entdecken, ohne ihre nationalen Identitäten aufzugeben.

Germany's future is in Europe: this statement is truer than ever before. European integration was one of the decisive preconditions of peaceful reunification, and it remains the decisive condition for peace and prosperity in Europe. A breakthrough to European union was achieved in the 1992 Maastricht Treaty. Europe is thus becoming a unified economic and monetary area which does not need to fear rivals from America or Asia in the competitive world economy. At the same time Europeans will discover to a greater extent than hitherto how much they have in common, but without abandoning their national identities.

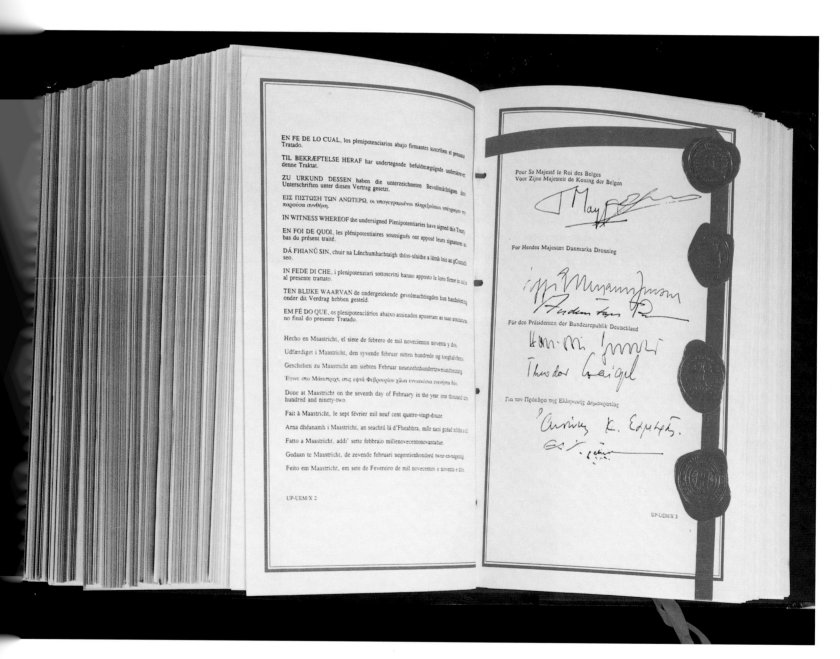

Der Vertrag von Maastricht. Das umfangreiche Abkommen wurde am 7.2. 1992 unterzeichnet und trat am 1.11.1993 in Kraft. Auf der rechten Seite sind in der Mitte stellvertretend »für den Präsidenten der Bundesrepublik Deutschland« die Unterschriften von Außenminister Hans-Dietrich Genscher und Finanzminister Theodor Waigel zu erkennen.

The Maastricht Treaty. The voluminous agreement was signed on February 7, 1992 and came into force on November 1, 1993. On the right-hand side in the center the signatures of Foreign Minister Hans-Dietrich Genscher and Finance Minister Theodor Waigel "on behalf of the President of the Federal Republic of Germany" can be discerned.

Als Aufsichtsbehörde für die neue europäische Währung wurde nach deutschen Vorschlägen die politisch unabhängige Europäische Zentralbank (EZB) mit Sitz in Frankfurt am Main gegründet. Beim Festakt zu ihrer Eröffnung am 30.6.1998 in der Alten Oper saß Bundeskanzler Helmut Kohl neben dem ersten EZB-Präsidenten Wim Duisenberg (rechts).

Following German proposals, the politically independent European Central Bank (ECB), was set up in Frankfurt am Main to supervise the new European currency. At the ceremony to mark its opening on June 30, 1998 in the Old Opera House, Chancellor Helmut Kohl sat next to the first ECB President Wim Duisenberg (right).

Druckstock für eine Münze im Wert eines Euro, aufgenommen am 7.8. 1998 anläßlich der ersten Probeprägung im Bayerischen Hauptmünzamt in München. Zum 1.1.1999 wurde der Euro als europäische Währung eingeführt und kann seitdem im bargeldlosen Zahlungsverkehr benutzt werden. Münzen und Scheine des Euro kommen vom 1.1.2002 an in Umlauf und ersetzen dann die Zahlungsmittel der einzelnen Mitgliedsstaaten.

Relief plate for a coin valued at 1 Euro, photographed on August 7, 1998 during the first trial minting at the head office of the Bavarian Mint in Munich. The Euro was introduced as the European currency with effect from January 1, 1999; since then it has been available for use in non-cash transactions. Euro coins and notes will be in circulation from January 1, 2002 and will replace the currencies of individual member states.

1998–1999

Bundestagswahl und die neue Regierung
Parliamentary Elections and the New Government

Bundeskanzler Gerhard Schröder eröffnet am Abend des 27.10.1998 die erste
Sitzung seines Kabinetts.

Chancellor Gerhard Schröder opens the first meeting of his cabinet on the
evening of October 27, 1998.

Aufbruch in die Zukunft

Ein halbes Jahrhundert nach dem Zweiten Weltkrieg sind die Deutschen wieder in einem Staat vereinigt. Sie haben die volle Souveränität über ihre inneren und äußeren Angelegenheiten übernommen und sind in die Mitte Europas zurückgekehrt.

Und doch ist nichts, wie es war. Seit der Wiedervereinigung existiert Deutschland erstmals in einem geographisch eindeutigen Staatsgebiet. Die Grenzen sind sämtlich sowohl von den Nachbarn als auch im eigenen Land unbestritten. Es kennt weder innerhalb noch außerhalb seines Territoriums ein nennenswertes Minderheitenproblem und besitzt keine machtpolitischen Interessen im Ausland. Die deutsche Souveränität ist unwiderruflich eingebunden in die integrierten Gemeinschaften der NATO und der Europäischen Union. Der zum 1.1.1999 eingeführte Euro wird als gemeinsame Währung der EU in absehbarer Zeit sogar die nationale Währung ersetzen und das Gebiet der D-Mark in einem einheitlichen europäischen Wirtschaftsraum aufgehen lassen. In diesem Raum bildet Deutschland die geographische, d.h. vor allem verkehrstechnische Mitte. Als politische Größe wird Mitteleuropa nach der Osterweiterung von NATO und EU endgültig verschwinden. Vor diesem Hintergrund zeichnet sich ab, daß die deutsche Geschichte als nationalstaatliche Geschichte im engeren Sinn zu Ende geht. Sie wird im europäischen Zusammenhang fortgeschrieben werden. So paradox es klingen mag: Mit der Wiederherstellung des Nationalstaats ist Deutschland endgültig in Europa angekommen.

Bei der Bundestagswahl am 27. 9. 1998 haben sich die Deutschen mit klarer Mehrheit für die Ablösung der Koalition von CDU/CSU und FDP entschieden. Die SPD wurde zum zweiten Mal nach 1972 stärkste Partei und bildete gemeinsam mit den Grünen, die erstmals in eine Bundesregierung eintraten, eine »rot-grüne« Koalition. Am 27.10.1998 wurde der bisherige Ministerpräsident des Landes Niedersachsen, Gerhard Schröder, zum Bundeskanzler gewählt. Nach 16 Jahren mußte Helmut Kohl dieses Amt abgeben. Er tat es mit Würde – und er trat ab als »Kanzler der Einheit«. Auch sein Nachfolger versagte ihm nicht den Respekt vor seiner historischen Leistung.

Der reibungslose Regierungswechsel hat gezeigt, daß die in 40 Jahren gewachsene demokratische Normalität der Bundesrepublik auch nach der Wiedervereinigung fortbesteht. Diese Normalität ist das Fundament, von dem aus das Land die Herausforderungen der Zukunft meistern kann. Mit guten Gründen stellte daher Bundeskanzler Schröder seine Regierungserklärung am 10.11.1998 unter das Motto: »Weil wir Deutschlands Kraft vertrauen«. Als wichtigste Ziele seiner Regierung der »neuen Mitte« nannte er die Beseitigung der Massenarbeitslosigkeit und die Vollendung der inneren Einheit Deutschlands.

Beide Aufgaben werden die Belastungs- und die Konsensfähigkeit der Deutschen auf eine harte Probe stellen. Der technologische Fortschritt, die Globalisierung der Märkte und der beschleunigte Wettbewerb unter den großen Wirtschaftsräumen erfordern mutige Anpassungsprozesse, deren soziale Folgen aufgefangen werden müssen. Zugleich werden die finanziellen Lasten des Aufbaus in Ostdeutschland und die in den Jahrzehnten der Teilung entstandenen Unterschiede der Gesellschaften und Mentalitäten in Ost und West noch länger bestehen bleiben.

Looking towards the Future

Half a century after the second world war the Germans are once more united in a single state. They now have full sovereignty over their internal and external affairs and have returned to the center of Europe.

And yet nothing is the same as it was. Since reunification the German state has for the first time occupied a geographically unambiguous territory. Its borders are all accepted without dispute both by its neighbors and in the country itself. Neither inside nor outside its territory does it have any problems worth speaking of with minorities, and it has no power-political interests abroad. German sovereignty is irrevocably tied into the integrated communities of NATO and the European Union.

The Euro, introduced with effect from January 1, 1999 as the EU common currency, will before long even replace the national currency, with the Deutschmark area being subsumed in a unified European economic area. Geographically, that is to say above all as regards questions of traffic and transport, Germany forms the center of this area. As NATO and the EU expand eastwards, Central Europe, as a political entity, will disappear for ever. Against this background it is becoming apparent that German history, as the history of a nation-state in the narrow sense, is coming to an end. It will continue within a European context. Paradoxical though it may sound, with its restoration as a nation-state Germany has finally arrived in Europe.

At the general election on September 27, 1998 the Germans opted by a clear majority for the dissolution of the CDU/CSU-FDP coalition. The SPD, now the strongest party for the second time since 1972, formed a "red-green" coalition with the Greens, who were included in a federal government for the first time. On October 27, 1998 Gerhard Schröder, who until then had been the Minister President of Lower Saxony, was elected Chancellor. Helmut Kohl had to relinquish this office after 16 years. He did so with dignity, and departed as the "Chancellor of unity." Nor did his successor deny Kohl his respect for that historic achievement.

The smooth change of government showed that after reunification the Federal Republic continues to be the normal democratic country that it had grown to be over a period of 40 years. This normality is the basis on which the country can rise to the challenges of the future.

Hence it was with good reason that for his inaugural government statement on November 10, 1998 Chancellor Schröder chose the motto: "Because we trust Germany's strength." He identified the elimination of mass unemployment and the completion of Germany's internal unity as the most important goals for his government of the "new center."

Both tasks will severely test the Germans' capacity for bearing burdens while sustaining a consensus. Technological advances, the globalization of markets and intensified competition between the major economic areas necessitate the courage to undergo processes of adjustment, and provision must be made to cushion the social consequences of these. At the same time the financial burden of reconstruction in eastern Germany, and the differences between East and West as regards society and mentality – the product of decades of division – will remain for some considerable time yet.

Der Sieger. Am Wahlabend trat ein strahlender Gerhard Schröder im Erich-Ollenhauer-Haus, der Parteizentrale der SPD in Bonn, vor seine Anhänger. Im Hintergrund: Ehefrau Doris Schröder-Köpf.

The victor. On the evening of election day a beaming Gerhard Schröder greeting his supporters in the Erich-Ollenhauer-House, the SPD party headquarters in Bonn. In the background is his wife, Doris Schröder-Köpf.

Ende einer Ära / The End of an Era

Am 27.9.1998 wählten die Bürger der Bundesrepublik Deutschland den 14. Deutschen Bundestag. Für die bisherigen Regierungsparteien CDU/CSU und FDP stimmten lediglich 35,2 bzw. 6,2 Prozent der Wähler. Dagegen erhielt die SPD mit ihrem Spitzenkandidaten Gerhard Schröder 40,9 Prozent der Stimmen und wurde erstmals seit 1972 wieder stärkste Fraktion im Parlament. Damit verfügten SPD und Bündnis 90/Die Grünen, die auf 6,7 Prozent der Stimmen kamen, über die absolute Mehrheit. Mit dem rot-grünen Wahlsieg zeichnete sich zum dritten Mal seit 1949 ein Regierungs- und Machtwechsel ab. Nach 16 Jahren mußte Helmut Kohl das Amt des Bundeskanzlers abgeben. Eine Ära ging zu Ende. Ein neuer Abschnitt begann.

On September 27, 1998 the citizens of the Federal Republic of Germany elected the 14th German parliament. As regards the previous government parties, only 35.2% of the voters voted for the CDU/CSU, only 6.2% for the FDP. The SPD in contrast, with its front-runner Gerhard Schröder, polled 40.9% of the vote, making it, for the first time since 1972, the strongest group in parliament. The SPD and the Bündnis 90/Greens, who polled 6.7% of the vote, thus had an absolute majority. The red-green election victory brought, for the third time since 1949, a change of government and a shift of power. After 16 years Helmut Kohl had to relinquish the office of Chancellor. An era was ending. A fresh start was imminent.

Nachdenklichkeit bei der FDP: Selbst dem sonst nicht auf den Mund gefallenen Generalsekretär Guido Westerwelle verschlug es angesichts des Wahlergebnisses vom 27. 9. 1998 die Sprache. Immerhin hatte jedoch die FDP ihr wichtigstes Wahlziel, den Verbleib im Parlament, erreicht. Ihre Stimmenverluste hielten sich in Grenzen.

Der Verlierer. Helmut Kohl gestand noch am Abend des 27.9.1998 die Niederlage seiner Partei ein, die auch für ihn persönlich eine bittere Niederlage war. Die Union hatte ihr schlechtestes Wahlergebnis seit der ersten Bundestagswahl von 1949 eingefahren.

A thoughtful FDP. General Secretary Guido Westerwelle, not generally at a loss for words, was left speechless by the outcome of the election on September 27, 1998. Even so, the FDP had achieved its most important goal: to remain in parliament. They had suffered only a limited drop in their share of the vote.

The loser. On the same evening of September 27, 1998, Helmut Kohl conceded his party's defeat, which was also a bitter personal defeat for him. It was the worst election result for the CDU/CSU since the first federal general election in 1949.

Am Tag nach der Wahl kündigte Gerhard Schröder (rechts) gemeinsam mit dem SPD-Vorsitzenden Oskar Lafontaine vor der Bundespressekonferenz in Bonn die Aufnahme von Koalitionsverhandlungen mit Bündnis 90/Die Grünen an.

On the day after the election Gerhard Schröder (right) together with SPD party chairman Oskar Lafontaine announced at the press conference in Bonn that they were opening coalition negotiations with the Bündnis 90/Greens.

(gegenüber) Die letzten Stunden auf der Regierungsbank. Am 16.10.1998 stimmte der Bundestag in seiner alten Zusammensetzung einem möglichen NATO-Einsatz wegen des Kosovo-Konflikts zu. Die Sitzung fand im Saal des ehemaligen Wasserwerks statt, weil im neuen Plenarsaal bereits der Umbau für die neue Sitzverteilung begonnen hatte. Erste Reihe (von links): Finanzminister Theo Waigel, Außenminister Klaus Kinkel, Bundeskanzler Helmut Kohl; zweite Reihe: Staatsminister im Bundeskanzleramt Bernd Schmidbauer und Kanzleramtschef Friedrich Bohl. Diesmal verraten die Gesichter der Beteiligten etwas vom Schmerz des Machtverlustes.

(opposite) The last hours on the government front bench. On October 16, 1998 parliament, with its old members, gave its consent for possible NATO military action in connection with the Kosovo conflict. The meeting took place in the hall of the former water plant because rearrangement of the new plenary chamber in accordance with the new distribution of seats had already begun. Front row (from left to right): Finance Minister Theo Waigel, Foreign Minister Klaus Kinkel, Chancellor Helmut Kohl; second row: Minister of State at the Chancellery Bernd Schmidbauer and Head of Chancellery Friedrich Bohl. This time the faces of those concerned do reveal something of the pain of losing power.

Vor dem Abstieg. Als nur noch amtierender Bundeskanzler auf Zeit verläßt Helmut Kohl nach der Pressekonferenz am 28.9.1998 nachdenklich und angespannt das Podium. Die Fröhlichkeit des CDU-Generalsekretärs Peter Hintze wirkt nicht echt – er wird wenig später zurücktreten und sein Amt an Angela Merkel übergeben,

Before stepping down. A tense and thoughtful Helmut Kohl, now only the temporary acting Chancellor, leaves the platform after the press conference on September 28, 1998. The cheerfulness of CDU General Secretary Peter Hintze does not seem genuine – he was to resign shortly afterwards and be replaced by Angela Merkel.

Abschied in Ehren. Sichtlich bewegt schritt der scheidende Bundeskanzler Helmut Kohl am 17. Oktober 1998 in Speyer die zum »Großen Zapfenstreich« angetretenen Reihen der Bundeswehr ab. Neben ihm: Bundesverteidigungsminister Volker Rühe und der Generalinspekteur der Bundeswehr, Hartmut Bagger.

Departing with honor. Visibly moved, the outgoing Chancellor Helmut Kohl taking the parade of troops drawn up for a Ceremonial Tattoo in Speyer on October 17, 1998. Beside him is Defense Minister Volker Rühe and the Chief of the Armed Forces Staff Hartmut Bagger.

Der immer irgendwie abrupte Abschied von der Macht ist allen Bundeskanzlern nicht leicht gefallen. Sie alle kamen sich vor, als ob man ihnen – wie Konrad Adenauer nach seinem Sturz einmal sagte – »Arme und Beine abgeschlagen,« als ob man sie in die Wüste geschickt hätte. Doch Helmut Kohl, dem hier Soldaten der Bundeswehr auf dem Truppenübungsplatz Jägerbrück bei Eggesin in Mecklenburg-Vorpommern ihr »Lebewohl« signalisieren, hat sich in der Rolle des »elder statesman« rasch zurechtgefunden.

There is always something abrupt about saying goodbye to power, and it has not been easy for any German Chancellor. They all felt – as Konrad Adenauer once said after his fall – as if their arms and legs had been cut off, as if they had been banished into the wilderness. But Helmut Kohl, from whom soldiers of the German army are here seen taking their leave at the Jägerbrück drill ground near Eggesin in Mecklenburg-Western Pomerania, was soon at ease in the role of "elder statesman."

Antrittsbesuche / Inaugural Visits

Kontinuität ist eine der wichtigsten Grundlagen deutscher Außenpolitik auch nach dem Regierungswechsel. Noch vor dem offiziellen Amtsantritt und während in Bonn die Koalitionsverhandlungen andauerten, reisten Gerhard Schröder und Joschka Fischer nach Washington, Paris und London, um die unveränderte Berechenbarkeit der Bundesrepublik in den Beziehungen zu den westlichen Partnern zu unterstreichen. Ihre Aufnahme war überall herzlich und unvoreingenommen. Die grundsätzliche Übereinstimmung in den zentralen Fragen der gemeinsamen Politik bildet weiterhin das Fundament für eine deutsche Außenpolitik, auch wenn diese in einzelnen Bereichen neue Akzente setzte und es etwa über den von deutscher Seite im Alleingang geplanten Ausstieg aus der Atomwirtschaft bald zu Irritationen bei den britischen und französischen Partnern kommen sollte.

Following the change of government, continuity is still one of the most important foundations of German foreign policy. Even before officially taking office amd while coalition negotiations were still in progress in Bonn, Gerhard Schröder and Joschka Fischer traveled to Washington, Paris and London in order to emphasize that the reliability of the Federal Republic in its relations with its western partners would remain unchanged. Their reception everywhere was cordial and free of prejudice. Basic agreement on central joint policy issues continues to provide the foundation for German foreign policy, even though there were shifts of emphasis in particular areas, and though friction was soon to arise between Germany and its French and British partners for instance over Germany's plan to go it alone in withdrawing from the nuclear energy industry.

8.10.1998: Der zukünftige Bundeskanzler und sein designierter Außenminister auf dem Flug in die USA. Während Gerhard Schröder mit ernster Miene das Feuilleton der »F.A.Z.« liest, studiert Joschka Fischer den englischen »Economist« – in beiden Blättern wird gegenüber der neuen Bundesregierung schon bald nicht mit Kritik gespart werden.

October 8, 1998: the future Chancellor and his Foreign Minister designate on their flight to the US. While Gerhard Schröder, looking serious, reads the feature pages of the Frankfurter Allgemeine Zeitung, Joschka Fischer studies the English "Economist" – before long both papers will be unsparing in their criticism of the new German government.

Der amerikanische Präsident Bill Clinton und der designierte Bundeskanzler Gerhard Schröder am 9.10.1998 vor dem Weißen Haus in Washington.

American President Bill Clinton and Chancellor designate Gerhard Schröder outside the White House in Washington on October 9, 1998.

Die »grünen Manager« der Bundesrepublik: Während ihres USA-Besuches am 9.10.1998 in Washington nutzen der zukünftige Außenminister Joschka Fischer und sein Staatsminister Ludger Volmer in der Halle des noblen Hotels Willard-Interconti eine kurze Pause zur Lektüre – doch auch hier sind aufmerksame Kameras nicht weit.

The "green managers" of the Federal Republic. In Washington on October 9, 1998, during their visit to the US, the future Foreign Minister Joschka Fischer and his Secretary of State Ludger Volmer take advantage of a short break to sit and read in the foyer of the elegant Willard-Interconti Hotel – but here too, attentive cameras are not far off.

Der erste Besuch des zukünftigen deutschen Bundeskanzlers führte traditionsgemäß in die französische Hauptstadt. Zwischen dem der Sozialistischen Partei angehörenden Premierminister Lionel Jospin und dem Sozialdemokraten Gerhard Schröder herrschte am 30.9.1998 offenkundig beste Stimmung.

Following tradition, the first visit by the future German Chancellor was to the French capital. There was obviously an excellent atmosphere between Prime Minister Lionel Jospin, a member of the Socialist Party, and Social Democrat Gerhard Schröder, on September 30, 1998.

Nicht minder freundschaftlich als in Paris war der Empfang in London. Auch in Downing Street No. 10 konnte Gerhard Schröder bei seinem zukünftigen Amtskollegen, Premierminister Tony Blair, auf breite politische Übereinstimmung zählen.

The reception in London was no less friendly than in Paris. Also at 10 Downing Street, Gerhard Schröder could count on broad political agreement with his future opposite number, Prime Minister Tony Blair.

Unmittelbar nach der Bundestagswahl vom 27.9.1998 nahmen Delegationen von SPD und Bündnis 90/Die Grünen Koalitionsgespräche auf. Am 20. Oktober konnten die Verhandlungsführer Gerhard Schröder und Joschka Fischer (rechts) der Presse den im wahrsten Sinne des Wortes rot-grünen Koalitionsvertrag präsentieren. Fünf Tage darauf wurden die Vereinbarungen auf Sonder-parteitagen beider Parteien mit überwältigender Mehrheit angenommen. Damit war das Funda-ment der Regierung der »Neuen Mitte« gelegt.

Immediately after the general election on September 27, 1998, delegations from the SPD and Alliance 90/The Greens began coalition talks. On October 20, Gerhard Schröder and Joschka Fischer (right), who had led the negotiations, were able to present to the press what was in the truest sense of the word a red-green coalition agreement. Five days later the terms of the agreement were accepted by an overwhelming majority at special conferences of the two parties. The basis was thereby laid for a government of the "new center."

Am 27.10.1998 wurde Gerhard Schröder im Bundestag zum siebten Bundeskanzler der Bundesrepublik Deutschland gewählt. Mit 351 von insge-samt 666 abgegebenen Stimmen erhielt er im ersten Wahlgang eine deutliche Mehrheit. Sogar mindestens sieben Abgeordnete der Opposition hatten für ihn votiert. Unter den Gratulanten waren auch sein Amtsvorgänger Helmut Kohl und der CDU/CSU-Fraktionsvorsitzende Wolfgang Schäuble, hier im Gespräch mit dem SPD-Vorsitzenden Oskar Lafontaine.

Gerhard Schröder was elected the seventh Chancellor of the Federal Republic by parliament on October 27, 1998. With 351 out of a total of 666 votes cast he won a clear majority at the first ballot. He even received the votes of at least seven Opposition members. Those offering their congratulations included his predecessor in office Helmut Kohl and the CDU/CSU party whip Wolfgang Schäuble, here in conversation with the SPD party chairman Oskar Lafontaine.

Die 1980 aus der Umwelt- und Friedensbewegung hervorgegangenen Grünen traten im Oktober 1998 erstmals in eine Bundesregierung ein. Zu den Strategen dieses Erfolgs gehörten (von rechts) der designierte Außenminister Joschka Fischer, der Fraktionssprecher Rezzo Schlauch sowie die zukünftige Vizepräsidentin des Bundestags Antje Vollmer, die schon dem vorherigen Bundestagspräsidium angehört hatte.

In October 1988 the Greens, who had emerged in 1980 from the ecological and peace movements, were included for the first time in a federal government. The strategic architects of this success included (from right to left) the Foreign Minister designate Joschka Fischer, the parliamentary group spokesman Rezzo Schlauch and the future Vice President of the Bundestag Antje Vollmer, who had already been a member of the presidential panel in the preceding Bundestag.

Ernennung des Bundesaußenministers: Aus der Hand von Bundespräsident Roman Herzog nahm Joschka Fischer (Mitte) am 27. Oktober 1998 im Beisein von Bundeskanzler Gerhard Schröder die Urkunde entgegen. Er wurde außerdem Stellvertreter des Bundeskanzlers.

The appointment of the Foreign Minister: Joschka Fischer (center) was handed his certificate of appointment by President Roman Herzog on October 27, 1998 in the presence of Chancellor Gerhard Schröder. He also became Deputy Chancellor.

Gruppenbild des neuen Kabinetts mit dem Bundespräsidenten. Erste Reihe (von links): Ministerin für wirtschaftliche Zusammenarbeit Heidemarie Wieczorek-Zeul (SPD), Bildungsministerin Edelgard Bulmahn (SPD), Bundespräsident Roman Herzog, Bundeskanzler Gerhard Schröder (SPD), Außenminister Joschka Fischer (Bündnis 90/Die Grünen), Innenminister Otto Schily (SPD), Justizministerin Herta Däubler-Gmelin (SPD); zweite Reihe: Bauminister Franz Müntefering (SPD), Gesundheitsministerin Andrea Fischer (Bündnis 90/Die Grünen), Chef des Bundeskanzleramtes Bodo Hombach (SPD), Finanzminister Oskar Lafontaine (SPD), Umweltminister Jürgen Trittin (Bündnis 90/Die Grünen), Verteidigungsminister Rudolf Scharping (SPD), Familienministerin Christine Bergmann (SPD); dritte Reihe: Arbeitsminister Walter Riester (SPD), Landwirtschaftsminister Karl-Heinz Funke (SPD), Wirtschaftsminister Werner Müller (parteilos).

A group photo of the new cabinet with the President. Front row (from left to right): Minister for Economic Cooperation Heidemarie Wieczorek-Zeul (SPD), Minister of Education Edelgard Bulmahn (SPD), President Roman Herzog, Chancellor Gerhard Schröder (SPD), Foreign Minister Joschka Fischer (Alliance 90/The Greens), Minister of the Interior Otto Schily (SPD), Minister of Justice Herta Däubler-Gmelin (SPD); second row: Minister of Construction Franz Müntefering (SPD), Minister of Health Andrea Fischer (Alliance 90/The Greens), Head of Chancellery Bodo Hombach (SPD), Finance Minister Oskar Lafontaine (SPD), Minister of the Environment Jürgen Trittin (Alliance 90/The Greens), Defense Minister Rudolf Scharping (SPD), Family Minister Christine Bergmann (SPD); third row: Minister of Labor Walter Riester (SPD), Minister of Agriculture Karl-Heinz Funke (SPD), Economics Minister Werner Müller (Independent).

Kanzler Gerhard Schröder / Chancellor Gerhard Schröder

Seinen Ehrgeiz, das höchste Regierungsamt zu übernehmen, hat er früh bekannt. Gern wird die Episode zitiert, als der junge Bundestagsabgeordnete Anfang der achtziger Jahre am Gitter des Bonner Bundeskanzleramtes ausrief: »Ich will da rein!« Doch der Weg nach oben war steinig. Gerhard Schröder war nie ein Mann der Partei. Schon als Vorsitzender der »Jusos«, der Jugendorganisation der SPD, rang er mit dem innerparteilichen Regelsystem der politischen Richtungen und Machtzentren. Als Pragmatiker setzte er stets auf die Wirkung bei den Wählern. Der Erfolg gab ihm recht. Schon als niedersächsischer Ministerpräsident gewann Schröder großes Ansehen in der Bevölkerung. Auch der Ausgang der Bundestagswahl im September 1998 war vor allem ein Erfolg des Kanzlerkandidaten. Mit dem Vertrauen der Wähler besitzt Gerhard Schröder als Bundeskanzler das Mandat, Deutschlands »Aufbruch und Erneuerung« durchzusetzen.

He admitted at an early stage to his ambition to occupy the highest government office. People like to cite the episode in which the young member of parliament, standing at the railings outside the Chancellery in Bonn in the early eighties, exclaimed: "I want to get in there!" But the path to the top was a rocky one. Gerhard Schröder was never a party man. Even as chairman of the Young Socialists ("Jusos"), the SPD youth organization, he battled against the system by which party policies and power centers were internally regulated. As a pragmatist he always looked to the voters' reactions. Results proved him right. As Minister President of Lower Saxony Schröder had already achieved a high standing among the people. The outcome of the general election in September 1998 was also primarily a success for the chancellor candidate. Trusted by the voters, Gerhard Schröder has a mandate as Chancellor to implement Germany's "fresh start and renewal."

(gegenüber) Die Muße für eine gute Zigarre ist dem Bundeskanzler allzu selten vergönnt. Dennoch machte Gerhard Schröder aus seiner langfristigen Lebensplanung nie ein Hehl. Bei seiner Ernennung am 27.10.1998 erwiderte er auf die Ansprache des Bundespräsidenten: »Ich habe mich besonders gefreut, daß Sie darauf hingewiesen haben, wie selten die Kanzlerwechsel in der Geschichte der Bundesrepublik waren. So wollen wir das auch in Zukunft halten.«

(opposite) All too rarely does the Chancellor have the time for a good cigar. Nonetheless Gerhard Schröder has never made a secret of his long-term plan for his life. When he was appointed on October 27, 1998 he replied to the President's address: "I was particularly pleased that you pointed out how seldom Chancellors have changed in the history of the Federal Republic. Let us keep it like that in future."

(rechts) Rückblende: Zwanzig Jahre früher. Gerhard Schröder am 3.12.1979 als Juso-Vorsitzender auf dem Bundesparteitag der SPD im Congress-Center in Berlin.

(right) Flashback: twenty years earlier. Gerhard Schröder as Chairman of the Young Socialists during the SPD federal party conference at the Congress Center in Berlin on December 3, 1979.

Bundeskanzler Schröder verdeutlicht dem Kabinett am 4.11.1998 noch einmal, wie groß die Regierungsmehrheit nach der Bundestagswahl ausgefallen ist. Die Frauen am Kabinettstisch amüsiert das beträchtlich: (von links) Ministerin für Gesundheit Andrea Fischer (Bündnis 90/Die Grünen); Ministerin für Familie, Senioren, Frauen und Jugend Christine Bergmann (SPD); Ministerin für Bildung, Wissenschaft, Forschung und Technologie Edelgard Bulmahn (SPD); Ministerin für wirtschaftliche Zusammenarbeit und Entwicklung Heidemarie Wieczorek-Zeul (SPD); Ministerin der Justiz Herta Däubler-Gmelin (SPD).

On November 4, 1998, Chancellor Schröder once more makes the size of the government majority, following the general election, clear to the cabinet. The women at the cabinet table are highly amused by this: (from left to right) Minister of Health Andrea Fischer (Alliance 90/The Greens), Minister for Family, Senior Citizens, Women and Youth Christine Bergmann (SPD); Minister of Education, Science, Research and Technology Edelgard Bulmahn (SPD), Minister for Economic Cooperation and Development Heidemarie Wieczorek-Zeul (SPD); Minister of Justice Herta Däubler-Gmelin (SPD).

Mit sichtbarem Stolz nahm der neue Außenminister der Bundesrepublik Deutschland am Abend des 27. 10. 1998 am Kabinettstisch auf dem Sessel des Vizekanzlers Platz. Lange hatte er auf diesen Moment gewartet und dabei nicht nur die Wähler, sondern auch viele Mitglieder seiner eigenen Partei von der Richtigkeit seines Weges in die Regierungsverantwortung überzeugen müssen.

With visible pride, the new German Foreign Minister took his place at the cabinet table in the Deputy Chancellor's seat on the evening of October 27, 1998. He had waited a long time for this moment, having had to convince not only the voters but also many members of his own party of the rightness of his chosen path to government responsibility.

Rückblende: Fünfzehn Jahre früher. Der Bundestagsabgeordnete der Grünen Joschka Fischer am 4. 5. 1983 am Rednerpult des alten Plenarsaals in Bonn.

Flashback: fifteen years earlier. The Green member of parliament Joschka Fischer on May 4, 1983 at the speaker's desk in the old plenary chamber in Bonn.

Der oberste Diplomat der Bundesrepublik und die NATO. Außenminister Fischer, der sich in den Jahren zuvor in der Erkenntnis, daß gegen Menschenrechtsverletzungen und Völkermord mit Pazifismus und Moralappellen wenig auszurichten ist, für einen begrenzten Militäreinsatz auf dem Balkan eingesetzt hatte, besuchte am 5.11.1998 das NATO-Hauptquartier. Seine öffentlich geäußerte Anregung, die NATO-Strategie zu überdenken und auf die Möglichkeit des atomaren Erstschlages prinzipiell zu verzichten, weckte allerdings Irritationen bei den Bündnispartnern. Zunächst hätte derlei intern vorbesprochen und beraten werden sollen, wurde Fischer vor allem von amerikanischer Seite bald vorgehalten.

The Federal Republic's top diplomat and NATO. A visit to NATO Headquarters on November 5, 1998 by Foreign Minister Fischer, who in previous years had supported limited military action in the Balkans, realizing that pacifism and moral appeals have little power against violations of human rights and genocide. But Germany's partners in the Alliance were displeased by his suggestion, made in public, that NATO should rethink its strategy and renounce, as a matter of principle, the possibility of an atomic first strike. Fischer was soon to hear the criticism, from the Americans in particular, that in a matter of this sort there should have been prior internal discussion and consultation.

Nur einen Tag nach seiner Ernennung begann für den Außenminister der strapaziöse Alltag seiner Amtsgeschäfte. Am 28. 10.1998 startete er seine Antrittsbesuche in den Hauptstädten der wichtigsten Nachbarstaaten Frankreich, Großbritannien und Polen, anschließend reiste Fischer in die USA. Der enge Kontakt zu den mitreisenden Journalisten, wie hier auf dem Flug nach Wahington am 2.11.1998, gehört in der modernen Medienwelt zu den unverzichtbaren Aufgaben der Regierungsarbeit.

Just one day after his appointment, the strenuous daily routine of official business began for the Foreign Minister. On October 28, 1998 he set off on his inaugural visits to the capitals of the most important neighboring states: France, Britain and Poland. Following this, Fischer went to the US. One of the indispensible aspects of the work of the government in the modern media world is close contact with the journalists who accompany politicians on their travels – as here during the flight to Washington on November 2, 1998.

Am Ende des Jahrhunderts kehrt die deutsche Politik wieder nach Berlin zurück. Doch die Rückkehr ist kein Weg in die Vergangenheit, sondern ein Aufbruch in die Zukunft. Die Baukräne im neuen Regierungsviertel zeugen nicht nur vom Wandel der Stadtarchitektur, sondern auch von der gewandelten Architektur Europas. Deutschland liegt, nachdem es jahrzehntelang an der Nahtstelle zweier feindlich gesonnener Blocksysteme geteilt war, wieder in der europäischen Mitte. Aber diese Position begründet nicht mehr jene Sonderrolle, die dem Kontinent seit Beginn des Jahrhunderts zum Verhängnis wurde. Die Bundesrepublik ist ein westliches Land, geistig, politisch und wirtschaftlich untrennbar mit den Demokratien des Westens verbunden. Das ist das Erbe jener Epoche, die als »Bonner Republik« bezeichnet wird. Der Abschied von Bonn ist ein Abschied von der Stadt am Rhein, nicht von den Grundlagen der deutschen Nachkriegspolitik.

At the end of the century German politics is returning to Berlin. However, this return does not lead back into the past, but forward into the future. The cranes in the new government quarter bear witness not only to architectural changes in the city but also to the changed architecture of Europe. After being divided for decades at the seam between two mutually hostile bloc systems, Germany is now once again located at the center of Europe. But this location is no longer a reason for that role which had fatal consequences for the continent from the beginning of the century onwards. The Federal Republic is a western country, inseparably bound up, intellectually, politically and economically, with the western democracies. That is the legacy of the era which we know as the "Bonn Republic." The departure from Bonn is the departure from the town on the Rhine, not from the foundations of German postwar politics.

(gegenüber) Auf den Fundamenten der Vergangenheit bereitet sich die deutsche Demokratie auf die Zukunft vor. Wie ein Symbol dieser Wandlung ruht auf dem ehrwürdigen Gemäuer des alten Reichtags die kühne Glaskuppel des Architekten Norman Foster. Im Mai 1998 war das markante Gesicht des neuen Bundestages in Berlin schon recht gut zu erkennen.

(opposite) On the foundations of the past, German democracy is preparing for the future. As a symbol of this change, the bold glass dome designed by the architect Norman Foster is supported by the venerable walls of the old Reichstag. By May 1998 the striking appearance of the new parliament building in Berlin was discernible.

Abschied aus Bonn. Ein halbes Jahrhundert lang war die Stadt am Rhein Schauplatz der hohen Politik der Bundesrepublik. Zahllose Staatsgäste wurden in der Villa Hammerschmidt, der Residenz des Bundespräsidenten, mit protokollarischen Ehren empfangen. Diese Epoche deutscher Zeitgeschichte ist beendet. Die roten Teppiche werden nun in der neuen Hauptstadt Berlin ausgerollt. Bonn aber bleibt das Synonym für die Erfolgsgeschichte der deutschen Nachkriegsdemokratie.

Departure from Bonn. For half a century the town on the Rhine was the scene of top-level politics in the Federal Republic. Countless guests on state visits were received with all due ceremony at the Villa Hammerschmidt, the President's official residence. This era of recent German history is at an end. The red carpets will now be put out in Berlin, the new capital. But Bonn will remain synonymous with the history of the success of postwar German democracy.

Personenverzeichnis

A

Acheson, Dean 1893–1971, Rechtsanwalt, US-Politiker (Demokrat), 1945–1947 Unterstaatssekretär, 1949–1953 Außenminister, ab 1961 außenpolit. Berater d. Präsidenten Kennedy und Johnson.

Acheson, Dean 1893–1971, lawyer, US politician (Democrat), 1945–1947 under-secretary of state, 1949–1953 secretary of state, from 1961 foreign policy adviser to Presidents Kennedy and Johnson.

Acker, Achille van 1898–1975, belgischer Politiker, Mitglied d. Sozialist. Arbeiterpartei bis 1940, 1926 Stadtverordneter von Brügge, ab 1927 Abgeord. im Parlament, ab 1936 Verwalter d. Finanzangelegenheiten d. Kammer, Mitbegründer einer illegalen Widerstands-Organisation in Belgien während d. II. Weltkrieges, 1944 Arbeits- Sozial- und Gesundheitsminister, 1945 und 1946 Regierungsvorsitz, 1947–1949 Verkehrsminister, 1954–1958 Leiter d. liberal-sozialist. Koalitionsregierung, 1961–1974 Präsident d. belgischen Abgeordnetenkammer.

Acker, Achille van 1898–1975, Belgian politician, member of Socialist Workers' Party until 1940, 1926 municipal government deputy in Bruges, from 1927 MP, from 1936 in charge of the financial affairs of the chamber, co-founder of an illegal resistance organization in Belgium during the second world war, 1944 minister of labor, social welfare and health, 1945 and 1946 president of government, 1947–1949 minister of transport, 1954–1958 leader of liberal-socialist coalition government, 1961–1974 president of Belgian chamber of deputies.

Adenauer, Emma geb. Weyer, 1880–1916, Konrad Adenauers erste Frau, verheiratet 1904–1916, Kinder: Konrad, Max und Maria.

Adenauer, Emma née Weyer, 1880–1916, Konrad Adenauer's first wife, married 1904–1916, children: Konrad, Max and Maria.

Adenauer, Gussie geb. Zinßer, 1895–1948, Konrad Adenauers zweite Frau, verheiratet 1919–1948, Kinder: Paul und Lotte.

Adenauer, Gussie née Zinßer, 1895–1948, Konrad Adenauer's second wife, married 1919–1948, children: Paul and Lotte.

Adenauer, Konrad, Dr. h.c. 1876–1967, 1917–1933 und Mai 1945–Oktober 1945 Oberbürgermeister von Köln, 1946–1950 Vorsitzender d. CDU in d. BBZ, 1948–1949 Präsident d. Parlament. Rates, 1949–1967 MdB, 15.9. 1949–15.10.1963 Bundeskanzler, 1951–1955 Außenminister, 1950–1966 Vorsitz. d. CDU.

Adenauer, Konrad, Dr. h.c. 1876–1967, 1917–1933 and May 1945–October 1945 mayor of Cologne, 1946–1950 chairman of CDU in British zone of occupation, 1948–1949 president of parliamentary council, 1949–1967 MdB, 15.9.1949–15.10.1963 federal chancellor, 1951–1955 foreign minister, 1950–1966 CDU party chairman.

Adenauer, Lotte, Dr. phil. geb. 1925, Tochter von Konrad Adenauer, ab 2.5.1950 verheiratet mit Heribert Multhaupt in Bonn.

Adenauer, Lotte, Dr. phil. b. 1925, daughter of Konrad Adenauer, married to Heribert Multhaupt in Bonn since 2.5.1950.

Ahlers, Conrad 1922–1980, von 1954–1957 außenpolit. Kommentator d. Zeitschrift »Die Welt«, 1957–1959 Bonner Korrespondent d. Zeitschrift »Der Spiegel«, 1959– 1962 innenpolit. Redakteur d. »Frankfurter Rundschau«, 1962–1966 stellvertr. Chefredakteur d. Zeitschrift »Der Spiegel«, 1962 während d. »Spiegel-Affäre« in Spanien verhaftet und nach Deutschl. überführt, 1966–1969 stellvertr. Leiter d. Presse- und Informationsamtes d. Bundesregierung, 1969–1972 Staatssekretär, 1972–1980 MdB für d. SPD, 1980 Intendant d. Dt. Welle.

Ahlers, Conrad 1922–1980, from 1954–1957 commentator on foreign affairs for *Die Welt,* 1957–1959 Bonn correspondent for *Der Spiegel,* 1959–1962 home affairs editor of the *Frankfurter Rundschau,* 1962–1966 deputy editor-in-chief of *Der Spiegel,* 1962 arrested in Spain and brought back to Germany during the *Spiegel* affair, 1966–1969 deputy head of government press and information office, 1969–1972 state secretary, 1972–1980 SPD MdB, 1980 general manager of *Deutsche Welle.*

Albert II, Prinz v. Belgien geb. 1934, seit 1976 Admiral, 1958 Senator u. Präsident d. Belgischen Roten Kreuzes, seit 1993 als Nachfolger seines verstorbenen Bruders Baudouin König v. Belgien

Albert II., Prince of Belgium b. 1934, since 1976 admiral, 1958 senator and president of Belgian Red Cross, 1993 succeeded his deceased brother Baudouin as King of Belgium.

Alphand, Hervé Jean-Charles 1907–1994, frz. Politiker und Diplomat, 1935 Kabinettschef im Handelsministerium, ab 1937 Finanzattaché d. Botschaft in Washington, Anfang d. 40er Direktor für Wirtschaftsangelegenheiten im 1. Nationalkomitee, leitete 1937 d. Verhandlungen zum dt.-frz. Handels- und Wirtschaftsabkommen, nahm 1946 an Außenministerkonferenzen teil, 1950 Vertreter Frankreichs im Rat d. Atlantikpaktmächte (NATO), Präsident d. Interimsausschusses für d. EVG und Vertreter bei d. OEEC, 1955 ständiger Vertreter im Sicherheitsrat d. UNO, 1956–1965 frz. Botschafter in Washington, 1965–1972 Generalsekretär im frz. Außenministerium.

Alphand, Hervé Jean-Charles 1907–1994, French politician and diplomat, 1935 cabinet head at the ministry of trade, from 1937 financial attaché at Washington embassy, early 1940s director of economic affairs in 1st national committee, 1937 led negotiations over the Franco-German trade and economic agreement, 1946 took part in foreign ministers' conferences, 1950 represented France on NATO council, president of EDC interim committee and representative at OEEC, 1955 permanent representative on UN security council, 1956–1965 French ambassador in Washington, 1965–1972 general secretary at French foreign office.

Andreotti, Giulio, Dr. h. c. geb. 1919, ital. Publizist und Politiker, 1942–1945 Präsident d. Vereinigung Katholischer Universitäten, 1944 Leiter d. Parteijugend d. Christl.-Demokr. Partei (DC), 1945 Mitglied in d. Verfassunggebenden Versammlung, 1947 in d. Kammer gewählt, 1947–1953 Unterstaatssekretär beim Ministerpräsidenten, bis 1968 Mitglied d. Regierung, 1959–1966 Leiter d. Verteidigungsministeriums, 1966–1968 Leiter d. Ministeriums für Industrie und Handel, 1972–1979 und 1989–1992 Ministerpräsident, 1983–1989 Außenminister, 1993 Ermittlungsverfahren gegen ihn wegen Verdacht »mafioser Tätigkeit« und Korruptionsvorwürfen.

Andreotti, Giulio, Dr. h. c. b. 1919, Italian publicist and politician, 1942–1945 president of association of catholic universities, 1944 head of Christian Democratic Party (DC) Youth, 1945 member of constitutive assembly, 1947 elected to chamber, 1947–1953 under state secretary with prime minister, until 1968 member of government, 1959–1966 head of ministry of defense, 1966–1968 head of ministry of trade and industry, 1972–1979 and 1989–1992 prime minister, 1983–1989 foreign minister, 1993 subject of legal proceedings on suspicion of mafia activity and corruption charges.

Arnold, Karl 1901–1958, ab 1920 Funktionär in d. christl. Arbeiterbewegung, 1945 Mitbegründer d. CDU, Beteiligung an d. Neugründung d. Gewerkschaften in d. BBZ, 1946 Oberbürgermeister von Düsseldorf und stellvertr. Ministerpräsident von Nordrhein-Westfalen, 1947–1956 Ministerpräsident von Nordrhein-Westfalen, 1949 zum 1. Bundesratspräsidenten d. BRD gewählt, 1956–1958 stellvertr. Bundesvorsitzender d. CDU, 1957–1958 MdB und stellvertr. Vorsitzender d. CDU/CSU-Fraktion, damit Gegenspieler Adenauers.

Arnold, Karl 1901–1958, from 1920 official in christian workers' movement, 1945 co-founder of CDU, involved in re-establishment of trade unions in British zone of occupation, 1946 mayor of Düsseldorf and deputy minister president of North Rhine-Westphalia, 1947–1956 minister president of North Rhine-Westphalia, 1949 elected 1st president of the FRG Bundesrat, 1956–1958 deputy CDU federal party chairman, 1957–1958 MdB and deputy CDU/CSU chief whip and hence Adenauer's antagonist.

Arendt, Hannah, Dr. phil. 1906–1975, amerik. polit. Philosophin und Publizistin aus Deutschl., 1933–1940 Leiterin einer Organisation in Paris, d. jüdische Waisenkinder nach Palästina brachte, ab 1940 Mitarbeiterin verschiedener Zeitschriften in d. USA, 1949–1952 Sekretärin d. Jewish Cultural Reconstruction Inc. In d. 50er und 60er Professorin für Polit. Theorie in Princeton und Chicago, 1967–1975 Professorin für Polit. Philosophie an d. New School for Social Research in New York City

Arendt, Hannah, Dr. phil. 1906–1975, American political philosopher and publicist from Germany, 1933–1940 head of an organization in Paris for settling Jewish orphans in Palestine, from 1940 worked for various US periodicals, 1949–1952 secretary of Jewish Cultural Reconstruction Inc. In 50s and 60s professor of political theory in Princeton and Chicago, 1967–1975 professor of political philosophy at New School for Social Research in New York City.

Arendt, Walter geb. 1925, Bergarbeiter, dt. SPD-Politiker, 1961–1980 MdB, 1964–1969 Vorsitzender d. IG Bergbau und Energie, 1967–1969 Präsident d. Internat. Bergarbeiterverbandes, 1968–1979 Mitglied im SPD-Parteivorstand, 1969–1976 Bundesminister für Arbeit und Sozialordnung, ab 1973 Mitglied d. SPD-Präsidiums, 1977 Stellvertr. SPD-Fraktionsvorsitzender.

Arendt, Walter b. 1925, miner, German SPD politician, 1961–1980 MdB, 1964–1964 chairman of IG mining und energy, 1967–1969 president of international miners' association, 1968–1979 member of SPD executive committee, 1969–1976 minister of labor and social order, from 1973 member of SPD presidium, 1977 SPD deputy whip.

Attlee, Clement Richard Earl (1955) 1883–1967, Anwalt und brit. Politiker, 1922–1945 Abgeordneter, 1935–1955 Führer d. Labour Party, 1945–1951 Ministerpräsident,1945–1945 zugleich Verteidigungsminister, 1951–1955 Oppositionsführer im Unterhaus, anschließend Mitglied d. Oberhauses.

Attlee, Clement Richard Earl (1955) 1883–1967, lawyer and British politician, 1922–1945 MP, 1935–1955 Labour Party leader, 1945–1951 prime minister, 1945–1945 at the same time minister of defense, 1951–1955 leader of the opposition in House of Commons, later member of House of Lords.

Augstein, Rudolf (Pseudonym: Jens Daniel), geb. 1923, Publizist, 1945 und 1946 Journalist d. Zeitschriften »Hannoversches Nachrichtenblatt« und »Die Woche« unter d. Leitung d. brit. Militärregierung. 1947 kam d. Magazin »Die Woche« durch ihn mit dem neuen Titel »Der Spiegel« heraus, d. Strafverfahren gegen ihn, aufgrund d. »Spiegel-Affäre« Ende Oktober 1962, wurde 1965 wegen Mangels an Beweisen eingestellt.

Augstein, Rudolf (pseudonym of Jens Daniel), b. 1923, publicist, 1945 und 1946 journalist with the *Hannoversche Nachrichtenblatt* and *Die Woche* under supervision of British military government. 1947 the periodical *Die Woche,* through his doing, acquired the new name *Der Spiegel,* criminal proceedings against him in the wake of the *Spiegel* affair in late October 1962 were dropped in 1965 due to lack of evidence.

Axen, Hermann 1916–1992, 1942 Mitglied d. KPD, nach Auslieferung aus Frankreich Einlieferung in d. KZ Auschwitz III, anschließend KZ Buchenwald, 1946 Mitbegründer d. FDJ, 1950 Chef d. Abteilung Agitation beim ZK d. SED, 1950–1953 Mitglied und Sekretär d. ZK und d. Parteisekretariats, seit 1954 Mitglied d. DDR-Volkskammer, 1956–1966 Chefredakteur d. SED-Zentralorgans »Neues Deutschland«, 1966 Sekretär d. ZK d. SED, u.a. verantwortlich für internat. Verbindungen, 1967– 1971 stellvertr. Vorsitzender, seit 1971 Vorsitzender d. Volkskammerausschusses für Auswärtige Angelegenheiten, seit 1970 Mitglied d. PBs, maßgeblich für d. außenpolit. Kurs d. DDR mitverantwortlich, 8.11.1989 Ausscheiden aus dem PB, 31.1.1990 Aufhebung d. Haftbefehls aus gesundheitlichen Gründen.

Axen, Hermann 1916–1992, 1942 member of KPD, after extradition from France sent to Auschwitz III KZ, then to Buchenwald KZ, 1946 co-founder of the FDJ, 1950 head of agitation section on SED central committee, 1950–1953 member and secretary of central committee and party secretariat, from 1954 member of GDR Volkskammer, 1956–1966 editor-in-chief of main SED party newspaper *Neues Deutschland,* 1966 secretary of SED central committee, responsible inter alia for international contacts, 1967–1971 deputy chairman, from 1971 chairman of *Volkskammer* foreign affairs committee, from 1970 member of PB, principally responsible for GDR foreign policy, 8.11.1989 left PB, 31.1.1990 arrest warrant cancelled on health grounds.

B

Backlund, Sven Einar geb. 1917, 1955–1961 Leiter d. Presseabteilung im schwed. Außenministerium, 1961– 1964 schwed. Botschafter in Belgrad, 1964–1967 Generalkonsul in Berlin, 1968–1972 Botschafter bei d. EG in Brüssel, 1972–1983 Botschafter in Bonn.

Backlund, Sven Einar b. 1917, 1955–1961 head of Swedish foreign ministry press department, 1961–1964 Swedish ambassador in Belgrade, 1964–1967 consul general in Berlin, 1968– 1972 ambassador to the EC in Brussels, 1972–1983 ambassador in Bonn.

Bagger, Hartmut geb. 1938, dt. General, ab 1958 Panzergrenadier und Offiziersanwärter in d. Bundeswehr, 1960 Beförderung zum Leutnant, 1969–1971 Generalstabsausbildung, danach Dozent für Militärpolitik an d. Führungsakademie d. Bundeswehr in Hamburg, 1978 als Referent im Bundesministerium d. Verteidigung in Bonn, 1992 stellvertr. Inspektor d. Heeres in Bonn, 1994 Inspektor, ab Februar 1996 Generalinspekteur d. Bundeswehr.

Bagger, Hartmut b. 1938, German general, from 1958 tank grenadier and officer cadet in German army, 1960 promoted to lieutenant, 1969–1971 general staff training, then lecturer in military politics at army command academy in Hamburg, 1978 adviser to ministry of defense in Bonn, 1992 deputy army inspector in Bonn, 1994 inspector, since February 1996 inspector general of the army.

Bahr, Egon Karl-Heinz geb. 1922, 1950–1960 Bonner Kommentator d. RIAS Berlin, 1960–1966 Leiter d. Presse- und Informationsamtes d. Landes Berlin, 1969–1972 Staatssekretär im Bundeskanzleramt, 1972–1992 MdB, 1972–1974 Bundesminister für besondere Aufgaben, 1974–1976 Bundesminister für wirtschaftl. Zusammenarbeit, 1976–1981 SPD-Bundesgeschäftsführer, ab 1982 Mitglied d. SPD-Parteivorstandes, ab 1987 Vorsitzender d. Sicherheitspolit. Kommission d. SPD, 1990 Berater d. DDR-Abrüstungs- und Verteidigungsministers R. Eppelmann.

Bahr, Egon Karl-Heinz b. 1922, 1950–1960 Bonn commentator with RIAS Berlin, 1960–1966 head of press and information office of the *Land* Berlin, 1969–1972 state secretary at chancellery, 1972–1992 MdB, 1972–1974 minister without portfolio, 1974–1976 minister for economic cooperation, 1976–1981 SPD parliamentary manager, from 1982 member of SPD party executive, from 1987 chairman of SPD security policy commission, 1990 adviser to GDR disarmament and defense minister R. Eppelmann.

Baker, James geb. 1930, amerik. Jurist und Politiker, 1957–1980 Anwalt, 1975/76 stellvertr. Handelsminister, 1976 Wahlkampfleiter für Präsident Ford, 1980, 1988 und 1992 Führung d. Präsidentschaftswahlkampfs für G. Bush, November 1980 Stabschef d. Weißen Hauses, 1984 Wahlkampfleiter für Präsident Reagan, 1985–1988 Finanzminister, Januar 1989 – August 1992 Außenminister, sodann kurzzeitig Stabschef im Weißen Haus.

Baker, James b. 1930, American lawyer and politician, 1957–1980 practised law, 1975/76 deputy minister of trade, 1976 election campaign manager for President Ford, 1980, 1988 und 1992 managed presidential election campaign for G. Bush, November 1980 chief of staff at the White House, 1984 election campaign manager for President Reagan, 1985–1988 minister of finance, Januar 1989 – August 1992 secretary of state, then briefly chief of staff at the White House.

Balke, Siegfried, Prof. Dr.-Ing. 1902–1984, dt. Chemiker und Ingenieur, 1953–1956 Bundesminister für d. Post- und Fernmeldewesen, 1956–1962 Bundesminister für Atomfragen bzw. für Atomkernenergie und Wasserwirtschaft, 1964–1969 Präsident d. Bundesvereinigung d. Dt. Arbeitgeberverbände, 1957–1969 MdB für d. CSU.

Balke, Siegfried, professor, Dr.-Ing. 1902–1984, German chemist and engineer, 1953–1956 minister of post and telecommunications, 1956–1962 minister for atomic issues/nuclear energy and waterways, 1964–1969 president of federal league of German employers associations, 1957–1969 CSU MdB.

Baring, Arnulf geb. 1932, Jurist, Publizist, 1962–1964 Redakteur beim WDR, 1969–1976 Professor für polit. Wissenschaft, ab 1976 für Zeitgeschichte und Internat. Beziehungen an d. FU-Berlin.

Baring, Arnulf b. 1932, lawyer, publicist, 1962–1964 editor at WDR, 1969–1976 professor of political science and from 1976 of contemporary history and international relations at Free University Berlin.

Barraclough, Sir John Ashworth geb. 1918, englischer Brigadier, 1946–1950 stellvertr. Militärgouverneur d. Landes Nordrhein-Westfalen, von 1938–1976 bei d. Royal Air Force, Rang: Air Chief Marshal, 1976–1979 stellvertr. Vorsitzender d. Air League Council, 1977–1980 Vizepräsident und 1980–1990 Präsident d. Air Public Relations Association.

Barraclough, Sir John Ashworth b. 1918, English brigadier, 1946–1950 deputy military governor of North Rhine-Westphalia, from 1938–1976 Royal Air Force with rank of air chief marshal, 1976–1979 deputy chairman of air league council, 1977–1980 vice president and 1980–1990 president of air public relations association.

Barschel, Uwe, Dr. jur. et phil. (1971) 1944–1987, CDU-Politiker, 1962 CDU-Eintritt, 1967–1971 Landesvorsitzender d. Jungen Union in Schleswig-Holstein, 1968 stellvertr., ab 1973 CDU-Kreisvorsitzender im Herzogtum Lauenburg, ab 1969 stellvertr. CDU-Landesvorsitzender, ab 1971 MdL in Schleswig-Holstein und stellvertr. Vorsitzender, ab 1973 Leiter d. CDU-Fraktion, ab 1979 Innenminister, 1982–1987 Ministerpräsident von Schleswig-Holstein (Rücktritt), wegen »Kieler-Affäre« vermutlich Freitod.

Barschel, Uwe, Dr. jur. et phil. (1971) 1944–1987, CDU politician, 1962 joined CDU, 1967–1971 *Land* chairman of Young Union in Schleswig-Holstein, 1968 CDU regional deputy chairman, from 1973 chairman, in Duchy of Lauenburg, from 1969 deputy CDU *Land* chairman, from 1971 MdL Schleswig-Holstein and deputy chairman, from 1973 CDU chief whip, from 1979 minister of the interior, 1982–1987 minister president of Schleswig-Holstein (resigned), probable suicide because of "Kiel affair."

Barzel, Rainer Candidus, Dr. jur. geb. 1924, Jurist, 1956 geschäftsführendes Mitglied im Landespräsidium d. CDU in Nordrhein-Westfalen, 1957–1987 MdB für d. CDU, 1963 stellvertr., 1964–1973 Fraktionsvorsitzender d. CDU/CSU, 1962/63 Bundesminister für Gesamtdt. Fragen, 1966–1971 stellvertr. und 1971–1973 CDU-Bundesvorsitzender, 1972 CDU/CSU-Kanzlerkandidat, 1976–1979 Vorsitz im Bundestagsausschuß für Wirtschaft, 1982/83 Bundesminister für innerdt. Beziehungen, 1983/84 Bundestagspräsident (Rücktritt).

Barzel, Rainer Candidus, Dr. jur. b. 1924, lawyer, 1956 managing member of the CDU *Land* executive body in North Rhine-Westphalia, 1957–1987 CDU MdB, 1963 CDU/CSU deputy whip, 1964–1973 chief whip, 1962/63 minister for all-German issues, 1966–1971 CDU deputy federal party chairman and 1971–1973 chairman, 1972 CDU/CSU chancellor candidate, 1976–1979 chairman of parliamentary economics committee, 1982/83 minister for inter-German relations, 1983/84 president of the Bundestag (resigned).

Bastian, Gert 1923–1992 (Freitod), Generalmajor a. D., Zug- und Kompanieführer eines Panzerpionierbataillons im Zweiten Weltkrieg, 1956 Eintritt als Oberleutnant in d. Bundeswehr, 1962–1967 Generalstabsoffizier, 1968–1971 Referent im Führungsstab d. Heeres, sodann Führung d. Jägerbrigade, dann bis 1976 Brigadegeneral, 1976 Generalmajor, Kommandeur d. 12. Panzerdivision in Veitshöchheim, 1980 vorzeitig pensioniert, 1954– 1963 CSU-Mitglied, 1983–1987 MdB für d. Grünen und Fraktionssprecher, 1992 erschoß er auch seine Freundin Petra Kelly

Register of Persons

Bastian, Gert 1923–1992, (suicide) major general (ret'd.), platoon and company leader of a tank pioneer batallion in second world war, 1956 joined army as first lieutenant, 1962–1967 general staff officer, 1968–1971 adviser to army command staff, then leader of a rifle brigade, then until 1976 brigadier general, 1976 major general commanding 12th tank division in Veitshöchheim, 1980 early retirement, 1954–1963 member of CSU, 1983–1987 MdB and parliamentary spokesman for Greens, 1992 shot himself and his companion Petra Kelly.

Beatrix Wilhelmine Armgard von Oranien-Nassau und von Lippe-Biesterfeld, Königin d. Niederlande seit 1980, geb. 1938, älteste Tochter von Königin Juliana, Promotion in Rechtswissenschaft, seit 1956 offizielle Thronerbin und Mitglied d. niederländischen Staatsrates, 1966 Heirat mit dem dt. Diplomaten Claus von Amsberg.

Beatrix Wilhelmine Armgard of Orange-Nassau and of Lippe-Biesterfeld, Queen of the Netherlands since 1980, b. 1938, eldest daughter of Queen Juliana, graduated in law, since 1956 official heir to the throne and member of Netherlands state council, 1966 married German diplomat Claus von Amsberg.

Beauvoir, Simone de 1908–1986, frz. Schriftstellerin, Lebensgefährtin von Jean-Paul Sartre, 1931–1943 Lehrerin, ab 1943 freie Schriftstellerin, zentrales Thema: d. Selbstbehauptung d. Frau, 1970/71 Direktorin einer linksradikalen Zeitschrift.

Beauvoir, Simone de 1908–1986, French writer, lifelong companion of Jean-Paul Sartre, 1931–1943 teacher, from 1943 freelance writer, central theme: woman's self-assertion, 1970/71 director of a radical left-wing periodical.

Bech, Joseph, Dr. jur. 1887–1975, luxemburg. Politiker, ab 1912 Rechtsanwalt, ab 1914 im Abgeordnetenhaus, 1921 Übernahme d. Unterrichts- und Innenministeriums, 1923 auch d. Justizministeriums, 1926–1937 und 1953–1958 Regierungschef, 1926–1959 Außenminister, 1929 Vizepräsident beim Völkerbund, 1953 auch Landwirtschafts- und Weinbauminister, 1957/58 Präsident d. Nordatlantik-Rats, 1964 Rückzug aus d. Politik.

Bech, Joseph, Dr. jur. 1887–1975, Luxembourg politician, from 1912 lawyer, from 1914 MP, 1921 took charge of ministry of the interior and education, 1923 also ministry of justice, 1926–1937 and 1953–1958 head of government, 1926–1959 foreign minister, 1929 vice president at league of nations, 1953 also minister of agriculture and viniculture, 1957/58 president of North Atlantic Council, 1964 retired from politics.

Beck, Marieluise geb. 1952, dt. Lehrerin u. Politikerin, ab 1980 Mitglied d. Grünen, 1991–1994 Mitglied d. Bremischen Bürgerschaft, 1983–1985, 1987–1990 und ab 1994 MdB, seit 1998 Ausländerbeauftragte d. Bundesregierung.

Beck, Marieluise b. 1952, German teacher and politician, since 1980 member of Greens, 1991–1994 member of Bremen city council, 1983–1985, 1987–1990 and since 1994 MdB, since 1998 member of government with responsibility for aliens.

Becker, Max, Dr. 1888–1960, Rechtsanwalt, Notar und Politiker, 1946 MdL in Hessen und 1948/49 Mitglied im Parlam. Rat, 1949–1960 MdB für d. FDP, 1956–1960 Vizepräsident d. Dt. Bundestages, 1957 FDP-Fraktionsvorsitzender

Becker, Max, Dr. 1888–1960, lawyer, notary and politician, 1946 MdL Hessen and 1948/49 MdPR, 1949–1960 FDP MdB, 1956–1960 vice president of Bundestag, 1957 FDP chief whip.

Beckmann, Lukas geb. 1950, Landwirtschaftslehre, März 1979 Gründungsmitglied d. Grünen in Frankfurt und deren Bundesgeschäftsführer, 1983 Aufbau d. Fraktion im Bundestag, 1987 Geschäftsführer d. Heinrich-Böll-Stiftung, Mitglied d. »Grünen Aufbruchs '88«, 1990 und 1994 zum Bundesfraktionsgeschäftsführer gewählt.

Beckmann, Lukas b. 1950, agricultural apprenticeship, March 1979 founding member of Greens in Frankfurt and their federal manager, 1983 built up federal parliamentary group, 1987 manager of Heinrich Böll foundation, member of "Green takeoff 88", 1990 und 1994 elected federal parliamentary manager.

Ben Gurion, David 1886–1973, 1905/06 nach Palästina, d. zionistischen Bewegung angehörig, 1915–1918 Organisation d. Jüdische Legion in d. USA, 1921 Mitbegründer d. Gewerkschaft Histadrut und 1921–1933 ihr Generalsekretär, 1930–1965 Vorsitzender d. sozialist. »Mapai«-Partei, 1935–1948 Leiter d. Jewish Agency for Palestine, am 14.5.1948 proklamierte er d. Gründung d. Staates Israel, 1948–1953 und 1955–1963 israelischer Ministerpräsident, 1948/49 und 1955–1963 Ministerpräsident und Verteidigungsminister, 1970 Rückzug aus d. Politik.

Ben Gurion, David 1886–1973, 1905/06 moved to Palestine, member of Zionist movement, 1915–1918 organized Jewish Legion in US, 1921 co-founder of Histadrut trade union and 1921–1923 its secretary general, 1930–1965 chairman of socialist *Mapai* party, 1935–1948 head of Jewish Agency for Palestine, on 14.5.1948 proclaimed the founding of the state of Israel, 1948– 1953 and 1955–1963 Israeli prime minister, 1948/49 and 1955– 1963 prime minister and defense minister, 1970 retired from politics.

Berger, Hans, Dr. jur. (1936) 1909–1985, Richter, dt. Diplomat, 1945–1949 Gerichtsrat, Ministerialrat und Richter in verschiedenen dt. Städten, 1949–1953 Landgerichtspräsident, 1954 Leiter d. Rechtsabteilung im Auswärtigen Amt, 1959–1965 Botschafter in Dänemark und Den Haag, 1965–1969 Staatssekretär und Chef d. Bundespräsidialamtes, 1969–1971 Botschafter d. BRD am Heiligen Stuhl in Rom, anschließend vorzeitig in d. Ruhestand.

Berger, Hans, Dr. jur. (1936) 1909–1985, judge, German diplomat, 1945–1949 judicial councillor, ministerial councillor and judge in various German cities, 1949–1953 president of *Land* court, 1954 head of foreign office legal department, 1959–1965 ambassador in Denmark and The Hague, 1965–1969 state secretary and head of federal president's office, 1969–1971 FRG ambassador to the Holy See in Rome, followed by early retirement.

Bergmann, Christine, Dr. rer. nat. (1989) geb. 1939, 1977–1990 Abteilungsleiterin im Institut für Arzneimittelwesen d. DDR, 1990 Präsidentin d. Stadtverordnetenversammlung, 1991–1998 Bürgermeisterin von Berlin und Senatorin für Arbeit, berufliche Bildung und Frauen, 1998 zur Bundesministerin für Familie, Senioren, Frauen und Jugend ernannt.

Bergmann, Christine, Dr. rer. nat. (1989) b. 1939, 1977–1990 head of department at GDR pharmacological institute, 1990 president of assembly of municipal deputies, 1991–1998 mayor of Berlin and senator for labor, vocational training and women, 1998 appointed minister of the family, senior citizens, women and youth.

Bernhard Leopold zur Lippe-Biesterfeld, Prinz d. Niederlande, geb. 1911, 1937 Heirat mit Prinzessin Juliana, Tochter Beatrix, 1954 in d. Generals- und Admiralsrang befördert, 1970–1976 Generalinspekteur d. Streitkräfte, übernahm mehrere Ehrenämter und Funktionen.

Bernhard Leopold of Lippe-Biesterfeld, Prince of the Netherlands, b. 1911, 1937 married Princess Juliana, daughter of Beatrix, 1954 promoted to rank of general and admiral, 1970– 1976 inspector general of armed forces, took on several honorary offices and functions.

Besson, Waldemar, Prof. Dr. (1954) 1929–1971, dt. Publizist, Historiker und Professor für Polit. Wissenschaften, 1954–1961 Assistent und Privatdozent an d. Universität Tübingen, danach Ordinarius und Dekan, ab 1966 Mitglied d. Gründungsausschusses d. Universität Konstanz und dort ordentlicher Professor, vier Buchveröffentlichungen zwischen 1955 und 1964.

Besson, Waldemar, professor, Dr. (1954) 1929–1971, German publicist, historian and professor of political science, 1954–1961 assistant and lecturer at Tübingen university, subsequently professor and dean, from 1966 member of founding committee of Constance university and professor and head of department there, four books published between 1955 and 1964.

Betancourt, Rómulo 1908–1981, 1940 Mitbegründer d. linksorientierten Acción Democrática, von 1945–1948 und 1959–1964 Staatspräsident von Venezuela, von 1948–1958 im Exil

Betancourt, Rómulo 1908–1981, 1940 co-founder of left-wing Acción Democrática, from 1945–1948 and 1959–1964 state president of Venezuela, from 1948–1958 in exile.

Beuys, Joseph 1921–1986, dt. Künstler, 1947–1952 Studium d. Malerei und Bildhauerei, 1961–1972 Professor an d. Düsseldorfer Akademie, 1978 Gastprofessur an d. Wiener Hochschule für Angewandte Kunst, 1980 an d. Frankfurter Städel-Schule, 1974 Gründung d. »Freien internat. Hochschule für Kreativität und interdisziplinäre Forschung« in Düsseldorf.

Beuys, Joseph 1921–1986, German artist, 1947–1952 studied painting and sculpture, 1961–1972 professor at Düsseldorf academy, 1978 visiting professor at college of applied art in Vienna, 1980 at Städel school in Frankfurt, 1974 founded "free international college for creativity and interdisiplinary research" in Düsseldorf.

Beyen, Johan Willem, Dr. (1918) 1897–1976, niederländischer Staats- und Finanzfachmann, 1918–1923 im Finanzministerium, 1924–1946 privat in d. Wirtschaft tätig, 1946 geschäftsführender Direktor d. Internat. Bank für Wiederaufbau und Entwicklung in Washington, 1948 Direktor d. Internat. Währungsfonds, daneben Sitz und Stimme in Verwaltungsräten weltbekannter Firmen, 1952–1956 Außenminister, sodann Leitung d. Staatskommissariats für dt. Angelegenheiten, 1958–1963 Botschafter in Paris.

Beyen, Johan Willem, Dr. (1918) 1897–1976, Dutch statesman and financial expert, 1918–1923 at finance ministry, 1924–1946 worked in private sector of economy, 1946 managing director of international reconstruction and development bank in Washington, 1948 director of international monetary fund, also seat and voting rights on adminstrative bodies of internationally well-known companies, 1952–1956 foreign minister, then head of state commissariat for German issues, 1958–1963 ambassador in Paris.

Bidault, Georges 1899–1983, 1936–1939 Journalist d. christl.-demokr. Zeitung »L'Aube«, 1941 Anschluß an d. Résistance, als Präsident d. Conseil National de la Résistance Leitung d. Pariser Aufstands im August 1944, 1944 Mitbegründer, 1949–1951 Vorsitzender d. Mouvement Républicain Populaire, 1944–1946 und 1947/48 und 1953/54 Außenminister, 1946 und 1949/50 Ministerpräsident, 1962 Mitglied d. Exekutivkomitees d. Organisation de l'Armée Secrète, 1962–1968 in Belgien bzw. Brasilien im Exil, 1968–1983 in Paris.

Bidault, Georges 1899–1983, 1936–1939 journalist for christian democratic newspaper *L'Aube*, 1941 joined the résistance, as president of the conseil national de la résistance led Paris rising in August 1944, 1944 co-founder and 1949–1951 chairman of the mouvement républicain populaire, 1944–1946 and 1947/48 and 1953/54 foreign minister, 1946 and 1949/50 prime minister, 1962 member of executive committee of the organisation de l'armée secrète, 1962–1968 exile in Belgium and Brazil, 1968–1983 in Paris.

Biermann, (Karl) Wolf geb. 1936 in Hamburg, 1953 Übersiedlung in d. DDR, zwischen 1959 und 1963 erste eigene Lieder, Vorbilder: Villon, Brecht, Heine, Brassens, wird »Liedermacher«, Dezember 1965 totales Auftritts- und Publikationsverbot in d. DDR, aber weitere Veröffentlichungen in d. BRD, 1976 Zwangsausbürgerung aus d. DDR.

Biermann, (Karl) Wolf b. 1936 in Hamburg, 1953 moved to GDR, between 1959 and 1963 wrote first songs, modelled on Villon, Brecht, Heine and Brassens, became "songmaker", December 1965 banned from all public appearances and forbidden to publish in GDR, but further publications in FRG, 1976 stripped of GDR citizenship.

Birke, Adolf M. geb 1939, Historiker, seit 1985 Leiter d. German Historical Institute in London, Mitglied d. Royal Historical Society und d. Kommission für d. Geschichte d. Parlamentarismus und d. polit. Parteien

Birke, Adolf M. b. 1939, historian, since 1985 head of German Historical Institute in London, member of Royal Historical Society and commission for history of parliamentarianism and political parties.

Bismarck, Otto von 1815–1898, Gründer und Kanzler d. Dt. Reiches, 1862–1890 preußischer Ministerpräsident, 1871–1890 Reichskanzler.

Bismarck, Otto von 1815–1898, founder and chancellor of the German Reich, 1862–1890 prime minister of Prussia, 1871–1890 Reich chancellor.

Blair, Tony geb. 1953, brit. Politiker, ab 1975 Mitglied d. Labour Party, ab 1976 Anwalt, ab 1983 ins Unterhaus, 1984–1987 Oppositionssprecher für Finanz- und Wirtschaftspolitik, 1987 stellvertr. Schattenminister für Industrie und Handel, 1988 Schattenminister für Energiepolitik, 1994 Parteivorsitzender, 1997 Premierminister.

Blair, Tony b. 1953, British politician, since 1975 member of Labour Party, since 1976 lawyer, MP since 1983, 1984–1987 opposition finance and economics spokesman, 1987 deputy shadow trade and industry minister, 1988 shadow minister for energy policy, 1994 party chairman, 1997 prime minister.

Blank, Theodor 1905–1972, dt. Politiker, 1949–1972 MdB für d. CDU, 1950 Beauftragter d. Bundesregierung für d. mit d. Vermehrung d. alliierten Truppen zusammenhängenden Fragen, 1955–1956 erster Bundesverteidigungsminister, 1957–1965 Bundesminister für Arbeit und Sozialordnung, 1965–1969 Stellvertr. Vorsitzender d. CDU/ CSU-Fraktion.

Blank, Theodor 1905–1972, German politician, 1949–1972 CDU MdB, 1950 member of government with responsibility for issues connected with the increase of Allied troops, 1955–1956 first federal defense minister, 1957–1965 minister of labor and social order, 1965–1969 deputy chairman of CDU/CSU parliamentary group.

Blankenhorn, Herbert 1904–1991, dt. Diplomat, Mitbegründer d. CDU in d. BBZ, 1948 Generalsekretär in d. BBZ, 1948/49 Adenauers persönlicher Referent, 1949 Ministerialdirektor im Bundeskanzleramt, 1950 Leiter d. Dienststelle für Auswärtige Angelegenheiten, dann im Auswärtigen Amt, 1955–1959 ständiger Vertreter bei d. NATO, 1958–1963 Botschafter in Paris, 1963–1965 Botschafter in Rom, 1965–1970 Botschafter in London, bis 1976 Vizepräsident d. Exekutivrates d. UNESCO.

Blankenhorn, Herbert 1904–1991, German diplomat, co-founder of CDU in British zone of occupation, 1948 secretary general in British zone of occupation, 1948/49 Adenauer's personal adviser, 1949 ministerial director at chancellery, 1950 head of department of foreign affairs, then at foreign office, 1955–1959 permanent representative at NATO, 1958–1963 ambassador in Paris, 1963–1965 ambassador in Rome, 1965–1970 ambassador in London, until 1976 vice president of UNESCO executive council.

Bloch, Ernst, Prof., Dr. phil. (1908) 1885–1977, freier Schriftsteller, 1938–1948 in d. USA, ab 1949–1957 Lehrstuhl für Philosophie in Leipzig, ab 1959 erschienen seine Bücher in d. BRD, 1961 in d. BRD übergesiedelt und bis 1977 Professor in Tübingen.

Bloch, Ernst, professor, Dr. phil. (1908) 1885–1977, freelance writer, 1938–1948 in US, from 1949–1957 professor of philosophy in Leipzig, from 1959 his books appeared in FRG, 1961 moved to FRG, professor in Tübingen until 1977.

Blücher, Franz 1896–1959, Bankdirektor, 1946–1947 Finanzminister von Nordrhein-Westfalen, 1948 Mitglied d. Frankfurter Wirtschaftsrats, ab 1949 MdB für d. FDP, 1949–1954 Erster Vorsitzender d. FDP, 1949–1957 Vizekanzler und Bundesminister für wirtschaftl. Zusammenarbeit.

Blücher, Franz 1896–1959, bank director, 1946–1947 finance minister of North Rhine-Westphalia, 1948 member of Frankfurt economic council, from 1949 FDP MdB, 1949–1954 first FDP party chairman, 1949–1957 deputy chancellor and minister for economic cooperation.

Blüm, Norbert, Dr. phil. (1967) geb. 1935, dt. Politiker, 1949–1957 Werkzeugmacher, 1949 Mitglied d. IG Metall, seit 1950 CDU-Mitglied, 1968–1975 Hauptgeschäftsführer d. Sozialausschüsse d. Christl.-Demokr. Arbeitnehmerschaft (CDA), 1974–1977 Landesvorsitzender d. Sozialausschüsse d. CDA Rheinland-Pfalz, 1972– 1981 und ab 1983 MdB, 1977–1987 Bundesvorsitzender d. Sozialausschüsse, 1980/81 mit stellvertr. Vorsitzender d. CDU/CSU-Bundestagsfraktion, 1972–1981 und seit 1983 MdB, Juni 1981– Oktober 1982 MdA von Berlin, Senator für Bundesangelegenheiten sowie Bevollmächtigter d. Landes Berlin beim Bund, 1982–1998 Bundesminister für Arbeit und Sozialordnung, ab 1987 CDU-Landesvorsitzender von Nordrhein-Westfalen.

Blüm, Norbert, Dr. phil. (1967) b. 1935, German politician, 1949–1957 toolmaker, 1949 member of IG Metal, since 1950 member of CDU, 1968–1975 manager-in-chief of social committees of association of christian democratic employees (CDA), 1974–1977 *Land* chairman of CDA social committees in Rhineland-Palatinate, 1972–1981 and from 1983 MdB, 1977–1987 federal chairman of social committees, 1980/81 deputy chairman of CDU/CSU federal parliamentary group, June 1981–October 1982 MdA Berlin, senator for federal issues and federal representative of the *Land* Berlin, 1982–1998 minister of labor and social order, from 1987 CDU party chairman in North Rhine-Westphalia.

Bohl, Friedrich geb. 1945, Rechtsanwalt, Notar und CDU-Politiker, CDU-Mitglied seit 1963, 1970–1980 MdL in Hessen, seit 1980 MdB, 1984–1991 parlam. Geschäftsführer d. CDU/CSU-Fraktion, 1991–1998 Bundesminister für besondere Aufgaben und Chef d. Bundeskanzleramtes.

Bohl, Friedrich b. 1945, lawyer, notary and CDU politician, member of CDU since 1963, 1970–1980 MdL Hessen, from 1980 MdB, 1984–1991 parliamentary manager of CDU/CSU group, 1991–1998 minister without portfolio and head of chancellery.

Böll, Heinrich 1917–1985, dt. Schriftsteller, 1970–1972 Präsident d. PEN-Zentrums in d. BRD, 1971–1974 Präsident d. internat. PEN-Clubs, 1972 Literatur-Nobelpreisträger.

Böll, Heinrich 1917–1985, German writer, 1970–1972 president of FRG branch of PEN, 1971–1974 president of international PEN Club, 1972 awarded Nobel Prize for literature.

Bölling, Klaus geb. 1928, Journalist, SPD (ab 1957), Redakteur d. Zeitschrift »Der Tagesspiegel«, RIAS, SFB, ARD-Korrespondent in Belgrad, WDR, 1966 Chefredakteur und Moderator d. ARD-Sendung »Weltspiegel«, 1969– 1973 Leiter d. ARD-Studios Washington und Chefkorrespondent in d. USA, 1973/74 Intendant von Radio Bremen, 1974–1980 und 1982 Leiter d. Presse- und Informationsamtes d. Bundesregierung (Staatssekretär), ab 1981/82 Ständiger Vertreter d. BRD in d. DDR.

Bölling, Klaus b. 1928, journalist, SPD (since 1957), editor of *Der Tagesspiegel*, RIAS, SFB and ARD correspondent in Belgrade, WDR, 1966 editor-in-chief and presenter of ARD program "Weltspiegel", 1969–1973 head of ARD Washington studio and chief US correspondent, 1973/74 general manager of Radio Bremen, 1974–1980 and 1982 head of government press and information office (state secretary), from 1981/82 permanent FRG representative in GDR.

Börner, Holger geb. 1931, Betonfacharbeiter, 1957–1976 MdB für d. SPD, 1961–1964 Bundesvorsitzender d. Jungsozialisten, 1967–1972 Staatssekretär im Bundesverkehrsministerium, 1972–1976 Bundesgeschäftsführer d. SPD, 1976–1987 (Rücktritt) Ministerpräsident von Hessen und Bundesratsmitglied, 1977–1987 (Rücktritt) SPD-Landesvorsitzender von Hessen, 1978–1987 MdL, seit 1987 Vorsitzender d. Friedrich-Ebert-Stiftung.

Börner, Holger b. 1931, skilled concrete worker, 1957–1976 SPD MdB, 1961–1964 JUSO federal chairman, 1967–1972 state secretary at ministry of transport, 1972–1976 SPD federal party manager, 1976–1987 (resigned) minister president of Hessen and member of Bundesrat, 1977–1987 (resigned) SPD *Land* chairman in Hessen, 1978–1987 MdL, since 1987 chairman of Friedrich Ebert foundation.

Brandt, Rut geb. Hansen, geb. 1920, norwegische Journalistin, ab 1948 Ehefrau von Willy Brandt, drei Kinder.

Brandt, Rut née Hansen, b. 1920, Norwegian journalist, from 1948 wife of Willy Brandt, three children.

Brandt, Willy (früher Herbert Ernst Karl Frahm) 1913–1992, ab 1930 SPD-Mitglied, zwischen 1933 und 1945 als Journalist in Norwegen und Schweden tätig, 1945–1947 Berichterstatter skandinavischer Zeitungen in Berlin, ab 1948 Vertreter d. SPD-Parteivorstands in Berlin, ab 1951 MdA von Berlin, dort 1955–1957 Präsident, 1949–1957 und ab 1969 MdB, 1957–1966 Regierender Bürgermeister von Berlin, 1961, 1965 und 1969 SPD-Kanzlerkandidat, 1962–1964 stellvertr. und 1964–1987 Vorsitzender d. SPD, 1966–1969 Außenminister und Vizekanzler, Oktober 1969– Mai 1974 Bundeskanzler (Rücktritt), 1976–1992 Präsident d. Sozialist. Internat., ab 1977 Vorsitzender d. unabhängigen internat. Nord-Süd-Kommission, 1979–1983 Abgeord. d. Europäischen Parlaments.

Brandt, Willy [formerly Herbert Ernst Karl Frahm] 1913–1992, since 1930 member of SPD, between 1933 and 1945 worked as journalist in Norway and Sweden, 1945–1947 reporter for Scandinavian newspapers in Berlin, from 1948 representaive of SPD party executive in Berlin, from 1951 MdA Berlin, 1955–1957 president there, 1949–1957 and from 1969 MdB, 1957–1966 mayor of (West) Berlin, 1961, 1965 and 1969 SPD chancellor candidate, 1962–1964 SPD deputy chairman and 1964–1987 chairman, 1966–1969 foreign minister und deputy chancellor, October 1969 – May 1974 federal chancellor (resigned), 1976–1992 president of socialist international, from 1977 chairman of independent international north-south commission, 1979–1983 MEP.

Brauer, Max 1887–1973, Facharbeiter, 1919 Bürgermeister und 1924 Oberbürgermeister von Altona, 1946–1953 und 1957–1961 Erster Bürgermeister von Hamburg, 1961– 1965 MdB für d. SPD.

Brauer, Max 1887–1973, skilled worker, 1919 mayor and 1924 mayor-in-chief of Altona, 1946–1953 and 1957–1961 first mayor of Hamburg, 1961–1965 SPD MdB.

Brecht, Bertolt 1898–1956, Schriftsteller und Bühnenautor, 1914/15 erste Veröffentlichung, Studium d. Literatur, Philosophie und Medizin bis 1923, dann Dramaturg bis 1926, 1928 erster großer Erfolg mit d. »Dreigroschenoper«, ab 1941 Exil in d. USA, 1949 Gründung d. Berliner Ensembles in Berlin.

Brecht, Bertolt 1898–1956, author and writer for the stage, 1914/15 first publication, studied literature, philosophy and medicine until 1923, then *Dramaturg* (artistic theatre manager) until 1926, 1928 first great success with the *Threepenny Opera*, from 1941 exile in US, 1949 founded Berlin Ensemble in Berlin.

Brentano, Heinrich von, Dr. 1904–1964, Rechtsanwalt und Notar, Mitbegründer d. CDU in Hessen, 1946–1949 MdL von Hessen, 1948/49 Mitglied im Parlam. Rat, 1949–1964 MdB, 1949–1955 und 1961–1964 Fraktionsvorsitzender d. CDU/CSU, 1955–1961 Bundesaußenminister.

Brentano, Heinrich von, Dr. 1904–1964, lawyer and notary, co-founder of the CDU in Hessen, 1946–1949 MdL Hessen, 1948/49 MdPR, 1949–1964 MdB, 1949–1955 and 1961–1964 CDU/CSU chief whip, 1955–1961 foreign minister.

Breschnew, Leonid Iljitsch 1906–1982, Ingenieur, seit 1931 Mitglied und ab 1937 hauptamtlicher Funktionär in d. KPdSU, 1938 Gebietssekretär, 1943 Aufstieg zum Generalmajor, 1950 Erster Sekretär d. ZK d. KP in Bessarabien, 1954 Stellvertreter, dann Parteichef von Kasachstan, 1952 Mitglied d. ZK d. KPdSU und 1952 sowie 1956–1960 dessen Sekretär, ab 1957 Vollmitglied im PB, 1960–1964 und ab 1977 Vorsitzender d. Präsidiums d. Obersten Sowjet, somit Staatsoberhaupt, 1964–1982 Generalsekretär d. KPdSU.

Brezhnev, Leonid Ilyich 1906–1982, engineer, from 1931 member and from 1937 full-time CPSU official, 1938 regional secretary, 1943 rose to rank of major general, 1950 first secretary of CP central committee in Bessarabia, 1954 deputy party leader, then party leader in Kazakhstan, 1952 member of CPSU central committee and its secretary 1952 and 1956–1960, from 1957 full member of PB, 1960–1964 and from 1977 chairman of the presidium of the supreme soviet and thereby head of state, 1964–1982 CPSU general secretary.

Breuel, Birgit geb. 1937, dt. Politikerin, 1966 CDU-Eintritt, 1970 in d. Hamburger Bürgerschaft, Mitglied d. CDU-Fraktionsvorstandes und d. geschäftsführenden Landesvorstandes, 1976 Wirtschaftssprecherin d. Hamburger CDU-Bürgerschaftsfraktion, 1978 Wirtschafts- und 1986–1990 Finanzministerin in Niedersachsen, sodann Vorstands- mitglied d. Treuhandanstalt (THA) in Ostberlin, April 1991 – Dezember 1994 Präsidentin d. THA, 1995 Expo-Generalkommissarin.

Breuel, Birgit b. 1937, German politician, 1966 joined CDU, 1970 in Hamburg city parliament, member of executive committee of CDU parliamentary group and of *Land* management committee, 1976 economic spokesperson for Hamburg CDU city parliament group, 1978 economics minister and 1986–1990 finance minister in Lower Saxony, then member of the executive committee of the *Treuhandanstalt* (THA) in East Berlin, April 1991 – December 1994 president of THA, 1995 Expo general commissioner.

Buback, Siegfried, Dr. jur. 1920–1977, (ermordet) dt. Jurist, 1953 Staatsanwalt, 1959 zum Ersten Staatsanwalt befördert und zur Bundesanwaltschaft beim Bundesgerichtshof abgeordnet, schließlich dort 1963 Oberstaatsanwalt und 1971 Bundesanwalt, ab 1974 Generalbundesanwalt.

Buback, Siegfried, Dr. jur. 1920–1977, (murdered) German lawyer, 1953 prosecuting attorney, 1959 promoted to senior prosecuting attorney and seconded as federal attorney to the German federal supreme court, finally in 1963 principal prosecuting attorney and 1971 federal attorney, from 1974 general federal attorney, assassinated.

Bucher, Ewald, Dr. jur. (1941) 1914–1991, Jurist und Politiker, Mitglied d. HJ und d. NSDAP, 1953–1969 MdB für d. FDP, 1956–1961 Geschäftsführer d. FDP-Bundestagsfraktion, 1961–1962 Stellvertr. Vorsitzender d. FDP-Bundestagsfraktion, 1962–1964 Bundesjustizminister (Rücktritt), 1964 Bundespräsidentenkandidat d. FDP, 1965–1966 Bundesminister für Wohnungswesen, Städtebau und Raumordnung (Rücktritt), sodann Wechsel in d. Privatwirtschaft, 1967–1991 Mitglied im Verbandsrat d. Dt. Verbandes für Wohnungswesen, Städtebau und Raumordnung, 1983 CDU-Eintritt.

Bucher, Ewald, Dr. jur. (1941) 1914–1991, lawyer and politician, member of Hitler Youth and NSDAP, 1953–1969 FDP MdB, 1956–1961 FDP federal parliamentary group manager, 1961–1962 deputy chairman of FDP parliamentary group, 1962–1964 minister of justice (resigned), 1964 FDP candidate for federal presidency, 1965–1966 minister of housing, urban construction and planning (resigned), then went into private sector, 1967–1991 member of council of association for German housing, urban construction and planning, 1983 joined CDU.

Bulganin, Nikolaj Alexandrowitsch 1895–1975, 1917 in d. »Sozialdemokr. Arbeiterpartei Rußlands«, dann in d. KPR, 1917–1922 Mitglied in d. Polit. Polizei (Tscheka), 1931–1937 Vorsitzender d. Moskauer Stadtsowjets, 1937 Mitglied d. ZK d. KPdSU, 1938–1941 stellvertr. Vorsitzender d. Rats d. Volkskommissare und Leiter d. Staatsbank, 1944 im Staatskomitee für Verteidigung, 1947 Marschall, ab 1948 Mitglied d. PBs, 1947–1949 und 1952–1955 Verteidigungsminister, 1955–1958 Ministerpräsident (Vorsitzende d. Ministerrates), 1958 amtsenthoben und aus dem PB, 1961 auch aus dem ZK, dann ganz aus d. KPdSU ausgeschlossen.

Bulganin, Nikolay Alexandrovich 1895–1975, 1917 in Russian social democratic workers' party, then in Russian CP, 1917–1922 member of political police (Cheka), 1931–1937 chairman of Moscow city soviet, 1937 member of CPSU central committee, 1938–1941 deputy chairman of council of people's commissars and head of state bank, 1944 on state defense committee, 1947 marshal, from 1948 member of PB, 1947–1949 and 1952–1955 minister of defense, 1955–1958 prime minister (chairman of council of ministers), 1958 removed and expelled from PB, 1961 also expelled from central committee, then expelled entirely from CPSU.

Bulmahn, Edelgard geb. 1951, SPD-Politikerin, ab 1980 Studienrätin, 1969 SPD-Eintritt, seit 1987 MdB für d. SPD und Mitglied im Bundestagsausschuß für Bildung, Wissenschaft, Forschung, Technologie, 1991 Mitglied d. SPD-Fraktionsvorstandes, 1993 in d. Parteivorstand gewählt, 1998 Bundesministerin für Bildung, Wissenschaft, Forschung und Technologie.

Bulmahn, Edelgard b. 1951, SPD politician, from 1980 teacher, 1969 joined SPD, since 1987 SPD MdB and member of parliamentary committee for education, science, research and technology, 1991 member of SPD parliamentary group executive, 1993 elected to party executive, 1998 minister of education, science, research and technology.

Burt, Richard geb. 1947, amerik. Journalist, Politiker, Diplomat, 1973–1975 Mitarbeiter d. Internat. Institute for Strategic Studies in London, ab 1975 dessen stellvertr. Direktor, 1977–1980 Korrespondent für nationale Sicherheitsfragen d. Washingtoner »New York Times«, 1981 Leiter d. Büros für politisch-militärische Angelegenheiten im State Departement, 1983 Unterstaatssekretär f. europ. Angelegenheiten, dabei Vorsitzender d. Beratungsgruppe d. NATO, 1985–1989 Botschafter in Bonn, 1991 Ausscheiden aus dem Staatsdienst.

Burt, Richard b. 1947, American journalist, politician, diplomat, 1973–1975 worked at International Institute for Strategic Studies in London, from 1975 its deputy director, 1977–1980 Washington New York Times correspondent for national security issues, 1981 head of office for military policy issues at the State Department, 1983 under-secretary of state for European affairs and chairman of NATO advisory group, 1985–1989 ambassador in Bonn, 1991 left public service.

Bush, George geb. 1924, ab 1966 Republikanischer Abgeord. im US-Repräsentantenhaus, 1970–1972 UNO-Delegierter, 1974 Leiter d. US-Verbindungsbüros in Peking, 1975/76 d. Geheimdienstes CIA, ab 1979 Bewerber um d. Republikanische Präsidentschaftskandidatur, ab 1980 Vizepräsident, 1988–1992 US-Präsident.

Bush, George b. 1924, from 1966 Republican member of US House of Representatives, 1970–1972 UN delegate, 1974 head of US liaison office in Beijing, 1975/76 head of CIA, from 1979 contender for Republican presidential candidacy, from 1980 vice president, 1988–1992 US President.

Byrnes, James Francis 1879–1972, amerik. Jurist und Politiker (Demokrat), 1911–1925 Mitglied d. Repräsentantenhauses, 1931–1941 Senator, 1941 Mitglied d. Obersten Bundesgerichts, 1942 Leiter d. Behörde für Nationale Wirtschaftsstabilisierung, 1943–1945 Leiter d. Rüstungsamtes, Mitglied d. US-Delegation auf d. Konferenz von Jalta, Juni 1945–Januar 1947 US-Außenminister, Teilnahme an d. Potsdamer Konferenz und Leiter d. US-Delegation bei d. alliierten Außenministertreffen, 1951– 1955 Gouverneur von South-Carolina.

Byrnes, James Francis 1879–1972, American lawyer and politician (Democrat), 1911–1925 member of House of Representatives, 1931–1941 senator, 1941 member of supreme court, 1942 head of national economic stabilization authority, 1943–1945 head of armaments office, member of US delegation at Yalta Conference, June 1945–January 1947 US secretary of state, took part in Potsdam Conference and led US delegation at meetings of Allied foreign ministers, 1951–1955 governor of South Carolina.

C

Caetano, Marcelo José das Neves Alves 1906–1980, 1968–1974 Ministerpräsident von Portugal, durch einen Militärputsch gestürzt, anschließend Exil in Rio de Janeiro, Brasilien.

Caetano, Marcelo José Das Neves Alves 1906–1980, 1968–1974 prime minister of Portugal, ousted by a military coup, subsequent exile in Rio de Janeiro, Brazil.

Calfa, Marián geb. 1946, tschechoslowakischer Politiker, 1972–1988 in d. Rechtsabteilung d. Amtes d. Regierungschefs, dann Minister ohne Geschäftsbereich, 1989–1992 Ministerpräsident d. CSSR bzw. CSFR, schied danach aus d. aktiven Politik aus und wählte d. tschechische Staatsbürgerschaft.

Calfa, Marián b. 1946, Czechoslovak politician, 1972–1988 in legal department of head of government's office, then minister without portfolio, 1989–1992 prime minister of CSSR and CSFR, then withdrew from active political life and chose Czech citizenship.

Carstens, Karl, Prof. Dr. jur. (1937) 1914–1992, dt. Rechtswissenschaftler und Politiker, 1945–1946 Rechtsanwalt und Landesanwalt beim Bremer Senat, ab 1950– 1973 Lehrtätigkeit, ab 1970 Direktor d. Instituts für d. Recht d. Europäischen Gemeinschaften, außerdem 1954/55 ständiger Vertreter d. BRD im Europarat, ab 1961 Stellvertreter d. Außenministers, 1967/68 Staatssekretär im Verteidigungsministerium, 1968/69 Staatssekretär d. Bundesregierung und Chef d. Bundeskanzleramtes, ab 1972 MdB für d. CDU, 1973–1976 Vorsitzender d. CDU/CSU-Bundestagsfraktion und Mitglied im CDU-Präsidium, 1976–1979 Bundestagspräsident, 1979–1984 Bundespräsident.

Carstens, Karl, professor, Dr. jur. (1937) 1914–1992, German legal expert and politician, 1945–1946 lawyer and regional attorney in the Bremen senate, from 1950–1973 worked in education, from 1970 director of institute for European Community law, in addition 1954/55 FRG permanent representative at Council of Europe, from 1961 deputy foreign minister, 1967/68 state secretary at ministry of defense, 1968/69 state secretary with federal government and head of chancellery, from 1972 CDU MdB, 1973–1976 CDU/CSU chief whip and member of CDU presidium, 1976–1979 president of the Bundestag, 1979–1984 federal president.

Carstens, Veronica, Dr. med. (1960) geb. Prior, 1923, Ärztin, ab 1944 Ehefrau von Karl Carstens, ab 1979 Schirmherrin d. Dt. Multiple Sklerose Gesellschaft, Vorstandsmitglied d. Stiftung zur Förderung d. Erfahrungsheilkunde.

Carstens, Veronica, Dr. med. (1960) née Prior, 1923, doctor, from 1944 wife of Karl Carstens, from 1979 patroness of German multiple sclerosis association, member of executive of foundation for the promotion of empirical medicine.

Carter, James Earl [Jimmy] geb. 1924, Nuklearingenieur und Kommandant eines Atom-U-Bootes, US-Demokrat, 1962 Senator und 1970–1974 Gouverneur von Georgia, 1976–1980 US-Präsident, 1979 Erfolge: Camp David Verhandlungen, sowie SALT II-Abkommen mit d. UdSSR.

Carter, James Earl [Jimmy] b. 1924, nuclear engineer and commander of American nuclear submarine, US Democrat, 1962 senator and 1970–1974 governer of Georgia, 1976–1980 US President, 1979 achievements: Camp David negotiations and SALT II agreement with USSR.

Charles Philip Arthur George, Prince of Wales (seit 1958) geb. 1948, Sohn v. Königin Elizabeth II. u. Prinz Philip, Herzog v. Edinburgh, seit 1952 Herzog v. Cornwall, seit 1970 Mitgl. im House of Lords, 1981–1996 mit Lady Diana Spencer verheiratet.

Charles Philip Arthur George, Prince of Wales (since 1958) b. 1948, son of Queen Elizabeth II. and Prince Philip, Duke of Edinburgh, since 1952 Duke of Cornwall, since 1970 member of House of Lords, 1981–1996 married to Lady Diana Spencer.

Chirac, Jacques René geb. 1932, frz. Politiker, 1967/68 in d. Nationalversammlung und zum Staatssekretär für soziale Angelegenheiten ernannt, 1968–1971 Staatssekretär im Wirtschafts- und Finanzministerium, 1971 Minister für Beziehungen zum Parlament, 1972 Landwirtschaftsminister, 1974–1976 Premierminister, 1976–1995 Abgeord. und Vorsitzender d. gaullistischen Partei (UDR bzw. RPR), 1977–1995 Bürgermeister von Paris, 1981, 1988 und 1995 Kandidatur bei d. Präsidentschaftswahlen, 1986–1988 (Rücktritt) Regierungschef, ab 1995 Staatspräsident.

Chirac, Jacques René b. 1932, French politician, 1967/68 entered national assembly and appointed state secretary for social issues, 1968–1971 state secretary at ministry of economics and finance, 1971 minister of relations with parliament, 1972 minister of agriculture, 1974–1976 prime minister, 1976–1995 delegate and chairman of Gaullist party (UDR/RPR), 1977–1995 mayor of Paris, 1981, 1988 and 1995 presidential candidate, 1986–1988 (resigned) head of government, since 1995 President.

Chrétien, Jean geb. 1934, kanadischer Jurist und Politiker, seit 1958 Anwalt, 1963–1986 Abgeord. im kanadischen Parlament für d. Liberale Partei, 1965/66 parlam. Sekretär, 1967/68 Minister ohne Geschäftsbereich, 1975–1976 Präsident d. kanadischen Schatzamtes, 1976–1977 Minister für Industrie und Handel, sodann bis 1979 Finanzminister, 1980–1982 Minister für Justiz und Staatsminister für Soziale Entwicklung, 1990 Parteivorsitz d. Liberalen, 1993 und 1997 zum Premierminister gewählt.

Chrétien, Jean b. 1934, Canadian lawyer and politician, from 1958 lawyer, 1963–1986 Liberal party member of Canadian parliament, 1965/66 parliamentary secretary, 1967/68 minister without portfolio, 1975–1976 president of Canadian treasury, 1976–1977 minister of trade and industry, then until 1979 finance minister, 1980–1982 justice minister and minister of state for social development, 1990 chairman of Liberal party.

Christo (eigentlich Christo Javachev) geb. 1935, bulgarisch-amerik. Künstler, 1952–1957 Kunstakademie in Sofia und Wien, ab 1964 in New York, Kunst d. Enthüllens durch Verhüllen in d. verschiedensten Ländern d. Welt, Juni 1995 Verhüllung d. Reichstages in Berlin in Polypropylengewebe, seit 1959 verheiratet mit Jeanne-Claude de Guillebon.

Christo (full name Christo Javachev) b. 1935, Bulgarian-American artist, 1952–1957 academy of art in Sofia and Vienna, from 1964 in New York, art of revelation by concealment in the most diverse countries throughout the world, June 1995 wrapped the Reichstag building in Berlin in polypropylene tissue, since 1959 married to Jeanne-Claude de Guillebon.

Chruschtschow, Nikita Sergejewitsch 1894–1971, 1939–1964 Mitglied d. PBs bzw. Präsidiums d. ZK d. KPdSU, 1953–1964 Erster Sekretär d. ZK d. KPdSU, 1958–1964 sowjetischer Ministerpräsident, am 14./ 15.10.1964 aller Ämter enthoben.

Khrushchev, Nikita Sergeyevich 1894–1971, 1939–1964 member of PB and presidium of CPSU central committee, 1953–1964 first secretary of CPSU central committee, 1958–1964 Soviet prime minister, removed from all offices on 14./15.10.1964.

Churchill, Sir (1953) Winston Leonard Spencer 1874–1965, 1896–1900 als Kavallerieleutnant und Kriegsberichterstatter in Kuba, dann in Indien, im Sudan und im Burenkrieg, ab 1900 konservatives Parlamentsmitglied, 1904 zu d. Liberalen, 1906 Unterstaatssekretär für d. Kolonien, 1908 Handels- und 1910 Innenminister, 1911 Erster Lord d. Admiralität, 1915/16 Teilnahme am 1. Weltkrieg als Offizier, 1917–1919 Munitionsminister, 1919–1921 Heeres- und Luftwaffenminister, 1924–1929 Schatzkanzler für d. Konservativen, 1939 erneut Erster Lord d. Admiralität, 1940 Verteidigungsminister, 1940–1945 und 1951– 1955 brit. Premierminister, danach weiter Unterhausabgeordneter.

Churchill, Sir (1953) Winston Leonard Spencer 1874–1965, 1896–1900 cavalry lieutenant and war reporter in Cuba, then in India, in Sudan and in the Boer War, from 1900 Conservative MP, 1904 went over to Liberals, 1906 under-secretary of state for the colonies, 1908 president of the board of trade and 1910 home secretary, 1911 first lord of the admiralty, 1915/16 served as officer in first world war, 1917–1919 munitions minister, 1919–1921 army and air force minister, 1924–1929 chancellor of the exchequer for the Conservatives, 1939 again first lord of the admiralty, 1940 minister of defense, 1940–1945 and 1951–1955 British prime minister, then remained an MP.

Clay, General Lucius Dubignon 1897–1978, ab 1945 stellvertr. und 1947–1949 Militärgouverneur in d. ABZ, Organisator d. Luftbrücke, 1949 aus dem Militärdienst ausgeschieden und in Führungsposten in US-Unternehmen, 1960/61 Sonderbeauftragter in Berlin.

Clay, General Lucius Dubignon 1897–1978, from 1945 deputy military governor and 1947–1949 military governer in American zone of occupation, oganized airlift, 1949 left military service and held leading posts in US companies, 1960/61 special envoy in Berlin.

Clinton, Bill geb. 1946, amerik. Jurist und Politiker (Demokrat), 1976 Justizminister in Arkansas, 1978–1980 und 1983–1992 dort Gouverneur, 1992 und 1996 zum US-Präsidenten gewählt, Erfolge:

GATT und NAFTA - Verträge; 1998/99 Amtsenthebungsverfahren gegen ihn.

Clinton, Bill b. 1946, American lawyer and politician (Democrat), 1976 minister of justice in Arkansas, 1978–1980 and 1983–1992 governor there, 1992 and 1996 elected US President, achievements: GATT und NAFTA treaties; 1998/99 subject of impeachment proceedings.

Conant, James Bryant, Dr. phil. (1916), Dr. h.c. 1893–1978, amerik. Professor für Chemie, 1933–1953 Präsident d. Harvard-Universität, 1946 Leiter d. beratenden Ausschusses für Atomenergie, 1953-1955 amerik. Hoher Kommissar in Bonn, 1955–1957 US-Botschafter in Bonn.

Conant, James Bryant, Dr. phil. (1916), Dr. h.c. 1893–1978, American professor of chemistry, 1933–1953 president of Harvard university, 1946 head of atomic energy advisory committee, 1953-1955 American high commissioner in Bonn, 1955–1957 US ambassador in Bonn.

Cossiga, Francesco, Dr. jur. geb. 1928, ital. Rechtswissenschaftler und Politiker, 1953 Professor, 1956 Provinzsekretär in d. Christl.-Demokr. Partei Italiens, 1966 Staatssekretär für Verteidigung, 1974 Minister für Verwaltungsreform, 1976–1978 Innenminister (Rücktritt) 1979/80 Ministerpräsident (Rücktritt), ab Juli 1983 Senatspräsident, 1985–1992 Staatspräsident, 1998 Gründer d. Partei »Demokratische Union der Republik« (UDR).

Cossiga, Francesco, Dr. jur. b. 1928, Italian legal expert and politician, 1953 professor, 1956 provincial secretary in Italian christian democratic party, 1966 state secretary of defense, 1974 minister for administrative reform, 1976–1978 minister of the interior (resigned), 1979/80 prime minister (resigned), from July 1983 president of senate, 1985–1992 President, 1998 founder of the party "Democratic Union of the Republic" (UDR).

Couve de Murville, Maurice, Dr. jur. geb. 1907, frz. Politiker u. Diplomat, 1940–1943 Leiter d. Abt. Auslandsfinanzen d. Finanzministeriums, 1945 Generaldirektor d. Polit. Abt. d. Außenministeriums, zugleich bis 1950 stellv. Minister im Alliierten Kontrollrat, 1950–1954 Botschafter in Ägypten, 1955/56 in Washington, sodann in Bonn, 1958–1968 Außenminister, 1968/69 Premierminister (Rücktritt), 1973– 1986 Mitgl. d. Nationalversammlung, 1986–1995 Senator.

Couve de Murville, Maurice, Dr. jur. b. 1907, French politician and diplomat, 1940–1943 head of foreign finance department at ministry of finance, 1945 director general of foreign ministry political department, at the same time until 1950 deputy minister in the Allied control council, 1950–1954 ambassador to Egypt, 1955/56 in Washington, then in Bonn, 1958–1968 foreign minister, 1968/69 prime minister (resigned), 1973–1986 member of the national assembly, 1986–1995 senator.

Cyrankiewicz, Josef 1911–1989, polnischer Politiker, ab 1935 Funktionär d. »Polnischen Sozialistischen Partei«, 1941–1945 im KZ, 1948–1971 Mitglied d. PBs d. Vereinigten Polnischen Arbeiterpartei, 1947–1952 und 1954–1971 poln. Ministerpräsident, 1970– 1972 Staatspräsident, 1973 Vorsitzender d. »Gesamtpolnischen Friedenskomitees«.

Cyrankiewicz, Josef 1911–1989, Polish politician, from 1935 Polish Socialist Party official, 1941–1945 in KZ, 1948–1971 member of PB of the United Polish Workers' Party, 1947–1952 and 1954–1971 Polish prime minister, 1970–1972 President, 1973 chairman of all-Polish peace committee.

D

Dahlgrün, Rolf, Dr. jur. (1937) 1908–1969, ab 1949 FDP-Mitglied, 1953–1957 Mitglied d. Hamburger Bürgerschaft, 1957–1969 MdB, 1961–1963 Vorsitzender d. Wirtschaftsausschusses, 1962–1966 Bundesfinanzminister (Rücktritt).

Dahlgrün, Rolf, Dr. jur. (1937) 1908–1969, from 1949 member of FDP, 1953–1957 member of Hamburg city parliament, 1957–1969 MdB, 1961–1963 chairman of economic committee, 1962–1966 minister of finance (resigned).

Daley, Richard Joseph 1902–1976, amerik. Politiker (Demokrat), 1936–1938 Landesabgeord. von Illinois, 1938–1946 Senator von Illinois, dabei 1941–1946 Minderheitsführer, 1949 state director, Revenue, ab 1953 Vorsitzender d. Demokr. Partei im Verwaltungsbezirk Cook, 1955–1976 Bürgermeister von Chicago, 1968 Delegierter auf d. »Democratic National Convention«.

Daley, Richard Joseph 1902–1976, American politician (Democrat), 1936–1938 regional delegate from Illinois, 1938–1946 senator from Illinois, also 1941–1946 minority leader, 1949 state revenue director, from 1953 chairman of Democratic Party in Cook administrative region, 1955–1976 mayor of Chicago, 1968 delegate at Democratic national convention.

Däubler-Gmelin, Herta geb. 1943, Rechtsanwältin, SPD-Politikerin, Mitglied d. SPD seit 1965, seit 1988 stellvertr. Bundesvorsitzende, seit 1972 MdB, 1980–1983 Vorsitzende d. Rechtsausschusses, 1983–1993 stellvertr. Vorsitzende d. SPD-Fraktion, seit 1998 Bundesministerin d. Justiz.

Däubler-Gemlin, Herta b. 1943, lawyer, SPD politician, SPD member since 1965, since 1988 deputy federal chairman, since 1972 MdB, 1980–1983 chairman of legal committee, 1983–1993 SPD deputy whip group, since 1998 minister of justice.

Degenhardt, Johannes Joachim, Dr. theol. (1964) geb. 1926, Erzbischof von Paderborn seit 1974, 1951 Priesterweihe, seit 1968 Weihbischof und Titularbischof von Vico di Pacato, 1973 Kapitularvikar d. Erzbistums.

Degenhardt, Johannes Joachim, Dr. theol. (1964) b. 1926, archbishop of Paderborn since 1974, 1951 ordained as priest, from 1968 suffragan bishop und titular bishop of Vico di Pacato, 1973 capitulary vicar of archbishopric.

Dehler, Thomas, Dr. jur. 1897–1967, FDP-Politiker, 1924 Mitbegründer d. »Reichsbanners Schwarz-Rot-Gold«, 1926–1933 Vorsitzender d. DDP Bamberg, 1944 Zwangsarbeiter, 1945 Landrat, 1946 Generalstaatsanwalt und Generalankläger zur Entnazifizierung in Bayern, 1947–1949 Oberlandesgerichtspräsident, gleichzeitig 1946–1949 Chef d. bayerischen FDP und Mitglied d. Parlam. Rates, 1946–1956 FDP-Landesvorsitzender in Bayern, 1949– 1967 MdB, 1949–1953 Bundesjustizminister, 1953–1957 FDP-Bundestagsfraktionsvorsitzender, 1954–1957 FDP-Vorsitzender, 1960–1967 Bundestagsvizepräsident.

Dehler, Thomas, Dr. jur. 1897–1967, FDP politician, 1924 co-founder of *Reichsbanner Schwarz-Rot-Gold*, 1926–1933 chairman of DDP Bamberg, 1944 forced labor, 1945 regional councillor, 1946 attorney and public prosecutor for denazification in Bavaria, 1947–1949 president of regional supreme court and at the same time 1946–1949 leader of Bavarian FDP and member of parliamentary council, 1946–1956 Bavarian regional FDP chairman, 1949–1967 MdB, 1949–1953 minister of justice, 1953–1957 FDP chief whip, 1954–1957 FDP party chairman, 1960–1967 vice president of Bundestag.

Delors, Jacques geb. 1925, frz. Wirtschaftspolitiker, 1945–1962 Abteilungsleiter bei d. Bank von Frankreich, 1959–1961 Mitglied d. Planungs- und Investmentabteilung d. Wirtschafts- und Sozialrats, 1969 Berater für soziale und kulturelle Angelegenheiten d. Ministerpräsidenten, ab 1974 Mitglied d. Sozialist. Partei, ab 1979 Präsident d. Wirtschafts- und Währungskommission im Europa-Parlament, ab 1981 Wirtschafts- und Finanz- sowie ab 1983 Budgetminister, 1983 Bürgermeister von Clichy, 1985–1994/95 Präsident d. EG/EU-Kommission.

Delors, Jacques b. 1925, French economist and politician, 1945–1962 head of department at Bank of France, 1959–1961 member of planning and investment department of economic and social council, 1969 adviser to prime minister on social and cultural matters, from 1974 member of Socialist Party, from 1979 president of European Parliament economic and currency commission, from 1981 minister of economics and finance and from 1983 budget minister, 1983 mayor of Clichy, 1985–1994/95 president of EC/EU Commission.

Deng Xiaoping 1904–1997, chinesischer Politiker, 1927–1929 im Sekretariat d. ZK d. KP, 1934/35 Gefolgsmann von Mao Zedong, ab 1945 Mitglied d. ZK d. KPCh, 1950 Chef d. Wirtschafts- und Finanzkommission, 1954 Generalsekretär d. ZK und 4. stellvertr. Ministerpräsident, 1956–1966, 1975/76 und ab 1977 Mitglied d. Ständigen Ausschusses d. PBs, 1973–1975 stellvertr. Ministerpräsident, 1975–1976 und 1977–1980 Erster stellvertr. Regierungschef (Rücktritt), 1981–1989 Vorsitzender d. Militärkommission d. ZK und Vorsitzender d. KPCh.

Deng Xiaoping 1904–1997, Chinese politician, 1927–1929 at CP central committee secretariat, 1934/35 follower of Mao Zedong, from 1945 member of Chinese CP central committee, 1950 head of economic and finance commission, 1954 general secretary of central committee and 4th deputy prime minister, 1956–1966, 1975/76 and from 1977 member of PB permanent committee, 1973–1975 deputy prime minister, 1975–1976 and 1977–1980 first deputy head of government (resigned), 1981–1989 chairman of central committee military commission and chairman of Chinese CP.

Diefenbaker, John George 1895–1979, kanadischer Jurist und Politiker, ab 1940 Abgeord. im Unterhaus Kanadas, 1956–1967 Vorsitzender d. Progressive Conservative Party, 1957–1963 kanadischer Premierminister, durch parlam. Mißtrauensvotum gestürzt.

Diefenbaker, John George 1895–1979, Canadian lawyer and politician, from 1940 member of Canadian parliament, 1956–1967 chairman of Progressive Conservative Party, 1957–1963 Canadian prime minister, brought down by parliamentary vote of no confidence.

Diehl, Günter geb. 1916, Diplom-Volkswirt, 1966–1967 Leiter d. Planungsstabs im Auswärtigen Amt, 1967–1969 Leiter d. Bundespresse- und Informationsamtes, 1968 Staatssekretär, 1970–1977 Botschafter d. BRD in Indien, 1977–1981 Botschafter in Japan.

Diehl, Günter b. 1916, graduate in economics, 1966–1967 head of foreign office planning staff, 1967–1969 head of federal press and information office, 1968 state secretary, 1970–1977 FRG ambassador to India, 1977–1981 ambassador to Japan.

Dienstbier, Jirí, Dr. phil.; Dr. h.c. geb. 1937, tschechoslowak. Journalist und Politiker, 1958 Eintritt in d. KPC, 1958–1969 Journalist, 1969 aus d. Partei und 1970 von allen gehobenen Berufen ausgeschlossen, 1989 Mitbegründer d.Organisation »Bürgerforum«, 1989–1992 tschechoslowak. Außenminister, 1991–1996 Mitbegründer und Vorsitzender d. Organisation »Bürgerliche Bewegung«, 1998 UN-Sonderermittler für Menschenrechte im ehemaligen Jugoslawien

Dienstbier, Jirí, Dr. phil.; Dr. h.c. b. 1937, Czech journalist and politician, 1958 joined Czech CP, 1958–1969 journalist, 1969 expelled from party and 1970 from all higher occupations, 1989 co-founder of "Civic Forum", 1989–1992 Czechoslovak foreign minister, 1991–1996 co-founder and chairman of a "Civic Movement", 1998 UN human rights special investigator in former Yugoslavia.

Diepgen, Eberhard geb. 1941, seit 1972 Rechtsanwalt, seit 1962 CDU-Mitglied, 1965/66 stellvertr. Vorsitzender d. Verbandes Dt. Studentenschaften (VDS), ab 1971 Mitglied d. Berliner CDU-Landesvorstandes und Geschäftsführender Landesvorsitzender, außerdem MdA von Berlin, 1980–1984 und 1989–1991 Berliner CDU-Fraktionsvorsitzender, seit 1983 Landesvorsitzender, 1984– 1989 Regierender Bürgermeister West-Berlins und seit 1991 Gesamtberlins, 1984–1989 und seit 1991 Mitglied d. Bundesrats.

Diepgen, Eberhard b. 1941, from 1972 lawyer, from 1962 member of CDU, 1965/66 deputy chairman of Association of German Student Bodies (VDS), from 1971 member of Berlin CDU *Land* executive and *Land* managing chairman, also MdA Berlin, 1980–1984 and 1989–1991 chief whip of Berlin CDU, from 1983 *Land* chairman, 1984–1989 mayor of West Berlin und from 1991 of all Berlin, 1984–1989 und since 1991 member of Bundesrat.

Dohnanyi, Klaus von, Dr. jur. (1949) geb. 1928, dt. Politiker und Wirtschaftsmanager, 1954–1967 in d. Industrie- und Marktforschung tätig, 1969–1981 MdB für d. SPD, 1968/69 Staatssekretär im Bundeswirtschaftsministerium, dann bis 1972 Staatssekretär im Bundesministerium für Bildung und Wissenschaft und 1972–1974 Bundesminister für Bildung und Wissenschaft, 1976–1981 Staatsminister im Auswärtigen Amt und 1979–1981 SPD-Landesvorsitzender Rheinland-Pfalz, 1981–1988 (Rücktritt) Erster Bürgermeister von Hamburg.

Dohnanyi, Klaus von, Dr. jur. (1949) b. 1928, German politician and economic manager, 1954–1967 worked in industry and market research, 1969–1981 SPD MdB, 1968/69 state secretary at economics ministry, then until 1972 state secretary at ministry of education and science and 1972–1974 minister of education and science, 1976–1981 minister of state at foreign office and 1979–1981 SPD *Land* chairman of Rhineland-Palatinate, 1981–1988 (resigned) mayor of Hamburg.

Dönhoff, Marion Gräfin, Dr. rer. pol. (1935) geb. 1909, Journalistin, ab 1946 Redaktionsmitglied, 1961 stellvertretende Chefredakteurin, 1968–1972 Chefredakteurin, ab 1973 Herausgeberin d. Wochenzeitung »Die Zeit«

Dönhoff, Marion Gräfin, Dr. rer. pol. (1935) b. 1909, journalist, from 1946 member of editorial board of weekly *Die Zeit*, 1961 deputy editor-in-chief, 1968–1972 editor-in-chief, from 1973 publisher.

Dönitz, Karl 1891–1980, dt. Großadmiral, 1912 Leutnant zur See, ab 1935 Befehl über d. Unterseebootwaffe, 1943 Oberbefehlshaber d. Kriegsmarine, Mai 1945 verhaftet, 1946 in Nürnberg zu 10 Jahren Gefängnis verurteilt.

Dönitz, Karl 1891–1980, German great admiral, 1912 naval lieutenant, from 1935 commander of submarine fleet, 1943 commander-in-chief of German navy, May 1945 arrested, 1946 sentenced to 10 years imprisonment at Nuremberg.

Döpfner, Julius, Dr. theol. (1939) 1913–1976, katholischer Theologe, 1948 Bischof von Würzburg, 1957 Bischof von Berlin, 1958 Kardinal, 1961–1976 Erzbischof von München-Freising.

Döpfner, Julius, Dr. theol. (1939) 1913–1976, Catholic theologian, 1948 bishop of Würzburg, 1957 bishop of Berlin, 1958 cardinal, 1961–1976 archbishop of Munich-Freising.

Dorn, Wolfram geb. 1924, dt. Politiker und seit 1985 Schriftsteller, 1954–1961 und wieder 1975–1980 MdL in Nordrhein-Westfalen für d. FDP, 1961–1972 MdB, 1968– 1969 und 1975 stellvertr. Fraktionsvorsitzender, 1969– 1972 Parlam. Staatssekretär im Bundesinnenministerium (Rücktritt).

Dorn, Wolfram b. 1924, German politician and since 1985 writer, 1954–1961 and again 1975–1980 FDP MdL North Rhine-Westphalia, 1961–1972 MdB, 1968–1969 and 1975 deputy whip, 1969–1972 parliamentary state secretary at ministry of interior (resigned).

Drechsel, Sammy 1925–1986, dt. Regisseur und Kabarettist, 1946–1950 als Zeitfunk- und Sensationsreporter beim RIAS, ab 1952 Reporter und Kommentator im Fernsehen, 1956 Mitbegründer d. »Münchner Lach- und Schießgesellschaft«, dort Organisator, Produzent und Regisseur.

Drechsel, Sammy 1925–1986, German theatre director and cabaret artist, 1946–1950 RIAS reporter for current affairs and sensational news items, from 1952 TV reporter and commentator, 1956 co-founder of Munich "Society for Laughter and Mirth", where he was organizer, producer and director.

Drenkmann, Günter von 1910–1974 (ermordet), Richter, 1964–1967 Direktor d. Senatsverwaltung für Justiz von Berlin, 1967–1974 Kammergerichtspräsident in Berlin.

Drenkmann, Günter von 1910–1974 (assassinated), judge, 1964–1967 director of senate justice administration department in Berlin, 1967–1974 president of the Berlin High Court.

Dubcek, Alexander, Dr. 1921–1992, Schlosser, tschechoslowak. Politiker, hilft nach dem Zweiten Weltkrieg beim Aufbau d. KP in d. Slowakei, 1951–1954 und ab 1960 Abgeord. d. Nationalversammlung, 1969–1970 d. Volkskammer, ab 1958 Mitglied d. ZK d. KPC (bis 1970) und d. ZK d. slowakischen KP, 1962–1969 Mitglied d. PBs d. KP d. CSR, 1968/69 Erster Sekretär d. ZK d. Gesamt-KPC, weiterhin Mitglied d. Präsidiums d. Gesamt-KP und Präsident d. Bundesversammlung, 1970 aus d. KP ausgeschlossen, 1989–1992 Präsident d. Bundesparlaments, 1992 Eintritt in d. Sozialdemokr. Partei d. Slowakei.

Dubcek, Alexander, Dr. 1921–1992, mechanic, Czechoslovak politician, after second world war helped to build up the CP in Slovakia, 1951–1954 and from 1960 member of national assembly 1969–1970 of people's chamber, from 1958 member of central committee of Czech CP (until 1970) and central committee of Slovak CP, 1962–1969 member of PB of CP of CSR, 1968/69 first secretary of central committee of CP of all Czechoslovakia, remained member of presidium of all-Czechoslovakia CP and president of federal assembly, 1970 expelled from CP, 1989–1992 president of federal parliament, 1992 joined Social Democratic Party of Slovakia.

Duckwitz, Georg Ferdinand 1904–1973, Diplomat, 1955–1958 dt. Botschafter in Kopenhagen, 1958–1961 Leiter d. Ostabteilung d. Auswärtigen Amtes, 1961–1965 Botschafter in Indien, 1967–1970 Staatssekretär im Auswärtigen Amt.

Duckwitz, Georg Ferdinand 1904–1973, diplomat, 1955–1958 German ambassador in Copenhagen, 1958–1961 head of foreign office eastern department, 1961–1965 ambassador to India, 1967–1970 state secretary at foreign office.

Duisenberg, Wim, Prof. Dr. (1965) geb. 1935, niederländ. Wirtschaftswissenschaftler, Bankmanager und Finanzpolitiker, 1966 beim Internat. Währungsfonds, 1970–1973 Professor für Makroökonomie, 1973–1977 Finanzminister für d. sozialdemokr. Partei d. Arbeit (PvdA), 1981 Direktoriumsmitglied, 1982 Präsident d. Niederländ. Zentralbank, 1997 Präsident d. Europäischen Währungsinstitutes in Frankfurt/M., ab Juli 1998 Präsident d. Europäischen Zentralbank.

Duisenberg, Wim, professor, Dr. (1965) b. 1935, Dutch economist, bank director and financial politician, 1966 at International Monetary Fund, 1970–1973 professor of macroeconomics, 1973–1977 finance minister for social democratic labor party (PvdA), 1981 member of directorate, 1982 president of Netherlands central bank, 1997 president of European Monetary Institute in Frankfurt am Main, since Juli 1998 president of European Central Bank.

Dulles, John Foster 1888–1959, Bankdirektor, Treuhänder und Vorsitzender großer Stiftungen, 1918/1919 Angehöriger d. US-Friedensdelegation in Versailles, 1945 Chefberater d. US-Delegation bei d. Gründung d. UNO, 1946– 1950 Delegierter bei d. Vereinten Nationen, setzte Friedensvertrag zwischen d. USA und Japan 1951 durch, 1953–1959 Außenminister (Rücktritt), verheiratet mit Janet Pomeroy Avery Dulles.

Dulles, John Foster 1888–1959, bank director, fiduciary and chairman of major foundations, 1918/1919 member of US peace delegation in Versailles, 1945 chief adviser to US delegation at founding of UN, 1946–1950 delegate to UN, achieved peace treaty between US and Japan in 1951, 1953–1959 secretary of state (resigned), married to Janet Pomeroy Avery Dulles.

Dumas, Roland geb. 1922, frz. Jurist und Politiker, 1956 frz. Abgeord. d. Mitterrand-Partei »Union démocratique et sociale de la Résistance« (UDSR), 1981–1993 in d. Nationalversammlung gewählt, 1983–1984 Europaminister, 1984 Regierungssprecher, 1984–1986 und 1988–1993 Außenminister.

Dumas, Roland b. 1922, French lawyer and politician, 1956 French delegate of the Mitterrand party "Union démocratique et sociale de la Résistance" (UDSR), 1981–1993 elected to national assembly, 1983–1984 minister for Europe, 1984 government spokesman, 1984–1986 and 1988–1993 foreign minister.

Dutschke, Rudi 1940–1979, 1961 von Ost- nach West-Berlin übergesiedelt, Soziologiestudent an d. FU Berlin, ab 1965 Mitglied d. SDS, Studentenführer und Sprecher d. APO, am 11.4.1968 durch ein Attentat schwer verletzt, 1971 Übersiedlung nach Dänemark.

Dutschke, Rudi 1940–1979, 1961 moved from East to West Berlin, studied sociology at FU Berlin, from 1965 member of SDS, student leader and APO spokesman, on 11.4.1968 seriously injured in an attempt on his life, 1971 moved to in Denmark.

E

Ebert, Friedrich 1894–1979, dt. Buchdrucker u. SED-Politiker, 1913 SPD-Mitgl., 1928–1933 MdR, 1945/46 MdL v. Brandenburg f. d. SPD, ab 1946 SED-Landesvorsitzender, Mitgl. d. ZK, ab 1949 Mitgl. d. PBs d. ZK, 1948–1967 Oberbürgermeister v. Ost-Berlin, 1950–1963 u. ab 1971 stellv. Präsident d. Volkskammer, 1951–1958 Präsident d. Gesellschaft f. »Deutsch-Sowjetische Freundschaft«, 1960–1979 Mitgl. d. DDR-Staatsrates, 1971–1979 Vorsitzender d. SED-Fraktion in d. Volkskammer.

Ebert, Friedrich 1894–1979, German book printer and SED politician, 1913 joined SPD, 1928–1933 member of Reichstag, 1945/46 SPD MdL Brandenburg, from 1946 SED *Land* chairman, member of ZK, from 1949 member of PB of ZK, 1948–1967 mayor of East Berlin, 1950–1963 and from 1971 deputy president of Volkskammer, 1951–1958 president of association for "German-Soviet friendship", 1960–1979 member of GDR council of state, 1971–1979 chairman of SED group in Volkskammer.

Eckardt, Felix von 1903–1979, dt. Politiker, 1952–1955 u. 1956–1962 Leiter d. Presse- u. Informationsamtes d. Bundesregierung, 1955–1956 dt. Botschafter bei d. UN, 1962–1965 Bundesbevollmächtigter f. Berlin, 1965–1972 MdB f. d. CDU.

Eckardt, Felix von 1903–1979, German politician, 1952–1955 and 1956–1962 head of government press and information office, 1955–1956 German ambassador to UN, 1962–1965 federal representative for Berlin, 1965–1972 CDU MdB.

Eden, Sir (1954) Anthony, Earl of Avon (1961) 1897–1977, ab 1923 konservativer Unterhausabgeord. in Großbritannien, 1931–1933 Unterstaatssekretär im Außenministerium, 1934/35 Lordsiegelbewahrer, 1935–1938 Außenminister (Rücktritt), 1940–1945, 1951– 1955 Außenminister Großbritanniens, 1940 Kriegsminister, 1955–1957 Premierminister (Rücktritt), 1961 Mitgl. d. Oberhauses.

Eden, Sir (1954) Anthony, Earl of Avon (1961) 1897–1977, from 1923 Conservative member of British House of Commons, 1931–1933 under-secretary of state at the foreign office, 1934/35 lord keeper of the privy seal, 1935–1938 (resigned), 1940–1945, 1951–1955 British foreign secretary, 1940 minister of war, 1955–1957 prime minister (resigned), 1961 member of House of Lords.

Ehard, Hans, Dr. jur. 1887–1980, dt. Jurist u. Politiker, ab 1919 im bayer. Justizdienst, 1931–1933 Ministerialrat, 1923 Vertreter d. Anklage im Hochverratsprozeß gegen Hitler, ab 1945 Staatssekretär im Bayer. Staatsministerium, MdL 1946–1954 u. 1960–1962 Ministerpräsident v. Bayern, 1949–1955 CSU-Vorsitzender, 1954– 1960 Landtagspräsident, 1950/51 u. 1961/62 Präsident d. Bundesrats, 1962–1966 Justizminister, ab 1969 Ehrenvorsitzender d. CSU.

Ehard, Hans, Dr. jur. 1887–1980, German lawyer and politician, from 1919 in Bavarian judiciary, 1931–1933 ministerial councillor, 1923 prosecuting counsel in trial of Adolf Hitler for high treason, from 1945 state secretary in Bavarian ministry of state, MdL 1946–1954 and 1960–1962 minister president of Bavaria, 1949–1955 CSU party chairman, 1954–1960 president of *Landtag*, 1950/51 and 1961/62 president of Bundesrat, 1962–1966 minister of justice, from 1969 honorary chairman of CSU.

Ehlers, Hermann 1904–1954, dt. Politiker, 1949–1954 MdB f. d. CDU, 1950–1954 Bundestagspräsident, 1952– 1954 Zweiter Vorsitzender d. CDU.

Ehlers, Hermannm 1904–1954, German politician, 1949–1954 CDU MdB, 1950–1954 president of Bundestag, 1952–1954 second chairman of CDU.

Ehmke, Horst, Dr. jur. (1952) geb. 1927, dt. Rechtsanwalt u. Professor, ab 1947 SPD-Mitgl., 1961–1967 Professor f. öffentl. Recht, 1967–1969 Staatssekretär im Bundesjustizministerium, 1969 Justizminister, 1969–1994 MdB f. d. SPD, 1969–1972 Bundesminister f. besondere Aufgaben u. Chef d. Bundeskanzleramtes, 1972–1974 Bundesminister f. Forschung u. Technologie u. f. d. Post- u. Fernmeldewesen, 1977–1991 stellv. Fraktionsvorsitzender.

Ehmke, Horst, Dr. jur. (1952) b. 1927, German lawyer and professor, from 1947 member of SPD, 1961–1967 professor of public law, 1967–1969 state secretary at ministry of justice, 1969 minister of justice, 1969–1994 SPD MdB, 1969–1972 minister without portfolio and head of chancellery, 1972–1974 minister of research and technology and of post and telecommunications, 1977–1991 deputy whip.

Eichel, Hans geb. 1941, SPD-Politiker, seit 1964 SPD-Mitgl, 1969–1972 stellv. JUSO-Bundesvorsitzender, 1970–1975 Fraktionsvorsitzender im Stadtparlam. Kassel, 1975–1991 Oberbürgermeister, ab 1989 SPD-Landesvorsitzender in Hessen, seit 1984 SPD-Vorstandsmitgl. 1991–1999 Ministerpräsident v. Hessen, ab April 1999 Bundesfinanzminister.

Eichel, Hans b. 1941, SPD politician, from 1964 member of SPD, 1969–1972 JUSO deputy federal chairman, 1970–1975 chief whip in Kassel municipal parliament, 1975–1991 mayor, from 1989 SPD *Land* chairman in Hessen, from 1984 member of SPD executive, 1991–1999 minister president of Hessen, since April 1999 federal finance minister.

Eichmann, Adolf 1906–1962, 1932 Eintritt in d. österr. NSDAP u. SS, 1934 beim Sicherheitsdienst im Juden-Referat II 112, 1939 Geschäftsführer d. »Reichszentrale f. jüdische Auswanderung« in Berlin, danach Versetzung ins Reichssicherheitshauptamt, ab 1941 Organisation d. Massentransporte d. Juden aus Deutschl. u. Böhmen, Beförderung zum SS-Obersturmbannführer, 1946 Flucht nach Argentinien, 1960 nach Israel gebracht, 1.6.1962 in Jerusalem hingerichtet.

Eichmann, Adolf 1906–1962, 1932 joined Austrian NSDAP and SS, 1934 with security service at Jewish Department II 112, 1939 director of Reich central office for Jewish emigration in Berlin, then transferred to Reich security head office, from 1941 organized mass transportation of Jews from Germany and Bohemia, promoted to SS "Obersturmbannführer", 1946 escaped to Argentina, 1960 taken to Israel, 1.6.1962 executed in Jerusalem.

Eisenhower, Dwight David 1890–1969, amerik. Politiker (Republikaner), 1941 Brigadegeneral, 1942 Oberbefehlshaber d. US-Verbände in Europa u. d. alliierten Truppen in Afrika, 1944 »General of the Army«, Juli-November 1945 Oberbefehlshaber d. Besatzungstruppen u. zeitweise Mitgl. d. Alliierten Kontrollrates in Deutschl., 1945–1948 Generalstabschef, 1950–1952 Oberbefehlshaber d. NATO-Streitkräfte (SACEUR), 1952–1960 Präsident d. USA.

Eisenhower, Dwight David 1890–1969, American politician (Republican), 1941 brigadier, 1942 supreme commander of US troops in Europe and Allied troops in Africa, 1944 general of the army, July-November 1945 supreme commander of occupying forces and sometime member of Allied control council in Germany, 1945–1948 chief of general staff, 1950–1952 supreme commander of NATO forces (SACEUR), 1952–1960 US President.

Elizabeth II., Königin geb. 1926 als Prinzessin Elizabeth Alexandra Mary, seit 1952 Königin bzw. Oberhaupt d. Commonwealth, 20.11.1947 Heirat mit Philip Mountbatten, Thronfolger ist ihr Sohn Prinz Charles.

Elizabeth II, Queen b. 1926 as Princess Elizabeth Alexandra Mary, since 1952 Queen and head of the Commonwealth, 20.11.1947 married Philip Mountbatten, their son Prince Charles is heir to the throne.

Engelhard, Hans Arnold geb. 1934, dt. Rechtsanwalt u. Politiker, seit 1954 FDP-Mitgl., 1970–1972 Fraktionsvorsitzender u. Parteivorsitzender in München, 1970–1982 Vorsitzender d. Münchner FDP u. Mitgl. d. Landes- u. Bundesvorstandes, 1972–1994 MdB, 1977– 1982 stellv. Vorsitzender d. FDP-Bundestagsfraktion, 1982–1990 Bundesjustizminister.

Engelhard, Hans Arnold b. 1934, German lawyer and politician, since 1954 member of FDP, 1970–1972 chief whip and party chairman in Munich, 1970–1982 chairman of Munich FDP and member of *Land* and federal executive, 1972–1994 MdB, 1977–1982 FDP deputy whip in federal parliament, 1982–1990 minister of justice.

Engholm, Björn geb. 1939, Schriftsetzer, dt. Politiker, seit 1962 SPD-Mitgl., 1965–1969 Vorsitzender d. Lübecker Jungsozialisten, 1969–1982 MdB f. d. SPD, 1977–1981 Parlam. Staatssekretär im Bundesministerium f. Bildung u. Wissenschaft, 1981–1982 Bundesminister f. Bildung u. Wissenschaft, ab 1983 MdL u. bis 1988 Fraktionsvorsitzender v. Schleswig-Holstein, ab 1984 Mitgl. d. SPD-Bundesvorstandes, 1988–1993 Ministerpräsident v. Schleswig-Holstein (Rücktritt), 1991–1993 Parteivorsitzender (Rücktritt).

Engholm, Björn b. 1939, typesetter, German politics graduate, since 1962 member of SPD, 1965–1969 chairman of Lübeck JUSOs, 1969–1982 SPD MdB, 1977–1981 parliamentary state secretary at ministry of education and science, 1981–1982 minister of education and science, from 1983 MdL and until 1988 chief whip in Schleswig-Holstein, from 1984 member of SPD federal executive, 1988–1993 minister president of Schleswig-Holstein (resigned), 1991–1993 party chairman (resigned).

Eppler, Erhard, Dr. phil., Dr. h.c. (1951) geb. 1926, dt. Politiker, 1952 Mitbegr. d. GVP (Gesamtdt. Volkspartei), seit 1956 SPD-Mitgl., 1961–1976 MdB f. d. SPD, 1967/68 außenpolit. Sprecher d. SPD-Fraktion, 1968–1974 Bundesminister f. wirtschaftl. Zusammenarbeit (Rücktritt), 1970–1991 SPD-Vorstandsmitgl., 1973–1982 u. 1984– 1989 Mitgl. im SPD-Parteipräsidiums, 1973–1981 SPD-Landesvorsitzender Baden-Württemberg, 1976–1982 MdL, 1976–1980 Vorsitzender d. SPD-Landtagsfraktion, 1977–1991 Leiter d. Grundwertekommission d. SPD, 1981–1983 u. 1989–1991 Kirchentagspräsident.

Eppler, Erhard, Dr. phil., Dr. h.c. (1951) b. 1926, German politician, 1952 co-founder of GVP, from 1956 member of SPD, 1961–1976 SPD MdB, 1967/68 foreign policy spokesman for SPD parliamentary group, 1968–1974 minister for economic cooperation (resigned), 1970–1991 member of SPD executive, 1973–1982 and 1984–1989 member of SPD presidium, 1973–1981 SPD *Land* chairman in Baden-Württemberg, 1976–1982 MdL, 1976–1980 SPD chief whip in *Landtag*, 1977–1991 head of SPD fundamental values commission, 1981–1983 and 1989–1991 president of church congress.

Erhard, Ludwig, Prof., Dr. rer. pol. (1925) 1897–1977, dt. Politiker, 1945/46 Wirtschaftsminister in Bayern, 1947 Leiter d. »Sonderstelle Geld u. Kredit« f. Geldreformpläne, 1948–1949 Direktor d. Verwaltung f. Wirtschaft d. Vereinigten Wirtschaftsgebietes, 1949–1977 MdB f. d. CDU, 1949–1963 Bundeswirtschaftsminister, 1957–1963 Vizekanzler, 1963–1966 Bundeskanzler (Rücktritt), 1966/ 67 Parteivorsitzender.

Erhard, Ludwig, professor, Dr. rer. pol. (1925) 1897–1977, German politician, 1945/46 economics minister in Bavaria, 1947 head of special section for money and credit to plan monetary reform, 1948–1949 director of economic administration of United Economic Area, 1949–1977 CDU MdB, 1949–1963 economics minister, 1957–1963 deputy chancellor, 1963–1966 chancellor (resigned), 1966/67 party chairman.

Ertl, Josef geb. 1925, Dipl.-Landwirt, 1961–1987 MdB f. d. FDP, 1968–1969 stellv. Fraktionsvorsitzender, 1969–1983 Bundesminister f. Ernährung, Landwirtschaft u. Forsten, 1971–1983 Vorsitzender d. FDP-Landesvorstandes Bayern.

Ertl, Josef b. 1925, graduated in agriculture, 1961–1987 FDP MdB, 1968–1969 deputy whip, 1969–1983 minister of food, agriculture and forestries, 1971–1983 chairman of FDP Bavarian *Land* executive.

Etzel, Franz 1902–1970, dt. Rechtsanwalt u. Politiker, ab 1945 CDU-Mitgl., 1946 Vorstandsmitgl. d. CDU Nordrhein u. Mitgl. d. Zonenausschusses d. Partei in d. BBZ, 1949–1953 u. 1957–1965 MdB, 1952–1957 Vizepräsident d. Hohen Behörde d. Montanunion, 1957–1961 Bundesfinanzminister.

Etzel, Franz 1902–1970, German lawyer and politician, from 1945 member of CDU, 1946 member of North Rhine CDU executive and member of zonal party committee in British zone of occupation, 1949–1953 and 1957–1965 MdB, 1952–1957 vice president of ECSC High Authority, 1957–1961 finance minister.

F

Faure, Maurice, Dr. jur. geb. 1922, frz. Politiker, 1947–1951 Staatsminister bzw. Staatssekretär im Kabinett, 1953–1955 Generalsekretär d. radikal-sozialist. Partei, 1956–1958 Staatssekretär im Auswärtigen Amt, 1959–1967 u. ab 1973 MdEP, 1961–1968 Präsident d. Europa-Bewegung, 1961– 1965 u. 1969–1971 Vorsitz. d. radikal-sozial. Partei, 1965–1990 Bürgermeister v. Cahors, 1979–1981 Abgeord. in d. Versammlung d. EG, 1981 Justizminister, 1988/89 Staatsminister f. Ausrüstung u. Wohnungsfragen.

Faure, Maurice, Dr. jur. b. 1922, French politician, 1947–1951 minister of state/state secretary in cabinet, 1953–1955 general secretary of radical socialist party, 1956–1958 state secretary at foreign office, 1959–1967 and from 1973 MEP, 1961–1968 president of Europe Movement, 1961–1965 and 1969–1971 chairman of radical socialist party, 1965–1990 majoy of Cahors, 1979–1981 delegate to EC assembly, 1981 minister of justice, 1988/89 minister of state for equipment and housing issues.

Fischer, Andrea geb. 1960, dt. Politikerin, Druckerin u. Volkswirtin, seit 1985 Mitgl. d. Grünen Partei, Mitgl. im Landesvorstand Berlin, Delegierte im Länderrat, seit 1994 MdB, Sozialpolit. Sprecherin d. Bundestagsfraktion, 1998 zur Bundesministerin f. Gesundheit ernannt

Fischer, Andrea b. 1960, German politician, printer and economics graduate, since 1985 member of Green party, member of executive for the *Land* Berlin, delegate to Länder council, since 1994 MdB, parliamentary group social policy spokesperson, 1998 appointed minister of health.

Fischer, Joseph (Joschka) geb. 1948, dt. Politiker, seit 1982 Mitgl. d. Grünen Partei, 1983–1985 u. seit 1994 MdB, 1987–1991 MdL Hessen, 1985–1987 Hessischer Minister f. Umwelt u. Energie, 1987–1991 Vorsitzender d. Landtagsfraktion, 1991–1994 Hessischer Minister f. Umwelt, Energie u. Bundesangelegenheiten, stellv. Ministerpräsident, 1994–1998 Sprecher d. Bundestagsfraktion v. Bündnis 90/Die Grünen, 1998 zum Bundesminister des Auswärtigen ernannt.

Fischer, Joseph (Joschka) b. 1948, German politician, since 1982 member of Green party, 1983–1985 and since 1994 MdB, 1987–1991 MdL Hessen, 1985–1987 environment and energy minister in Hessen, 1987–1991 party chief whip in *Landtag*, 1991–1994 minister for environemt, energy and federal isues in Hessen, deputy minister president, 1994–1998 spokesman for parliamentary group Alliance 90/Greens, 1998 appointed foreign minister.

Focke, Katharina, Dr. phil. (1954) (geb. Friedlaender) geb. 1922, seit 1964 SPD-Mitgl., 1969–1972 Parlam. Staatssekretärin im Bundeskanzleramt, 1972–1976 Bundesministerin f. Jugend, Familie u. Gesundheit, 1966–1969 MdL Nordrhein-Westfalen, 1969–1980 MdB, 1979–1989 MdEP.

Focke, Katharina, Dr. phil. (1954) (née Friedlaender) b. 1922, since 1964 member of SPD, 1969–1972 parliamentary state secretary at chancellery, 1972–1976 minister of youth, family and health, 1966–1969 MdL North Rhine-Westphalia, 1969–1980 MdB, 1979–1989 MEP.

Foertsch, Friedrich 1900–1976, dt. General, 1922 Leutnant, 1940–1945 Generalstabschef, bis 1955 in sowjet. Gefangenschaft, ab 1956 Mitgl. d. dt. Bundeswehr, 1961– 1964 Generalinspekteur d. Bundeswehr.

Foertsch, Friedrich, 1900–1976, German general, 1922 lieutenant, 1940–1945 chief of general staff, until 1955 imprisoned by Russians, from 1956 member of German armed forces, 1961–1964 inspector general of the armed forces.

Ford, Gerald Rudolph geb. 1913, amerik. Rechtsanwalt u. Politiker, ab 1948 Republikanischer Abgeord. v. Michigan im Repräsentantenhaus, 1965 Fraktionsführer, Ende 1973 Vizepräsident, Aug. 1974 – Jan. 1977 US-Präsident.

Ford, Gerald Rudolph b. 1913, American lawyer and politician, from 1948 Republican member of House of Representatives for Michigan, 1965 floor leader, late 1973 vice president, Aug. 1974–Jan. 1977 US President.

Foster, Sir Norman geb. 1935, brit. Architekt, 1994 mit dem Umbau d. Reichstags beauftragt.

Foster, Sir Norman b. 1935, British architect, 1994 commissioned to rebuild the Reichstag.

François-Poncet, Jean André, Dr. geb. 1928, frz. Diplomat, Politiker u. Wirtschaftswissenschaftler, Mitarbeit an d. Formulierung d. EG-Verträge, 1956–1958 Generalsekretär d. frz. Delegation bei EWG u. EURATOM, dann im Außenministerium, 1969–1971 frz. Botschafter im Iran, 1976 Staatssekretär im Außenministerium, dann als Generalsekretär im Elysée-Palast enger Mitarbeiter v. Giscard d'Estaing, 1978–1981 Außenminister, 1983 u. 1992 zum Senator gewählt.

François-Poncet, Jean André, Dr. b. 1928, French diplomat, politician and economist, involved in drafting the EC treaties, 1956–1958 general secretary of French delegation to EEC and EURATOM, then at foreign ministry, 1969–1971 French ambassador to Iran, 1976 state secretary at foreign ministry, then as general secretary at Elysée Palace close cooperation with Giscard d'Estaing, 1978–1981 foreign minister, 1983 and 1992 elected senator.

François-Poncet, André 1887–1978, frz. Publizist u. Diplomat, 1931–1938 frz. Botschafter in Berlin, 1938–1940 in Rom, 1940–1943 Mitgl. d. Nationalrats, anschließend v. Dt. deportiert u. bis 1945 interniert, 1949–1953 frz. Hochkommissar in Deutschl., 1953–1955 Botschafter in Bonn, 1955–1957 Präsident d. Frz. Roten Kreuzes, 1952–1978 Mitgl. d. Academie Francaise.

François-Poncet, André 1887–1978, French publicist and diplomat, 1931–1938 French ambassador in Berlin, 1938–1940 in Rome, 1940–1943 member of national council, subsequently deported by Germans and interned until 1945, 1949–1953 French High Commissioner in Germany, 1953–1955 ambassador in Bonn, 1955–1957 president of French Red Cross, 1952–1978 member of Academie Française.

Frank, Hans, Dr. (1924) 1900–1946, dt. Anwalt, 1923 Eintritt in d. Dt. AP u. in d. SA, Beteiligung am Hitlerputsch, 1929 oberster Rechtsberater d. NSDAP u. Leiter d. rechtspolit. Abt. d. NS-Reichsleitung, 1933 bayer. Justizminister, Leiter d. Rechtsamts d. NSDAP (bis 1942) u. Reichsführer d. NS-Juristenbundes, Reichsminister ohne Geschäftsbereich, Präsident d. Akademie f. Dt. Recht u. 1940 d. Internat. Rechtskammer, Generalgouverneur f. Polen, in Nürnberg hingerichtet.

Frank, Hans, Dr. (1924) 1900–1946, German lawyer, 1923 joined German Workers' party (DAP) and SA, involved in Munich putsch, 1929 top legal adviser to NSDAP and head of legal policy department at NS Reich headquarters, 1933 Bavarian minister of justice, head of NSDAP legal office (until 1942) and Reich leader of league of NS lawyers, Reich minister without portfolio, president of academy for German law and 1940 of chamber of international law, governor general of Poland, executed at Nuremberg.

Franke, Egon 1913–1995, dt. Politiker, ab 1929 SPD-Mitgl., 1945 Mitbegr. d. SPD in Stadt u. Bezirk Hannover, 1947– 1952 Mitgl. im SPD-Parteivorstand, bis 1970 Landes vorsitzender in Niedersachsen, 1964–1973 Mitgl. im SPD-Präsidium, 1947–1951 MdL Niedersachsen, 1951– 1995 MdB, 1969–1982 Bundesminister f. innerdt. Beziehungen.

Franke, Egon 1913–1995, German politician, from 1929 member of SPD, 1945 co-founder of SPD in city and region of Hanover, 1947–1952 member of SPD executive, until 1970 Land chairman of Lower Saxony, 1964–1973 member of SPD presidium, 1947–1951 MdL Lower Saxony, 1951–1995 MdB, 1969–1982 minister of inter-German relations.

Frick, Wilhelm, Dr. 1877–1946, 1919 Leiter d. Abt. polit. Polizei, 1923 Teilnahme am Hitlerputsch, 1924 Mitgl. im Reichstag f. d. NSDAP, 1928 Fraktionschef, 1930/31 thüringischer Innenminister, 1933–1943 Reichsinnenminister, verantwortlich f. d. Nürnberger

Rassengesetze, 1943 Reichsprotektor v. Böhmen u. Mähren, in Nürnberg hingerichtet.

Frick, Wilhelm, Dr. 1877–1946, 1919 head of political police department, 1923 involved in Munich putsch, 1924 NSDAP member of Reichstag, 1928 chief whip, 1930/31 Thuringian minister of the interior, 1933–1943 Reich minister of the interior, responsible for Nuremberg race laws, 1943 Reich protector of Bohemia and Moravia, executed at Nuremberg.

Friederike, Luise, Königin v. Griechenland 1917–1981, Tochter d. Herzogs Ernst August v. Braunschweig u. Lüneburg u. v. Prinzessin Viktoria Luise v. Preußen, 1938 Heirat mit dem griech. Thronfolger Prinz Paul, ab 1967 in Rom im Exil.

Friederike, Luise, Queen of Greece 1917–1981, daughter of Duke Ernst August of Braunschweig and Lüneburg and Princess Victoria Luise of Prussia, 1938 married Greek heir to throne Prince Paul, from 1967 in exile in Rome.

Frings, Joseph, Dr. theol. (1922) 1887–1978, 1910 Priesterweihe, 1942–1969 Erzbischof v. Köln, 1945–1967 Vorsitzender d. Fuldaer Bischofskonferenz, 1946 Kardinal, Mitbegr. d. kathol. Spendenhilfswerke »Misereor« u. »Adveniat«.

Frings, Joseph, Dr. theol. (1922) 1887–1978, 1910 ordained as priest, 1942–1969 archbishop of Cologne, 1945–1967 chairman of Fulda bishops' conference, 1946 cardinal, co-founder of catholic aid organizations "Misereor" and "Adveniat".

Fritzsche, Hans 1900–1953, 1923 DNVP-Eintritt, 1932 Leiter des drahtlosen Nachrichtendienstes beim Dt. Rundfunk, 1933 Leiter des Nachrichtenwesens in d. Presseabt. d. Reichspropagandaministeriums, NSDAP-Eintritt, Verantwortung f. d. Gleichschaltung d. Nachrichtenkanäle in NS-Deutschl., 1938 Leiter d. Abt. Dt. Presse, 1942 d. Abt. Rundfunk im Propagandaministerium, 1946 Freispruch in Nürnberg.

Fritzsche, Hans 1900–1953, 1923 joined DNVP, 1932 head of wireless news broadcasting with German Radio, 1933 head of news service of Reich propaganda ministry press department, joined NSDAP, responsible for standardization (*Gleichschaltung*) of news channels in NS Germany, 1938 head of German press department, 1942 head of propaganda ministry broadcasting department, 1946 acquitted at Nuremberg.

Frohne, Edmund, Dr., Dr. (1926) 1891–1971, 1938 Abteilungspräsident in d. Reichsbahndirektion Hannover, 1947–1949 Direktor d. Hauptverwaltung f. Verkehr d. Vereinigten Wirtschaftsgebietes, 1950–1952 Staatssekretär im Bundesverkehrsministerium, 1952–1957 Präsident u. Vorsitzender d. Vorstandes d. Dt. Bundesbahn.

Frohne, Edmund, Dr. Dr. (1926) 1891–1971, 1938 departmental president at Reich railway directorate in Hanover, 1947–1949 director of main traffic administration in United Economic Area, 1950–1952 state secretary at ministry of transport, 1952–1957 president and chairman of German federal railway executive.

Frondizi, Arturo, Prof., Dr. jur. (1930) 1908–1995, argentin. Rechtsanwalt u. Politiker, 1946–1952 MdP in Argentinien, 1958–1962 Staatspräsident, am 29.3.1962 durch Militärrevolte gestürtzt u. verbannt, 1964 Gründer d. Movimiento de Integración y Desarrollo (MID), Chefredakteur d. Tageszeitung »Clarín«.

Frondizi, Arturo, professor, Dr. jur. (1930) 1908–1995, Argentinian lawyer and politician, 1946–1952 MP in Argentinia, 1958–1962 President, 29.3.1962 ousted and exiled following military revolt, 1964 founder of Movimiento de Integración y Desarrollo (MID), editor-in-chief of daily paper *Clarín*.

Funk, Walther 1890–1960, 1931 NSDAP-Eintritt, Hitlers persönl. Wirtschaftsberater, Leiter d. Amtes f. Wirtschaftspolitik in d. Reichsleitung, 1933 Pressechef d. Reichsregierung u. Staatssekretär im Propagandaministerium, dann auch Vizepräsident d. Reichskulturkammer, 1937–1945 Reichswirtschaftsminister u. Generalbevollmächtigter f. d. Kriegswirtsch., 1939 Präsident d. Dt. Reichsbank, bis 1958 im Spandauer Kriegsverbrechergefängnis.

Funk, Walther 1890–1960, 1931 joined NSDAP, Hitler's personal economic adviser, head of economic policy office at Reich headquarters, 1933 Reich government press director and state secretary at propaganda ministry, then also vice president of Reich chamber of culture, 1937–1945 Reich economics minister with overall responsibility for war economy, 1939 president of German Reich bank, until 1958 imprisoned as war criminal in Spandau.

Funke, Karl-Heinz geb. 1946, dt. Landwirt u. Politiker, seit 1964 SPD-Mitgl., seit 1972 Kreistagsabgeordn. im Landkreis Friesland, ab 1978 MdL v. Niedersachsen, ab 1981 Bürgermeister d. Stadt Varel, 1990–1998 Minister f. Ernährung, Landwirtsch. u. Forsten in Niedersachsen. Seit 1998 Bundeslandwirtschaftsminister.

Funke, Karl-Heinz b. 1946, German economist and politician, since 1964 member of SPD, from 1972 member of Friesland district assembly, from 1978 MdL Lower Saxony, from 1981 mayor of the town of Varel, 1990–1998 minister of food, agriculture and forestries in Lower Saxony.

Furtwängler, Wilhelm, Dr. h.c. 1886–1954, Dirigent, Chordirigent u. Kapellmeister ab 1911 in Deutschl., 1922–1945 u. 1949–1954 Leiter d. Berliner Philharmoniker, 1922–1940 auch Leiter d. Leipziger Gewandhausorchesters u. d. Wiener Philharmoniker.

Furtwängler, Wilhelm, Dr. h.c. 1886–1954, conductor, choirmaster and bandmaster in Germany from 1911, 1922–1945 and 1949–1954 principal conductor of Berlin Philharmonic, 1922–1940 also of Leipzig Gewandhaus orchestra and of Vienna Philharmonic.

G

Gaillard, Félix 1919–1970, frz. Finanzwirtschaftler, 1943 Mitgl. d. provisor. Regierung in Frankreich, ab 1946 Abgeord., 1951–1953 im Regierungskabinett tätig, 1957 Finanz- u. Wirtschaftsminister u. 1957–1958 Regierungschef, 1958–1961 Vorsitzender d. Radikal-sozialist. Partei.

Gaillard, Félix 1919–1970, French financial expert, 1943 member of French provisional government, from 1946 MP, 1951–1953 cabinet minister, 1957 finance and economics minister and 1957–1958 head of government, 1958–1961 chairman of radical socialist party.

Galinski, Heinz 1912–1992, kaufmännische Lehre, 1940–1943 Zwangsarbeiter, dann nach Auschwitz deportiert, 1945 KZ Buchenwald u. Bergen-Belsen, nach dem Krieg am Wiederaufbau d. Jüdischen Gemeinde in Berlin beteiligt, ab 1949 Vorsitzender d. Gemeindevorstandes, Direktoriumsmitgl. im Zentralrat d. Juden in Deutschl. sowie u.a. Vorstandsmitgl. d. Zentralwohlfahrtsstelle d. Juden in Deutschl., ab 1988 Vorsitzender d. Zentralrates d. Juden.

Galinski, Heinz 1912–1992, commercial apprenticeship, 1940–1943 forced labor, then deported to Auschwitz, 1945 KZ Buchenwald and Bergen-Belsen, after the war involved in reconstruction of Jewish community in Berlin, from 1949 chairman of community executive, member of directorate of central council of Jews in Germany and inter alia member of executive of central welfare office for Jews in Germany, from 1988 chairman of Jewish central council.

Gauck, Joachim geb. 1940, 1965 Diensteintritt in d. Ev.-Lutherische Landeskirche Mecklenburgs, 1990 MdVK in Mecklenburg-Vorpommern f. d. Neue Forum, 1990 u. 1995 zum »Sonderbeauftragten f. d. Unterlagen d. Staatssicherheitsdienstes d. ehemal. DDR« gewählt (»Gauck-Behörde«)

Gauck, Joachim b. 1940, 1965 entered service of evangelical-Lutheran church of *Land* Mecklenburg, 1990 New Forum member of Volkskammer in Mecklenburg-Vorpommern, 1990 and 1995 elected "official with special responsibility for the documents of the state security service of the former GDR" ("Gauck office").

Gaulle, Charles de 1890–1970, 1940 General u. Unterstaatssekretär f. Verteidigung, Gründer d. Londoner Komitees »Freies Frankreich« u. sodann Führer d. Résistance, November 1944 – Januar 1946 Chef d. provisor. Regierung, 1947 Gründung d. »Rassemblement du Peuple Francais«, 1958 erneut Ministerpräsident, 1959–1969 Staatspräsident (Rücktritt), veranlaßte 1966 Frankreichs Austritt aus d. militärischen Integration d. NATO.

Gaulle, Charles de 1890–1970, 1940 general and under-secretary of state for defense, founder of London "Free French" committee and then leader of résistance, November 1944 – January 1946 head of provisional government, 1947 founded "Rassemblement du Peuple Français", 1958 again prime minister, 1959–1969 President (resigned), 1966 brought about France's withdrawal from the military structure of NATO.

Gaus, Günter geb. 1929, dt. Publizist, Diplomat u. Politiker, seit 1976 SPD-Mitgl., 1953–1965 Redakteur bei verschied. Zeitungen, 1965–1969 Programmdirektor u. stellv. Intendant d. Südwestfunks, 1966–1968 Interviewreihe »Zur Person« (ZDF), 1969–1973 Chefredakteur d. Zeitschrift »Der Spiegel«, 1973 Staatssekretär im Bundeskanzleramt, 1974–1981 Leiter d. Ständigen Vertretung d. BRD in d. DDR, dann deutschl.- u. außenpolit. Berater d. Internat. Kommission beim SPD-Vorstand, ab 1990 Fernseh-interview-Reihe »Zur Person« (Neuauflage).

Gaus, Günter b. 1929, German publicist, diplomat and politician, since 1976 member of SPD, 1953–1965 editor of various newspapers, 1965–1969 program director and deputy general manager of German South West Radio, 1966–1968 ZDF interview series "Zur Person", 1969–1973 editor-in-chief of *Der Spiegel*, 1973 state secretary at chancellery, 1974–1981 head of FRG permanent mission in GDR, then adviser on foreign policy and inter-German relations to international commission of SPD executive, from 1990 new series of TV interviews "Zur Person".

Geiger, Hansjörg, Dr. jur. (1971) geb. 1942, dt. Jurist, 1975 Richter am Münchner Amtsgericht, ab 1990 stellv. Sonderbeauftragter d. »Gauck-Behörde«, 1996 Präsident d. Bundesnachrichtendienstes (BND) u. d. Bundesamtes f. Verfassungsschutz in Köln.

Geiger, Hansjörg, Dr. jur.(1971) b. 1942, German lawyer, 1975 judge at Munich district court, from 1990 deputy head of "Gauck office", 1996 president of federal intelligence service and of federal office for the protection of the constitution in Cologne.

Geißler, Heiner, Dr. jur. (1960) geb. 1930, dt. Politiker, 1962 Richter, 1961–1965 Vorsitzender d. JU Baden-Württemberg, 1962–1965 Leiter d. Büros d. Arbeits- u. Sozialministers v. Baden-Württemberg, 1965–1967 u. seit 1980 MdB f. d. CDU, 1967–1977 Minister f. Soziales, Gesundheit u. Sport in Rheinland-Pfalz, 1971–1979 MdL Rheinland-Pfalz, 1977–1989 Generalsekretär d. CDU, bis 1998 Mitgl. im CDU-Präsidium, 1982–1985 Bundesminister f. Jugend, Familie u. Gesundheit, 1986–1993 Vizepräsident d. Christl.-Demokr. Internationale, 1991–1998 stellv. CDU/CSU-Fraktionsvorsitzender, seit 1994 Mitgl. d. CDU-Bundesvorstandes u. d. Sozialausschüsse CDA.

Geißler, Heiner, Dr. jur. (1960) b. 1930, German politician, 1962 judge, 1961–1965 chairman of Young Union in Baden-Württemberg, 1962–1965 head of the office of minister of labor and welfare in Baden–Württemberg, 1965–1967 and since 1980 CDU MdB, 1967–1977 minister of welfare issues, health and sport in Rhineland-Palatinate, 1971–1979 MdL Rhineland-Palatinate, 1977–1989 general secretary of CDU, until 1998 member of CDU presidium, 1982–1985 federal minister of youth, family and health, 1986–1993 vice president pf Christian Democrat International, 1991–1998 CDU/CSU deputy whip, since 1994 member of CDU federal executive and of CDA welfare committees.

Genscher, Hans-Dietrich geb. 1927, Jurist, dt. Politiker, 1944 Reichsarbeitsdienst, 1946–1952 Mitgl. d. Liberal-Demokr. Partei, ab 1952 FDP-Mitgl., 1959–1965 Geschäftsführer d. FDP-Bundestagsfraktion, daneben 1962–1964 FDP-Bundesgeschäftsführer, ab 1965 MdB, 1968–1974 stellv. Parteivorsitzender, 1969–1974 Bundesinnenminister, 1974–1992 Bundesminister d. Auswärtigen Amtes sowie Vizekanzler, 1984–1985 Präsident d. NATO-Rates, 1984 Präsident d. Europarates.

Genscher, Hans-Dietrich b. 1927, lawyer, German politician, 1944 Reich labor service, 1946–1952 member of Liberal Democratic Party, from 1952 member of FDP, 1959–1965 manager of FDP parliamentary group, also 1962–1964 FDP federal manager, from 1965 MdB, 1968–1974 deputy party chairman, 1969–1974 minister of the interior, 1974–1992 foreign minister and deputy chancellor, 1984–1985 president of NATO Council, 1984 president of Council of Europe.

George-Brown, Lord Alfred (seit 1970) 1914–1985, kaufmännische Lehre, ab 1945 Abgeord. d. brit. Labour Party, dann bis 1951 parlam. Staatssekretär, sodann Minister f. öffentliche Arbeiten u. Mitgl. d. Geheimen Staatsrates, 1951–1953 u. 1960–1964 brit. Vertreter im Europarat, 1964–1966 Vizepremier u. Wirtschaftsminister, 1966–1968 Außenminister, 1976 Ausscheiden aus d. Partei, 1980 Eintritt in d. Social and Democratic Party.

George-Brown, Lord Alfred (from 1970) 1914–1985, trained in commerce, from 1945 British Labour Party MP, then until 1951 parliamentary secretary, then minister of public works and member of privy council, 1951–1953 and 1960–1964 British representative at Council of Europe, 1964–1966 deputy prime minister and economics minister, 1966–1968 foreign secretary, 1976 left Labour Party, joined Social Democratic Party in 1980s.

Gerhardsen, Einar 1897–1987, norweg. Politiker, 1919 Vorsitzender d. Straßenarbeitergewerkschaft Norwegens, 1922 Sekretär d. norweg. AP, 1925–1935 Parteisekretär in Oslo, 1935–1945 Generalsekretär u. Mitgl. d. Stadtrats v. Oslo, 1942–1944 KZ Sachsenhausen, 1940 u. 1945 Bürgermeister v. Oslo, 1945 bis 1965 Vorsitzender d. AP, 1945–1951 u. 1955–1965 Ministerpräsident.

Gerhardsen, Einar 1897–1987, Norwegian politician, 1919 chairman of Norwegian road workers' trade union, 1922 secretary of Norwegian Workers' Party, 1925–1935 party secretary in Oslo, 1935–1945 general secretary and member of Oslo town council, 1942–1944 KZ Sachsenhausen, 1940 and 1945 mayor of Oslo, 1945-1965 chairman of Workers' Party, 1945–1951 and 1955–1965 prime minister.

Gerstenmaier, Eugen 1906–1986, ev. Theologe u. Politiker, 1936–1944 hauptamtlicher Mitarbeiter im Kirchlichen Außenamt d. Dt. Evangelischen Kirche, 1945 Mitbegr. u. bis 1951 Leiter d. Hilfswerks d. Evangelischen Kirche in Deutschl. (EKD), 1948 Mitgl. d. Synode d. EKD, 1949–1969 MdB, 1954–1969 Bundestagspräsident (Rücktritt), 1956–1969 stellv. CDU-Vorsitzender.

Gerstenmaier, Eugen 1906–1986, protestant theologian and politician, 1936–1944 worked full-time at the external ecclesiastical office of the German protestant church, 1945 co-founder and until 1951 head of German protestant church aid organization (EKD), 1948 member of EKD synod, 1949–1969 MdB, 1954–1969 president of Bundestag (resigned), 1956–1969 CDU deputy party chairman.

Gierek, Edward geb. 1913, Bergarbeiter, poln. Politiker, 1946 Vorsitzender d. Nationalrats der Polen in Belgien, 1948 in Polen Funktionär im ZK d. Poln. Vereinigten AP (PVAP), 1952–1980 Abgeord. d. Sejm, 1954 ZK-Mitgl. d. PVAP, 1956–1964 einer d. ZK-Sekretäre, ab 1956 Mitgl. d. PBs, 1970–1980 Parteichef, 1980 aus PB, ZK u. Staatsrat enthoben u. Sejm-Mandat entzogen, 1981 aus d. Partei ausgeschlossen, bis 1982 interniert.

Gierek, Edward b. 1913, miner, Polish politician, 1946 chairman of national council of Poles in Belgium, 1948 in Poland party official on central committee of Polish United Workers' Party (PVAP), 1952–1980 MP (Sejm), 1954 member of PVAP central committee, 1956–1964 one of the central committee secretaries, from 1956 member of PB, 1970–1980 party leader, 1980 removed from PB, central committee and council of state and Sejm mandate withdrawn, 1981 expelled from party and interned until 1982.

Giscard d'Estaing, Valéry geb. 1926, Finanz- u. Wirtschaftsexperte, 1956–1974, 1984–1989 u. 1993 MdP f. d. Republikaner, 1956–1958 Mitgl. d. frz. UNO-Delegation, 1959 Staatssekretär im Finanzministerium, 1962–1965 u. 1969–1974 Finanz- u. Wirtschaftsminister, 1964–1974 Bürgermeister v. Chamalière, 1974–1981 Staatspräsident, 1988–1996 UDF-Präsident (Union pour la démocratie francaise), 1989–1993 MdEP

Giscard d'Estaing, Valéry b. 1926, finance and economics expert, 1956–1974, 1984–1989 and 1993 Republican MP, 1956–1958 member of French delegation to UN, 1959 state secretary at finance ministry, 1962–1965 and 1969–1974 finance and economics minister, 1964–1974 mayor of Chamalière, 1974–1981 President, 1988–1996 president of UDF (Union pour la démocratie française), 1989–1993 MEP.

Globke, Hans, Dr. jur. 1898–1973, dt. Verwaltungsbeamter, 1929 Ministerialrat im preuß. Innenministerium, 1932–1945 im Reichsinnenministerium tätig, beteiligt an den Gesetzen zur Gleichschaltung parlam. Gremien in Preußen, Mitarbeit an d. Kommentaren zu den Nürnberger Rassengesetzen, 1949 Ministerialdirigent im Bundeskanzleramt, 1950 Leitung d. Hauptabt. f. innere Angelegenheiten, 1953–1963 Staatssekretär im Bundeskanzleramt.

Globke, Hans, Dr. jur. 1898–1973, German civil servant, 1929 ministerial councillor at Prussian ministry of the interior, 1932–1945 worked in Reich ministry of the interior, involved in laws for the standardization (*Gleichschaltung*) of parliamentary bodies in Prussia, contributed to commentaries on Nuremberg race laws, 1949 ministerial director at chancellery, 1950 head of main department of internal affairs, 1953–1963 state secretary at chancellery.

Goebbels, Joseph 1897–1945 (Freitod), 1924 NSDAP-Eintritt, 1925 Geschäftsführer d. Partei im Gau Rheinland-Nord, 1926 zum Gauleiter v. Berlin-Brandenburg ernannt, 1927 Gründung d. NS-Wochenblattes »Der Angriff«, 1929 v. Hitler zum Reichspropagandaleiter ernannt, ab 1928 Reichstagsabgeordneter, 13.3.1933 Reichsminister f. Volksaufklärung u. Propaganda, ordnete 1942 d. Deportation d. Berliner Juden an, Juli 1944/45 Generalbevollmächtigter f. den totalen Krieg, ließ seine Kinder vergiften u. wählte mit seiner Frau den Freitod.

Goebbels, Joseph 1897–1945 (suicide), 1924 joined NSDAP, 1925 party manager in North Rhineland region (*Gau*), 1926 appointed regional leader (*Gauleiter*) of Berlin-Brandenburg, 1927 founded NS weekly *Der Angriff*, 1929 appointed head of Reich propaganda by Hitler, from 1928 member of Reichstag, 13.3.1933 Reich minister of public enlightenment and propaganda, 1942 ordered deportation of Jews from Berlin, July 1944/45 overall responsibility for total war, had his children poisoned and committed suicide with his wife.

Gomulka, Wladyslaw 1905–1982, poln. Politiker, ab 1926 Mitgl. d. poln. KP, 1943–1948 Generalsekretär d. poln. AP, 1945–1949 stellv. Ministerpräsident u. Minister f. d. »wiedergewonnenen Gebiete«, 1948/49 aus allen Ämtern u. d. Partei ausgeschlossen, 1951–1955 in Haft, 1956–1970 wieder Erster Sekretär d. »Poln. Vereinigten AP« (Rücktritt), 1971 Ausschluß aus dem ZK.

Gomulka, Wladyslaw 1905–1982, Polish politician, from 1926 member of Polish CP, 1943–1948 general secretary of Polish Workers' Party, 1945–1949 deputy prime minister and minister for the "regained territories", 1948/49 expelled from all offices and from the party, 1951–1955 in prison, 1956–1970 again first secretary of Polish United Workers' Party (resigned), 1971 removed from central committee.

Gonzáles, Carmen Romero Lopez, seit 1968 d. Ehefrau v. Felipe Gonzáles, aktiv in d. Gewerkschaft UGT u. in d. Frauenbewegung »Frente de Liberación de la Mujer«.

Gonzáles, Carmen Romero Lopez, since 1968 wife of Felipe Gonzáles, active in the trade union UGT and in women's movement "Frente de Liberación de la Mujer".

Gonzáles Márquez, Felipe geb. 1942, span. Jurist u. Politiker, 1965–1970 Mitgl. d. Provinzialkomitees u. d. Nationalen Komitees d. Partido Socialista Obrero Espanol (PSOE), ab 1970 im Exekutivausschuß, 1974 Generalsekretär d. PSOE, 1982–1996 Ministerpräsident, ab 1996 Fraktionsvorsitzender.

Gonzáles Márquez, Felipe b. 1942, Spanish lawyer and politician, 1965–1970 member of provincial committee and national committee of Partido Socialista Obrero Espanol (PSOE), from 1970 on executive committee, 1974 general secretary of PSOE, 1982–1996 prime minister, since 1996 chief whip.

Goppel, Alfons, Dr. h.c. (1964) 1905–1991, dt. Rechtsanwalt, 1934 Staatsanwalt in Kaiserslautern, 1930–1933 Mitgl. d. Bayer. Volkspartei, 1945 Mitbegr. d. CSU, 1954 MdL, 1957 Staats-

sekretär im Justizministerium Bayerns, 1958 Innenminister, 1962–1978 Ministerpräsident, 1979–1984 MdEP.

Goppel, Alfons, Dr. h.c. (1964) 1905–1991, German lawyer, 1934 prosecuting attorney in Kaiserslautern, 1930–1933 member of Bavarian People's Party, 1945 co-founder of CSU, 1954 MdL, 1957 state secretary at Bavarian ministry of justice, 1958 minister of the interior, 1962–1978 minister president, 1979–1984 MEP.

Gorbatschow, Michail Sergejewitsch geb. 1931, sowjet. Diplomagraring., ab 1952 Mitgl. d. KPdSU, ab 1970 Mitgl. d. Obersten Sowjets d. UdSSR, 1971 Vollmitgl. im ZK, 1978 ZK-Sekretär u. Übernahme d. Abt. Agrarwirtschaft, 1980 Vollmitgl. d. PB, 1985–1991 Generalsekretär d. KPdSU u. Vorsitzender d. Verteidigungsrates, 1989 Präsidiumsvorsitzender d. Obersten Sowjets, 1990–1991 erster sowjet. Präsident.

Gorbachev, Mikhail Sergeyevich b. 1931, Soviet agricultural engineering graduate, from 1952 member of CPSU, from 1970 member of USSR supreme soviet, 1971 full member of central committee, 1978 secretary of central committee with responsibility for agriculture, 1980 full member of PB, 1985–1991 CPSU general secretary and chairman of defense council, 1989 chairman of supreme soviet presidium, 1990–1991 first Soviet president.

Gorbatschowa, Raissa Maximowna, Prof. Dr. (1967) (geb. Titorenko) geb. 1932, sowjet. Soziologin, seit 1953 Ehefrau v. Michail Gorbatschow

Gorbacheva, Raissa Maximovna, professor, Dr. (1967) (née Titorenko) b. 1932, Soviet sociologist, since 1953 married to Mikhail Gorbachev.

Göring, Hermann 1893–1946 (Freitod), 1922 Kommandeur d. SA, 1923 Teilnahme am Hitlerputsch, 1927 NSDAP-Eintritt, 1928 MdR f. d. NSDAP, 1932 Reichstagspräsident, ab 30.1.1933 preuß. Innenminister, Chef d. Polizei, Reichskommissar f. Luftfahrt u. Reichsminister ohne Geschäftsbereich, errichtet erste KZs f. polit. Gegner, April 1933 preuß. Ministerpräsident, Mai 1935 Oberbefehlshaber d. Luftwaffe, 1939 Vorsitzender d. Reichsverteidigungsrates, 1.9.1939 zu Hitlers Nachfolger ernannt, 1940 Reichsmarschall, April 1945 seiner Ämter enthoben, aus d. Partei ausgestoßen u. inhaftiert, vom Nürnberger Gericht 1946 zum Tode verurteilt.

Göring, Hermann 1893–1946 (suicide), 1922 SA commander, 1923 involved in Munich putsch, 1927 joined NSDAP, 1928 NSDAP member of Reichstag, 1932 president of Reichstag, from 30.1.1933 Prussian minister of the interior, chief of police, Reich commissioner for aviation and Reich minister without portfolio, set up first concentration camps for political opponents, April 1933 prime minister of Prussia, May 1935 supreme commander of German air force, 1939 chairman of Reich defense council, 1.9.1939 appointed Hitler's successor, 1940 Reich Marshal, April 1945 removed from his posts, expelled from party and imprisoned, condemned to death by Nuremberg court in 1946.

Grewe, Wilhelm, Dr. jur. (1936) geb. 1911, dt. Völkerrechtler, Diplomat u. Publizist, 1955–1958 Leiter d. Rechtsabt. d. Auswärtigen Amtes, 1958–1962 Botschafter in Washington, 1962–1971 NATO-Botschafter in Brüssel, 1971–1976 Botschafter in Tokio.

Grewe, Wilhelm, Dr. jur. (1936) b. 1911, German expert on international law, diplomat and publicist, 1955–1958 head of foreign office legal department, 1958–1962 ambassador in Washington, 1962–1971 NATO ambassador in Brussels, 1971–1976 ambassador in Tokyo.

Gromyko, Andrej Andrejewitsch, Dr. geb. 1909–1989, sowjet. Politiker, ab 1931 Mitgl. d. KPdSU, 1943–1946 sowjet. Botschafter in Washington u. Gesandter in Kuba, 1946–1948 ständiger sowjet. Vertreter im Weltsicherheitsrat, 1948–1952 u. 1953–1957 Erster stellv. Außenminister, 1952/53 Botschafter in London, ab 1956 Mitgl. d. ZK, 1957–1985 Außenminister d. UdSSR, 1985–1988 Vorsitzender d. Präsidiums d. Obersten Sowjets d. UdSSR.

Gromyko, Andrey Andreyevich, Dr. 1909–1989, Soviet politician, from 1931 member of CPSU, 1943–1946 Soviet ambassador in Washington and envoy to Cuba, 1946–1948 permanent Soviet representative on UN security council, 1948–1952 and 1953–1957 first deputy foreign minister, 1952/53 ambassador in London, from 1956 member of central committee, 1957–1985 USSR foreign minister, 1985–1988 chairman of USSR supreme soviet presidium.

Gross, Johannes, Dr. h.c. geb. 1932, dt. Publizist, 1974 Chefredakteur, ab 1980 Hrsg. d. Wirtschaftsmagazine »Capital« u. »Impulse«.

Gross, Johannes, Dr. h.c. b. 1932, German publicist, 1974 editor-in-chief, from 1980 publisher of economics periodicals *Capital* and *Impulse*.

Grotewohl, Otto Heinrich 1894–1964, Drucker, 1920–1926 MdL v. Braunschweig, 1921/22 Innen- u. Bildungsminister in Braunschweig, 1923/24 Minister f. Justiz, ab 1945 Vorsitzender d. Zentralausschusses d. SPD in d. SBZ, 1946–1954 SED-Vorsitzender, 1946–1950 MdL v. Sachsen, 1947 Präsident d. Volkskongresses, 1948/49 Mitgl. d. Dt. Volksrates, ab 7.10.1949 Ministerpräsident bzw. Vorsitzender d. Ministerrats d. DDR, ab 1960 stellv. Vorsitzender d. Staatsrats.

Grotewohl, Otto Heinrich 1894–1964, printer, 1920–1926 MdL Braunschweig, 1921/22 minister of the interior and education in Braunschweig, 1923/24 minister of justice, from 1945 chairman of central committee of SPD in SBZ, 1946–1954 chairman of SED, 1946–1950 MdL Saxony, 1947 president of people's congress, 1948/49 member of German people's council, from 7.10.1949 GDR prime minister, i.e. chairman of council of ministers, from 1960 deputy chairman of state council.

Gudmundsson, Kristinn geb. 1897, isländischer Politiker, Diplomat, 1953–1956 Außenminister, 1957–1960 Botschafter in LaHaye u. Großbritannien, ab 1961 Botschafter in d. UdSSR, Rumänien, Bulgarien u. Ungarn.

Gudmundsson, Kristinn b. 1897, Icelandic politician, diplomat, 1953–1956 foreign minister, 1957–1960 ambassador in The Hague and Britain, from 1961 ambassador to USSR, Romania, Bulgaria and Hungary.

Guillaume, Günter 1927–1995, dt. Journalist, Spion d. DDR, 1956 Übersiedlung in d. BRD, 1957 SPD-Eintritt, 1964 Parteisekretär d. SPD-Unterbezirks Frankfurt, 1970 Referent im Bundeskanzleramt, 1974 verhaftet, 1975 zu 13 Jahren Haft verurteilt, 1981 nach Begnadigung in d. DDR abgeschoben.

Guillaume, Günter 1927–1995, German journalist, GDR spy, 1956 moved to FRG, 1957 joined SPD, 1964 party secretary of SPD sub-district Frankfurt, 1970 adviser at chancellery, 1974 arrested, 1975 sentenced to 13 years imprisonment, 1981 pardoned and deported to GDR.

Guttenberg, Karl Theodor Freiherr von und zu 1921–1972, 1957–1972 MdB f. d. CSU, 1961–1972 Mitgl. d. CSU-Landesvorstandes, 1967–1972 Parlam. Staatssekretär im Bundeskanzleramt.

Guttenberg, Karl Theodor Freiherr of 1921–1972, 1957–1972 CSU MdB, 1961–1972 member of CSU *Land* executive, 1967– 1972 parliamentary state secretary at chancellery.

Gysi, Gregor, Dr. jur. (1976) geb. 1948, Diplomjurist, PDS-Politiker, Dez. 1989 – Jan. 1990 Vorsitzender d. SED/PDS, März-Oktober 1990 MdVK, 1990–1993 Bundesvorsitzender d. PDS, 1990–1998 Vorsitzender d. Gruppe d. PDS, seit 1990 MdB, seit 1998 Vorsitzender d. PDS-Fraktion.

Gysi, Gregor, Dr. jur. (1976) b. 1948, law graduate, politician (PDS), Dec. 1989 – Jan. 1990 chairman of SED/PDS, March-October 1990 member of Volkskammer, 1990–1993 PDS federal chairman, 1990–1998 leader of Bundestag PDS group, since 1990 MdB, since 1998 PDS chief whip.

H

Hacke, Christian geb. 1943, Professor f. internat. Politik, Mitgl. d. Dt. Gesellschaft f. Auswärtige Politik in Bonn u. d. Internat. Instituts f. Strategische Studien in London.

Hacke, Christian b. 1943, professor of international politics, member of German foreign policy association in Bonn and of International Institute for Strategic Studies in London.

Haffner, Sebastian 1907–1999, 1938 Emigration nach England, journalist. Tätigkeit u.a. beim »Observer«, ab 1961 polit. Kolumnist f. »Die Welt«, 1963–1976 f. d. »Stern«, Verfasser zahlreicher polit. Essays, u.a. »Anmerkungen zu Hitler«

Haffner, Sebastian 1907–1999, 1938 exiled to England, worked as journalist inter alia for the *Observer*, from 1961 political columnist for *Die Welt*, 1963–1976 for *Stern*, author of numerous political essays, including *Anmerkungen zu Hitler* [Notes on Hitler].

Haile Selassie I. 1892–1975, 1930–1974 Kaiser v. Äthiopien (abgesetzt), ab 1916 Regent u. Thronfolger, ab 1928 König, 1936–1941 im Exil in Großbritannien, 1963 Mitbegr. d. Organisation f. Afrikanische Einheit.

Haile Selassie I, 1892-1975, 1930-1974 Emperor of Ethiopia (deposed). In 1916 named prince and heir to the throne, in 1928 king, 1936-1941 in exile in Great Britain. Founding member of the Organization of African Unity.

Hallstein, Walter 1901–1982, 1949/50 dt. Leiter d. UNESCO-Kommission, 1950/51 Verhandlungsführer zur Bildung d. Montanunion, 1950 Staatssekretär im Bundeskanzleramt, 1951– 1957 Staatssekretär im Auswärtigen Amt, 1958–1967 Präsident d. EWG-Kommission, 1968–1974 Präsident d. Europ. Bewegung, 1969–1972 MdB f. d. CDU.

Hallstein, Walter 1901–1982, 1949/50 German head of UNESCO commission, 1950/51 led negotiations leading to creation of ECSC, 1950 state secretary at chancellery, 1951–1957 state secretary at foreign office, 1958–1967 president of EEC Commission, 1968–1974 president of European movement, 1969–1972 CDU MdB.

Hamm-Brücher, Hildegard, Dr. rer. nat. (1945) geb. 1921, dt. Politikerin, seit 1948 FDP-Mitgl., 1950–1966 u. 1969–1976 MdL v. Bayern, 1967–1969 Staatssekretärin im Kultusministerium v. Hessen, 1969–1972 Staatssekretärin im Bundesministerium f. Bildung u. Wissenschaft (Rücktritt), 1972–1976 stellv. Bundesvorsitzende, 1976–1990 MdB, 1994 Bundespräsidentschaftskandidatin d. FDP.

Hamm-Brücher, Hildegard, Dr. rer. nat. (1945) b. 1921, German politician, since 1948 member of FDP, 1950–1966 and 1979–1976 MdL Bavaria, 1967–1969 state secretary at ministry of education in Hessen, 1969–1972 state secretary at federal ministry of education and science (resigned), 1972–1976 FDP deputy federal chairperson, 1976–1990 MdB, 1994 federal presidential candidate.

Hansen, Hans-Christian Svane 1906–1960, dänischer Politiker, 1945 u. 1947–1950 Finanz-, 1953–1958 Außenminister, 1955–1960 Parteivorsitzender u. Ministerpräsident.

Hansen, Hans-Christian Svane 1906–1960, Danish politician, 1945 and 1947–1950 finance minister, 1953–1958 foreign minister, 1955–1960 party chairman and prime minister.

Hartmann, Alfred 1894–1967, 1942/43 im Rechnungshof d. Dt. Reiches in Potsdam, 1947 Ministerialdirigent u. Leiter d. Haushaltsabt. im Bayer. Finanzministerium, sodann Direktor d. Verwaltung f. Finanzen beim Zweizonenwirtschaftsrat in Frankfurt/M., 1949–1959 Staatssekretär im Bundesfinanzministerium, anschließend bis 1965 u. a. Vorstandssprecher der VEBA.

Hartmann, Alfred 1894–1967, 1942/43 worked at audit office of German Reich in Potsdam, 1947 ministerial director and head of budget department of Bavarian finance ministry, then director of financial administration of bizonal economic council in Frankfurt am Main, 1949–1959 state secretary at federal ministry of finance, then until 1965 inter alia spokesman for VEBA board.

Hase, Karl-Günther von geb. 1917, ZDF-Intendant u. Diplomat, 1953–1956 Gesandtschaftsrat an d. dt. Botschaft in Ottawa, 1958 Leitung d. Pressereferats d. Auswärtigen Amts, 1961 Ministerialdirektor, 1962–1967 Staatssekretär u. Leitung d. Presse- u. Informationsamtes d. Bundesregierung, 1967–1969 Staatssekretär im Bundesministerium f. Verteidigung, 1970–1977 Botschafter in Großbritannien.

Hase, Karl-Günther von b. 1917, general manager of ZDF and diplomat, 1953–1956 councillor at German embassy in Ottawa, 1958 head of foreign office press section, 1961 ministerial director, 1962–1967 state secretary and head of government press and information office, 1967–1969 state secretary at defense ministry, 1970–1977 ambassador to Britain.

Hashimoto, Ryutaro geb. 1937, japan. Politiker, 1963– 1993 MdP, 1970 Staatssekretär im Gesundheitsministerium, 1978/79 Minister f. Gesundheit u. Soziales, 1986/87 Verkehrsminster, sodann bis 1989 Generalsekretär d. LDP, 1989–1991 Finanzminister, 1994 Leitung d. Ministeriums f. Internationalen Handel u. Industrie, 1995 Vorsitzender d. LDP u. Vizepremier, 1996 japan. Ministerpräsident.

Hashimoto, Ryutaro b. 1937, Japanese politician, 1963–1993 MP, 1970 state secretary at ministry of health, 1978/79 minister of health and welfare, 1986/87 minister of transport, then until 1989 general secretary of LDP, 1989–1991 finance minister, 1994 head of ministry of international trade and industry, 1995 LPD chairman and deputy prime minister.

Hassan II. geb. 1929, seit 1961 König v. Marokko, 1956 Oberbefehlshaber, 1957 Kronprinz, 1960/61 stellv. Ministerpräsident u. Verteidigungsminister, 1961–1963 u. 1965–1967 Übernahme d. Regierung, 1972 Übernahme d. Verteidigungsministeriums.

Hassan II. b. 1929, since 1961 King of Morocco, 1956 supreme commander, 1957 crown prince, 1960/61 deputy prime minister and defense minister, 1961–1963 and 1965–1967 took over government, 1972 took over ministry of defense.

Hassel, Kai-Uwe von, Dr. phil. h.c. 1913–1997, dt. Politiker, 1950–1965 MdL f. d. CDU, 1954–1963 Ministerpräsident v. Schleswig-Holstein, 1955–1964 CDU-Landesvorsitzender, 1956–1969 stellv. Bundesvorsitzender, 1953/ 1954 sowie 1965–1980 MdB, 1963–1966 Bundesminister f. Verteidigung, 1966–1969 f. Vertriebene, Flüchtlinge u. Kriegsgeschädigte, 1969–1972 Bundestagspräsident, bis 1980 Vizepräsident, 1973 Präsident d. EUCD, ab 1977 Vizepräsident d. Parlam. Versammlung d. Europarates u. Präsident d. Parlam. Versammlung d. WEU (bis 1980), 1979–1984 MdEP.

Hassel, Kai-Uwe von, Dr. phil. h.c. 1913–1997, German politician, 1950–1965 CDU MdL, 1954–1963 minister president of Schleswig-Holstein, 1955–1964 CDU-*Land* chairman, 1956–1969 deputy federal chairman, 1953/1954 and 1965–1980 MdB, 1963–1966 minister of defense, 1966–1969 minister for expellees, refugees and the war-disabled, 1969–1972 president of Bundestag, until 1980 deputy president and 1973 president of EUCD, from 1977 deputy president of parliamentary assembly of Council of Europe and president of parliamentary assembly of WEU (until 1980), 1979–1984 MEP.

Hasselfeldt, Gerda geb. 1950, dt. Diplomvolkswirtin u. Politikerin, seit 1969 CSU-Mitgl., seit 1987 MdB, 1989–1991 Bundesministerin f. Raumordnung, Bauwesen u. Städtebau, 1991–1992 Bundesministerin f. Gesundheit, seit 1995 Kreisvorsitzende d. CSU Fürstenfeldbruck, seit 1996 Kreisrätin.

Hasselfeldt, Gerda b. 1950, German economics graduate and politician, since 1969 member of CSU, since 1987 MdB, 1989–1991 minister of planning, construction and urban construction, 1991–1992 minister of health, since 1995 district chairperson of CSU in Fürstenfeldbruck, since 1996 district councillor.

Havel, Vaclav, Dr. h.c. geb. 1936, tschech. Schriftsteller, Dramaturg u. Politiker, 1968 Vorsitzender d. »Klubs unabhängiger Schriftsteller«, 1977 Mitbegr. u. Sprecher d. Menschen- u. Bürgerrechtsbewegung »Charta 77«, 1979– 1983 inhaftiert, 1989 Vorsitzender d. »Bürgerforums«, 1989–1992 Staatspräsident d. CSFR, 1993 u. 1998 zum Staatspräsidenten d. Tschech. Republik gewählt.

Havel, Vaclav, Dr. h.c. b. 1936, Czech writer, artistic theatre manager and politician, 1968 chairman of "independent writers club", 1977 co-founder and spokesman of human and civil rights movement "Charter 77", 1979–1983 imprisoned, 1989 chairman of "Civic Forum", 1989–1992 President of CSFR, 1993 and 1998 elected President of Czech Republic.

Heck, Bruno, Prof., Dr. phil. (1950) 1917–1989, dt. Politiker, ab 1946 CDU-Mitgl., 1952–1958 Bundesgeschäftsführer d. CDU, 1952–1976 MdB, ab 1961 Parlam. Geschäftsführer d. CDU/CSU-Bundestagsfraktion, 1962– 1968 Bundesminister f. Familie u. Jugend (Rücktritt), 1961–1989 Vorsitzender d. Konrad-Adenauer-Stiftung, 1967–1971 Generalsekretär d. CDU.

Heck, Bruno, professor, Dr. phil. (1950) 1917–1989, German politician, from 1946 member of CDU, 1952–1958 CDU federal manager, 1952–1976 MdB, from 1961 parliamentary manager of CDU/CSU group, 1962–1968 minister for family and youth (resigned), 1961–1989 chairman of Konrad Adenauer foundation, 1967–1971 CDU general secretary.

Heinemann, Gustav, Dr. (1922 u. 1929) 1899–1976, dt. Rechtsanwalt, zuerst f. d. DDP, dann 1930-1933 f. d. Christl.-Sozialen Volksdienst tätig, 1945 Mitbegr. d. CDU, 1946–1949 Oberbürgermeister in Essen, 1947–1950 MdL, 1947/48 Justizminister v. Nordrhein-Westfalen, 1949/1950 Bundesinnenminister (Rücktritt), 1952 Gründer d. GVP, 1957 SPD-Eintritt, 1957–1969 MdB f. d. SPD, 1966–1969 Justizminister, 1969–1974 Bundespräsident.

Heinemann, Gustav, Dr. (1922 and 1929) 1899–1976, German lawyer, active at first on behalf of DDP, then 1930-1933 of christian-social "Volksdienst" ["serving the people"], 1945 co-founder of CDU, 1946–1949 mayor of Essen, 1947–1950 MdL, 1947/48 justice minister of North Rhine-Westphalia, 1949/1950 federal minister of the interior (resigned), 1952 founder of GVP, 1957 joined SPD, 1957–1969 SPD MdB, 1966–1969 justice minister, 1969–1974 federal president.

Heinemann, Hilda (geb. Ordemann) 1896–1979, ab 1926 Ehefrau v. Gustav Heinemann, 1970 Gründung der nach ihr benannten Stiftung zur Eingliederung geistig behinderter Erwachsener in d. Berufswelt.

Heinemann, Hilda (née Ordemann) 1896–1979, from 1926 wife of Gustav Heinemann, 1970 set up foundation named after her for the integration of mentally handicapped adults into the world of work.

Heitmann, Steffen geb. 1944, dt. Theologe, Jurist u. Politiker, 1982–1990 Leiter d. Bezirkskirchenamtes Dresden, 1991 CDU-Eintritt u. Justizminister v. Sachsen, 1993 kurzzeitig Bundespräsidentschaftskandidat (Rücktritt), seit 1995 Mithrsg. d. Bonner Wochenzeitung »Rheinischer Merkur«.

Heitmann, Steffen b. 1944, German theologian, lawyer and politician, 1982–1990 head of Dresden district church office, 1991 joined CDU and was justice minister of Saxony, 1993 briefly federal presidential candidate (stood down), since 1995 co-editor of Bonn weekly *Rheinischer Merkur*.

Hellwege, Heinrich Peter 1908–1991 dt. Außenhandelskaufmann u. Politiker, 1945 Mitbegr. d. Niedersächsischen Landespartei (1947 umbenannt in DP), 1947–1961 DP-Vorsitzender, 1947–1950 MdL v. Niedersachsen, 1949– 1955 MdB u. Bundesminister f. Angelegenheiten d. Bundesrates, 1955–1959 Ministerpräsident v. Niedersachsen, 1961–1979 CDU-Mitgl.

Hellwege, Heinrich Peter 1908–1991 German foreign trade merchant and politician, 1945 co-founder of Lower Saxony "Landespartei" (1947 renamed DP), 1947–1961 chairman of DP, 1947–1950 MdL Lower Saxony, 1949–1955 MdB and minister for Bundesrat affairs, 1955–1959 minister president of Lower Saxony, 1961–1979 member of CDU.

Herold, Horst, Dr. jur. (1951) geb. 1923, dt. Polizeibeamter, 1964 Kriminaldirektor u. Vertreter d. Polizeipräsidenten in Nürnberg,

1967 Polizeipräsident in Nürnberg, 1971–1981 Präsident d. Bundeskriminalamtes in Wiesbaden (Rücktritt), Einführung des INPOL-Systems (zentrale elektr. Datenbank).

Herold, Horst, Dr. jur. (1951) b. 1923, German police officer, 1964 director of criminal investigations and deputy chief of police of Nuremberg, 1967 chief of police of Nuremberg, 1971–1981 president of federal criminal investigation department in Wiesbaden (resigned), introduced INPOL system (central computer data base).

Herwarth von Bittenfeld, Hans geb. 1904, dt. Diplomat, 1930 an d. dt. Botschaft in Paris, 1931–1939 in Moskau, 1951–1954 Chef d. Protokolls im Auswärtigen Amt, 1955–1961 Botschafter in London, 1961–1964 Staatssekretär im Bundespräsidialamt, 1965–1969 Botschafter in Rom, 1971–1977 Präsident d. Goethe-Instituts.

Herwarth von Bittenfeld, Hans b. 1904, German diplomat, 1930 at German embassy in Paris, 1931–1939 in Moscow, 1951–1954 chief of protocol at foreign office, 1955–1961 ambassador in London, 1961–1964 state secretary at federal president's office, 1965–1969 ambassador in Rome, 1971–1977 president of Goethe Institute.

Herzog, Roman, Prof., Dr. jur. (1958) geb. 1934, dt. Jurist u. Politiker, 1970 CDU-Eintritt, 1973–1978 Leiter d. rheinland-pfälzischen Landesvertretung in Bonn, 1978–1980 Minister f. Kultus u. Sport, 1980–1983 MdL u. Innenminister v. Baden-Württemberg, 1979– 1983 Mitgl. im CDU-Bundesvorstand, 1983–1987 Vizepräsident, 1987–1994 Präsident d. Bundesverfassungsgerichts, 1994-1999 Bundespräsident.

Herzog, Roman, professor, Dr. jur. (1958) b. 1934, German lawyer and politician, 1970 joined CDU, 1973–1978 leader of representatives from Rhineland-Palatinate in Bonn, 1978–1980 minister of education and sport, 1980–1983 MdL and minister of the interior of Baden-Württemberg, 1979–1983 member of CDU federal executive, 1983–1987 deputy president and 1987–1994 president of federal constitutional court.

Heß, Rudolf 1894–1987 (Freitod), 1920 NSDAP-Eintritt, Teilnahme am Hitlerputsch 1923, sodann in Haft mit Hitler, 1925–1932 Hitlers Privatsekretär, 1933 »Stellvertreter d. Führers« als Parteiführer sowie Reichsminister ohne Geschäftsbereich, 1939 Mitgl. d. Ministerrates f. d. Reichsverteidigung u. Hitlers zweiter Nachfolger, 1941 Flucht nach England, 1946 in Nürnberg zu lebenslanger Haft verurteilt.

Heß, Rudolf 1894–1987 (suicide), 1920 joined NSDAP, involved in Munich putsch 1923, then in prison with Hitler, 1925–1932 Hitler's private secretary, 1933 "representative of the Führer" as party leader, and Reich minister without portfolio, 1939 member of council of ministers for the defense of the Reich and Hitler's second successor-designate, 1941 flight to England, 1946 sentenced to life imprisonment at Nuremberg.

Heusinger, Adolf 1897–1982, dt. General, ab 1931 tätig im Reichswehrministerium, 1937 Major, 1941 Generalmajor, 1943 Generalleutnant, 1944 v. seinen Ämtern u. Pflichten als Offizier entbunden, 1949 Adenauers militärischer Berater, 1951 Militärexperte, 1952 Mitwirkung bei d. Planung d. Bundeswehr, später Chef d. Abt. Streitkräfte im Bundesverteidigungsministerium, 1957–1960 Generalinspekteur d. Bundeswehr, 1960–1964 Vorsitzender d. Ständigen Militärausschusses d. NATO in Washington.

Heusinger, Adolf 1897–1982, German general, from 1931 employed at army ministry, 1937 major, 1941 major general, 1943 lieutenant general, 1944 removed from his posts and relieved of duties as an officer, 1949 Adenauer's military adviser, 1951 military expert, 1952 involved in planning for federal German army, later head of defense ministry armed forces department, 1957–1960 inspector general of the army, 1960–1964 chairman of NATO permanent military committee in Washington.

Heuss, Theodor, Prof. Dr. rer. pol. (1905) 1884–1963, dt. Politiker u. Publizist, 1924–1928 u. 1930–1933 MdR f. d. DDP, 1946 Mitgl. d. Württemberg-Badischen Landtags f. d. DVP, 1946 Vorsitzender d. DVP in der ABZ, 1947 im Vorstand d. DPD, 1948/49 MdPR, dort Fraktionsvorsitzender d. Liberalen, 1948/49 1. Bundesvorsitzender d. FDP, 1949–1959 erster Bundespräsident.

Heuss, Theodor, professor, Dr. rer. pol. (1905) 1884–1963, German politician and publicist, 1924–1928 and 1930–1933 DDP member of Reichstag, 1946 DVP MdL Württemberg-Baden, 1946 DVP chairman in ABZ, 1947 member of DPD executive, 1948/49 member of parliamentary council where he was chairman of Liberal group, 1948/49 first FDP federal chairman, 1949–1959 first federal president.

Heuss-Knapp, Elly 1881–1952, ab 1908 Ehefrau v. Theodor Heuss, Gründerin d. dt. Genesungswerkes.

Heuss-Knapp, Elly 1881–1952, from 1908 wife of Theodor Heuss, founder of German support organization for convalescent mothers.

Hintze, Peter geb. 1950, dt. ev. Theologe, 1977–1979 Vikar, 1980–1983 Pfarrer, 1983–1990 Bundesbeauftragter f. d.

Zivildienst, seit 1990 MdB, 1990–1992 Bundesvorsitzender d. ev. Arbeitskreises d. CDU/CSU, 1991–1992 Parlam. Staatssekretär beim Bundesministerium f. Frauen u. Jugend, 1992–1998 CDU-Generalsekretär.

Hintze, Peter b. 1950, German protestant theologian, 1977–1979 curate, 1980–1983 vicar, 1983–1990 federal official in charge of community service, since 1990 MdB, 1990–1992 federal chairman of protestant working party of CDU/CSU, 1991–1992 parliamentary state secretary at ministry for women and youth, 1992–1998 CDU general secretary.

Hitler, Adolf 1889–1945 (Freitod), 18.9.1919 Eintritt in d. Deutsche. Arbeiterpartei, Juli 1921 Parteivorsitzender, wegen Putschversuchs im Nov. 1923 bis Dez. 1924 inhaftiert, Feb. 1925 Führer d. Partei, 1932 Annahme d. dt. Staatsangehörigkeit, Reichspräsidentschaftskandidat, 30.1.1933 Reichskanzler, 2.8.1934 Reichskanzler u. Reichspräsident, 1938 Oberkommandeur d. Wehrmacht, 29.4.1945 Heirat mit Eva Braun, anschließend Freitod.

Hitler, Adolf 1889–1945 (suicide), 18.9.1919 joined German Workers' Party, July 1921 party chairman, imprisoned Nov. 1923 to Dec. 1924 for attempted putsch, Feb. 1925 party leader, 1932 took German citizenship, Reich presidential candidate, 30.1.1933 Reich chancellor, 2.8.1934 Reich chancellor and Reich president, 1938 Army supreme commander, 29.4.1945 married Eva Braun, then committed suicide.

Höcherl, Hermann 1912–1989, dt. Jurist u. Politiker, 1950/51 Staatsanwalt, 1953–1976 MdB f. d. CSU, 1957– 1961 Vorsitzender d. CSU-Landesgruppe im Bundestag u. stellv. Vorsitzender d. Unionsbundestagsfraktion, 1961– 1965 Bundesinnenminister, 1965–1969 Bundesminister f. Ernährung, Landwirtsch. u. Forsten, 1970–1976 Leitung d. Arbeitskreises Haushalt, Steuern u. Finanzen d. CDU/CSU- Bundestagsfraktion.

Höcherl, Hermann 1912–1989, German lawyer and politician, 1950/51 prosecuting attorney, 1953–1976 CSU MdB, 1957–1961 chairman of CSU regional group in parliament and deputy CDU/CSU chief whip, 1961–1965 minister of the interior, 1965–1969 minister of food, agriculture and forestries, 1970–1976 head of CDU/CSU parliamentary group budget, taxes and finances working party.

Höffner, Joseph, Dr. 1906–1987, 1932 dt. Priester, Mitgl. d. wissenschaftl. Beirats beim Bundesministerium f. Arbeit u. Sozialordnung, f. Familie u. Jugend u. f. Wohnungswesen, Städtebau u. Raumordnung, 1962 Bischof v. Münster, 1969 Erzbischof v. Köln u. Kardinal, 1976–1987 Vorsitzender d. Dt. Bischofskonferenz.

Höffner, Joseph, Dr. 1906–1987, 1932 German priest, member of scientific advisory body at ministries of labor and social order, family and youth, and housing, urban construction and planning, 1962 bishop of Münster, 1969 archbishop of Cologne and cardinal, 1976–1987 chairman of German bishops' conference.

Holleben, Ehrenfried von 1909–1988, dt. Jurist u. Diplomat, 1953–1956 Konsul in Glasgow, 1956–1959 Leiter d. Rechts- u. Konsularabt. d. dt. Botschaft in London, 1960 stellv., 1962 Chef d. Protokolls in Bonn, 1966–1970 Botschafter in Rio de Janeiro, 1971–1974 dt. Botschafter in Lissabon.

Holleben, Ehrenfried von 1909–1988, German lawyer and diplomat, 1953–1956 consul in Glasgow, 1956–1959 head of legal and consular department of German embassy in London, 1960 deputy chief and 1962 chief of protocol in Bonn, 1966–1970 ambassador in Rio de Janeiro, 1971–1974 German ambassador in Lisbon.

Hombach, Bodo geb. 1952, dt. Manager u. Politiker, seit 1971 SPD-Mitgl., Wahlkampfberater, 1979–1981 stellv., 1981–1991 SPD-Landesgeschäftsführer in Nordrhein-Westfalen, 1990 MdL, dort bis 1998 wirtschaftspolit. Sprecher d. SPD-Landtagsfraktion, seit 1998 Wirtschafts- u. Verkehrsminister in Nordrhein-Westfalen, 1998 zum Kanzleramtsminister ernannt.

Hombach, Bodo b. 1952, German manager and politician, since 1971 member of SPD, election campaign adviser, 1979–1981 SPD *Land* deputy manager and 1981–1991 manager for North Rhine-Westphalia, 1990 MdL and until 1998 economic policy spokesman for SPD *Landtag* group, 1998 minister of economics and transport in North Rhine-Westphalia, also 1998 appointed minister at chancellery.

Honecker, Erich 1912–1994, DDR-Politiker, 1926 Mitgl. im Kommunist. Jugendverband Deutschl., 1929 KPD-Mitgl., 1937–1945 Zuchthaus, 1946–1955 Vorsitzender d. FDJ, ab 1946 Mitgl. im ZK d. SED, 1950 Mitgl. im SED-PB, 1958 Sekretär d. ZK f. Sicherheitsfragen, 1971 Leiter d. Nationalen Verteidigungsrates, 1971–1989 1. Sekretär d. ZK, 1976–1989 Staatsratsvorsitzender, 1991–1992 Asyl in d. chilen. Botschaft, 1993 Exil in Chile.

Honecker, Erich 1912–1994, GDR politician, 1926 member of German communist youth association, 1929 member of KPD, 1937–1945 penitentiary, 1946–1955 FDJ chairman, from 1946 member of SED central committee, 1950 member of SED PB, 1958 central committee secretary for security matters, 1971 head of national defense council, 1971–1989 first secretary of central

---

committee, 1976–1989 chairman of state council, 1991–1992 political asylum at Chilean embassy, 1993 exile in Chile.

Hupka, Herbert, Dr. phil. (1939) 1915–1997, dt. Journalist u. Politiker, 1958–1964 Pressereferent d. Kuratoriums »Unteilbares Deutschl«. in Bonn, 1955–1972 SPD-Mitgl., 1969 f. d. SPD, 1972–1987 f. d. CDU MdB, 1976–1990 Vorsitzender d. Kommission f. Volksgruppenrecht u. Aussiedlerfragen d. CDU/CSU-Bundestagsfraktion.

Hupka, Herbert, Dr. phil. (1939) b. 1915, German journalist and politician, 1958–1964 press adviser at committee for "indivisible Germany" in Bonn, 1955–1972 member of SPD, 1969 SPD MdB, 1972–1987 CDU MdB, 1976–1990 chairman of CDU/CSU parliamentary group commission for ethnic group rights and issues relating to repatriated ethnic Germans.

Hurd, Douglas geb. 1930, brit. Politiker u. Diplomat, 1954 als 3. Sekretär Vertreter in Beijing, 1956 Vertreter bei d. UN, 1963–1966 in d. brit. Botschaft in Rom, 1970 Polit. Sekretär d. Premierministers, ab 1974 Mitgl. d. Unterhauses, 1979 Staatsminister im Außenministerium, 1983 im Innenministerium, 1984 Secretary of State f. Nordirland, 1985 Innenminister, 1989–1995 Außenminister.

Hurd, Douglas b. 1930, British politician and diplomat, 1954 representative in Beijing (third secretary), 1956 UN representative, 1963–1966 at British embassy in Rome, 1970 prime minister's political secretary, from 1974 member of House of Commons, 1979 minister of state at foreign office, 1983 at home office, 1984 secretary of state for Northern Ireland, 1985 home secretary, 1989–1995 foreign secretary.

J

Jahn, Gerhard geb. 1927, dt. Politiker u. Jurist, 1956–1962 Leiter d. Marburger SPD-Fraktion im Stadtrat, 1962–1974 Stadtverordnetenvorsteher, 1957–1990 MdB f. d. SPD, 1961, 1965–1967 u. 1974–1990 Parlam. Geschäftsführer d. SPD-Fraktion, 1967–1969 Parlam. Staatssekretär im Auswärtigen Amt, 1969–1974 Bundesjustizminister, 1975–1979 u. 1981/82 Vertreter d. BRD in d. UN-Menschenrechtskommission.

Jahn, Gerhard b. 1927, German politician and lawyer, 1956–1962 leader of Marburg town council SPD group, 1962–1974 chairman of town council, 1957–1990 SPD MdB, 1961, 1965–1967 and 1974–1990 SPD parliamentary group manager, 1967–1969 parliamentary state secretary at foreign office, 1969–1974 justice minister, 1975–1979 and 1981/82 FRG representative on UN commission on human rights.

Jedrychowski, Stefan, Dr. jur. 1910, poln. Politiker u. Diplomat, 1940 Abgeord. d. litauischen Nationalversammlung, 1944 diplom. Vertreter Polens bei d. Sowjetregierung, 1944 Leitung d. Informations- u. Propagandaabt., 1944/45 Vertreter Polens in Frankr., 1945–1947 Minister f. Schiffahrt u. Außenhandel, 1945– 1975 Mitgl. d. ZK d. AP,1952–1957 stellv. Ministerpräsident, 1968–1971 poln. Außenminister, sodann bis 1974 Finanzminister, 1975 poln. Botschafter in Ungarn.

Jedrychowski, Stefan, Dr. jur. 1910, Polish politician and diplomat, 1940 member of Lithuanian national assembly, 1944 Poland's diplomatic representative to the Soviet government, 1944 head of information and propaganda department, 1944/45 Poland's representative in France, 1945–1947 minister of shipping and foreign trade, 1945–1975 member of AP central committee, 1952–1957 deputy prime minister, 1968–1971 Polish foreign minister, then until 1974 finance minister, 1975 Polish ambassador to Hungary.

Jelzin, Boris Nikolajewitsch geb. 1931, russ. Politiker u. Ing., 1961–1990 Mitgl. d. KPdSU, 1981 Mitgl. d. ZK d. KPdSU, ab 1984 Mitgl. d. Präsidiums d. Obersten Sowjet d. UdSSR, 1985 Leiter d. ZK-Abt. f. Bauwesen, ebenso Moskauer Parteichef, 1989 in d. »Kongreß d. Volksdeputierten« gewählt, März 1991 u. 1996 zum ersten direkt gewählten Präsidenten d. Russ. Föderation gewählt, ab Nov. 1991/1992 Regierungschef, 1992 auch Verteidigungsminister.

Yeltsin, Boris Nikolayevich b. 1931, Russian politician and engineer, 1961–1990 member of CPSU, 1981 member of CPSU central committee, from 1984 member of presidium of USSR supreme soviet, 1985 head of central committee construction department, and party chief in Moscow, 1989 elected to "congress of people's deputies", March 1991 and 1996 first directly elected president of the Russian federation, from Nov. 1991/1992 head of government, 1992 also defense minister.

Jenninger, Philipp, Dr. jur. (1957) geb. 1932, dt. Jurist, Politiker u. Diplomat, 1969–1990 MdB f. d. CDU, 1975–1982 1. Parlam. Geschäftsführer d. CDU/CSU-Bundestagsfraktion, 1982–1984 Staatsminister im Bundeskanzleramt, 1984–1988 Bundestagspräsident (Rücktritt), 1991–1995 dt. Botschafter in Österr., 1995–1997 beim Heiligen Stuhl in Rom.

Jenninger, Philipp, Dr. jur. (1957) b. 1932, German lawyer, politician and diplomat, 1969–1990 CDU MdB, 1975–1982 CDU/CSU senior parliamentary manager, 1982–1984 minister of state at chancellery, 1984–1988 president of Bundestag (resigned), 1991–1995 German ambassador to Austria, 1995–1997 at Holy See in Rome.

Jodl, Alfred 1890–1946, ab 1912 dt. Leutnant, 1935 Oberst, 1939 Generalmajor, 1940 Chef d. Wehrmachtführungsstabes, General d. Artillerie, 1944 Generaloberst, 1946 in Nürnberg zum Tode verurteilt

Jodl, Alfred 1890–1946, from 1912 German lieutenant, 1935 colonel, 1939 major general, 1940 chief of army command staff, artillery general, 1944 general, 1946 sentenced to death at Nuremberg.

Johnson, Lyndon Baines 1908–1973, amerik. Politiker (Demokrat), 1937–1949 Abgeord. im Repräsentantenhaus, 1949–1961 Senator, 1951–1961 Fraktionsvorsitzender d. Demokraten, Nov. 1960 zum Vizepräsidenten gewählt, Nov. 1963–1969 US-Präsident.

Johnson, Lyndon Baines 1908–1973, American politician (Democrat), 1937–1949 member of House of Representatives, 1949–1961 senator, 1951–1961 Democrat floor leader, Nov. 1960 elected vice president, Nov. 1963–1969 US President.

Jonasson, Hermann 1896–1976, isländ. Rechtsanwalt u. Politiker, 1928–1934 Polizeichef v. Reykjavik, 1934 MdP f. d. Fortschrittspartei, 1934–1942 Premierminister, ab 1944 Vorsitzender d. Partei, 1950–1953 Landwirtschaftsminister, 1956–1958 Ministerpräsident

Jonasson, Hermann 1896–1976, Icelandic lawyer and politician, 1928–1934 chief of police of Reykjavik, 1934 Progressive Party MP, 1934–1942 prime minister, from 1944 party chairman, 1950–1953 agriculture minister, 1956–1958 minister president.

Jospin, Lionel Robert geb. 1937, frz. Politiker, 1965–1970 Sekretär im Außenministerium, 1971 Mitgl. d. PS, 1975 Minister f. »Beziehungen zur Dritten Welt«, 1979 Minister f. außenpolit. Beziehungen, 1981–1988 Mitgl. d. Nationalversammlung, 1981–1987 u. ab 1995 Parteivorsitzender, 1988–1992 Ressortchef f. Erziehung, Forschung u. Sport, 1995 Präsidentschaftskandidat, 1997 zum Ministerpräsidenten gewählt.

Jospin, Lionel Robert b. 1937, French politician, 1965–1970 secretary at foreign ministry, 1971 member of PS, 1975 minister for "third world relations", 1979 Minister of foreign affairs, 1981–1988 member of national assembly, 1981–1987 and from 1995 party chairman, 1988–1992 in charge of education, research and sport, 1995 presidential candidate.

Juliana Louise Emma Marie Wilhelmina von Oranien-Nassau, Dr. phil. geb. 1909, 1948–1980 Königin d. Niederlande, seit 1937 mit Prinz Bernhard zu Lippe-Biesterfeld verheiratet.

Juliana Louise Emma Marie Wilhelmina of Orange-Nassau (Dr. phil.), b. 1909, 1948–1980 Queen of the Netherlands, since 1937 married to Prince Bernhard of Lippe-Biesterfeld.

K

Kaisen, Wilhelm 1887–1979, dt. Politiker, 1905 Mitgl. d. sozialdemokrat. Partei in Hamburg, 1919–1926 Parteijournalist in Bremen, 1921 Mitgl. d. Bremer Bürgerschaft, 1927–1933 u. ab 1945 Senator f. Wohlfahrt, 1945–1965 Bürgermeister v. Bremen, ab 1946 Senats-Präsident u. bis 1950 Mitgl. im SPD-Bundesvorstand.

Kaisen, Wilhelm 1887–1979, German politician, 1905 member of Social Democratic Party in Hamburg, 1919–1926 party journalist in Bremen, 1921 member of Bremen city parliament, 1927–1933 and from 1945 senator for welfare, 1945–1965 mayor of Bremen, from 1946 president of senate and until 1950 member of SPD party executive.

Kaiser, Jakob 1888–1961, dt. Buchbinder u. Politiker, 1912 Mitgl. d. Zentrums, 1928–1933 Mitgl. d. Zentrum-Reichsvorstandes, 1932/33 MdR, 1945 Mitbegr. d. CDU in Berlin u. d. SBZ, 1945 1. Vorsitzender d. CDU in d. SBZ, 1946–1949 Stadtverordneter, 1948/49 MdPR f. West-Berlin, 1949–1957 MdB, Bundesminister f. Gesamtdeutsche Fragen, 1950– 1961 Vorsitzender d. Exil-CDU, 1950–1958 stellv. CDU-Vorsitzender d. BRD, 1958–1961 Ehrenvorsitzender.

Kaiser, Jakob 1888–1961, German bookbinder and politician, 1912 member of Center Party, 1928–1933 member of Reich Center Party executive, 1932/33 MdR, 1945 co-founder of CDU in Berlin and SBZ, 1945 first party chairman of CDU in SBZ, 1946–1949 member of city parliament, 1948/49 MdPR for West Berlin, 1949–1957 MdB, minister for all-German affairs, 1950–1961 chairman of exiled CDU, 1950–1958 deputy chairman of CDU in FRG, 1958–1961 honorary chairman.

Kaltenbrunner, Ernst, Dr. (1926) 1903–1946, österr. Anwalt bis 1935, 1932 Eintritt in d. österr. NSDAP u. SS, 1938 Staatssekretär f. öffentl. Sicherheit, SS-Gruppenführer u. MdR, 1941 Generalleutnant d. Polizei, 1943 Führung d. Reichssicherheitshauptamtes in Berlin, 1944 Übernahme d. Nachrichten- u. Abwehrdienstes, 1946 in Nürnberg hingerichtet

Kaltenbrunner, Ernst, Dr. (1926) 1903–1946, Austrian lawyer until 1935, 1932 joined Austrian NSDAP and SS, 1938 state secretary for public security, SS group leader and MdR, 1941 lieutenant general of police, 1943 in charge of Reich security head office in

Berlin, 1944 took over intelligence services, executed 1946 at Nuremberg.

Karamanlis, Konstantin 1907–1998, griech. Rechtsanwalt u. Staatsmann, 1935–1952 MdP f. d. Volkspartei, 1946 Arbeitsminister, 1947 Transportminister, 1948 Minister f. Verkehr, dann Wohlfahrts- u. Sozialminister, 1952 Leiter d. Ministeriums f. öffentl. Arbeiten, 1954 Minister f. Verkehr, 1956 Gründer d. Nationalradikalen Union (ERE), bis 1963 Regierungschef, 1974 Gründer d. ND, bis 1980 Regierungschef, 1980–1985 sowie 1990–1995 Staatspräsident.

Karamanlis, Konstantin 1907–1998, Greek lawyer and statesman, 1935–1952 People's party MP, 1946 minister of labor, 1947 minister of transport, 1948 minister of road traffic, then social and welfare minister, 1952 head of ministry of public works, 1954 minister of road traffic, 1956 founder of National Radical Union (ERE), until 1963 head of government, 1974 founder of ND, until 1980 head of government, 1980–1985 and 1990–1995 President.

Katzer, Hans 1919–1996, dt. Politiker, ab 1945 CDU-Mitgl., 1950–1957 Mitgl. d. Kölner Stadtrats f. d. CDU, 1957–1980 MdB, 1963–1977 Vorsitzender d. CDU-Sozialausschüsse d. CDA, 1965–1969 Bundesminister f. Arbeit u. Sozialordnung, ab 1969 stellv. Fraktionsvorsitzender, bis 1981 CDU-Präsidiumsmitgl., 1977 erster Präsident d. EUCDA, 1979–1982 MdEP.

Katzer, Hans 1919–1996, German politician, from 1945 member of CDU, 1950–1957 CDU member of Cologne city council, 1957–1980 MdB, 1963–1977 chairman of CDU social committees of CDA, 1965–1969 minister of labor and social order, from 1969 deputy whip, until 1981 member of CDU presidium, 1977 first president of EUCDA, 1979–1982 MEP.

Keita, Modibo 1915–1977, afrikan. Politiker, 1946 Mitgl. d. linken RDA, 1948 Mitgl. d. ersten Territorialversammlung d. Frz. Sudan, später dort Vizepräsident, mehrfacher Bürgermeister v. Bamako, 1956 als Sudan-Abgeord. Mitgl. u. kurz Vizepräsident d. frz. Nationalversammlung, 1956 Staatssekretär f. d. Überseeischen Gebiete, 1959 Regierungschef d. Sudan u. Ministerpräsident d. Mali-Föderation, 1960–1968 Staats- u. Regierungschef v. Mali.

Keita, Modibo 1915–1977, African politician, 1946 member of left-wing RDA, 1948 member of first territorial assembly of French Sudan, later vice president there, several times mayor of Bamako, 1956 as Sudanese delegate member, and briefly vice president of French national assembly, 1956 state secretary for the overseas territories, 1959 head of government of Sudan and prime minister of Mali federation, 1960–1968 head of state and government of Mali.

Keitel, Wilhelm 1882–1946, 1930–1934 Leiter d. Heeresorganisationsabt. im Truppenamt, 1934 Generalmajor, 1934–1938 Chef d. Wehrmachtamtes im Reichskriegsministerium, 1936 Generalleutnant, 1937 General d. Artillerie, 1938–1945 Chef d. Oberkommandos d. Wehrmacht, 1940 Generalfeldmarschall, 1946 in Nürnberg hingerichtet.

Keitel, Wilhelm 1882–1946, 1930–1934 head of army organization department of armed forces office, 1934 major general, 1934–1938 head of Reich war ministry army office, 1936 lieutenant general, 1937 artillery general, 1938–1945 chief of army supreme commandt, 1940 general field marshal, executed at Nuremberg.

Kelly, Petra 1947–1992, Politologin u. dt. Politikerin, 1971–1982 Mitarbeiterin d. EG in Brüssel, 1973 Gründerin d. »G.P. Kelly-Vereinigung zur Unterstützung d. Krebsforschung f. Kinder e.V.«, 1979 Gründungsmitgl. d. Grünen, 1980–1982 Sprecherin d. Bundesvorstandes, 1983–1985 MdB u. Fraktionssprecherin, 1987–1990 Parteivorsitzende d. Grünen, vermutlich Freitod zusammen mit Gert Bastian.

Kelly, Petra 1947–1992, German political scientist and politician, 1971–1982 worked at EC in Brussels, 1973 founder of "G.P. Kelly Union for the promotion of research into child cancer Inc.", 1979 founding member of the Greens, 1980–1982 federal executive spokesperson, 1983–1985 MdB and parliamentary group spokesperson, 1987–1990 Green party chairman, suspected suicide together with Gert Bastian.

Kennedy, Edward Moore geb. 1932, amerik. Anwalt u. Politiker (Demokrat), Bruder v. John F. Kennedy, seit 1962 Senator v. Massachusetts.

Kennedy, Edward Moore b. 1932, American lawyer and politician (Democrat), brother of John F. Kennedy, since 1962 senator from Massachusetts.

Kennedy, John Fitzgerald, Dr. jur. h.c. 1917–1963 (ermordet), amerik. Politiker (Demokrat), ab 1946 Kongreßabgeord., ab 1953 Senator v. Massachusetts, Jan. 1961– Nov. 1963 US-Präsident.

Kennedy, John Fitzgerald, Dr. jur. h.c. 1917–1963 (assassinated), American politician (Democrat), from 1946 member of Congress, from 1953 senator from Massachusetts, Jan. 1961– Nov. 1963 US President.

Kennedy, Robert Francis 1925–1968 (ermordet), amerik. Jurist u. Politiker (Demokrat), Bruder v. John F. Kennedy, 1955 Anwalt beim Obersten US-Gerichtshof, 1960 Wahlkampfleiter für J.F.K., sodann Justizminister (Rücktritt im Sept. 1964) u. engster Berater von J.F.K., 1964 Senator im Kongreß f. New York, 1968 Bewerber f. d. Präsidentschaft.

Kennedy, Robert Francis 1925–1968 (assassinated), American lawyer and politician (Democrat), brother of John F. Kennedy, 1955 lawyer at US supreme court, 1960 election campaign manager for J.F.K., then attorney general (resigned Sept. 1964) and closest adviser to J.F.K., 1964 senator for New York in Congress, 1968 presidential candidate.

Kiechle, Ignaz geb. 1930, dt. Landwirtschaftspolitiker, seit 1953 CSU-Mitgl., 1960–1972 Ortsvorsitzender d. CSU in St. Mang, 1972–1982 Kreisvorsitzender v. Oberallgäu, 1969– 1995 MdB, 1982/83 stellv. Vorsitzender d. CDU/ CSU-Fraktion, 1983–1993 Bundesminister f. Ernährung, Landwirtsch. u. Forsten.

Kiechle, Ignaz b. 1930, German agricultural politician, since 1953 member of CSU, 1960–1972 local CDU chairman in St. Mang, 1972–1982 district chairman of Oberallgäu, 1969–1995 MdB, 1982/83 CDU/CSU deputy whip, 1983–1993 minister of food, agriculture and forestries.

Kiesinger, Kurt Georg 1904–1988, dt. Rechtsanwalt u. Politiker, 1933–1945 NSDAP-Mitgl., 1943 stellv. Abteilungsleiter in d. Rundfunkabt. d. Reichsaußenministeriums, 1949–1958 u. 1969–1980 MdB f. d. CDU, ab 1950 Parteivorstandsmitgl., 1950–1958 Mitgl. d. Parlam. Versammlung d. Europarats, 1958–1966 Ministerpräsident v. Baden-Württemberg, 1960–1966 MdL, 1966–1969 Bundeskanzler, 1967–1971 CDU-Bundesvorsitzender

Kiesinger, Kurt Georg, 1904–1988, German lawyer and politician, 1933–1945 member of NSDAP, 1943 deputy head of Reich foreign ministry broadcasting department, 1949–1958 and 1969–1980 CDU MdB, from 1950 member of party executive, 1950–1958 member of Council of Europe parliamentary assembly, 1958–1966 minister president of Baden-Württemberg, 1960–1966 MdL, 1966–1969 federal chancellor, 1967–1971 federal CDU party chairman.

Kießling, Günter, Dr. rer. pol. geb. 1925, 1956 Eintritt in d. dt. Bundeswehr, 1971 General, 1976 Generalmajor, 1979 Generalleutnant, 1982–1984 Stellv. d. Obersten Alliierten Befehlshabers in Europa

Kießling, Günter, Dr. rer. pol. b. 1925, 1956 joined German army, 1971 general, 1976 major general, 1979 lieutenant general, 1982–1984 deputy supreme Allied commander in Europe.

Kinkel, Klaus, Dr. (1964) geb. 1936, dt. Jurist u. Politiker, 1991 FDP-Mitglied, 1970–1974 persönl. Referent d. Bundesministers d. Innern u. Leiter seines Ministerbüros, 1974–1977 Leiter des Leitungsstabes, 1977–1979 Leiter d. Planungsstabes im Auswärtigen Amt, 1979–1982 Präsident d. Bundesnachrichtendienstes, 1982–1991 Staatssekretär im Bundesministerium d. Justiz, 1991/92 Bundesminister d. Justiz, 1993–1995 Bundesvorsitzender d. FDP, 1992– 1998 Bundesminister d. Auswärtigen, 1993–1998 Vizekanzler, seit 1994 MdB, seit 1998 stellv. Vorsitzender d. Bundestagsfraktion.

Kinkel, Klaus, Dr. (1964) b. 1936, German lawyer and politician, 1991 member of FDP, 1970–1974 personal adviser to minister of the interior and head of his ministerial office, 1974–1977 head of management staff, 1977–1979 head of foreign office planning staff, 1979–1982 president of federal intelligence service, 1982–1991 state secretary at ministry of justice, 1991/92 minister of justice, 1993–1995 FDP federal party chairman, 1992–1998 foreign minister, 1993–1998 deputy chancellor, since 1994 MdB, since 1998 deputy whip and parliamentary group spokesman on sports policy.

Kirchbach, Hans-Peter von geb. 1941, dt. General, 1960 Eintritt in d. Bundeswehr, 1962 Leutnant, 1974–1976 Hilfsreferent im Führungsstab d. Heeres im Verteidigungsministerium in Bonn, anschließend Generalstabsoffizier, 1992–1994 Abteilungsleiter im Führungsstab d. Heeres in Bonn, dann Generalmajor, 1997 Befehlshaber u. Einsatzleiter während d. Oder-Hochwassers, 1998 Generalleutnant, zum 1.4.99 als Generalinspektor d. Bundeswehr vorgesehen.

Kirchbach, Hans-Peter von b. 1941, German general, 1960 joined army, 1962 lieutenant, 1974–1976 assistant adviser to army command staff at defense ministry in Bonn, subsequently general staff officer, 1992–1994 departmental head at army command staff in Bonn, then major general, 1997 commander and head of operations during the Oder flood, 1998 lieutenant general, from 1.4.99 in mind for inspector general of the army.

Kirchner, Martin geb. 1949, dt. Diplom-Jurist u. Politiker, 1967–1990 CDU-Mitgl. d. DDR, 1989/90 CDU-Generalsekretär, 1990 MdVK.

Kirchner, Martin b. 1949, German law graduate and politician, 1967–1990 member of GDR CDU, 1989/90 CDU general secretary, 1990 member of Volkskammer.

Kirkpatrick, Sir (1948) Ivone 1897–1964, brit. Diplomat, 1919/20 als 3. Sekretär in d. brit. Botschaft in Rio de Janeiro, 1921 als 2. u. ab 1928 als 1. Sekretär im Foreign Office, 1933–1938 1. Sekretär in d. brit. Botschaft in Berlin, 1940/41 Leiter d. Auslandsabt. d. Informationsministeriums in London, 1945 stellv. Untersekretär im Foreign Office, 1948 Leiter d. Deutschlandabt., 1950– 1953 Hoher brit. Kommissar in Deutschl., sodann bis 1957 ständiger Untersekretär im Foreign Office.

Kirkpatrick, Sir (1948) Ivone 1897–1964, British diplomat, 1919/20 third secretary at British embassy in Rio de Janeiro, 1921 second and from 1928 first secretary at Foreign Office, 1933–1938 first secretary at British embassy in Berlin, 1940/41 head of ministry of information aliens department in London, 1945 deputy under-secretary at Foreign Office, 1948 head of German department, 1950–1953 British High Commissioner in Germany, then until 1957 permanent under-secretary at Foreign Office.

Kissinger, Henry Alfred, Prof., Ph. D. (1954) geb. 1923 in Deutschl., amerik. Politiker u. Hochschullehrer, 1938 Auswanderung in d. USA, 1950–1960 Berater d. Behörde f. Waffenentwicklung beim Vereinigten Generalstab, 1961– 1968 Berater d. US-Agentur f. Waffenkontrolle u. Abrüstungsfragen, 1968 Außen- u. Sicherheitspolit. Berater d. US-Präsidenten, außerdem Sept. 1973–1977 Außenminister, 1983 Leiter d. überparteil. Mittelamerika-Kommission.

Kissinger, Henry Alfred, professor, Ph. D. (1954) b. 1923 in Germany, American politician and university lecturer, 1938 emigrated to US, 1950–1960 adviser to joint general staff weapons development authority, 1961–1968 adviser to US weapons control and disarmament issues agency, 1968 foreign and security policy adviser to US President, also Sept. 1973–1977 secretary of state, 1983 head of non-party Central American Commission.

Klein, Hans 1931–1996, dt. Journalist u. Politiker, 1959– 1965 Presseattaché an d. dt. Botschaften in Jordanien, Syrien, Irak u. Indonesien, 1972 CSU-Eintritt, 1976–1996 MdB, 1982–1987 Außenpolit. Sprecher d. CDU/CSU-Fraktion, 1987–1990 Bundesminister f. besondere Aufgaben u. Chef d. Presse- u. Informationsamtes d. Bundesregierung, 1990–1996 Bundestagsvizepräsident.

Klein, Hans 1931–1996, German journalist and politician, 1959–1965 press attaché at German embassies in Jordan, Syria, Iraq and Indonesia, 1972 joined CSU, 1976–1996 MdB, 1982– 1987 CDU/CSU parliamentary group foreign policy spokesman, 1987–1990 minister without portfolio and head of government press and information office, 1990–1996 deputy president of *Bundestag.*

Kohl, Hannelore, (geb. Renner) geb. 1933, dt. Diplomdolmetscherin, Präsidentin d. »Kuratoriums ZNS« (f. Unfallverletzte mit Schäden d. Zentralnervensystems), seit 1960 Ehefrau v. Helmut Kohl.

Kohl, Hannelore, (née Renner) b. 1933, German graduate interpreter, president of "ZNS Committee" (for accident victims with injuries to central nervous system), since 1960 married to Helmut Kohl.

Kohl, Helmut, Dr. phil. (1958) geb. 1930, Politiker, seit 1947 CDU-Mitgl., 1954 stellv. Landesvorsitzender d. JU Rheinland-Pfalz, 1960–1966 Vorsitzender d. CDU-Stadtratsfraktion Ludwigshafen, 1959 MdL v. Rheinland-Pfalz, 1961 stellv. Vorsitzender, 1963–1969 Vorsitzender d. CDU-Landtagsfraktion, Mitgl. d. Bundesvorstandes, 1966–1973 Landesvorsitzender d. CDU v. Rheinland-Pfalz, 1969 stellv. u. 1973–1998 Bundesvorsitzender, 1969–1976 Ministerpräsident v. Rheinland-Pfalz, seit 1976 MdB, 1976–1982 Vorsitzender d. CDU/CSU-Fraktion, 1982–1998 Bundeskanzler, seit Nov. 1998 Ehrenvorsitzender d. CDU.

Kohl, Helmut, Dr. phil. (1958) b. 1930, politician, since 1947 member of CDU, 1954 deputy *Land* chairman of Young Union in Rhineland-Palatinate, 1960–1966 chairman of Ludwigshafen CDU city council group, 1959 MdL Rhineland-Palatinate, 1961 CDU deputy whip and 1963–1969 chief whip in *Landtag,* member of federal executive, 1966–1973 *Land* CDU chairman of Rhineland-Palatinate, 1969 deputy federal chairman and 1973–1998 chairman, 1969–1976 minister president of Rhineland-Palatinate, since 1976 MdB, 1976–1982 CDU/CSU chief whip, 1982–1998 federal chancellor, since Nov. 1998 honorary chairman of CDU.

Kohl, Michael, Dr. jur. (1956) 1929–1981, dt. Politiker u. Diplomat, ab 1948 SED-Mitgl., 1958–1963 Abgeord. d. Bezirkstags Gera, 1961–1965 Abteilungsleiter u. Kollegiumsmitgl. im Ministerium f. Auswärtige Angelegenheiten, 1965–1973 Staatssekretär beim Ministerrat, ab 1971 Mitgl. d. Außenpolit. Kommission u. Westkommission beim PB d. ZK d. SED, 1974–1978 Leiter d. Ständigen Vertretung d. DDR in d. BRD, 1978 stellv. Außenminister.

Kohl, Michael, Dr. jur. (1956) 1929–1981, German politician and diplomat, from 1948 member of SED, 1958–1963 member of Gera district council, 1961–1965 departmental head and member of ministry of foreign affairs administrative staff, 1965–1973 state secretary at council of ministers, from 1971 member of foreign policy commission and Western commission of PB of SED central committee, 1974–1978 head of GDR permanent mission in FRG, 1978 deputy foreign minister.

Kokoschka, Oskar, Prof. 1886–1980, österr. Maler, Graphiker u. Schriftsteller, 1919–1924 Professor d. Kunstakademie, 1947 Annahme d. brit. Staatsbürgerschaft.

Kokoschka, Oskar, professor, 1886–1980, Austrian painter, graphic artist and writer, 1919–1924 professor at academy of art, 1947 took British citizenship.

Kopf, Hinrich Wilhelm 1893–1961, dt. Politiker, 1945 Oberpräsident d. Provinz Hannover, ab 1946 MdL f. d. SPD, 1946–1955 u. 1959– 1961 Ministerpräsident d. Landes Hannover bzw. v. Niedersachsen, 1957–1959 niedersächs. Innenminister u. stellv. Ministerpräsident.

Kopf, Hinrich Wilhelm 1893–1961, German politician, 1945 senior president of Hanover province, from 1946 SPD MdL, 1946–1955 and 1959–1961 minister president of the *Land* Hanover, subsequently Lower Saxony, 1957–1959 minister of the interior and deputy minister president of Lower Saxony.

Köprülü, Mehmed Fuat, Dr. 1890–1966, türk. Wissenschaftler u. Politiker, 1925 Berater d. Ministeriums f. Erziehung, 1935 in d. Nationalversammlung gewählt, 1946 Mitbegr. d. DP, 1950–1956 Außenminister (Rücktritt).

Köprülü, Mehmed Fuat, Dr. 1890–1966, Turkish scientist and politician, 1925 adviser to ministry of education, 1935 elected to national assembly, 1946 co-founder of DP, 1950–1956 foreign minister (resigned).

Koschnick, Hans geb. 1929, dt. SPD-Politiker, 1955–1963 Mitgl. d. Bremer Bürgerschaft, 1963 Innensenator v. Bremen, 1965 2. Bürgermeister u. stellv. Senatspräsident, 1967–1985 Bürgermeister u. Präsident d. Senats, 1975–1979 stellv. SPD-Bundesvorsitzender, 1987–1994 MdB, 1994–1996 EU-Administrator in Mostar.

Koschnick, Hans b. 1929, German politician (SPD), 1955–1963 member of Bremen city parliament, 1963 Bremen senator for the interior, 1965 second mayor and deputy president of senate, 1967–1985 mayor and president of senate, 1975–1979 SPD deputy federal chairman, 1987–1994 MdB, 1994–1996 EU administrator in Mostar.

Kossygin, Alexej Nikolajewitsch 1904–1980, sowjetruss. Politiker, 1927 KPdSU-Eintritt, 1938–1939 Oberbürgermeister v. Leningrad, 1939 Minister f. d. Textilindustrie, 1939–1980 Mitgl. d. ZK d. KPdSU, 1940–1946 u. 1957–1960 stellv. Ministerpräsident (stellv. Vorsitz. im Rat d. Volkskommissare), 1948–1952 Mitgl. d. PBs, 1956/57 1. stellv. Vorsitzender d. Staatl. Wirtschaftskommission d. Ministerrates d. UdSSR, 1960–1980 1. stellv. Ministerpräsident u. Vollmitgl. im PB, 1964–1980 Vorsitzender d. Ministerrates d. UdSSR.

Kosygin, Aleksey Nikolayevich 1904–1980, Soviet Russian politician, 1927 joined CPSU, 1938–1939 mayor of Leningrad, 1939 minister for textile industry, 1939–1980 member of CPSU central committee, 1940–1946 and 1957–1960 deputy prime minister (deputy chairman of council of people's commissars), 1948–1952 PB member, 1956/57 first deputy chairman of state economic commission of USSR council of ministers, 1960–1980 first deputy prime minister and full member of PB, 1964–1980 chairman of USSR council of ministers.

Kraske, Konrad, Dr. phil. (1951) geb. 1926, dt. Politiker, 1953 stellv., 1958–1970 Bundesgeschäftsführer d. CDU, 1965–1980 MdB, 1969 Mitgl. d. CDU-Bundesvorstands, 1971–1973 Generalsekretär, ab 1992 Vorsitzender d. ZDF-Fernsehrates, Vorstandsmitgl. d. Konrad-Adenauer-Stiftung.

Kraske, Konrad, Dr. phil. (1951) b. 1926, German politician, 1953 CDU deputy federal manager, then 1958–1970 manager, 1965–1980 MdB, 1969 member of CDU federal executive, 1971– 1973 general secretary, from 1992 chairman of ZDF TV council, member of management board of Konrad Adenauer foundation.

Krause, Günther, Dr. (1987) geb. 1953, Dipl.-Bauing. in d. DDR, 1987 Vorsitzender d. Kreisverbandes Bad Doberan, 1990 Vorsitzender d. CDU-Landesverbandes Mecklenburg-Vorpommern, MdVK u. Vorsitzender d. CDU-Fraktion, März-Okt. 1990 Parlam. Staatssekretär im Amt d. Ministerpräsidenten d. DDR, 1990–1994 MdB, 1990/91 Minister f. besondere Aufgaben, 1991–1993 Minister f. Verkehr (Rücktritt).

Krause, Günther, Dr. (1987) b. 1953, civil engineering graduate in GDR, from 1975 member of CDU, 1987 chairman of Bad Doberan district association, 1990 chairman of CDU *Land* association of Mecklenburg-Vorpommern, member of Volkskammer and CDU chief whip, March-Oct. 1990 parliamentary state secretary at GDR prime minister's office, 1990–1994 MdB, 1990/91 minister without portfolio, 1991–1993 minister of transport (resigned).

Krenz, Egon geb. 1937, SED-Politiker, Staatsratsvorsitzender, ab 1955 SED-Mitgl., 1973–1989 Mitgl. d. ZK d. SED, 1971–1990 MdVK, 1971–1976 Vorsitzender d. FDJ-Fraktion, 1971–1981 Mitgl. d. Präsidiums d. Volkskammer, 1974–1983 1. Sekretär d. Zentralrats d. FDJ, 1983–1989 Mitgl. d. PB u. Sekretär f. Sicherheit u. Kaderfragen d. ZK d. SED, 1981–1984 Mitgl. d. Staatsrats, Ende 1989 Generalsekretär d. ZK d. SED, Vorsitzender

d. Staatsrats u. d. Nationalen Verteidigungsrats, 1990 Ausschluß aus d. SED-PDS.

Krenz, Egon b. 1937, SED politician, from 1955 member of SED, 1973–1989 member of SED central committee, 1971–1990 member of Volkskammer, 1971–1976 FDJ chief whip, 1971–1981 member of Volkskammer presidium, 1974–1983 first secretary of FDJ central council, 1983–1989 PB member and SED central committee secretary for security and cadre matters, 1981–1984 member of state council, late 1989 general secretary of SED central committee, chairman of state council and of national defense council, 1990 expelled from SED-PDS.

Krone, Heinrich, Dr. phil. (1923) 1895–1989, dt. Lehrer u. Politiker, 1923 stellv. Generalsekretär d. Dt. Zentrumspartei, 1925–1933 MdR, ab 1934 Mitbegr. u. Organisator d. Caritas-Notwerks, 1945 Mitbegr. d. CDU, 1949–1969 MdB, 1955–1961 Vorsitzender d. CDU/CSU-Bundestagsfraktion, 1958–1964 stellv. Parteivorsitzender d. CDU, 1961–1966 Bundesminister f. besondere Aufgaben, 1967–1969 Sonderberater d. Kanzlers f. Schulfragen.

Krone, Heinrich, Dr. phil. (1923) 1895–1989, German teacher and politician, 1923 deputy general secretary of Center Party, 1925–1933 member of Reichstag, 1934 co-founder and organizer of Caritas aid organization, 1945 co-founder of CDU, 1949–1969 MdB, 1955–1961 CDU/CSU chief whip, 1958–1964 CDU deputy party chairman, 1961–1966 minister without portfolio, 1967–1969 special adviser to chancellor on school matters.

L

Lafontaine, Oskar geb. 1943, dt. Diplom-Physiker u. Politiker, 1966 SPD-Eintritt, 1974–1976 Bürgermeister, 1976–1985 Oberbürgermeister v. Saarbrücken, 1977–1996 Landesvorsitzender d. SPD Saarland, 1979 Mitgl. d. SPD-Bundesvorstandes, 1985–1998 Ministerpräsident v. Saarland, 1987 stellv. Bundesvorsitzender u. Geschäftsführender Vorsitzender d. SPD-Programmkommission, 1990 Spitzenkandidat, 1994–1999 MdB, 1995–1999 Bundesvorsitzender d. SPD (Rücktritt), Okt. 1998– März 1999 Bundesminister d. Finanzen (Rücktritt).

Lafontaine, Oskar b. 1943, German physics graduate and politician, 1966 joined SPD, 1974–1976 mayor and 1976–1985 senior mayor of Saarbrücken, 1977–1996 SPD *Land* chairman in Saarland, 1979 member of SPD federal executive, 1985–1998 minister president of Saarland, 1987 deputy federal chairman and managing chairman of SPD party program commission, 1990 front runner for leadership, 1994–1999 MdB, 1995–1999 SPD federal chairman (resigned), Oct. 1998–March 1999 federal finance minister (resigned).

Lahnstein, Manfred geb. 1937, dt. Dipl.-Kaufmann, Medienmanager, ab 1959 SPD-Mitgl., 1971–1973 Kabinettschef beim dt. EG-Vizepräsidenten, sodann Leiter d. wirtschaftspolit. Abt. im Bundeskanzleramt, dann 1974 Leiter d. finanzpolit. Grundsatzabt. im Finanzministerium, 1977 Staatssekretär f. Grundsatzfragen d. Finanzpolitik u. f. internat. u. nat. Währungspol., 1980–1982 Chef d. Bundeskanzleramtes, Apr.-Okt. 1982 Bundesminister d. Finanzen.

Lahnstein, Manfred b. 1937, German business studies graduate, media manager, from 1959 member of SPD, 1971–1973 cabinet chief for German EC vice president, then head of chancellery economic policy department, 1974 head of finance ministry department of fundamental financial policy, 1977 state secretary for fundamental financial policy issues and for international and national currency policy, 1980–1982 head of chancellery, Apr.-Oct. 1982 finance minister.

Lahr, Rolf 1908–1985, dt. Diplomat, ab 1953 im Auswärtigen Amt, Leiter d. Sonderreferats f. dt.-frz. Beziehungen, 1960/61 Vertreter d. BRD bei d. EG, sodann Staatssekretär im Auswärtigen Amt, 1969–1973 Botschafter in Rom.

Lahr, Rolf 1908–1985, German diplomat, from 1953 at foreign office, head of special section for Franco-German relations, 1960/61 FRG representative at EC, then state secretary at foreign office, 1969–1973 ambassador in Rome.

Lambsdorff, Otto Graf, Dr. jur. (1952) geb. 1926, dt. Rechtsanwalt u. Politiker, seit 1951 FDP-Mitgl., 1968–1978 Landesschatzmeister d. FDP in Nordrhein-Westfalen, 1972 Mitgl. d. FDP-Bundesvorstands, 1972–1998 MdB u. wirtschaftspolit. Sprecher d. FDP-Bundestagsfraktion, 1977–1984 Bundeswirtschaftsminister (Rücktritt), 1988–1993 Bundesvorsitzender.

Lambsdorff, Otto Count, Dr. jur. (1952) b. 1926, German lawyer and politician, since 1951 member of FDP, 1968–1978 FDP *Land* treasurer in North Rhine-Westphalia, 1972 member of FDP federal executive, 1972–1998 MdB and economic policy spokesman for FDP parliamentary group, 1977–1984 economics minister (resigned), 1988–1993 federal party chairman.

Lange, Halvard, Dr. h.c. (1955) 1902–1970, norweg. Politiker, 1933–1939 Mitgl. d. Exekutivkomitees d. norweg. AP, 1942–1945 in dt. KZs deportiert, 1946–1965 Leiter d. norweg. Außenministeriums, 1950–1969 MdP, 1962 Präsident d. OECD-Rates.

Lange, Halvard, Dr. h.c. (1955) 1902–1970, Norwegian politician, 1933–1939 member of executive committee of Norwegian Labor Party, 1942–1945 deported to German KZs, 1946–1965 head of Norwegian foreign ministry, 1950–1969 MP, 1962 president of OECD council.

Lauritzen, Lauritz, Dr. jur. (1936) 1910–1980, dt. Politiker, ab 1929 SPD-Mitgl., 1963 Minister f. Justiz u. Bundesangelegenheiten in Hessen, 1966/67 MdL v. Hessen, 1966–1974 Bundesminister f. Wohnungswesen u. Städtebau, 1969–1980 MdB, 1972–1974 Bundesminister f. Verkehr.

Lauritzen, Lauritz, Dr. jur. (1936) 1910–1980, German politician, since 1929 member of SPD, 1963 minister of justice and federal issues in Hessen, 1966/67 MdL Hessen, 1966–1974 federal minister of housing and urban construction, 1969–1980 MdB, 1972–1974 minister of transport.

Lattre de Tassigny, Jean-Joseph-Marie-Gabriel 1889–1952, frz. Marschall, ab 1943 Führer d. I. frz. Armee unter de Gaulle, 1945 Oberbefehlshaber d. frz. Besatzungstruppen in Deutschl.

Lattre de Tassigny, Jean-Joseph-Marie-Gabriel 1889–1952, French marshal, from 1943 head of I. French army under de Gaulle, 1945 supreme commander of French occupying forces in Germany.

Leber, Georg, Dr. jur. h.c. geb. 1920, dt. Politiker, 1947 SPD-Eintritt, 1957–1983 MdB, 1968–1973 Mitgl. im SPD-Präsidium, 1966–1978 Bundesminister f. Verkehr (Rücktritt), 1969 auch Minister f. d. Post- u. Fernmeldewesen, 1972–1978 Bundesverteidigungsminister, 1978–1982 Mitgl. d. Fraktionsvorstandes, 1979–1983 Vizepräsident d. Bundestage.

Leber, Georg, Dr. jur. h.c. b. 1920, German politician, 1947 joined SPD, 1957–1983 MdB, 1968–1973 member of SPD presidium, 1966–1978 minister of transport (resigned), 1969 also minister of post and telecommunications, 1972–1978 defense minister, 1978–1982 member of parliamentary group executive, 1979–1983 vice president of the Bundestag.

Lemmer, Ernst 1898–1970, dt. Journalist u. Politiker, 1924–1933 MdR f. d. DDP bzw. dt. Staatspartei, 1945 Mitbegr. d. CDU in d. SBZ, 1950–1969 MdA in Berlin, bis 1957 Fraktionsvorsitzender, 1952–1970 MdB (Berlin), 1956–1961 CDU-Landesvorsitzender Berlin, 1956–1962 Bundesminister f. d. Post- u. Fernmeldewesen, 1957 f. gesamtdt. Fragen, 1964/65 Bundesminister f. Vertriebene u Flüchtlinge, 1965–1969 Sonderbeauftragter d. Bundeskanzlers f. Berlin.

Lemmer, Ernst 1898–1970, German journalist and politician, 1924–1933 DDP/German State Party MdR, 1945 co-founder of CDU in SBZ, 1950–1969 MdA in Berlin, until 1957 chief whip, 1952–1970 MdB (Berlin), 1956–1961 CDU-*Land* chairman for Berlin, 1956–1962 federal minister of post and telecommunications, 1957 minister for all-German issues, 1964/65 minister for expellees and refugees, 1965–1969 chancellor's special envoy to Berlin.

Lenin, Wladimir Iljitsch (Deckname v.: W. I. Ulijanow) 1870–1924, russ. Revolutionär, Politiker u. Rechtsanwalt, Bolschewiki, ab 1917 Vorsitzender d. Rats d. Volkskommissare

Lenin, Vladimir Ilyitch (assumed name of V. I. Uljanov) 1870– 1924, Russian revolutionary, politician and lawyer, bolshevik, from 1917 chairman of soviet of people's commissars.

Leussink, Hans, Dr. h.c., Dr.-Ing. geb. 1912, dt. Ing. u. Rektor, 1960–1962 Präsident d. Westdt. Rektorenkonferenz, 1969–1972 Bundesminister f. Bildung u. Wissenschaft.

Leussink, Hans, Dr. h.c., Dr.-Ing. b. 1912, German engineer and university president, 1960–1962 president of conference of West German university presidents, 1969–1972 minister of education and science.

Lindrath, Hermann 1896–1960, Dr. d. Staatswissenschaft, Prokurist, Universitätsdozent, 1928–1933 Mitgl. d. DVP, 1929–1939 Direktor d. städt. Steuerverwaltung Halle, 1939–1945 Stadtoberverwaltungsrat, 1952 stellv. CDU-Vorsitzender, 1953–1960 MdB, 1957–1960 Bundesminister f. wirtschaftl. Besitz d. Bundes.

Lindrath, Hermann 1896–1960, Doctorate in politics, company secretary, university lecturer, 1928–1933 member of DVP, 1929–1939 director of municipal tax administration in Halle, 1939–1945 municipal chief councillor, 1952 CDU deputy chairman, 1953–1960 MdB, 1957–1960 minister for economic property of the *Bund*.

Linthorst Homan, Johannes 1903–1967, 1952–1958 Direktor im Amt f. Bauwesen, ab 1958 niederl. Vertreter bei d. EWG u. EURATOM.

Linthorst Homan, Johannes 1903–1967, 1952–1958 director at office of construction industry, from 1958 Netherlands EEC and EURATOM representative.

Lionaes, Aase geb. 1907, norweg. Politikerin, ab 1949 Mitgl. d. norweg. »Nobel Committee«, 1969–1979 Vorsitzende, 1946–1965 Mitgl. d. norweg. UN-Delegation.

Lionaes, Aase b. 1907, Norwegian politician, from 1949 member of Norwegian "Nobel Committee", 1969–1979 chairperson, 1946–1965 member of Norwegian UN delegation.

Lloyd, Selwyn 1904–1978, brit. Politiker u. Anwalt, 1945 Abgeord. im Unterhaus (Konservativer), 1951 Staatsminister im Foreign Office, 1954 Versorgungsminister, 1955 Verteidigungsminister, sodann bis 1960 Außenminister, 1960–1962 Schatzkanzler, 1963/64 Lordsiegelbewahrer, 1971–1976 Sprecher d. Unterhauses, anschließend Mitgl. d. Oberhauses.

Lloyd, Selwyn 1904–1978, British politician and lawyer, 1945 MP (Conservative), 1951 minister of state at the Foreign Office, 1954 minister of supply, 1955 defense minister, then until 1960 foreign secretary, 1960–1962 chancellor of the exchequer, 1963/64 lord keeper of the privy seal, 1971–1976 speaker of the House of Commons, then member of House of Lords.

Loewe, Lothar geb. 1929, dt. Fernsehjournalist, 1961–1967 u. 1978–1983 Rundfunk- u. Fernsehkorrespondent f. ARD in Washington, 1967–1970 ARD-Fernsehkorrespondent in Moskau, 1971–1974 Fernseh-Sonderkorrespondent f. aktuelle Berichterstattung (ARD), 1974–1976 Leiter d. DDR-Studios d. ARD in Ost-Berlin, 1983–1986 Intendant d. SFB in West-Berlin.

Loewe, Lothar b. 1929, German TV journalist, 1961–1967 and 1978–1983 ARD radio and TV correspondent in Washington, 1967–1970 ARD TV correspondent in Moscow, 1971–1974 ARD special current affairs correspondent, 1974–1976 head of ARD GDR studio in East Berlin, 1983–1986 general manager of SFB in West Berlin.

Löbe, Paul 1875–1967, dt. Schriftsetzer, Journalist u. Politiker, 1919 Mitgl. d. Weimarer Nationalversammlung u. Vizepräsident, 1920–1932 MdR u. Reichstagspräsident, 1945 SPD-Mitgl., 1948/49 MdPR, 1949 Präsident d. dt. Rates d. »Europa-Bewegung«.

Löbe, Paul 1875–1967, German typesetter, journalist and politician, 1919 member and vice president of Weimar national assembly, 1920–1932 member and president of Reichstag, 1945 member of SPD, 1948/49 MdPR, 1949 president of German council of "Europe movement".

Lorenz, Peter, Dr. h.c. 1922–1987, dt. Politiker, Rechtsanwalt u. Notar, ab 1945 CDU-Mitgl., 1946–1959 Vorsitzende d. JU in Berlin, ab 1954 MdA u. d. Fraktionsvorstands, 1961–1965 u. 1967–1969 stellv., ab 1969 CDU-Landesvorsitzender, 1967–1975 Vizepräsident 1975–1980 Präsident d. Abgeordnetenhauses, 1976–1987 MdB, 1982–1987 Parlam. Staatssekrtär im Bundeskanzleramt.

Lorenz, Peter, Dr. h.c. 1922–1987, German politician, lawyer and notary, from 1945 member of CDU, 1946–1959 chairman of Young Union in Berlin, from 1954 MdA and member of parliamentary group executive, 1961–1965 and 1967–1969 CDU *Land* deputy chairman and from 1969 chairman, 1967–1975 vice president and 1975–1980 president of Chamber of Deputies, 1976–1987 MdB, 1982–1987 parliamentary state secretary at chancellery.

Lubbers, Rudolphus (»Ruud«) Frans Marie geb. 1939, niederl. Wirtschaftsfachmann u. Politiker, 1973 Wirtschaftsminister, 1977 MdP f. d. Christl. Demokr. Appell, 1979 Fraktionsvorsitzender, 1982–1994 Ministerpräsident

Lubbers, Rudolphus ("Ruud") Frans Marie b. 1939, Netherlands economics expert and politician, 1973 economics minister, 1977 Christian Democrat Appeal MP, 1979 chief whip, 1982–1994 prime minister.

Lübke, Heinrich, Dr. h.c.1894–1972, dt. Vermessungs- u. Kulturing., Politiker, 1931–1935 MdL v. Preußen f. d. Zentrum, 1945 CDU-Eintritt, 1946 MdL v. Westfalen, 1947–1952 Minister f. Ernährung, Landwirtsch. u. Forsten in Nordrhein-Westfalen, 1949/50 u. 1953 MdB, 1953 Bundesminister f. Ernährung, Landwirtsch. u. Forsten, 1959–1969 Bundespräsident (Rücktritt).

Lübke, Heinrich, Dr. h.c. 1894–1972, German land surveyor and agricultural engineer, politician, 1931–1935 Center Party MdL Prussia, 1945 joined CDU, 1946 MdL Westphalia, 1947–1952 minister of food, agriculture and forestries in North Rhine-Westphalia, 1949/50 and 1953 MdB, 1953 federal minister of food, agriculture and forestries, 1959–1969 federal president (resigned).

Lübke, Wilhelmine (geb. Keuthen) 1885–1981, dt. Lehrerin u. Studienrätin, ab 1929 verheiratet mit Heinrich Lübke.

Lübke, Wilhelmine (née Keuthen) 1885–1981, German school and grammar school teacher, from 1929 married to Heinrich Lübke.

Lücke, Paul 1914–1976, dt. Maschinening u. Politiker, ab 1945 CDU-Mitgl., 1949–1972 MdB, 1957–1965 Bundesminister f. Wohnungsbau, 1965–1968 Bundesminister d. Innern.

Lücke, Paul 1914–1976, German mechanical engineer and politician, from 1945 member of CDU, 1949–1972 MdB, 1957–1965 minister of housing construction, 1965–1968 minister of the interior.

Lüdemann, Hermann 1880–1959, dt. Ing. u. Politiker, 1915–1922 Berliner Stadtverordneter f. d. SPD, 1920–1929 MdL v. Preußen, 1920/21 preuß. Finanzminister, 1928–1932 Oberpräsident v. Schlesien, 1945 SPD-Landesgeschäftsführer in Mecklenburg u. Parteisekretär in Berlin, 1946–1949 Innenminister u. Ministerpräsident v. Schleswig-Holstein, ab 1947 MdL.

Lüdemann, Hermann 1880–1959, German engineer and politician, 1915–1922 SPD member of Berlin city council, 1920–1929 MdL Prussia, 1920/21 Prussian finance minister, 1928–1932 president of Silesia, 1945 SPD Land party manager in Mecklenburg and party secretary in Berlin, 1946–1949 minister of the interior and minister president of Schleswig-Holstein, from 1947 MdL.

Lukaschek, Hans, Dr. jur. 1885–1960, dt. Politiker u. Rechtsanwalt, 1916 Bürgermeister v. Berlin, 1927–1929 Oberbürgermeister v. Hindenburg, 1929–1933 Oberpräsident Oberschlesien, 1945 Mitbegr. d. CDU Berlin, 1949–1953 Bundesminister f. Vertriebene.

Lukaschek, Hans, Dr. jur. 1885–1960, German politician and lawyer, 1916 mayor of Berlin, 1927–1929 senior mayor of Hindenburg, 1929–1933 president of Upper Silesia, 1945 co-founder of Berlin CDU, 1949–1953 federal minister for expellees.

Luns, Joseph Marie Antoine Hubert, Dr. jur. (1937) geb. 1911, niederl. Politiker u. Diplomat, 1933–1936 Mitgl. d. niederl. Nationalsozialist. Bewegung, 1938 Attaché in d. Zentrale d. Auswärtigen Dienstes in Den Haag, 1940 Gesandtschaftsattaché in Bern, 1943–1949 als Botschaftssekretär in London, 1949–1952 niederl. Vertreter bei d. UN, 1956–1971 Außenminister, 1958/59 Präsident d. NATO-Rates, 1971–1984 NATO-Generalsekretär.

Luns, Joseph Marie Antoine Hubert, Dr. jur. (1937) b. 1911, Netherlands politician and diplomat, 1933–1936 member of Netherlands national socialist movement, 1938 attaché at foreign service central office in The Hague, 1940 attaché at legation in Berne, 1943–1949 secretary at London embassy, 1949–1952 Netherlands UN representative, 1956–1971 foreign minister, 1958/59 president of NATO council, 1971–1984 NATO general secretary.

M

Macmillan, Harold Maurice 1894–1986, brit. Staatsmann u. Verleger, 1924–1929 u. 1931–1964 Mitgl. d. Unterhauses (Konservativer), 1940 parlam. Staatssekretär im Beschaffungsministerium, 1942 parlam. Unterstaatssekretär im Kolonialministerium, 1942–1945 als brit. Minister-Resident in Nordwestafrika, 1945 Luftwaffenminister, 1951–1954 Minister f. Wohnungsbau, dann Verteidigungsminister, 1955 Schatzamtsminister, 1957–1963 Premierminister (Rücktritt), 1984 Mitgl. d. Oberhauses.

Macmillan, Harold Maurice 1894–1986, British statesman and publisher, 1924–1929 and 1931–1964 MP (Conservative), 1940 parliamentary secretary of state at ministry of supply, 1942 parliamentary under-secretary of state at colonial office, 1942–1945 British resident minister in North-West Africa, 1945 minister of the air force, 1951–1954 minister of housing construction, then defense minister, 1955 treasury minister, 1957–1963 prime minister (resigned), 1984 member of House of Lords.

Mahler, Horst geb. 1936, dt. Jurist, Mitgl. d. SDS, APO-Anwalt, Mitbegr. d. »Sozialistischen Anwaltkollektivs«, 1970 zu 10 Monaten Gefängnis, 1974 zu 14 Jahren Freiheitsentzug verurteilt.

Mahler, Horst b. 1936, German lawyer, member of SDS, APO lawyer, co-founder of "socialist lawyers collective", 1970 sentenced to 10 months and 1974 to 14 years imprisonment.

Maier, Reinhold, Dr. jur. (1921) 1889–1971, dt. Rechtsanwalt u. Politiker, 1924–1933 MdL v. Württemberg, 1924 Landesvorsitzender d. DDP, 1929–1933 württemb. Wirtschaftsminister, 1932/33 MdR, 1945–1953 Ministerpräsident v. Württemberg-Baden, 1946–1963 MdL (DVP/FDP), 1953–1956 u. 1957–1959 MdB f. d. FDP, 1957– 1960 Bundesvorsitzender d. FDP.

Maier, Reinhold, Dr. jur. (1921) 1889–1971, German lawyer and politician, 1924–1933 MdL Württemberg, 1924 DDP Land chairman, 1929–1933 Württemberg economics minister, 1932/33 MdR, 1945–1953 minister president of Württemberg-Baden, 1946–1963 MdL (DVP/FDP), 1953–1956 and 1957–1959 FDP MdB, 1957–1960 FDP federal chairman.

Maihofer, Werner, Dr. jur., Dr. h.c. (1950, 1953) geb. 1918, dt. Politiker, Rektor u. Prof. f. Strafrecht, 1969 FDP-Eintritt, 1970–1978 Präsidiumsmitgl., 1972–1980 MdB, 1972 Bundesminister f. besondere Aufgaben, 1974–1978 Bundesminister d. Innern.

Maihofer, Werner, Dr. jur., Dr. h.c. (1950, 1953) b. 1918, German politician, university president and professor of criminal law, 1969 joined FDP, 1970–1978 member of presidium, 1972–1980 MdB, 1972 minister without portfolio, 1974–1978 minister of the interior.

Maizière, Lothar de geb. 1940, dt. Politiker u. Rechtsanwalt, ab 1956 CDU-Mitgl. in d. DDR, Nov. 1989 Vorsitzender d. CDU, 1990 MdVK u. Ministerpräsident, Nov. 1990 Mitgl. im Landesvorstand

d. CDU Brandenburg, 1990/1991 MdB, Minister f. besondere Aufgaben u. stellv. CDU-Vorsitzender.

Maizière, Lothar de b. 1940, German politician and lawyer, from 1956 member of CDU in GDR, Nov. 1989 CDU chairman, 1990 member of Volkskammer and prime minister, Nov. 1990 member of *Land* CDU executive in Brandenburg, 1990/1991 MdB, minister without portfolio and CDU deputy chairman.

Major, John geb. 1943, brit. Politiker u. Bankier, 1979 Mitgl. im Unterhaus (Konservativer), 1981 persönl. Sekretär d. Innenministers, 1987 Schatzamtsminister, 1989 Schatzkanzler, 1990–1997 Premierminister.

Major, John b. 1943, British politician and banker, 1979 MP (Conservative), 1981 personal secretary to Home Secretary, 1987 treasury minister, 1989 chanceller of the exchequer, 1990–1997 prime minister.

Mao Tse-tung [Mao Zedong], 1893–1976, 1921 Mitbegr. d. chin. KP, ab 1923 Mitgl. d. ZK u. d. PB d. KPCh, ab 1924 Leiter d. Organisationsabt. beim ZK d. KPCh, 1927–1935 aus dem PB ausgeschlossen, ab 1928 Führer d. kommun. Partisanen- u. Rätebewegung in Süd-China, 1931 u. 1935/36 Vorsitzender d. Regierung d. »chinesischen Sowjetrepublik«, 1934/35 Anführer d. »Langen Marsches«, 1935 Vorsitzender d. Militärkommission d. ZK d. KPCh, Bildung d. chin. »Roten Armee«, ab 1945 Vorsitzender d. ZK u. d. PB, 1949–1954 Vorsitzender d. Zentralen Volksregierungsrates u. Vorsitzender d. Revolutionären Militärrates, 1954–1958 Staatsoberhaupt.

Mao Tse-tung [Mao Zedong], 1893–1976, 1921 co-founder of Chinese CP, from 1923 member of central committee and PB of Chinese CP, from 1924 head of organization department of central committee of Chinese CP, 1927–1935 expelled from PB, from 1928 leader of Communist partisan and soviet movement in South China, 1931 and 1935/36 chairman of government of "Chinese Soviet Republic", 1934/35 leader of the "long march", 1935 chairman of military commission of the central committee of the Chinese CP, formation of Chinese "Red Army", from 1945 chairman of central committee and PB, 1949–1954 chairman of central council of people's governments and chairman of revolutionary military council, 1954–1958 head of state.

Marcuse, Herbert, Prof., Dr. phil. (1922) 1898–1979, dt. »neomarxistischer« Philosoph, ab 1934 in Amerika, 1942–1950 Sektionschef im Office of Strategic Services, 1965 Honorarprofessor an d. Freien Universität Berlin.

Marcuse, Herbert, professor, Dr. phil. (1922) 1898–1979, German "neo-Marxist" philosopher, from 1934 in America, 1942–1950 section head at Office of Strategic Services, 1965 honorary professor at the Free University of Berlin.

Marshall, George Catlett 1880–1959, amerik. General u. Staatsmann, 1939–1945 Stabschef d. US-Armee, Dez. 1944 General d. US-Armee, 1944–1947 als Botschafter in China, 1947–1949 US-Außenminister, 1950/51 Verteidigungsminister.

Marshall, George Catlett 1880–1959, American general and statesman, 1939–1945 US army chief of staff, Dec. 1944 general of US army, 1944–1947 ambassador in China, 1947–1949 US secretary of state, 1950/51 defense minister.

Martino, Gaetano, Dr. med. (1923) 1900–1967, ital. Physiologe u. Politiker, Universitätsprofessor u. Rektor, ab 1945 Mitgl. d. Liberalen Partei Italiens, 1946 Mitgl. d. Verfassunggebenden Nationalversammlung, 1954–1957 Außenminister, 1962–1964 Präsident d. EP.

Martino, Gaetano, Dr. med. (1923) 1900–1967, Italian physiologist and politician, university professor and president, from 1945 member of Liberal Party of Italy, 1946 member of constitutive national assembly, 1954–1957 foreign minister, 1962–1964 president of EP.

Marty, François, Dr. theol. 1904–1994, 1930 Priesterweihe, 1952 Bischof v. Saint-Flour, 1959 Titularbischof v. Emesa, 1960 Erzbischof v. Reims, 1968–1981 Erzbischof v. Paris, 1969 Kardinal, 1969–1975 Präsident d. frz. Bischofskonferenz.

Marty, François, Dr. theol. 1904–1994, 1930 ordained as priest, 1952 bishop of Saint-Flour, 1959 titular bishop of Emesa, 1960 archbishop of Reims, 1968–1981 archbishop of Paris, 1969 cardinal, 1969–1975 president of conference of French bishops.

Marx, Karl Heinrich, Dr. (1841) 1818–1883, dt. Philosoph, Historiker u. Journalist, mit F. Engels Begründer d. Marxismus.
Marx, Karl Heinrich, Dr. (1841) 1818–1883, German philosopher, historian and journalist, with F. Engels founder of Marxism.

Matthäus-Maier, Ingrid geb. 1945, dt. Politikerin u. Juristin, 1966–1969 Mitgl. d. APO, 1969–1982 FDP-Mitgl., 1976–1982 f. d. FDP u. seit 1983 f. d. SPD MdB, seit 1988 stellv. Fraktionsvorsitzende d. SPD-Bundestagsfraktion.

Matthäus-Maier, Ingrid b. 1945, German politician and lawyer, 1966–1969 member of APO, 1969–1982 member of FDP, 1976–1982 FDP MdB and since 1983 SPD MdB, since 1988 SPD deputy whip.

Mazowiecki, Tadeusz, Dr. h.c. geb. 1927, poln. Reformpolitiker u. Journalist, 1961–1971 MdP, 1989/90 Ministerpräsident, 1991 Begründer d. »Demokrat. Union«, 1992–1995 Sonderberichterstatter d. UNO in Bosnien-Herzegowina, 1994/95 Führer d. Reformer »Union d. Freiheit«.

Mazowiecki, Tadeusz, Dr. h.c. b. 1927, Polish reform politician and journalist, 1961–1971 MP, 1989/90 prime minister, 1991 founder of "Democratic Union", 1992–1995 UN special investigator in Bosnia-Herzegovina, 1994/95 leader of reformist "Liberty Union".

McCloy, John Jay 1895–1989, amerik. Jurist, Politiker u. Verwaltungsfachmann, 1941–1945 Unterstaatssekretär im Kriegsministerium, 1946/47 Mitgl. d. Atomenergie-Komitees d. Außenministeriums, 1947 Präsident d. Weltbank, 1949–1952 als Militärgouverneur u. Hoher Kommissar in Deutschl., 1961–1974 Mitgl. d. Beraterkomitees in Abrüstungsfragen f. d. US-Präsidenten.

McCloy, John Jay 1895–1989, American lawyer, politician and administrator, 1941–1945 unter-secretary of state at ministry of war, 1946/47 member of foreign ministry atomic energy committee, 1947 president of World Bank, 1949–1952 military governor and High Commissioner in Germany, 1961–1974 member of US presidential advisory committee on disarmament issues.

Meckel, Markus geb. 1952, dt. Pfarrer u. SPD-Politiker, 1989 Mitbegr. d. SPD in d. DDR, 1990 stellv. Vorsitzender d. Ost-SPD, MdVK, DDR-Außenminister, seit Dez. 1990 MdB

Meckel, Markus b. 1952, German vicar and SPD politician, 1989 co-founder of SPD in GDR, 1990 deputy chairman of East German SPD, member of Volkskammer, GDR foreign minister, since Dec. 1990 MdB.

Meir, Golda 1898–1978, israel. Politikerin, ab 1921 in Palästina, ab 1923 Mitgl. d. Gewerkschaft Histadrut, Mitgl. d. Arbeiterpartei Mapai, 1948/49 isr. Gesandte in Moskau, 1949–1974 MdP, 1949–1956 Ministerin f. Arbeit u. soziale Sicherheit, 1956–1965 Außenministerin, 1966–1968 Generalsekretärin d. Mapai-Partei, 1969–1974 Ministerpräsidentin (Rücktritt).

Meir, Golda 1898–1978, Israeli politician, from 1921 in Palestine, from 1923 member of Histadrut trade union, member of Mapai labor party, 1948/49 Israeli envoy to Moscow, 1949–1974 MP, 1949–1956 minister of labor and social security, 1956–1965 foreign minister, 1966–1968 Mapai Party general secretary, 1969–1974 prime minister (resigned).

Mende, Erich, Dr. jur. 1916–1998, dt. Politiker, 1945 FDP-Eintritt, ab 1949 Bundesvorstandsmitgl. d. FDP, 1949–1970 f. d. FDP, dann bis 1980 f. d. CDU MdB, 1950–1953 Fraktionsgeschäftsführer, 1953–1957 stellv., 1957–1963 Fraktionsvorsitzender, 1960–1967 FDP-Bundesvorsitzender, 1963–1966 Bundesminister f. gesamtdt. Fragen u. Vizekanzler, 1970 Wechsel in d. CDU.

Mende, Erich, Dr. jur. 1916–1998, German politician, 1945 joined FDP, from 1949 member of FDP federal executive, 1949–1970 FDP MdB, then until 1980 CDU MdB, 1950–1953 parliamentary group manager, 1953–1957 deputy whip and 1957–1963 chief whip, 1960–1967 FDP federal chairman, 1963–1966 minister for all-German issues and deputy chancellor, 1970 went over to CDU.

Menderes, Adnan 1899–1961, türk. Politiker, 1946 Mitbegr. u. Vorsitzender d. DP, 1950–1960 Regierungschef (gestürzt u. hingerichtet).

Menderes, Adnan 1899–1961, Turkish politician, 1946 co-founder and chairman of DP, 1950–1960 head of government (deposed and executed).

Mendès-France, Pierre, Dr. jur. 1907–1982 , frz. Politiker, Journalist u. Publizist, ab 1932 Paralmentsabgeord. f. d. radikalsozialist. Partei, 1935–1958 Bürgermeister v. Louviers, 1944/45 Wirtschaftsminister, 1954/55 Ministerpräsident u. Außenminister, 1955/56 stellv. Parteivorsitzender, 1956 Staatsminister, 1959 Parteiausschluß, 1960–1969 Mitgl. d. »Vereinigten Sozialist. Partei«

Mendès-France, Pierre, Dr. jur. 1907–1982, French politician, journalist and publicist, from 1932 radical socialist party MP, 1935–1958 mayor of Louviers, 1944/45 economics minister, 1954/55 prime minister and foreign minister, 1955/56 deputy party chairman, 1956 minister of state, 1959 expelled from party, 1960–1969 member of united socialist party.

Merkel, Angela, Dr. (1986) geb. 1954, dt. Diplomphysikerin u. Politikerin, 1989 Mitgl. d. »Demokr. Aufbruchs«, 1990 stellv. Regierungssprecherin d. Regierung de Maizière, Referentin im Bundespresseamt, seit Dez. 1990 CDU-Mitgl. u. MdB, 1991–1994 Bundesministerin f. Frauen u. Jugend, 1991–1998 stellv. Vorsitzende d. CDU Deutschl., seit 1993 Vorsitzende d. CDU Mecklenburg-Vorpommern, 1994–1998 Bundesministerin f. Umwelt, Naturschutz u. Reaktorsicherheit, seit Nov. 1998 Generalsekretärin d. CDU.

Merkel, Angela, Dr. (1986) b. 1954, German physics graduate and politician, 1989 member of "Democratic Beginning", 1990 deputy government spokesperson in the de Maizière government, adviser at federal press office, since Dec. 1990 member of CDU and MdB, 1991–1994 minister for women and youth, 1991–1998 deputy chairperson of CDU (Germany), since 1993 chairperson of CDU (Mecklenburg-Vorpommern), 1994–1998 minister for the environment, the protection of nature and reactor safety, since Nov. 1998 CDU general secretary.

Merkle, Hans L., Prof., Dr. h.c. geb. 1913, dt. Industriemanager, 1958 Mitgl. d. Geschäftsführung d. Robert Bosch GmbH in Stuttgart, 1963–1984 dort Vorsitzender, 1984–1988 Vorsitzender d. Aufsichtsrats, 1986 Vorsitzender d. Fritz-Thyssen-Stiftung, 1967–1979 CDU-Mitgl., wirtschaftspolit. Berater v. Spitzenpolitikern.

Merkle, Hans L., professor, Dr. h.c. b. 1913, German industrial manager, 1958 member of board of management of Robert Bosch Ltd. in Stuttgart, 1963–1984 chairman of board, 1984–1988 chairman of supervisory board, 1986 chairman of Fritz Thyssen foundation, 1967–1979 member of CDU, economic policy adviser to leading politicians.

Merseburger, Peter geb. 1928, dt. Fernsehjournalist u. Publizist, seit 1950 Mitgl. d. SPD, 1960–1965 Korrespondent f. d. »Spiegel«, 1967–1975 Chefredakteur beim NDR (»Panorama«), 1977 ARD-Korrespondent in Washington, 1982–1987 in Ost-Berlin, 1987–1991 Fernsehkorrespondent u. ARD-Studioleiter in London, ab 1991 freier Publizist.

Merseburger, Peter b. 1928, German TV journalist and publicist, since 1950 member of SPD, 1960–1965 correspondent for *Der Spiegel*, 1967–1975 editor-in-chief at NDR ("Panorama"), 1977 ARD correspondent in Washington, 1982–1987 in East Berlin, 1987–1991 TV correspondent and head of ARD studio London, from 1991 freelance publicist.

Messmer, Pierre, Dr. jur. geb. 1916, frz. Politiker, 1950 Kabinettschef beim Hochkommissar f. Indochina, 1951 Verwaltungschef f. d. überseeische Frankr., 1952 Gouverneur v. Mauretanien, 1954 d. Elfenbeinküste, 1956 Hochkommissar in Kamerun, 1958/59 in Dakar, 1960–1969 Verteidigungsminister, 1968–1988 Mitgl. d. Nationalversammlung, 1971 Staatsminister f. d. Überseegebiete, 1972–1974 Ministerpräsident, 1979/80 MdEP.

Messmer, Pierre, Dr. jur. b. 1916, French politician, 1950 cabinet chief of High Commissioner of Indochina, 1951 administrative head for French overseas territories, 1952 governor of Mauritania, 1954 of the Ivory Coast, 1956 High Commissioner in Cameroon, 1958/59 in Dakar, 1960–1969 defense minister, 1968–1988 member of national assembly, 1971 minister of state for the overseas territories, 1972–1974 prime minister, 1979/80 MEP.

Meyers, Franz, Dr. jur. (1933) geb. 1908, dt. Politiker u. Rechtsanwalt, ab 1948 CDU-Mitgl., 1950–1970 MdL v. Nordrhein-Westfalen, 1952–1956 Innenminister, 1957/58 MdB, 1958–1966 Ministerpräsident v. Nordrhein-Westfalen.

Meyers, Franz, Dr. jur. (1933) b. 1908, German politician and lawyer, from 1948 member of CDU, 1950–1970 MdL North Rhine-Westphalia, 1952–1956 minister of the interior, 1957/58 MdB, 1958–1966 minister president of North Rhine-Westphalia.

Mielke, Erich geb. 1907, dt. Speditionskaufmann, 1927 KPD-Eintritt, 1931 Flucht ins Ausland, 1945 KPD-Mitgl. u. 1946 SED-Mitgl., 1946–1949 Vizepräsident d. Dt. Verwaltung d. Innern, 1950–1989 Mitgl. d. ZK d. SED, 1950–1953 Staatssekretär im Ministerium f. Staatssicherheit, 1953–1955 stellv. Staatssekretär, 1955–1957 stellv. Minister f. Staatssicherheit, dann bis 1989 Minister f. Staatssicherheit, 1958–1989 MdVK, ab 1976 Mitgl. d. PB d. ZK d. SED, 1989 Ausschluß aus ZK u. SED, 1993 Verurteilung zu 6 Jahren Gefängnis.

Mielke, Erich b. 1907, German haulage contractor, 1927 joined KPD, 1931 fled abroad, 1945 member of KPD and 1946 SED, 1946–1949 vice president of German internal administration, 1950–1989 SED central committee member, 1950–1953 state secretary at ministry of state security, 1953–1955 deputy state secretary, 1955–1957 deputy minister for state security, then until 1989 minister for state security, 1958–1989 member of Volkskammer, from 1976 member of PB of SED central committee, 1989 expelled from central committee and SED, 1993 sentenced to six years imprisonment.

Mischnick, Wolfgang geb. 1921, dt. Politiker, 1945 Mitbegr. d. LDP in Dresden, 1946–1948 Stadtverordneter, 1954–1957 MdL v. Hessen f. d. FDP sowie Bundesvorsitzender d. Dt. Jungdemokraten, 1956–1961 u. 1964–1968 Fraktionsvorsitzender im Landtag, 1957–1994 MdB, 1968–1991 Fraktionsvorsitzender, 1961–1963 Bundesminister f. Vertriebene, Flüchtlinge u. Kriegsgeschädigte (Rücktritt), 1964–1988 stellv. Parteivorsitzender, 1967–1977 FDP-Landesvorsitzender v. Hessen.

Mischnick, Wolfgang b. 1921, German politician, 1945 co-founder of LDP in Dresden, 1946–1948 member of municipal council, 1954–1957 FDP MdL Hessen and federal chairman of German Young Democrats, 1956–1961 and 1964–1968 chief whip in *Landtag*, 1957–1994 MdB, 1968–1991 chief whip, 1961–1963 federal minister for expellees, refugees and the war-disabled (resigned), 1964–1988 deputy party chairman, 1967–1977 FDP-*Land* chairman of Hessen.

Mitterrand, François 1916–1996, frz. Politiker, 1945 Mitgl. d. UDSR, 1946–1981 MdP, 1947/48 Minister f. Frontkämpfer u. Kriegsopfer, 1950/51 Leiter d. Überseeminsteriums, 1953 Parteivorsitzender, 1954/55 Innenminister, 1956/57 Justizminister, 1959–1981 Bürgermeister v. Château-Chinon, 1971– 1981 1. Sekretär d. PS, 1981–1995 Staatspräsident.

Mitterrand, François 1916–1996, French politician, 1945 member of UDSR, 1946–1981 MP, 1947/48 minister for frontline soldiers and victims of war, 1950/51 head of overseas ministry, 1953 party chairman, 1954/55 minister of the interior, 1956/57 justice minister, 1959–1981 mayor of Château-Chinon, 1971–1981 first secretary of PS, 1981–1995 President.

Modrow, Hans, Dr. (1966) geb. 1928, dt. Maschinenschlosser u. Politiker, ab 1949 SED-Mitgl., 1949–1951 Abteilungsleiter u. Sekretär d. FDJ-Landesvorstandes v. Brandenburg, 1953–1961 1. Sekretär d. Bezirksleitung v. Berlin u. Sekretär d. Zentralrats d. FDJ, 1958–1967 MdVK, 1967–1989 Mitgl. d. ZK d. SED, 1971–1973 Leiter d. Abt. Agitation d. ZK, Nov. 1989–März 1990 Vorsitzender d. DDR-Ministerrats, 1989/90 stellv. Vorsitzender d. SED/PDS, 1990–1994 MdB f. d. Linke Liste/PDS.

Modrow, Hans, Dr. (1966) b. 1928, German mechanic and politician, from 1949 member of SED, 1949–1951 head of department and secretary of FDJ *Land* executive in Brandenburg, 1953–1961 first secretary of Berlin district administration and secretary to FDJ central council, 1958–1967 member of Volkskammer, 1967–1989 member of SED central committee, 1971–1973 head of central committee department of agitation, Nov. 1989 - March 1990 chairman of GDR council of ministers, 1989/90 deputy chairman of SED/PDS, 1990–1994 MdB (Left List/PDS).

Möllemann, Jürgen geb. 1945, dt. Lehrer u. Politiker, seit 1970 FDP-Mitgl., seit 1972 MdB, 1975–1984 Vorsitzender d. FDP Bezirksverbands Münsterland, 1982–1983 stellv., 1983–1994 u. seit 1996 Landesvorsitzender v. Nordrhein-Westfalen, 1981–1997 Mitgl. d. Bundesvorstandes, 1982–1987 Staatsminister im Auswärtigen Amt, 1987–1991 Bundesminister f. Bildung u. Wissenschaft, 1991–1993 Bundesminister f. Wirtschaft, 1992/93 Vizekanzler, seit Nov. 1998 Vorsitzender im Ausschuß f. Bildung, Forschung u. Technikfolgenabschätzung.

Möllemann, Jürgen b. 1945, German teacher and politician, since 1970 member of FDP, since 1972 MdB, 1975–1984 chairman of FDP district association in Münsterland, 1982–1983 *Land* deputy chairman and 1983–1994 and since 1996 chairman in North Rhine-Westphalia, 1981–1997 member of federal executive, 1982–1987 minister of state at foreign office, 1987–1991 minister of education and science, 1991–1993 economics minister, 1992/93 deputy chancellor, since Nov. 1998 chairman of committee for education, research and the estimation of the consequences of technology.

Möller, Alex (Alexander) 1903–1985, dt. Politiker, 1922 SPD-Eintritt, 1928–1933 MdL v. Preußen, 1946–1961 MdL v. Baden-Württemberg, 1950–1961 Landtagsfraktionsvorsitzender, 1961–1976 MdB, 1962–1966 SPD-Vorsitzender in Baden-Württemberg, 1964–1969 u. 1972–1976 stellv. Bundesfraktionsvorsitzender, 1969–1971 Bundesfinanzminister (Rücktritt).

Möller, Alex (Alexander) 1903–1985, German politician, 1922 joined SPD, 1928–1933 MdL Prussia, 1946–1961 MdL Baden-Württemberg, 1950–1961 *Landtag* chief whip, 1961–1976 MdB, 1962–1966 SPD party chairman in Baden-Württemberg, 1964–1969 and 1972–1976 federal deputy whip, 1969–1971 finance minister (resigned).

Mollet, Guy 1905–1975, frz. Lehrer u. Politiker, 1923 Mitgl. d. PS, 1944–1975 Bürgermeister v. Arras, 1946–1969 Parteivorsitzender, 1949–1956 Mitgl. d. Beratenden Versammlung d. Europarates, 1956/57 Ministerpräsident, 1958/59 Staatsminister.

Mollet, Guy 1905–1975, French teacher and politician, 1923 member of PS, 1944–1975 mayor of Arras, 1946–1969 party chairman, 1949–1956 member of Council of Europe advisory assembly, 1956/57 prime minister, 1958/59 minister of state.

Molotow, Wjatscheslaw Michailowitsch (vorher W. M. Skrjabin) 1890–1986, sowjet. Politiker, ab 1906 Sozialist, 1916 Eintritt in d. ZK d. Bolschewiki, 1921–1957 Mitgl. d. ZK d. KPdSU, 1926–1952 Mitgl. d. PB, 1930–1941 Vorsitzender d. Rates d. Volkskommissare (sowjet. Ministerpräsident) 1939–1949 u. 1953–1956 Außenminister, ab 1942 1. Stellvertreter d. Ministerpräsidenten, 1956 Minister f. Staatskontrolle, 1957 aller Ämter enthoben, 1984 Wiederaufnahme in d. Partei.

Molotov, Vyacheslav Mikhaylovich (formerly V. M. Skriabin) 1890–1986, Soviet politician, from 1906 socialist, 1916 joined bolshevik central committee, 1921–1957 member of CPSU central committee, 1926–1952 member of PB, 1930–1941 chairman of soviet of people's commissars (Soviet prime minister) 1939–1949 and 1953–1956 foreign minister, from 1942 1st deputy prime minister, 1956 minister for state control, 1957 removed from all his posts, 1984 readmitted to party.

Moltke, Helmuth James Graf von 1907–1945, dt. Widerstands-

kämpfer während d. II. Weltkrieges, wegen »Hochverrats« in Plötzensee bei Berlin hingerichtet.

Moltke, Helmuth James Count von 1907–1945, German resistance fighter during second world war, executed for "high treason" at Plötzensee near Berlin.

Momper, Walter geb. 1945, dt. Politiker u. Wirtschaftsmanager, 1967 SPD-Eintritt, 1978 Mitgl. im SPD-Landesvorstand Berlin, 1975–1995 MdA v. Berlin, 1980–1985 stellv., 1985–1989 SPD-Fraktionsvorsitzender, 1986–1992 Landesvorsitzender, 1989–1991 Regier. Bürgermeister v. Berlin, 1999 SPD-Spitzenkandidat.

Momper, Walter b. 1945, German politician and economic manager, 1967 joined SPD, 1978 member of SPD Berlin *Land* executive, 1975–1995 MdA Berlin, 1980–1985 SPD deputy whip and 1985–1989 chief whip, 1986–1992 *Land* chairman, 1989–1991 governing mayor of Berlin, 1999 SPD front runner.

Müller, Werner geb. 1946, dt. Dipl.-Volkswirt u. Manager, parteilos, Staatssekretär im Ministerium d. Innern in Brandenburg, seit 1998 Bundesminister f. Wirtschaft u. Technologie.

Müller, Werner b. 1946, German economics graduate and manager, no party, state secretary at ministry of the interior in Brandenburg, since 1998 minister of economics and technology.

Müntefering, Franz geb. 1940, Industriekaufmann, seit 1966 SPD-Mitgl., 1975–1992 u. seit 1998 MdB, 1990–1992 Parlam. Geschäftsführer d. SPD-Fraktion, 1992–1995 Minister f. Arbeit, Gesundheit u. Soziales v. Nordrhein-Westfalen, 1995–1998 SPD-Bundesgeschäftsführer, seit 1996 MdL, seit 1998 Vorsitzender d. Landesverbands Nordrhein-Westfalen u. Bundesminister f. Verkehr, Bau- u. Wohnungswesen.

Müntefering, Franz b. 1940, industrial manager, since 1966 member of SPD, 1975–1992 and since 1998 MdB, 1990–1992 SPD parliamentary group manager, 1992–1995 minister of labor, health and welfare in North Rhine-Westphalia, 1995–1998 SPD federal manager, since 1996 MdL, since 1998 chairman of *Land* association in North Rhine-Westphalia and minister of transport, construction and housing.

N

Nadig, Friederike (Frieda) 1897–1970, dt. Wohlfahrtspflegerin, ab 1916 SPD-Mitgl., ab 1945 Geschäftsführerin d. Arbeiterwohlfahrt d. Bezirks Ostwestfalen, 1947–1950 MdL v. Nordrhein-Westfalen f. d. SPD, 1948/49 MdPR, 1949–1961 MdB.

Nadig, Friederike (Frieda) 1897-1970, German welfare worker, from 1916 member of SPD, from 1945 workers' welfare manager in district of East Westphalia, 1947–1950 SPD MdL North Rhine-Westphalia, 1948/49 MdPR, 1949-1961 MdB.

Nakasone, Yasuhiro geb. 1918, japan. Politiker, ab 1947 Unterhausmitgl. f. d. LDP, 1959–1961 Generaldirektor d. Amtes f. Wissensch. u. Technik, 1967/68 Verkehrsminister, 1970/71 u. 1980–1982 Staatsminister, 1972–1974 Minister f. Außenhandel u. Industrie, 1974–1976 Parteigeneralsekretär, 1982–1987 Ministerpräsident u. Parteivorsitzender, 1989–1991 Parteiaustritt.

Nakasone, Yasuhiro b. 1918, Japanese politician, from 1947 LDP MP, 1959–1961 general director of science and technology office, 1967/68 minister of transport, 1970/71 and 1980–1982 minister of state, 1972–1974 minister of foreign trade and industry, 1974–1976 party general secretary, 1982–1987 prime minister and party chairman, 1989–1991 left party.

Nasser, Gamal Abd el 1918–1970, ägypt. Staatsmann, 1953 stellv. Ministerpräsident u. Innenminister, 1954–1956 Ministerpräsident u. Militärführer, 1956–1958 Staatspräsident v. Ägypten, 1958–1970 Präsident d. Vereinigt. Arab. Republik, 1967–1970 ebenso Ministerpräsident.

Nasser, Gamal Abd el 1918–1970, Egyptian statesman, 1953 deputy prime minister and minister of the interior, 1954–1956 prime minister and leader of the army, 1956–1958 President of Egypt, 1958–1970 President and 1967–1970 prime minister of United Arab Republic.

Ne Win (eigentl. Maung Shu Maung), geb. 1911, birman. Politiker, ab 1947 MdP, 1956 General, 1949/50, 1958–1960, 1962–1974 Ministerpräsident, 1962–1974 zusätzl. Vorsitzender d. Revolutionsrates, 1974–1981 Staatspräsident, 1958/60 u. 1962–1974 Verteidigungs-, 1962/63 Finanz- u. Justizminister, 1962–1965 Planungsminister, 1962 Gründer d. »Partei d. Birmanischen Weges zum Sozialismus« (BSPP), 1973–1988 Parteivorsitzender.

Ne Win (originally Maung Shu Maung), b. 1911, Burmese politician, from 1947 MP, 1956 general, 1949/50, 1958–1960, 1962–1974 prime minister, 1962–1974 in addition chairman of revolutionary council, 1974–1981 President, 1958/60 and 1962–1974 defense minister, 1962/63 finance and justice minister, 1962–1965 minister of planning, 1962 founder of "Party of the Burmese road to socialism" (BSPP), 1973–1988 party chairman.

Nehru, Jawaharlal, Dr. h.c., Dr. h.c. 1889–1964, indisch. Rechtsanwalt u. Staatsmann, ab 1918 Sitz im All-Indischen Kongreß, 1947–1964 Ministerpräsident u. Außenminister, Leiter d. indisch. Kongreßpartei bis 1957.

Nehru, Jawaharlal, Dr. h.c., Dr. h.c. 1889–1964, Indian lawyer and statesman, from 1918 member of All-Indian congress, 1947–1964 prime minister and foreign minister, leader of Indian Congress Party until 1957.

Neurath, Konstantin Freiherr von 1873–1956, dt. Diplomat, 1914–1916 Botschaftsrat in Konstantinopel, 1919 Gesandter in Kopenhagen, 1921–1930 Botschafter in Rom, 1930–1932 Botschafter in London, 1937 NSDAP-Eintritt, 1932–1938 Reichsaußenminister, sodann Reichsminister ohne Geschäftsbereich, 1939–1941 Reichsprotektor v. Böhmen u. Mähren, 1943 SS-Obergruppenführer, 1946 in Nürnberg zu 15 Jahren Haft verurteilt.

Neurath, Konstantin Freiherr von 1873–1956, German diplomat, 1914–1916 councillor at embassy in Constantinople, 1919 envoy in Copenhagen, 1921–1930 ambassador in Rome, 1930–1932 ambassador in London, 1937 joined NSDAP, 1932–1938 Reich foreign minister, then Reich minister without portfolio, 1939–1941 Reich protecter of Bohemia and Moravia, 1943 SS "Obergruppenführer", 1946 sentenced to 15 years imprisonment at Nuremberg.

Nickels, Christa (geb. Kleuters) geb. 1952, dt. Krankenschwester u. Politikerin, Gründungsmitgl. d. Grünen in Nordrhein-Westfalen, 1983–1985, 1987–1990 u. seit 1994 MdB, seit 1998 Parlam. Staatssekretärin beim Bundesministerium f. Gesundheit.

Nickels, Christa (née Kleuters) b. 1952, German nurse and politician, founding member of Greens in North Rhine-Westphalia, 1983–1985, 1987–1990 and since 1994 MdB, since 1998 parliamentary state secretary at federal ministry of health.

Niklas, Wilhelm, Dr.-Ing., Dr. med. vet. h.c. 1887–1957, dt. Dipl.-Landwirt u. CSU-Politiker, 1945 Staatsrat im Bayer. Landwirtschaftsministerium, 1948/49 stellv. Direktor d. Verwaltung f. Ernährung, Landwirtsch. u. Forsten d. Vereinigten Wirtschaftsgebietes in Frankfurt/M., 1949–1953 Bundesminister f. Ernährung, Landwirtsch. u. Forsten, 1951–1953 MdB f. d. CSU.

Niklas, Wilhelm, Dr.-Ing., Dr. med. vet. h.c. 1887–1957, German agriculture graduate and CSU politician, 1945 state councillor at Bavarian ministry of agriculture, 1948/49 deputy director of administration for food, agriculture and forestries of United Economic Area in Frankfurt am Main, 1949–1953 federal minister of food, agriculture and forestries, 1951–1953 CSU MdB.

Nixon, Pat (Patricia), Dr. (1961) (geb. Ryan) 1912–1993, Amerikanerin, ab 1940 Ehefrau v. Richard Nixon.

Nixon, Pat (Patricia), Dr. (1961) (née Ryan) 1912–1993, American, from 1940 wife of Richard Nixon.

Nixon, Richard Milhous 1913–1994, amerik. Anwalt u. Politiker (Republikaner), 1947–1953 Kongreßmitgl., 1953–1961 Vizepräsident, 1960 Republikan. Präsidentschaftskandidat, 1969–1974 US-Präsident (Rücktritt wegen d. Watergate-Affäre).

Nixon, Richard Milhous 1913–1994, American lawyer and politician (Republican), 1947–1953 member of Congress, 1953–1961 vice president, 1960 Republican presidential candidate, 1969–1974 US President (resigned over Watergate affair).

Nowottny, Friedrich geb. 1929, dt. Fernsehjournalist u. Medienberater, 1967–1973 stellv., 1973 Leiter d. WDR-Fernsehstudios in Bonn u. Chefkorrespondent d. ARD, 1973–1985 »Bericht aus Bonn«, 1985–1995 Intendant d. WDR.

Nowottny, Friedrich b. 1929, German TV journalist and media adviser, 1967–1973 deputy head and 1973 head of WDR Bonn TV studio and ARD chief correspondent, 1973–1985 "Bericht aus Bonn" [Report from Bonn], 1985–1995 general manager of WDR.

O

Oberländer, Theodor, Dr. 1905–1998, dt. Politiker u. Prof. f. Landwirtschaftspolit., 1933 NSDAP-Eintritt, 1934–1937 Leiter d. »Bundes deutscher Osten«, 1950 Gründer u. bayer. Landesvorsitzender d. BHE, 1954 Bundesvorsitzender, 1950–1953 Staatssekretär d. bayer. Regierung, 1953–1955 MdB, 1953–1960 Bundesminister f. Vertriebene, Flüchtlinge u. Kriegsgeschädigte (Rücktritt), 1956 CDU-Eintritt, 1957–1961 u. 1963–1965 MdB f. d. CDU.

Oberländer, Theodor, Dr. 1905–1998, German politician and professor of agricultural policy, 1933 joined NSDAP, 1934–1937 head of "Eastern League", 1950 founder and Bavarian Land chairman of BHE, 1954 federal chairman, 1950–1953 Bavarian government state secretary, 1953–1955 MdB, 1953–1960 minister for expellees, refugees and the war-disabled (resigned), 1956 joined CDU, 1957–1961 and 1963–1965 CDU MdB.

Ohnesorg, Benno 1941–1967, Student d. Freien Universität Berlin, bei einer Demonstration gegen d. Besuch d. Schahs v. Persien v. einem Polizisten erschossen.

Ohnesorg, Benno 1941–1967, student at Free University of Berlin, shot dead by a policeman during a demonstration against the visit by the Shah of Persia.

Ollenhauer, Erich 1901–1963, dt. Politiker, 1916 Mitgl. d. Sozialist. Arbeiterjugend, 1933 Mitgl. im SPD-Vorstand, 1946–1952 stellv. SPD-Vorsitzender, 1949–1963 MdB, 1949–1952 stellv., 1952–1963 Fraktionsvorsitzender sowie Parteivorsitzender, 1963 Präsident d. Sozialist. Internat.

Ollenhauer, Erich 1901–1963, German politician, 1916 member of Young Socialist Workers, 1933 member of SPD executive, 1946–1952 deputy SPD party chairman, 1949–1963 MdB, 1949–1952 deputy whip and 1952–1963 chief whip and party chairman, 1963 president of Socialist International.

Ortleb, Rainer, Prof., Dr., Dr. (1971 u. 1983) geb. 1944, dt. Computerfachmann u. Politiker, 1968 Mitgl. d. LDPD d. DDR, 1990 MdVK, Vorsitzender d. LDP, dann stellv. Vorsitzender d. FDP, 1990/91 Bundesminister f. besondere Aufgaben, 1990–1998 MdB, 1991– 1994 Bundesminister f. Bildung u. Wissenschaft, 1991–1994 FDP-Landesvorsitzender in Mecklenburg-Vorpommern.

Ortleb, Rainer, professor, Dr., Dr. (1971 and 1983) b. 1944, German computer expert and politician, 1968 member of GDR LDPD, 1990 member of Volkskammer, LDP party chairman, then FDP deputy chairman, 1990/91 minister without portfolio, 1990–1998 MdB, 1991–1994 minister of education and science, 1991–1994 FDP *Land* chairman in Mecklenburg-Vorpommern.

Ossietzky, Carl von 1889–1938, dt. Publizist u. Pazifist, ab 1920 Redakteur linksliberaler Zeitungen u. Zeitschriften, 1931 wegen Landesverrat verurteilt, 1932 amnestiert, 1933 als Staatsfeind erneut verhaftet, KZ, 1935 Friedensnobelpreis (Annahme durch NS verboten).

Ossietzky, Carl von 1889–1938, German publicist and pacifist, from 1920 editor of left-liberal newspapers and periodicals, 1931 convicted of treason, 1932 amnestied, 1933 re-imprisoned as enemy of the state, KZ, 1935 Nobel peace prize (forbidden by NS to accept).

Osswald, Albert 1919–1996, dt. Kaufmann u. Politiker, 1945 SPD-Eintritt, 1949 Stadtverordneter in Gießen, 1954 Bürgermeister, 1957 Oberbürgermeister, 1954–1978 MdL v. Hessen, 1962 Landeswirtschaftsminister, 1964 Finanzminister, 1969–1977 SPD-Landesvorsitzender, 1969–1976 hessischer Ministerpräsident (Rücktritt).

Osswald, Albert 1919–1996, German businessman and politician, 1945 joined SPD, 1949 member of town council in Gießen, 1954 mayor, 1957 senior mayor, 1954–1978 MdL Hessen, 1962 *Land* agriculture minister, 1964 finance minister, 1969–1977 SPD *Land* chairman, 1969–1976 minister president of Hessen (resigned).

Osterheld, Horst, Dr. 1919–1998, dt. Jurist, 1960–1969 Leiter d. außenpolit. Büros im Bundeskanzleramt, ab 1966 Abteilungsleiter, dt. Botschafter in Chile, 1980–1984 Abteilungsleiter im Bundespräsidialamt.

Osterheld, Horst, Dr. 1919–1998 German lawyer, 1960–1969 head of chancellery foreign policy office, from 1966 departmental head, German ambassador in Chile, 1980–1984 departmental head at federal president's office.

P

Pahlevi, Mohammed Reza 1919–1980, 1941–1979 Schah d. Iran, 1963 Gründer d. Regierungspartei »Neues Iran«, 1979 in Abwesenheit zu Tode verurteilt, Zuflucht in Ägypten.

Pahlevi, Mohammed Reza 1919–1980, 1941–1979 Shah of Iran, 1963 founder of governing party "New Iran", 1979 sentenced to death in absentia, refuge in Egypt.

Palme, Olof 1927–1986 (ermordet), schwed. Politiker (Sozialdemokrat), 1953 persönl. Sekretär d. Ministerpräsidenten, 1957 MdP, 1963 Mitgl. d. Parteivorstands, 1965 Minister f. Verkehr, Post u. Fernmeldewesen, 1967 Unterrichtsminister, 1969 Parteivorsitzender, 1969–1976 u. 1982–1986 Regierungschef.

Palme, Olof 1927–1986 (assassinated), Swedish politician (Social Democrat), 1953 prime minister's personal secretary, 1957 MP, 1963 member of party executive, 1965 minister of transport, post and telecommunications, 1967 minister of education, 1969 party chairman, 1969–1976 and 1982–1986 head of government.

Papen, Franz von 1879–1969, dt. Offizier, 1920–1932 MdL v. Preußen f. d. Zentrumsfraktion, 1932 Reichskanzler (Rücktritt), 1932 Reichskommissar v. Preußen (Preußenschlag), 1933/34 Hitlers Vizekanzler, 1936–1938 Botschafter in Wien, 1939–1944 in Ankara, 1946 in Nürnberg freigesprochen.

Papen, Franz von 1879–1969, German officer, 1920–1932 Center Party MdL Prussia, 1932 Reich chancellor (resigned), 1932 Reich Commissar for Prussia (the "strike against Prussia"), 1933/34 Hitler's deputy chancellor, 1936–1938 ambassador in Vienna, 1939–1944 in Ankara, 1946 acquitted at Nuremberg.

Paul I. 1901–1964, König v. Griechenland, Ing., seit 1938 verheiratet mit Prinzessin Friederike Luise v. Braunschweig.
Paul I. 1901–1964, King of Greece, engineer, from 1938 married to Princess Friederike Luise of Brunswick.

Paul II., Johannes (Karol Wojtyla), Dr. h.c. geb. 1920 in Polen, Schauspieler, 1946 Priesterweihe, 1958 Weihbischof, 1964 Erzbischof von Krakau, 1967 Kardinal, seit 1978 Papst

Paul II., John (Karol Wojtyla), Dr. h.c. b. 1920 in Poland, actor, 1946 ordained as priest, 1958 suffragan bishop, 1964 archbishop of Krakow, 1967 cardinal, since 1978 Pope.

Paul, Hugo 1905–1962, dt. Werkzeugmacher u. Politiker, 1932/33 MdR u. Unterbezirkssekretär d. KPD, bis 1939 KZ-Haft, 1946–1948 Minister f. Wiederaufbau v. Nordrhein-Westfalen, Landesvorsitzender d. KPD, ab 1947 MdL, ab 1949 MdB.

Paul, Hugo 1905–1962, German toolmaker and politician, 1932/33 MdR and KPD district under-secretary, imprisoned in KZ until 1939, 1946–1948 minister of reconstruction in North Rhine-Westphalia, KPD *Land* chairman, from 1947 MdL, from 1949 MdB.

Pearson, Lester 1897–1972, kanad. Politiker d. Liberalen Partei, 1935–1941 1. Sekretär beim kanad. Botschafter in England, 1942 Botschaftsrat in Washington, 1946 Unterstaatssekretär in Ottawa, 1948–1968 Mitgl. d. Unterhauses, 1948–1957 Außenminister, 1951 Präsident d. NATO-Rates, 1958–1968 Parteiführer, 1963–1968 Premierminister.

Pearson, Lester 1897–1972, Canadian politician (Liberal Party), 1935–1941 first secretary to Canadian ambasssador in England, 1942 councillor at Washington embassy, 1946 under-secretary of state in Ottawa, 1948–1968 MP, 1948–1957 foreign minister, 1951 president of NATO council, 1958–1968 party leader, 1963–1968 prime minister.

Peres, Shimon (eigentl. S. Persky) geb. 1923, israel. Politiker, seit 1933 in Palästina, Mitgl. d. Haganah, bis 1965 Mitgl. d. Mapai Partei, 1941–1945 Generalsekretär d. Gewerkschaft Histadrut, 1948 Leiter d. Marineabt. im Verteidigungsministerium, 1953 dort Generaldirektor, 1959–1965 stellv. Verteidigungsminister, 1968 Mitgl. d. AP, 1969 Minister f. Einwanderung u. verwaltete Gebiete, 1970 Transport- u. Postminister, 1974–1977 Verteidigungsminister, 1984–1986 u. 1995/1996 Regierungschef, 1986–1988 u. 1992– 1995 Außenminister, 1988–1990 Finanzminister.

Peres, Shimon (originally S. Persky) b. 1923, Israeli politician, from 1933 in Palestine, member of Haganah, until 1965 member of Mapai party, 1941–1945 general secretary of Histadrut trade union, 1948 head of naval department at defense ministry, 1953 director general there, 1959–1965 deputy defense minister, 1968 member of Labor Party, 1969 minister of immigration and administered territories, 1970 minister of transport and post, 1974–1977 defense minister, 1984–1986 and 1995/1996 head of government, 1986–1988 and 1992–1995 foreign minister, 1988–1990 finance minister.

Perwuchin, Michail Georgijewitsch 1904–1978, sowjet. Elektro-Ing., Wirtschaftspolitiker u. Diplomat, 1919 KP-Mitgl., 1939 ZK-Mitgl., 1942–1950 Verwalter d. Volkskommissariats bzw. d. Ministeriums f. chem. Industrie d. UdSSR, 1950–1957 stellv. Vorsitzender d. Ministerrats d. UdSSR, 1952–1957 Präsidiumsmitgl. d. ZK, 1953–1955 Leiter d. Mininsteriums f. Elektroindustrie, 1957 Leiter d. Ministeriums f. mittleren Maschinenbau, 1958–1962 sowjet. Botschafter in Ost-Berlin.

Pervuchin, Mikhail Georgeyevich 1904–1978, Soviet electrical engineer, economist, politician and diplomat, 1919 member of CP, 1939 member of central committee, 1942–1950 administrator of people's commissariat/ministry for the USSR chemical industry, 1950–1957 deputy chairman of USSR council of ministers, 1952–1957 member of central committee presidium, 1953–1955 head of ministry for the electrical industry, 1957 head of ministry of medium-scale engineering, 1958–1962 Soviet ambassador in East Berlin.

Philip Mountbatten, geb. 1921, seit 1947 Herzog v. Edinburgh, seit 1957 Prinz v. Großbritannien u. Nordirland, seit 1947 mit Königin Elizabeth II. verheiratet.

Philip Mountbatten, b. 1921, since 1947 Duke of Edinburgh, since 1957 Prince of Great Britain and Northern Ireland, since 1947 married to Queen Elizabeth II.

Pieck, Wilhelm 1876–1960, dt. Tischler u. Politiker, 1917 Mitbegr. d. Spartakusbundes, 1918 d. KPD, 1935 Vorsitzender d. Exil-KPD, 1938–1943 Generalsekretär d. Komintern, 1943 Mitbegr. d. Nationalkomitees Freies Deutschl., ab 1945 KPD-Vorsitzender, 1946–1954 SED-Vorsitzender, 1949–1960 Präsident d. DDR.

Pieck, Wilhelm 1876–1960, German joiner, 1917 co-founder of Spartacus League and 1918 of KPD, 1935 chairman of KPD in exile, 1938–1943 Comintern general secretary, 1943 co-founder of national committee Free Germany, from 1945 KPD party chairman, 1946–1954 SED party chairman, 1949–1960 president of GDR.

Pineau, Christian 1904–1995, frz. Politiker, Wirtschaftler u. Schriftsteller, 1934–1936 Sekretär d. Wirtschaftsrats d. CGT, 1945 Leiter d. Ernährungsministeriums, 1946–1958 Mitgl. d. Nationalversammlung f. d. Sozialist. Partei SFIO, 1947–1950 Minister f. öffentl. Arbeiten u. Transportwesen, 1956–1958 Außenminister.

Pineau, Christian 1904–1995, French politician, economist and writer, 1934–1936 secretary of CGT economic council, 1945 head of ministry of food, 1946–1958 member of national assembly for the socialist party SFIO, 1947–1950 minister of public works and transport, 1956–1958 foreign minister.

Pleitgen, Fritz Ferdinand geb. 1938, dt. Fernsehjournalist, 1963–1970 Reporter f. d. »Tagesschau« beim WDR, 1970 ARD-Fernsehkorrespondent in Moskau, 1977–1982 in Ost-Berlin, 1982–1987 in Washington, dann in New York, ab 1988 WDR-Chefredakteur, 1994 WDR-Hörfunkdirektor, ab 1995 WDR-Intendant.

Pleitgen, Fritz Ferdinand b. 1938, German TV journalist, 1963–1970 WDR news and current affairs reporter, 1970 ARD TV correspondent in Moscow, 1977–1982 in East Berlin, 1982–1987 in Washington, then in New York, from 1988 WDR editor-in-chief, 1994 WDR director of radio, from 1995 WDR general manager.

Pompidou, George 1911–1974, frz. Politiker, 1948–1954 u. 1958/59 Kabinettschef, 1959-1962 Mitgl. d. Verfassungsrats, 1962–1968 Ministerpräsident, 1969–1974 Staatspräsident.

Pompidou, George 1911–1974, French politician, 1948–1954 and 1958/59 head of cabinet, 1959-1962 member of constitutive council, 1962–1968 prime minister, 1969–1974 President.

Ponto, Jürgen 1923–1977 (ermordet), dt. Bankier, 1959 Chefsyndikus d. Dresdner Bank, ab 1969 Vorstandssprecher.

Ponto, Jürgen 1923–1977 (assassinated), German banker, 1959 principal company lawyer for Dresdner Bank, from 1969 board spokesman.

Prodi, Romano, Prof. geb. 1939, ital. Wirtschaftswissenschaftler, Industriemanager, Publizist u. Politiker, 1978/79 Industrieminister, 1982–1989 u. 1993/94 Präsident d. ital. Instituts f. Industriellen Wiederaufbau, 1996–1998 Ministerpräsident u. Führer d. Mitte-Links-Allianz »Olivenbaum«, 1999 Kandidat f. d. Präsidentschaft d. EU-Kommission.

Prodi, Romano, professor, b. 1939, Italian economist, industrial manager, publicist and politician, 1978/79 industry minister, 1982–1989 and 1993/94 president of Italian institute of industrial reconstruction, 1996–1998 prime minister and leader of center-left "olive tree" alliance, 1999 president of EU commission.

Pünder, Hermann Josef, Dr., Dr. jur. h.c. (1910) 1888–1976, dt. Jurist u. Politiker, 1919 Regierungsrat im Finanzministerium, bis 1933 Zentrumsmitgl., 1926–1932 Chef d. Reichskanzlei, 1945 Mitbegr. d. CDU in Münster, 1945–1948 Oberbürgermeister v. Köln, 1948 Oberdirektor u. Vorsitzender d. Verwaltungsrates d. Vereinigten Wirtschaftsgebietes, 1949–1957 MdB, ab 1952 mehrmals Vizepräsident d. beratenden Versammlung d. Europarates.

Pünder, Hermann Josef, Dr., Dr. jur. h.c. (1910) 1888–1976, German lawyer and politician, 1919 government councillor at finance ministry, until 1933 member of Center Party, 1926–1932 head of Reich chancellery, 1945 co-founder of CDU in Münster, 1945–1948 mayor of Cologne, 1948 senior director and chairman of administrative council of the United Economic Area, 1949–1957 MdB, from 1952 several times vice president of Council of Europe consultative assembly.

Q

Quidde, Ludwig 1858–1941, dt. Historiker u. Politiker, Ratsmitgl. u. Vizepräsident d. internat. Friedensbureaus, 1914 Vorsitz d. dt. Friedensgesellschaft, Mitgl. d. DDP, 1927 Träger d. Friedensnobelpreises f. seinen Verdienst um eine dt.-frz. Verständigung, 1921–1929 Präsident d. Dt. Friedenskartells, 1933 Flucht in d. Schweiz.

Quidde, Ludwig 1858–-1941, German historian and politician, council member and vice president of International Peace Bureau, 1914 chairman of German Peace Association, member of DDP, 1927 awarded Nobel peace prize for his contribution to Franco-German understanding, 1921–1929 president of German Peace Alliance, 1933 fled to Switzerland.

R

Rabin, Yitzhak [Jitzhak] 1922–1995 (ermordet), israel. Politiker u. General, 1941 Mitgl. d. »Palmach«, 1944 stellv. Befehlshaber, 1960–1964 stellv. u. 1964–1967 Generalstabschef, 1968–1973 israel. Vertreter in Washington, 1973 MdP f. d. AP, Arbeitsminister, 1974–1977 u. 1992–1995 Ministerpräsident, 1984–1990 u. 1992–1995 Verteidigungsminister.

Rabin, Yitzhak 1922–1995 (assassinated), Israeli politician and general, 1941 member of "Palmach", 1944 deputy commander, 1960–1964 deputy and 1964–1967 chief of general staff, 1968–1973 Israeli representative in Washington, 1973 Labor Party MP, minister of labor, 1974–1977 and 1992–1995 prime minister, 1984–1990 and 1992–1995 defense minister.

Raeder, Erich, Dr. phil. h.c. 1876–1960, dt. Großadmiral, 1894 Eintritt in d. Marine, 1897 Seeoffizier, 1928 Marine-Admiral, 1934 Generaladmiral, 1935–1943 Oberbefehlshaber d. Kriegsmarine, 1939 Großadmiral, 1946 in Nürnberg zu lebenslanger Haft verurteilt, 1955 freigelassen.

Raeder, Erich Dr. phil. h.c. 1876–1960, German great admiral, 1894 joined Navy, 1897 naval officer, 1928 naval admiral, 1934 general admiral, 1935–1943 naval supreme commander, 1939 great admiral, 1946 sentenced to life imprisonment at Nuremberg, released in 1955.

Rathke, Arthur, Dr. med. (1944) 1920–1980, dt. Arzt u. Politiker, ab 1956 CDU-Mitgl., 1963–1970 Sprecher d. CDU-Bundesvorstandes, ab 1970 Staatssekretär f. d. Informations- u. Presseamt d. Landesregierung Schleswig-Holstein, ab 1970 Mitgl. d. Fernsehrates d. ZDF.

Rathke, Arthur, Dr. med. (1944) 1920–1980, German doctor and politician, from 1956 member of CDU, 1963–1970 CDU federal executive spokesman, from 1970 state secretary at press and information office of *Land* government in Schleswig-Holstein, 1970 member of ZDF TV council.

Rau, Johannes, Dr. h.c. geb. 1931, dt. Verlagsbuchhändler u. Politiker, 1952–1957 GVP-Mitgl., 1957 SPD-Eintritt, 1964–1978 Stadtverordneter v. Wuppertal, 1969–1970 Oberbürgermeister, seit 1958 MdL v. Nordrhein-Westfalen, 1967–1970 Fraktionsvorsitzender, 1970–1978 Minister f. Wissensch. u. Forschung, 1978–1998 Ministerpräsident von Nordrhein-Westfalen, 1990–1995 zugleich Minister f. Bundesangelegenheiten, 1977–1998 SPD-Landesvorsitzender, seit 1968 Mitgl. d. Bundesparteivorstandes, seit 1978 Mitgl. d. Präsidiums, seit 1982 stellv. SPD-Vorsitzender, 1986/87 SPD-Kanzlerkandidat, 1999 Präsidentschaftskandidat.

Rau, Johannes, Dr. h.c. b. 1931, German publisher and politician, 1952–1957 member of GVP, 1957 joined SPD, 1964–1978 member of Wuppertal town council, 1969–1970 mayor, from 1958 MdL North Rhine-Westphalia, 1967–1970 chief whip, 1970–1978 minister of science and research, 1978–1998 minister president of North Rhine-Westphalia, 1990–1995 also minister for federal affairs, 1977–1998 SPD Land chairman, since 1968 member of federal party executive, since 1978 member of presidium, since 1982 deputy SPD party chairman, 1986/87 SPD chancellor candidate, 1999 presidential candidate.

Reagan, Nancy (geb. Ann Francis Robbins) geb. 1921, amerik. Schauspielerin, seit 1951 Ronald Reagans Ehefrau, 1967–1974 »First Lady« v. Kalifornien, 1981–1989 »US-First Lady«.

Reagan, Nancy (née Ann Francis Robbins) b. 1921, American actress, since 1951 wife of Ronald Reagan, 1967–1974 "First Lady" of California, 1981–1989 "US First Lady".

Reagan, Ronald Wilson geb. 1911, amerik. Schauspieler u. Politiker (Republikaner), 1967–1974 Gouverneur v. Kalifornien, 1981–1989 US-Präsident.

Reagan, Ronald Wilson b. 1911, American actor and politician (Republican), 1967–1974 Governor of California, 1981–1989 US President.

Reimann, Max 1898–1977, dt. Bergmann u. Politiker, 1916 Mitgl. d. Spartakusbundes, 1919 Mitbegr. d. KPD, 1928–1932 Parteisekretär im Bezirk Hamm, 1936–1939 Mitgl. d. Auslandbüros d. ZK d. KPD, 1939–1945 Zuchthaus u. KZ, 1947 1. Vorsitzender d. Landesverbandes Nordrhein-Westfalen u. Vorsitzender in d. BBZ, 1948– 1956 1. Parteivorsitzender d. KPD, MdPR sowie d. bizonalen Wirtschaftsrates, 1949–1953 MdB u. Fraktionsvorsitzender, 1971 DKP-Eintritt u. Präsidiumsmitgl.

Reimann, Max 1898–1977, German miner and politician, 1916 member of Spartacus League, 1919 co-founder of KPD, 1928–1932 Hamm district party secretary, 1936–1939 member of foreign bureau of KPD central committee, 1939–1945 penitentiary and KZ, 1947 first chairman of Land association in North Rhine-Westphalia and chairman in British zone of occupation, 1948–1956 first party chairman of KPD, MdPR and member of bizonal economic council, 1949–1953 MdB and chief whip, 1971 joined DKP, member of presidium.

Renger, Annemarie (geb. Wildung) geb. 1919, dt. Politikerin, seit 1945 SPD-Mitgl., 1945–1952 Privatsekretärin d. SPD-Vorsitzenden Kurt Schumacher, 1953–1990 MdB, 1961–1973 Parteivorstandsmitgl., 1970–1973 Präsidiumsmitgl., 1972–1976 Bundestagspräsidentin, 1976–1990 Bundestagsvizepräsidentin, 1990 Präsidentin d. Dt. Rates d. Europ. Bewegung.

Renger, Annemarie (née Wildung) b. 1919, German politician, from 1945 member of SPD, 1945–1952 private secretary of SPD party chairman Kurt Schumacher, 1953–1990 MdB, 1961–1973 member of party executive, 1970–1973 member of presidium, 1972–1976 president of Bundestag, 1976–1990 vice president of Bundestag, 1990 president of German council of Europe Movement.

Renner, Heinz 1892–1964, dt. Journalist u. Politiker (KPD), 1942–1945 KZ, 1946–1950 MdL v. Nordrhein-Westfalen, 1946 Sozialminister, Oberbürgermeister v. Essen, 1947/48 Verkehrsminister, 1948/49 MdPR, 1949–1953 MdB.

Renner, Heinz 1892–1964, German journalist and politician (KPD), 1942–1945 KZ, 1946–1950 MdL North Rhine-Westphalia, 1946 welfare minister, mayor of Essen, 1947/48 transport minister, 1948/49 MdPR, 1949–1953 MdB.

Reuter, Ernst 1889–1953, dt. Politiker, 1912 u. 1922 SPD-Eintritt, 1918–1922 KPD-Mitgl., 1921 Generalsekretär, 1926 Mitschöpfer d. BVG, 1931–1933 Oberbürgermeister v. Magdeburg, 1932/33 MdR, dann in d. Türkei Berater d. Wirtschafts- u. Verkehrsministeriums, 1947 zum Oberbürgermeister gewählt, 1948 Amtsantritt, 1951– 1953 Regierender Bürgermeister v. Berlin.

Reuter, Ernst 1889–1953, German politician, 1912 and 1922 joined SPD, 1918–1922 member of KPD, 1921 general secretary, 1926 co-creator of BVG, 1931–1933 mayor of Magdeburg, 1932/33 MdR, then adviser at ministry of economics and transport in Turkey, 1947 elected mayor of Berlin, took up office in 1948, 1951–1953 governing mayor of Berlin.

Ribbentrop, Joachim von 1863–1946, dt. NS-Politiker, 1932 NSDAP-Eintritt, 1933 MdR, Hitlers außenpolit. Berater, 1936–1938 Botschafter in London, 1938–1945 Reichsaußenminister, in Nürnberg hingerichtet.

Ribbentrop, Joachim 1863–1946, German NS politician, 1932 joined NSDAP, 1933 MdR, Hitler's foreign policy adviser, 1936–1938 ambassador in London, 1938–1945 Reich foreign minister, executed at Nuremberg.

Ridgway, Matthew Bunker 1895–1993, amerik. General, 1939–1942 in d. War Plans Division im Verteidigungsministerium, 1942–1944 Kommando über d. 82. Infanteriedivision bzw. Luftlandedivision, 1949 stellv. Chef d. Stabes d. US Army in Washington, 1951 Oberster Befehlshaber d. alliierten Truppen im Fernen Osten, 1952/53 NATO-Oberbefehlshaber, 1953–1955 Generalstabschef d. Heeres

Ridgway, Matthew Bunker 1895–1993, American general, 1939–1942 at war plans division of defense ministry, 1942–1944 in command of 82nd infantry division/air landing division, 1949 US army deputy chief of staff in Washington, 1951 supreme commander of Allied forces in the Far East, 1952/53 NATO supreme commander, 1953–1955 chief of army general staff.

Riesenhuber, Heinz, Prof. Dr. rer. nat. (1965) geb. 1935, dt. Dipl.-Chemiker u. Politiker, 1961 CDU-Eintritt, 1965-1969 Landesvorsitzender d. JU in Hessen, 1968 stellv. JU-Vorsitzender, 1968 Mitgl. im Präsidium d. CDU Hessen, 1973-1978 Kreisvorsitzender in Frankfurt, seit 1976 MdB, 1982-1993 Bundesminister f. Forschung u. Technologie.

Riesenhuber, Heinz, professor, Dr. rer. nat. (1965) b. 1935, German chemistry graduate and politician, 1961 joined CDU, 1965-1969 *Land* chairman of Young Union in Hessen, 1968 deputy chairman of Young Union, 1968 member of CDU presidium in Hessen, 1973-1978 Frankfurt district chairman, since 1976 MdB, 1982-1993 minister of research and technology.

Riester, Walter geb. 1943, dt. Fliesenleger u. Gewerkschaftsfunktionär, 1957 Mitgl. d. IG Bau-Steine-Erden, ab 1970 DGB-Mitgl., ab 1977 Mitgl. d. IG Metall, seit 1993 2. IG-Metall-Vorsitzender, seit 1966 SPD-Mitgl., seit 1998 Bundesminister f. Arbeit u. Sozialhilfe.

Riester, Walter b. 1943, German tiler and trade union official, 1957 member of IG construction, from 1970 member of DGB, from 1977 member of IG metal, since 1993 second chairman of IG metal, since 1966 member of SPD, since 1998 minister of labor and welfare assistance.

Rohwedder, Detlev Karsten, Dr. jur. (1961) 1932–1991, (ermordet) dt. Industriemanager, 1969 SPD-Eintritt, 1969–1978 Staatssekretär im Wirtschaftsministerium, 1980–1990 Vorstandsvorsitzender d. Hoesch Werke AG, 1990/91 Vorstandsvorsitzender d. Treuhandanstalt, ermordet durch RAF-Anschlag.

Rohwedder, Detlev Karsten, Dr. jur. (1961) 1932–1991, German industrial manager, 1969 joined SPD, 1969–1978 state secretary at economics ministry, 1980–1990 member of board of management of Hoesch Werke & Co, 1990/91 member of executive of "Treuhandanstalt", assassinated by RAF.

Romberg, Walter, Dr. (1965) geb. 1928, dt. Mathematiker u. Politiker, 1989 SPD-Eintritt, Mitgl. d. Grundsatzkommission, 1990 DDR-Finanzminister, 1990 MdEP.

Romberg, Walter, Dr. (1965) b. 1928 German mathematician and politician, 1989 joined SPD, member of fundamental values commission, 1990 GDR finance minister, 1990 MEP.

Rönsch, Hannelore geb. 1942, dt. Politikerin, 1963 CDU-Eintritt, 1974–1980 Stadtverordnete in Wiesbaden, 1980–1983 Stadträtin, seit 1983 MdB, seit 1988 Mitgl. d. CDU-Präsidiums in Hessen, 1991–1994 Bundesmininsterin f. Familie u. Senioren, seit 1994 stellv. CDU/CSU-Fraktionsvorsitzende.

Rönsch, Hannelore b. 1942, German politician, 1963 joined CDU, 1974–1980 member of Wiesbaden town council, 1980–1983 municiapl councillor, since 1983 MdB, since 1988 member of CDU presidium in Hessen, 1991–1994 minister for the family and senior citizens, since 1994 CDU/CSU deputy whip.

Rosenberg, Alfred 1893–1946, 1919 Eintritt in d. Dt. AP, 1923 Hauptschriftleiter d. Zeitschrift »Völkischer Beobachter«, Teilnahme am Hitlerputsch, 1924 Gründer d. Org. »Großdeutsche Volksgemeinschaft«, 1930 MdR f. d. NSDAP, 1933–1945 Leiter d. Außenpolit. Amtes, 1934 Beauftragter f. d. Überwachung d. gesamten geistigen u. weltanschaul. Schulung u. Erziehung d. NSDAP, 1941 Reichsminister f. d. besetzten Ostgebiete, in Nürnberg hingerichtet.

Rosenberg, Alfred 1893–1946, 1919 joined German Workers' party, 1923 chief editor of the *Völkischer Beobachter*, involved in Munich putsch, 1924 founder of "Greater German People's Community", 1930 NSDAP MdR, 1933–1945 head of foreign affairs office, 1934 NSDAP official with responsibility for supervising intellectual and philosophical schooling and education in its entirety, 1941 Reich minister for the occupied eastern territories, executed at Nuremberg.

Rühe, Volker geb. 1942, dt. Lehrer u. Politiker, seit 1963 CDU-Mitgl., 1970-1976 Mitgl. d. Hamburger Bürgerschaft, 1973 stellv. Fraktionsvorsitzender, 1973-1975 Mitgl. d. Bundesvorstandes d. JU, seit 1976 MdB, 1982-1989 u. seit 1998 stellv. Vorsitzender d. CDU/CSU-Fraktion, 1989-1992 Generalsekretär, seit 1990 Mitgl. d. Präsidiums, 1992-1998 Bundesminister d. Verteidigung, seit 1998 stellv. Parteivorsitzender.

Rühe, Volker b. 1942, German teacher and politician, since 1963 member of CDU, 1970-1976 member of Hamburg city parliament, 1973 deputy whip, 1973-1975 member of Young Union federal executive, since 1976 MdB, 1982-1989 and since 1998 CDU/CSU deputy whip, 1989-1992 general secretary, since 1990 member of presidium, 1992-1998 defense minister, since 1998 deputy party chairman.

S

Sadat, Anwar el 1918–1981 (ermordet), ägypt. Staatsmann, 1938 Gründer d. Organisation »Freie Offiziere«, 1952 Oberst, 1954–1956 Informationsminister, 1957–1961 Generalsekretär, 1960–1969 Präsident d. Nationalversammlung, 1969 Vizepräsident d. Ägyptisch-Syrischen Union (VAR), 1970–1981 Staatspräsident, 1973/74 u. 1980/81 ebenso Regierungschef, 1979 Friedensvertrag mit Israel.

Sadat, Anwar el 1918–1981 (assassinated), Egyptian statesman, 1938 founder of the organization "Free Officers", 1952 colonel, 1954–1956 minister of information, 1957–1961 general secretary, 1960–1969 president of national assembly, 1969 vice president of Union of Egypt and Syria (United Arab Republic), 1970–1981 President, 1973/74 and 1980/81 also head of government, 1979 peace treaty with Israel.

Santer, Jacques, Dr. jur. geb. 1937, luxemb. Jurist u. Politiker, 1963 Attaché im Ministerium f. Arbeit u. Soziales, 1972 Staatssekretär im Arbeitsministerium u. im Ministerium f. kulturelle Angelegenheiten, 1974–1982 CSV-Präsident, 1975–1979 Vizepräsident d. EP, Mitbegr. d. EVP (1987–1990 Präsident), 1979–1984 Minister f. Finanzen, Arbeit u. Soziales, 1984–1994 zum Ministerpräsidenten gewählt, 1984–1989 zugleich Minister f. d. Finanzen, 1995–1999 Präsident d. EU-Kommission.

Santer, Jacques, Dr. jur. b. 1937, Luxembourgian lawyer and politician, 1963 attaché at ministry of labor and welfare, 1972 state secretary at ministry of labor and ministry of cultural affairs, 1974–1982 CSV president, 1975–1979 vice president of EP, co-founder of EVP (1987–1990 president), 1979–1984 minister of finance, labor and welfare, 1984–1994 elected prime minister, 1984–1989 also minister of finance, 1995–1999 president of EU Commission.

Sauckel, Fritz 1894–1946, NS-Beamter u. Politiker, 1942–1945 Generalbevollmächtigter f. d. Arbeitseinsatz, in Nürnberg hingerichtet.

Sauckel, Fritz 1894–1946, NS civil servant and politician, 1942–1945 "Official with overall responsibility for the employment of labor", executed at Nuremberg.

Schabowski, Günter geb. 1929, dt. Journalist u. DDR-Politiker, 1952 SED-Eintritt, 1978–1985 Mitgl. d. Agitationskommission beim PB d. ZK d. SED,1981–1990 MdVK, 1981–1989 ZK-Mitgl., ab 1984 Mitgl. d. PB, ab 1986 Sekretär d. ZK d. SED, 1984–1989 Mitgl. d. PB, 1990 Parteiausschluß.

Schabowski, Günter b. 1929, German journalist and GDR politician, 1952 joined SED, 1978–1985 member of agitation commission of SED central committee PB, 1981–1990 member of Volkskammer, 1981–1989 member of central committee, from 1984 member of PB, from 1986 secretary of SED central committee, 1984–1989 member of PB, 1990 expelled from party.

Schacht, Hjalmar, Dr. phil. (1900) 1877–1970, dt. Finanzfachmann, 1908 stellv. Direktor d. Dresdner Bank, 1923–1930 u. 1933–1938 Reichsbankpräsident, 1934–1937 Reichswirtschaftsminister, sodann Reichsminister ohne Geschäftsbereich, 1944/45 KZ, 1948 in Nürnberg freigesprochen.

Schacht, Hjalmar, Dr. phil. (1900) 1877–1970, German financial expert, 1908 deputy director of Dresdner Bank, 1923–1930 and 1933–1938 president of Reichsbank, 1934–1937 Reich economics minister, then Reich minister without portfolio, 1944/45 KZ, 1948 acquitted at Nuremberg.

Schäfer, Hermann, Dr. phil. (1914) 1892–1966, dt. Politiker, 1920 Mitgl. d. DDP, 1925–1933 Mitgl. im Reichsvorstand, 1946 stellv. FDP-Vorsitzender d. Landesverbandes Hamburg, 1948/49 MdPR u. Vizepräsident, 1949–1957 MdB, Vizepräsident d. Bundestages, 1949–1956 Vorsitzender d. FDP-Fraktion, 1950–1955 stellv. Parteivorsitzender, 1953–1956 Minister f. Sonderaufgaben, 1956–1960 Mitbegr. u. stellv. Parteivorsitzender d. FVP, 1961 wieder FDP-Mitgl.

Schäfer, Hermann, Dr. phil. (1914) 1892–1966, German politician, 1920 member of DDP, 1925–1933 member of Reich executive, 1946 deputy chairman of Hamburg FDP *Land* association, 1948/49 member and vice president of parliamentary council, 1949–1957 MdB, vice president of the Bundestag, 1949–1956 FDP chief whip, 1950–1955 deputy party chairman, 1953–1956 minister without portfolio, 1956–1960 co-founder and deputy chairman of FVP, 1961 again member of FDP.

Schäffer, Fritz 1888–1967, dt. Jurist u. Politiker, 1920 Oberregierungsrat im Ministerium f. Unterricht u. Kultus in Bayern, MdL f. d. Bayer. Volkspartei, 1929 Parteiführer 1931–1933 Staatsrat u. Leiter d. bayer. Finanzministeriums, 1945 kurz bayer. Ministerpräsident, Mitbegr. d. CSU, 1946–1948 v. d. Militärregierung v. polit. Tätigkeiten ausgeschlossen, 1949–1961 MdB f. d. CSU, 1949–1957 Bundesfinanzminister, 1957–1961 Bundesjustizminister.

Schäffer, Fritz 1888–1967, German lawyer and politician, 1920 senior government councillor at Bavarian ministry of education and culture, MdL (Bavarian People's Party), 1929 party leader, 1931–1933 state councillor and head of Bavarian finance ministry, 1945 briefly minister president of Bavaria, co-founder of CSU, 1946–1948 banned from political activity by the military government, 1949–1961 CSU MdB, 1949–1957 federal finance minister, 1957–1961 justice minister.

Scharping, Rudolf geb. 1947, dt. Politiker, seit 1966 SPD-Mitgl., 1975–1994 MdL v. Rheinland-Pfalz, 1991-1994 Ministerpräsident, 1993-1995 SPD-Vorsitzender, seit 1994 MdB, 1994–1998 Vorsitzender d. SPD-Fraktion, seit 1998 Bundesminister d. Verteidigung.

Scharping, Rudolf b. 1947, German politician, since 1966 member of SPD, 1975–1994 MdL Rhineland-Palatinate, 1991-1994 minister president, 1993-1995 SPD party chairman, since 1994 MdB, 1994–1998 SPD chief whip, since 1998 defense minister.

Schäuble, Wolfgang, Dr. (1971) geb. 1942, dt. Rechtsanwalt u. Politiker, seit 1961 Mitgl. d. JU, seit 1965 CDU-Mitgl., seit 1972 MdB, 1981-1984 Parlam. Geschäftsführer d. CDU/CSU-Fraktion, 1984-1989 Bundesminister f. besondere Aufgaben u. Chef d. Bundeskanzleramtes, 1989-1991 Bundesminister d. Innern, seit 1991 Vorsitzender d. CDU/CSU-Fraktion, seit Nov. 1998 CDU-Bundesvorsitzender.

Schäuble, Wolfgang, Dr. (1971) b. 1942, German lawyer and politician, from 1961 member of Young Union, since 1965 member of CDU, since 1972 MdB, 1981-1984 CDU/CSU parliamentary group manager, 1984-1989 minister without portfolio and head of chancellery, 1989-1991 minister of the interior, since 1991 CDU/CSU chief whip, since Nov. 1998 CDU federal chairman.

Scheel, Walter, Dr. h.c. geb. 1919, dt. Politiker, seit 1946 Mitgl. d. FDP, 1950–1953 MdL v. Nordrhein-Westfalen, 1953–1974 MdB, 1967–1969 Bundestagsvizepräsident, 1961–1966 Bundesminister f. wirtschaftl. Zusammenarbeit, 1968–1974 FDP-Bundesvorsitzender, 1969–1974 Außenminister u. Vizekanzler, 1974–1979 Bundespräsident.

Scheel, Walter, Dr. h.c. b. 1919, German politician, since 1946 member of FDP, 1950–1953 MdL North Rhine-Westphalia, 1953–1974 MdB, 1967–1969 deputy president of Bundestag, 1961–1966 minister for economic cooperation, 1968–1974 FDP federal party chairman, 1969–1974 foreign minister and deputy chancellor, 1974–1979 President.

Scheel, Mildred, Dr. med. (geb. Wirtz) 1932–1985, dt. Ärztin, seit 1969 mit Walter Scheel verheiratet.

Scheel, Mildred, Dr. med. (née Wirtz) 1932–1985, German doctor, from 1969 married to Walter Scheel.

Scheidemann, Philipp 1865–1939, dt. Buchdrucker u. Politiker, 1883 SPD-Eintritt, 1906–1911 Stadtverordneter v. Kassel, 1903–1918 MdR, 1911 Mitgl. d. Parteivorstandes, 1918 Proklamation d. dt. Republik, 1919 Ministerpräsident d. Reichsregierung, 1920–1925 Oberbürgermeister v. Kassel, 1920–1933 MdR, 1933 Flucht ins Ausland.

Scheidemann, Philipp 1865–1939, German bookprinter and politician, 1883 joined SPD, 1906–1911 member of Kassel town council, 1903–1918 MdR, 1911 member of party executive, 1918 proclaimed German Republic, 1919 Reich prime minister, 1920–1925 mayor of Kassel, 1920–1933 MdR, 1933 fled abroad.

Scherpenberg, Albert Hilger van, Dr. jur. (1926) 1899–1969, dt. Diplomat, 1928–1935 Legationssekretär in d. Botschaft in London, 1945–1949 Bayer. Wirtschaftsminister, 1949–1953 Bundeswirtschaftsminister, 1953–1961 f. d. Auswärtige Amt in Bonn tätig, ab 1955 Ministerialdirektor, ab 1958 Staatssekretär, 1961–1964 Botschafter beim Heiligen Stuhl in Rom.

Scherpenberg, Albert Hilger van, Dr. jur. (1926) 1899–1969, German diplomat, 1928–1935 legation secretary at London embassy, 1945–1949 Bavarian economics minister, 1949–1953 federal economics minister, 1953–1961 worked for the foreign office in Bonn, from 1955 ministerial director, from 1958 state secretary, 1961–1964 ambassador to Holy See in Rome.

Schewardnadse, Eduard Ambrosewitsch geb. 1928, sowjet. Politiker, ab 1948 Mitgl. d. KPdSU, 1957–1961 1. Sekretär d. ZK d. Komsomol Georgiens, 1959 Mitgl. d. Obersten Sowjet Georgiens, 1965–1972 Minister f. öffentl. Sicherheit bzw. Innenminister, 1966 Vollmitgl. d. PB, 1969 General, 1972–1985 Parteichef in Georgien, ab 1974 Mitgl. d. Obersten Sowjet d. UdSSR, 1976 Vollmitgl. d. ZK d. KPdSU, 1985 Vollmitgl. d. PB, 1985–1991 Außenminister d. UdSSR, seit 1992 Staatsoberhaupt Georgiens.

Shevardnadze, Eduard Amvrosiyevich b. 1928, Soviet politician, from 1948 member of CPSU, 1957–1961 first secretary of Georgian comsomol central committee, 1959 member of Georgian supreme soviet, 1965–1972 minister of public security/minister of the interior, 1966 full member of PB, 1969 general, 1972–1985 party chief in Georgia, from 1974 member of USSR supreme soviet, 1976 full member of CPSU central committee, 1985 full member of PB, 1985–1991 USSR foreign minister, since 1992 Georgian head of state.

Schiller, Karl, Dr. h.c. (1935/1939) 1911–1994, dt. Wirtschaftswissenschaftler u. Politiker, 1946–1972 u. ab 1980 Mitgl. d. SPD, 1948–1953 Senator f. Wirtschaft u. Verkehr in Hamburg u. 1961–1965 in Berlin, 1949–1957 Mitgl. d. Hamburger Bürgerschaft, 1965–1972 MdB, 1966–1972 Bundesminister f. Wirtschaft u. Finanzen.

Schiller, Karl, Dr. h.c. (1935/1939) b. 1911–1994, German economist and politician, 1946–1972 and from 1980 member of SPD, 1948–1953 senator for economics and transport in Hamburg and 1961–1965 in Berlin, 1949–1957 member of Hamburg city parliament, 1965–1972 MdB, 1966–1972 minister of economics and finance.

Schily, Otto geb. 1932, dt. Rechtsanwalt u. Politiker, Gründungsmitgl. d. Grünen Partei, 1983-1986 u. 1987-1989 MdB, seit 1990 MdB f. d. SPD, 1993/94 Vorsitzender d. Treuhand-Untersuchungsausschusses, 1994–1998 stellv. Vorsitzender d. SPD-Fraktion, 1998 zum Bundesminister des Innern ernannt.

Schily, Otto b. 1932, German lawyer and politician, founding member of Green Party, 1983-1986 and 1987-1989 MdB, since 1990 SPD MdB, 1993/94 chairman of "Treuhand" investigative committee, 1994–1998 SPD deputy whip, 1998 appointed minister of the interior.

Schirach, Baldur von 1907–1974, dt. NS-Politiker, 1925 NSDAP-Eintritt, 1929 Führer d. NS Dt. Studentenbundes, 1931–1940 Reichsjugendführer d. NSDAP, 1933 Jugendführer d. Dt. Reiches, 1940 Gauleiter u. Reichsstatthalter in Wien, 1946 in Nürnberg zu 20 Jahren Haft verurteilt.

Schirach, Baldur von 1907–1974, German NS politician, 1925 joined NSDAP, 1929 leader of NS league of German students, 1931–1940 Reich NSDAP youth leader, 1933 German Reich youth leader, 1940 regional leader (*Gauleiter* and Reich governor in Vienna, 1946 sentenced to 20 years imprisonment at Nuremberg.

Schlauch, Rezzo geb. 1947, dt. Rechtsanwalt u. Politiker, 1980 Grünen-Eintritt, 1984–1994 MdL v. Baden-Württemberg, 1990-1992 Vorsitzender d. Grünen-Fraktion, seit 1994 MdB, ab Okt. 1998 Fraktionsvorsitzender.

Schlauch, Rezzo b. 1947, German lawyer and politician, 1980 joined Green Party, 1984–1994 MdL Baden-Württemberg, 1990-1992 Green Party chief whip, since 1994 MdB, from Oct. 1998 chief whip.

Schlei, Marie (geb. Stabenow) 1919–1983, dt. Lehrerin, Rektorin u. Politikerin, ab 1949 SPD-Mitgl., 1969–1981 MdB, 1974–1976 Parlam. Staatssekretärin beim Bundeskanzler, 1976–1978 Bundesministerin f. wirtschaftl. Zusammenarbeit, 1980/81 stellv. Vorsitzende d. SPD-Bundestagsfraktion

Schlei, Marie (née Stabenow) 1919–1983, German teacher, university president and politician, from 1949 member of SPD, 1969–1981 MdB, 1974–1976 parliamentary state secretary to chancellor, 1976–1978 minister for economic cooperation, 1980/81 SPD deputy whip.

Schleyer, Hanns Martin, Dr. jur. 1915–1977, dt. Industriemanager, ab 1963 Vorstandsmitgl. d. Stuttgarter Automobilkonzerns Daimler-Benz AG, ab 1973 Präsident d. BdA, ab 1977 Präsident d. BDI, ermordet durch RAF-Terroristen.

Schleyer, Hanns Martin, Dr. jur. 1915–1977, German industrial manager, from 1963 member of board of management of the Stuttgart automobil company Daimler-Benz, from 1973 president of BdA, from 1977 president of BDI, assassinated by RAF terrorists.

Schmid, Carlo, Dr. h.c. (1923/1929) 1896–1979, dt. Jurist u. Politiker, ab 1945 SPD-Mitgl., 1945 SPD-Landesvorsitzender v. Südwürttemberg, 1947–1950 Staatssekretär f. Justiz in Württemberg-Hohenzollern, MdL, 1947 Parteivorstandsmitgl., 1948/49 MdPR (Fraktionsvorsitzender), 1949–1972 MdB, 1949–1966 u. 1969–1972 Bundestagsvizepräsident, 1957–1966 stellv. Fraktionsvorsitzender, 1966–1969 Bundesminister f. Angelegenheiten d. Bundesrates u. d. Länder.

Schmid, Carlo, Dr. h.c. (1923/1929) 1896–1979, German lawyer and politician, from 1945 member of SPD, 1945 SPD Land chairman of South Württemberg, 1947–1950 state secretary for justice in Württemberg-Hohenzollern, MdL, 1947 member of party executive, 1948/49 MdPR (chief whip), 1949–1972 MdB, 1949–1966 and 1969–1972 vice president of the Bundestag, 1957–1966 deputy whip, 1966–1969 minister for Bundesrat and *Länder* affairs.

Schmidbauer, Bernd geb. 1939, dt. CDU-Politiker, seit 1983 MdB, 1991 Parlam. Staatssekretär beim Bundesministerium f. Umwelt, Naturschutz u. Reaktorsicherheit, 1991–1998 Staatsminister beim Bundeskanzler.

Schmidbauer, Bernd b. 1939, German CDU politician, since 1983 MdB, 1991 parliamentary state secretary at ministry of the environment, the protection of nature and reactor safety, 1991–1998 minister of state with the chancellor.

Schmidt, Hannelore (Loki) (geb. Glaser) geb. 1919, dt. Lehrerin, seit 1942 Ehefrau v. Helmut Schmidt.

Schmidt, Hannelore (Loki) (née Glaser), b. 1919, German teacher, since 1942 wife of Helmut Schmidt.

Schmidt, Helmut, Dr. h.c. geb. 1918, dt. Dipl.-Volkswirt, Publizist u. Politiker, seit 1946 SPD-Mitgl., 1953–1961 u. 1965–1987 MdB, 1961–1965 Innensenator v. Hamburg, 1965/66 stellv. u. 1967–1969 Fraktionsvorsitzender, 1968–1984 stellv. Parteivorsitzender, 1969–1972 Bundesverteidigungsminister, 1972–1974 Bundesfinanzminister, 1974–1982 Bundeskanzler, ab 1985 Mithrsg. d. Wochenzeitung »Die Zeit«.

Schmidt, Helmut, Dr. h.c. b. 1918, German economics graduate, publicist and politician, since 1946 member of SPD, 1953–1961 and 1965–1987 MdB, 1961–1965 Hamburg senator for the interior, 1965/66 deputy whip and 1967–1969 chief whip, 1968–1984 deputy party chairman, 1969–1972 defense minister, 1972–1974 finance minister, 1974–1982 chancellor, from 1985 co-editor of weekly *Die Zeit.*

Schmückle, Gerd geb. 1917, dt. General u. Publizist, 1956 Bundeswehr-Eintritt, 1957–1962 Pressesprecher d. Bundesverteidigungsministeriums, 1964 Brigadegeneral, 1964–1968 militär. Berater d. dt. NATO-Vertretung, 1970–1973 stellv. Chef d. Operationsabt. im NATO-Hauptquartier (SHAPE), 1970 Generalmajor, 1974–1978 Direktor d. IMS d. NATO, Generalleutnant, 1978–1980 stellv. NATO-Oberbefehlshaber, General.

Schmückle, Gerd b. 1917, German general and publicist, 1956 joined army, 1957–1962 defense ministry press spokesman, 1964 brigadier, 1964–1968 military adviser to German representatives at NATO, 1970–1973 deputy head of department of operations at NATO headquarters (SHAPE), 1970 major general, 1974–1978 director of NATO IMS, lieutenant general, 1978–1980 deputy supreme commander of NATO, general.

Schmücker, Kurt, Dr. h.c. 1919–1996, dt. Verleger u. Wirtschaftspolitiker, Mitbegr. d. JU in Oldenburg (1948–1954 Landesvorsitzender), 1949–1972 MdB, 1961–1963 stellv. CDU/CSU Fraktionsvorsitzender, 1963–1966 Bundeswirtschaftsminister, 1966–1969 Bundesschatzminister, 1968–1971 CDU-Schatzmeister.

Schmücker, Kurt, Dr. h.c. 1919–1996, German publisher, economist and politician, co-founder of CDU Young Union in Oldenburg (1948–1954 *Land* chairman), 1949–1972 MdB, 1961–1963 CDU/CSU deputy whip, 1963–1966 economics minister, 1966–1969 treasury minister, 1968–1971 CDU treasurer.

Schoeler, Andreas von geb. 1948, dt. Politiker, 1966–1982 FDP-Mitgl., ab 1982 SPD-Mitgl., 1972–1983 MdB, 1976–1982 Parlam. Staatssekretär beim Bundesminister d. Innern, 1976–1987 Staatssekretär im Innenministerium v. Hessen, 1991–1995 Oberbürgermeister v. Frankfurt/M.

Schoeler, Andreas von b. 1948, German politician, 1966–1982 member of FDP, from 1982 member of SPD, 1972–1983 MdB, 1976–1982 parliamentary state secretary with the minister of the interior, 1976–1987 state secretary at ministry of the interior in Hessen, 1991–1995 mayor of Frankfurt am Main.

Schönfelder, Adolf 1875–1966, dt. Zimmermann u. Politiker, ab 1919 Mitgl. d. Hamburger Bürgerschaft (SPD), 1920–1933 Mitgl. im SPD-Parteivorstand, 1925–1933 Senator, 1945/46 2. Bürgermeister, 1946–1960 Präsident d. Bürgerschaft, 1948/49 MdPR (Alters- u. Vizepräsident)

Schönfelder, Adolf 1875–1966, German carpenter and politician, from 1919 SPD member of Hamburg city parliament, 1920–1933 member of SPD party executive, 1925–1933 senator, 1945/46 second mayor, 1946–1960 president of city parliament, 1948/49 MdPR (senior member and vice president).

Schrempp, Jürgen geb. 1944, dt. Dipl.-Ing., 1989–1995 Vorstandsvorsitzender d. Daimler-Benz-Aerospace AG (DASA), ab 1995 Vorstandsvorsitzender d. Daimler-Benz AG.

Schrempp, Jürgen b. 1944, German engineering graduate, 1989–1995 chairman of board of DASA, from 1995 chairman of board of Daimler Benz & Co.

Schröder, Gerhard 1910–1989, dt. Jurist u. Politiker, 1949–1980 MdB f. d. CDU, 1952/53 stellv. Fraktionsvorsitzender, 1953–1961 Bundesinnenminister, 1961–1966 Bundesaußenminister, 1966–1969 Verteidigungsminister, 1967–1973 stellv. CDU-Bundesvorsitzender.

Schröder, Gerhard 1910–1989, German lawyer and politician, 1949–1980 CDU MdB, 1952/53 deputy whip, 1953–1961 minister of the interior, 1961–1966 foreign minister, 1966–1969 defense minister, 1967–1973 CDU deputy federal chairman.

Schröder, Gerhard geb. 1944, dt. Einzelhandelskaufmann, Rechtsanwalt u. Politiker, seit 1973 Mitglied d. ÖTV, seit 1963 SPD-Mitgl., 1978–1980 Juso-Bundesvorsitzender, 1980–1986 u. seit 1998 MdB, 1986–1998 MdL v. Niedersachsen, seit 1986 Parteivorstandsmitgl., seit 1989 Präsidiumsmitgl., 1986–1990 Vorsitzender d. SPD-Landtagsfraktion, 1990–1998 Ministerpräsident v. Niedersachsen, 1994–1998 Landesvorsitzender d. SPD Niedersachsen, 1998 zum Bundeskanzler gewählt.

Schröder, Gerhard b. 1944, German retail salesman, lawyer and politician, since 1973 member of ÖTV, since 1963 member of SPD, 1978–1980 JUSO federal chairman, 1980–1986 and since 1998 MdB, 1986–1998 MdL Lower Saxony, since 1986 member of party executive, since 1989 member of presidium, 1986–1990 SPD chief whip in *Landtag,* 1990–1998 minister president of Lower Saxony, 1994–1998 SPD *Land* chairman in Lower Saxony, 1998 elected federal chancellor.

Schröder-Köpf, Doris geb. 1963, dt. Journalistin, seit 1997 Ehefrau v. Gerhard Schröder.

Schröder-Köpf, Doris b. 1963, German journalist, since 1997 wife of Gerhard Schröder.

Schtscharanski, Anatoli geb. 1948, sowjet. jüdischer Dissident, 1978 wegen »antisowjet. Agitation, Propaganda u. Landesverrat« zu 3 Jahren Haft u. 10 Jahren Arbeitslager verurteilt, 1986 gegen Ost-Agenten ausgetauscht.

Schtscharanski, Anatoli, born 1948, Jewish-Soviet dissident. In 1978, sentenced to three years in prison and ten years in a work camp for "anti-Soviet agitation, propaganda and treason." In 1986 exchanged for Eastern European spies.

Schuberth, Hans, Dr. Ing. 1897–1976, dt. Dipl.-Ing., 1945 in Regensburg u. 1947 in München Präsident d. Oberpostdirektion, CSU-Mitgl., 1947–1949 Direktor d. Verwaltung f. Post- u. Fernmeldewesen in Frankfurt/M., 1949–1953 Bundesminister f. Post- u. Fernmeldewesen, 1953–1957 MdB.

Schuberth, Hans, Dr. Ing. 1897–1976, German engineering graduate, 1945 head of postal services administration in Regensburg, 1947 ditto in Munich, member of CSU, 1947–1949 administrative director of post and telecommunications in Frankfurt am Main, 1949–1953 federal minister of post and telecommunications, 1953–1957 MdB.

Schüler, Manfred, Dr. rer. pol. geb. 1932, dt. Wirtschafts- u. Verwaltungsfachmann, seit 1959 SPD-Mitgl., 1969 Ministerialdirektor im Finanzministerium, 1972–1974 Staatssekretär im Finanzministerium, 1974–1980 Chef d. Bundeskanzleramtes, ab 1981 Vorstandsmitgl. in d. Kreditanstalt für Wiederaufbau (KfW).

Schüler, Manfred, Dr. rer. pol. b. 1932, German economist and administrator, since 1959 member of SPD, 1969 ministerial director at finance ministry, 1972–1974 state secretary at finance ministry, 1974–1980 head of chancellery, from 1981 member of KfW executive.

Schulze-Vorberg, Max, Dr. jur. geb. 1919, dt. Journalist, ab 1948 Bonner Korrespondent f. d. Bayer. Rundfunk, 1965–1976 MdB f. d. CSU.

Schulze-Vorberg, Max, Dr. jur. b. 1919, German journalist, from 1948 Bavarian Radio Bonn correspondent, 1965–1976 CSU MdB.

Schukow, Georgij Konstantinowitsch 1896–1974, sowj. Marschall seit 1942, 1944/45 Generalstabschef d. Roten Armee, 1945/46 Oberbefehlshaber d. sowjet. Truppen in Deutschl. sowie Vertreter d. UdSSR im Alliierten Kontrollrat, ab 1950 Mitgl. d. Obersten Sowjet, 1953 Vollmitgl. d. ZK d. KPdSU, 1955–1957 sowjet. Verteidigungsminister, 1957 aller Partei- u. Regierungsfunktionen enthoben.

Schukow, Georgij Konstantinowitsch 1896–1974, sowj. Marschall seit 1942, 1944/45 Generalstabschef d. Roten Armee, 1945/46 Oberbefehlshaber d. sowjet. Truppen in Deutschl. sowie Vertreter

d. UdSSR im Alliierten Kontrollrat, ab 1950 Mitgl. d. Obersten Sowjet, 1953 Vollmitgl. d. ZK d. KPdSU, 1955–1957 sowjet. Verteidigungsminister, 1957 aller Partei- u. Regierungsfunktionen enthoben.

Schumacher, Kurt 1895–1952, dt. Journalist u. Politiker, 1930–1933 MdR f. d. SPD, 1933–1944 im KZ, 1946–1952 SPD-Vorsitzender, 1948/49 MdPR, 1949–1952 MdB u. Vorsitzender d. Bundestagsfraktion.

Schumacher, Kurt 1895–1952, German journalist and politician, 1930–1933 SPD MdR, 1933–1944 in KZ, 1946–1952 SPD party chairman, 1948/49 MdPR, 1949–1952 MdB and chief whip.

Schumann, Jürgen 1940-1977 (ermordet), dt. Flugkapitän, Pilot d. im Okt. 1977 v. Terroristen entführten Lufthansamaschine »Landshut«.

Schumann, Jürgen 1940-1977 (murdered), German aircraft captain, pilot of "Landshut", the Lufthansa plane hijacked by terrorists in Oct. 1977.

Schuman, Robert 1886–1963, frz. Jurist u. Politiker, 1946–1962 Mitgl. d. frz. Nationalversammlung, 1946/47 Finanzminister, 1947/48 Ministerpräsident, 1948–1953 Außenminister, 1955/56 Justizminister, 1956 Präsident d. Europ. Bewegung, 1958–1960 Präsident d. Versammlung d. EP.

Schuman, Robert 1886–1963, French lawyer and politician, 1946–1962 member of French national assembly, 1946/47 finance minister, 1947/48 prime minister, 1948–1953 foreign minister, 1955/56 justice minister, 1956 president of European Movement, 1958–1960 president of EP assembly.

Schwaetzer, Irmgard, Dr. (1971) geb. 1942, dt. FDP-Politikerin, seit 1975 FDP-Mitgl., 1982–1984 Generalsekretärin, 1984–1987 Bundesschatzmeisterin d. FDP, 1988–1994 stellv. Bundesvorsitzende, 1990–1995 Vorsitzende d. Bundesvereinigung »Liberale Frauen« e.V., seit 1980 MdB, 1987–1991 Staatsministerin im Auswärtigen Amt, 1991–1994 Bundesministerin f. Raumordnung, Bauwesen u. Städtebau.

Schwaetzer, Irmgard, Dr. (1971) b. 1942, German politician (FDP), since 1975 member of FDP, 1982-1984 general secretary, 1984-1987 FDP federal treasurer, 1988-1994 deputy federal chairperson, 1990–1995 chairperson of federal association "Liberal Women" Inc., since 1980 MdB, 1987-1991 minister of state at foreign office, 1991-1994 minister of planning, construction and urban construction.

Schwarz, Werner, 1900–1982, dt. Landwirt u. Politiker, ab 1952 CDU-Mitgl., 1953–1965 MdB, 1959–1965 Bundesminister f. Ernährung, Landwirtsch. u. Forsten.

Schwarz, Werner, 1900-1982, German farmer and politician, since 1952 member of CDU, 1953-1965 MdB, 1959-1965 minister of food, agriculture and forestries.

Schwarz-Schilling, Christian, Dr. phil. (1956) geb. 1930, dt. Sinologe, Unternehmer u. Politiker, 1960 CDU-Eintritt, 1966–1976 MdL v. Hessen, 1967–1980 Generalsekretär d. CDU in Hessen, 1967–1996 stellv. CDU-Landesvorsitzender, 1971—1982 Mitgl. d. ZDF-Fernsehrats, seit 1976 MdB, 1982–1992 Bundesminister f. Post- u. Telekommunikation.

Schwarz-Schilling, Christian, Dr. phil. (1956) b. 1930, German Sinologist, entrepreneur and politician, 1960 joined CDU, 1966–1976 MdL Hessen, 1967–1980 general secretary of CDU in Hessen, 1967–1996 deputy CDU *Land* chairman, 1971—1982 member of ZDF TV council, since 1976 MdB, 1982–1992 minister of post and telecommunications.

Seebacher-Brandt, Brigitte, Dr. phil. (1984; geb. Seebacher) geb. 1946, dt. Publizistin u. Journalistin, seit 1965 SPD-Mitgl., 1973–1977 Chefredakteurin d. Parteizeitung »Berliner Stimme«, seit 1983 mit Willy Brandt verheiratet

Seebacher-Brandt, Brigitte, Dr. phil. (1984); (née Seebacher) b. 1946, German publicist and journalist, since 1965 member of SPD, 1973–1977 editor-in-chief of party paper *Berliner Stimme* ["Voice of Berlin"], since 1983 married to Willy Brandt.

Seebohm, Hans-Christoph, Dr. (1933) 1903–1967, dt. Politiker, 1946–1948 Minister f. Aufbau u. Arbeit in Niedersachsen, 1948/49 MdPR, 1949–1967 MdB, 1949–1966 Bundesminister f. Verkehr, bis 1960 DP-Mitgl., ab 1960 CDU-Mitgl., 1966/67 CDU-Schatzmeister.

Seebohm, Hans-Christoph, Dr. (1933) 1903–1967, German politician, 1946–1948 minister of reconstruction and labor in Lower Saxony, 1948/49 MdPR, 1949–1967 MdB, 1949–1966 federal minister of transport, until 1960 member of DP, from 1960 member of CDU, 1966/67 CDU treasurer.

Segni, Antonio 1891–1972, ital. Politiker, Anwalt, Universitätsprofessor u. Schriftsteller, 1946–1951 Landwirtschaftsminister, 1955–1957 u. 1959/60 Ministerpräsident, 1958/59 zugleich Verteidigungsminister, 1959/60 Innenminister, 1960–1962 Außenminister, 1962–1964 Staatspräsident.

Segni, Antonio 1891–1972, Italian politician, lawyer, university professor and writer, 1946–1951 minister of agriculture, 1955–1957 and 1959/60 prime minister, 1958/59 also defense minister, 1959/60 minister of the interior, 1960–1962 foreign minister, 1962–1964 President.

Seibt, Dankmar, Dr. jur. 1911–1977, dt. Rechtsanwalt u. Politiker, ab 1949 im Bundeswirtschaftsministerium tätig, 1952–1966 persönl. Referent v. Ludwig Erhard.

Seibt, Dankmar, Dr. jur. 1911–1977, German lawyer and politician, from 1949 worked at federal economics ministry, 1952–1966 personal adviser to Ludwig Erhard.

Seite, Berndt, Dr. med. vet. geb. 1940, dt. Tierarzt u. Politiker, ab 1975 Mitgl. d. ev. Landessynode Mecklenburgs, 1990 CDU-Eintritt, 1991/92 Generalsekretär d. CDU-Mecklenburg-Vorpommern, 1992–1998 Ministerpräsident, seit 1994 MdL.

Seite, Berndt, Dr. med. vet. b. 1940, German veterinary surgeon and politician, from 1975 member of protestant synod of the *Land* Mecklenburg, 1990 joined CDU, 1991/92 general secretary of CDU in Mecklenburg-Vorpommern, 1992–1998 minister president, since 1994 MdL.

Seiters, Rudolf geb. 1937, dt. Jurist u. Politiker, seit 1958 CDU-Mitgl., 1965–1970 JU-Landesvorsitzender v. Niedersachsen, seit 1972 stellv. Landesvorsitzender d. CDU, 1992–1998 CDU-Präsidiumsmitgl., seit 1969 MdB, 1969-1976 u. 1982–1989 Parlam. Geschäftsführer d. CDU/CSU-Fraktion, 1989–1991 Bundesminister f. besondere Aufgaben u. Chef d. Bundeskanzleramtes, 1991–1993 Bundesminister d. Innern, 1994–1998 stellv. Vorsitzender d. CDU/CSU-Fraktion, seit 1998 Vizepräsident d. Bundestages.

Seiters, Rudolf b. 1937, German lawyer and politician, since 1958 member of CDU, 1965–1970 Young Union Land chairman in Lower Saxony, from 1972 CDU deputy Land chairman, 1992–1998 member of CDU presidium, since 1969 MdB, 1969-1976 and 1982–1989 parliamentary CDU/CSU group manager, 1989–1991 minister without portfolio and head of chancellery, 1991–1993 minister of the interior, 1994–1998 CDU/CSU deputy whip, since 1998 vice president of the Bundestag.

Selbert, Elisabeth, Dr. jur. geb. 1896, dt. Rechtsanwältin u. Notarin, 1918 SPD-Eintritt, 1. Wahlperiode MdL in Hessen, 1948/49 MdPR.

Selbert, Elisabeth, Dr. jur. b. 1896, German lawyer and notary, 1918 joined SPD, first electoral term MdL in Hessen, 1948/49 MdPR.

Seydoux Fornier de Clausonne, François geb. 1905, frz. Diplomat, 1945 Botschaftsrat in Brüssel sowie Generalsekretär d. frz. Delegation bei d. Pariser Friedenskonferenz, 1946 Sonderberater d. Staatskommissariats, 1949–1955 Chef d. Europa-Abt. im Außenministerium, 1955–1958 Botschafter in Wien, 1958–1962 u. 1965–1970 in Bonn, 1962–1965 NATO-Botschafter, 1970–1976 Staatsrat.

Seydoux Fornier de Clausonne, François b. 1905, French diplomat, 1945 councillor at embassy in Brussels and general secretary of French delegation at Paris peace conference, 1946 special adviser to state commissariat, 1949–1955 head of foreign office European department, 1955–1958 ambassador in Vienna, 1958–1962 and 1965–1970 in Bonn, 1962–1965 ambassador to NATO, 1970–1976 state councillor.

Seyß-Inquart, Arthur 1892–1946, österr. Rechtsanwalt u. NS-Politiker, 1938 österr. Innenminister, dann Bundeskanzler u. Bundespräsident, sodann SS-Obergruppenführer, bis 1939 Reichsstatthalter d. »Ostmark«, 1939 Reichsminister ohne Geschäftsbereich, dann stellv. Generalgouverneur v. Hans Frank, 1940–1945 Reichskommissar f. d. niederl. Gebiete, in Nürnberg hingerichtet.

Seyß-Inquart, Arthur, 1892–1946, Austrian lawyer and NS politician, 1938 Austrian minister of the interior, then chancellor and President, then SS "Obergruppenführer", until 1939 Reich governor of the *Ostmark*, 1939 Reich minister without portfolio, then deputy to governor-general Hans Frank, 1940–1945 Reich commissar for the Netherlands territories, executed at Nuremberg.

Sforza, Carlo, Graf 1873–1952, ital. Publizist, Diplomat u. Senator, 1896–1905 Botschaftssekretär u. a. in Paris.

Sforza, Carlo, Count 1873–1952, Italian publicist, diplomat, senator, 1896–1905 secretary at embassies in Paris and elsewhere.

Sharett (bis 1949 Shertok), Moshe 1894–1965, israel. Politiker, seit 1906 in Palästina, 1931–1933 Sekretär u. 1933–1948 Leiter d. polit. Abt. d. Jewish Agency, Mitgl. d. israel. AP »Mapai«, 1947 Hauptdelegierter d. UN-Kommission f. d. Jewish Agency, 1948– 1956 Außenminister (Rücktritt), 1953–1955 Ministerpräsident.

Sharett (until 1949 Shertok), Moshe 1894–1965, Israeli politician, from 1906 in Palestine, 1931–1933 secretary and 1933–1948 head of political department of Jewish Agency, member of Israeli "Mapai" workers' party, 1947 Jewish Agency chief delegate to the UN commission, 1948–1956 foreign minister (resigned), 1953–1955 prime minister.

Simonis, Heide (geb. Steinhardt) geb. 1943, dt. Dipl.-Volkswirtin u. Politikerin, seit 1969 SPD-Mitgl., 1976–1988 MdB, 1988–1991 u. seit 1993 Mitgl. d. SPD-Bundesvorstandes, 1988–1993 Finanzministerin v. Schleswig-Holstein, 1990–1994 Vorsitzende d. Tarifgemeinschaft deutscher Länder (TdL), seit 1992 MdL, seit 1993 Ministerpräsidentin.

Simonis, Heide (née Steinhardt) b. 1943, German economics graduate and politician, since 1969 member of SPD, 1976–1988 MdB, 1988–1991 and since 1993 member of SPD federal executive, 1988–1993 finance minister of Schleswig-Holstein, 1990–1994 chairperson of TdL, since 1992 MdL, since 1993 minister president.

Snoy et d'Oppuers, (Baron) Jean-Charles geb. 1907, 1939–1960 Staatssekretär im belg. Wirtschaftsministerium, 1958/59 belg. Vertreter in d. EWG, 1968–1971 Mitgl. d. Repräsentantenkammer, 1968–1972 Finanzminister, 1947–1960 Präsident d. Rates d. Benelux-Union.

Snoy et d'Oppuers, (Baron) Jean-Charles b. 1907, 1939–1960 state secretary at Belgian economics ministry, 1958/59 Belgian representative at EEC, 1968–1971 member of chamber of representatives, 1968–1972 finance minister, 1947–1960 president of Benelux Union council.

Soraya Esfandiary Bakhtiary, geb. 1932, 1951–1958 Kaiserin v. Persien, 1951–1958 mit Mohammed Reza Pahlewi, Schah v. Persien, verheiratet.

Soraya Esfandiary Bakhtiary, b. 1932, 1951–1958 Empress of Persia, 1951–1958 married to Mohammed Reza Pahlavi, Shah of Persia.

Spaak, Paul Henri 1899–1972, belg. Jurist u. Staatsmann, 1925 polit. Sekretär d. Arbeitsministers, 1946 u. 1947–1949 belg. Ministerpräsident, 1936–1940, 1946–1949, 1954–1957 u. 1961–1966 Außenminister, 1949–1951 Präsident d. Beratenden Versammlung d. Europarates, 1952–1954 Präsident d. Montanunion, 1957–1961 NATO-Generalsekretär, 1961–1965 stellv. Ministerpräsident.

Spaak, Paul Henri 1899–1972, Belgian lawyer and statesman, 1925 political secretary to minister of labor, 1946 and 1947–1949 Belgian prime minister, 1936–1940, 1946–1949, 1954–1957 and 1961–1966 foreign minister, 1949–1951 president of Council of Europe consultative assembly, 1952–1954 president of ECSC, 1957–1961 NATO general secretary, 1961–1965 deputy prime minister.

Speer, Albert 1905–1981, dt. Architekt u. NS-Politiker, 1931 SA-Eintritt, 1932 NSDAP-Eintritt, ab 1933 verantwortlich f. d. Gestaltung d. NS-Massenkundgebungen, entwarf d. Neue Berliner Reichskanzlei u. d. Nürnberger Parteitagsgelände, 1937 Generalbauinspektor f. Berlin, 1938 Preuß. Staatsrat, ab 1941 MdR, 1942 Reichsminister f. Bewaffnung u. Munition, Generalinspekteur f. d. Straßenwesen, Wasser u. Energie, 1943–1945 Reichsminister f. Rüstung u. Kriegsproduktion, 1946 zu 20 Jahren Haft verurteilt.

Speer, Albert 1905–1981, German architect and NS politician, 1931 joined SA, 1932 joined NSDAP, from 1933 responsible for organization of NS mass rallies, designed new Reich chancellery in Berlin and party rally arena in Nuremberg, 1937 inspector-general of buildings for Berlin, 1938 Prussian state councillor, from 1941 MdR, 1942 Reich minister of armaments and munitions, inspector-general of highways, waterways and energy, 1943–1945 Reich minister for armaments and war production, 1946 sentenced to 20 years imprisonment.

Spöri, Dieter, Dr. rer. soc. (1973) geb. 1943, dt. Dipl.-Volkswirt u. Politiker, seit 1970 SPD-Mitgl., 1976–1988 MdB, 1983–1988 Vorsitzender d. baden-württemb. SPD-Landesgruppe, 1983–1988 Mitgl. im Vorstand d. Bundestagsfraktion, 1988–1997 MdL, ab 1988 Vorsitzender d. Landtagsfraktion u. Mitgl. d. Bundesparteivorstandes, 1992–1996 Wirtschaftsminister u. stellv. Ministerpräsident.

Spöri, Dieter, Dr. rer. soc. (1973) b. 1943, German economics graduate and politician, since 1970 member of SPD, 1976–1988 MdB, 1983–1988 chairman of SPD Land group in Baden-Württemberg, 1983–1988 member of federal party group executive, 1988–1997 MdL, from 1988 Landtag chief whip and member of federal party executive, 1992–1996 economics minister and deputy minister president.

Spranger, Carl-Dieter geb. 1939, dt. Rechtsanwalt u. Politiker, seit 1972 MdB f. d. CSU, ab 1973 stellv. u. seit 1989 Vorsitzender d. CSU-Bezirksverbands Mittelfranken, seit 1977 Mitgl. d. Landesvorstandes d. CSU, 1982-1991 Parlam. Staatssekretär im Bundesministerium d. Innern, 1991-1998 Bundesminister f. wirtschaftl. Zusammenarbeit u. Entwicklung.

Spranger, Carl-Dieter b. 1939, German lawyer and politician, since 1972 CSU MdB, from 1973 deputy chairman and since 1989 chairman of CSU district association in Central Franconia, since 1977 member of CSU Land executive, 1982-1991 parliamentary state secretary at federal ministry of the interior, 1991-1998 minister for economic cooperation and development.

Stalin, Jossif Wissarinowitsch (eigentl. J. W. Dschugaschwili) 1879–1953, sowjet. Revolutionär u. Politiker, 1898 Eintritt in d. Sozialdemokr. AP Rußlands, ab 1903 Bolschewik, sodann nach Sibirien verbannt, 1912 Mitgl. d. ZK d. Bolschewiki, 1919 Mitgl. d. PB d. KPR(B) u. d. Organisationsbüros, 1919–1923 Volkskommissar f. Nationalitätenfragen u. f. d. Arbeiter u. Bauerninspektion, ab 1922 Generalsekretär d. ZK d. KPdSU, ab 1929 Partei- u. Staatsoberhaupt, 1941 Vorsitzender d. Rates d. Volkskommissare u. ab 1945 d. Ministerrates, ab 1941 Führer d. Staatskomitees f. Verteidigung, 1943 Marschall, 1945 »Generalissimus«.

Stalin, Iosif Vissarionovich (originally J. W. Dzhugashvili) 1879–1953, Soviet revolutionary and politician, 1898 joined Russian Social Democratic Workers' Party, from 1903 bolshevik, then exiled to Siberia, 1912 member of bolshevik central committee, 1919 member of PB and organizational office of CPR(B), 1919–1923 people's commissar for nationality issues and for inspection of workers and peasants, from 1922 general secretary of CPSU central committee, from 1929 head of party and state, 1941 chairman of council of people's commissars and from 1945 of council of ministers, from 1941 leader of state defense committee, 1943 marshal, 1945 "Generalissimo".

Steiner, Julius geb. 1924, dt. Politiker, 1952 Landesgeschäftsführer d. CDU in Württemberg-Hohenzollern, 1969–1972 MdB, 1973 Parteiaustritt.

Steiner, Julius b. 1924, German politician, 1952 CDU Land manager in Württemberg-Hohenzollern, 1969–1972 MdB, 1973 left party.

Steinhoff, Johannes 1913–1994, dt. General, 1934 Eintritt in d. Kriegsmarine, 1945 Oberst, 1960–1963 Vertreter d. BRD im NATO-Militärausschuß, 1965 Chef d. Stabes d. alliierten Luftstreitkräfte Europa Mitte, 1966–1970 Luftwaffeninspektor d. dt. Bundeswehr, 1971–1974 Vorsitzender d. NATO-Militärausschusses.

Steinhoff, Johannes 1913–1994, German general, 1934 joined navy, 1945 colonel, 1960–1963 FRG representative on NATO military committee, 1965 chief of staff of allied air forces in Europe (central), 1966–1970 German armed forces air force inspector, 1971–1974 chairman of NATO military committee.

Stephanopoulos, Stephan, Dr. 1898–1982, griech. Jurist u. Politiker, Mitgl. d. Populisten-Partei bis 1950, 1930 MdP, 1932 Unterstaatssekretär im Arbeitsministerium, 1933 Wirtschaftsminister, 1944 Transportminister, 1946–1950 Minister f. wirtschaftl. Koordination, 1951 Eintritt in d. Papagos-Partei, 1952–1955 Außenminister, 1954/55 stellv. Ministerpräsident, 1963–1965 stellv. Premierminister u. Koordinator f. Wirtschaftspolitik.

Stephanopoulos, Stephan, Dr. 1898–1982, Greek lawyer and politician, member of Populist Party until 1950, 1930 MP, 1932 undersecretary of state at ministry of labor, 1933 economics minister, 1944 minister of transport, 1946–1950 minister of economic coordination, 1951 joined Papagos Party, 1952–1955 foreign minister, 1954/55 deputy prime minister, 1963–1965 deputy prime minister and economic policy coordinator.

Stikker, Dirk Uipko, Dr. jur. 1897–1979, niederl. Manager, Politiker u. Diplomat, Gründer d. »Volkspartei für Freiheit und Demokratie«, 1948–1951 Außenminister, 1950–1952 Vorsitzender d. Ministerrats d. OEEC, 1952–1958 Botschafter in London, 1958–1961 bei d. NATO, 1961–1964 NATO-Generalsekretär

Stikker, Dirk Uipko, Dr. jur. 1897–1979, Netherlands manager, politician and diplomat, founder of "People's Party for Freedom and Democracy", 1948–1951 foreign minister, 1950–1952 chairman of OEEC council of ministers, 1952–1958 ambassador in London, 1958–1961 with NATO, 1961–1964 NATO general secretary.

Stock, Jean 1893–1965, dt. Buchdrucker u. Politiker, ab 1911 SPD-Mitgl., ab 1919 Mitgl. d. Stadtrats in Aschaffenburg, MdL v. Bayern, 1944/45 KZ, 1945 Oberbürgermeister u. Landrat, Regierungspräsident v. Unterfranken,1946–1962 MdL, 1946–1950 Fraktionsvorsitzender, 1948/49 MdPR.

Stock, Jean 1893–1965, German book printer and politician, from 1911 member of SPD, from 1919 member of Aschaffenburg town council, MdL Bavaria, 1944/45 KZ, 1945 mayor and Land councillor, president of government in Lower Franconia, 1946–1962 MdL, 1946–1950 chief whip, 1948/49 MdPR.

Stoiber, Edmund, Dr. jur. geb. 1941, dt. Jurist u. Politiker, seit 1975 Mitgl. d. Bezirksvorstandes d. CSU Oberbayern, seit 1974 MdL v. Bayern, 1978–1983 CSU-Generalsekretär, seit 1989 stellv. CSU-Vorsitzender, 1983–1986 Staatssekretär, 1986–1988 Staatsminister d. Bayer. Staatskanzlei, 1988–1993 Staatsminister d. Innern, seit 1993 Ministerpräsident.

Stoiber, Edmund, Dr. jur. b. 1941, German lawyer and politician, since 1975 member of CSU Upper Bavaria district executive, since 1974 MdL Bavaria, 1978–1983 CSU general secretary, since 1989 CSU deputy chairman, 1983–1986 state secretary, 1986–1988 minister of state at Bavarian state chancellery, 1988–1993 Bavarian minister of the interior, since 1993 minister president.

Stoltenberg, Gerhard, Dr. phil. (1954) geb. 1928, seit 1947 CDU-Mitgl., 1955–1961 Bundesvorsitzender d. JU, 1957–1971 u. 1982–1998 MdB, 1965–1969 Bundesminister f. Wissenschaft u. Forschung, 1954–1957 u. 1971–1982 MdL v. Schleswig-Holstein, 1971–1982 Ministerpräsident, 1971–1989 CDU-Landesvorsitzender, 1982–1989 Bundesminister d. Finanzen, 1989–1992 Bundesminister d. Verteidigung.

Stoltenberg, Gerhard, Dr. phil. (1954) b. 1928, since 1947 member of CDU, 1955–1961 federal chairman of Young Union, 1957–1971 and 1982–1998 MdB, 1965–1969 minister of science and research, 1954–1957 and 1971–1982 MdL Schleswig-Holstein, 1971–1982 minister president, 1971–1989 CDU Land chairman, 1982–1989 finance minister, 1989–1992 defense minister.

Stoph, Willi geb. 1914, DDR-Politiker, 1931 KPD-Eintritt, 1950–1989 MdVK f. d. SED, ab 1950 Mitgl. d. ZK d. SED, 1952–1955 Innenminister, 1953–1989 Mitgl. d. PB d. ZK, ab 1954 stellv. Ministerpräsident, 1956–1960 Verteidigungsminister u. Oberkommandierender d. Streitkräfte d. Warschauer Paktstaaten, 1964–1973 u. 1976–1989 (Rücktritt) Vorsitzender d. Ministerrats (Ministerpräsident) sowie stellv. Staatsratsvorsitzender, 1973–1976 Vorsitzender d. Staatsrats (Staatsoberhaupt), 1989 Parteiausschluß, 1992 Haftverschonung.

Stoph, Willi b. 1914, GDR politician, 1931 joined KPD, 1950–1989 SED MdVK, from 1950 member of SED central committee, 1952–1955 minister of the interior, 1953–1989 member of central committee PB, from 1954 deputy minister president, 1956–1960 defense minister and supreme commander of the armed forces of the Warsaw Pact states, 1964–1973 and 1976–1989 (resigned) chairman of council of ministers (prime minister) and deputy chairman of state council, 1973–1976 chairman of state council (head of state), 1989 expelled from party, 1992 exempted from imprisonment.

Storch, Anton Valentin, 1892–1975, dt. Politiker, 1946–1948 Leiter d. Hauptabt. Sozialpolitik beim DGB, 1946–1949 Mitgl. d. Wirtschaftsrates d. Bizone, 1948/49 Direktor d. Amtes f. Arbeit im Wirtschaftsrat, 1949–1965 MdB f. d. CDU, 1949–1957 Bundesminister f. Arbeit, ab 1958 MdEP.

Storch, Anton Valentin, 1892–1975, German politician, 1946–1948 head of DGB main department of welfare policy, 1946–1949 member of economic council of Bizone, 1948/49 director of economic council labor office, 1949–1965 CDU MdB, 1949–1957 minister of labor, from 1958 MEP.

Strauß, Franz Josef, Dr. h.c. 1915–1988, dt. Politiker, 1948 Bayer. Mitbegr. d. CSU, 1949–1952 Generalsekretär, 1949–1978 MdB, 1950–1953 u. 1963–1966 stellv. Vorsitzender d. CDU/CSU-Fraktion, 1953 Bundesminister f. besondere Aufgaben u. 1955 f. Atomfragen, 1956–1962 Bundesminister d. Verteidigung, 1961–1988 CSU-Vorsitzender, 1966–1969 Bundesminister f. Finanzen, ab 1978 MdL, 1978–1988 Bayer. Ministerpräsident, 1979 Kanzlerkandidat.

Strauß, Franz Josef, Dr. h.c. 1915–1988, German politician, 1948–1952 CSU general secretary, 1949–1978 MdB, 1950–1953 and 1963–1966 CDU/CSU deputy whip, 1953 minister without portfolio, 1955 minister for atomic issues, 1956–1962 defense minister, 1961– 1988 CSU party chairman, 1966–1969 finance minister, from 1978 MdL, 1978–1988 minister president of Bavaria, 1979 chancellor candidate.

Strauss-Kahn, Dominique, Prof., Dr. (1975) geb. 1949, frz. Wirtschaftsanwalt u. Politiker, 1978–1980 UNO-Konsultant, 1982– 1984 Finanzchef d. Generalkommissars f. d. Wirtschaftsplan u. 1984–1986 stellv. Generalkommissar f. d. Wirtschaftsplan, 1984–1989 Nationalsekretär d. PS, 1986–1991 Mitgl. d. Nationalversammlung, 1992/93 Minister f. Industrie u. Außenhandel, 1995–1997 Bürgermeister v. Sarcelles, seit 1997 Minister f. Wirtschaft, Finanzen u. Industrie.

Strauss-Kahn, Dominique, professor, Dr. (1975) b. 1949, French business lawyer and politician, 1978–1980 UN consultant, 1982–1984 chief of finance of the commissar-general for the economic plan and 1984–1986 deputy commissar-general for the economic plan, 1984–1989 PS national secretary, 1986–1991 member of national assembly, 1992/93 minister of industry and foreign trade, 1995–1997 mayor of Sarcelles, since 1997 minister of economics, finance and industry.

Streicher, Julius 1885–1946, dt. Volksschullehrer u. NS-Politiker, 1919 Mitbegr. d. Dt.-Sozialen Partei, 1921 NSDAP-Eintritt, 1923 Teilnahme am Hitlerputsch, 1925–1939 Gauleiter in Franken, 1924 MdL v. Bayern, 1923–1945 Hrsg. u. Begründer d. Hetzblattes »Der Stürmer«, 1933 Leiter d. Zentralkomitees zur Abwehr jüdischer Greuel- u. Boykotthetze, 1933 MdR, 1934 SA-Gruppenführer, 1940 seiner Parteiämter enthoben, in Nürnberg hingerichtet.

Streicher, Julius 1885–1946, German primary school teacher and NS politician, 1919 co-founder of German Social Party, 1921 joined NSDAP, 1923 involved in Munich putsch, 1925–1939 regional leader (Gauleiter) of Franconia, 1924 MdL Bavaria, 1923–1945 founder and publisher of demagogic paper *Der Stürmer,* 1933 head of central committee to combat Jewish boycott and atrocity propaganda campaign, 1933 MdR, 1934 SA "Gruppenführer", 1940 removed from his party posts, executed at Nuremberg.

Stresemann, Gustav 1878–1929, dt. Nationalökonom u. Politiker, ab 1914 MdR f. d. Nationalliberalen, 1918/1919 Gründer u. Vorsitzender d. DVP, ab 1920 MdR f. d. DVP, 1923 Reichskanzler, 1923–1929 Reichsaußenminister.

Stresemann, Gustav 1878–1929, German political economist and politician, from 1914 National Liberal MdR, 1918/1919 founder and chairman of DVP, from 1920 DVP MdR, 1923 Reich chancellor, 1923–1929 Reich foreign minister.

Strobel, Käte (geb. Müller) 1907–1996, dt. Politikerin, ab 1925 SPD-Mitgl.,1949–1972 MdB f. d. SPD, 1958–1966 MdEP, 1962–1964 Vizepräsidentin, 1964–1966 Vorsitzende d. Sozialist. Fraktion im EP, 1966–1969 Bundesministerin f. Gesundheitswesen, 1969–1972 f. Jugend, Familie u. Gesundheit, 1972–1978 Mitgl. d. SPD-Fraktion im Nürnberger Stadtrat, bis 1990 Vorsitzende d. SPD-Seniorenrates.

Strobel, Käte (née Müller) 1907–1996, German politician, from 1925 member of SPD, 1949–1972 SPD MdB, 1958–1966 MEP, 1962–1964 vice president and 1964–1966 chairperson of EP socialist group, 1966–1969 minister of health, 1969–1972 minister of youth, family and health, 1972–1978 member of SPD group on Nuremberg town council, until 1990 chairperson of SPD senior citizens' council.

Stücklen, Richard geb. 1916, dt. Elektro-Ing. u. Politiker, seit 1945 CSU-Mitgl., 1949–1990 MdB, 1953–1957 u. 1966–1976 stellv. Vorsitzender d. CDU/CSU-Fraktion, 1957–1966 Bundesminister f. d. Post- u. Fernmeldewesen, 1966–1976 Vorsitzender d. CSU-Landesgruppe im Bundestag, 1976–1979 u. 1983–1990 Bundestagsvizepräsident, 1979–1983 Bundestagspräsident.

Stücklen, Richard b. 1916, German electrical engineer and politician, since 1945 member of CSU, 1949–1990 MdB, 1953–1957 and 1966–1976 CDU/CSU deputy whip, 1957–1966 minister of post and telecommunications, 1966–1976 chairman of CSU Land group in federal parliament, 1976–1979 and 1983–1990 vice president of Bundestag, 1979–1983 president of Bundestag.

Süssmuth, Rita, Dr. phil. (1964 geb. Kickuth) geb. 1937, dt. Universitätsprofessorin u. Politikerin, seit 1981 CDU-Mitgl., 1986 im Bundesvorstand d. Frauen-Union d. CDU, seit 1987 MdB, 1985/86 Bundesministerin f. Jugend, Familie u. Gesundheit, 1986–1988 f. Jugend, Familie, Frauen u. Gesundheit, bis Nov. 1998 Mitgl. im CDU-Präsidium, 1988-1998 Präsidentin d. Bundestages.

Süssmuth, Rita, Dr. phil. (1964; née Kickuth) b. 1937, German university professor and politician, since 1981 member of CDU, 1986 member of federal executive of CDU Women's Union, since 1987 MdB, 1985/86 minister of youth, family and health and 1986-1988 of youth, family, women and health, until Nov. 1998 member of CDU presidium, 1988-1998 president of the Bundestag.

T

Teitgen, Pierre-Henri 1908–1997, Professor d. Rechts u. frz. Politiker, 1944 Minister f. Informationen, 1945/46 Justizminister, 1945–1958 Mitgl. d. frz. Nationalversammlung f. d. MRP, 1947/48 Minister d. Streitkräfte, 1952–1956 Vorsitzender d. MRP, 1955/56 Minister f. d. überseeischen Gebiete.

Teitgen, Pierre-Henri 1908–1997, French politician and professor of law, 1944 minister of information, 1945/46 justice minister, 1945–1958 MRP member of French national assembly, 1947/48 minister for the armed forces, 1952–1956 chairman of MRP, 1955/56 minister for the overseas territories.

Teufel, Fritz geb. 1943, dt. Student d. Publizistik in Berlin, 1967 Mitgl. d. Kommune I in Berlin, APO-Aktivität, 1971 wegen versuchter Brandstiftung zu 2 Jahren Freiheitsstrafe verurteilt.

Teufel, Fritz b. 1943, German student (media studies) in Berlin, 1967 member of Commune I in Berlin, active in APO, 1971 sentenced to two years imprisonment for attempted arson.

Thadden, Adolf von geb. 1921, dt. Journalist, Publizist u. Politiker, 1947 Eintritt in d. Dt. Rechtspartei, 1948–1960 Stadtverordneter v. Göttingen, 1949–1953 MdB, 1955–1959 u. 1967–1970 MdL v. Niedersachsen, 1961 Bundesvorsitzender d. DRP, 1964 Landesvorsitzender, 1967–1971 Bundesvorsitzender d. NPD, 1970 MdL f. d. NPD.

Thadden, Adolf von b. 1921, German journalist, publicist and politician, 1947 joined "Deutsche Rechtspartei" (DRP), 1948– 1960 member of Göttingen town council, 1949–1953 MdB, 1955–1959 and 1967–1970 MdL Lower Saxony, 1961 DRP federal chairman, 1964 Land chairman and 1967–1971 federal chairman of NPD, 1970 NPD MdL.

Thatcher, Margaret Hilda (geb. Roberts) geb. 1925, brit. Chemikerin, Juristin u. Politikerin, 1959–1992 Mitgl. d. Unterhauses f. d. Konservativen, 1964–1970 Parteisprecherin, 1970–1974 Ministerin f. Erziehung u. Wissenschaft, 1975 Parteivorsitzende, 1979–1990 Premierministerin, ab 1992 Mitgl. d. Oberhauses, somit »Baroness of Kesteven«.

Thatcher, Margaret Hilda (née Roberts), b. 1925, British chemistry graduate, lawyer and politician, 1959–1992 Conservative MP, 1964–1970 party spokesperson, 1970–1974 minister of education and science, 1975 party chairperson, 1979–1990 prime minister, from 1992 member of House of Lords as "Baroness of Kesteven".

Tietmeyer, Hans, Dr. rer. pol. (1961) geb. 1931, dt. Finanz- u. Wirtschaftsfachmann, 1962–1967 Hilfsreferent im Bundeswirtschaftsministerium, 1967–1970 Leiter d. Grundsatzreferates, 1973 Ministerialdirektor d. Abt. Wirtschaftspolitik, 1972–1982 Vertreter d. BRD im Ausschuß f. Wirtschaftspolitik d. OECD u. d. EG, 1982–1989 Staatssekretär im Bundesfinanzministerium, 1990 Architekt d. WWSU, seit 1993 Präsident d. Dt. Bundesbank.

Tietmeyer, Hans, Dr. rer. pol. (1961) b. 1931, German finance and economics expert, 1962–1967 assistant adviser at economics ministry, 1967–1970 head of fundamental issues office, 1973 ministerial director in economic policy department, 1972–1982 FRG representative on OECD and EC economic policy committees, 1982–1989 state secretary at finance ministry, 1990 architect of WWSU, since 1993 president of the Bundesbank.

Tito, Josip (eigentl. J. Broz) 1892–1980, jugosl. Politiker, 1934 Mitgl. d. ZK d. KPJ, 1937 Zentralsekretär d. KPJ, 1943 Marschall, 1945–1953 Ministerpräsident u. Verteidigungsminister, ab 1966 Parteipräsident d. Exekutivkomitees, 1953–1980 Staatspräsident u. Regierungschef.

Tito, Josip (originally J. Broz) 1892–1980, Yugoslav politician, 1934 member of Yugoslav CP central committee, 1937 central secretary of Yugloslav KPJ, 1943 marshal, 1945–1953 prime minister and defense minister, from 1966 president of party executive committee, 1953–1980 President and head of government.

Töpfer, Klaus, Dr. rer. pol. (1968) geb. 1938, dt. Volkswirt u. Politiker, 1972 CDU-Eintritt, 1978–1985 Staatssekretär im Ministerium f. Soziales, Gesundheit u. Umwelt in Rheinland-Pfalz, 1985–1987 Minister f. Umwelt u. Gesundheit, 1990–1995 Landesvorsitzender d. CDU im Saarland, 1987–1994 Bundesminister f. Umwelt, Naturschutz u. Reaktorsicherheit, ab 1989 Bundesvorstandsmitgl., ab 1992 Präsidiumsmitgl., 1990–1998 MdB, 1994–1998 Bundesminister f. Raumordnung, Bauwesen u. Städtebau, 1998 Exekutiv-Direktor d. UNEP.

Töpfer, Klaus, Dr. per. pol. (1968) b. 1938, German economist and politician, 1972 joined CDU, 1978–1985 state secretary at ministry of welfare, health and environment in Rhineland-Palatinate, 1985–1987 minister of environment and health, 1990–1995 Land CDU chairman in Saarland, 1987–1994 federal minister of the environment, the protection of nature and reactor safety, from 1989 member of federal executive, from 1992 member of presidium, 1990–1998 MdB, 1994–1998 minister of planning, construction and urban construction, 1998 executive director of UNEP.

Touré, Sekou 1922–1984, Politiker v. Guinea, 1946 Mitbegr. d. Rassemblement Démocratique Africain (RDA), 1948 Generalsekretär d. Gewerkschaftsverbandes CGT in Guinea, 1952–1984 Generalsekretär d. Parti Démocratique de Guinée (PDG), 1956 Generalsekretär u. 1959 Präsident d. Union Générale des Travailleurs d'Afrique Noire (UGTAN), 1956 Abgeord. d. frz. Nationalversammlung, 1958–1984 Präsident v. Guinea,. bis 1972 Premierminister.

Touré, Sekou 1922–1984, politician in Guinea, 1946 co-founder of RDA, 1948 general secretary of association of trade unions (CGT) in Guinea, 1952–1984 general secretary of PDG, 1956 general secretary and 1959 president of UGTAN, 1956 member of French national assembly, 1958–1984 President of Guinea and prime minister until 1972.

Trichet, Jean-Claude, Prof. Dr. geb. 1942, frz. Wirtschaftswissenschaftler, Verwaltungsbeamter u. Politiker, 1976 Generalsekretär d. Interministeriellen Komitees zur Gestaltung d. Industriestrukturen, 1978 Berater f. Industrie, Energie u. Forschung d. Wirtschaftsministers u. d. Staatspräsidenten, ab 1986 Kabinettsdirektor d. Führungsstabes d. Wirtschafts-, Finanz- u. Privatisierungsministers, seit 1994 Präsident d. Banque de France.

Trichet, Jean-Claude, professor, b. 1942, French economist, administrative official and politician, 1976 general secretary of interministerial industrial structure planning committee, 1978 adviser to the economics minister and the President on industry, energy and research, from 1986 cabinet director of management staff of minister of economics, finance and privatisation, since 1994 president of the Banque de France.

Trittin, Jürgen geb. 1954, dt. Diplomsozialwirt u. Politiker, seit 1980 Mitgl. d. Grünen, 1985/86 u. 1988–1990 Vorsitzender d. Fraktion d. Grünen in Niedersachsen, 1990–1994 Niedersächsischer Minister f. Bundes- u. Europaangelegenheiten, 1994–1998 Sprecher d. Bundesvorstands v. Bündnis 90/Die Grünen, seit 1998 MdB sowie Bundesminister f. Umwelt, Naturschutz u. Reaktorsicherheit.

Trittin, Jürgen b. 1954 German social studies graduate and politician, since 1980 member of the Greens, 1985/86 and 1988–1990 Greens chief whip in Lower Saxony, 1990–1994 minister of federal and European affairs in Lower Saxony, 1994–1998 federal executive spokesman for Alliance 90/The Greens, since 1998 MdB and federal minister of the environment, the protection of nature and reactor safety.

Truman, Harry Spencer 1884–1972, amerik. Jurist u. Politiker (Demokrat), 1934–1944 US-Senator, 1945 Vizepräsident, 1945–1953 US-Präsident.

Truman, Harry Spencer 1884–1972, American lawyer and politician (Democrat), 1934–1944 US senator, 1945 vice president, 1945–1953 US President.

U

Ulbricht, Walter 1893–1973, dt. Tischler u. DDR-Politiker, 1912 SPD-Eintritt, 1919 Mitbegr. d. KPD in Leipzig, ab 1923 Mitgl. d. ZK d. KPD, 1926–1929 MdL v. Sachsen, 1928 MdR, 1929–1946 Mitgl. d. PB d. ZK, 1933–1945 Emigration,1946–1973 Mitgl. d. ZK d. SED, 1946–1950 stellv. SED-Vorsitzender, 1949–1973 Mitgl. d. PB d. ZK, 1946–1951 MdL v. Sachsen-Anhalt, ab 1949 MdVK, 1949–1960 Stellv. d. Ministerratsvorsitzenden, 1950–1953 SED-Generalsekretär, 1953–1971 1. Sekretär d. ZK, 1960–1971 Vorsitzender d. Nationalen Verteidigungsrates, 1960–1973 Staatsratsvorsitzender, 1971–1973 SED-Vorsitzender.

Ulbricht, Walter 1893–1973, German joiner and GDR politician, 1912 joined SPD, 1919 co-founder of KPD in Leipzig, from 1923 member of KPD central committee, 1926–1929 MdL Saxony, 1928 MdR, 1929–1946 member of central committee PB, 1933–1945 exile, 1946–1973 member of SED central committee, 1946–1950 deputy SED party chairman, 1949–1973 member of central committee PB, 1946–1951 MdL Saxony-Anhalt, from 1949 member of Volkskammer, 1949–1960 deputy to chairman of council of ministers, 1950–1953 SED general secretary, 1953–1971 first secretary of central committee, 1960–1971 chairman of national defense council, 1960–1973 chairman of council of state, 1971–1973 SED party chairman.

V

Verheugen, Günter geb. 1944, dt. Journalist u. Politiker, 1960-1982 FDP-Mitgl., 1977–1978 FDP-Bundesgeschäftsführer, 1978–1982 Generalsekretär, seit 1982 SPD-Mitgl., seit 1983 Bundesgeschäftsführer d. SPD u. MdB, seit 1998 Staatsminister im Auswärtigen Amt.

Verheugen, Günter b. 1944, German journalist and politician, 1960-1982 member of FDP, 1977–1978 FDP federal manager, 1978–1982 general secretary, since 1982 member of SPD, since 1983 SPD federal manager and MdB, since 1998 minister of state at foreign office.

Vogel, Hans-Jochen, Dr. jur. (1950) geb. 1926, dt. Jurist u. Politiker, 1950 SPD-Eintritt, 1960–1972 Oberbürgermeister v. München, 1972–1977 Bayer. SPD-Landesvorsitzender, 1972–1981 u. 1983–1 994 MdB, bis 1991 SPD-Fraktionsvorsitzender, 1972–1974 Bundesminister f. Raumordnung, Bauwesen u. Städtebau, 1974– 1981 Bundesminister d. Justiz, 1981–1983 MdA v. Berlin u. kurz Regierender Bürgermeister, 1983 SPD-Kanzlerkandidat.

Vogel, Hans-Jochen, Dr. jur. (1950) b. 1926, German lawyer and politician, 1950 joined SPD, 1960–1972 mayor of Munich, 1972–1977 Bavarian SPD Land chairman, 1972–1981 and 1983–1994 MdB, until 1991 SPD chief whip, 1972–1974 minister of planning, construction and urban construction, 1974–1981 minister of justice, 1981–1983 MdA in Berlin and briefly governing mayor, 1983 SPD chancellor candidate.

Vollmer, Antje, Dr. phil. geb. 1943, dt. Theologin, Pädagogin, Publizistin u. Politikerin, seit 1985 Mitgl. d. Grünen, 1983-1985, 1987-1990 u. seit 1994 MdB, seit 1994 Bundestagsvizepräsidentin.

Vollmer, Antje, Dr. phil. b. 1943, German theologian, educationist, publicist and politician, since 1985 member of Greens, 1983-1985, 1987-1990 and since 1994 MdB, since 1994 vice president of Bundestag.

Volmer, Ludger, Dr. geb. 1952, dt. Dipl.-Sozialwissenschaftler u. Politiker, 1979 Mitbegr. d. Grünen, 1983–1990 u. seit 1994 MdB, 1988 Gründer d. Gruppe »Linkes Forum«, 1991–1994 Bundesvorstandssprecher, seit 1998 Staatsminister im Auswärtigen Amt.

Volmer, Ludger, Dr. b. 1952, German sociology graduate and politician, 1979 co-founder of Greens, 1983–1990 and since 1994 MdB, 1988 founder of group "Linkes Forum" ["Left-wing Forum"], 1991–1994 federal executive spokesman, since 1998 minister of state at foreign office.

W

Waigel, Theodor, Dr. (1967) geb. 1939, dt. Jurist u. Politiker, 1971–1975 Landesvorsitzender d. JU Bayern, 1973–1988 Vorsitzender d. CSU-Gundsatzkommission, seit 1972 MdB, 1982–1989 Vorsitzender d. CSU-Landesgruppe u. 1. stellv. Vorsitzender d. CDU/CSU-Fraktion, 1988–1999 CSU-Vorsitzender, 1989–1998 Bundesminister d. Finanzen.

Waigel, Theodor, Dr. (1967) b. 1939, German lawyer and politician, 1971–1975 Bavarian Young Union Land chairman, 1973–1988 chairman of CSU fundamental issues commission, since 1972 MdB, 1982-1989 chairman of CSU Land group and CDU/CSU first deputy whip, 1988-1999 CSU party chairman, 1989-1998 minister of finance.

Waldheim, Kurt, Dr. jur. (1944) geb. 1918, österr. Politiker u. Diplomat, 1948–1951 1. Botschafter in Paris, 1951–1955 Legationsrat im Außenministerium, 1956–1960 Botschafter in Kanada, 1960–1964 Leiter d. Polit. Abt. im Außenministerium, 1955–1968 u. 1970/71 Mitgl. d. UN-Generalversammlung, 1968–1970 Außenminister, 1972–1981 Generalsekretär d. UNO, 1986–1992 österr. Bundespräsident.

Waldheim, Kurt, Dr. jur. (1944) b. 1918, Austrian politician and diplomat, 1948–1951 first ambassador in Paris, 1951–1955 legation councillor at foreign ministry, 1956–1960 ambassador to Canada, 1960–1964 head of foreign ministry political department, 1955–1968 and 1970/71 member of UN general assembly, 1968–1970 foreign minister, 1972–1981 UN secretary-general, 1986–1992 Austrian President.

Walesa, Lech geb. 1943, Gewerkschafter u. poln. Politiker, 1970 u. 1980 Streikführer d. Danziger Lenin-Werftarbeiter, 1980–1991 Vorsitzender d. Gewerkschaftsorganisation »Solidarität«, 1990–1995 Staatspräsident, 1992 Austritt aus d. »Solidarität«.

Walesa, Lech b. 1943, Polish politician and trade unionist, 1970 and 1980 strike leader at Lenin shipyard in Gdansk, 1980–1991 chairman of trade union organization "Solidarity", 1990–1995 President, 1992 left "Solidarity".

Weber, Helene, Dr. h.c. 1881–1962, dt. Sozialpädagogin u. Politikerin, 1918–1933 Referentin u. Ministerialrätin im Preuß. Wohlfahrtsministerium, 1919–1933 Mitgl. d. Naitonalversammlung u. MdR f. d. Zentrum, 1946–1947 MdL v. Nordrhein-Westfalen, 1948/49 MdPR, ab 1949 MdB u. stellv. Delegierte im Europarat.

Weber, Helene, Dr. h.c. 1881–1962, German welfare educationist and politician, 1918–1933 adviser and ministerial councillor at Prussian ministry of welfare, 1919–1933 member of national assembly and Center Party MdR, 1946–1947 MdL North Rhine-Westphalia, 1948/49 MdPR, from 1949 MdB and deputy delegate to Council of Europe.

Wechmar, Rüdiger Freiherr von geb. 1923, dt. Diplomat u. Journalist, 1948–1958 Leiter d. Bonner Büros d. UP, 1958–1963 Presseattaché d. dt. Generalkonsulates in New York, 1963–1968 Leiter d. ZDF-Osteuropa-Studios in Wien, 1968–1970 Leiter d. German Information Center in New York, 1970 stellv., 1972–1974 Leiter d. Presse- u. Informationsamtes sowie Sprecher d. Bundesregierung, 1971 FDP-Eintritt, 1974–1981 Botschafter u. Vertreter d. BRD bei d. UNO, 1981–1983 Botschafter in Italien, 1983–1988 Botschafter in Großbrit., 1989–1994 MdEP.

Wechmar, Rüdiger Freiherr von b. 1923, German diplomat and journalist, 1948–1958 head of UP Bonn office, 1958–1963 press attaché at German general consulate in New York, 1963–1968 head of ZDF Eastern Europe studio in Vienna, 1968–1970 head of German Information Center in New York, 1970 deputy head and 1972–1974 head of press and information office and government spokesman, 1971 joined FDP, 1974–1981 ambassador and FRG representative at UN, 1981–1983 ambassador to Italy, 1983–1988 ambassador to Britain, 1989–1994 MEP.

Wegener, Ulrich geb. 1929, Kommandeur beim Bundesgrenzschutz, erster Chef d. »GSG 9«.

Wegener, Ulrich b. 1929, commander of federal border guard, first head of "GSG 9".

Wehner, Herbert 1906–1990, dt. Politiker, 1923 u. 1946 SPD-Eintritt, 1927 KPD-Eintritt, 1930/31 MdL v. Sachsen, 1935–1946 Emigration, 1942 KPD-Ausschluß, 1949–1983 MdB, 1958–1973 stellv. SPD-Vorsitzender, bis 1982 Mitgl. d. Parteivorstandes, 1966–1969 Bundesminister f. gesamtdt. Fragen, 1969–1983 SPD-Bundestagsfraktionsvorsitzender.

Wehner, Herbert 1906–1990, German politician, 1923 and 1946 joined SPD, 1927 joined KPD, 1930/31 MdL Saxony, 1935–1946 exile, 1942 expelled from KPD, 1949–1983 MdB, 1958–1973 SPD deputy party chairman, until 1982 member of party executive, 1966–1969 minister for all-German issues, 1969–1983 SPD chief whip.

Weizsäcker, Marianne Freifrau von (geb. Kretschmann) geb. 1932, Hausfrau, seit 1953 mit Dr. Richard von Weizsäcker verheiratet, 1989 Gründerin d. »Stiftung Integrationshilfe ehemals Drogenabhängiger e.V«.

Weizsäcker, Marianne Freifrau von (née Kretschmann) b. 1932, German housewife, since 1953 married to Dr. Richard von Weizsäcker, 1989 set up foundation to assist in social reintegration of former drug addicts.

Weizsäcker, Richard Freiherr von, Dr. jur. (1954) geb. 1920, dt. Politiker, seit 1954 CDU-Mitgl., ab 1966 Mitgl. d. CDU-Bundesvorstandes, 1969–1981 MdB, 1972–1979 stellv. Vorsitzender d. CDU/CSU Bundestagsfraktion, 1979–1981 Bundestagsvizepräsident, 1981–1984 Regierender Bürgermeister Berlins (Rücktritt), 1981–1984 CDU-Landesvorsitzender, 1984–1994 Bundespräsident.

Weizsäcker, Richard Freiherr von, Dr. jur. (1954) b. 1920, German politician, since 1954 member of CDU, from 1966 member of CDU federal executive, 1969–1981 MdB, 1972–1979 CDU/CSU deputy whip, 1979–1981 vice president of Bundestag, 1981–1984 governing mayor of Berlin (resigned), 1981–1984 CDU Land chairman, 1984–1994 federal President.

Wessel, Helene 1898–1969, dt. Fürsorgerin u. Politikerin, 1928–1933 MdL v. Preußen f. d. Zentrum, 1946–1950 MdL v. Nordrhein-Westfalen, 1948/49 MdPR, 1949–1953 f. d. Zentrum u. 1957–1969 MdB f. d. SPD, 1949–1951 Vorsitzende d. Dt. Zentrumspartei, 1952 Mitbegr. d. GVP.

Wessel, Helene 1898–1969, German welfare worker and politician, 1928–1933 Center Party MdL Prussia, 1946–1950 MdL North Rhine-Westphalia, 1948/49 MdPR, 1949–1953 Center Party MdB, 1957–1969 SPD MdB, 1949–1951 chairperson of German Center Party, 1952 co-founder of GVP.

Westerwelle, Guido, Dr. jur. (1994) geb. 1961, dt. Rechtsanwalt u. Politiker, seit 1980 FDP-Mitgl., 1983-1988 Bundesvorsitzender d. Jungen Liberalen, seit 1988 Mitgl. d. Bundesvorstandes d. FDP, seit 1993 Kreisvorsitzender d. Bonner FDP, seit 1994 FDP-Generalsekretär, seit 1996 MdB.

Westerwelle, Guido, Dr. jur. (1994) b. 1961, German lawyer and politician, since 1980 member of FDP, 1983-1988 federal chairman of Young Liberals, since 1988 member of FDP federal executive, since 1993 FDP Bonn district chairman, since 1994 FDP general secretary, since 1996 MdB.

Westrick, Ludger, Dr. jur. 1894–1990, dt. Wirtschaftspolitiker, 1951–1963 Staatssekretär im Bundeswirtschaftsministerium, 1963 Staatssekretär im Bundeskanzleramt sowie 1964–1966 Bundesminister f. besondere Aufgaben (Rücktritt).

Westrick, Ludger, Dr. jur. 1894–1990, German economist and politician, 1951–1963 state secretary at economics ministry, 1963 state secretary at chancellery and 1964–1966 minister without portfolio (resigned).

Weyer, Willi, Dr. h.c. 1917–1987, Sportfunktionär u. dt. Politiker, 1945 FDP-Eintritt, 1950 stellv. u. 1956–1972 Landesvorsitzender v. Nordrhein-Westfalen, 1950–1954 u. 1958–1975 MdL, ab 1952 Mitgl. d. FDP-Bundesvorstandes, 1953/54 MdB, 1954–1956 Wiederaufbauminister, 1956–1958 Finanzminister u. stellv. Ministerpräsident, 1962–1975 Innenminister u. stellv. Ministerpräsident, 1963–1968 stellv. Bundesvorsitzender, 1974–1986 DSB-Präsident.

Weyer, Willi, Dr. h.c. 1917–1987, German politician and sports official, 1945 joined FDP, 1950 Land deputy chairman and 1956–1972 chairman in North Rhine-Westphalia, 1950–1954 and 1958–1975 MdL, from 1952 member of FDP federal executive, 1953/54 MdB, 1954–1956 Land minister of reconstruction, 1956–1958 finance minister and deputy minister president, 1962–1975 minister of the interior and deputy minister president, 1963–1968 federal deputy chairman, 1974–1986 president of DSB.

Wickert, Ulrich geb. 1942, dt. Fernsehjournalist, 1969–1977 Redakteur d. WDR-Fernsehmagazins »Monitor«, 1977/78 ARD-Korrespondent in Washington, 1978–1981 in Paris, 1981–1984 ARD-Studioleiter in New York, 1984–1991 ARD-Studioleiter in Paris, seit 1991 Moderator d. »Tagesthemen«.

Wickert, Ulrich b. 1942, German TV journalist, 1969–1977 editor of WDR TV magazine "Monitor", 1977/78 ARD correspondent in Washington, 1978–1981 in Paris, 1981–1984 head of ARD studio in New York, 1984–1991 head of ARD studio in Paris, since 1991 presenter of "Tagesthemen" [Topics of the Day].

Wieczorek-Zeul, Heidemarie geb. 1942, dt. Lehrerin u. Politikerin, 1965 SPD-Eintritt, 1974–1977 Juso-Bundesvorsitzende, 1979-1987 MdEP, seit 1987 MdB, 1987-1998 europapolit. Sprecherin d. SPD-Fraktion, 1993 stellv. SPD-Vorsitzende u. europapolit. Sprecherin der SPD, seit 1998 Bundesministerin f. wirtschaftl. Zusammenarbeit u. Entwicklung.

Wieczorek-Zeul, Heidemarie b. 1942, German teacher and politician, 1965 joined SPD, 1974–1977 JUSO federal chairperson, 1979-1987 MEP, since 1987 MdB, 1987-1998 SPD parliamentary group spokesperson on European policy, 1993 SPD deputy chairperson and SPD spokesperson on European policy, since 1998 minister for economic cooperation and development.

Wienand, Karl geb. 1926, dt. Politiker u. Unternehmensberater, 1947 SPD-Eintritt, 1952 Bürgermeister v. Rosbach, 1953–1974 MdB, 1967–1974 Parlam. Geschäftsführer d. SPD-Fraktion.

Wienand, Karl b. 1926, German politician and business consultant, 1947 joined SPD, 1952 mayor of Rosbach, 1953–1974 MdB, 1967–1974 SPD parliamentary group manager.

Wildermuth, Eberhard Hermann 1890–1952, dt. Wirtschaftspolitiker, 1919–1933 DDP-Mitgl., 1946 Leiter d. Staatssekretariats f. Wirtsch. v. Württemberg-Hohenzollern, MdL f. d. DVP/FDP, 1947–1949 Wirtschaftsminister, ab 1949 MdB u. Bundesminister f. Wohnungsbau.

Wildermuth, Eberhard Hermann 1890–1952, German economist and politician, 1919–1933 member of DDP, 1946 head of state economics secretariat in Württemberg-Hohenzollern, DVP/FDP MdL, 1947–1949 economics minister, from 1949 MdB and federal minister of housing construction.

Wilhelm II. 1859–1941, 1888–1918 letzter preuß. König u. Dt. Kaiser, anschließend im Exil in d. Niederlanden.

Wilhelm II. 1859–1941, 1888–1918 last King of Prussia and German emperor, subsequently exiled to the Netherlands.

Wilson, Sir (1976) Harold 1916–1995, brit. Politiker, 1945–1983 Mitgl. d. Unterhauses f. Labour, 1945–1947 Parlam. Sekretär d. Ministers f. Öffentl. Arbeiten, 1947–1951 brit. Handelsminister (Rücktritt), ab 1952 Mitgl. d. Parteivorstandes, 1963–1976 Parteiführer, 1964–1970 u. 1974–1976 Premierminister (Rücktritt), 1967–1970 zusätzl. Wirtschaftsminister, ab 1983 Mitgl. d. Oberhauses.

Wilson, Sir (1976) Harold, 1916–1995, British politician, 1945–1983 Labour MP, 1945–1947 parliamentary secretary to minister of public works, 1947–1951 president of board of trade (resigned), from 1952 member of party executive, 1963–1976 party leader, 1964–1970 and 1974–1976 (resigned) prime minister, 1967–1970 also economics minister, from 1983 member of House of Lords.

Winzer, Otto 1902–1975, dt. Schriftsetzer u. DDR-Politiker, 1919 KPD-Eintritt, 1925–1927 Mitgl. d. Kommunist. Partei Österr., 1928– 1930 Mitgl. d. KPdSU, 1945 Mitgl. d. ZK d. KPD, ab 1947 Mitgl. d. ZK d. SED, 1949–1956 Staatssekretär u. Chef d. Privatkanzlei d. DDR-Präsidenten, ab 1950 MdVK, 1956–1965 stellv. Außenminister, 1959–1965 Staatssekretär im Außenministerium, 1965–1975 Außenminister.

Winzer, Otto 1902–1975, German typesetter and GDR politician, 1919 joined KPD, 1925–1927 member of Austrian CP, 1928–1930 member of CPSU, 1945 member of KPD central committee, from 1947 member of SED central committee, 1949–1956 state secretary and head of GDR president's private chancellery, from 1950 member of Volkskammer, 1956–1965 deputy foreign minister, 1959–1965 state secretary at foreign ministry, 1965–1975 foreign minister.

Wischnewski, Hans-Jürgen geb. 1922, dt. Politiker, 1946 SPD-Eintritt, 1957–1990 MdB, 1959–1961 Bundesvorsitzender d. Jusos, 1961–1965 MdEP, 1966–1968 Bundesminister f. wirtschaftl. Zusammenarbeit, 1968–1972 SPD-Bundesgeschäftsführer, ab 1970 Mitgl. d. Parteivorstandes u. Präsidiums, 1974–1976 Parlam. Staatssekretär im Auswärtigen Amt, 1976–1979 u. 1982 im Bundeskanzleramt, 1979–1982 stellv. Parteivorsitzender, 1984/85 SPD-Bundesschatzmeister.

Wischnewski, Hans-Jürgen b. 1922, German politician, 1946 joined SPD, 1957–1990 MdB, 1959–1961 JUSO federal chairman, 1961–1965 MEP, 1966–1968 minister of economic cooperation, 1968–1972 SPD federal manager, from 1970 member of party executive and presidium, 1974–1976 parliamentary state secretary at foreign office, 1976–1979 and 1982 at chancellery, 1979–1982 deputy party chairman, 1984/85 SPD federal treasurer.

Wörner, Manfred, Dr. jur. 1934–1994, dt. Politiker u. Jurist, 1953 Eintritt in d. JU, 1956 CDU-Eintritt, 1965–1988 MdB, 1969–1972 stellv. Vorsitzender d. Unionsfraktion, 1973 Mitgl. d. Bundesvorstandes, 1982–1988 Bundesminister d. Verteidigung, 1988–1994 NATO-Generalsekretär.

Wörner, Manfred, Dr. jur. 1934–1994, German politician and lawyer, 1953 joined Young Union, 1956 joined CDU, 1965–1988 MdB, 1969–1972 CDU/CSU deputy whip, 1973 member of federal executive, 1982–1988 defense minister, 1988–1994 NATO general secretary.

Wuermeling, Franz-Josef, Dr. rer. pol. (1921) 1900–1986, dt. Politiker, 1926–1931 Regierungsreferendar u. -assessor im Preuß. Innenministerium, 1931–1938 Landesrat in Kassel, 1945 CDU-Eintritt, 1947–1951 MdL, 1947–1949 Staatssekretär im Innenministerium v. Rheinland-Pfalz, 1949–1969 MdB, 1953–1962 Bundesminister f. Familien- u. Jugendfragen.

Wuermeling, Franz-Josef, Dr. rer. pol. (1921) 1900–1986, German politician, 1926–1931 civil service training at Prussian ministry of the interior, 1931–1938 *Land* councillor in Kassel, 1945 joined CDU, 1947–1951 MdL, 1947–1949 state secretary at ministry of interior in Rhineland-Palatinate, 1949–1969 MdB, 1953–1962 federal minister for family and youth issues.

Z

Zarapkin, Semjon Konstantinowitsch 1906–1984, sowjet. Diplomat, ab 1945 Mitgl. d. Ministeriums f. Auswärtige Angelegenheiten, 1946 Geschäftsträger d. Sowjetbotschaft in Washington, 1948–1952 Delegierter im UN-Sicherheitsrat u. in d. UN-Abrüstungskommission, 1963 Chefdelegierter d. Genfer Abrüstungskonferenz, 1966–1971 Botschafter in Bonn.

Zarapkin, Semyon Konstantinovich 1906–1984, Soviet diplomat, from 1945 member of ministry of foreign affairs, 1946 Soviet embassy manager in Washington, 1948–1952 delegate on UN security council and on UN disarmament commission, 1963 chief delegate at Geneva disarmament conference, 1966–1971 ambassador in Bonn.

Zeeland, Paul van, Dr. geb. 1893, belg. Finanzpolitiker, 1934 Minister ohne Geschäftsbereich, 1935–1938 Ministerpräsident, 1935 u. 1949–1954 Außenminister.

Zeeland, Paul van, Dr. b. 1893, Belgian financial expert and politician, 1934 minister without portfolio, 1935–1938 prime minister, 1935 and 1949–1954 foreign minister.

Zimmermann, Friedrich, Dr. jur. (1950) geb. 1925, dt. Rechtsanwalt u. Politiker, 1948 CSU-Eintritt, 1955 Hauptgeschäftsführer u. 1956–1963 Generalsekretär d. CSU, 1957– 1990 MdB, 1972 stellv. u. 1976–1982 Vorsitzender d. CSU-Landesgruppe sowie stellv. Fraktionsvorsitzender, 1982–1989 Bundesinnenminister, 1989–1991 Bundesminister f. Verkehr.

Zimmermann, Friedrich, Dr. jur. (1950) b. 1925, German lawyer and politician, 1948 joined CSU, 1955 chief manager and 1956–1963 general secretary, 1957–1990 MdB, 1972 deputy chairman and 1976–1982 chairman of CSU *Land* group and deputy whip, 1982–1989 federal minister of the interior, 1989–1991 minister of transport.

Zinn, Georg August, Dr. h.c. 1901–1976, dt. Rechtsanwalt u. Politiker, 1920 SPD-Eintritt, 1945–1959 u. 1960–1963 hessischer Justizminister, 1945–1970 MdL, 1947 Mitgl. u. Vizepräsident d. Frankfurter Wirtschaftsrates, 1948/49 MdPR, 1949–1951 u. 1961 MdB, 1950–1969 hessischer Ministerpräsident (Rücktritt).

Zinn, Georg August, Dr. h.c. 1901–1976, German lawyer and politician, 1920 joined SPD, 1945–1959 and 1950–1963 minister of justice in Hessen, 1945–1970 MdL, 1947 member and vice president of Frankfurt economic council, 1948/49 MdPR, 1949–1951 and 1961 MdB, 1950–1969 minister president of Hessen (resigned).

Zoli, Adone, Dr. jur. geb. 1887, ital. Rechtsanwalt u. Politiker, Nationalberater, in d. 1. u. 2. Legislaturperiode Senator, 1951 Justizminister, 1954 Finanzminister, 1957/58 Ministerpräsident.

Zoli, Adone, Dr. jur. b. 1887, Italian lawyer and politician, national adviser, senator in first and second legislative period, 1951 minister of justice, 1954 minister of finance, 1957/58 prime minister.

Zundel, Rolf, Dr. rer. nat. geb. 1929, dt. Journalist, ab 1959 Redakteur u. ab 1965 Bonner Korrespondent bei d. Wochenzeitung »Die Zeit«.

Zundel, Rolf, Dr. rer. nat. b. 1929, German journalist, from 1959 editor and from 1965 Bonn correspondent of weekly *Die Zeit*.

Deutschlandkarte / Map of Germany

Nordsee

DÄNEMARK

Ostsee

Nord-friesische
Inseln
Sylt
Helgoland
Ostfriesische Inseln
Westfriesische Inseln

Tondern
Flensburg
Schleswig
Neumünster
Schleswig-
Holstein
Kiel
Fehmarn
Lübeck
Wismar
Laaland
Mon
Falster
Gedser
Rügen
Stralsund
Rostock
Greifswald
Usedom
Kolobrzeg
(Kolberg)
Schwerin
Mecklenburg-
Vorpommern
Neubrandenburg
Neustrelitz
Swinoujscie
(Swinemünde)
Szczecin
(Stettin)
Stargard Szczeciński
(Stargard)

NIEDER-
LANDE

Leeuwarden
Groningen
Deventer
Utrecht
Arnheim
Nimwegen
Eindhoven
Maast-richt
Lüttich
BELGIEN
Eupen
Aachen

Cuxhaven
Wilhelmshaven
Bremerhaven
Emden
Oldenburg
Delmenhorst
Bremen
Wesermünde
Ems
Weser
Niedersachsen
Osnabrück
Minden
Herford
Münster
Bielefeld
Paderborn
BUNDESREPUBLIK
Nordrhein-
Gelsenkirchen
Oberhausen
Dortmund
Duisburg
Bochum
Essen
Krefeld
Hagen
Düsseldorf
Wuppertal
Mönchen-Gladbach
Remscheid
Solingen
Westfalen
Köln
Siegen
Bonn

Hamburg
Lüneburg
Aller
Celle
Hannover
Braunschweig
Hildesheim
Salzgitter
Wolfsburg
Göttingen
Kassel
Marburg
Gießen
Hessen
DEUTSCHLAND
Koblenz
Mosel

Elbe
Wittenberge
Uelzen
Stendal
Havel
Brandenburg
Ehemalige
DEUTSCHE
Berlin
Potsdam
Branden-burg
Frankfurt/Oder
DEMOKRATISCHE
Magdeburg
Sachsen-
Anhalt
Halberstadt
Bernburg
Dessau
REPUBLIK
Saale
Halle
Nordhausen
Weißenfels
Leipzig
Altenburg
Spree
Cottbus
Dresden
Sachsen
Görlitz
Bautzen
Oder
Gorzow-Wielkopolski
(Landsberg)
Küstrin
(Kostryn)
Wartha
Gubin
(Guben)
Grünberg
Zagan
(Sagan)
Neiße

Eisenach
Gotha
Erfurt
Weimar
Jena
Gera
Thüringen
Suhl
Chemnitz
Zwickau
Plauen
Hof
Coburg
Liberec
(Reichenbach)
Usti nad Labem
(Aussig)
Teplice
(Teplitz)
Eger
Karlovy Vary
(Karlsbad)
Cheb
(Eger)
TSCHECHISCHE
REPUBLIK
Pilzen
(Pilsen)
Praha
(Prag)

Rheinland-
Pfalz
Trier
LUXEM-BURG
Luxemburg
Frankfurt
a. Main
Wiesbaden
Mainz
Offenbach
Main
Darmstadt
Aschaffenburg
Worms
Ludwigshafen
Mannheim
Schweinfurt
Würzburg
Bamberg
Main
Bayreuth
Erlangen
Nürnberg
Fürth
Ansbach
Bayern

Saarland
Saarbrücken
Kaiserslautern
Pirmasens
Speyer
Heidelberg
Baden-
Heilbronn
Karlsruhe
Pforzheim
Stuttgart
Esslingen
Regensburg
Ceske Budejovice
(Budweis)
Moldau

Verdun
Metz
Nancy
FRANKREICH
Epinal
Colmar
Mühlhausen
(Mulhouse)
Vesoul
Belfort
Doubs
Besancon
Rhein
Maas

Straßburg
(Straßbourg)
Baden-Baden
Tübingen
Würtemberg
Ulm
Donau
Ingolstadt
Augsburg
Lech
München
Rosenheim
Isar
Landshut
Passau
Linz
Wels
Steyr
Enns
Salzburg
ÖSTERREICH
Inn

Sigmaringen
Freiburg
i.Br.
Schaffhausen
Konstanz
Bodensee
Lindau
Kempten
Kufstein
Mur

Basel
Zürich
St. Gallen
Bregenz
SCHWEIZ

Register

Index

Abkürzungen / Abbreviations   Bildnachweis / Photographic credit

ABZ – Amerikanische Besatzungszone (American Zone of Occupation)
AP – Arbeiterpartei (Workers' Party)
APO – Außerparlamentarische Opposition (Extra-Parliamentary Opposition)
ARD – Arbeitsgemeinschaft der öffentlich-rechtlichen Rundfunkanstalten Deutschlands (Association of German public radio corporations)
ASEM – Asia-Europe Meeting (Asien-Europa Treffen)
BBZ – Britische Besatzungszone (British Zone of Occupation)
BDA – Bundesvereinigung der Deutschen Arbeitgeberverbände (Confederation of the German Employee's Federation)
BdD – Bund der Deutschen. Partei für Einheit, Frieden und Freiheit (German League: Party of Unity, Peace and Freedom)
BDI – Bundesverband der Deutschen Industrie (Confederation of the German Industry)
BHE – Bund der Heimatvertriebenen und Entrechteten (League of the Displaced and Dispossessed)
BRD – Bundesrepublik Deutschland (Federal Republic of Germany)
CDA – Christlich-Demokratische Arbeitnehmerschaft (Christian Democratic Employees)
CDU – Christlich-Demokratische Union (Christian Democratic Union)
CSFR – Ceskoslovenská Federativní Republika (Tschechische und Slowakische Föderative Republik, Czechoslovakian Federation)
CS(S)R – Ceskoslovenská (Socialistická) Republika (Tschechoslowakische (Sozialistische) Republik, Czechoslovak Socialist Republic)
CSU – Christlich-Soziale Union (Christian Social Union)
DDP – Deutsche Demokratische Partei (German Democratic Party)
DDR – Deutsche Demokratische Republik (German Democratic Republic)
DG – Deutsche Gemeinschaft (German Community)
DGB – Deutscher Gewerkschaftsbund (German Trade Unions Association)
DKP – Deutsche Kommunistische Partei (German Communist Party)
DM – Deutsche Mark (German Mark)
DNVP – Deutschnationale Volkspartei (German National People's Party)
DP – Demokratische Partei / Deutsche Partei (Democratic Party / German Party)
DPD – Demokratische Partei Deutschlands (Democratic Party of Germany)
DSB – Deutscher Sportbund (German Sports Association)

DVP – Demokratische Volkspartei (Democratic People's Party)
ECU – European Currency Unit (Europäische Währungseinheit)
EEA – Einheitliche Europäische Akte (Single European Act)
EFTA – European Free Trade Association (Europäisches Freihandelsabkommen)
EG – Europäische Gemeinschaft (European Community)
EGKS – Europäische Gemeinschaft für Kohle und Stahl (European Coal and Steel Community)
EP – Europäisches Parlament (European Parliament)
EPG – Europäische Politische Gemeinschaft (European Political Community)
ERP – European Recovery Program (Europäisches Wiedergutmachungsprogramm)
EU – Europäische Union (European Union)
EUCD – Europäische Union Christlicher Demokraten (European Union of Christian Democrats)
EUCDA – Europäische Union Christlich-Demokratischer Arbeitnehmer (European Union of Christian Democratic Employees)
EURATOM – Europäische Atomgemeinschaft (European Atomic Energy Community)
ev. – evangelisch (evangelical, Protestant)
EVG – Europäische Verteidigungsgemeinschaft (European Defense Community)
EVP – Europäische Volkspartei (European People's Party)
EWG – Europäische Wirtschaftsgemeinschaft (European Economic Community)
EWS – Europäisches Währungssystem (European Monetary System)
EZB – Europäische Zentralbank (European Central Bank)
FBZ – Französische Besatzungszone (French Zone of Occupation)
FDJ – Freie Deutsche Jugend (Free German Youth)
FDP – Freie Demokratische Partei (Free Democratic Party)
GATT – General Agreement on Tariffs and Trade (Generalabkommen für Preise und Handel)
GSG 9 – Grenzschutz-Gruppe-9 (Spezialeinheit des Bundesgrenzschutzes) (Special Unit of the Federal Border Gard)
GUS – Gemeinschaft Unabhängiger Staaten (Community of Independent States)
GVP – Gesamtdeutsche Volkspartei (All-German People's Party)
HJ – Hitlerjugend (Hitler Youth)
IFOR – Implementation Force (seit Dez. 1995, eine multinationale Streitmacht der NATO, Funktion: Frieden durchsetzen)
IG – Industrie-Gewerkschaft (Industrial Trade Union)
JU – Junge Union (Young Union)
Jusos – Jungsozialisten (Young Socialists)

KfW – Kreditanstalt für Wiederaufbau (Credit institution for Reconstruction)
KP – Kommunistische Partei (Communist Party)
KPD – Kommunistische Partei Deutschlands (Communist Party of Germany)
KPdSU – Kommunistische Partei der Sowjetunion (Communist Party of the Sowjet Union)
KSZE – Konferenz über Sicherheit und Zusammenarbeit in Europa (Conference of Security and Co-operation in Europe)
KZ – Konzentrationslager (Concentration Camp)
LDP – Liberal-Demokratische Partei (Liberal Democratic Party)
LDPD – Liberal-Demokratische Partei Deutschlands (Liberal Demokratic Party of Germany)
MdA – Mitglied des Abgeordnetenhauses (Member of Chamber of Deputies)
MdB – Mitglied des Bundestages (Member of (German) Parliament)
MdEP – Mitglied des Europäischen Parlaments (Member of the European Parliament)
MdL – Mitglied des Landtages (Member of the *Land* Parliament)
MdP – Mitglied des Parlaments (Member of Parliament)
MdPR – Mitglied des Parlamentarischen Rates (Member of the Parliamentary Council)
MdR – Mitglied des Reichstages (Member of the Reichstag)
MdVK – Mitglied der Volkskammer (Member of the Volkskammer)
MLF – Multilateral (Nuclear) Force (Multilaterale [Atom-] Streitmacht)
NAFTA – North-Atlantic Free Trade Agreement (Nordatlantisches Freihandelsabkommen)
NATO – North Atlantic Treaty Organization (Nordatlantikpaktorganisation)
ND – Nea Dimokratia (Neue Demokratie, New Democracy)
NDR – Norddeutscher Rundfunk (North German Radio)
NPD – Nationaldemokratische Partei Deutschland (National Democratic Party of Germany)
NS – Nationalsozialismus (National Socialism)
NSDAP – Nationalsozialistische Deutsche Arbeiterpartei (National Socialist German Workers' Party)
NVA – Nationale Volksarmee (National People's Army)
OEEC – Organization of European Economic Cooperation (Organisation für wirtschaftliche Zusammenarbeit in Europa)
OSZE – Organisation für Sicherheit und Zusammenarbeit in Europa (bis 1994 KSZE) (Organization for Security and Cooperation in Europe (until 1994 CSCE))

ÖTV – Gewerkschaft für öffentliche Transporte und Verkehr (Public Transport Trade Union)
PB – Politbüro (Politburo)
PDS – Partei des Demokratischen Sozialismus (Democratic Socialist Party)
PEN – (International Association of) Poets, Playwrights, Editors, Essayists and Novelists (Internationale Vereinigung von Dichtern, Schriftstellern, Herausgebern, Essayisten und Romanschreibern)
PLO – Palestine Liberation Organization (Palästinensische Freiheitsorganisation)
PS – Partie Socialiste (Sozialistische Partei, Socialistic Party)
RAF – Rote Armee Fraktion (Red Army Faction)
RM – Reichsmark (Reichsmark)
SA – Sturmabteilung (Storm Troops)
SALT – Strategic Arms Limitation Talks (Gespräche zur Einschränkung strategischer Waffen)
SBZ – Sowjetische Besatzungszone (Soviet Zone of Occupation)
SDI – Strategic Defense Initiative (Strategische Verteidigungsinitiative)
SDS – Sozialistischer Deutscher Studentenbund (Association of German Socialist Students)
SED – Sozialistische Einheitspartei Deutschlands (Socialist Unity Party of Germany)
SFB – Sender Freies Berlin (Radio Free Berlin)
SFOR – Stabilisation Force (seit Dez. 1996 die Nachfolgeorganisation von IFOR, Funktion: Frieden stabilisieren)
SMAD – Sowjetische Militäradministration in Deutschland (Soviet Military Administration in Germany)
SPD – Sozialdemokratische Partei Deutschlands (Social Democratic Party of Germany)
SS – Schutzstaffel (National Socialist organization)
Stasi – Ministerium für Staatssicherheit (GDR Ministry of State Security)
UdSSR – Union der Sozialistischen Sowjetrepublik (Union of Soviet Socialist Republics)
UN(0) – United Nations (Organization)
UNESCO – United Nations Educational, Scientific and Cultural Organization (Organisation der Vereinten Nationen für Bildung, Wissenschaft und Kultur)
VEBA – Vereinigte Elektrizitäts- und Bergwerks-Aktiengesellschaft (United Electricity and Mining Company)
WDR – Westdeutscher Rundfunk (West German Radio)
WEU – Westeuropäische Union (West European Union)
ZDF – Zweites Deutsches Fernsehen (Second German Television Channel)
ZK – Zentralkomitee (Central Committee)